THE EVOLUTION
OF THE
GRAND TOUR

Frontispiece: Inigo Jones, *The Castel Sant'Angelo* (Rome, 1614).
Jones inscribed his pen and ink sketch: 'Roma 29 magio 1614 / this[?] night I saw againe y^e girandolo and focci artifiszalle / The Prosesion Corpus domine at Corronation di P Paulo V.' A hundred and sixty years later, Joseph Wright of Derby would paint a more glamorous, Grand Tourist's version of this scene, in which the famous papal fireworks erupt from the *girandola*, or giant wheel, on top of what had been Hadrian's Tomb. [Devonshire Collection, Chatsworth; reproduced by permission of the Chatsworth Settlement Trustees; photograph: E. Chaney]

THE
EVOLUTION
OF THE
GRAND TOUR

Anglo-Italian Cultural Relations
since the Renaissance

EDWARD CHANEY

FRANK CASS
LONDON • PORTLAND, OR

First published in 1998
First published in paperback in Great Britain by
FRANK CASS PUBLISHERS
Newbury House, 900 Eastern Avenue
London IG2 7HH,

and in the United States of America by
FRANK CASS PUBLISHERS
c/o ISBS. 5824 N.E. Hassalo Street
Portland, Oregon 97213-3644

Website: www.frankcass.com

British Library Cataloguing in Publication data

Chaney, Edward
    The evolution of the Grand Tour: Anglo-Italian cultural
    relations since the Renaissance
    1. Great Britain – Relations – Italy – History   2. Italy –
    Relations – Great Britain – History
    I. Title
    303.4'82'41'045

            ISBN 0-7146-4577-x (cloth)
            ISBN 0-7146-4474-9 (paper)

Library of Congress Cataloging in Publication data

Chaney, Edward.
    The evolution of the grand tour: Anglo-Italian cultural relations
since the Renaissance / Edward Chaney.
        p.   cm.
    Includes bibliographical references and index.
    ISBN 0-7146-4577-X (cloth) ISBN 0-7146-4474-9 (paper)
    1. Great Britain – Civilization – Italian influences.   2. England –
Civilization – Italian influences.   3. Americans – Travel – Italy –
History.   4. Great Britain – Relations – Italy.   5. Italy – Relations –
Great Britain.   6. British – Travel – Italy – History.   7. Travelers –
Italy – History.   I. Title.
    DA47.9.I8C48   1998
    941—dc21   98-5404
                                                                    CIP

Typeset in 11/13pt Photina by Regent Typesetting, London
Printed in Great Britain by
Bookcraft (Bath) Ltd, Midsomer Norton, Somerset

For my family,
with love and gratitude

Contents

∽👁️∽

List of Illustrations

❧

Introduction

❦

WITH MONOGRAPHS and exhibitions on the Grand Tour now materializing at regular intervals there seems to be a more widespread acknowledgement of the interest and importance of this subject. Although the academic custom of dividing the humanities into distinct 'disciplines' still militates against the Grand Tour, there are even signs that universities, which for so long have preached the virtues of inter-disciplinary or cultural history, are adopting the Grand Tour – or Anglo-Italian cultural relations – as a subject that illuminates significant aspects of literature, art and architectural history, the history of science and medicine, archaeology, musicology and many another 'construction'. There can surely be few topics more worthy of study than the history of how contact with Italy (almost?) civilized Britain and much of its empire, including America.

Having hosted the Roman modification of ancient Greek civilization as well as the revival of this hybrid during the Renaissance, Italy became the focus of extraordinary fascination for the emerging nations of Northern Europe after the disintegration of medieval Christendom. The way in which the English became conscious of the Italian Renaissance – and thereby discovered classical antiquity itself – is the principal subject of this book. Unlike most works on the Grand Tour, it therefore deals not so much with the fully-fledged eighteenth-century phenomenon, when young men from perhaps the most powerful nation on earth patronized a museum set in a picturesque landscape, but rather with the sixteenth and seventeenth centuries, when the English travelled to a country whose contemporary culture was as impressive as its past and in many respects still outshone their own.

When Milton and Hobbes visited Italy in the 1630s, though

Protestant and sceptic respectively, they still conformed to the social requirements of a supremely sophisticated civilization. They gratefully accepted invitations to grand academic functions, to dine at the Jesuit-run English College or attend the unrivalled musical soirées sponsored by Cardinal Barberini. The Baroque Rome of the universally talented Gianlorenzo Bernini attracted the greatest living artists, from Velázquez to Poussin, who drew inspiration from fashions set by Caravaggio and the Carracci. Meanwhile the universities trained native scientists such as Galileo and Malpighi, as well as Englishmen such as William Harvey, who is unlikely to have 'discovered' the circulation of the blood had he not studied at Padua. Our literature, music, mathematics, science, art, architecture, politics, banking, philosophy, historiography and much else were derived more or less directly from our experience of Italy. At the time, the Italian influence in equitation, fencing, fortification, tennis, dancing and 'politeness' generally would have been considered no less significant. Whether or not Shakespeare travelled to the country in which he chose to set so many of his plays, from John Donne to John Dowland, from Inigo Jones to the Earl and Countess of Arundel, those who required a more immediate rapport than that available through imported books found the voyage of Italy irresistible.

Although most of the essays in this volume have been published previously in some form or other, thanks to Frank Cass I have been able to revise all of them, some substantially, for re-presentation here as a unified collection. All retain their original format, however, and thus convey something of their *raison d'être*. Chapter 1, the essay on 'British and American Travellers in Sicily' began life as an introduction to the third edition of the *Blue Guide Sicily* (ed. Alta Macadam, London and New York, 1988). Because it was published without footnotes, I integrated citation of most of the literary sources into the text so that they would be traceable by anyone interested in pursuing them. I have not therefore annotated this revised and expanded version but merely clarified a few of the references and added an endnote in order to facilitate the same procedure. This should now be enhanced by use of the index via which one can cross-refer to relevant footnotes in other articles if required. R.S. Pine-Coffin's *Bibliography of British and American Travel in Italy to 1860* (Florence, 1974), together with its supplement in *La Bibliofilia*, LXXIII (1981), pp. 237–61, may be used as the standard catalogue of published primary sources here and elsewhere in this book.

If an introductory survey attempting to cover more than a millennium of travel to one Mediterranean island runs the risk of overemphasizing continuity, Chapter 2, on 'Early Tudor Tombs', provides a corrective, focusing as it does on a period in which relations between England and Italy waxed and waned rapidly. Enthusiasm for all things Italian burgeoned in the conditions of peace established by the first Tudor king, but the increasingly irresponsible policies of his son led to an unprecedented decline in Anglo-Roman relations. This had profound consequences for English culture. Enhanced access to a vernacular bible encouraged an unprecedented level of literacy, which culminated in Shakespeare. Where the visual arts were concerned, however, the consequences of the Reformation were largely negative, direct access to the achievement of Renaissance Italy being essential for their development. With the crucial encouragement of Cardinal Wolsey, Henry VIII had made significant efforts to patronize the new style but, largely owing to the break with Rome, inadequate consolidation of such efforts left England lagging behind its classicizing rivals France and Spain. Although the increasingly tyrannical men who governed England in the name of Henry's invalid son Edward VI personally favoured Italianate culture, their political and religious policies encouraged iconoclasm and further isolation from the Catholic continent. The excommunication of Elizabeth in 1570 and war with Spain in the 1580s confirmed this isolation and rendered travel to Italy a clandestine activity, engendering danger abroad and suspicion at one's return home. Under these uncertain conditions, the visual arts came to be monopolized by foreigners who tended to re-emigrate in times of difficulty. In sculpture and painting (though a case may be made for the miniature) the achievement of Torrigiano and Holbein was only to be matched a century later by fellow foreigners, Dieussart and Van Dyck. Thanks to his travels in Italy, Inigo Jones was the only British architect (and theatre designer) capable of matching continental standards for more than a century.

I am fully aware of the alternative, more relativist (multicultural?) view of such matters, most recently articulated in the collection of essays edited by Lucy Gent: *Albion's Classicism: The Visual Arts in Britain, 1550–1660* (New Haven and London, 1995). I remain unpersuaded, however, that choice, as distinct from incomplete familiarity with Renaissance Italy (and the strength of local traditions) determined the development of British art and architecture in this period. When Dr Gent writes that 'access to classicism for the educated elite was via reading rather than seeing' (p. 5) she is confirming that it was the limitations on travel to Italy that determined the distinctive styles developed in Tudor England. When she warns that 'twentieth-century perceptions of the classicism embodied in the Italian Renaissance are inappropriate to sixteenth- and early seventeenth-century Britain' (p. 6) she may unwittingly be condemning most of her contributors, for it is their late twentieth-century anxiety to eschew the canonical that encourages them to praise or overinterpret British artefacts which sophisticated sixteenth-century Italians and their seventeenth-century successors in belatedly classicizing Britain ridiculed as parochial. Long before Lord Burlington and the Rule of Taste, the cosmopolitan Roger Pratt regarded the handful of buildings by Inigo Jones as the only models worthy of imitation in Britain, insisting that an aspiring architect travel to Italy. His contemporary John Aubrey, painfully conscious of having failed to tour Italy himself, concluded that: 'in Queen Elizabeth's time architecture . . . went backwards.'

By 1617 the future bishop, Joseph Hall, was borrowing Christ's question to St Peter, '*Quo Vadis?*', not to ask why anyone was leaving Rome, but to censure the new craze for travelling to this source of religious and moral corruption. As James I's 1604 treaty with Spain began to render Spanish-dominated Italy accessible again, so Hall emphasized the benefits of touring Protestant Britain instead. Chapter 3 investigates the sixteenth-century origins of Hall's anxiety and documents the lengths to which the young 'Gentlemen of our Nation' of his subtitle went in order to see Italy for themselves. What might be termed 'the Italian imperative' encouraged an ever-deepening commitment to Renaissance culture. This was to be so thoroughly assimilated that by the nineteenth century it was as if the Romans had never abandoned us.

Returning to travel in Southern Italy, Chapter 4 examines the evolution of travel to Naples and beyond. Inevitably, we meet again some of the travellers encountered in Sicily, notably the enterprising Thomas Hoby who is here confirmed as the prototypical Grand Tourist, a corrective to our exclusively eighteenth-century idea of this phenomenon. George Berkeley also re-emerges, now in greater detail, documenting in his letters and journals a more extensive tour of Italy than any British traveller since Hoby. Berkeley's better-known successors, the more orthodox, city-hopping tourists, remain on the margin of this account (they are dealt with in greater detail in the Tate Gallery's 1996 exhibition catalogue and in John Ingamells's *Dictionary of British and Irish Travellers in Italy 1701–1800*). By the nineteenth century, with the top-heavy Grand Tour associated too closely with the grand-parental *ancien régime* and Cook's Tourism (as it was soon to be known) all too intimately with the egalitarian shape of things to come, an alternative breed of traveller revived the tradition of Hoby and Berkeley to roam again through romantic but classical and rural Italy. Albeit unaware of these predecessors, from Ramage and Edward Lear to Norman Douglas and D.H. Lawrence, their self-consciously individualistic writings nonetheless echo the entire tradition of Northern travel to the South.

During Elizabeth's reign, the cult of Italy had flourished despite (to some extent because of) restricted access. Following the failure of the Armada, fear of Italy's Spanish masters waned and more enterprising travellers, such as the 5th Earl of Rutland and his brothers, ventured at least as far as Florence. (The Privy Council vetoed visits to Rome until well into the seventeenth century.) For Rutland's scholarly servant, Robert Dallington, the subject of Chapter 5, Tuscany seems to have proved something of an anti-climax. At the turn of the sixteenth century, the educated Englishman was not expected to be as familiar with the visual arts as with the literary. In Dallington's view therefore, the extraordinary cultural achievement we now associate so particularly with Florence, failed to compensate for Medici tyranny, for Popery (already identified with tyrannical government), for declining scholarly standards (again associated with autocracy) and for incentive-stifling and harshly exacted taxation. When Dallington published his highly critical *Survey of Tuscany* in 1605, the Grand Duke Ferdinand insisted that James I destroy the edition, a demand which was fortunately met merely by a token gesture. Dallington's subsequently successful career demonstrates that his 'aristodemocraticall' politics – based in part on his experience of Italy – did not hold him back.

The first of the two documentary items which make up Chapter 6 provides a reminder of Spanish dominance not merely over Italy but, albeit briefly, over England under Philip and Mary. It was Philip, 'Re d'Inghilterra', rather than Mary who was sent the miniature of the Three Magi mentioned by Lewis Einstein in his pioneering work on *The Italian Renaissance in England* (1902). This was, moreover,

painted by the celebrated Giulio Clovio and though featuring that
favorite subject of the Medici (long-standing devotees of the cult of
the Magi), it was commissioned by Eleanor of Toledo rather than her
husband Cosimo I. Dealing still with art and diplomacy, the second
item publishes two letters written by Henry Wotton to the Duke of
Mantua. These provide new information on Wotton's patronage of
that intriguing artist Odoardo Fialetti and early evidence of a link
between England and Mantua in the period of Gonzaga decline.

When the Catholic Countess of Arundel resided in the Veneto in
the early 1620s, one result of her fraught dealings with ambassador
Wotton may have been Charles I's acquisition of the Gonzaga
collections. Her first experience of Italy, however, had been in 1613–
14 when she and her husband, the great 'Collector Earl', employed
Inigo Jones as their *cicerone*. Jones and the Earl surveyed Roman
antiquities and Palladian buildings and imbibed the knowledge
which provided the foundations for that extraordinary flourishing of
Renaissance visual culture under the first two Stuarts. Chapter 7
focuses on the least studied part of this most significant of all Grand
Tours, their 1614 visit to Naples and in particular on Jones's fascination with the once prominent Roman temple of Castor and Pollux.

Chapter 8, 'Pilgrims to Pictures', summarizes some of what has
gone before and places Wotton's embassies and the travels of
Jones and the Arundels into the broader context of the seventeenth-
century Grand Tour, emphasizing the crucial role of English
Catholics in the growth of interest in art and collecting. After the
diplomatic, military, and linguistic educational priorities of the sixteenth century, art and architecture finally joined these justifications
for travel during the seventeenth. Where pilgrims of all ages and
both sexes had once justified travelling thousands of miles in terms
of seeing, perhaps touching, and occasionally acquiring a sacred
object, with the rise of the virtuoso and then the connoisseur, the
gentlemen travellers of post-Reformation Britain went to see and
eventually to acquire a Raphael, Carracci or piece of antique sculpture. Given that their patrons now tended to go on the Grand Tour,
the artists and architects found themselves obliged to study their
sources ever more assiduously, some becoming professional *ciceroni*
or bear-leaders. They also discovered the world of dealing, pro-
fessionalizing and greatly enlarging a trade which had previously
been conducted either by ambassadors such as Dudley Carleton and
Henry Wotton as a useful sideline, or by the likes of Tobie Matthew,

George Gage and Peter Fitton, Catholic double-agents whose artistic expertise provided a cover for political and religious intrigue. Arundel's apparently Anglican agent, William Petty, was unusual in his disinterested (and more exclusive) pursuit of works of art: his secretiveness was maintained primarily in the interests of a bargain. The king's agent, Nicholas Lanier, disguised his intentions both for this reason and for reasons of state when negotiating the controversial acquisition of the Gonzaga collections. In the denuding of bankrupt Mantua by English purchasing power we glimpse the shape of things to come in the age of the mature Grand Tour.

If Wotton was a diplomat first who exploited a secondary interest in art in order to ingratiate himself with his patrons, Balthazar Gerbier began his career as an artist, then became an art agent and finally emerged in the unlikely and more or less disastrous role of fully-fledged diplomat. His travels in Italy during the 1620s in search of pictures for the Duke of Buckingham (desperate to catch up with the likes of Lord Arundel) led directly to political missions in Spain and Brussels. It would be worth publishing Gerbier's fascinating letters, the bulk of them now in the Public Record Office. The frustration of condensing a considerable amount of material into a short entry for Macmillan's *Dictionary of Art* accounts for Gerbier featuring as Chapter 9. It also explains the unorthodox format which seemed more appropriate to the non-definitive nature of these notes towards a more definitive biography.

Similarly non-definitive is Chapter 10 on 'English Catholic Poets in mid-Seventeenth Century Rome', originally written as an appendix to my dissertation on Richard Lassels. If Gerbier flirted with Catholicism when it suited, the more devout English recusants suffered persecution and exile. This short survey offers glimpses into lives which were obscure but sheds light upon the careers of fellow poets-in-exile such as Richard Crashaw whose reputations survived in better shape and in this sense came home.

Returning to matters less overtly artistic (for hospitals were in some sense works of art in this period), the Protestant view of Italian charitable institutions was necessarily a complex one. The great polychrome terracotta frieze, which completed the hospital portico at Pistoia in the early sixteenth century, confirms that 'Good Works' still contributed to salvation and reduced one's time in Purgatory. But while the Italians consolidated their commitment to such beliefs both artistically and via the dictates of the Council of Trent, most

Northern Europeans were abandoning Purgatory and demoting good works except as manifestations of predestined election. The Calvinists who so profoundly influenced the English Church considered personal salvation too important to leave to the free will of mere mortals. In Reformation England, standards of care for the poor and the sick suffered accordingly. Henry VIII shut down the largely monastic hospitals and failed to replace the facilities they had provided on anything approaching the scale required, even in London. Although first-time travellers from the Protestant North arrived in Italy keen to cite evidence of superstition, they were so impressed by the facilities for inmates of the Catholic hospitals that only the most cynical followed Luther in commenting adversely on the longer-term motives of the donors.

Myth and legend can be at least as creative as superstition. The legend of Milton's visit to Vallombrosa took more than a century to mature, but by the time of William Beckford's Grand Tour it was apparently powerful enough to prompt a pilgrimage in the poet's honour to this out-of-the-way monastery. The nineteenth century, in some ways so rationalist, was also pervaded by romantic belief, if not in God (though He too was revived) at least in Culture. Milton's reputation grew to a point where even Masson's six-volume *Life* could not satisfy Victorian curiosity. The mere mention of the poetic Italian name for a shady valley in *Paradise Lost*, doubtless derived from Ariosto, had meanwhile sufficed to transform it into one of the most significant sojourns of Milton's otherwise well-documented tour of Italy. His inherently unlikely visit to a remote Catholic monastery became a credo not merely for travellers who 'followed' him there but for a Fascist government wishing to remind foreigners of their indebtedness to Italy. And so to some extent apparently it still was with many of the American academics who attended the Third International Milton Symposium held in Vallombrosa in June 1988. Having cast doubt on the visit in *The Grand Tour and the Great Rebellion* (Geneva, 1985), I was asked to re-examine the evidence in my paper to the conference. The more I looked, the clearer it seemed – to me at least, and short of proving a negative – that Milton never visited Vallombrosa. The legend that he did, however, spawned a literature worthy of investigation in itself, though this apparently failed to console the Miltonists.

Compared to students of literature (as distinct from 'texts'), philosophers tend to be less interested in the history of their subject and still less in the lives of their predecessors. Even so it is remarkable how little the four years that George Berkeley spent in Italy have been studied. No annotated edition of his travel journals and related correspondence has yet been produced in English. Although necessarily incomplete, in Chapter 13 I have attempted to survey both Berkeley's Grand Tours, the second of which was one of the most extensive tours of Italy ever undertaken. Berkeley's originality both in his choice of itinerary, which included Sicily, Ischia and Puglia (though not Vallombrosa), as well as his aesthetic and anthropological judgement, is set against the more conventional aspects of his Grand Tour, illustrated by his commentary on Rome. With the conclusion of the wars with Louis XIV, the British Grand Tour had come to full maturity and its essential character altered relatively little during the rest of the century.

Finally, by way of tribute to a friend who since his death in 1994 seems to have received less than his due, this collection ends with a revised version of my obituary of Sir Harold Acton, first published in *Apollo*. Although he was not keen on footnotes, I hope he would have found something of interest in those chapters he did not live long enough to read. I hope also that his great bequest, the Villa La Pietra, its contents and its beautiful gardens, will always reflect something of his charm and meritocratic generosity and will honour his devotion to all that was creative in the conjunction between England and Italy.

I have thanked many individuals in the footnotes to each chapter. Here it remains to thank those who have helped in preparing this volume. Above all I wish to thank my daughter Jessica who encouraged me to persevere with this project in a period fraught with difficulties for us both. She has shown a generosity of spirit and maturity of judgement far beyond her years. My parents Tim and Malise and my brother Philip were no less supportive; my younger daughter Olivia meanwhile providing a brilliant musical accompaniment. I remain profoundly grateful to them all. Many others have helped, some also in ways too profound to detail; they include Dr Malcolm Airs, Dr Brian Allen, Professor David Berman, Dr John and Sarah Bold, John and Berenice Bonallack, Anne Brookes, Charles and Suzie Chafyn-Grove, Dr D.S. Chambers, Sir Howard Colvin, Professoressa Anna Maria Crinò, Lord Dacre of Glanton, Professor Kerry Downes, Robert Easton, Dr Nicola Figgis, Professor Vittorio Gabrieli, Dr Richard and Barbara Gardner, Drs Ole and Helen Grell,

Professor Francis Haskell, Dr Gordon Higgott, Professor K.J. Höltgen, Dr Charles Hope, Andrew Humphrys, Keith and Sira Jacka, Dr Hilton Kelliher, Dr Helen Langdon, Professor Michael McCarthy, Dr Elizabeth McGrath, Dr Noel Malcolm, Giles Mandelbrote, John Newman, Richard and Mary Ollard, John Peacock, Dr Dennis Rhodes, Professor Andrew Saint, Robin and Joanna Simon, Dr John Stoye, Linda Tieri, Professor J.B. Trapp, Michael and Katherine Thomson-Glover, Mark and Heather Roberts, Jonathan and Julie Weeks, Dr Linda Whiteley, Dr Timothy Wilks, Jeremy Wood, and Drs Clifford and Valerie Yorke.

Finally, among those institutions that have given crucial support during the past two decades, in the order that I attended them I would like to thank: the Warburg Institute, University of London; the European University Institute, Florence; the Harvard University Center for Italian Renaissance Studies, Villa I Tatti, Florence; Lincoln College, Oxford; the Paul Mellon Centre for Studies in British Art, London; and the Huntington Library, San Marino, California. I have received funding from the Leverhulme Trust, Lincoln College, the British Academy, and the Alice Krieble Delmas Foundation.

Morcombelake, Dorset, July 1996

After a further period of revision, picture research and proof-reading, I should like to add my warmest thanks to Professor Peter Coupe, Dean of the Built Environment Faculty, and to my new colleagues in Fine Arts Valuation at the Southampton Institute.

Oxford/Southampton, November 1997

The opportunity to incorporate minor improvements and corrections has been taken in this second, paperback edition. A longer note has been added to the chapter on Milton and Vallombrosa. More significantly, in response to one particular reviewer, a critical bibliography has been appended as Chapter 15. This concentrates on the twentieth-century historiography of the evolution of the Grand Tour. It is hoped that this functions as a contribution to the history of publishing as well as shedding light on the historiography of travel *per se*. In the preparation of this second edition I should like to thank, as before, my editor, Andrew Humphrys, and also Ray Green, Cass's expert (and very accommodating) production manager.

Southampton, May 2000

1 *The Kingdom of the Two Sicilies*, from Henry Swinburne, *Travel in the Two Sicilies*, 2 vols (London, 1783–85).

2 The 5th-century BC Greek quarries at Syracuse (The Latomie) from John Durant Breval, *Remarks on Several Parts of Europe, Relating Chiefly to Their Antiquities and History* . . . (London, 1738), vol. I, opposite p. 23 (cop engraving by Pierre Fourdrinier). [E. Chaney]

British and American Travellers in Sicily from the Eighth to the Twentieth Century

To have seen Italy without having seen Sicily is not to have seen Italy
at all, for Sicily is the clue to everything.

J.W. von Goethe, *Italian Journey: 1786–1788*, transl.
W.H. Auden and E. Mayer (London, 1962), p. 240

O N 18 APRIL 1955, less than a fortnight after resigning as Prime Minister, the 80-year-old Sir Winston Churchill wrote to the young Queen Elizabeth II. Presumably because he wanted somewhere relatively remote but essentially civilized, somewhere steeped in history, warmed and well-lit by the Mediterranean sun (so he could paint out of doors), he had headed straight for Sicily and for Siracusa in particular. He informed Her Majesty that:

> The historical atmosphere of Syracuse grows perceptibly upon me and my companions here as the days pass. Our hotel rises out of the sinister quarries [Fig. 2] in which six thousand Athenian prisoners of war were toiled and starved to death in 413 BC, and I am trying to paint a picture of a cavern's mouth near the listening gallery whose echoes brought secrets to the ears of Dionysius. All this is agreeable to the mental and psychological processes of laying down direct responsibility for the guidance of great affairs and falling back upon the comforting reflection 'I have done my best'.

Not much is known of what was happening in Britain in 413 BC; no doubt very little compared with what was undoubtedly happening in Athens and Syracuse, then the two greatest cities in (at least) the western world. The earliest British accounts of Sicily date from more than a millennium later and are very sketchy. The first I have found was written in Latin by a nun to whom the aged St Willibald dictated his memoirs. Unfortunately, while he (and perhaps she) elaborated interestingly on the subjects of Syria, Jerusalem and Constantinople in the narrative of his pilgrimage, posterity was left to guess at most of what he saw during the three weeks he spent in Catania in 723, or his overnight stop in Syracuse. Only the Mediterranean volcanoes seem to have aroused any real enthusiasm in him. Even when he describes the miraculous powers of Catania's Sant' Agata (whom he misremembers as St Agnes), he is interested primarily because those powers included the capacity to halt Etna's lava flow. On his return journey from the east six years later, it was the island of Vulcano which fascinated him as it had fascinated Thucydides more than a millennium earlier:

> Thence they sailed to the island Vulcano: there is the inferno of Theodoric. And when they arrived, they went up from the ship to see what the inferno was like. Willibald was very curious to see what was inside the inferno, and would have climbed to the mountain top above it: but he could not. For the ashes blew up from the black hell and lay piled in heaps on the edge and . . . prevented Willibald's ascent. But he saw the flames belching black and terrible and horrifying from the pit like resounding thunder, and he watched the great flame and the vapor from the smoke mounting terribly but awfully on high. That pumice which writers use he saw rising from the inferno and blown out in flame and hurled into the sea and thence cast ashore and men take it up and carry it away.

For most of the rest of the Anglo-Saxon period Sicily was ruled by the Saracens and there was even less 'English' contact with the island. In the wake of the Norman conquests of both England and Sicily in the latter part of the eleventh century, however, Anglo-Sicilian relations flourished as never before nor since. In particular, Anglo-Norman scholars and administrators of all kinds visited or established their careers in Sicily, jostling for promotion with rival Italian, Greek and Arab bureaucrats. Most eminent among those who made the long journey in the first half of the twelfth century were John of Salisbury (the most learned classical writer of the Middle Ages), Adelard of Bath (pioneer of Arab studies), John of Lincoln (Canon of Agrigento), Robert of Selby (who became King Roger's Chancellor) and Master Thomas Brown (who after serving in Roger's civil service for 21 years – organizing the Sicilian treasury along English lines – returned home to help Henry II organize Angevin England, using his Sicilian experience). Under Roger's 'Bad' son, William I, and 'Good' grandson, William II, in the second half of the century, the Anglo-Sicilian connection was at its strongest. The international reputation of the court at Palermo for cosmopolitan culture and good career prospects attracted learned prelates such as Richard Palmer, eventually Archbishop of Messina, whose epitaph is still in his Cathedral (albeit somewhat damaged by the 1908 earthquake) and Robert Cricklade, Chancellor of the University of Oxford and biographer of Thomas Becket. The somewhat sinister Walter 'Ophamil', who rose to become Archbishop of Palermo, and his brother, Bartholomew, who succeeded him as Archbishop in 1190, do not seem to have been English, the quaint notion that their surname was derived from 'of the Mill' being now discredited.

In the early years of William II's reign, during the period leading up to Becket's assassination in December 1170, rival emissaries from the opposed camps of the English King and this 'turbulent' Archbishop of Canterbury arrived in droves, each trying to enlist powerful Sicilian support for their respective causes. Together with Louis VII of France, Becket was particularly opposed to the proposed marriage between the young King of Sicily and a daughter of Henry II. In the event, not even his assassination and subsequent canonization prevented this great alliance, Henry's profession of innocence and his public penance persuading the Sicilians to forgive and forget the sacrilege at the same time they were naming churches and decorating their cathedrals with mosaics commemorating the new English saint. The tall figure of St Thomas in the apse of Monreale dates from the 1180s, but approval to convert a mosque at Catania into a church of St Thomas of Canterbury was granted as early as January 1179. Later, Marsala would even dedicate its Cathedral to the English saint.

John of Oxford, Bishop of Norwich, was despatched by Henry II in the summer of 1176 to finalize arrangements for the marriage of his third daughter, Joanna, to King William and we have a record of his difficult journey, at first 'troubled by a great shortage of bread and of fodder', then by danger from the Lombards who supported an anti-pope, and eventually by the 'excess of heat', the rocks and whirlpool of Scylla and Charybdis, where 'the sea frequently turns upside down in an instant', and the 'notable filth of the oarsmen [which] produced nausea'. The royal progress of the 10-year-old Princess herself, starting from Southampton on 26 September 1176, was evidently more comfortable, her nausea being brought on merely by the motion of the ship. She was escorted initially by her eldest brother, Henry, and then by another brother, Richard Coeur de Lion, later to make the journey to Sicily himself on his way to the Crusades. On reaching the port of St Gilles, at the mouth of the Rhône, she was met by 25 of her future husband's ships. The Sicilians decided to play safe with their precious cargo, all the more so when news arrived that two ships transporting William's gifts to Henry II had foundered. They clung close to the French coast and down most of the western shore of Italy as far as Naples, at which point the Princess's seasickness necessitated continuing the journey by land most of the way down to the Straits of Messina and then due west along the north coast of Sicily, via Cefalù, to Palermo. Here the 23-year-old William met his fellow French-speaking bride at the city gates, had her mounted on one of his finest horses, and escorted her to the palace (which must surely have been the recently completed Zisa) where she and her household were to stay for the 11 days which remained until her wedding. A contemporary wrote that 'the stars in the heavens could scarcely be seen for the brilliance of the lights' which illuminated Palermo for the state entry. The couple were married on St Valentine's Eve 1177 and, immediately after, Joanna was crowned Queen of Sicily by 'Emir and Archbishop' Walter in the Cappella Palatina.

William the Good died in 1189, without a legitimate heir and genuinely mourned by most of his subjects, perhaps because they sensed that Sicily's prosperity might not endure under his com-promise successor, Tancred. William's tutor, Peter of Blois, had indeed left the island 20 years earlier, urging his friend, Richard Palmer, to likewise 'Flee . . . the mountains which vomit flame' and the land which 'devours its inhabitants'.

In the spring of 1191, Catania was the scene of an extraordinary meeting between Queen Joanna, her brother Richard I (who had just caused havoc by occupying Messina), his mother, the 69-year-old Eleanor of Aquitaine and his bride-to-be, Berengaria. Despite the recent prohibition against Crusading women he took her with him and his sister to the Holy Land. Though there is no evidence as to what Richard and the English crusaders thought of Sicilian volcanoes, there is ample negative testimony on 'the wicked citizens, commonly called Griffons, . . . many of them born of Saracen fathers'. The *Itinerarium Ricardi* admits that 'the city of Messina . . . is filled with many varieties of good things in a region which is pleasant and most satisfying . . . It stands first in Sicily, rich in essential supplies and in all good things: but it has cruel and evil men.' Clearly both factors lay behind the English occupation of Messina. Three years later the Western Emperor, Henry VI of Hohenstaufen, invaded Sicily with the help of 50 ships taken as ransom for Richard's release from post-crusading captivity and on Christmas Day 1194 he was crowned King of Sicily in Archbishop Walter's Cathedral in Palermo. Sicily would flourish again under Henry's son Frederick II, 'Stupor Mundi', but the golden age of its intimacy with that Norman-dominated island in the north was over, even if the continued presence of outstanding individuals such as Gervase of Tilbury and Michael Scot perpetuated some of the traditional cultural connections.

Though the Spaniard, Pero Tafur, was capable of providing posterity with a coherent description of the cities of Sicily in the 1430s, it was not until the first half of the sixteenth century that we notice signs of the Holy Land pilgrimage being replaced by something resembling the Grand Tour and the first reasonably coherent English accounts of Sicily. In general, the 1517–18 diary of the priest, Richard Torkynton, depends heavily on the printed *Pylgrymage of Sir Richard Guylforde Knygth* of 1511. Guylforde, however, seems not to have stopped in Sicily and died in Jerusalem so we can assume that the little Torkynton says on this subject is more or less original.

Returning from the Holy Land, via Cyprus, Rhodes and Corfu, 'the fairest ground that ever I saw in my life', Torkynton and his party arrived after much difficulty at Messina on Saint Gregory's Day (March) 1518 and spent five days relaxing in the city:

> Thys Missena, in Cecyll, ys a fayer Cite and well wallyd wt many fayer towers and Div[er]se castell, the fayrest havyn for Shippes that ev I saw, ther ys also plente of all maner of thyngs that ys necessari for man, except clothe, that ys very Dere ther, ffor englyssh men brynge it theyr by watyr owt of . . . Enlong [England], it ys a grett long wey.

Hakluyt tells us that the English wool merchants made regular journeys between London and Sicily in the early sixteenth century but this is a rare contemporary reference to the trade, though it

was not long before there were English consuls in Trapani and
Messina.

Richard Torkynton must have been one of the last pilgrims to visit
the Holy Land whilst it was still governed by the relatively tolerant
Egyptian Mameluke dynasty. While he was on his way home,
Jerusalem fell to the Ottoman Sultan Selim I and henceforth Palestine
was ruled by the Turks. Increasingly, Rome and Loreto became the
two major substitute destinations for pilgrims, and though the
merchants continued to trade in Sicily and southern Italy, the south
was visited, if at all, out of curiosity. The 'curiositas poetica', which
Petrarch had feared might replace 'devotione catolica' as early as the
mid-fourteenth century, became ever more dominant during the
Renaissance and eventually triumphed in the mentality which mani-
fested itself in the Grand Tour. That Sicily never fully established itself
as an essential ingredient of a Grand Tour itinerary is for the present
purposes all to the good. Those who bothered to break off or extend
their tours to include it, tended to be the more imaginative, eccentric
or adventurous, and thus, where they record their journeys, reveal
far more than the conventional tourist about both themselves and
the fascinating island they were visiting.

Much the most remarkable of the surviving sixteenth-century
accounts of Sicily is that to be found in the autobiographical *Booke
of the Travaile and Lief of me Thomas Hoby* which, despite its intrinsic
interest and its importance as the work of the translator of
Castiglione's *Il Cortegiano*, remained unpublished until 1902 and is
still inadequately known [Fig. 3]. On 11 February 1550, having
explored Naples and its environs with a group of English friends, the
20-year-old Hoby decided to set off on his own, 'throwghe the dukedom of Calabria by land into Cicilia, both to have a sight of the
countrey and also to absent my self for while owt of Englishemenne's
companie for the tung's sake.'

From Reggio, recently ravaged by the Turkish pirate-cum-admiral,
Barbarossa, Hoby crossed over to Messina which he considered
'on[e] of the fairest portes in Europe'. He was equally impressed by
both its ancient and modern features; on the one hand by 'the
heades of Scipio and Hannibal, when they were yong menn, in
stone', and on the other by the recently rebuilt royal palace, the
three Spanish castles and, most recent of all, the exquisite Orion
fountain upon which the great Florentine sculptor, Giovanni
Montorsoli, was then still working:

3 Sir Thomas Hoby (foreground) and his half-brother Sir Philip: the Hoby tomb at Bisham Church, Berkshire (*c.*1566). [E. Chaney]

> For a new worke and that not finisshed at my being there, I saw a fountaine of verie white marble graven with the storie of Acteon and such other, by on[e] Giovan Angelo, a florentine, which to my eyes is on[e] of the fairest peece of worke that ever I sawe. This fountain was appointed to be sett uppe before the hige churche where there is an old on[e] alreadie.

In 1563 Hoby set up his own fountain at Bisham Abbey, while at Nonsuch, the Ovidian Actaeon story features prominently in the fountain sculpture created by the Italophile 12th Earl of Arundel (whom Hoby entertained to dinner in 1560) [Fig. 4] and his son-in-law, Lord Lumley. In 1566, either Hoby or his widow – stranded in France when he died – commissioned a tomb featuring Italianate effigies of him and his brother which were in advance of any other contemporary sculpture in England [Fig. 3].

After two days in Messina, Hoby 'departed from thense towardes Siracuse'. *En route*, at Taormina, it was again the classical associations with which he dealt first, noting that: 'Cicero makethe oft mention of this towne in his orations against Verres' and that 'abowt yt are verie auntient ruines' [Fig. 10]. He then continued

4 Hans Eworth, probably of Henry Fitzalan, 12th Earl of Arundel (1512–1580). Oak tondo
of 65cm diameter signed and dated 1550, inscribed with sitter's age (38) and Horatian
inscription signifying 'Let Envy be turned upon its Author'. Arundel was the only peer aged
38 in 1550. He remained a Roman Catholic and toured Italy in 1566–7. [Lane Fine Art]

south, past fields of sugar cane, through 'a plain country full of
marisshes', until he came upon 'the rootes of Mongibello, called in
old time Ætna'. The once 'famous citie' of Catania now seemed to
depend above all upon its fishermen, 'that travail the seea day and
night'. Though he was visiting the city prior to more than one post-
earthquake rebuilding, like the modern visitor he particularly noticed
the fact that it was 'built with ruggie heavie stone' full of little holes,
which the 'inhabitants saye have in times past bine cast owt of
Mongibello'.

He had intended climbing Etna, but:

> th' inhabitants persuaded me to the contrarie, saing that the snowe was so thick, the way so troublesom, and the cold so extreme, that I shuld not be able to bring my purpose to passe. (And againe which was worst of all) there was no lodging to be had: and to goo and com back again but from the hither most part of the snowe which liethe upon the hill, they said it was not possible in a daye.

As a sceptical humanist and Protestant to boot, Hoby invents a complex pseudo-scientific explanation for Etna's inactivity rather than accept – as previous travellers from St Willibald to Torkynton had done – 'th'inhabitants'' assertion that Sant'Agata's 'holie bodie' had prevented the volcano 'from annoying the towne in suche sort as it was accustomed in time to fore'.

Having crossed the Simeto, which he describes as 'on[e] of the fairest rivers in all Sicilia', Hoby finally arrived in Syracuse: 'the towne so famous in all writers both greeke and latin, which hath bine esteemed on[e] of the principallest cities of all Greece.' 'The name of it doth still remaine', writes Hoby, 'but the bewtee and majestie of it is cleane decayed. No part of it is now inhabited but onlie that which was wont to be the least part of the citie, called the iland [Ortygia].' Here, as 'the auntientist thing within the towne', Hoby admired the Duomo, whose Norman façade was to collapse during the 1693 earthquake, but whose massive Doric columns – what he calls its 'olde great pillars' – have continued to hold up the rest of the structure to the present day. Next he admired the so-called Fountain of Arethuse, from which Nelson was to water his fleet 250 years later. For Hoby, as for Milton, who never got as far as Sicily, this was the 'sacer fons' of Ovid among others, and as such was described in detail. On the mainland, most impressive among the 'sundrie ruines', was the great 'theater cutt by force of hand owt of the verie rock . . . in the toppe wherof yssuethe owt at a hole owt of the rocke a faire spring of freshe water'. The Latomie and 'Ear of Dionysius' were also described, though the latter had to wait another 50 years for Caravaggio to give it its picturesque name [Fig. 2].

After three days' sightseeing in Syracuse, Hoby was waiting for a boat to take him on to Malta, when:

> ther arrived sodainlie in a night the galies of Malta, upon the whiche I

met with an Englishman called Richard Lucas a gonner . . . who persuaded me to goo back again to Messina with them by seea, saing I shuld find nothing at Malta worth the sight, withowt it were the knigts there.

Agreeing that Malta's main tourist attraction might indeed be the Knights of St John, Hoby boarded Lucas's galley and joined the fleet – on its way to meet up with Andrea Doria in his attack on Tunis – as far as Messina. Before entering the port, the slaves had to row vigorously in order to pass the treacherous whirlpool of Charybdis. Having then taken another ship for Naples, Hoby:

> cam by the other jeapardous place called in times past Scylla, which is nothing elles but a great rocke that leaneth owt into the seea on the side of Calabria, against the which the salt water, driven by the violence of the windes, reboundeth backe again with great force, not without the hasard oftentimes of manie vessells.

Hoby finally reached Naples, via the islands of Lipari, Vulcano, Panarea and Stromboli, on 25 March 1550. Back in England he began the task of translating the *Cortegiano* into English, while his travelling companion, Peter Whitehorne, with whom he had shared a room as guests of a latter-day Duchess of Malfi, prepared his almost equally influential translation of Machiavelli's *Arte of Warre*.

During the Elizabethan period Machiavelli's more controversial works, *Il Principe* and the *Discorsi*, had to be published surreptitiously in England in the original Italian, and it is interesting that John Wolfe, their publisher, selected the Spanish-dominated Sicilian capital of Palermo, which even Hoby had not visited, for his false imprint. If he assumed that no Englishman would have been able to check up on him in this period, however, he would have been mistaken, for another English gunner, Edward Webbe, galley-slave and victim of torture at the hands of both Turks and Spaniards, had not only been to Palermo himself, but had seen there and described in his *Rare and Most Wonderfull Things* (1590), a far more distinguished Englishman:

> One thing did greatly comfort me which I saw long since in Sicilia, in the citie of Palermo, a thing worthie of memorie, where the right honourable the Earle of Oxenford [Fig. 5] a famous man for Chivalrie, at what time he travailed into forraine countries, being then personally present, made there a challeng against al maner of persons whatsoever,

5 Unknown artist, *Edward de Vere, 17th Earl of Oxford*, 1575. [National Portrait Gallery, London]

& at all manner of weapons, as Turniments, Barriors with Horse and armour, to fight and combat with any whatsoever, in the defence of his Prince and countrey: for which he was verie highly commended, and yet no man durst be so hardie to encounter with him, so that al Italy over, he is acknowledged ever since for the same, the onely Chivallier and Noble man of England.

John Aubrey's explanation for the Earl of Oxford's abrupt departure for the continent in 1572 was that: 'making of his Low Obeisance to Queen Elizabeth [he] happened to let a Fart, at which he was so abashed and ashamed that he went to Travell, 7 yeares. On his return, the Queene welcomed him home and sayd, My Lord, I had forgott the Fart.' Though this unusual motive for going on a Grand Tour is otherwise undocumented, what was notorious at the time is that when the Earl returned, he was led to believe that his wife, Anne Cecil, had cuckolded him in his absence and that her daughter was therefore not his. If it were also known that he had visited Sicily, this must surely have been in Robert Greene's mind when, in 1588, he published his popular novella *Pandosto*. This story of a falsely accused queen obliged to abandon her daughter, who is then brought up by shepherds in Sicily, in turn inspired Greene's younger collaborator and rival, that 'upstart crow' William Shakespeare, to write *The Winter's Tale*, which is also partly set in Sicily.

In a similar genre to Webbe's true-adventure story, first published in 1590, was that of another English galley-slave: *A True Relation of the Travailes and most miserable Captivitie of William Davies, Barber–Surgion of London, under the Duke of Florence*. Like Webbe, Davies had called in at Palermo and perhaps also ascended the hill to Monreale:

> At this Citie I have beene very often in the time of my slaverie in the Dukes Gallies, also, neere this Citie there is a monasterie wherein they affirme, that the Pillar of Salt that Lots Wife was turned into, comming out of Sodome is. They professe the Romish Religion through out this Iland both Men and Women, speakng the Italian tongue generally . . . and are called Sicilianes. Mercina being another famous Citie, lyeth close upon the Sea, and is scituated upon high ground, under the foote of a great Mountayne. This City is strongly fortified and planted with Ordnance: also there is a great store of Gallies and shipping belonging to this place, which doth much offend the Turke, but chefely they are employed in Marchandize.

Unfortunately, the last but most distinguished Englishman to be made a galley-slave, this time by the Sicilians themselves, did not have time to write his autobiography. Thanks to an unscrupulous step-mother, Francis Verney was effectively disinherited in the early years of the seventeenth century and, despite being knighted by James I in 1604, became so incensed at his failure to reacquire his estates on coming of age that he left England and his family for ever to earn his living as a mercenary. Failing to make his fortune in this capacity, he 'turned *Turke* in *Tunnis*' and became a notorious pirate, to the extent that when he was captured by the Sicilian galleys, the British government did not protest at his reduction to the status of slave, as it had done a few years earlier when the captain and crew of a British merchant ship were caught in a relatively petty act of piracy and imprisoned in Palermo. Verney's pathetic end is vividly recorded by William Lithgow [Fig. 6], writing of his second (1615) visit to the island:

> Here in *Messina* I found the (sometimes) great English Gallant Sr. *Frances Verny* lying sick in a Hospitall [the same in which Cervantes had lain after Lepanto], whom six weekes before I had met in *Palermo* . . . here in the extreamest calamity of extreame miseries [he] contracted Death: whose dead corps I charitably interred in the best manner time could affoord me strength, bewailing sorrowfully the miserable mutability of Fortune, who from so great a birth, had given him so meane a Buriall; and truely so may I say, *Sic transit gloria mundi.*

Despite the sympathetic rhetoric, if Verney had possessed any spare cash at the time of his death, the far from scrupulous, hyperactive eccentric, Lithgow, would probably have pocketed it himself, if we may judge from other anecdotes quite unselfconsciously recorded in his *Most delectable, and True Discourse, of an admired and painefull peregrination from Scotland, to the most famous Kingdomes in Europe, Asia and Affricke.* First published in 1614 and several times revised and reprinted, this book, like its near contemporary *Coryat's Crudities*, is misleadingly jocular in tone. Just as Coryate's often comic travelogue turns out on close reading to contain some of the best early descriptions of architecture in the English language, so Lithgow's often crude and bombastic prose provides us with our first useful accounts of social and economic conditions in, among other places, early modern Sicily:

> The most of the Townes and Villages within land, are builded on the highest hills and greatest heights in the Countrie; the reason is two-fold; first it serveth them for strength, and a great defence in time of cursarary invasions. . . . The second is, because their dwellings being farre above the parching Plaines, these situations are good preservative for their health, whereon they have a sweet and cooling ayre, which in such a hot climat, is the soveraigne salve to prevent sicknesse.

Loe here's mine Effigie, *and* Turkiſh ſuite ;
My Staffe, *my* Shaſſe, *as I did* Aſia *foote* :
'Plac'd in *old* Ilium'; P riam s *Scepter thralles*:
The Grecian *Campe deſign'd ; loſt* Dardan *falles*
Gird'd with ſmall Simois : Idaes *tops, a Gate*;
Two fatall Tombes, *an* Eagle, ſackt Troyes *State.*

6 William Lithgow from *The Total Discourse of the Rare Adventures & Painefull Peregrinations*
(London, 1632).

The Villages be farre distant, some sixe, ten, fifteene, twenty miles one
from another; in all which grounds there is no sequestrate house,
unlesse (being a high way) it be a Fundaco or Inne. About the sides of
the hills whereon their Townes stand, grow all their Wines, and on the
Plaines, nothing but red Wheat, which for goodnesse is unparalelled,
and the best bread and abundance of it in the world is here. . .

Interestingly, Lithgow was struck by the fact that, though he had
'thrice traversed the middle parts [of Sicily] from Sea to Sea, [he]

never saw any of that selfe Nation, to begge bread, or seeke almes; so great is the beatitude of their plenty'. He was no less impressed by the prosperity of the urban environment, as for example, when he describes Palermo in the 1632 edition of his book: 'It is a spacious City, and well Watered with delicate Fountaynes, having goodly buildings, and large streetes, whereof Strado reale is principall, beeing a mile long. In which I have seene in an evening march along for Recreation above 60 Coaches.'

On his second visit to Sicily, Lithgow noticed that the seventeenth-century version of the Mafia had been all but eliminated by methods equivalent to those exploited by Mussolini and Cesare Mori with similar success in the late 1920s.

> This Countrey was ever sore oppressed with Rebells and Bandits, until such time that the military Duke of Sona [Osuna], came to rule as Vice-roy, Anno 1611. Where in the first yeare he brought in five hundred, some whereof were hanged, some pardoned, and some committed to the Gallies: so that within two yeares of his foure yeares government, there was no Bandit left at random in all Sicilia.

An arranged marriage which went wrong may have encouraged the son of the Archbishop of York, George Sandys, to leave England in 1610. Like Verney and Lithgow, he headed first for the Holy Land on what may still be defined as a pilgrimage, albeit a scholarly and a respectably Protestant one. If Lithgow's *True Discourse* achieved popular success for its sensationalist and anecdotal style, Sandys' *Relation of a Journey* must surely have appealed above all for its measured classical learning, exploited even when describing tunny fishing near Messina. A not unrelated quality, also to be found in Sandys' travelogue but not in Lithgow's, is its proto-Romantic poeticism, our first glimpse of the great translation in rhyming couplets of Ovid's *Metamorphoses* which he eventually completed in America. All the relevant authors are not merely cited *in situ* but quoted at length alongside excellent parallel text translations. His *Aeneid*-based commentary on that 'so-chanted Fountain of Arethusa' would surely have encouraged Milton's unfulfilled wish to visit Sicily in the 1630s.

The accounts of Lithgow and Sandys thus complement each other; on the subject of Etna, for example, though Sandys' catalogue of classical references satisfies one side of our curiosity, Lithgow's almost Baconian empiricism completes the picture. Characteristically, he is unique among these early travellers in having taken the trouble to 'view the Mountayne more strictly. Ascending on the East and Passable part, with tedious toyle, and curious climbing . . .' until he felt his feet getting hot but could honestly report that he had seen the 'upmost Fornace, that Empedocles the Phylospher cast himself in, to be reputed for a god'. Sandys plays safe, merely quoting Lucretius on the fate of Empedocles instead. He is not unobservant, however, as his account of Messina reveals, confirming Lithgow's view of Sicilian prosperity:

> Here they live in all abundance and delicacy, having more then enough of Food, and Fruits of all kinds; excellent Wines, and Snow in the Summer [from Etna] to qualifie the heat thereof, at a contemptible rate. The better sort are Spanish in attire; and the meanest artificers wife is clothed in silk.

Unfortunately, a city bank was necessary in which to deposit money because 'they dare not venture to keep it in their houses, so ordinarily broken open by Thieves (as are the shops and warehouses) for all their cross-bar'd Windows, Iron Doors, Locks, Bolts, and Bars on the in-side . . .' This was the negative side of prosperous life in what nevertheless struck Sandys as an extremely sophisticated and attractive society. Judging by the Messinese setting of Shakespeare's *Much Ado about Nothing*, this was an impression which even untravelled Jacobeans received. There were compensations for the security-conscious citizens, however, including then, as now, the long evening promenade, providing ample opportunity 'per far'una bella figura':

> Every evening they solace themselves along the Marine (a place left throughout between the City wall and the haven) the men on horseback, and the women in large Carosses, being drawn with the slowest procession. There is to be seen the pride and beauties of the City. There have they their Playhouses, where the parts of women are acted by women, and too naturally passionate; which they forbear not to frequent upon Sundays.

By the mid-seventeenth century, however, Messina was showing signs of economic decline. In March 1634, Bullen Reymes [Fig. 7], who with Wat Montagu, Lord Carnarvon and three other Englishmen lodged 'dans la maison de Mr Garroway', described Messina's port as one of the best he had ever seen. He considered the area

7 Samuel van Hoogstraten (attrib.), *Colonel Bullen Reymes*, c.1666. [Private collection; photo E. Chaney]

immediately around the harbour, with its fountains and bronze statue of Philip IV, 'fort belle' but noted ominously that the rest of the city's streets were very ugly (MS in author's possession). Robert Bargrave, son of the Dean of Canterbury, called in at the 'Regall City' of Palermo on his way to Constantinople in 1646, but acknowledged in his manuscript journal that 'ye Greatest Mart is Messina, wherein there is very great trade driven by ye English & other Nations' (Bodleian Library, Rawlinson MS C. 799). He considered it 'a durty toune', however, 'despicable as to itselfe, were it not for ye front of it, which affords a faire (though a false) prospect'. Syracuse he described as 'famous formerly for many Galantries, but now only for wine, & for some old Ruins of Antiquity, & remarkable Caverns under Ground'. Returning from a journey to Spain in March 1655, Bargrave revisited Messina. Only after he had been subjected to 'a strict search over all parts of our Bodies yt were suspicious, if we had any Plague-Sores, or tokens from the Spanish Ladies' could he and his travelling companions obtain permission to disembark and thus 'have the pleasant freedom of walking in a very delicat Garden a mile distant from ye Toune call'd from its curiositie: il Paradiso'. The fascinating drawings done by the Dutch artist and bear-leader, Willem Schellinks, in the mid-1660s (and published in 1983) testify to Messina's decline. By the mid-nineteenth century, Messina was, according to Edward Lear, 'dirtyissimo'.

The now forgotten Catholic poet and physician, James Gibbes, spent many years in Italy, where he acquired a reputation as the 'Horace of this age', eventually being appointed Poet Laureate by the Emperor Leopold (see below, pp. 227-30). In February 1659 he set off from Rome for Naples in the company of William Cavendish, future Duke of Devonshire and builder of Chatsworth, and Dryden's friend, Lord Roscommon. Though he seems to have liked Naples enough to stay there for several years, when he spent a few months in Sicily in 1661 he wrote to a friend that his only pleasure there was 'the remembrance of our beloved Italy'. Messina, in particular, must have declined dramatically since Sandys and Lithgow had described it half a century earlier:

> For although it is the stateliest situation, I think in the whole world, yet it is very nasty, smells intolerably bad, and looks as if it was but a half-built town, fit only for the inhabitants, whose language, with their manners, consists one half of heathen Greek, and the other half of

barbarous Spanish, somewhat Italianised . . . learning or the polite arts have scarce ever been heard of.

Within a few months of Gibbes writing this letter, as if responding to the latter criticism, the University of Messina appointed the great Bolognese physiologist and discoverer of capillary circulation, Marcello Malpighi, Professor Primarius for four years at a salary of 1000 scudi. When the great naturalist John Ray visited Malpighi's native Bologna in 1663, and then published a complete list of the University staff in his *Observations, Topographical, Moral, & Physiological*, he noted that Malpighi was on an extended sabbatical. It is disappointing therefore that when Ray arrived in Messina in the spring of the following year, neither he nor his friend Philip Skippon, who wrote a livelier account of their journey, seem to have made any attempt to meet the great Italian who eventually joined them as a Fellow of the Royal Society. Otherwise the accounts of Ray and Skippon of their Sicilian experiences far outdo those of Lithgow and Sandys in their scientific scrupulousness. Unlike Lithgow, who climbed Etna from lava-built Randazzo, Ray and Skippon attempted the ascent from Catania on 20 May 1664, but reached only as far as 'the conservatories of snow'. 'Seeing the mountain above us all covered with snow, we did not, nor indeed could we ascend any higher.' They fully compensated for this, however, by recording for the first time the plant life on the upper slopes of the volcano. 'At the highest village upon Mount Etna', Ray found 'stalks of a tall prickling thistle' and, nearby, '*Tragacantha* C.B. Towards the top of the Mountain we observed *Barberry-trees* growing plentifully, which we found no where else in *Italy* or *Sicily*.'

Six years later, in May 1669, Heneage Finch, second Earl of Winchelsea, returning home after almost a decade as British Ambassador in Constantinople, witnessed the destruction of the natural landscape and much else on the Catania side of Etna. He saw 'a River of Fire' flood down from the volcano, 'of a terrible fiery or red colour and stones of paper Red to swim thereon . . . some as big as an ordinary Table'. Enclosing a sketch which was immediately published together with his account, he reported to Charles II that in 40 days the eruption 'destroyed the inhabitations of 27 thousand persons, made two Hills of one . . . one [of] four miles in compass'. The frequent reprinting of Winchelsea's pamphlet may have encouraged John Dennis to include volcanoes in *The Grounds of*

Criticism of 1704 among prodigies such as witches, monsters, lions and tigers which inspired 'Sublime' emotion. Thenceforth volcanoes in general and Etna in particular were to become standard features of the vast eighteenth-century literature on 'the Sublime and the Beautiful'.

Where Sandys had described tunny fishing with reference to classical precedent, Ray describes 'the Manner of taking Tortoises' (that is, turtles) and swordfish in more mundanely technical terms. Ellis Veryard, whose *Account of Divers Choice Remarks* describes a world tour begun in 1682, though it was not published until 1701, had clearly read Ray's description of swordfishing but improves upon it by adopting an anthropological approach to the fishermen he observes. One way of taking the fish, he writes:

> . . . is by certain Huers, who discovering the Fish from the Clifts on the Sea side, advertize the Boatmen who are at Sea, and by certain Signs and Gestures guide them to the place, which is much like our Pilchard-fishing in the West of England. In the Seasons when the Fish keep so far from the shoare that the Huers cannot be serviceable, they draw them to the Boat's side by the following Song, which is sung by the whole Crew, but understood by none. I have been at Sea with them, and taken it verbatim.

Veryard then prints in full the Sicilian dialect fishermen's song and describes its devastating effect on the fish.

Thanks to his father's fame, John Dryden Junior received superior hospitality when he arrived in Messina in November 1700. He stayed there with the British Consul, Thomas Chamberlain, who in turn recommended him to the Baron Camulio in Syracuse. Here, despite being 'bit and tormented with a sort of stinging fly, with which Syracuse abounds', Dryden managed to complete a thorough survey of the city accompanied by Camulio's brother-in-law and fellow senator, the young Baron Carcaccia. He described the Fountain of Arethusa as 'foul':

> 'tis become the resort of all the laundresses, who, standing up to their knees in the water, beat and wring all their foul linen in this poetical fountain, which certainly were Ovid alive to see, it wou'd greive him to the very heart.

A Catholic like his father (his brother was a priest), Dryden included an unusually detailed account of Santa Lucia, the recently rebuilt Norman church dedicated to the patron saint of Syracuse, who was martyred in 304. He also visited the adjacent Chapel of San Sepolcro, though he does not mention the dramatically sinister painting of *The Burial of St Lucy*, which the artist in exile, Caravaggio, had painted for it a century earlier. Dryden next moved on to the early Christian Catacombs of San Giovanni which, on discovering 'very good antient Greek characters engraven in the walls', he concluded must have been pre-Roman. He seemed unaware of the existence of the genuinely Greek theatre but did visit the Roman amphitheatre, complaining that it was overgrown with bushes and briars and far smaller than the Colosseum. At Palermo, it was the wealthy English merchant, Mr William Gifford, son of the former consul, who played host to Dryden and his friends. This city is described far more favourably than Syracuse, though the catacombs of the Capuccini evidently surprised Dryden as much as they tend to shock the visitor today [Fig. 8]. In January 1701, he and his friends already found there:

> abundance of Cappuchins standing in a row one by another against the wall, seemingly in a devout posture; when coming near to them, we found they were so many dead men, all dry'd up, but with all the flesh

8 Corpses in Capuccini catacombs of Palermo [E. Chaney]

and skin on their hands and faces entire, nor were the nerves rotted
. . . notwithstanding the bodys are all cloath'd in Cappuchins habits, yet
an abundance of them had been laymen and persons of the best quality
in Palermo . . . many of an hundred years standing . . . were as entire
as the newest, and you might handle their faces and hands without
damageing them.

Evelyn Waugh was to respond more facetiously 250 years later,
ordering his garrulous Franciscan guide to 'shut up' so he could con-
centrate on what he described as the 'delicious' perfume emanating
from the desiccated corpses.

If the whole of Dryden's manuscript genuinely dates from the first
years of the eighteenth century (it was not published until 1776), it
deserves wider recognition as a key document in the history of taste.
His feeling for natural landscape was vividly expressed when he
'rowed quite round the island [of Capri] whose high rocks make a
terrible, yet pleasing prospect'. On discovering a 'Dark Grotto' which
sounds remarkably like the now famous 'Blue' one, he enthused:
'this cavern looks so romantique, that we cou'd not but fancy it
belong'd to some sea god, as his court or palace.' No less remarkable was his ability to appreciate art and architecture that was
neither 'modern' nor classical. Thus he praised Monreale not just for
its view – 'the best prospect of any valley I ever saw in my life' –
but for its 'venerable and majestick' Norman cathedral. In defining
its style without a hint of prejudice as 'of Gothick architecture', he
seems an aesthetic survivor rather than pioneering reviver. In
describing its magnificent mosaics (which few other travellers
mention), however, his judicious historicism makes one wonder:

The mosaic work on the walls on high is well done for those times
they were done in, and deserves observation, as it contains the whole
history of Genesis . . . A little higher . . . you may turn into a very fine
and neat chappel [the baroque *Cappella del Crocifisso*], built by the
present Archbishop, who has erected a noble monument in it for himself. The gilt ironwork of the doores, I think, was made in England; and
I am sure the lock and keys were English, and, as Mr William Coldgrave
told us, a present which Mr Gifford had made to the Archbishop.

Even more anthropological in tone than Veryard's *Account* were
the journals of the great Anglo–Irish philosopher, George Berkeley,
who travelled twice to Italy, both times primarily in order to visit

Sicily, to which he was no doubt attracted as a result of his extensive reading in Greek and Roman literature [Fig. 9]. On 15 October 1713 he wrote to his friend and patron, Sir John Percival, that he was 'on the point of going to Sicily where I propose to see the new King's coronation'. He continued: 'I go Chaplain to my Lord Peter-

9 John Smibert, *George Berkeley*, probably painted in Italy, *c.*1720. [Ex collection Mrs Maurice Berkeley, Glos. – photo Prof. David Berman]

borough who is the ambassador extraordinary sent thither on this occasion. . . There is not any place that I have a greater curiosity to see than Sicily.'

Unfortunately, on this occasion, Berkeley only got as far as Tuscany when plans were changed and the ambassador had to travel ahead incognito and without him. Berkeley did not abandon his plans, however, and though he had to return home in the spring of 1714, by the autumn of 1716 he had found another form of employment which would enable him to see Rome, southern Italy and Sicily, this time as travelling tutor to the son of the Bishop of Clogher. Thomas Coke, the future Earl of Leicester and builder of Holkham, had visited Sicily earlier in the year, but although he purchased several topographical and historical books on the island, he had restricted his sightseeing to the major cities. Had Berkeley been his bear-leader, he would have seen considerably more. By late January 1717, the great philosopher had completed a rigorous inspection of the sights of Rome. He then dragged his delicate pupil further south to Naples, across the peninsula to Puglia, down into the heel as far as Lecce and back up to Naples again. He was meanwhile taking detailed notes and writing more polished letters back to friends in England. Together, these provide us with a record of the most extensive and most intelligently observed Italian tour of the period. It is thus particularly unfortunate that the notebook documenting the four or five months he spent in Sicily after he arrived there in late 1717 was lost overboard on the journey back to Naples.

From scattered hints, however, and his occasional references to Sicily later in life, we can deduce something of Berkeley's movements and priorities while on the island. He had already demonstrated a sophisticated knowledge of art and architecture in his detailed notes on Rome. He developed this in Puglia where, for all his bias in favour of the classical, he was able to appreciate the southern Baroque, eulogizing Lecce in particular as 'the most beautiful city in Italy'. Here he also outdid Veryard in his anthropological approach, assiduously tracking down the tarantula and the malady and curative dances associated with the spider whose bite supposedly produced pathological disorders, constantly testing superstition and hypothesis against first-hand observation. But above all, despite the scattered nature of the evidence, Berkeley's long winter sojourn in Sicily should be recognized for its pioneering appreciation of Greek Doric architecture. By July 1718 Berkeley was looking forward to returning home so that he could help Percival design the house he was intending to build the following winter:

> for you must know I pretend to an uncommon skill in architecture . . . This gusto of mine is formed on the remains of antiquity that I have met with in my travels, particularly in Sicily, which convince me that the old Romans were inferior to the Greeks, and that the moderns fall infinitely short of both in the grandeur and simplicity of taste.

Berkeley would certainly have sought out the classical remains in and around Syracuse and Taormina, which were already part of the tourist's Sicilian itinerary. It is clear, however, that he also visited Agrigento in order to see the now famous 'Valley of the Temples' [Fig. 11]. Writing on the subject of petrifaction to his friend Thomas Prior some 20 years later, Berkeley observed that 'the air is in many places impregnated with . . . salts' and recalled that 'I have seen at Agrigentum in Sicily the pillars of stone in an ancient temple corroded and consumed by the air, while the shells which entered into the composition of the stone remained intire and untouched.' Read in conjunction with what he had written to Percival in 1718, this isolated reference reveals Berkeley as the first person known to have inspected a Doric temple in that neoclassical spirit which was to dominate European taste in the second half of the eighteenth century (for this and his probable Virgil-inspired visit to Selinunte, see below, p. 358, n. 46).

In the same letter to Prior, Berkeley also recalled having seen 'Sciara' or volcanic rock 'hewed and employed at Catania and other places adjacent'. In the winter of 1717, this 'ponderous, hard, grey stone, used for the most part in the basements and coinage of buildings', was still being extensively exploited in the massive rebuilding programme which had been launched in the wake of the great earthquake of 1693 when Catania was almost entirely destroyed. In 1750 Berkeley published an article 'On Earthquakes' in the *Gentleman's Magazine*, in which he paraphrased an eyewitness account of this disaster by Count Tezzani who had been 'dug out of the ruins of his own house':

> . . . some hours [before the earthquake] he observed a line in the air . . . [and] heard a hollow frightful murmur about a minute before the shock. Of 25,000 inhabitants 18,000 absolutely perished, not to mention others who were miserably bruised and wounded. There did not

escape so much as one single house. The streets were narrow and the buildings high, so there was no safety in running into the streets.

Although the Count rebuilt his house in stone, Berkeley reports, 'yet he ever after lay in a small adjoyning apartment made of reeds plastered over'. 'Catanea was rebuilt more regular and beautiful than ever. The houses indeed are lower, and the streets broader than before, for security against future shock.'

John Breval was slightly older than Berkeley but visited Sicily for the first time in the spring of 1725, seven years after him. He had probably heard about Berkeley's expedition and the great philosopher's novel enthusiasm for the Greek antiquities, if only through mutual acquaintance with Percival, who was tutored by Dr Breval senior at Westminster. A former Fellow of Trinity College, Cambridge, expelled for cudgelling the husband of a woman with whom he was having an affair, Breval left England in about 1710 to seek his fortune, first as a soldier and eventually as a freelance writer of controversial poems and plays and well-illustrated travel books. In the 1720s he worked as a travelling tutor, fraternised with the Jacobites in Rome and married a Milanese nun 'of great beauty'. It is in the second set of his two-volume *Remarks on Several Parts of Europe*, which appeared in the year of his death in 1738, that we find not merely the first detailed English account of the Greek and Roman remains in Sicily, but the first engravings of them ever published. That Breval was conscious of his originality in this respect is apparent from his preface:

> SICILY is a Ground very few *Englishmen* have trod before me as *Observers*; and tho' I am far from pretending to the Learning and Merit of some now living, who have made that *Tour* [and here he may have been thinking of Berkeley], yet, I hope, my Account of that Island . . . will not send the Curious away unsatisfy'd. The Views of the Temples, and other principal Ruins, are just as I found them.

Reminiscent of Addison (and anticipating Gibbon), Breval was scornful of what he called the 'Mists of the Monkish Ignorance', rejoiced in the fact that England now had 'a dozen Arundels at least for one she had a Century ago', and boasted of travelling Sicily 'in Company with all the Antients, as well as Moderns, that have left any thing memorable concerning it'.

His classically oriented itinerary involved a complete circum-

10 The remains of the Graeco-Roman Theatre at Taormina, Sicily; from John Breval, *Remarks* (London, 1738), vol. 1, p. 9. Copper engraving by Pierre Fourdrinier. [E. Chaney]

navigation of the island, starting in Messina. Calling first at Taormina, Breval stayed overnight in the port:

> We took Horse to the Town itself next Morning, where upon a very steep and rugged Eminence we met with some Vestiges of the Greatness of the *Tauromenians*, a People who made no small Figure among the *Greek* Colonies in Sicily. These consist in a *Theater* of Brick (still pretty entire, all but the *Corridor* which faces to the Southward) in a *Reservoir* of Water; and some Tracks of a *Naumachia*, that was supply'd by it [Fig. 10].

As he had 'so often heard and read of the total Subversion of Catanea in the general Calamity of 1693, I was not a little surpriz'd, on my Arrival there, to find it not only repeopled, but rebuilt also in that pretty and regular Manner that it is'. After an interesting account of the few classical structures to have survived the earthquake and interviews with eyewitnesses similar to those which Berkeley had conducted, Breval and his companions sailed across the

gulf to Augusta where they spent the night in what is now the
largest oil port in Italy. The next morning they visited Megara
Hyblaea, finding 'large Plantations of Sugar' where today the oil
refineries have created one of the most polluted coastlines in the
world. They arrived that evening at what Breval calls 'the miserable
Remains of antient *Syracusa*', where he indulged his curiosity for
almost a week, 'meeting with great Hospitality at the Hands of the
Governor', General Diespach. 'Among the numberless Accounts . . .
of this City's former Splendour', he recommends above all that to be
found in Cicero's *Orations against Verres* but refers also to
Thucydides, Theocritus, Livy, Plutarch, Fazello and Clüver. On the
basis of Cicero's description of the Fountain of Arethusa, with its
'strong marble barriers' built to protect the city from flooding, Breval
doubts the authenticity of the present one, which, he says, 'might
be taken rather for a Puddle than a Fountain so far is it from
coming up to that noble Description'. He is more respectful towards
the massive Temple of Athene which forms the basic structure of the
Duomo:

> The fatal Earthquake of 1693 threw down the Portico [it is usually
> thought that only the Norman west front collapsed] and the Fragments
> of it still lie scatter'd upon the Ground; I measured the Diameter of one
> of the Pillars full six *English* Foot: There are about four and twenty
> others still in their upright [sic] that support the modern Roof of the
> *Church*, but are half bury'd in the new Side Walls.

The standard survey of the Greek Revival begins in 1760, while
as recently as 1979, Arnaldo Momigliano wrote that the temples of
Paestum, which were discovered in the mid-eighteenth century,
'gave the first taste of pure Doric style'. It is clear, however, that
Berkeley and Breval had developed a taste for this style two and a
half decades earlier. The latter describes the columns of the Temple
of Athene as '*Doric*, (an Order common to most of the old Buildings
in *Sicily*; their first *Greek* Colonies having come from *Doris*) with
Flutings and some *Triglyphs* still visible; about one-third of the Height
is under Ground'. He was informed by 'the Fathers who officiate
here' that 'some very beautiful Fragments . . . were carry'd off
privately from hence by King *Victor Amadeus*', presumably between
1713, when, with English help, the former Duke of Savoy became
King of Sicily, and 1720, when the treaties of London and The
Hague obliged him to hand over his kingdom to the Habsburg

Emperor Charles. It is interesting to read Breval, three years before Andrea Palma began his monumental Baroque façade, quoting these same Fathers as saying that 'before the Earthquake a round Hole was yet to be seen in the Facade of this old Building which was suposed to have been contrived by Archimedes to shew when the Sun was in the Equinox'.

After inspecting the 'house' (probably the tomb) of Archimedes on the mainland, as well as the nearby Latomiae [Fig. 2] and Ear of Dionysius, Breval set out in search of more examples of Doric architecture. He returned to his felucca and sailed round the south-eastern corner of Sicily via Avola, failing to comment on the post-1693 hexagonal town plan, and Licata, which he wrongly argues was the site of ancient Gela, finally arriving at the port of Girgenti, now Agrigento. Here, his sense of discovery must have been some-what diminished by finding 'English Vessels in abundance loading Corn', and 'a Priest who had been apprized of our coming [who] met us very obligingly with Horses'. Breval and his travelling companions took a brief 'Survey' of the 'new city' up on Monte Camico, before descending into the old one, 'but scarce met with any thing Remark-worthy, except the Battesimo or Font in the Choir of their Cathedral':

> It is a noble *Greek Sarcophagus*, carved on all the four Sides with Bas-Relievos of a fine Taste, from which it appears that the Ashes contained in it belong'd to some Huntsman of Quality, slain in the Pursuit of a wild Boar. At first sight I mistook it for the Story of *Meleager*, which is so obvious upon *Greek* or *Roman* Monuments of this kind; but upon a strict Survey found the Circumstances differ'd in many Respects. (I, p. 32)

They were so impressed with this sarcophagus, now on display in the thirteenth-century church of San Nicola, that they 'employ'd a Painter of the Town to make a Draught of it, which was sent after us to *Rome*, but lost by the Way'. The fame of the sarcophagus was much enhanced by its lavish illustration in Giuseppe Pancrazzi's *Antichità Siciliane* of 1751, most of whose etched plates, including those of the temples of Agrigento, were prominently dedicated to British Grand Tourists who visited Naples around 1750. Enthused over by almost all subsequent travellers from Brydone to Bernard Berenson, who judged it 'poor in execution but excellent as composition', the Sarcophagus of Phaedra is now thought to be

Roman and no earlier than the second century AD. Goethe, who was one of the first to recognize the huntsman as Hippolytus, also observed that it was thanks to having been 'converted into an altar' that the sarcophagus was in such a good state of preservation. Less tolerantly, Breval concluded his account by commenting on the 'scandalous impropriety' of the 'Christians of former Ages, when they bury'd their Dead in these antient *Sarcophagi*'. From the 'new' city, the travellers now 'took Horse . . . to the Platform of the old Agrigentum, (which may be twelve or thirteen Miles in Circumference) under the Conduct of two or three well arm'd Banditti, (a Caution which we understood was necessary)'.

Given the loss of Berkeley's Sicilian notebooks, Breval's detailed if inevitably somewhat incoherent survey of the ruins of Agrigento is one of the earliest in English and certainly the first to be published. The only earlier traveller's account I know was first published in 1987 and described by its editors as anonymous. In fact, this remarkable 1647-9 travelogue is clearly that of the Royalist clergyman in exile, Isaac Basire, and his pupils (see below, p. 87, n. 2). This describes Agrigento's 'ruines of the so famous castell [the Temple of Zeus], built upon the shouldiers of 3 gyants of stones, of an incredable bignes' and 'the Temple of Concord, a brave piece of antiquity as is in Sicily: it hath 36 pillars' [Fig. 11]. To judge from the impressive list of subscribers which prefaces Breval's book, it must have been extremely influential, not least for its engravings of the so-called Temple of Concord:

> as in the *Dome* of *Syracusa*, the Doric Pillars appear in their primitive Simplicity, (the Flutings only excepted) for they have neither Base nor Plinth . . . The Number of them is thirteen by six; they consist of four Cylinders each, have a little Swelling in the Middle, and a proportionable Diminution at the Top. There was not the least appearance of Cement in any Part these Building. (I, p. 34)

On the Temple of Zeus, Breval was less impressive, finding no other reason for its being called the *Castello de Tre Giganti* 'but only because these Ruins lie in three distinct Heaps'.

After a further four hours sailing west along the southern coast of Sicily, Breval next visited and described Selinunte. Like Basire, he notes that the ruins were clearly visible to passing ships: 'They cover, as near as I could guess, between fifty and sixty Acres of Ground . . . and (the Bulk of the Stones which compose them con-

11 The Temple of Concord, Agrigento, Sicily; from John Breval, *Remarks* (London, 1738)
vol I, p. 34. Copper engraving by Pierre Fourdrinier. [E. Chaney]

sider'd) are what I believe one shall scarce meet with in any other
Part of Europe.'

He measured the broken columns, thereby guessing at the vast
height of the temples, and concluded his account with a eulogy of
the ancients, remarkably reminiscent of what Berkeley had written
regarding the formation of his architectural taste:

I had seen no Ruin in any Part of my Travels that could furnish an Artist
in that Stile (such as *Panini* may be now, or *Viviano* was formerly) with
more sublime or Pinturesque Ideas [*sic*], especially if he took them in
such a point of View as would inclose a little Portion of the adjoining
Sea. The Cylinders had been join'd, I observ'd, at the Center by huge
Bars of Iron . . . but otherwise uncemented . . . The Proportion of some
few of these was rather *Tuscan* than *Doric* . . . The Ruins of [Selinunte's]
amazing Temples, and other publick Structures, have not their Equal, in
all likelihood, in our Age, on this Side *Palmyra* or *Egypt*, and are a
Demonstration beyond any other that *Europe* affords, how far the
Antients exceeded the Moderns, not only in a great Taste of Archi-

tecture, but likewise in their Skill in Mechanicks, by raising to such an Height such unwieldly and ponderous Bodies.

Via Marsala and Trápani, Breval proceeded 'directly for Palermo, the Wind setting in so strong from the Levant, that it was impossible for us to turn (as we fain would have done) into the Gulf of Castella Mare, there to see the fine Doric Temple of old Segesta which is esteem'd the best preserv'd Antiquity in the Island'.

Published in 1738, Breval's *Remarks* set a high standard for the rest of the eighteenth century and a good deal of the nineteenth. Their originality was inadequately acknowledged, however, by those who wanted to appear to have discovered Sicily for themselves. There can be little doubt, for example, that the 20-year-old John Montagu, 4th Earl of Sandwich, who started out on an extended Mediterranean cruise a few weeks after the first appearance of Breval's illustrated volumes, knew them well. At Syracuse he refers to the Duomo in strikingly similar terms to those used by Breval. Breval's enthusiasm for the Doric was clearly lost on Lord Sandwich, however, for he dismisses this and the nearby Temple of Diana as 'neither of them any otherwise remarkable than for their antiquity, being of but ordinary workmanship and appearing to have been built in an age when architecture was in no great perfection'. In his famous 1759 book on the temples of Agrigento, Winckelmann had to acknowledge his use of the Scots architect Robert Mylne's 1757 notes and drawings of 'The Antiquities of Sicily', as it was well known he had never been there himself. Mylne, on the other hand, whose Breval-like appreciation of both the architectural taste and the mechanical skills of the ancients won him the commission to build Blackfriars Bridge on his return to Britain, was less forthcoming about his source.

'Had there been any book in our language on the subject of the following Letters', boasts the misleading 'Advertisement' which prefaces the most widely-read of all eighteenth-century travelogues, Patrick Brydone's *Tour through Sicily and Malta*, 'they would never have been published.' There is no denying that Brydone's book is considerably more entertaining than Breval's, however, and in many instances more informative. On Agrigento, for example, he manages to expand Breval's account partly by re-reading one of the latter's primary sources, Fazello's remarkable *De rebus Siculis*. It is worth recalling, while on the subject of the 'discovery' of Doric architecture, that the Sicilian Dominican, Tommaso Fazello, who was born in the fifteenth century, had celebrated in print 'the marvellous public temples of Agrigento', 'the three very ancient, sumptuous and magnificent temples of Selinunte' and the 'stupendous' ruins of Segesta more than a century before Northern Europeans first noticed them.

Owing to a severe storm which arose soon after his boat left Agrigento, Brydone never saw Selinunte and despite his subsequent decision to travel north to Palermo overland, like Breval he never visited Segesta either, though he must have passed within a few miles of it. In 1786, 13 years after Brydone published his book, its most famous fan, Goethe, compensated for this omission by writing one of the clearest descriptions of the temple to date, failing to visit Syracuse instead. Like Winckelmann, Goethe too drew upon the unpublished notes of an English traveller, Richard Payne Knight's *Expedition into Sicily*. Goethe's interest in the artist Jakob Philipp Hackert, who, together with the wealthy amateur Charles Gore, had accompanied Payne Knight, was such that he acquired a copy of the latter's account of their 1777 journey together and published it in German in 1811. The original manuscript remained at Weimar and was not published until 1986, when it was reunited with Gore and Hackert's exquisite watercolours.

Just as Brydone writes as if Breval had not existed, so Payne Knight was far from forthcoming about his familiarity with Brydone's book in his stuffier account. He gives himself away, however, when he quite falsely claims that 'The trifling Indiscretion of a British Travellor, in publishing part of a private conversation had like to have ruined the learned Canon Recupero of Catania, & will probably prevent his valuable Work upon Mount Aetna from ever appearing to the World.' The learned Canon Giuseppe Recupero had acted as Brydone's guide in Catania, and had told him that by counting the layers of lava and measuring the depth of earth which had formed above each layer, he had come to the conclusion that Etna was at least 14,000 years old. In typically facetious form, Brydone commented that the Catholic scholar was 'exceedingly embarrassed by these discoveries' for 'in writing the history of the mountain . . . Moses hangs like a dead weight upon him . . . really he has not the conscience to make his mountain so young, as that prophet makes the world.'

Payne Knight misleads his readers into believing that it was as a result of Brydone's indiscretion that 'The Bishop gave [Recupero] a very severe admonition, & an absolute injunction, not to mention any thing for the future, that could possibly invalidate the Authority of Moses. Thus is a Man of real learning & Genius render'd useless to the World.' In fact the bishop's admonitory reaction to Recupero's theory not only pre-dated Brydone's book but actually featured prominently in his witty account of the whole affair. As this account clearly represented the sum total of Payne Knight's knowledge of the matter, it is a measure of his irritation with the book which may have inspired him to visit Sicily in the first place that he should have attempted to discredit its author in this way. Dr Johnson's stricture that Brydone should have been 'more attentive to his Bible' is at least more straightforward.

The Catholic travel-writer, Henry Swinburne, author of the well-illustrated two-volume *Travels in the Two Sicilies* (1783–85), was only slightly more candid about his English sources. In a letter from Palermo dated 25 December 1777, he had written:

> I went to a soiree at the Prince of Patagonia's [*sic* for 'Palagonia's] country-house, where was assembled a collection of frightful women, being the principal belles of Palermo. I am sorry I left Brydone's book at Naples by mistake, for it would have amused me on the road, and I should be glad to see how far he deserves the reputation of lying that most travellers have bestowed on his work. However, he is certainly right in what he says of the scarcity of female beauty in this part of the world.

Although he presents a more sober and in some ways more comprehensive account of Sicily (based in part on his 1574 edition of Diodorus Siculus), it is evident throughout that by the time Swinburne was writing up his *Travels*, he had Brydone's 'inaccurate' book to hand. The extent of his indebtedness becomes apparent when one compares the neutral tone he had adopted a few days after visiting the Villa Palagonia with the lurid account he published of this extraordinary building seven years later. The latter is indeed little more than a paraphrase of Brydone's rich and more entertaining 1773 description. This highly original set-piece instantly established the Villa as one of the key tourist sights of Sicily, becoming familiar even to contemporaries who would never see it. When, in his youth, the great architect Sir John Soane toured Sicily with two friends, he followed Brydone precisely, merely adding Selinunte and Segesta to his itinerary, as Swinburne had done. Soane's movements in 1779 are documented by the detailed letters which one of these friends, John Patteson, sent back to his mother. To involve her more fully and save himself the trouble of copying out long descriptions, Patteson persuaded his mother to acquire a copy of Brydone's *Tour* so he could merely refer her to the relevant passages. Thus when he wrote that 'The Prince of Palagonia's Monsters are nothing more than the most extravagant caricatures in stone', he assumed that his mother would have read the following:

The amazing crowd of statues that surround his house, appear at a distance like a little army drawn up for its defence; but when you get amongst them, and every one assumes his true likeness, you imagine you have got into the regions of delusion and enchantment . . . for there is not one made to represent any one object in nature . . . [The Prince] has put the heads of men to the bodies of every sort of animal, and the heads of every other animal to the bodies of men. Sometimes he makes a compound of five or six animals that have no sort of resemblance in nature . . . it is truly unaccountable that he has not been shut up many years ago; but he is perfectly innocent, and troubles nobody by the indulgence of his frenzy; on the contrary he gives bread to a vast number of statuaries and other workmen whom he rewards in pro-portion as they can bring their imaginations to coincide with his own . . . The inside of this inchanted castle corresponds exactly with the out; it is in every respect as whimsical and fantastical . . . Some of the apart-ments are exceedingly spacious and magnificent, with vast arch'd roofs; which instead of plaister or stucco, are composed entirely of large mirrors, nicely joined together. The effect that these produce, (as each of them make a small angle with the other,) is exactly that of a multiply-ing glass, so that when three or four people are walking below, there is always the appearance of three or four hundred walking above. The whole of the doors are likewise covered over with small pieces of mirror, cut into the most ridiculous shapes and intermixed with a vast variety of chrystal and glass of different colours. All the chimney-pieces, windows, and side-boards are crouded with pyramids and pillars of tea-pots, caudle-cups, bowls, cups, saucers, &c. strongly cemented together . . . The windows of this inchanted castle are composed of a variety of glass of every different colour, mixed without any sort of order or regularity. Blue, red, yellow, purple, violet, – So that at each window, you may have the heavens and earth of whatever colour you chuse, only by looking through that pane that pleases you. The house clock is cased in the body of a statue; the eyes of the figure move with the pendulum, turning up their white and black alternately, and make a hideous appearance.

While features such as the clock with the swivelling eyes, the pillar of tea-pots, or the bed-chamber made like an apartment in Noah's Ark which Brydone goes on to describe, would no doubt have been an inspiration to the surrealists (had they looked beyond their immediate past), the Villa's more tastefully eccentric features seem to have inspired Soane as much as the Greek temples inspired his enthusiasm for 'the primitive Manner of Building'. Two copies of Brydone's book are still to be found in the library of the highly original London house he built for his old age. With this extraordinary description to help him remember the 'wonderful performances' he had admired decades earlier in the Villa Palagonia, Soane installed 'arch'd roofs', angled mirrors and coloured glass throughout his own home, purchasing the neighbouring house, altering and expanding the rooms to accommodate his ever-growing collections, and finally leaving the finished product to the nation as a museum for 'the study of Architecture and the Allied Arts'.

Soon after their first publication, both Brydone and Swinburne appeared in print in French and German, a hitherto rare compliment for an English travel book. A millennium of British travel-writing had finally evolved into something which the rest of Europe might learn from. With the rest of Italy dominated by Napoleon, the enlightened regime of Lord William Bentinck helped Sicily flourish briefly under a liberal constitution. Archaeology flourished also. The relative failure of the digs conducted by the artist, art dealer and Consul-General, Robert Fagan, was followed by the successful discovery by William Harris and Samuel Angell of the great sculptured metopes of Selinunte, which Angell published after his friend died of malaria in Palermo in 1823. An almost contemporary discovery was that of Marsala wine, to be monopolized for well over a century by trading families such as the Inghams and Whitakers. These created enormous wealth for themselves and that particular brand of Anglo-Sicilianism celebrated in *Sicily and England*, a remarkable synthesis of 'political and social reminiscences', discreetly recorded by the formidable Tina Whitaker, née Scalia, who married the great-nephew of the multi-millionaire, Benjamin Ingham, and died aged 97 in 1957.

Late eighteenth-century visitors such as Swinburne (who illustrated Palermo's La Zisa) and Cornelia Knight had already begun to
appreciate what the latter called 'the fanciful singularity of [Sicily's]
remaining Saracenic architecture'. By the 1830s Saracen and
Norman buildings were being accorded the sort of specialised attention hitherto reserved for the Greek. Henry Gally Knight's *The
Normans in Sicily* of 1838 was most remarkable in this respect,
arguing that a post-crusading combination of these styles was
responsible for the pointed arch. The owner of Stourhead, Sir
Richard Colt Hoare, had retained eighteenth-century priorities in
his *Classical Tour* of 1819, but in 1827–8 the owner of equally
picturesque Stowe, Richard, Duke of Buckingham and Chandos,
responded more eclectically in his vivid *Diary*. The Cappella Palatina
was eulogized as 'the most superb specimen of Saracenic architecture I ever saw' but he was no less enthusiastic about Baron
Pisano's extraordinarily enlightened lunatic asylum in Palermo.
Sicily soon became an almost routine part of the Grand Tour,
visited by Gladstone, J.S. Mill, Newman, the Marquis of Ormonde,
Edward Cheney (who set his novel *Malvagna* on the island) and
William Sharp (who eventually died there); Americans such as
Henry Adams, Andrew Biglow and Washington Irving; 'unprotected
females' (Emily Lowe in 1859) and Cook's tourists alike. In response
to the new demand, George Dennis finally published his still useful
Murray's Handbook for Travellers in Sicily in 1864. In the wake of
Garibaldi's 1860 liberation of the island, Dennis had had to rewrite
parts of his text, but he seems to have been equally busy excavating
at Gela and Agrigento, his wife hiding their most precious finds from
the tombs under her crinoline. In 1870 he was appointed Consul in
Palermo, and had to act as *cicerone* to distinguished visitors such as
the Duke and Duchess of Edinburgh.

By now, skilfully illustrated coffee-table books such as William
Bartlett's *Pictures from Sicily* (1853) were familiarizing those who
never visited the island with the full range of its beauties. Lord
Leighton and his architect, George Aitchison, were inspired by La
Zisa (which Bartlett had illustrated) when designing the Arab Hall
extension to Leighton House in the late 1870s. Though more
rational and reliable than their predecessors, if only because of
their comprehensiveness, the new guidebooks encouraged a more
standardized response. Exceptional individuals such as Samuel Butler
and his friend, Festing Jones, however, still managed to maintain an

unpredictable approach. Butler's belief that *The Authoress of the Odyssey* was a young woman who had lived at Trápani endeared him to Sicilians everywhere, but especially in the hilltop town of Calatafimi, where both a street and the hotel in which he wrote much of his book were named in his honour. 'Enrico' Festing Jones meanwhile became a world expert on Sicilian puppet theatre.

Sicily's heyday, so far as the British visitor is concerned, was the Edwardian era. In the wake of Douglas Sladen's 1000-page *In Sicily*, published in two massive illustrated volumes in 1901, and his more portable *Sicily: The New Winter Resort*, King Edward VII himself and cousin Kaiser Wilhelm both called in on their cruises. Edward was entertained by the Whitakers at their luxurious Villa Malfitano in Palermo in 1907. Prime Minister Asquith followed in 1912. His secretary, Edwin Montagu, future husband of Asquith's beloved Venetia Stanley (who arrived in Sicily a day or two later), entertainingly described 'the Prime's' equestrian visit to the 'Roman' temple at Segesta and their return journey to Palermo in a car whose broken spring 'had been repaired by a log of wood'. In 1908 Aubrey Waterfield, Bertrand Russell, Charles and G.M. Trevelyan (who was collecting material for his three-volume history of the Risorgimento) walked from Marsala to Palermo in Garibaldi's footsteps. Though fellow Garibaldians, Trevelyan's parents were anxious about his safety as 'the whole island was talking of Mrs Cacciola's will' in which the young historian was known to be a major beneficiary.

Indirectly the will of Signora Cacciola, née Florence Trevelyan, also benefitted Taormina, for the extensive gardens which she had acquired there and improved during the 1890s were eventually donated to the town. Another notable Edwardian garden was the Honourable Albert Stopford's, in which the Stopford rose was developed. Yet another, described by both Sladen and the *Seekers in Sicily* (two American ladies whose 1908 book of that title has as its frontispiece a photograph of two nude Sicilian men), was that belonging to Mabel Hill, a philanthropist who revived the art of lace-making in Taormina. Let in this period to the Duchess of Sutherland, but effectively open to the public, this property included the lovely Renaissance cloister of Santa Caterina, whose adjoining chapel functioned as the English church.

Despite the daunting number of respectable females and Sladen's assurance that 'nobody goes about naked, as might be imagined from the photographs', Taormina increasingly attracted male refugees from more repressive climates, several of whom found temporary accommodation, even at the luxurious 'artists' hotel', the Victoria, inadequate and decided to settle permanently. Having waxed lyrical about the 'fair daughters' whom Germany, England and America 'send over to sample the island' each spring, Norma Lorimer contrasted them with the 'German and English contingents who winter in Sicily', about whom 'there is nothing either youthful or beautiful'. In the less euphemistic words of Harold Acton [Fig. 60], Taormina had become 'a polite synonym for Sodom'. As on Capri, however, the community of exiles was characterized by a creativity which even the Great War failed to destroy. Some of the wealthier aesthetes became serious patrons of art and architecture. On an exquisite site, 260 metres above sea-level and just outside the ancient walls, the talented watercolourist, Robert Kitson, built a beautiful villa for himself, commissioning his friend, Frank Brangwyn, to decorate and furnish it. In 1907, when Kitson's Casa Cuseni was nearing completion, the elderly eccentric, Colonel Shaw-Heller, commissioned C.R. Ashbee to design the self-consciously Anglo-Sicilian Villa San Giorgio, the foundations of which provided finds which the great classical archaeologist John Beazley came to inspect in the following year. After a brief tour of the island, Ashbee wrote that: 'I doubt whether there is anywhere else in the world such a record of stupendous building contained in so small a compass as here in Sicily.'

When, soon after the First World War, via Florence and Capri, the Nottinghamshire miner's son and his German wife, D.H. and Frieda Lawrence, moved into a villa on the outskirts of Taormina, they found themselves surrounded by almost as many compatriots (including 'a parterre of English weeds') as on the island they had just left. Fascism and the Second World War, however, were more permanently destructive of these international resorts. When peace returned, the exotic exiles were replaced by tourists of the kind Lawrence Durrell accompanies in his *Sicilian Carousel*. Guiding the hilariously grumpy Evelyn Waugh around the sights, Harold Acton complained that Taormina was now 'quite as respectable as Bournemouth . . . a shop window displaying an aspidistra and a placard inscribed "Nice Cuppa Tea" in Gothic letters'.

When Bernard Berenson first visited Taormina more than a century ago, 'the only inn was a small pink house just under the

Greek theatre.' By 1904 there were already seven hotels; now it boasts more than a hundred. Returning in 1953, the 87-year-old art historian still found it difficult to leave 'this so beautiful, so comfortable, so restful place'. Not everywhere had expanded so unobtrusively, however. Despite the Sitwellian celebration of Noto, this 'fascinating town' was as sleepy as ever, but: 'What a different Syracuse from the one I knew in 1888! The town was then confined entirely to Ortygia . . . Now a vast modern city has gathered on both sides of the narrow water, spanned by a bridge so wide that it appears to be an ordinary street.' He acknowledges that the water-front, with its 'delightful terraces leading up to the papyrus-filled spring of Arethusa', was unchanged and that nothing could be 'more classical than the view, across the great harbour, of Plemyrion and the Iblean hills', but he records his elderly waiter's regret for the time when travellers 'stayed, dressed for dinner, took time to enjoy the place': 'Now they mostly come in huge buses and see the whole of Sicily in six days. "What do they see?" the old waiter asked. "They make sure the town they have heard of has not run away."'

And yet it could be argued that it is thanks to tourism that Ortygia, Cefalù and even Taormina remain relatively pleasant places. Against the nineteenth-century background of grinding poverty, crime and emigration, Mrs Alec-Tweedie's 1904 condemnation of 'officialism' for being 'too blind to make Sicily the holiday resort of Europe' was entirely convincing. Today, Sicily's great cities, Palermo, Messina and Catania, could still absorb a much expanded tourist industry with little ill-effect and considerable gains, both social and economic.

NOTE

This essay started life as an introduction to the third edition of the *Blue Guide Sicily* (ed. Alta Macadam, London and New York, 1988). It was reprinted with minor corrections in 1990 but omitted from the fourth edition in 1993. The quotation with which I begin this revised version comes from the last volume of Martin Gilbert's masterly biography of Winston Churchill (London, 1988). There are some relevant essays in volume 1 of the three-volume *Viaggio nel Sud*, ed. E. Kanceff and R. Rampone, *Viaggiatori stranieri in Sicilia* (Moncalieri and Geneva, 1991). Most recently, Raleigh Trevelyan, author of that fascinating account of the Anglo-Sicilian Inghams and Whitakers, *Princes under the Volcano* (London, 1972) has completed the new *Companion Guide to Sicily* (Woodbridge, 1996).

2

Early Tudor Tombs and the Rise and Fall of Anglo-Italian Relations

꿍

Among all the Sepulchurs that I have seene in Europe, or in Turkey, that in Westminster erected to Henrie the seventh, King of England, of Copper mettall, adorned with vulgar precious stones, is the fairest, especially considering the Stately Chappell built over it. The next to that in my opinion is the Sepulcher at Winsore, made of the same mettall curiously carved, at the charge of Cardinall Wolsye, had he not left it unperfected, so as none hath yet been buried under it.

Fynes Moryson, *An Itinerary containing his ten yeeres travell . . .* (London, 1617), III, ii, p. 63

ALTHOUGH THERE was no English cardinal in the Curia from the death of Adam Easton in 1398 until the reign of Henry VIII, throughout the fifteenth century a growing number of English students travelled to Italy as would-be humanists. With the advent of the Tudor dynasty, while returned humanists such as Grocyn, Urswick, Latimer, Linacre, Lily, Colet, Tunstall and Pace began to exercise the most profound influence on our culture and institutions, our diplomatic representation in Rome 'increased in vigour and prestige'.[1]

The English delegation which thanked Innocent VIII for a dispensation permitting Henry VII to marry and recognizing the right of his heir to inherit the throne consisted of ten clerical and lay Englishmen, half of whom were already resident in Rome.[2] Thenceforth, after a series of no doubt more competent Italians, including Giovanni and Silvestro Gigli (both of whom obtained bishoprics in England) and the wealthy Adriano Castellesi, who became not merely Bishop of Bath and Wells but a palazzo-building cardinal as well, from 1509 our interests at the Papal Court were forcefully represented by a native (Francophobic) Englishman, Christopher Bainbridge. Notwithstanding his title of Archbishop of York, Bainbridge functioned in a largely secular capacity.[3] Three years before his death at Rome by poisoning, he also became a cardinal, acting as the belligerent Julius II's legate in the war against Ferrara and foreign 'barbarians' in return for the privilege. During the papacy of Leo X, Cardinal Giulio de' Medici – the future Clement VII – was made Protector of the English, while the Pope's brother was made a Knight of the Garter. Anglo-Roman relations reached their (albeit ambivalent) apogee with Lorenzo Campeggio, the cardinal who became Bishop of Salisbury, and with Bainbridge's successor as Cardinal Archbishop of York, Thomas Wolsey.[4] Not satisfied with even these rapid strides upwards in England's international status, Henry VIII, now 'Defender of the (Roman Catholic) Faith', twice attempted to have Wolsey elected Pope. The almost hysterical intensification of Anglo-Roman diplomatic relations, which preceded their sudden decline, and Wolsey's dismissal, were both the result of Henry's impossible, divorce-related demands.

Having sent three distinguished ambassadors to swear obedience to Julius II in 1504, Henry VII was given the Bramantean palace in which they were accommodated by the man who had built it, Cardinal Adriano Castellesi. Now known as the Palazzo Giraud–Torlonia, this was to be the only truly Renaissance building owned by an English monarch before the age of Inigo Jones.[5] In the same year, having been dissuaded from marrying his eldest son's Spanish widow, Henry obtained a portrait of the Dowager Queen of Naples with a view to marrying her. Though compared to his son he pursued a relatively isolationist foreign policy, Henry VII had lived in France, spoke some Italian and was familiar with a great variety of Italians, including musicians, the wealthier merchants, envoys, Latin secretaries and courtiers such as Pietro Carmeliano, the Giglis, Johannes Michael Nagonius and Polydore Vergil (whom he chose to record his reign for posterity). Via Italian merchants he may have employed the sculptor Benedetto da Maiano in the 1490s, and certainly employed Guido Mazzoni (Master Paganino or Pageny) to design an early version of his tomb. When, perhaps encouraged by the Italophile Thomas Linacre, he decided to build a Utopian hospital in London, he sent for a detailed account of the functioning of Florence's then famous Arcispedale di Santa Maria Nuova and had the Savoy designed on the same cruciform plan.[6] Henry was thus sufficiently conscious of the cultural achievement of Italy's competing city-states to have been correspondingly conscious of Britain's relative backwardness, a backwardness which may have been prolonged by the dynastic wars he had brought to an end.

A Machiavellian *avant la lettre*, he had gained the throne by force of arms but had to continue exploiting his *virtù* in order to render it secure for his heirs. The Italian envoys envied him his enormous wealth ('and what is more he never spends anything') and admired his political acumen. But there was little for the classically orientated Italian to admire in our cultural achievement, still less in the xenophobic man (and woman) in the street who, 'with the malevolent look of pigs', periodically rose up to assault all foreigners and wreck their property.[7] 'Whenever they see a handsome foreigner', records Andrea Trevisano in 1498, 'they say that "he looks like an Englishman".' Trying hard to praise, he recognized that London was the only city in the island comparable in beauty or size with the great Italian cities and that although its citizens prospered, even London had 'no buildings in the Italian style [all'usanza Italiana] but of timber and brick [legnami e terra] like the French'.[8] Even the northern European, Erasmus, who eventually found much to admire among a handful of scholars in England, was disgusted by the state of English houses, their rush-covered clay floors nursing 20 years' worth of 'spittle, vomit, dog and human excrement, spilt beer, fish bones, and other filth [from all of which] is exhaled a vapour . . . by no means beneficial to the human condition'. Referring more metaphorically to houses in a 1499 letter to a young Englishman studying in Italy, he wrote from London that: 'You are in a country where the very walls are more scholarly and articulate than human beings are with us, so that things which men in these parts regard as beautifully finished, elegant, and charming, in Italy cannot escape seeming vulgar, and lacking in wit.'[9]

Thus Baldassare Castiglione – traditionally believed to have presented Henry VII with Raphael's St George as a diplomatic gift from his patron, the Duke of Urbino – praised Prince Henry's 'many virtues' in his *Cortegiano*. On the other hand, he found as little to say in praise of English art, architecture, arms, armour, literature, history-writing, furniture, riding, fencing, cooking, clothing or courtiership, as Poggio Bracciolini or Aeneas Sylvius Piccolomini had in the previous century. To compare Raphael's small but superb St George slaying the dragon with the large but ludicrous panel

depicting the same scene frozen above a clumsy group of the kneeling Henry VII and family is to appreciate the extent of the gap
between the two cultures.[10]

After accepting the Order of the Garter on his master's behalf in
the Gothic chapel at Windsor, Castiglione received from Henry not
pictures but dogs and horses. When he was also presented with a
gold collar of Lancastrians Ss (like that worn by Thomas More in his
portrait by Holbein) he was delighted, passing it on with particular
pride to his heirs.[11] Its value to one who was soon to be painted by
Raphael was, however, symbolic rather than artistic. Ironically, if
Castiglione returned to Italy with anything that he might have considered of artistic value it is likely to have been of Italian manu-
facture: a large bronze medal featuring the motto of the Garter in
Gothic letters and depicting the ruler he was to eulogize in the
Cortegiano, his patron's father, Federigo da Montefeltro.[12] If, as has
been suggested – partly because of its similarity to the Lovell roundel
which also features the Garter motto – this handsome object were
by Torrigiano and dated from 1506,[13] it would be his first known
work in England. This would bring forward the date of his arrival
here by several years. Torrigiano is documented as having worked
in Fossombrone in 1500, where the Duke of Urbino held his court,
which included Castiglione before his departure for England and
after his return. In 1508, Castiglione attended the duke at his death-
bed there.[14] In 1501 Torrigiano carved the marble St Francis for
Francesco Piccolomini's monumental tomb in the Duomo at Siena.
Before his brief reign as Pope in 1503, Piccolomini was Cardinal
Protector of England and actively involved in trade with this
country.[15] Torrigiano's whereabouts between his presence in
Avignon in 1504 and his repairing a 'figure' of Mary Tudor in
Flanders in April 1510 are still unknown. Given the Federigo medal,
however, and the possibility of earlier work on both this figure and
the bust of Henry VII (now in the Victoria and Albert Museum and
generally considered to have been done from the death mask after
1509), it is conceivable that Henry VII rather than his son (or
Wolsey) deserves the credit for recruiting Torrigiano. Though Vasari
says that he was led ('condotto') to England by certain Florentine
merchants (for whom he had made many small bronze and marble
figures), it is even possible that Torrigiano came to England with
Castiglione's much postponed embassy in 1506.[16]

Once the 17-year-old Henry VIII was securely established on his father's hard-won throne, Julius II courted him assiduously in order to recruit him as perhaps his wealthiest ally against the French. At this time, Julius was having the chapel of his uncle, Sixtus IV, redecorated by Michelangelo Buonarotti. As poet, painter, architect and sculptor, Michelangelo was the product of several centuries of an intensely refined and classically inclined urban civilization without parallel in 'waning' medieval England. Indeed, despite the attempts of both Henrys and variously civilized kings, queens, aristocrats and millionaires since, the interested Briton still has to travel to Rome to see the likes of the Sistine ceiling; for even now we have nothing to compare with those newly cleaned frescoes, or those with which Raphael adorned Julius's apartments in the Vatican, or the colossal church of St Peter's, begun by Bramante to accommodate Julius's tomb. Even in its drastically scaled-down form in a much smaller church, this tomb is without its artistic equal in Britain, if only thanks to Michelangelo's Moses.[17]

And yet, as planned by Torrigiano and revised by Baccio Bandinelli, Henry VIII's tomb would have out-monumentalized even Julius's megalomaniac memorial. It was, however, to be compromised still more radically. While what remains of Michelangelo's grandiose project perhaps epitomizes the Pope's imperfections (including his ultimate failure to keep the barbarian French and Spanish out of Italy) and while Gilg Sesselschreiber's similarly scaled-down monument for the Emperor Maximilian may epitomize Habsburg continuity,[18] the fate of Henry's tomb symbolizes the literally dreadful disappointment of his regime and the destructive legacy he bequeathed his successors, down to the terrible 1640s. Having been most enthusiastically welcomed, in the words of Thomas More, as 'the beginning of our joy', Henry's reign began prosperously but eventually degenerated into a faction-torn era of Stalinist-style revolution from above, characterized by savage and unpredictable persecution. Henry managed to secure the throne for his three isolated children but did so at the expense of cultural continuity, provoking an unprecedentedly traumatic break with the Catholic continent just when interest in things Italian (and thus the urge to visit the source of Renaissance civilization) was reaching unprecedented levels.[19] Paul III was paying Michelangelo to complete the Sistine Chapel with a Last Judgement – thereby preventing him from completing Julius's tomb – when the Pope confirmed Henry's excommunication.[20] When Paul III died, the young Thomas Hoby

[Fig. 3], who would later translate Castiglione's *Cortegiano* into English, rushed to Rome from Siena to witness a papal election. Commenting that an 'honourable sepulture' had been commissioned by the deceased Pope's nephews, Hoby reports that this had been 'taken in hand for him by Michael Angelo'. Though probably the first reference to the artist in English, this would also prove to be the last until peace with Spain in the next century permitted the revival of Italian travel.[21]

Via the early Tudor tombs we can trace the rise, the attempt at consolidation, and the sharp decline of sixteenth-century England's relationship with Italian art. The relationship's tentative beginnings are suggested by a lost, pre-1497 bust of Henry VII by Benedetto da Maiano, which Vasari records as having been modelled on the basis of drawings conveyed to the artist by Florentine merchants.[22] By 1503, with the death of the queen, we hear of Henry's unfinished tomb being conveyed from the Lady Chapel at Windsor to his recently begun chantry chapel at Westminster.[23] By the winter of 1505-6 Henry VII had progressed to the point of employing the sensational Modenese sculptor, Guido Mazzoni, on what must have been a completely revised version of his still unfinished tomb.[24] Mazzoni's design also seems to have proved unsatisfactory, however, perhaps because he had depicted the king in a kneeling posture adapted from his recently completed tomb of Charles VIII at St Denis. It should be remembered, however, that Henry is depicted kneeling in the St George altarpiece referred to above, and his son, who is said to have 'misliked' Mazzoni's design for this reason, is likewise depicted 'priant' in the Black Book of the Order of the Garter.[25]

Torrigiano's first recorded English commission (November 1511) was for the tomb of Henry's mother, Lady Margaret Beaufort, the inscription for which was composed by Erasmus. If Torrigiano was recruited before 1509, Henry evidently failed to finalize arrangements for his own tomb, bequeathing funds and precise instructions for the placing of the post-Mazzoni monument in the centre of his now completed Gothic chapel. With whatever native and foreign help he could gather into his rapidly expanding Westminster workshop, Torrigiano designed, carved, modelled, cast and gilded Henry's tomb (1512-18) while completing his mother's.[26] Now in great demand, Torrigiano is thought to have received several other commissions in this period though none is documented. Another tomb, for the Master of the Rolls, Dr John Young, who died in 1516, was probably designed and in part carried out by Torrigiano. The terracotta busts of Bishop Fisher (principal executor of Lady Margaret's will) and that said to portray the beardless Henry VIII are also considered to have been completed in this period. The roundel of the Master of the Rolls, Sir Thomas Lovell (d. 1524), may have been done later, as may the bust of Dean Colet (d. 1519), which could have been done from a death mask after Torrigiano's return from Italy in 1520.

Torrigiano's next major commission (March 1517) was for the high altar and baldacchino which Henry VII had requested for his chapel.[27] As agreed in a contract he doubtless helped to draw up, Torrigiano designed a magnificent canopied structure of bronze, and black and white marble. Beyond even the late king's tomb, this was entirely Italianate in character, reminiscent in particular of Michelozzo's great tabernacles in SS. Annunziata and San Miniato in Florence and topped with glazed polychrome angels in the manner of Della Robbia. Having half completed it, Torrigiano indeed wished to return to Florence, mainly in order to recruit the skilled assistants unavailable in England. To finance the journey, however, he first required, as in 1512 and 1517, that he should be given a major new commission whilst completing the previous one. From a surviving letter to Wolsey it is clear that the cardinal had promised to obtain from the king just such a commission.[28] By January 1519 an indenture was drafted for the commissioning of a £2,000 tomb in white marble and black touchstone for:

> our . . . most dradd soveraign Lorde the Kyng and the most excellent princesse Kateryn his most derist Quene & wife . . . the which nowe [*sic*: new?] tomb shalbe more grettir by the iiijth parte than ys the said Tombe whiche the same Petre before made & fynysshed for the same King Henry the viith.[29]

The most influential inspiration for Torrigiano's tomb of Henry VII was Antonio Pollaiuolo's extraordinary tomb for Julius II's uncle, Sixtus IV.[30] The argument that the inspiration for Henry VIII's tomb as planned was Julius's great project is reinforced by Henry's choice (or rather Wolsey's and, as we shall see, the papal datary's) of Michelangelo's two most aggressive rivals to design it.

Notorious throughout Italy, and effectively exiled from Florence after the event, even in England the few who had heard of Michelangelo would also have heard that it was Torrigiano who had

broken the great man's nose. Indeed, it seems Torrigiano could not
resist boasting of the occasion on which, in response to critical
comments from this younger rival protégé of Lorenzo de' Medici, he
'gave [Michelangelo] so violent a blow upon the nose, that [he] felt
the bone and the cartilage of the nose break under the stroke, as if
it had been a wafer [un cialdone]'.[31] Torrigiano boasted at least once
too often of this incident, and in particular during his 1519 recruitment drive in Florence, concluding the version he told the young
Benvenuto Cellini with: 'thus marked by me he will remain as long
as he lives'. This proved a tactical disaster for, having already
bragged of his 'bold deeds among those beasts of Englishmen', he
had hoped to persuade Cellini to return with him to England to
execute 'a great work for my King', a work which would include
'vast works in bronze'. Cellini writes that 'These words begat in me
so great a hatred, since I saw continually the works of the divine
Michelagniolo, that notwithstanding that I had conceived a desire to
go with him to England, I could not bear even to see him.'[32] Though
he thus failed to recruit the man who would have been the greatest
sculptor and goldsmith ever to work in Britain, in the autumn of the
same year, 1519, Torrigiano enrolled several other 'Florentine
fellow citizens', 'to stay with him for four years and half, and to
work at the trade in Italy, France, Flanders, England, Germany, or
in any other part of the world whatsoever'. One of these was the
21-year-old Antonio Toto del Nunziata, variously described as a
painter and architect, whom Vasari records as having made for
Henry VIII his 'principale palazzo'.[33]

Julius not only sent Henry VIII a golden rose, a hundred
Parmesan cheeses and several barrels of wine to encourage loyalty
to his Holy League against France; in March 1512 he wrote a brief
authorizing the transference of all Louis XII's dominions and titles to
the 20-year-old king once the French were defeated.[34] Although
Julius died in February of the following year, Henry would not let
the papacy forget this promise. Beyond the traditional aspiration to
the French throne, Henry was soon attempting to succeed
Maximilian as Emperor and announcing that he had 'no superior on
earth'. Martin Luther commented: 'Junker Heinz thinks he is God'
and for the time being, Europe's most distinguished anti-Lutheran
indeed found himself flattered by the new Emperor, the King of
France, Luther himself (albeit briefly) and the Pope, whom he wished
Wolsey to succeed. All such illusions and aspirations are implicit in

the tomb as planned, just as their collapse – Henry's failure to win the Empire, France, even a divorce, culminating in his excommuni-cation by a now hostile and Habsburg-dominated papacy – lie behind the abandonment of his Italianate triumphal monument.

Though it is usually said that the primary purpose of Torrigiano's year-long visit to Italy was to recruit skilled artists to help him complete the great altar for Henry VII's chapel, he was probably at least as concerned with Henry VIII's tomb. This tends to be confirmed by a comparison of the contracts he drew up with the artists he recruited and the draft indenture retained by Wolsey. In particular, the latter specifies a time-limit of four years for the completion of the tomb. The altar was scheduled for completion in November 1519, yet in September and October 1519 Torrigiano committed his new assistants to four-and-a-half-year contracts. The usual view is that Torrigiano's tomb design was in any case abandoned: that he returned to England, completed the altar and then left for Spain, where he died in prison in 1528.[35]

According to his sixteenth-century biographer, on the night he died – 30 November 1521 – Pope Leo X was shown an extra-ordinary wooden model of a tomb which 'was being prepared in carved marble' for Henry VIII in Britain.[36] A fortnight later, Michelangelo's assistant, Leonardo Sellaio, wrote from Rome (where he guarded Julius's incomplete tomb in Michelangelo's workshop) and described this model to his master in Florence.[37] Commissioned by Giovanni Cavalcanti from Baccio Bandinelli, it represented an enormous ensemble which would feature 142 gilt-bronze, life-size figures and bas-relief panels arranged around a triumphal arch on a massive stepped platform, the whole (Hawkwood-like) surmounted by an equestrian statue of the king. The cost of gilding alone was estimated at 40,000 gold ducats. Having explained in his first letter that the papal datary had obliged Cavalcanti to award the commission to Bandinelli, when referring to the model again three weeks later Sellaio confirms to Michelangelo that 'there is no work for you in it . . . I am doubtful whether Baccio will embark upon it.' In his life of Bandinelli, Vasari records that he made a 'bellissimo modello di legno, e le figure di cera, per una sepoltura al re d'Inghilterra', but abridges the rest of the story by concluding that the commission was given to Benedetto da Rovezzano, 'who made it of metal'.[38]

Those who have written on this subject seem to concur in the

belief that this model was an entirely separate project from
Torrigiano's and was commissioned by Leo X as Henry's reward –
apparently in addition to his title as 'Defender of the Faith' – for
having defended the sacraments. We are even told that Henry may
have known nothing of the plan.[39] A more plausible scenario is that
in 1519 the extrovert Torrigiano, who had agreed in his January
contract to produce a model for Henry's tomb, began to design this
'great work for my King', including 'vast works in bronze', while in
Italy and discussed it widely with potential associates and assistants.
He would no doubt have obtained all the details he could regarding
Julius's tomb – perhaps glimpsing the completed lower portion – and
have sought to outdo it in every way possible. Michelangelo's
second most notorious rival was his fellow Florentine Bandinelli,
whom Vasari accuses of tearing up the celebrated cartoon for the
Battle of Cascina out of jealousy.[40] Bandinelli and Torrigiano are in
any case likely to have met and discussed Henry's tomb during the
year, but a documented link between all the parties involved was
the Florentine merchant banker, Giovanni Cavalcanti. He it was,
rather than Leo X, according to my reading of Sellaio's letter, who
actually commissioned the 1521 model, choosing Bandinelli because
of pressure from the datary, who may himself have been under
pressure from Giulio de' Medici, Protector of the English and long-
term patron of Bandinelli. Whether Torrigiano had amicably passed
on the job, had already absconded to Spain, or had been dismissed,
it would have been up to Cavalcanti as one of his guarantors to try
to fulfil the requirements specified in the Wolsey indenture within
the 1519–22 time-limit. In other words, the Bandinelli commission
was contiguous with Torrigiano's and no doubt reflected English
rather than Roman requirements, albeit in High Renaissance taste.[41]

Neither Bandinelli nor Cellini came to England (though, like
Leonardo, the latter did work in France); nor for that matter did
Jacopo Sansovino (who was given a 75,000 ducat commission by
Henry in 1527) or Michelangelo (who was nevertheless awarded a
£20 life annuity by the Edwardian government).[42] Benedetto da
Rovezzano and Giovanni da Maiano arrived soon after, perhaps as
a result of Torrigiano's recruitment campaign, and set to work on
a vast tomb for Cardinal Wolsey in the Lady Chapel (now the
Albert Memorial Chapel) at Windsor. Having still not succeeded in
finalizing his own tomb by the time he engineered Wolsey's downfall, Henry commandeered his servant's half-completed one and

abandoned his intention of building his own tomb in the centre of the Lady Chapel at Westminster (the position he seems to have been reserving for himself, thereby failing to comply with his father's request that his tomb be placed there).[43] But even this major compromise could not be carried through, despite a large contingent of Italian craftsmen. With Wolsey gone, Fisher, More and countless other patrons executed, with the monasteries being sacked, pictures, sculpture and stained glass being destroyed in the name of a religious reformation Henry had half-wittingly promoted, the Italian Catholics began to return home. These included the sculptors da Rovezzano and da Maiano.

In 1531, in *The Boke named the Governor*, Sir Thomas Elyot had regretted that the English 'be constrayned, if we wyll have any thinge well paynted, kerved, or embrawdred, to abandon our own countraymen and resort unto straungers'. Ambassador Sir John Wallop's report from Fontainebleau in 1540 epitomizes this dependency. Francis I conducted him around the château in person, helping him mount a bench in order to examine the 'antycall borders' and offering to forward to Henry 'divers moulds of antique personages that he hath now coming out of Italy, with which he shall have done within three or four months'.[44] By 1545, however, Lord Cobham was receiving instructions 'to send over no more strangers, and move the rest there to send none, for the king is not content'.[45] Niccolo da Modena, a refugee from French justice, was hired to complete the tomb but seems to have failed owing to inadequate support.[46]

When Henry died, still some sort of Catholic, he was buried with Jane Seymour beneath a plain cloth in the choir of St George's, Windsor, pending the completion of his tomb in the adjoining chapel. His heirs never completed it and of them, indeed, only Elizabeth has a tomb of her own, and that thanks to James I.[47] It has even been argued that Henry's daughter Mary, together with Cardinal Pole (whose aged mother Henry had judicially murdered), dug up his body and burned it.[48] In the 1640s, as well as destroying Torrigiano's beautiful altar, the Puritans destroyed even the scaled-down version of Henry's tomb, leaving only the almost indestructible sarcophagus. Had it been built as planned, with its giant 'image of sculpture of God the Father' holding Henry's soul in one hand while blessing it with the other, the colossal Bandinelli version would no doubt have been destroyed within his son's lifetime.

Knowledge of Bandinelli's great model (or something very like it) nevertheless survived into the seventeenth century. In 1623, John Speed published a detailed 'Description of a Model of a Tomb for Henry VIII' which had been forwarded to him by that 'industrious' Lancaster Herald, Nicholas Charles. The original manuscript seems to have been accompanied by a drawing.[49] A conscious echo of Henry's imperial tomb design may thus be present in Van Dyck's more subtly imperial image of Charles I on horseback (now in Buckingham Palace), for the Speed account has the equestrian figure *under* 'an Arch triumphall, of white Marble . . . as the patterne sheweth'.[50] When Inigo Jones designed his imperial monument for Charles I, the Temple Bar Gate, he produced something closer to the Bandinelli model in that his equestrian figure was to be placed above the triumphal arch.[51] The Puritans sold the Van Dyck and destroyed Charles, together with his noble projects. The sarcophagus, which Wolsey, Henry and Elizabeth never used, can be seen today in the crypt of St Paul's Cathedral, where it preserves the remains of Horatio, Viscount Nelson.

NOTES

This is an expanded version of an article which first appeared in *Apollo*, CXXXIV (October 1991), pp. 234–38, as 'Henry VIII's Tombs: "Plus Catholique que le Pape"?'

1. G.B. Parks, *The English Traveler to Italy*. Vol. I. *The Middle Ages (to 1525)* (Rome, 1954), p. 310; see also Lewis Einstein, *The Italian Renaissance in England* (New York, 1902). For Colet, Urswick, More and much else, see J.B. Trapp, *Essays on the Renaissance and the Classical Tradition* (Aldershot, 1990) and idem, *Erasmus, Colet and More: The Early Tudor Humanists and their Books* (London, 1991).

2. Ugo Balzani, 'Un'ambasciata inglese a Roma', *Archivio della Società Romana di Storia Patria*, III (1880), pp. 175–211; J. Burckard, *Liber Notarum, 1483–1506*, in Muratori, *Rerum Italicarum Scriptores*, ed. E. Celani (1906), I, pp. 195–6; and Parks, op. cit., p. 305.

3. D.S. Chambers, *Cardinal Bainbridge in the Court of Rome, 1509 to 1514* (Oxford, 1965).

4. P. Gwyn, *The King's Cardinal: The Rise and Fall of Thomas Wolsey* (London, 1990). Neither this otherwise inclusive biography nor those of Henry VIII by J.J. Scarisbrick (1968) and J. Ridley (1984) mentions Torrigiano.

5. Henry VIII gave this Palazzo (in the Borgo Nuovo near St Peter's) to his legate, Cardinal Campeggio, who promptly complained about its 'unfinished' state; see the note dated 12 March 1519 in *Letters and Papers, Foreign and Domestic, of*

the *Reign of Henry VIII*, 1509–47, ed. J.S. Brewer, J. Gairdner and R.H. Brodie, 21 vols and addenda (London, 1862–1932), I, i, pp. 3817f.; also W.M. Brady, *Anglo-Roman Papers* (1890), pp. 9–91; corrections in Parks, op. cit., pp. 332–4.

6. E. Chaney, '"Philanthropy in Italy": English Obervations on Italian Hospitals, 1549–1789', in *Aspects of Poverty in Early Modern Europe*, ed. T. Riis (Florence and Stuttgart, 1981), pp. 182 and 211; and Chapter 11 in this volume. The account of S. Maria Nuova which the hospital's hereditary patron, Francesco de' Portinari, sent to Henry VII is Bodleian Library, MS Bodley 488. It is handsomely illuminated with the Royal Arms of England. Ironically, this Portinari, himself related to Dante's Beatrice, was probably a relation of the Giovanni de' Portinari who acted as Cromwell's monastery breaker in the 1530s. The latter went on to oversee the production of Henry VIII's tomb and, if it is still the same Giovanni, to become a sought-after military engineer under Elizabeth; see H. Colvin (ed.), *The History of the King's Works*, IV, ii (London, 1982), p. 409, and III, i (1975), pp. 196–206, for the Savoy Hospital. In view of Linacre's medical training and his years in Florence, and the acknowledged influence of Italian institutions on his foundation of the College of Physicians in 1518, he is the obvious person to have suggested S. Maria Nuova as a model to Henry, whose children he tutored. As Thomas More's teacher, he is also the most obvious source for the ideal (Italianate) hospital described in *Utopia* (1516). In 1493, Colet's name had been registered in the *Liber fraternitatis* of the no less exemplary hospital of Santo Spirito in Rome; see J.B. Trapp, op. cit., p. 213.

7. J. Lees-Milne, *Tudor Renaissance* (London, 1951), p. 12 (quoting a Venetian ambassador).

8. *A Relation . . . of the Island of England*, ed. C.A. Sneyd (Camden Society, 1847), pp. 21 and 42.

9. See below, pp. 61 and 89, n. 15.

10. C. Clough, 'The Relations between the English and Urbino Courts, 1474–1508', *Studies in in the Renaissance*, XIV (1967), pp. 202–18; and C. Clough, 'Sir Gilbert Talbot and Raphael's Washington "St George"', *Report of the Society of the Friends of St George's and the Descendants of the Knights of the Garter*, VI, No. 6 (1985), pp. 242–53 (I thank Timothy Wilson for this reference). See also C. Clough, 'Il "San Giorgio" di Washington: Fonti e Fortuna', *Studi su Raffaello*, ed. M.S. Hamoud and M.L. Strocchi (Urbino, 1987).

11. J. Cartwright, *The Perfect Courtier: Baldassare Castiglione, his Life and Letters, 1478–1529*, 2 vols (London, 1908), I, pp. 183–7.

12. G.F. Hill, *A Corpus of Italian Medals of the Renaissance before the Cellini* (London, 1930). No. 1118; and J.G. Pollard, 'England and the Italian Medal', in *England and the Continental Renaissance: Essays in Honour of J.B. Trapp*, ed. E. Chaney and P. Mack (Woodbridge, 1990), p. 192.

13. A.P. Darr, *Pietro Torrigiano and his Sculpture for the Henry VII Chapel, Westminster Abbey*, unpublished PhD thesis, New York University, 1980, pp. 47–8.

14. J. Cartwright, op. cit., I, pp. 231–4.

15. W.E. Wilkie, *The Cardinal Protectors of England: Rome and the Tudors before the Reformation* (Cambridge, 1974), pp. 10–28; and Darr, op. cit., pp. 48–9. This magnificent tomb, on which Michelangelo also worked, was begun by Andrea Bregno (to whom Adriano Castellesi's Roman Palazzo is attributed). Though eventually completed as an altar, it must have influenced Torrigiano's ideas on tomb design.

16. G. Vasari, *Le opere . . .*, ed. G. Milanesi, 9 vols (Florence, 1906), IV, p. 260.

17. For a reconstruction of the Julius tomb as planned, see C. de Tolnay, *Michelangelo*, IV (Princeton, 1954).

18. H.R. Trevor-Roper, 'The Emperor Maximilian I, as patron of the arts', *Renaissance Essays* (London 1985), pp. 22–3: the Nuremberg sculptors Peter Vischer and Veit Stoss were both employed on the tomb but after the emperor's death work was suspended: 'But the heirs of Maximilian, to the fourth generation, honoured his wishes and revered his name', and under Archduke Ferdinand of Tyrol the scaled-down version was completed. For more detail, see Vincenz Oberhammer, *Die Bronzestatuen am Grabmal Maximilians I* (Innsbruck, 1943).

19. The almost millenarian quality of the eulogies of Henry in the early years of his reign remind one of Giles of Viterbo's 'Golden Age' eulogies of Julius.

20. See Scarisbrick, op. cit., pp. 318, 320 and 334, for the various stages of threatened excommunication from Clement VII in 1533, and their effect in England.

21. 'A Book of the Travaile and Life of me Thomas Hoby', ed. E. Powell (Camden Society, X, 1902), pp. 24–5. Thomas Wyatt seems to refer to Michelangelo's *David* in one of his sonnets. For the rapid secularization of travel and travel literature, after the pilgrimage accounts of Sir Richard Guylforde (1506) and Sir Richard Torkington, epitomized by the mid-century writings of Hoby and William Thomas, see Chapter 3 in this volume.

22. G. Vasari, *Le opere . . .*, ed. G. Milanesi, 9 vols (Florence, 1906), III, p. 339. If this was ever obtained by the King, it would have been the most important precedent for the employment of Mazzoni and Torrigiano and further evidence that Henry VII's patronage was at least as discriminating as that of his son; for the most recent bibliography in context, see C. Galvin and P. Lindley, 'Pietro Torrigiano's portrait bust of King Henry VII', *Burlington Magazine*, CXXX (1988), pp. 892–902.

23. Colvin, *King's Works*, III, i, pp. 219–20. In his otherwise excellent article, 'On the Work of Florentine Sculptors in England in the early part of the sixteenth century . . .', *Archaeological Journal*, LI (1894), pp. 129–220, Alfred Higgins is mistaken (p. 136) in supposing 'Master Esterfelde' to be the maker of the uncompleted 1501–3 tomb; he is John Esterfeld, Canon of Windsor, to whom payments were made in these years.

24. *The History of the King's Works, III, 1485–1660*, ed. H. Colvin (London, 1975), i, p. 220. For recent literature on Mazzoni, see John Larson, 'A polychrome terracotta bust of a laughing child at Windsor Castle', *Burlington Magazine*, CXXXI (1989), pp. 618–24. Darr, op. cit. (pp. 186 and 288) doubts that Mazzoni came to England, but from the wording of payments to 'Master Paganyne that werks abowte the king's towmbe', it is obvious that he did. *King's Works*, III, i, p. 219, records September 1505–April 1506 payments to a 'Dutch' smith called Thomas for 'certen coperwerke to be made for the king's tombe'. In her 'Two Italian Portrait-Busts of Henry VIII' (*Art Bulletin*, XLII (1960), pp. 291–4, H.J. Dow argues that the terracotta bust of a smiling child at Windsor depicts the young Henry VIII. That the 'images' on the tomb were to be polychromed is clear from the 'remembrance' published as Appendix A by B.H. Meyer, 'The First Tomb of Henry VII of England', *Art Bulletin*, LVIII (1976), pp. 358–67; cf. T. Verdon, *The Art of Guido Mazzoni* (New York, 1980), fig. 91. In 1511 Torrigiano followed a design for Lady Margaret's tomb drawn on cloth by Meynard Vewicke, probably John Maynard, 'the king's painter' cited in *King's Works*, op. cit., p. 218. He may represent an important element of continuity between the Mazzoni and Torrigiano projects.

25. Oliver Millar, *Pictures in the Royal Collection: Tudor, Stuart and Early Georgian Pictures*, 2 vols (London, 1963), cat. no. 19; D. Starkey, *The Reign of Henry VIII*

(London, 1985), fig. 58, and entry in ibid., *Henry VIII: A European Court in England*, National Maritime Museum, Greenwich (exhibition catalogue) (London, 1991), p. 95. As will now be clear, Dr Starkey is mistaken in his belief that Torrigiano was 'the first to practise the Renaissance style in England' (ibid., p. 32). See on this also, P.G. Lindley, 'Playing check-mate with royal majesty? Wolsey's patronage of Italian sculpture', in *Cardinal Wolsey: Church, State and Art*, ed. S.J. Gunn and P.G. Lindley (Cambridge, 1991), pp. 261–2, n. 3.

26. Darr, op. cit., pp. 54–6, and his 'The Sculptures of Torrigiano: the Westminster Abbey Tombs', *Connoisseur*, CC (1979), pp. 177–242.

27. For the tomb of John Young, or Yonge, and the Lovell roundel, see E. Chaney in *Henry VIII: A European Court in England*, op. cit., pp. 32–3. For an illustration of the high altar, see idem, *Apollo*, CXXXIV (1991), p. 234.

28. Torrigiano's Latin letter to Wolsey is printed by Higgins, op. cit., Appendix I, pp. 199–200.

29. The 'Transcription of a Draft of an Indenture of Covenants for the erecting of a Tomb . . . ' is printed in *Archaeologia*, XVI (1812), pp. 84–8.

30. M. Whinney, *Sculpture in England: 1530–1830*, rev. edn by J. Physick (Harmondsworth, 1988), pp. 31–3; J. Pope-Hennessy, *Italian Renaissance Sculpture* (London, 1971), pp. 44–5, and his 'The Tombs and Monuments', in A.L. Rowse (ed.), *Westminster Abbey* (London, 1979), pp. 214–15.

31. R.H.H. Cust (ed.), *The Life of Benvenuto Cellini*, 2 vols (London, 1935), I, pp. 39–44.

32. Ibid., p. 44.

33. Vasari, op. cit, IV, p. 262n (originals now transcribed in Darr, op. cit., documents 18, 19 and 20) and p. 590; *King's Works*, III, *passim*; E. Auerbach, *Tudor Artists* (London, 1954); and A.E. Popham, 'Hans Holbein's Italian contemporaries in England', *Burlington Magazine*, LXXXIV (1944), pp. 12–17. A pupil of Ridolfo Ghirlandaio, Toto not only painted Old Testament subjects for the Royal Library at Hampton Court in 1530 but presented a 'Calumny of Apelles' and 'story of King Alexander' as New Year's gifts to Henry in 1538 and 1541 respectively. Since he seems not to have returned to Italy, and was naturalized in 1538, he may have become a Protestant. By 'particolarmente il suo principale palazzo', Vasari may mean Nonsuch.

34. Scarisbrick, op. cit., p. 27. For the gifts, see ed. J.S. Brewer *et al.*, *Letters and Papers* (cit. note 5 above) I. i. p. 842; meanwhile Julius was sending his 'Galleas into England for tin to cover the church of St Peter'.

35. Darr, op. cit., pp. 58–61.

36. P. Giovio, *De vita Leonis Pont. Max.* (Florence, 1584), IV, p. 113, cited in M. Mitchell, 'Works of Art from Rome for Henry VIII', *Journal of the Warburg and Courtauld Institutes*, XXIV (1971), p. 178.

37. Mitchell, op. cit., p. 201 (Appendix I).

38. Vasari, op. cit., VI, pp. 144–5. As noted by Higgins (op. cit., p. 185), John Speed (*History of Britain* (London, 1623), pp. 796–7) transcribed a very detailed account of the same project which he had received from Nicholas Charles, shortly before 1613.

39. Mitchell, op. cit., p. 190, and most recently N. Llewellyn, 'The Royal Body: Monuments to the Dead, for the Living', in L. Gent and N. Llewellyn (eds), *Renaissance Bodies: the Human Figure in English Culture c. 1540–1660* (London, 1990), pp. 234–5. It seems to me more likely that the tomb project would have been exploited by Henry (or Wolsey) as additional means for furthering his international ambitions. Like M. Howard on 'Self-fashioning and the Classical

Moment in mid-sixteenth-century Architecture' in the same volume, Dr Llewellyn articulates very different views to those presented here. Where Dr Howard (p. 205) states that 'the building style of mid-sixteenth-century England was not a false dawn before the arrival of Inigo Jones half a century and more later', I would argue that this was effectively what it was. Dr Llewellyn asserts that 'Monuments were not designed to show off an artist's Italian training or a patron's taste: they were functional objects designed to mark permanently the site of a funeral.'

40. Vasari, op. cit., V, p. 133.
41. The 'John Canalchanty' in the transcription of the Torrigiano–Wolsey indenture cited in n. 28 above is clearly the Giovanni Cavalcanti mentioned in the Sellaio letter cited in n. 37.
42. For Sansovino, see Mitchell, op. cit., p. 203 (Appendix III); for the mysterious annuity paid to 'Michaell Angelo of Florence' in November 1551 (under the Italianate Northumberland, who patronized William Thomas and sent John Shute to Italy to study classical architecture), see *King's Works*, IV, ii, p. 24.
43. Darr, op. cit., pp. 289–94.
44. C. Brown, 'British Painting and the Low Countries 1530-1630', in *Dynasties: Painting in Tudor and Jacobean England 1530-1630*, ed. K. Hearn (Tate Gallery, London, 1995), p. 27 and Colvin, *King's Works*, IV, i, pp. 22–3.
45. Lees-Milne, op. cit., p. 71. Cobham received these instructions (from Sir William Paget) in Calais, not in Rome as stated by Lees-Milne; see *King's Works*, IV, ii, pp. 24 and 388.
46. R.W. Carden, 'The Italian Artists in England during the 16th Century', *Proceedings of the Society of Antiquaries*, XXIV (1911–12), p. 189; and M. Biddle, 'Nicholas Bellin of Modena: an Italian Artificer at the Courts of Francis I and Henry VIII', *Journal of the British Archaeological Association*, XXIX (1966), pp. 199–201. He had been involved in defrauding the French king. Indicative of the decline of even imported sculpture since Torrigiano is Margaret Whinney's praise of the 1566 Hoby effigies at Bisham [Fig. 3] as 'far in advance of current English work'; op. cit. (n. 30 above), p. 41.
47. In 1602, the Duke of Stettin commented: 'The sepulchre of King Henricus octavus was not quite finished; it is to stand in the centre of the choir. The monument itself was of good Lydian stone [Probirsteine], the emblemata of brass and bell-metal, a work so large that it would take not less than 40 carts to remove it' ('Diary of the Journey of Philip Julius, Duke of Stettin-Pomerania, through England in the year 1602', ed. G. von Bülow, *Transactions of the Royal Historical Society*, NS VI (1892), p. 49. After the paucity of Tudor tombs, James's lavishness in this area reflects his (and Anne of Denmark's) general readiness to spend on display. Between 1605 and 1609 four royal tombs were erected in Henry VII's Chapel: that for Elizabeth by Maximilian Colt, those for James's infant daughters, Sophia and Mary, also by Colt, and that for his mother, Mary Queen of Scots, by Cornelius Cure and his son William; see *King's Works*, III, i, p. 120. The highly decorated altar which was placed over that most Puritan of our monarchs, Edward VI, was destroyed by Sir Robert Harley's Parliamentary commission in the 1640s; A.P. Stanley, *Historical Memorials of Westminster Abbey* (London, 1869), p. 504.
48. Scarisbrick, op. cit., p. 497.
49. See n. 38 above.
50. Mitchell, op. cit., p. 202.
51. John Harris, *Catalogue of the Drawings of the RIBA: Inigo Jones and John Webb* (London, 1972), no. 53. For the imperial theme, see Roy Strong, *Charles I on*

Horseback (London, 1972), pp. 46–57, who stresses 'the enormous time lag' between the use of the 'imperial' style *à l'antique* in Renaissance Italy and its arrival in England in the seventeenth century but does not remark on how, but for the Reformation, this time lag would have been minimal.

3

Quo Vadis? Travel as Education and the Impact of Italy in the Sixteenth Century

IT MUST SURELY have amused the 20-year-old Sir Thomas Isham and his friends at Rome to be informed by a correspondent in January 1678 that in far-away Oxford:

> One of the prime questions at the encaenia . . . was whether travelling be good for English Gentlmn.[1]

Busily squandering his recently inherited fortune on pictures by Salvator Rosa and exotic Italian mistresses (one of whom he shared with an exiled English priest), Isham would have assumed the debate long since settled. And indeed, for better or worse, the Grand Tour was already a fully established social convention and educational institution by this date, nowhere more so than among Royalist families such as his own, many of whom had been 'doom'd to wander' during the Civil War and Interregnum, utilizing their enforced leisure as pleasurably or profitably as possible.[2]

Pleasure and profit, or 'voluptas' and 'utilitas', were the twin poles around which the great European debate on the pros and cons of foreign travel had revolved since the early Renaissance, though England had been characteristically slow to catch up with the continent in the development of both the theory and practice of secular travel.

Although Jerusalem was still placed at the centre of the world in Hereford Cathedral's great thirteenth-century Mappa Mundi, after the institution of the Jubilee Year and the subsequent return of the Popes from Avignon, Rome steadily regained its predominant position, eventually replacing the Holy Land and all other rivals as Europe's most popular place of pilgrimage.[3] Even before this consolidation, however, Petrarch, referring to his 1350 Holy Year visit, was expressing concern lest Rome's secular cultural attractions might distract the pilgrim from his true purpose. Writing to a friend, he concluded it to have been providential that they had not been there together:

> Otherwise, instead of visiting the churches out of Catholic devotion [devotione Catholica], they would, careless of their souls, have wandered about the city with the curiosity of poets [curiositate poetica]; for however delightful intellectual pursuits might be, they are as nothing unless they tend to the one great end.[4]

In one of his late, influential letters to Boccaccio, Petrarch wrote that as a result of adopting such a pious approach, this, his post-Black Death visit to Rome, had certainly been 'the most happy of all'.[5] But it was Petrarch's earlier visits of 1337 and 1341, when he was crowned Poet Laureate on the Capitoline Hill, which would have appealed most to Geoffrey Chaucer, who if he sought out Petrarch and Boccaccio during his travels in Italy would have done so in a spirit of 'poetic curiosity', for the sake of their early works, rather than one of Catholic devotion for their repentant old age.[6] Chaucer's attitude to pilgrimage may be deduced from the Canterbury Tales in general and his Prologue portrayal of the worldly Wife of Bath in particular. With characteristic good humour he catalogues the latter's journeys to Jerusalem, Rome, Compostella and Cologne, as if they somehow complemented the list of her husbands and love-affairs.[7] Though all were ostensibly classic pilgrimage destinations and she had travelled thrice to the Holy Land, there is not a hint of religious conviction behind her fondness 'of wandrynge by the weye'.

When the Florentine government invited Petrarch to settle down and teach at their new university, they wrote: 'Surely you have travelled enough, and the manners and cities of foreign peoples are an open book to you.'[8] A hundred and fifty years later, ambassador Francesco Vettori composed an enjoyably Boccaccesque travelogue on the basis of a journey through Germany and Switzerland, concluding that 'Among the honest pleasures that men can experience, I believe that of travelling to be the greatest; he who has not known many men and seen many places cannot be truly wise.'[9]

In both instances the justification for travel was derived from
Homer's tribute to Ulysses as echoed by Horace. As eventually taken
up in sixteenth-century England this became: 'All travellers do
gladly report great prayse of Ulysses, / For that he knew mens
maners, and saw many Cities'.[10]

But by the early seventeenth century, Ben Jonson was mocking
this dictum through the ludicrous medium of Sir Politic Would-Be.
It was not, the latter explained,

> That idle, antique, stale, grey-headed project
> Of knowing men's minds, and manners, with Ulysees;
> But a peculiar humour of my wife's,
> Laid for this height of Venice, to observe,
> To quote, to learn the language, and so forth.[11]

In 1507, writing in an exclusively secular vein, Vettori had advised
that 'to profit from journeys several factors must combine: a good
and robust constitution, wealth, and companions of a cheerful and
relaxed character. If one of these is missing, travel is no longer a
pleasure.' It seems we northerners took longer to unburden our guilt
and travel without ostensible religious justification. Meanwhile,
however, provoked by the still flourishing Wife of Bath syndrome,
with uncharacteristic (and un-Chaucerian) severity, even Erasmus
felt obliged to re-emphasize Jerome's point about the non-essential
nature of pilgrimage, warning his readers of the moral dangers
inherent in young men and women travelling too far from home;
they did so, he wrote, 'non sine gravi discrimine morum et integri-
tatis'.[12]

Despite such warnings, during the course of the sixteenth
century pilgrimage continued to thrive in Catholic countries.[13] If
Palestine became an increasingly unpleasant and dangerous place in
which to travel, especially after the Turkish takeover of Jerusalem
from the relatively tolerant Egyptian Mameluke dynasty in 1517,
hitherto little-known European centres such as Loreto grew from
strength to strength. The Santa Casa or Holy House of the Virgin
was indeed especially flown over to the east coast of Italy from
Palestine by four angels and soon rivalled Rome itself in wealth
and prestige, receiving gifts and visits even from the likes of
Montaigne and – in the following century – Galileo and Descartes.[14]
In northern Europe, however, the Reformation radically undermined
the respect for the relics, legends and papally approved indulgences

which were the basis for the sacred status of such centres. But since no Reformation could be so thorough as to eliminate the desire to travel, alongside the disintegration of unified Christendom, the development of hostile Protestant and Catholic nation-states with great centralized courts, the spread of humanism and the expansion of the profession of diplomacy, new justifications for travel were evolved to replace the old.

Changing practice seems none the less to have preceded articulated theory. Alongside the pilgrims, ambassadors and ecclesiastics, during the fifteenth century increasing numbers of influential Englishmen had travelled to Italy, principally in order to study at one of the many universities or with one of the great humanist teachers. This educational phenomenon proved so successful that by 1499, Erasmus, writing from London to one such student, implied that this specific reason for crossing the Alps might be becoming unnecessary. He conceded that 'you are in a country where the very walls are more scholarly and articulate than human beings are with us', and that 'England looks to find you not only accomplished in the science of law but also equally fluent in Latin and Greek.'[15] It is clear from the same letter, however, that we were now unprecedentedly capable of valuing such accomplishments. Since Erasmus also describes the English weather as 'at once agreeable and extremely healthy', he may well be exaggerating here; but even allowing for the customary quota of epideictic rhetoric, his praise of the 'quantity of intellectual refinement and scholarship . . . profound and learned and truly classical', is striking, not least because he concludes that standards are so high that he himself has 'little longing left for Italy, except for visiting it. When I listen to Colet', he writes of his new friend, the future founder of St Paul's School, 'it seems to me that I am listening to Plato himself.' A few years later he went still further, confirming that 'there are indeed five or six men in London profoundly versed in Greek, and I doubt if Italy contains such good ones at this present'.[16]

Just as Henry VII was inspired by travellers' tales of the utopian Florentine hospital of S. Maria Nuova to found London's Savoy Hospital, so surely must Colet have been inspired by his first-hand experience of scholarly institutions in Italy to found a school in London which would instruct 153 boys, free of charge, in 'good Maners and litterature . . . both laten and greke'.[17] Whether this latecomer to Greek studies attended the lectures of Poliziano in Florence is not known. His friend, Thomas Linacre, however, had certainly done so and would have had the Studio Fiorentino in mind when he endowed the lectureships at Oxford and Cambridge which were named after him. (Both Colet and Linacre placed the management of their respective foundations – Italian-style – in secular hands, in the care of the Mercers' Company.) In the same way, Linacre's foundation of the College of Physicians in 1518 was specifically inspired by Italian example, a debt acknowledged in the opening lines of the foundation charter: 'Itaque partim bene institutarum civitatum in Italia, et aliis multis nationibus exemplum imitati.'[18]

Given the relatively recent discovery of humanism in England, it is remarkable testimony to the success of humanistic education under the Tudors and the relative decline of the same in Italy, that by the end of the sixteenth century, the travelling tutor, Robert Dallington, could write indignantly that in the University of Florence 'yee shall scarce finde two that are good *Grecians*, without the which tongue, they holde in our Schooles in England a man never deserveth the reputation of learned.'[19]

In his *Areopagitica* of 1644, Milton lamented the decline of Florentine scholarship as well as the silencing of Galileo, noting that Italian scholars had counted him happy 'to be born in such a place of *Philosophic* freedom as they supposed England was'.[20] Finally, Gilbert, the future Bishop Burnet, was told in 1686, by none other than the great Florentine librarian, Antonio Magliabechi, that 'there was not one man in Florence that either understood Greek, or that examined Manuscripts.'[21]

We shall see that the nouveau-cultured English were so successful in their campaign to establish Greek and Latin as the norm 'in our Schooles' that as early as the mid-sixteenth century some were concerned that the vernacular was suffering as a result and began consciously promoting modern languages. But moving on from the vast subject of those who travelled to specific locations in Italy in order to study there, to those who went, in the words of Erasmus, 'for the sake of visiting it', the first well-documented European tours undertaken in an entirely secular spirit date from the late 1540s. Suggestive that the two phenomena were not unrelated is the fact that those who undertook such tours included our most prominent promoters of the vernacular, both Italian and English.

Thomas Hoby, eventually to achieve fame as the translator of Castiglione's *Cortegiano*, was encouraged to travel by his elder half-brother Sir Philip in order to complete his education and gain experience of foreign courts, manners and languages so as to equip himself for a career in the diplomatic service [Fig. 3].[22] The success of this plan – and of the 1561 publication which directly resulted from it – is demonstrated by the younger Hoby's knighthood and his appointment as ambassador to France in 1566.[23] He had first spent two years at St John's College, Cambridge, studying with John Cheke, the scholar immortalized by Milton as the man who 'taught Cambridge, and King Edward, Greek', but one who would also – after exile in Padua – write the important, vernacular-promoting letter which prefaces Hoby's *Courtyer*.[24] In August 1547, Hoby left Cambridge without graduating and moved to Strasbourg, where for almost a year he studied with Martin Bucer (in whose house he lodged) and with several other distinguished Protestant teachers, including Paulus Fagius and the Florentine exile, Peter Martyr Vermigli.[25] After a few months, the latter left Germany to become Professor of Divinity at Oxford and, in the following year, Bucer (accompanied by Fagius) also emigrated to England, where he was appointed Regius Professor of Divinity at Cambridge.

Though still in his teens, Hoby had meanwhile contributed to Bucer's reputation in England by translating his controversial treatise against Stephen Gardiner's epistles on the celibacy of the clergy and sending the translation to his brother to be printed.[26] In the summer of 1548, Sir Philip, sent by Edward VI and Protector Somerset to treat with the Emperor Charles V, arrived at Augsburg and arranged for Thomas to tour Italy. Throughout this period Hoby kept a fascinating diary which he wrote up in finished form a few years later, perhaps encouraged by the publication of Leandro Alberti's encyclopaedic *Descrittione di tutta Italia* in 1550, which he plagiarized extensively. Having identified this major source for the Italian section of his diary, it is now possible to distinguish what is first-hand observation in his account from what is merely para-phrased or translated. While the autobiographical or eye-witness passages are of greater immediate appeal and historical value, in this instance the borrowings are also of interest in providing us with opportunities to observe the trainee translator at work, practising on Alberti's mundane prose an art he would soon be perfecting in turn-ing Castiglione's far more sophisticated text into one of the most influential publications of the Elizabethan period.[27]

Almost as influential, and equally a direct product of travel in

Italy, was the soldier-scholar Peter Whitehorne's translation of Machiavelli's *Arte della Guerra*, published, according to its title-page, in July 1560, a year before the *Courtyer*, but more probably in April 1562, the date we find in the colophon. If this ambiguity suggests avant-garde rivalry with Thomas Hoby's launch of another major Renaissance text, it tends to confirm that the translator of the *Arte of Warre* was the same Peter Whitehorne who features as one of Hoby's travelling companions in the latter's autobiography.[28] On arrival in Padua in July 1548, Hoby had settled down to attend lectures in civil law, logic, 'humanitie' and Italian at the university. In June of the following year, he decided to 'travaile into the middes of Italye, as well as to have a better knowleg in the tung, as to see the countrey of Tuscane, so much renowmed [*sic*] in all places'.[29] The best Italian was (and is still) thought to be spoken in Siena, and it was here that Hoby next based himself. Having recorded the names of several Englishmen in Padua, including that of Sir Thomas Wyatt (son of the poet and future rebel), Hoby found another nine or ten in Siena, including a 'Mr Peter Whitehorne' who was one of those who refused to accompany Hoby, Edward Stradling, Francis Peto and others to a dinner given by Don Diego di Mendoza, the Imperial Ambassador.[30] From his preface to the *Arte of Warre*, we know the Machiavellian Whitehorne to have been in both Italy and North Africa, campaigning with Charles V, little more than a year after this refusal, which suggests that if the two Whitehornes are one and the same, his anti-imperial attitude must have softened somewhat during the intervening period abroad.

On 16 November 1549, after hearing of the death of Paul III – the Farnese Pope who more than a decade earlier had excommunicated Henry VIII – Hoby, Whitehorne, Henry Parker and William Barker joined the train of Cardinal Salviati on its way to Rome in order to observe a papal election.[31] After a few weeks in Rome, during which the same foursome 'throwghlie searched owt suche antiquities as were here to bee seene' and were informed that the Farnese were commissioning a papal tomb from Michelangelo (probably the first English reference to this artist), they finally grew impatient with what, after the sabotage of Cardinal Pole's allegedly 'Lutherian' candidature, became one of the longest conclaves in history, and 'determined in the meane time to make a journeye to Naples'.[32] Once he had 'well vewed whatsoever was to bee seene bothe within the citie of Naples and in the countrey abowt the same', Hoby then 'tooke a journey upon mee to goo throwghe the dukedome of Calabria by land into Cicillia, both to have a sight of the countrey and also to absent my self for a while owt of Englishemenne's companie for the tung's sake'.[33]

On his return from this extraordinary journey, not to be paralleled until Isaac Basire and his pupils covered equivalent ground a century later, Hoby met up with his companions again in Naples and, perhaps inspired by his adventures, they persuaded him to head south again in their company. They travelled overland to Salerno and 'When we had seen Salerno sufficientlie we entred into a bote to go a long the faire coost of Amalfi, which is praysed to be on[e] of the pleasantest peices of ground in all Italie' (by English standards a pioneering expression of enthusiasm for natural landscape).[34] Here, thanks to a former acquaintance in Siena, the entire party was entertained by the Duchess of Amalfi and her son, Innico, in the castle in which a better-known Duchess of Malfi and her children were probably murdered some 37 years earlier. Hoby's account of their reception is worth quoting in view of the influence such courtly, Renaissance-style hospitality seems to have had on the less sophisticated English tradition via a combination of this kind of direct personal experience and the Platonic praise of 'grace', *sprezzatura* and perfect manners to be found in the increasingly fashionable courtesy books. It is a sad irony that, in 1600, Hoby's unpleasantly puritanical second son, Sir Thomas Posthumus Hoby, brought a legal action against guests who had alledgedly abused 'the laws of hospitality' in his house but who justified their brutish behaviour in terms of the grudging reception and 'limited diet' they had been offered by their host:[35]

When [Innico, Marquis of Capistrano] sawe me and Whitehorn cumming into the castle to him he did not onlie gentlie receave us with loving entertainement, but also browght us in to the Dutchesse his mother to do the like towardes us. And while we were sitting in communication together, he had privilie willed on[e] of his menn to bring uppe into the castle to him the rest of owr companie remaining benethe in the towne, where we supped all together, everie mann served his mess severallie at the table to himself in sylver verie honorablie. And there had he with him at supper the Captain of the towne the better to entertain us all. When suppar was done everie mann was browght to his rest: Whitehorn and I were had [led?] into a chamber hanged with clothe of gold and vellett, wherein were two beddes, th'on[e] of silver worke and the other of vellett, with pillowes bolsters and the shetes curiouslie wrowght with neelde [needle] worke. In another chamber hard bie lay Stradlinge and Grinwaye. And bicause there was not provision sufficient within the castle, Handford and Frauns Williams were ledd to the Captain's howse of the towne, where they laye sumptuouslie, and were greatlie feasted.[36]

In view of the vividly positive impression such first-hand experiences made on Hoby, no less ironic than his son's reputation for 'seldome interteyning of strangers' was Roger Ascham's recommendation, published in *The Scholemaster* in 1570, that a careful reading of Castiglione's *Cortegiano* – 'so well translated into English by a worthie ientleman Syr *Th. Hobbie*, who was many wayes well furnished with learnyng, and very expert in knowledge of divers tongues' – followed by a year's careful practice of its precepts in England 'would do a yong ientlemen more good, I wisse, then three yeares travell abroad spent in *Italie*'.[37]

Ascham's influentially negative view of Italy was based on a total experience of nine days in Venice in 1552, though they must have been very busy ones, for he 'saw in that litle tyme, in one Citie, more libertie to sinne, than ever I hard tell of in our noble Citie of London in ix. yeare'.[38] It is clear from what he says elsewhere, that as well as the powerful threat of 'Papistrie or worse' to the integrity of young Englishmen, Ascham was no less alarmed by 'the maners of Italie', or what he calls her 'filthy living'. Venice's legendary 30–40,000 taxed and registered prostitutes cannot have helped here. He writes euphemistically of knowing those 'that never had gone out of England, but onelie to serve *Circes*, in Italie'.[39] Sent to Venice in 1587 by Sir Francis Walsingham to report on Spanish preparations to invade England, the intrepid Stephen Powle meanwhile reported to his friend John Chamberlain on his neighbours, in which he considered himself 'highly fortunate':

for I am lodged amongst a great number of Signoras: Isabella Bellochia in the next house on my right hand: and Virginia Padoana, that honoreth all our nation for my Lord of Oxford's sake, is my neighbour on the lefte side: Over my head hath Lodovica Gonzaga, the French King's mistress, her house. You think it peradventure preposterous in Architecture to have hir lye over me.[40]

By the end of the sixteenth century there was a brothel in London which went simply by the name of 'Venice'. Ben Jonson exploited the legend in *Volpone*, as did his rival, John Day, whose *Humour out of Breath* defined Venice as 'the best flesh-shambles in Italy'.[41] No doubt stimulated by such accounts, 'Traveller and Gentleman author' Thomas Coryate decided to investigate the legend for himself, and in his *Crudities* of 1611 published a detailed, somewhat Gladstonian report on the Venetian courtesans, many of whom, he wrote, were 'esteemed so loose that they are said to open their quivers to every arrow'. Citing classical precedent, he claims to have attempted the conversion of one of these wantons 'to a holy and religious woman', though his high moral tone here is not entirely consistent with the accompanying engraving, which depicts him being enthusiastically greeted by the bare-breasted 'Margarita Emiliana bella Cortesana di Venetia' [Fig. 12].[42]

Later in the seventeenth century, in recommending travel as an essential part of good breeding, Catholic priest and coiner of the phrase 'Grand Tour', Richard Lassels, nevertheless warned against those who 'travel a whole month together, to *Venice*, for a nights lodgeing with an impudent woman. And thus by a false ayming at breeding abroad, they returne with those diseases which hinder them from breeding at home.'[43] But by the second half of the eighteenth century only Bishop Hurd still seemed seriously worried.[44] In *A Modest Defence of Public Stews* of 1724, Bernard Mandeville had sarcastically affected to support the anti-Grand Tourists by recommending the recruitment of foreign prostitutes into legalized brothels so as to keep English girls moral and save young Englishmen from the trouble of travelling abroad merely to satisfy their lustful curiosity.[45]

Another early admirer of 'the book named the Courtyer', but one who spent considerably longer in Italy than Ascham, travelling as far as Naples and back and forming a much more positive view as a result, was Thomas Whythorne (no relation, it seems, to the Machiavellian).[46] Rediscovered in this century by Peter Warlock, who acclaimed him as 'a composer of real genius', Whythorne is now generally acknowledged as having been 'an important pioneer' in English music, particularly for his major contribution to the development of the madrigal.[47] There can be no doubt that it was Whythorne's encounter with the madrigal as performed and, no less significantly, as published in Italy that inspired him to popularize the

12 Thomas Coryate visiting the Venetian courtesan Margarita Emiliana in 1608; engraving
by William Hole from *Coryat's Crudities* (London, 1611). [E. Chaney]

same at home, publishing in 1571 his own *Triplex of Songes*, 'the
earliest example we possess of a book of secular music printed in
England'.[48] In his autobiography, Whythorne says he went abroad
initially 'as well to know the customs and manners of the people
where I came, as also to learne their speech and languages'.[49]

Looking back, however, it was clearly the continental respect for music and musicians that impressed him most, and he cites this phenomenon and its positive consequences when condemning the philistine attitude of those 'blockheads, and dolts, who will so utterly condemn' the art of music in his own country, thus encouraging its general decay, which, he strongly implies, began with the dissolution of the monasteries.[50] Regarding 'the general estimation of music in foreign realms', Whythorne says he knows the situation 'In Italy, France and the Dutchland':

> But chiefly in Italy where I perceived that, among such as were of any account, they were esteemed to be but rudely and basely brought up who had no knowledge of music, or at the least able to play or sound on some musical instrument, or else to sing pricksong [that is, from a score] . . . And for that cause ye shall find in that country, in most men's houses that be of any reputation or account, not only instruments of music, but also all sorts of music in print; having sets of books in their houses for singing and for instruments that be of two, three, four, five, six, seven and also of eight parts and upward. Because that when there be many in one company together who can sing pricksong perfectly, ye shall in those books find songs of divers trades for them to sing. And for that the printers would have every day new songs to print, they do fee the best musicians that they can retain, to the end that when they do make any new songs their printers may have the only copies of them to print; which encourageth the musicians to employ and give his mind and endeavour the more to his study therein.[51]

Like Hoby, John Shute was also sent abroad for specifically educational reasons.[52] Vaguely aware perhaps that English architecture was a century or two behind the times and that this might relate to ignorance of the Italian revival of classical antiquity, in 1550 John Dudley, Earl of Warwick, soon to be Duke of Northumberland, sent Shute to Italy. Dudley was clearly a major patron of Italian travel in the mid-century, his travelling or travelled protégés including, besides Shute (and, as we shall see, William Thomas): Francis Yaxley, Francis Peto and Thomas Wilson. Before his downfall it seems he was also about to employ Whythorne, the loss of this anticipated patronage prompting Whythorne's departure for Italy, though other members of the Dudley family supported him on his return.[53] In the dedication to Queen Elizabeth of the fruits of his journey, the illustrated folio entitled *The First and Chief Groundes of*

Architecture, published in 1563, Shute, now able to call himself 'Paynter and Archytecte', recalls that:

> It pleased his grace for my forther knowledg to maintaine me in Italie ther to confer with the doinges of ye skilful maisters in architectur, & also to view such auncient Monumentes hereof as are yet extant, where-upon at my retourne, presenting his grace with the fruites of my travailes, it pleased the same to shewe them unto that noble king Edward the vi. your maiesties most deare brother of famous memorie, whose delectation and pleasure was to see it.[54]

A far more remarkable protégé of Dudley's, but tragically, one who was to follow his patron to the scaffold, was William Thomas, author of *The Historie of Italie* [Fig. 13]. In early 1548, when Hoby was still studying in Strasbourg, he recorded in his diary that 'William Thomas cam this waye owt of Italye towards England. Also Sr Thomas Wyat arrived here to go towards Italye.'[55]

Five years later, Thomas was to involve himself in Wyatt's insurrection to prevent the marriage of Queen Mary with Philip of Spain, and both Protestant Italophiles were executed.[56] Though his original reasons for leaving England had been considerably less respectable than either Hoby's or Shute's, the fruits of Thomas's travels are of such importance that he not only secures a place beside them but may be described as having done more to introduce an awareness and appreciation of Italian life, language and culture into this country than any other sixteenth-century Englishman (and he was Welsh). His only rival in this respect was John Florio (and he was Italian).[57]

As a bankrupt gambler and Protestant, early in 1545 Thomas embezzled some of his Catholic master's money and fled to Venice. Unfortunately, news of his crime arrived the morning he did, so that he was welcomed to the city by a brief period of imprisonment arranged for him by the English ambassador, Edmund Harvell.[58] After the money was paid back, Thomas was released but effective-ly became an exile for the next three years. Via Padua he first trav-elled south to Bologna, where he later claimed (in a work called *Perygrine*) to have defended Henry VIII in a political and religious debate. He seems somehow to have earned a living, for he next moved down to Florence where 'he continued a certain space at mine owne charges and laie a good while with *Maister Bartholomew Panciatico*, one of the notablest citizens.' This could only be the

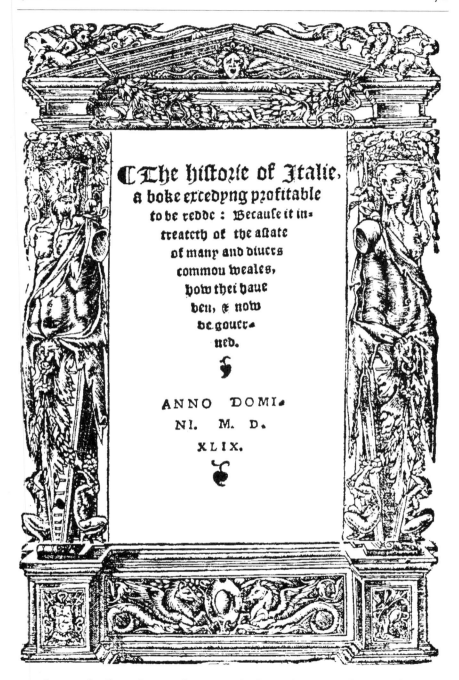

¶The hiſtorie of Italie,
a boke excedyng profitable
to be redde : Becauſe it in=
treateth of the aſtate
of many and diuers
commou weales,
how thei haue
ben, & now
be.gouer=
ned.

ANNO DOMI=
NI. M. D.
XLIX.

13 Title page of William Thomas, *The Historie of Italie* (London, 1549). [E. Chaney]

Bartolomeo Panciatichi whose striking portrait by Bronzino now hangs in the Uffizi and who was not only a distinguished diplomat, poet and patron of the arts, but, in this still relatively liberal period, a discreet Protestant also.[59] Probably it was Panciatichi who introduced his foreign guest to the recently founded Florentine Academy, 'one of the goodliest ordres that I have seene'. Thomas's attendance at one of its Italian language '*Haranges*', almost a century before Milton attended the equivalent, clearly enhanced his Vives-influenced respect for the vernacular. 'I never heard reader in schole, nor preacher in pulpitte handle theim selfes better', he wrote of this impressive performance.[60] As such it can only have encouraged the attitude he reveals in the preface to his manuscript translation of Sacrobosco's *De Sphaera* where he argues – 30 years before Richard Mulcaster was to argue likewise – that the schoolchild should be taught his own language properly before 'his maister putteth the Latin grammer in his hande'. One would thus avoid the absurd but presumably common situation whereby, 'the childe consumeth the flowre of his learning youth' in learning to write a Latin epistle, 'though well he can not write half a pistle in Englishe'.[61] Thomas concludes that 'if our nation desier to triumphe in Civile knoledge, as other nations do, the meane must be that eche man first covett to florishe in his owne naturall tongue, w'oute the whiche he shal have much ado to be excellent in any other tongue.'[62]

Thomas probably travelled as far south as Naples during the winter of 1547–8. He certainly spent Christmas Day 1547 in Rome, for he provides us with a brilliant account of the cardinals' procession across the Ponte Sant' Angelo and up the *Borgo* to Saint Peter's (to the sound of fifes, drums, trumpets and shawms) and finally, the Papal Mass itself, 'sang so sweetly that methought I never heard the like'.[63] By comparison with most later and some earlier Protestant indictments of the Whore of Babylon and her court, his account of Paul III and the College of Cardinals is refreshingly moderate, even if he condemns the extent of papal pomp, 'pride and abomination' more vigorously than Hoby, makes delightfully crude insinuations about the cardinals' taste for their well 'trimmed' page-boys, and insists, like Lord Morley before him, on referring to the Pope as the Bishop of Rome.[64] Thomas's description of the city itself is the first coherent one in English; a vast improvement on Andrew Borde's then newly published notice. As well as succinct descriptions of Rome's gates, hills, arches, porches, baths, temples, theatres and the ancient rubbish dump or Monte Testaccio, which Thomas thought too conspicuous to have been merely a depository for broken pots, the *Historie* includes our first account of the architectural orders. Given that this short Vitruvian treatise, entitled 'Of the Pyllers', was published prior to Shute's journey and that the *Historie* was dedicated to the man who sent Shute to Italy, Thomas may well have been the inspiration behind the entire project.[65]

Before his return journey via Strasbourg, Thomas wintered in Padua, where the still prevalent Pomponazzian scepticism concerning the immortality of the soul would have encouraged him to accept the 'naturalist' ethics of Machiavelli he had imbibed in Florence. 'With diligent searche', he learned that in Padua, 'the noumbre of scholers there was little lesse than fifteen hundreth: wherof I dare saie, a thousande at the lest were gentilmen.'[66] One such newly arrived gentleman, John Tamworth, 'beeying desirouse to learne the tongue, intreated the saied William Thomas to drawe himself out in Englishe some of the principall rules that might leade him to the true knowledge thereof'.[67]

The result of this request was the first Italian grammar in English, published in London in 1550, complete with a pioneering dictionary 'for the bettre understandynge of Boccace, Petrarcha and Dante', a work which went through three editions in the 1560s.[68] But it must have been before this, most likely in grand-ducal Florence, that Thomas began compiling materials for his most remarkable achievement, *The Historie of Italie*, which he would publish before the dictionary, within a year of returning to Edwardian England.[69] This somewhat misleadingly entitled work contains not merely a sophisticated chronicle of every major Italian city-state, but in each instance concludes with a fascinating summary of that city's current political and economic situation, and an almost invariably enthusiastic account of its social customs, 'civilitee', physical setting and major buildings. As such it has been praised as 'the first, and for a long time the only, introduction to [Italy] in English'.[70] Given that it appeared a year before Leandro Alberti's *Descrittione d'Italia*, however, it deserves more inclusive recognition as the first and best account of Italy in any language since Flavio Biondo's almost century-old *Italia illustrata*, which it effectively superseded.[71]

If Thomas's observations on the high proportion of gentry at the University of Padua might have encouraged the gradual gentrification of Oxford and Cambridge noted by Hexter and others in the

second half of the sixteenth century,[72] in the shorter term, his
eulogy of the more broadly based, secularized educational opportunities available throughout Italy as a whole must have encouraged
many a frustrated Oxbridge student to leave England without further
ado:

> And I thinke verilie, that in one region of all the worlde againe, are not
> halfe so many straungers as in Italie: specially of gentlemen, whose
> resorte thither is principallie under pretence of studie. For there are
> divers famous cittees, that be privileged with great libertees for all
> scholers that come: as Padoa, Bonogna, Pavia, Ferrara, Pisa, and
> others: in every one of the which, are excellente learned men, waged for
> the readyng of philosophie, of the civile lawes, and of all the liberall
> sciences. Besides excellent maisters of musicke to syng and plaie on all
> maner of instruments, and the beste maisters of fence at all weapons that
> can be founde.
>
> So that all kyndes of vertue maie there be learned: and therfore are
> those places accordyngly furnished: not of suche studentes alone, as
> moste commonly are brought up in our universitees (meane mens
> children set to schole in hope to live upon hyred learnyng) but for the
> more parte of noble mens sonnes, and of the best gentilmen: that
> studie more for knowlage and pleasure, than for curiositee or luker. For
> lightly [that is, commonly] there passeth no shroftide without renning at
> the tilte, tourneiyng, fighting at the barriers, and other like feates of
> armes, handled and furnished after the best sorte; the greatest dooers
> whereof are scholers.[73]

It was this same non-specialist or gentlemanly bias which prevailed
in Italy that encouraged Hoby's travelling companion, William
Barker, to add 'an experience of travell' to his learning in 1549.
After taking his MA at Cambridge, he left England because he was
unenthusiastic about the limited alternatives available for further
study (though to judge from his later career as a Catholic plotter, the
Edwardian regime would in any case have been antipathetic). Barker
was delighted to discover that in Italy, just as Thomas had described,
'the Stodye of a gentleman is supposed to consyst in knowledge for
his own contentacion'.[74]

One of the many remarkable features of the *Historie of Italie* is
the all-pervading influence of Machiavelli's historical and political
writings. Not merely the account of Florence, which Thomas
openly admits is indebted to 'Nicholas Macchiavegli, a notable

learned man', but the tone of the entire book is conditioned by
unmistakably Machiavellian priorities: an overriding concern with
the origin of states, the effects of good and bad government, the fates
and reputations of rulers as resulting from their virtue or lack of it,
and the mutability of fortune. Above all, as Felix Raab observed,
'in all this there is (literally) no mention of God', a phenomenon
which may have encouraged Bishop Ridley to denounce Thomas as
'ungodly'.[75] Consistent with this is Thomas's praise for Venetian
toleration, not so much of personal vice – as Ascham would propa-
gandize – but of political opinion, religious belief and even non-belief.
While this account – in its later editions – might have encouraged
recusant exiles from Elizabethan England to visit or settle in the
Veneto, in the shorter term it was, ironically, the Marian exiles who
would find their fellow Protestant's praise of 'The Libertee of
Straungers' in 'The Venetian Astate' most relevant:

> Al men, specially strangers, have so muche libertee there, that though
> they speake verie ill by the Venetians, so they attempt nothyng in effecte
> against theyr astate, no man shall controll theim for it . . .
> Further, he that dwelleth in Venice, maie recken him selfe exempt
> from subjection. For no man there marketh an others dooynges, or that
> meddleth with an other mans livyng. If thou be a papist, there shalt thou
> want no kinde of supersticion to feede upon. If thou be a gospeller, no
> man shall aske why thou comest not to churche. If thou be a Jewe, a
> Turke, or beleevest in the divell (so thou spreade not thyne opinions
> abroade) thou arte free from all controllement. To lyve maried or
> unmaried, no man shall aske the why.[76]

Given that the *Historie* was dedicated to Dudley and, as we have
seen, it was the latter who introduced the works of John Shute to
Edward VI, it seems likely it was Dudley who introduced Thomas to
the 11-year-old king. Little more than a year after returning to
England – his former patron dead and his misdemeanours forgotten
– Thomas not only became Clerk to the Privy Council, but more discreetly he also became the king's personal adviser, managing, by
1551, to acquire substantial estates in Hereford and Sussex.[77] It was
at the royal pleasure that Thomas composed a series of *Discourses* on
subjects such as 'whether it be better for a commonwealth that the
power be in the nobility or in the commonalty'. Although most are
intelligently translated paraphrases of Machiavelli's *Discorsi* and *The
Prince*, most also address themselves usefully to the specific problems

of mid-sixteenth-century England, in particular, the essay 'touching the reformation of the coin', which seems to have directly influenced the king.[78]

Sadly, the positively Italianate works of Thomas, Hoby, Peter Whitehorne and Shute, published – or in Thomas's case, republished – in almost every year throughout the 1560s, reached a peak of popularity on the eve of an unprecedented period of isolation from the Catholic continent, a period in which the adjective 'Italianate' would become a devastating pejorative. The book which would have updated and partially superseded Thomas's *Historie*, which the remarkable papal organist and chief musician to the Cardinal of Ferrara, Thomas Shakerley, outlined to Sir Nicholas Throckmorton in 1562, was never written. Fortunately, Shakerley's pioneering three-day *Guida Romana* was completed and published before the decade opened and – since its use was far from restricted to English tourists – it survived through numerous editions as an appendix to the equally popular *Le Cose Maravigliose dell' Alma Città di Roma*.[79] The period in which these young men had travelled was one in which moderate Erasmians were still managing to hold back the extremist advocates of Reform and Counter-Reform. By the end of the 1560s, however, uncompromising Calvinists and their 'Jesuitical' opposite numbers were moving into the major positions of influence throughout Europe, working behind the scenes to promote those religious and civil wars which were to plague Europe for almost a century.

In particular, the publication in 1567 of Pius V's bull *In coena domini* (which confirmed the exclusion of heretics from Italian states); the Northern Rising of 1569, the excommunication of 'Elizabeth, Pretended Queen of England' in 1570; Italian-connected conspiracies such as the Ridolfi Plot and, in the following decade, war with Spain, which dominated most of the Italian peninsula, had the effect of rendering the country which Thomas had defined as flourishing 'in civilitee moste of all other', unprecedentedly inaccessible to English travellers. The travel licences which all but merchants were obliged to obtain from the Privy Council specified that Rome and all territories 'not with us in league or amity' were out of bounds and threatened the confiscation of property if impromptu orders to return were not obeyed. Thus while the good Protestant travelled abroad in terror of the Inquisition, the good Catholic or merely curious returned home in fear of Elizabeth's secret

service. If Shakespeare filled part of his 'lost years' with a journey to
Italy – 'a harmless fantasy' allowed us even by Samuel Schoenbaum
– he would have been careful not to leave any evidence of having
done so.[80] Izaak Walton convinces us that in this period the more
overtly Catholic John Donne, 'staid some years first in Italy, and
then in Spain, where he made many useful observations of those
Countreys, their Laws and manner of Government, and returned
perfect in their Languages'. Were it not for Walton's *Life*, however,
we would never have known of these travels, for no documentary
evidence of them has come to light. More or less the same applies to
the first Italian journey of Donne's friend, Inigo Jones. Given his
reputation (by 1605) as 'a great traveller' and the spelling of his
Christian name (and that of his father) as 'Yñigo', it is likely that
Jones would also have visited Spain in this period.[81]

Had it not been for this Reformation-related era of intolerance,
there is every reason to suppose that the example of Hoby and the
like, and indeed of those whom Erasmus had chaperoned through
northern Italy, would have led to the establishment of the Grand
Tour as a fully developed social and educational phenomenon in the
second half of the sixteenth century instead of the seventeenth, after
its re-establishment had been postponed again by the so-called
Puritan Revolution.[82] In 1555, a member of Mary's embassy to
Paul IV journeyed to Rome and back in the spirit of a tourist and,
apparently oblivious of Thomas's recent fate, praised his 'truly and
notably set forth . . . book of the Description of Italy' in enthusiastic
terms, especially for its account of Rome (even whilst silently
repromoting the 'Bishop of Rome' to the status of Pope).[83] Neither
did this relatively relaxed state of things alter with the advent of
Elizabeth. In 1559, proposals laid before Parliament included a
recommendation that 'the nobilitie . . . bryng up their children in
lernyng, at some universitie in Englonde, or beyonde the sea from
xii yeres of their age until xvii at the lest'.[84] The reprinting of
Thomas's *Historie* in 1561 and his Italian grammar a year later
suggests a still flourishing demand on the part of as yet untroubled
travellers. In 1562 Hoby's brother-in-law, Sir William Cecil, who
may have initiated the parliamentary proposal himself, was urging
his son's tutor, Thomas Windebank, to leave Germany and conduct
his charge into Italy, where he 'wolde have him see moste part of
the Contrey as farre as Rome and Naples'.[85] As late as 1563, almost
five years into the reign of Elizabeth, we find a certain Richard Smith
accompanying an apparently nonchalant Sir Edward Unton on a

tour of Italy and writing up a rather thin diary which criticizes Thomas's enthusiasm for Venice.⁸⁶ Smith praised Pius IV's great building projects in Rome and recorded without undue emphasis that 'the whole dukedome of myllane is under king philip.' Unton himself acquired a standard guidebook and, perhaps inspired by Thomas's enthusiasm, purchased a Venetian edition of the '*Historie of Nicolo Machiavelli*'. This copy of the 1541 edition of the *Istorie fiorentine*, bound in with the *Arte della Guerra* (1537), survives, complete with an inscription by Unton.⁸⁷ Symptomatic of what was to come, however, was the brief but ominous imprisonment in Rome little more than a year later of Thomas Sackville, future Baron Buckhurst and first Earl of Dorset.⁸⁸ In 1559, at the Peace of Cateau-Cambrésis, Spain had finally confirmed its control over most of Italy. In 1563 the Council of Trent, called by Paul III before Thomas and Hoby arrived in Italy, concluded its deliberations too late and too dogmatically to unify Christendom, providing instead a powerful set of certainties to revitalize Roman Catholicism and deal effectively with heresy. Sackville's 1565 visit may in fact have represented a secret attempt on the part of Elizabeth to prevent a total break with the papacy, and indeed on his release he was granted interviews with the Pope and several leading cardinals.⁸⁹ Nothing of any significance was achieved however, and as if to fulfil the worst fears of the growing anti-travel lobby – many of whom were former Marian exiles who had seen Italy for themselves – Sackville seems to have begun the abandonment of his religion in favour of his mother's Roman Catholicism as a result of the journey.⁹⁰

Soon, suspect Catholics, such as Sir Francis Englefield, were being penalized by confiscation of their property if they stayed too long in Italy. A Privy Councillor under Mary, Englefield had left England in 1559 with a licence to travel for one year. In 1562 he ignored Elizabeth's order to return home and his property was confiscated. Henry Fitzalan, 12th Earl of Arundel [Fig. 4], may have had this precedent in mind when in April 1566, on the eve of his Italian tour, he transferred his estate (including Nonsuch) to his fellow Catholic son-in-law, Lord Lumley. In 1564, Sir Robert Peckham went on a foreign tour 'for his farther encrese of knowledge and for the remedie of certaine diseases', according to his epitaph in Denham, but his epitaph in San Gregorio Magno in Rome (where all but his heart was buried in 1569) states that he exiled himself 'on account of the final triumph of protestantism under Elizabeth'.

Knighted by Arundel in 1553, Edward Lord Windsor died in Venice in 1575, where his prominent tomb and epitaph in SS Giovanni e Paolo clearly confirm his Catholicism.[91]

By the beginning of 1567 we find Edward Moorcrofte, recently returned from Italy to Paris, writing an 18-page report to Cecil, disparaging Italy as if he had the positive aspects of Thomas's *Historie* specifically in mind. In defensively chauvinistic terms, he claimed that, 'for provision of scholars, set France, Italy and Germany together, they are all as farre inferyour to oure universytes, as owre halles for the moste parte are fayrer then theyre colledges.' His educational priorities were implicit in his particular condemnation of the inadequate emphasis accorded the study of divinity in the Italian universities. Moorcrofte concluded that 'none shall lyke of Italye unlesse he be Italyzate, & howe he is to be lyked of, ye generall proverbe proveth, Anglus Italizatus demon Incarnatus'.[92]

Though on the whole it was the Catholics who kept the lines of communication open in these years, even they occasionally resorted to negative clichés about the evils of Italian travel. In 1571, William Barker, Catholic author and MP whom we encountered more than 20 years earlier, betrayed his master, the Duke of Norfolk, for whom he had acted as go-between in the Ridolfi Plot. The Duke, apparently disregarding the fact that Barker had spoken under torture, bitterly labelled him as 'ane Italianifyd Inglyschemane'.[93]

On the positive side, Sackville's fame as co-author of *Gorboduc*, the first blank-verse drama in English, his widely acknowledged virtue as diplomat and politician, his poetic endorsement of Hoby's *Courtier*, his patronage of Italianate music and, eventually, his lavish expenditure on Knole, must all have encouraged a discriminating minority of the younger generation to associate *l'inglese italianato* with culture and courtesy rather than with the *diabolo incarnato* of the antitravel propaganda.[94] So too must the examples of distinguished former travellers in Italy such as the Protestant, Sir Thomas Smith, author of *De Republica Anglorum*, or the Catholic, John Caius of Caius College fame. Despite the increasing dangers and difficulties, therefore, and occasionally perhaps because of them, 'the Siren song' of Italy continued to attract if not increasing numbers, at least a core of key personalities who maintained the Hobyan tradition.

In May 1572, having obtained his licence to leave England 'with three servants and four horses to remain the space of two years', Philip Sidney managed to persuade his Huguenot tutor, Languet, to approve his travelling to Italy only on condition he went no further south than Padua.[95] That Sidney, like Richard Smith, must have written to Languet of being disappointed in Venice when he got there is apparent from his anxious tutor's relieved reply: 'I judge from your letter that the splendour of Venice does not equal your expectation; nevertheless Italy has nothing fit to be compared to it, so that if this does not please you, the rest will disgust you.' The full extent of Languet's loathing for Italy – and his successful encouragement of Sidney to feel likewise – is revealed by a letter dating from just four months later: 'You judge rightly about Italy; whenever the Turks gain possession of it, all the ancient virtues that remains in them will soon be lost, and so the rest of Christendom will reap a double benefit from its fall.'[96]

Though there is an unattractive, xenophobic quality about the ever more vehemently articulated hostility to Italian travel in these years, the anxiety of fathers, guardians and tutors was not entirely unjustified. If it seemed so later, this was partly due to the over-stating of the case by the likes of Joseph Hall, whose influential *Quo Vadis? Or a Just Censure of Travell* appeared in 1617, when the more progressive minds in Europe were trying to re-establish greater inter-national understanding and an eclectically ecumenical or Arminian church.[97] No doubt a rival travelling tutor, Henry Peacham, had Hall in mind when he wrote his essay 'Of Travaile' which he included in *The Compleat Gentleman* of 1622. 'Travaile', he remarked, 'many dis-allow in Gentleman, yea and some great travellers themselves; but me thinkes they are as one who hath filled his own belly, and denieth the dish to his fellow.'[98] But the most prominent Elizabethan campaigners against Italian travel, Ascham, Languet and, in his old age, William Cecil, all of whom had travelled in safer, more civilized times, cannot entirely be blamed for changing their minds in the light of such drastically changed circumstances.

Fortunately – in contrast to more recent cold wars – in this case the native tongue of the antagonist had established itself as the principal language of diplomacy before the iron curtains were drawn, a factor which facilitated a vital minimum of continued com-munication. In February 1575 William Cecil, now Lord Burghley, together with the seven other members of the Privy Council, enter-tained four Venetian noblemen to dinner and greatly impressed their guests by 'almost all of them speaking our Italian tongue or at least understanding it'. The Venetians in turn endeavoured to convince their hosts of the vast esteem in which the Queen – also fluent in Italian – and 'all their Lordships, as well as the entire kingdom were held at Venice, and vowed that when any Englishman arrived there they met with very good greeting and every mark of respect'.[99] Eventually, however, Burghley – who had wanted his eldest son, Thomas, the future Earl of Exeter, to travel as far as Naples and had allowed his ward and son-in-law, the Earl of Oxford, to wander still further afield – no doubt partly because of the unfortunate results of these tours, considered the language unnecessary and even Venice beyond the pale. In ominous instructions to his children, written not long before his death in 1598, he wrote: 'Suffer not thy sonnes to pass the Alps, for they shall learn nothing there but pride, blasphemy, and atheism. And if by travel they get a few broken languages, that shal profit them nothing more than to have one meat served on divers dishes.'[100]

In 1585, Burghley failed to prevent his grandson and namesake, William Cecil, later 3rd Baron Burghley and 2nd Earl of Exeter, from visiting Rome. Although he forwarded thanks to Cardinal Savelli for his grandson's safe return in 1586, it was thought he had become a Catholic. William junior married Baroness Roos, daughter of the 3rd Earl of Rutland, and their son, William, Lord Roos, not only converted to Catholicism in Italy, he connived in the betrayal of his Protestant tutor to the Inquisition, with the effect that the poor man spent the rest of his life in a Roman prison.[101] Nor did the danger remain restricted to beyond the Alps. In 1572, less than two years after Burghley had written a *Memoryall* advising Roos's grandfather Rutland what to see in France, Philip Sidney had to take refuge in the English Embassy at Paris to escape the Massacre of St Bartholomew.[102] In Venice Sidney saw much of his cousin, Richard Shelley, 'a man of erudition, who knows Greek, Latin, and Italian well, but is sadly addicted to Popery'. On 10 March 1575, Languet warned his protégé that, by fraternizing with the likes of Shelley, friends were beginning to suspect him 'on the score of religion'.[103] It is ironic that Languet wrote this from Prague for it was here, in 1577, that Sidney met a far more dangerous papist, Edmund Campion. Campion had been at Oxford at the same time as Sidney and had left England just before him, but had gone via Douai to Rome where he had joined the Jesuits. He was now Professor of Rhetoric at the Jesuit College at Prague, an exemplary young member of that order's elite educational reform movement and soon to be martyred for his faith in England.[104] From what he wrote about his interview with Sidney a few months later, it seems to have gone very amicably. The reason for Protestant alarm at such meetings, however, is manifest in what Campion recommends should be done to follow through his good work:

> if any one of the labourers sent into the vineyard [that is, England] from the Douai seminary has an opportunity of watering this plant, he may watch the occasion for helping a poor wavering soul. If this young man, so wonderfully beloved and admired by his countrymen, chances to be converted, he will astonish his noble father, the Deputy of Ireland, his uncles the Dudleys, and all the young courtiers and Cecil himself. Let it be kept secret.[105]

In the second half of the seventeenth century, John Aubrey recorded the legend that Edward de Vere, the 17th Earl of Oxford [Fig. 5], 'making of his Low Obeisance to Queen Elizabeth happened to let a Fart, at which he was so abashed and ashamed that he went to Travell, 7 yeares'.[106] A more likely (partial) explanation for Oxford's insistence on leaving England in 1575 was his rivalry with Philip Sidney. Sidney had competed with Oxford for the hand of Burghley's daughter, Anne; they were rival leaders of opposed literary and political factions at court, and they were to become notorious rivals on the tennis court, where Oxford called Sidney a puppy and Sidney broke with etiquette by challenging his social superior to a duel.[107] On his Grand Tour, Oxford outdid Sidney to the extent of visiting Sicily (as few but Hoby had done) and issuing a challenge to all-comers in the style of the Admirable Crichton.[108] Soon after his return to England, however, he secretly 'made profession of the Catholic faith' with some of his friends, only to betray them all four years later. Not surprisingly, this provoked the government into issuing a 'Proclamation . . . for the revocation of sundry of the Queen's Majesty's subjects remaining beyond the seas under the colour of study, and living contrary to the laws of God and of the Realm'.[109] Meanwhile sermons were preached at St Paul's Cross, warning the public of the moral and political threat from 'Oure Italienated Papistes'.[110] One such was the wealthy young tourist George Gilbert. Robert Persons 'reconciled' him in Rome and in 1579 sent him home to become 'the true founder of the English Jesuit mission'. Cashing in on all this, in 1582 Anthony Munday published a sensationalized report of his successful infiltration of the

Jesuit-run English College in Rome, *The English Romayne Lyfe*.[111] Meanwhile, Charles Arundel was accusing the Italianated Oxford of 'buggering a boy that is his cook and many other boys' and Oxford was accusing Burghley's daughter of cuckolding him during his absence abroad. The latter slander may, via Robert Greene's *Pandosto*, have inspired *The Winter's Tale* (see above, p. 12). But anyone now daring to profess a positive interest in things Italians felt obliged to explain themselves. Greene himself, like Munday a known protégé of Oxford's, announced that he was English born and had English thoughts and was not 'a devill incarnate because I am italianate'.[112]

Only after the defeat of the Armada and the election of the Gorbachevian Clement VIII in 1592 did Italy begin to become more accessible again. Though anti-Italianism continued to keep the conformist away during the 1590s, curiosity eventually broke down the effectiveness of negative topoi even where loyal Protestants were concerned. Meanwhile, the fact that it had been the often less-than-loyal Catholics who had remained in touch with a superior culture proved to be of fundamental importance in the formation of those networks of patronage which would condition many key aspects of late Elizabethan and Jacobean culture.[113]

First the exiles, then more patriotic Catholics such as John Donne, Henry Piers and John Dowland, and eventually Protestant and Catholic alike defied both legal and conventional restrictions.[114] A report dating from July 1582 had stated that, excluding those in Catholic seminaries, there were not more than 20 Englishmen in the whole of Italy, 'and those in dread of their lives from the Inquisition'. In the early 1580s generally, reported arrests of Englishmen by the Inquisition were frequent, in January 1584 some 15 being sent from the 'Holy House' at Rome to the galleys in Naples.[115] In 1581, while the French Catholic, Montaigne, was enjoying his leisurely tour through the length of Italy, Arthur Throckmorton, son of Sir Nicholas, was finding even Florence – where he encountered the Catholic double-agent, Anthony Standen – too dangerous a place to stay in.[116] On a special travelling Fellowship from Peterhouse, Cambridge, whilst in Italy between 1593–95, Fynes Moryson disguised himself as a French Catholic, yet by 1597 the Earl of Essex's agent, Sir Thomas Chaloner, himself safely resident in Tuscany, reported on the increased tendency by an expanding range of Englishmen to ignore all impediments to travel:

14 Daniel Mytens, *Thomas Howard, 14th Earl of Arundel* (1585–1646), *c.*1618.
[National Portrait Gallery, London]

15 Daniel Mytens, *Aletheia, Countess of Arundel* (1590–1654), *c.*1618. [National Portrait Gallery, London]

Those who have charge of the sea coast of England must be either negligent or slothful. Every week fugitives from that country arrive in vast numbers, so as it is no longer true, as Lucan says, *Penitus divisos orbe Britannos*; while such a rabble of English roam now in Italy that it would seem as though the English laws did not forbid the voyage.[117]

After the 1604 Peace Treaty with Spain, the last major legal barriers were removed and travellers such as the collector Earl of Arundel – at this stage still a known Catholic – together with his wealthy Catholic wife [Figs 14 and 15] and brilliant servant, Inigo Jones [Fig. 29], defied the remaining restrictions by visiting Rome and Naples. When Arundel returned home, he was interviewed by the Calvinist Archbishop of Canterbury, and had to arrange for a servant to return to Italy to establish his innocence of involvement in alleged plots against the king. James was meanwhile becoming so alarmed by such developments that he renewed instructions to his ambassador in Venice, Sir Henry Wotton, to forbid British subjects from venturing 'beyond the bounds of the Dukedom of Florence'.[118]

The government, however, was completely unable to halt the travel boom. Under Charles I it was more or less encouraged. By 1637 the Venetian ambassador observed that the Pope so appreciated the good treatment of Catholics in England 'that whereas Englishmen were previously in great danger in Rome, they are now as safe there as in their own country'.[119] During the years of isolation from the Catholic continent, an image of Italy, evolved out of the relatively raw material produced by Thomas and Hoby, modified by numerous translations, was ultimately moulded by the variously sophisticated or sensational works of Nashe, Greene, Shakespeare, Jonson, Marston, Fletcher and Webster. However anachronistic or distorted, this image proved irresistible.[120] Ironically, the same period had also seen the development of a significant body of theoretical literature which sought to promote the educational value of travel.[121] The steady growth of interest in antiquity and in the visual arts – whose incipient development had been stunted by the effects of the Reformation – as well as in the natural sciences – an area in which otherwise decadent Italy continued to flourish – guaranteed the ever expanding success of the Grand Tour. By the early eighteenth century, the 3rd Earl of Shaftesbury, who would return to Italy to die in Naples, provided the ultimate justification for travel: by studying the arts and sciences in a European context one could become not merely a 'virtuoso', but *virtuous* in the modern sense of the word also.[122]

NOTES

This chapter was first published in *International Currents in Educational Ideas and Practices: Proceedings of the 1987 Annual Conference of the History of Education Society*, ed. P. Cunningham and C. Brook (London, 1988). I thank Professor J.B. Trapp and Lord Dacre of Glanton for their most helpful comments on the draft version of this essay.

1. Gerald Burdon, 'Sir Thomas Isham: an English Collector in Rome in 1677-8', *Italian Studies*, XV (1960), pp. 1-25. Isham also acquired art-history books in Italy, including the works of Bellori, Boschini, Marino, Ridolfi and Vasari; see Dennis E. Rhodes, 'Some English, Welsh, Scottish and Irish Book-Collectors in Italy, 1467-1850' in D.E. Rhodes (ed.), *Bookbindings & other Bibliophily: Essays in honour of Anthony Hobson* (Verona, 1994), pp. 247-76.

2. E. Chaney, *The Grand Tour and the Great Rebellion* (Geneva and Turin, 1985), Chapter IV. 'Twas usefully done, since so many of us are doom'd to wander' were the words used by Sir John Berkenhead to introduce the young Royalist John Raymond's *Itinerary* (1649). The latter seems to have been written by Raymond with help from his tutor and uncle, Dr John Bargrave, an expelled Fellow of Peterhouse, Cambridge [Fig. 17]. Contemporary with this is the more extensive account of *Travels through France and Italy* (1647-49), recently published as anonymous, on the basis of Folger Library MS V.a. 428, by Professor Luigi Monga with assistance from Chris Hassel (Geneva and Turin, 1987). It is clear, however, that this manuscript is a slightly abridged version of the one in Durham, Dean and Chapter Library (MS Hunter 134) and was co-authored by the expelled Archdeacon of Northumberland, Dr Isaac Basire, and his pupils, the 14-year-old William Ashburnham, Thomas Lambton, John Lawrence and possibly a Master Ashworth (identified on p. 331 of my *Grand Tour*; see also pp. 17, 58, 299, 334 and 400). This is deducible from *The Correspondence of Isaac Basire . . .*, ed. W.N. Darnell (London, 1831), but for confirmatory photocopies from the Folger, Durham and a microfilm of the University of Padua visitors' book in the Istituto Universitario Europeo, Florence, I thank Laetitia Yeandle, Roger Norris and Linda Tieri. I have since discovered the BPhil (equivalent to MPhil) dissertation by David F. Jones, *An Itinerary of Fraunce and Italy in the yeares 1647 and 1648 by Isaac Basire*, edited with introduction, notes and bibliography (St Andrew's University, 1974), based on the correct Durham MS. More recently, Isaac Basire was the subject of a Durham University PhD thesis (1988) by Canon Colin Brennen whom I also thank for his views on this matter. For further references to Basire and particularly to his pioneering account of the Greek remains at Agrigento and Selinunte, see above Chapter 1, p. 30 and below Chapter 13, note 46. (For brevity's sake, I have referred to Basire as the author, despite Hunter 134 being in several hands, as the content would largely have been based on information supplied by him and the section describing the journey from Rome, Naples, Sicily and Malta and back is entirely in Basire's hand.)

3. J.-G. Arentzen, *Imago Mundi Cartographica* (London, 1984); H. Thurston, *The Holy Year of Jubilee* (London, 1900); and J. Sumption, *Pilgrimage: An Image of Mediaeval Religion* (London, 1975), all *passim*. See now also R.B. Tate and T. Turville-Petre, *Two Pilgrim Itineraries of the Later Middle Ages* (Santiago, 1995). For some instances of the changing use of the term pilgrimage, see Anthony Parr, 'Thomas Coryat and the Discovery of Europe', *Huntington Library Quarterly*, LV (1992), pp. 579-602.

4. *Epistolae de Rebus Familiaribus*, XII, 7, as quoted in Thurston, op. cit., p. 139.

5. Ibid., p. 138.

6. For the likelihood of such meetings, see the essays in *Chaucer and the Italian Trecento*, ed. Piero Boitani (Cambridge, 1983), though the discussion in G.B. Parks, *The English Traveller to Italy . . . (to 1525)* (Rome, 1954), pp. 511-17, is still useful.

7. Muriel Bowden, 'The Good Wife of *Juxta Bathon*', in *A Commentary on the General Prologue to the Canterbury Tales*, 2nd edn (London, 1967), pp. 214-29; but compare the slightly later but hysterically pious pilgrimages documented in *The Book of Margery Kempe*, ed. S.B. Meech, Early English Text Society, os 212 (1940).

8. G.B. Parks, 'Travel as Education', in *The Seventeenth Century*, ed. R.F. Jones (Stanford, CA, 1951), pp. 264-91.

9. Vettori, 'Viaggio in Alemagna', in *Scritti*, ed. E. Niccolini (Bari, 1972), pp. 122, 203-4; compare the version in a useful essay on Renaissance travel in John Hale (ed.) *The Travel Journal of Antonio de Beatis . . . 1517-1518*, Hakluyt Society (1979), p. 20. For Vettori, see the biography by R.D. Jones (London, 1972). For what was probably the more standard, complaining attitude to a journey to Pavia, Siena and Rome on ecclesiastical business, see L. Monga, ' "Inter infectionem pestis et caloris intemperiem": The Voyage to the Council of Pavia-Siena (1423) of the Abbot of St Albans', *Bulletin of the Society for Renaissance Studies*, IV (1986), pp. 7-17.

10. *The English Works of Roger Ascham*, ed. W.A. Wright (Cambridge, 1904), p. 224. This English rendering of the Greek and Latin precedents (also provided) is that of 'M. Watson, myne olde frend, somtime Bishop of Lincolne', the Catholic humanist, Thomas Watson, who was deprived of his see in 1559 and was kept in custody until his death in 1584. Ascham's regard for him seems to have survived his condemnation of Hoby's now deceased teachers, Bucer and Fagius, as heretics and the exhumation and burning of their bodies during the 1556-7 visitation of Cambridge. Sir Philip Sidney also cited Ulysses in encouraging his brother Robert to travel: 'whoe travails with the eye of Ulisses doth take one of the most excellent waies of worldlie wisdome, for hard sure it is to knowe England, without you knowe it by comparing it with others'; *Prose Works*, ed. A. Feuillerat (Cambridge, 1962), III, p. 125.

11. *Volpone* (London, 1606), Act II, Scene i, lines 9-12.

12. *Colloquies*, as quoted in Clare Howard, *English Travellers of the Renaissance* (London, 1914), p. 6. For the context of objections, see the concluding chapter of Sumption, op. cit., the proceedings of the conference on pilgrimage held at the Roehampton Institute and Sara Warneke, *Images of the Educational Traveller in Early Modern England* (Leiden, 1995), esp. Chapter 1.

13. And, of course, among numerous post-Reformation English Catholics; see especially, Gregory Martin, *Roma Sancta (1581)*, ed. G.B. Parks (Rome, 1969) and Thomas Frank, *An Edition of A Discourse of HP His Travelles* (*MS Rawlinson D 83*), (unpublished B.Litt. thesis, St Catherine's Society, Oxford, 1954). (I thank Professor Frank for the loan of his copy of this work.) The Holy Land

continued to attract Protestant visitors, notably Fynes Moryson, William Lithgow and George Sandys, the three most popular travel writers of the Jacobean period; for their works, see R.S. Pine-Coffin, *Bibliography of British and American Travel in Italy to 1860* (Florence, 1974), and supplement, *La Bibliofilia*, LXXIII (1981), pp. 237-61. For Martin, see below, pp. 251-5.

14. In 1581 Montaigne presented a silver statuette of himself, his wife and daughter to the Santa Casa and considered himself fortunate when it was temporarily hung on a wall within the shrine. Galileo visited it in 1618 and again in November 1624 when Descartes also came, thereby fulfilling a vow made some years earlier. Erasmus commented ironically on the Santa Casa; Fynes Moryson and Lithgow were more scathing in their travel accounts but in 1639 Henrietta Maria donated a precious gift to the shrine while the Catholic convert poet, Richard Crashaw, went so far as to become a 'beneficiatus' at Loreto, dying there a few months later in 1649; see my 'Van Dyck, John Hoskins, Jean Petitot and the Ex-Voto of Queen Henrietta Maria', *Burlington Magazine*, CXXII (1980), pp. 837-8 and below, pp. 230-1.

15. *The Correspondence of Erasmus*, ed. R.A.B. Mynors, D.F.S. Thomson and A. Dalzell (Toronto, 1974), I, p. 235 (letter to Robert Fisher who had been a pupil of Erasmus in Paris but had gone to Italy in early 1498 to study law). The literature on Anglo-Italian humanism is too large to cite here, but I mention Roberto Weiss, *Humanism in England during the fifteenth century*, 3rd edn (Oxford, 1967) and the welcome appearance of Denys Hay, *Renaissance Essays* (London and Ronceverte, 1988). See also the masterly essays on Erasmus and More in H.R. Trevor-Roper's volume of the same title (London, 1985).

16. Ibid., p. 235. The most reliable and up-to-date life of Colet is the entry by J.B. Trapp in *Contemporaries of Erasmus*, ed. P.G. Bietenholz and T.B. Deutscher (Toronto, 1985), I, pp. 324-8 though now see also, John B. Gleason, *John Colet* (Berkeley, 1989). Professor Trapp points out that Colet was Greekless until the age of nearly 50, citing the 1516 letter in which Colet writes to Erasmus 'I am sorry I never learnt Greek' (*Correspondence of Erasmus*, ed. cit., No. 423). Later letters (ibid., 468 and 471) contain references to Colet's efforts to learn the language. He is known to have been in Rome in early 1493, however, and to have corresponded with Ficino in the later 1490s. It is therefore probable that he, like Linacre, Grocyn and others, would have visited Florence and was fully aware of the revival of Greek studies before Erasmus met him in England.

17. Henry's request for details on the running of S. Maria Nuova resulted in the presentation, by a descendant of its founder, Francesco Portinari, of a MS *regolamento* (Bodleian Library, MS. Bodley 488). For this and documentation of the Florentine hospital's status as the prototype for the Savoy's design, see H. Colvin (ed.), *The King's Works*, III, pt. i (London, 1975), pp. 196-206. See also for this and later enthusiastic English responses to Italian hospitals Chapter 11 below. More's *Utopia*, which includes a description of an ideal hospital resembling sixteenth-century accounts of Italian hospitals, was first published in 1516. For his likely involvement and other Italian influences, see Paul Slack, *The Impact of Plague in Tudor and Stuart England* (London, 1985), pp. 46, 201, 207-8.

18. Charles Webster, 'Thomas Linacre and the Foundation of the College of Physicians', *Linacre Studies*, ed. F. Maddison, M. Pelling and C. Webster (Oxford, 1977), p. 213. In view of Linacre's medical expertise, his close connections with the court in this period and his tutorship of Prince Arthur

and Princess Mary, he may well have been instrumental in advising Henry on the foundation of the Savoy and on adopting S. Maria Nuova as its model. For qualifications to the inevitably straightforward-seeming Italianate progress presented here, see A. Grafton and L. Jardine, *From Humanism to the Humanities* (London, 1986) and the essays by D. Gray and J.B. Trapp in *Italy and the English Renaissance*, ed. S. Rossi and D. Savoia (Milan, 1989). But Professor Trapp's consciousness of native precedents (e.g. the pre-St Paul's trusteeship by the Mercers' Company of Farthinghoe grammar school; loc. cit., p. 46) does not lead him to abandon an 'innovatory' Colet, creator of 'the first English school that we know of to prescribe the teaching of Greek'.

19. *A Survey of the Great Dukes State of Tuscany in . . . 1596* (London, 1605), p. 62. For Dallington, see A.M. Crinò, 'Documenti relativi al libro di Sir Robert Dallington sulla Toscana', *Fatti e Figure del Seicento Anglo-Toscano* (Florence, 1957), pp. 41-8, K.J. Höltgen, 'Sir Robert Dallington (1561-1637)', *Huntington Library Quarterly*, LIV (1984), pp. 147-77 and Chapter 5 below. For an Italian edition of the *Survey*, see *Descrizione dello Stato del Granduca di Toscana*, ed. N.F. Onesti and L. Rombai (Florence, 1983). Dudley Wilson's article on '*The Strife of Love in a Dreame*, an Elizabethan Translation of Part of the First Book of Francesco Colonna's *Hypnerotomachia*' (*Bulletin of the Society for Renaissance Studies*, IV (1986), pp. 41-53) seems to have been written too soon to accommodate Professor Höltgen's arguments in favour of the translator 'R.D.' being Dallington. For Tudor education, see Joan Simon, *Education and Society in Tudor England* (Cambridge, 1966).

20. See Appendix III of my *Grand Tour*, op. cit., and Chapter 12 below. Milton had to emphasize that the Italians he encountered in 1638-9 merely 'supposed' England was a place of philosophic freedom, as he knew they were referring to a period which he (along with the majority of twentieth-century historians) wished to believe was an 11-year 'Tyranny', necessarily less free than the witch-burning and priest-disembowelling Britain of the Puritan-dominated 1640s.

21. *Some Letters containing an Account of what seemed most remarkable in Switzerland, Italy, &c.* (Rotterdam, 1686), p. 175. For George Berkeley's negative views on scholarship in Genoa and Turin in 1714, see below p. 358, note 56.

22. For Sir Philip, see *Dictionary of National Biography* (DNB), an entry by P.S. Edwards in *History of Parliament. The House of Commons, 1509-1558*, ed. S.T. Bindoff, II (London, 1982), pp. 366-8 and S. Brigden, 'The Letters of Richard Scudamore to Sir Philip Hoby September 1549-March 1555', *Camden Miscellany*, XXX (1990), pp. 67-148. He was well acquainted with Holbein, Aretino and Titian, the latter including a message for Aretino from Hoby in a letter dated 11 November 1550, 'the only known record of an encounter between Titian and an Englishman'; see Charles Hope, 'Titian, Philip II and Mary Tudor', in *England and the Continental Renaissance: Essays for J.B. Trapp*, ed. E. Chaney and P. Mack (Woodbridge, 1990), p. 55, n. 10. Sir Philip was clearly the dominant influence on his brother, for whom the principal source is his autobiography (Camden Society, X (1902), ed. Edgar Powell, *A Booke of the Travaile and life of me Thomas Hoby* (henceforth cited as Hoby). Folios 186-204 of the original MS in the British Library (Egerton 2148) consist of 'A Description of the State of Italy' which remains unpublished. In the absence of any monograph on Hoby, I cite Maria Grazia Padovan's important *tesi de laurea* (University of Pisa, 1982), *Il primo viaggio in Italia di Sir Thomas Hoby*. I have discussed other aspects of his travels in Chapters 1, 4 and 11. One of A.L. Rowse's best essays is devoted to 'Bisham and the Hobys' (*Times,*

Persons and Places (London, 1965), pp. 188–218) while his survey of the effect of Italy on Hoby, William Thomas and others in Part 1, Chapter 1 of *The Elizabethan Renaissance* (London, 1971), pp. 17–26, is very useful. For Hoby as translator, see F.O. Matthiessen, *Translation, an Elizabethan Art* (New York, 1965). Much the best survey of mid-sixteenth-century travel in Italy is E.J. Baskerville's 1967 Columbia University PhD dissertation, *The English Traveller to Italy, 1547–1560* (now available from University Microfilms International, Ann Arbor, Michigan), but see also Lewis Einstein, *The Italian Renaissance in England* (New York, 1902). Other relevant works include: Clare Howard, *English Travellers of the Renaissance* (New York, 1914, reprint 1968); John Hale, *England and the Italian Renaissance*, 2nd edn (London, 1963); A. Lytton Sells, *The Italian Influence in English Poetry from Chaucer to Southwell* (London, 1955); and the 'Italia fuori l'Italia' essays by Le Goff, De Seta and Venturi in the relevant volumes of the *Storia d'Italia* published by Einaudi. Cesare de Seta's essay now forms the basis of the illustrated book *L'Italia del Grand Tour: Da Montaigne a Goethe* (Naples, 1991). For completeness' sake I mention K.R. Bartlett, 'Profit by travelling therein: three mid-sixteenth century views of Italy', *Bollettino del C.I.R.V.I.*, III, ii (1982), pp. 247–59, idem 'Dangers and Delights . . .' *Forestieri e Stranieri* (Florence, 1988), and now idem, *The English in Italy 1525–1558: A Study in Culture and Politics* (Geneva and Turin, 1992), though Professor Bartlett's bibliography lacks Baskerville's *English Traveller to Italy*, cit. As almost all his contemporaries, including Sir Thomas Wyatt, Roger Ascham and Thomas Whythorne, spell Hoby's name with two b's, and the family arms include the falcon known as a hobby, it should clearly be pronounced with a short 'o'.

23. Hoby, p. xiii.
24. Hoby, p. x. Roger Ascham was to praise Cheke and St John's College for educating 'so many learned men . . . at one time, as I believe, the whole Universitie of Louvaine, in many years was never able to affourd' (*The Scholemaster*, in *English Works*, ed. W.A. Wright (Cambridge, 1904), p. 219). For Cheke's Italian exile, see Baskerville, pp. 97–104, also Christina Garrett, *The Marian Exiles* (Cambridge, 1939) and K.R. Bartlett, 'The Strangeness of Strangers', *Quaderni d'Italianistica*, I (1980), pp. 46–63.
25. Hoby, p. 4.
26. Hoby, pp. 5–6. Bucer's treatise was published in 1549 as *The Gratulation of the mooste famous clerk M. Bucer* . . . For his posthumous fate, see n. 10.
27. Chapter 4, n. 56. For a perhaps overenthusiastic survey of the *Courtyer's* impact, see Mary A. Scott, *Elizabethan Translations from the Italian* (New York, 1916), pp. 445–51; cf. P. Burke, *The Fortunes of the Courtier: The European Reception of Castiglione's Cortegiano* (Oxford, 1995). Hoby seems to have done the bulk of his translating after settling in France in July 1552 following the execution of Somerset. It is interesting to note the *Courtyer's* feminist inspiration (given the subject of the third book): 'After I had convayed my stuff to Paris and settled myself there, the first thing I did was to translate into Englishe the third booke of the "Cowrtisan", which my Ladie Marquess [of Northampton] had often willed me to do, and for the lacke of time ever differred it.' Hoby continues: 'And from thense I sent unto Sir Henry Sidney the epitome of the Italian tung which I drue owt there for him' (Hoby, p. 78).
28. For Whitehorne, see *DNB*. The *Arte of Warre* was republished in 1573 and, appropriately, in 1588. He also translated Fabio Cotta's Italian version of Onosandro Platonico's *Of the Generall Captain, and of his Office* (London, 1563) and invented a soldier's life-preserver to be used in fording rivers; see

Baskerville, pp. 8–9 and 14. The title-page of *Arte of Warre* describes
Whitehorne as 'studient of Graies Inne', while the later colophon at the end
of his appended *Certaine Wayes* describes him as a 'felow' of the same institution. His fellow traveller, Francis Peto (below n. 30) was likewise a Fellow
of Gray's Inn (Hoby, p. 19).

29. Hoby, p. 17.
30. Hoby, p. 19. For Stradling and Peto, see Baskerville, *passim*. See also Jonathan
    M. Woolfson *English Students at Padua 1480–1580* (unpublished PhD disser-
    tation, University of London, 1994) which includes a very useful 'Bio-
    graphical Register of English Students at Padua'. Peto's travels were
    subsidized by the government: 'The late King Edward sixte gave him towardes
    his fynding at lerning in Italy a pension yerely during pleasure . . .' (letter
    sent to Philip II, dated 10 September 1556, PRO SP Dom., Mary, IX, cited by
    Baskerville, p. 245). If, as I suspect, the 'Francisco Freitto anglus', entered
    under the date 1546 in J.L. Andrich, *De Natione Anglica et Scota Iuristarum
    Universitatis Patavinae* (Padua, 1892), p. 40, is one of Andrich's numerous
    misreadings (compare note on 'Ignes' for Fynes Moryson in my *Grand Tour*,
    p. 330), and actually refers to Francis Peto (Peyto/Peitto), then the latter's
    arrival in Italy may be put back by more than a year; compare Baskerville,
    who says he arrived in Italy in 1547 and that 'there is no record of his being
    a student at Padua'. For 'Freitto' as advance guard in a new wave of post-
    Poleian English in Padua, see G.B. Parks, 'The First Italianate Englishmen',
    Studies in the Renaissance, VIII (1961), pp. 197–216. Woolfson's entry for Peto
    (op. cit., p. 170), implies that the original manuscript has 'Freitto'.
31. Hoby, p. 21 and below, p. 118. Henry Parker was presumably the grandson
    of Henry, Lord Morley, the translator of Petrarch's *Trionfi*. This Henry became
    still more fervently Catholic than his father and lived as an exile from 1569.
    For William Barker, see note 74 below.
32. Hoby, pp. 24–5. Cf. the implicit reference to Michelangelo's *David* by Thomas
    Wyatt quoted by Lewis Einstein, *Tudor Ideals* (New York, 1921), p. 274.
    Hoby's most interesting account of a work of art is that of Montorsoli's then
    still incomplete Orion Fountain in Messina, 'on[e] of the fairest peece of worke
    that ever I sawe' (p. 45); cf. Birgit Laschke, *Fra Giovan Angelo da Montorsoli*
    (Berlin, 1993). In 1563 Hoby completed a fountain of his own at Bisham
    (p. 129). Public sculpture other than in tombs remained rare in England until
    the 1620s.
33. Hoby, p. 37. For Hoby's Sicilian journey, see above, Chapter 1.
34. Hoby, pp. 52–3.
35. *Diary of Lady Margaret Hoby 1599–1605*, ed. D.M. Meads (London, 1930),
    pp. 269–72 and, for an analysis of implications, Felicity Heal, 'Hospitality and
    Honor in Early Modern England', *Food and Foodways*, 1 (1987), pp. 321–50.
36. Hoby, p. 54. In the *Courtyer's* dedicatory letter to Lord Henry Hastings, Hoby
    expressed the wish that 'we alone in the world may not be still counted
    barbarous in our tongue, as in time out of mind we have been in our
    manners. And so shall we perchance in time become as famous in England
    as the learned men of other nations have been and presently are.'
37. Ascham, *The Scholemaster*, op. cit., p. 218. The best discussion of these
    passages and the MS notes for them is in Parks, 'The first Italianate English-
    men', op. cit., pp. 200–3. See also S. Warneke (op. cit. above, note 12) who
    rightly cites the link between Ascham's 1570 anti-Italianism and Elizabeth's
    excommunication.
38. Ascham, op. cit., p. 234. Sir John Cheke was to write a similar letter after just

ten days in Padua in 1554; see Parks, op. cit., p. 206.

39. Ascham, pp. 228-9. In some ways Ascham's ambivalence towards Italian culture resembles Cato the Elder's attitude to the more ancient (and decadent) civilization of 2nd-century BC Greece on the eve of Rome's rise to supreme power in the Mediterranean.

40. Bodleian Library, Tanner MS 309 fols 54v-55r (dated 27 September 1587). This and Tanner MS 130, also by Powle, have been well exploited by Anton Mączak in his *Travel in Early Modern Europe* (Oxford, 1995) but unfortunately without reference to Virginia F. Stern's *Sir Stephen Powle of Court and Country* (London and Toronto, 1992) which quotes a modernized transcription of the full text of this and other letters from an impressive range of sources.

41. E.H. Sugden, *A Topographical Dictionary to the Works of Shakespeare* . . . (Manchester, 1925), pp. 545-6.

42. *Coryats Crudities hastily gobled up in five moneths travells* . . . (London, 1611), pp. 260-72. Coryate explains that he was imitating Panutius who visited the courtesan Thais 'to persuade her to the feare of God and religion, and the reformation of her licentious life'. Perhaps fellow classicist Gladstone had the same precedent in mind when he visited the wanton courtesans of nineteenth-century London. In a somewhat exaggerated thesis, G.B. Parks places the *Crudities* into a context of 'books in praise of Italy' restarting in 1599 only to be followed by 'The Decline and Fall of the English Renaissance Admiration of Italy' (*Huntington Library Quarterly*, X (1968), pp. 341-57).

43. *The Voyage of Italy: or a Compleat Iourney t[h]rough Italy* (Paris, 1670). For a biography of Lassels, who first used the expression 'Grand Tour' in an English context, see my *Grand Tour*, op. cit.

44. Richard Hurd, *On the Uses of Foreign Travel* (London, 1763), *passim*. For the debate on travel as education in the eighteenth century, see George C. Brauer, *The Education of a Gentleman* (New York, 1959), Chapter VI.

45. Vern L. Bullough, 'Prostitution and Reform in Eighteenth-Century England', *Eighteenth Century Life*, IX, NS III (May 1985), p. 67. See also in the same issue the Grand Tour as an 'erotic tour', in G.S. Rousseau, 'The Pursuit of Homosexuality in the Eighteenth Century'.

46. *The Autobiography of Thomas Whythorne*, ed. James M. Osborn (Oxford, 1961) (henceforth *Autobiography*). Despite the existence of a modern-spelling edition of Whythorne's sixteenth-century phonetic text, also by Osborn (Oxford, 1982), I cite the original edition as it is unabridged. Whythorne says he spent 'ny half A yeer' in Italy (p. 62). He also 'wrote in prose a book of my travel' which unfortunately does not survive; see Introduction, p. xxvii.

47. Philip Heseltine (alias Peter Warlock), *Thomas Whythorne, an unknown Elizabethan Composer* (Oxford, 1925), p. 11, and E.H. Fellowes, *The English Madrigal Composers*, 2nd edn (London, 1948), pp. 34-6.

48. Heseltine, op. cit., p. 5. Compare Kenneth Charlton's claim for Nicholas Yonge's *Musicae Transalpinae* of 1588, in *Education in Renaissance England* (London, 1965), p. 211 and Thomas Watson's own claims for his *First Sett of Italian Madrigals Englished*, published in 1590 (which includes two madrigals by William Byrd).

49. *Autobiography*, p. 60.

50. Ibid., pp. 245 and 248.

51. Ibid., p. 247.

52. For Shute, see the *DNB* and the somewhat speculative introduction by Lawrence Weaver to the facsimile of the 1563 *The First and Chief Grounds*

of Architecture (London, 1912). Shute's connections with Dudley building projects are hypothesized in W. Douglas Simpson's 'Dudley Castle, the Renaissance Buildings', *Archaeological Journal*, CL (1944), pp. 119-25, and, in more general terms, in J. Lees-Milne, *Tudor Renaissance* (London, 1951), pp. 56-7. Most recently, see Maurice Howard, *The Early Tudor Country House* (London, 1987), p. 187, and his 'The Ideal House and Healthy Life: the Origins of Architectural Theory in England', *Les Traités d'Architecture de la Renaissance* (Tours, 1988), pp. 425-31.

53. See preceding note and E. Rosenberg, *Leicester: Patron of Letters* (New York, 1958), pp. 21 and 31; also Baskerville, op. cit., pp. 227, 245 and 248. For Whythorne's fortunes with the Dudleys, see *Autobiography*, pp. xxviii–xxx, 55, 60, 85 and 297-9. Thomas Wilson dedicated his *Arte of Rhetorique* to Northumberland's equally ill-fated son and heir in 1553; see V. Gabrieli, 'Thomas Wilson fra Retorica ed Eresia', *La Cultura*, XII (1974), pp. 381-413 (I thank Lord Dacre for informing me of this article and for the loan of his copy). Given that John Dudley Jr was Edward VI's Master of the Horse from 1552, it was probably he or his father who sent John Parker (of the King's Stables) to Italy in February 1553 (*Acts of the Privy Council*, IV, 212 and 248, cited in Baskerville, p. 7). Ostensibly undertaken in order to buy £400 worth of horses in Naples, Parker may also have been expected to study the latest equestrian fashions. In *The Italian Renaissance in England* (New York, 1905), p. 69, Lewis Einstein points out that Edward VI had an Italian riding master. Although this journey is not mentioned by Peter Edwards in *The Horse Trade of Tudor and Stuart England* (Cambridge, 1988), several other interesting Italian connections are. The French Ambassador, De Noailles, described Northumberland as 'avide de gloire', which was no doubt the principal explanation for his apparently enlightened artistic patronage in this period (H. Chapman, *The Last Tudor King* (London, 1958), p. 156). Like Henry VIII, he died a Catholic.

54. Op. cit., sig. Aii r. With Dudley, Somerset and Sir William Sharrington, Sir John Thynne, builder of Longleat, was one of an elite group of Italianate Edwardians. Applying to work for Thynne in August 1547, Charles Williams boasted of having travelled through Italy as far as Sicily for 12 years. He writes that he is a 'Maker of Gally disshis, and pavements for the same after the manner of Italye: And also can make Style glasses, fynally can both paynt and also write both the maner of Italye; and this said realme of Englande'; Lees-Milne, op. cit., p. 100. Inigo Jones could offer patrons the choice of Italic or Secretary hand more than half a century later.

55. Hoby, p.4. There is a problem with this information as it is supposed to date from January but Thomas dates the preface to his *Principal Rules of the Italian Grammar* '3 February 1548'. For Thomas's biography and other writings, see E.R. Adair, 'William Thomas', in *Tudor Studies Presented to A.F. Pollard*, ed. R.W. Seton-Watson (London, 1924), pp. 132-60; P.J. Laven, *The Life and Writings of William Thomas* (unpublished MA thesis, University of London, 1954); Baskerville, op. cit., *passim*; Sergio Rossi, 'Un "Italianista" nel Cinquecento Inglese: William Thomas', *Aevum*, XL (1966), pp. 281-314; Margie M. Hankinson, 'William Thomas: Italianate Englishman' (unpublished PhD dissertation, Columbia University, 1967); the entry by T.F.T. Baker in *The House of Commons, 1509-1558*, ed. S.T. Bindoff (London, 1982), III, pp. 439-43; Sydney Anglo, 'Our Extremist Shift is to Work by Policy: William Thomas and Early Tudor Machiavellianism', *Transactions of the Honourable Society of Cymmrodorion* (1984), pp. 35-50 and A.J. Carlson 'Mundus Muliebris: The

World of Women Reviled and Defended ca. 195 B.C. and 1551 A.D. . . .',
Sixteenth Century Journal, XXIV (1993), pp. 541-60. See also Felix Raab, *The English Face of Machiavelli* (London, 1965), pp. 40-9. There is a useful modern edition of the *Historie* by G.B. Parks (Ithaca, NY, 1963), but since the text is abridged and spelling modernized I cite the original, now available in facsimile (Amsterdam and Norwood, NJ, 1977).
56. David Loades, *Two Tudor Conspiracies* (1965), 2nd edn (Bangor, 1992).
57. For Florio, see Frances Yates's biography (London, 1934). Thomas was alleged to have planned the assassination of Mary to render Wyatt's rebellion unnecessary. In prison he attempted suicide with a bread knife; at his trial he protested that an esquire should not be tried by a jury of common merchants; at Tyburn he declared that he was dying for his country; see Baker, cit., pp. 442-3.
58. The letter informing Harvell of Thomas's crime, dated 25 March 1545, arrived on the 10 April, having taken less than a fortnight to get to Venice from London. It is not clear why Laven (op. cit., pp. 14 and 24) dates Thomas's flight as far back as 'the end of the year 1544, old style'; see the relevant correspondence in *Letters and Papers Henry VIII*, XX, i, *passim*. Thomas Hoby was to stay with Harvell on his outward journey three years later, paying his respects to Harvell's widow on the way back. Two years after this, Thomas was being considered for the post which Harvell had held. Eventually Peter Vannes was to have it (for whom see Baskerville, *passim*).
59. *Historie*, fol. 138v. For Panciatichi see Janet Ross, *Florentine Palaces* (London, 1905), p. 162; though cf. L. Ginori Lisci, *The Palazzi of Florence* (Florence, 1985), I, pp. 383-5, who argues that the Palazzo Panciatichi in Via Cavour still belonged to Giovanni della Casa of *Galateo* fame, but fails to mention Bartolomeo. In 1544 he was commissioned by Cosimo I to help recruit intellectual talent for Florence (E. Cochrane, *Florence in the Forgotten Centuries* (London and Chicago, 1973), p. 71). According to the *Perygrine*, Thomas heard of the death of Henry VIII in Florence before his debate in Bologna; cf. Laven, op. cit., pp. 29-30, 75-112.
60. *Historie*, fol. 139r. For bibliography, see notes to Frances Yates, 'The Italian Academies', *Renaissance and Reform: The Italian Contribution*, II (London, 1983), pp. 6-29, 223-5. See also Chapter I of idem, *The French Academies of the Sixteenth Century* (London, 1947, 1988). Among other things Thomas might have seen in Florence was the first performance in 1547 of Nicolo Secchi's *Gli Inganni* (published 1562), Shakespeare's source for *Twelfth Night*. For 'The Genesis of Tudor Interest in Italian', see the article by G.B. Parks in *PMLA*, LXXXVII (1962), pp. 529-35.
61. British Library, MS Egerton 837, cited by Adair, pp. 156-60.
62. Ibid., p. 160. The translation of *De Sphaera* was dedicated to Henry Brandon, Duke of Suffolk. For rivalry between the classical and the vernacular, the views of Mulcaster, and the eventual *Triumph of the English Language* (a century or more after the equivalent triumph in Italy), see the book of this title by R.F. Jones (Stanford, CA, 1953). For an excellent summary of the issue in context, see J.B. Trapp, 'Education in the Renaissance' in *Background to the English Renaissance*, ed. J.B. Trapp (London 1974), pp. 67-89.
63. Adair (p. 136) states that Thomas's account of Naples 'makes it abundantly clear that he had never visited that city', but this is not so; see below, p. 109. Adair also states that Thomas 'must have been in Padua' during the winter of 1547-8 but he is more likely to have wintered there a year later.
64. Bartlett (op. cit., p. 253) greatly overstates the case when he says that

Thomas 'could not escape his committed advanced Protestantism and violent hatred of the Roman Church'. Interestingly, Hoby seems to use the disrespectful term only when paraphrasing the Marian abrogation of all statutes against 'the Bisshoppe of Rome's usurped authoritie' on 28 November 1554 (Hoby, p. 119). As early as 1539, on the other hand, Lord Morley (who had never been to Italy but was a fervent admirer of Machiavelli) exhorted Cromwell to 'note well what the Florantyns dyd agaynst the Romysche Bysshop and how lyttle they reputyd his cursynges'. In a published book of the same year, he rounded off his dedication to Henry VIII by wishing him prosperity and 'to your ennemye the Babylonnical byshoppe of Rome, reproufe, shame, and utter ruine'; see *Forty-six Lives translated from Boccaccio's De Claris Mulieribus*, by Henry Parker, Lord Morley, ed. H.G. Wright, Early English Text Society, os 214 (1934), pp. xxxi–iii. Parker's son and grandson both became notorious Catholic exiles.

65. *Historie*, fols 32v–33r. Thomas describes the 'iiii. sundrie facions, *Ionici, Dorici, Italici, and Corinthii, or Tusculani*, as Vitruvius writeth. These kyndes of pyllers were so common amongeste the Romaynes, that almost he was no man, that had not a numbre of pyllers in his house, of white, red, or divers coloured marble, or of porphyrie, or other like riche stone for the graie is not accoumpted marble in Italie, but graie stone.' Thomas's sources for this account include Biondo's *Roma Instaurata* and Andrea Fulvio's *Antiquitates urbis* (1527), Book III. Inigo Jones owned the Italian edition of Fulvio, published in Venice in 1543 (now at Worcester College, Oxford).

66. *Historie*, fol. 3r.

67. Berthelet's preface to the *Principal Rules of the Italian Grammar* (London, 1550), though cf. Laven, op. cit., p. 31.

68. 1560, 1562 and 1567. Best on this is Sergio Rossi, 'Un "Italianista" nel Cinquecento Inglese: William Thomas', *Aevum*, XL (1966), pp. 281–314; see also T.G. Griffith, *Avventure linguistiche del Cinquecento* (Florence, 1961).

69. The preface is signed 'At London the .xx. daie of September. 1549'.

70. G.B. Parks' introduction to Folger edition, op. cit., p. xxvii.

71. For Biondo and Alberti, see essays 3 and 8 in Denys Hay, op. cit., and respective entries in vol. I of the *Dizionario Biografico degli Italiani* (Rome, 1966). On the (limited) extent to which Thomas uses Biondo, see S. Rossi (cit. above in note 55), pp. 296–7.

72. J.H. Hexter, 'The Education of the Aristocracy in the Renaissance', *Reappraisals in History* (London, 1961), pp. 45–70. See also Ruth Kelso, *The Doctrine of the English Gentleman in the Sixteenth Century* (Urbana, IL, 1929), M.H. Curtis, *Oxford and Cambridge in Transition: 1558–1642* (Oxford, 1959), K. Charlton, op. cit., Hugh Kearney, *Scholars and Gentlemen: 1500–1700* (London, 1970) and L. Stone (ed.), *The University in Society*. Vol. I. *Oxford and Cambridge from the 14th century to the early 19th century* (Princeton, 1974). Oxford's 'monkish' clerical bias was still being complained of in the seventeenth century by Aubrey and in the eighteenth by Gibbon. In the early eighteenth century, 30–40 per cent of graduates still became clergymen. By the 1750s, the Grand Tour was threatening to become a substitute for university, with standards drastically in decline and the number of students at Oxford lower than it had been in the 1660s. John Towner's statistical research confirms that between 1547 and 1840 a decreasing percentage of tourists had attended university. Over the same period the increased number of middle-class tourists led to a rise in the average age of the same sample; see 'The Grand Tour: A Key phase in the History of Tourism', *Annals of*

Tourism Research, XII, 3 (1985), pp. 297-33; cf. idem, *The European Grand Tour, c.1550-1840* (unpublished PhD dissertation, University of Birmingham, 1984).

73. *Historie*, fol. 2v-3r.
74. Barker, *The Nobility of Women*, ed. R.W. Bond (Roxburghe Club, I, 1904), p. 88, cited by Baskerville, p. 36. See also ibid., pp. 82-3; G.B. Parks, 'William Barker, Tudor Translator', *Papers of the Bibliographical Society of America*, LI (1957), pp. 126-40 and P.W. Hasler (ed.), *History of Parliament: The House of Commons, 1558-1603*, 3 vols (London, 1981), I, p. 396.
75. Raab, op. cit., p. 40 and Adair, p. 145. For the most detailed survey of the influence of Machiavelli in this period, see Emile Casquet, *Le Courant Machiavélien dans la pensée et la littérature anglaises du XVIe siècle* (Paris, 1974), though cf. my entry on Machiavelli in *The Spenser Encyclopedia*, ed. A.C. Hamilton (Toronto, 1992).
76. *Historie*, fol. 85r-v. See the discussion in Parks, 'The First Italianate Englishmen', op. cit., pp. 205-6. Thomas was evidently familiar with Contarini's *Republica ei magistrati di Vinegia*, mentioning the 'great Contarene' in *Perygrine* (D'Aubant ed., p. 99); cf. Laven, op. cit., pp. 185-6. Confirmation that even 'gospellers' (or Protestants) were protected by the Venetian state became manifest in the 1550s when Marian exiles obtained asylum from prosecution by their own ambassador; see K. Bartlett, op. cit. (n. 22), pp. 133-35.
77. Baker, op. cit., p. 441. It is interesting to note that Hoby travelled with Thomas among the Marquis of Northampton's embassy to France in 1551, both of them seeing the major French renaissance châteaux in the process (Hoby, pp. 66-9).
78. Laven, op. cit., pp. 48-54, 389-91 and *The Chronicle of Edward VI*, ed. W.K. Jordan (London, 1966), pp. xx-xxi.
79. Shakerley's *Guida* first appeared as an appendix to the 1557 edition of *Le Cose Maravigliose*; see Ludwig Schudt, *Le Guide di Roma* (Vienna and Augsburg, 1930), pp. 28-31, 166 and 198-9, though Baskerville, who presents the best survey of Shakerley's career, mentions only the 1562 version which he transcribes in full from the detached British Library copy. Also appended to *Le Cose* was Palladio's *L'Antichità di Roma* (Venice, 1588) which was the source for the notes jotted down by Inigo Jones in his *Roman Sketchbook* in February 1614.
80. S. Schoenbaum, *William Shakespeare: A Compact Documentary Life* (Oxford, 1977), pp. 169-70. See the case of John Cotton, cited in my *Grand Tour*, p. 352. For the Marian exiles and their role in the increased restrictions, see Baskerville, pp. x-xi and 139-42.
81. See John Sparrow, 'The Dating of Donne's Travels', in Theodore Spencer (ed.), *A Garland for John Donne: 1631-1931* (Oxford, 1931), pp. 121-51 and R.C. Bald, *John Donne: A Life* (Oxford, 1970), pp. 50-2. For an analysis of the travels in the context of Donne's Catholicism, see the first chapter of John Carey's *John Donne: Life, Mind and Art* (London, 1981). For Jones's travels, see below, Chapter 7.
82. For Erasmus sharing responsibility for the supervision of the sons of Giovanni Battista Boerio, the king's physician, on their 1506 tour to Italy, see his letter to Linacre and accompanying note in *Correspondence*, ed. cit., II, No. 194. On arrival in Padua, Erasmus also tutored Alexander Stuart, the illegitimate son of James IV, who was already Archbishop of St Andrews; see J.D. Tracy, *Erasmus: the Growth of a Mind* (Geneva, 1972), p. 111-14.
83. 'The Journey of the Queen's Ambassadors unto Rome, anno 1555' (British

Library, Harleian MS. 252, fols 49r–74v partially published in *Miscellaneous State Papers, 1501-1762*, 2 vols (London, 1778), I, p. 99. Another reference to Thomas is on p. 97. This interesting account is not listed in Pine-Coffin's *Bibliography*, cit.

84. Baskerville, p. 34.

85. Ibid., p. 51–52. See also, Sara Warneke, *Images* (cit., above note 12), pp. 37–39 though she does not cite Baskerville.

86. 'The Grand Tour of an Elizabethan', ed. A.H.S. Yeames, *Papers of the British School at Rome*, VII, No. 3 (1914), p. 106: 'it semeth unto me as well as to others that hath ben there that he speketh more in the prayse of itt than it dothe deserve.' John Dee also visited northern Italy in 1563.

87. On the final endpaper a previous reader has inscribed: 'Machiavelli Maxima/Qui nescit dissimulare/nescit vivere'; to which Unton has added his own coment: 'Vive et vivas/Edw. Unton.'; see *The Unton Inventories*, ed. J.G. Nichols, p. xxxviii, and C. Howard, op.cit, p. 56 but both of these provide inaccurate accounts of the inscriptions which are clearly in two different hands. I am very grateful to the late Professor J.H. Whitfield for showing me this book which was in his possession.

88. For the most detailed discussion, see Paul Bacquet, *Un contemporain d'Elisabeth I: Thomas Sackville, l'homme et l'oeuvre* (Geneva, 1966); also C. Wilson, 'Thomas Sackville: An Elizabethan Poet as Citizen', in *Ten Studies in Anglo-Dutch Relations*, ed. J. Van Dorsten (Leiden, 1974), pp. 40–50. Apparently the only surviving poem to justify Jasper Heywood's praise of 'Sackvyldes' sonnets sweetly sauste' is that prefacing Hoby's *Courtyer*. Between 1558 and 1559, Thomas Wilson had also been imprisoned in Rome, being, as he put it in the 1562 edition of his *Arte of Rhetorique*, 'counted an heretic'. The circumstances of his arrest are, however, even more obscure than Sackville's and may have been arranged from Mary's England; see V. Gabrieli, op. cit., pp. 399–401; cf. Barlett, op. cit. *passim*.

89. Bacquet, pp. 39–43.

90. Ibid., pp. 45–9 and for Richard Blount SJ's role in Sackville's conversion, J. Morris, *Troubles of our Catholic Forefathers* (London, 1872), p. 197 citing a letter from Blount in Stonyhurst MSS, Collectanea M, fols. 95–6. Sackville's younger son, also Thomas, converted during his 1602 tour of Italy.

91. For Windsor's Catholic funeral, see *Cal SP Rome*, II (1926), pp. 194–5. For Peckham, see *DNB*, s.v. Sir Edmund Peckham. In 1561, fellow Catholic Sir Edward Carne was also buried in San Gregorio, whence S. Augustine set out for England in 597. For Englefield, see Baskerville, op. cit., pp. 137–42 and A.J. Loomie, *The Spanish Elizabethans* (New York, 1963), pp. 14–51. Arundel's ostensible reason for travelling to Italy was to take the waters, the same given by his Catholic great-nephew, the collector earl, in 1612. The *DNB*'s assertion, followed by Roy Strong and others, that Lord Lumley travelled to Italy in this period, is convincingly rejected by Kathryn Barron in *Classicism and Antiquarianism in Elizabethan Patronage: The Case of John, Lord Lumley* (unpublished M.Litt. dissertation, University of Oxford, 1996), Appendix.

92. Parks, 'The Italianate Englishman', op. cit., p. 209. Parks records the earliest known use of the expression 'ung Inglese Italianato e ung diavolo incarnato' as being that by Sir William Paget in a letter to the Privy Council dated 1546 (ibid., p. 200); see also Baskerville, op. cit., p. 37.

93. Ibid., pp. 211–12; compare Clare Howard, op. cit., p. 63. For Barker's involvement, see F. Edwards, *The Marvellous Chance: Thomas Howard and the Ridolphi Plot* (London, 1968), *passim*.

94. Bacquet, *passim*.

95. *The Correspondence of Sir Philip Sidney and Hubert Languet*, ed. S.A. Pears (London, 1845), pp. 1–3.

96. Ibid., pp. 12 and 61. In his presumably less anti-Italian youth, Languet had been painted by Titian who was considered too old to do the same for Sidney, Paolo Veronese being employed instead; see James M. Osborn, *Young Philip Sidney 1572–77* (New Haven and London, 1972), pp. 151–7, where the extension of Sidney's travels to Genoa and Florence is also discussed; see also below, notes 104–5.

97. See, for example, the background to the publication in London in 1619 of 'Paolo Sarpi's *History of the Council of Trent*' as described by Frances Yates in the article now republished in *Renaissance and Reform*, cit., pp. 189–217. The future Bishop Hall was not yet 'the defiant assertor of episcopacy' he was to become; see H.R. Trevor-Roper, 'Laudianism and Political Power', in *Catholics, Anglicans and Puritans* (London, 1987), p. 59. F.L. Huntley, *Bishop Joseph Hall* (Cambridge, 1979), has disappointingly little on *Quo vadis?*

98. *Compleat Gentleman*, 1633 edn, p. 229. Peacham continues: 'in my opinion nothing rectifieth and confirmeth more the judgement of a Gentleman in forraine affaires, teacheth him knowledge of himselfe, and setleth his affection more sure to his owne Country, then travaile doth.' Unfortunately, the dedicatee of Peacham's book, Lord Arundel's son, William Howard, later Viscount Stafford, was executed during the Popish Plot.

99. *Cal. S.P. Ven. 1558–80*, VI, p. 524.

100. C. Howard, op. cit., p. 73 and Baskerville (cit. above, note 22), pp. 45–54. After causing scandal in France, Thomas never got as far as Italy, partly because Cecil lost his other son in the meantime, which rendered Thomas more precious. 'Fayne i wold he shold see Italy and loth to object hym to hazard', he now wrote in poignant despondency to Windebank, leaving the decision to the tutor who considered 'the Inticement to pleasure and wantones' they would find in Italy too much of a risk; see G. Ravenscroft Dennis, *The House of Cecil* (London, 1914), chapter V.

101. R.W. Lightbown, 'The Protestant Confessor, or the Tragic History of Mr Mole', in *England and the Continental Renaissance . . .*, ed. E. Chaney and P. Mack (Woodbridge, 1990), pp. 239–56. John P. Feil, *Sir Tobie Matthew and his Collection of Letters* (unpublished PhD dissertation, University of Chicago, 1962), pp. 59–70, contains a good account of the Mole scandal and of the key role played by the Archbishop of York's son, Tobie Matthew, who had converted to Catholicism in Florence in 1605. For the 3rd Baron Burghley and his son, see G.E.C., *Complete Peerage*, and J. Irene Whalley, 'Italian Art and English Taste: an early-seventeenth-century letter', *Apollo*, XCIV (1971), pp. 184–91, though the latter incorrectly identifies the author of the letter as the 'great' Lord Burghley's nephew. William Jr wrote to his grandfather from Padua on 20 July and 8 and 24 November 1585 (see *Cal. S.P. Dom.*). His second licence to travel was issued in June 1599 (*Cal. S.P. Dom., 1598–1601*, p. 223). Though he may have returned to Italy after the 1604 Spanish treaty, he had already developed a taste for art and architecture which was extremely sophisticated by English standards. See the brief discussion of him and Roos in D. Howarth, *Lord Arundel and his Circle* (New Haven and London, 1985), pp. 20–1, but beware Howarth's exacerbation of Whalley's confusion over identity.

102. John Buxton, *Sir Philip Sidney and the English Renaissance* (London, 1966), p. 66. Cecil's *Memoryall for the Erle of Rutland* is PRO SP Dom. Elizabeth LXXVII,

no. 6 (20 Jan. 1571).

103. Roger Howell, *Sir Philip Sidney, the Shepherd Knight* (London, 1968), p. 146 and Richard Simpson, *Edmund Campion: A Biography* (1867), corrected edn (London, 1896), p. 114.

104. Simpson, op. cit., *passim*. K.J. Höltgen has recently confirmed that George More, Donne's future father-in-law, accompanied Sidney on this 1577 embassy to Germany; 'Why there are no Wolves in England', *Anglia*, XCIV (1981), pp. 60–82. See now T.M. McCoog (ed.), *The Reckoned Expense: Edmund Campion and the English Jesuits* (Oxford, 1996).

105. Simpson, op. cit., p. 123. Thomas Fitzherbert, SJ, the Rector of the English College, Rome, who was to entertain an ungrateful Milton in 1638, remembered in a letter of February 1628 that Sidney confessed that 'one of the most memorable things he had witnessed abroad was a sermon by Campion, at which he had assisted with the Emperor in Prague' (Simpson, op. cit., pp. 115–16). See also Katherine Duncan-Jones, *Sir Philip Sidney: Courtier Poet* (London, 1991); she develops this theme and concludes that: 'Perhaps Sidney was a discreet Catholic fellow traveller for a while after his meetings with Campion', op. cit., p. 127; cf. idem, 'Sir Philip Sidney's debt to Edmund Campion' in T.M. McCoog (ed. cit.), pp. 85–102.

106. For this, and its connection with other 'unfortunate explosions', including Ben Jonson's great Parliamentary fart of 1610, see the hilarious account in H.R. Trevor-Roper, 'Nicholas Hill, the English Atomist', *Catholics, Anglicans and Puritans*, op. cit., pp. 3–9.

107. B.M. Ward, *The Seventeenth Earl of Oxford, 1550–1604, from contemporary documents* (London, 1928), pp. 164–77.

108. See above pp. 10–11. A little-known account of the death of the Admirable Crichton is to be found in Fynes Moryson's *Fourth Part of an Itinerary*, Corpus Christi College (Oxford) MS 94, fol. 153. As early as 1567, Oxford had killed a servant of Burghley's in a sword fight.

109. Ward, op. cit., pp. 206–14.

110. Parks, 'The First Italianate Englishmen', op. cit., p. 215. For Gilbert, see B. Basset, *The English Jesuits* (London, 1967), pp. 25–6.

111. Modern edition by P.J. Ayres (Oxford, 1980).

112. See A.L. Rowse, 'Edward de Vere 17th Earl of Oxford', *Eminent Elizabethans* (London, 1983), pp. 88–9 and under 'Italianate' in the *OED*.

113. See note 81 above and, for the establishment of Trinity College, Dublin, in 1591 as an alternative to the corruption of foreign travel, p. 320 below.

114. Dowland demonstrated his patriotism by forwarding the names of compatriots encountered in Italy in 1595 and, in at least one instance, enclosing a letter written in Florence by the Catholic priest John Scudamore recommending him to Father Fitzherbert in Rome (though in the event he did not dare go this far south); see Diana Poulton, *John Dowland* (London, 1972, rev. edn, 1982), pp. 35–41. One of the two men he reported meeting at Bologna, 'Pierce an Irishman', was surely the Catholic convert, Henry Piers, for whom see, T. Franks (ed.), *An Edition of A Discourse of HP his Travelles* (unpublished BLitt thesis, University of Oxford, 1954).

115. Franks, op. cit., p. 3p1 and 46.

116. See the account based on Throckmorton's unpublished diary in A.L. Rowse, *Ralegh and the Throckmortons* (London, 1962), pp. 91–3. Before being frightened home by a 'warning to depart out of Florence', following news of arrests in Rome, Throckmorton had socialized with Florentine nobility and studied music with Galileo's father, Vincenzo. For Standen being loaned to

Thomas Arundel as a guide and travelling companion in 1580 when his own fell ill, see A.M. Crinò, 'Contatti tosco-britannici nel Seicento', *English Miscellany*, XII (1961), pp. 151–2.

117. *HMC Salisbury MSS*, VII, (1899), p. 10, letter dated Pisa, 8 January 1597.

118. L. Pearsall Smith, *The Life and Letters of Sir Henry Wotton*, 2 vols (Oxford, 1907), I, p. 70n, below p. 197, n. 30, and Howarth, op. cit., p. 231, n. 57, who, however, also quotes Winwood on Arundel, reporting that the King 'doth find the matter most ridiculous'.

119. *Cal. S. P. Ven. 1636–1639*, XXIV, p. 303.

120. J.L. Lievsay, *The Elizabethan Image of Italy* (Ithaca, NY, 1964).

121. For example: *The Traveiler of Jerome Turler* (London, 1575), an anonymous translation of H. Turler's *De peregrinatione*; William Bourne's *Treasure for Traveilers . . .* (London, 1578) (not much on Italy); *A Direction for Travailers. Taken out of Iustus Lipsius, and enlarged for the behoofe of the right honorable Lord, the yong Earle of Bedford, being now ready to travell* (London, 1592), a free translation of Lipsius's *Epistola de peregrinatione italica*, by the adopted son of Hoby's fellow traveller, Sir Edward Stradling; the significantly titled *A Discourse not altogether unprofitable, nor unpleasant for such as are desirous to know the situation and customes of forraine Cities without travelling to see them*, by Samuel Lewkenor; and the introductory chapter of Robert Dallington's *Method for Travell* (London, 1605), based on his travels in France and Italy with the Earl of Rutland and his brothers (and probably Inigo Jones) in 1596–1600. As well as these, there are innumerable unpublished manuscripts in this genre. Although Francis Bacon's 'Of Travel' should be mentioned here, the genre may be said to have reached its witty climax in Richard Lassels's 'Preface to the Reader, concerning Travelling', published posthumously in *The Voyage of Italy* (Paris, 1670). A good survey of some of these is in Charlton, op. cit., pp. 215–19.

122. Brinsley Ford, 'The Englishman in Italy', in *The Treasure Houses of Britain*, ed. G. Jackson-Stops (New Haven and London, 1986), p. 41. For Shaftesbury, see below, Chapter 13.

4

The Grand Tour and Beyond:
British and American Travellers in
Southern Italy, 1545-1960

ᴇᴏᴇᴏ

NAPLES: THE RISE AND FALL OF AN
INTERNATIONAL REPUTATION

WHEN, IN 1705, Joseph Addison declared that there was 'certainly no Place in the World where a Man may Travel with greater Pleasure and Advantage than in Italy', he was referring to a country whose southernmost point, as far as the tourists were concerned, was still Naples.[1] More heavily biased than his predecessors towards the 'classic ground' of Italy, Addison was unusual in having also visited Capri, 'being very desirous to see a Place that had been the Retirement of *Augustus* for some time, and the Residence of *Tiberius* for several Years'.[2] In October 1700 John Dryden junior, son of the poet, had 'rowed quite around the island' with some friends, describing a marine cavern he called the 'Grotta Cieca' as 'so romantique, that we cou'd not but fancy it belong'd to some sea god, as his court or palace'.[3]

The majority of early eighteenth-century Grand Tourists, however, did not include even this brief excursion off the beaten track, assuming no doubt, as a French traveller was still doing a century later, that: 'L'Europe finit à Naples . . . La Calabre, la Sicile, tout le reste est de l'Afrique.'[4] The standard *Giro d'Italia* was still very much that which the mid-seventeenth-century travel writers had formulated. 'Sufficiently sated with rolling up and downe', in the words of John Evelyn [Fig. 16], they had regarded Naples, or more precisely

16 Robert Walker, *John Evelyn* (1648). [National Portrait Gallery, London]

Vesuvius, up which an afternoon's clamber was already obligatory, as 'the Non ultra of [their] Travells'.[5] The relatively superficial nature of their acquaintance even with Naples and its environs is suggested by a manuscript *Description of Italy*, written in 1654 by the Catholic priest and travelling tutor, Richard Lassels, at the request of a young Scottish aristocrat, David Murray, Lord Balvaird:

> Being thus come to Rome about the midle of November (if you sett out of Paris about the midle of September), while yet the weather is good, and whiles some freind furnish you a house; and whiles your Tayler is makeing you clothes sutable to that Court, your Lordship may go to Naples, a journey which will cost you onely fifteen dayes; that is, five in going, five in comeing, and five in staying there . . . you may either go with the Procaccio, or els take a Vetturino of your owne who will horse you and defray you to Naples; lett you have his horses two dayes there, to see Vesuvius and Puzzolo, and bring you home againe, for thirteen or fourteen crownes a man.[6]

Lassels's recommended route, that taken by almost all seventeenth-century travellers, involved leaving Rome by the Porta di S. Giovanni on the Via Appia Nuova. Having spent the first night at Piperno (Priverno), one set out in convoy through bandit-infested country, soon passing Fossanova and the Cistercian Abbey in which Aquinas, 'going to the Councel of Lions by ordre of Gregorie the Tenth, fell sick and dyed' in 1274.[7] Descending into the Agro Pontino, one joined the ancient Appian Way – 'smooth and shyne-ing . . . like a sylver highway' – and came 'at last . . . to Terracina to dinnar and to Fundi to Supper in the Kingdome of Naples'.[8] It was at this stage of their journey, having passed the admonitory marble plaque proclaiming the 'Fines Regni Neopolitani', that the travellers began to recognize the fertile landscape which classical texts, familiar since their school-days, led them to expect. In 1647 the teenage Royalist, John Raymond, compiling what was to be the first English guidebook to Italy, quoted Cicero on the now 'spoild' city of Fondi and a neo-Latinizing predecessor of Goethe on its still flourishing situation:

> Collibus hinc atque; inde Lacu simul aequore cinctum
> Citria cui florent hortis e littore Myrti.[9]

Then as if to bring these lines to life Raymond recalls how, together with his uncle, John Bargrave, and fellow student, Alexander Chap-

17 Matteo Bolognini, *Alexander Chapman, Dr John Bargrave and John Raymond* (painted in Siena, 1647). [Canterbury Cathedral Library]

man, he 'went into an Orchard, and for twenty Citrons & about thirty Oranges, . . . gave the Owner a *Julio* (that comes to an English sixpence), which very well contented him' [Fig. 17].[10] Two years earlier Evelyn had helped himself to 'Oranges & Citrons for nothing'. 'I shall never forget', he wrote later:

> how exceedingly I was delighted with the Sweetnesse of this passage, the Sepulchers mixed amongst the verdures of all Sorts; besides being now come within sight of that noble Citty Cajeta [Gaeta] which gives a surprizing Prospect along the Tyrhen Sea, in manner of a Theater; & here we beheld that strangly cleft Rock, an hideous & frightfull spectacle; which they have a tradition hapn'd upon the Passion of our B: Saviour [Fig. 18]: But the hast of our Procaccio suffer'd us not to dwell so long on these objects, and the many antiquities of this Towne as we desired.[11]

Continuing along the Appian Way, past the so-called 'Tomb of Cicero' and wondering meanwhile at 'a world of Corke Trees', one eventually arrived at the ruined amphitheatre and aqueduct of ancient Minturnae and took the ferry across the Garigliano:

> Passing the ferry you ride along the fine green feilds which at last shew

18 *Gaeta*; from John Breval, *Remarks* (London, 1738), vol. 1, p. 76. Copper engraving by
Pierre Fourdrinier. [E. Chaney]

> you the Mons Massicus [Monte Massica or Garo] famous anciently for
> Vinum Massicum and by and by to Santa Agatha; from thence a mile
> further to Cascana.[12]

Having stayed the night at S. Agata or Cascana, one rose early 'to
come to dinnar to Capua . . . and at night (having passed by Aversa
a pleasant litle towne) to Naples'.[13] The road from 'once mighty'
Capua to Naples, was, according to Evelyn, 'as straight as a line
could lay it, & of a huge breadth, swarming with travellers more
than ever I remember any of our greatest, & most frequented roads
neere London'.[14]

On arrival in the city, most seventeenth-century visitors stayed
either at the 'Aquila Nera' or at the 'Tre Re'. John Evelyn, who spent
about a week at the latter in 1645, remembered it as 'a Place of
treatement to excesse . . . where provisions are miraculously cheape,
& we seldome sat downe to fewer than 18 or 20 dishes of the most
exquisite meate & fruites.'[15]

In January 1639, John Milton [Fig. 19] had as his guide around
Naples and the viceroy's court, Tasso's former friend and biographer,
Giambattista Manso. From the poetic but scholarly description of the

19 Unknown artist,
John Milton. [National
Portrait Gallery, London]

city with which the latter introduced his *Vita di Tasso* in 1621 we
may realize how fortunate Milton was in having got himself introduced (by the mysterious 'hermit' with whom he had travelled down
from Rome) to this aristocratic man of letters. In calling on Manso
at his villa near Posillipo, incidentally, Milton would also have
visited the Solfatara, an experience which may well have influenced
his description of Hell.[16]

Though in Rome Evelyn and his friends had hired a 'Sightsman'
to show them round, in Naples they seem to have relied on their
Latin and Italian guidebooks and 'hired a Coach to carry [them]
about the Towne'. After several days' sightseeing, during which
certain of his companions 'did purchase their repentance at a deare
rate, after their returne' as a consequence of encounters with some
of the city's '30000 registered sinners', Evelyn felt he was in a
position to sum up:

> The building of the Citty is for the quantity the most magnificent of
> Europe, the streetes exceeding large, well paved, having many Vaults,

and conveyances under them for the sullage which renders them very sweete and cleane even in the midst of winter: To it belongeth more than 3000 churches and monasteries, and those the best built & adornd in Italy: they greately affect the Spanish gravity in their habite, delight in good horses; the streetes are full of Gallants, in their Coaches, on horse-back, & sedans, from hence brought first into England by Sir Sanders Duncomb: The Women are generaly well featur'd, but excessively libidinous; the Country people so jovial and addicted to Musick, that the very husbandmen almost universaly play on the guitarr, singing and composing songs in prayse of their Sweete-hearts.[17]

Before three accounts which appeared between 1614 and 1617, only two coherent English descriptions of Naples, or indeed Italy, had ever been written: William Thomas's *Historie*, first published in 1549, and the one found in the manuscript autobiography of Sir Thomas Hoby [Fig. 3], dating from the following year.[18] The long lacuna which lay between this pair of mid-sixteenth-century accounts and the sudden crop of Jacobean publications was primarily the result of the breakdown of England's political relations with Spain, which then dominated most of Italy, including the vast kingdom of Naples. Whatever Marlowe, Shakespeare and their Italian-obsessed contemporaries lacked in first-hand familiarity, they more than made up for in fantasy, but it was not until 1604 that peace between the two countries was re-established, and even then it took a long time before English Protestants felt confident of not being molested by the Inquisition on their travels. Only in the 1630s, after Charles I and Philip IV signed a treaty of peace and friendship, could the Grand Tour finally establish itself in the form it was to retain for the next two centuries.[19]

The publication of Edward Webbe's *Rare and most wonderfull things* in 1590 had meanwhile done little to encourage his fellow country-men to explore southern Italy. Having been ransomed from the Turks, Webbe had the misfortune to be almost immediately recap-tured and imprisoned in the year of the Armada by the Spanish at Naples. He was given the *strappado*, that is, 'hoysted up backward with my handes bound behind me which strocke all the iointes in my armes out of ioint', and then 'constrained to drinke salte water and quicklyme and then fine lawne or callico [was] thruste downe my throate and pluckt up again readie to pluck my hart out of my belly, al to make me confesse that I was an English spye.'[20]

It is not surprising that in the following decade, when Fynes Moryson and the future ambassador to Venice, Henry Wotton, visited Naples, they went about disguised, the former as a French Catholic, the latter as a German.[21] As late as 1639 Milton claims that he was tipped off by English merchants at Naples that a Jesuit plot awaited him at Rome, but by this date such a story is unconvincing and he probably published it partly in order to enhance his prestige in Puritan England and partly to disguise the extent to which he had in fact fraternized with Catholics whilst in Italy.[22]

It is a sad irony that William Thomas, author of the first English book on Italy and the first Anglo-Italian grammar-cum-dictionary, should have been executed within five years of his return to England for treasonable opposition to the marriage of Mary Tudor and Philip II of Spain, for this sophisticated but fiery Welshman's active Protestantism had not prevented his being a great admirer of Catholic Italy in general and Spanish Naples, 'one of the fayrest citees of the worlde', in particular. There seems no reason to doubt that Thomas visited Naples, whose 'goodly streetes and beautifull buildyng of temples and houses' he praised enthusiastically'; 'specially the Castell Novo, wherin the kynges were wonte (as the Vicere now is) to be most commonly resident: beyng one of the rarest buildyngs for greatnesse and strength, that any where is lightly to be founde.'[23]

In late 1549, a few months after Thomas published his *Historie of Italie*, the 19-year-old Thomas Hoby left Siena for Rome on hearing of the death of Pope Paul III. At first it seemed that Reginald Pole would be elected his successor, but 'he . . . lost by the Cardinall of Ferrara his meanes the voice of manie cardinalls of the French partie, persuading them that Cardinall Poole was both Imperiall and also a verie Lutherian.' Impatient with what then became one of the longest papal conclaves in history, Hoby and three companions 'determined in the meane time to make a journeye to Naples'.[24] Despite so apparently casual a beginning, this journey turned out to be the first leg of the first extensive tour of southern Italy on record:

> We sett owt of Roome in a vessell . . . the X of Januarye [1550]; the same night we laye upon the Tever. The next morning we cam to Ostia, a verie auntient citie . . . After we were . . . cum into the see, we sayled all that night after and passed Monte Circello . . . In a litle port under the hill lye manie times Moores and Turks with their foistes and other

> vesselles to take the passinger vesselles that goo betwixt Roome and
> Naples . . . yf we had cum bye yt by daye . . . we had bine all taken
> slaves. From hense we sayled to Gaieta [Fig. 18] an auntient towne
> taking his name of Eneas' nurse so named and buried there, as Virgil
> makethe mention.[25]

Here Hoby and his friends disembarked to inspect the castle which
made Gaeta 'on[e] of the strongest holdes in all christendom'.
Thanks to not having a pre-paid *procaccio* constantly urging him on
– as Evelyn was to have a century later – Hoby was able to contemplate Gaeta's 'antiquities' at his leisure. Partly as a result of such
visits, it is interesting to note that Hoby's sea route to Naples took
just as long as the standard overland one:

> Betwext Gaieta and Naples we were sailing two dayes, which is lx miles
> by seea: we passed by the iland of Pontia [Ponza], whiche they saye was
> Pontius Pilate's inheritance. And we sailed by Ischia and Procida, and
> so cam to the citie of Naples, where we arrived the fift day after owr
> setting furthe of Roome.[26]

Hoby described Naples in detail. In this 'verie beawtifull citie
situated betwext the seea and verie pleasant hilles', he particularly
admired the 'howses', the flourishing university, the fortifications
(which the Emperor Charles V was in the process of extending), the
'sumptious palaces, delicious gardines, and sundrie divises of fountaynes round abowt it'. At this period, somewhat exceptionally, the
Spanish Viceroy (Don Pedro di Toledo) was 'verie well beloved both
in the citie and throwghowt the realm'.[27] Like most of his travelling
compatriots during the next two centuries, Hoby also praised the
'very bewtifull and large hospitall', the Annunziata. Even the anti-
papist Gilbert, later Bishop Burnet, conceded that this was 'the
greatest Hospital in the World' and went on to describe it in some
detail, probably hoping that English readers might improve their
own relatively backward facilities for the poor and sick along
similar lines.[28]

Rare before the eighteenth century were general observations on
Neapolitan daily life of the kind supplied by John Ray who, in 1664,
also visited Sicily, Malta and Gozo in his quest for rare botanical and
geological specimens:

> To cool the streets in the afternoon they draw about a tun filled with
> cold water, and bored with several holes, whence the water gushes out

as it goes along. The Dialect of the common people is much different from the *Tuscane*, and not to be understood but by one who hath a long time conversed with them. This City is well served with all provisions, especially fruit which is very cheap heer . . . *Macarones* and *Vermicelle* (which are nothing but a kind of paste cut into the figure of worms or thongs) boil'd in broth or water, are a great dish heer as well as at *Messina*, and as much esteemed by the vulgar, as Frumenty by the Countrey people in *England*. All the *Neopolitans* and *Sicilians*, and generally the *Italians* drink their Wine and water snowed [iced]; and you shall see many stalls in the streets where there is snowed water to be sold: many also you shall meet, with a barrel at their backs and glasses in their hands, crying *Acqua ghiacciata*, or *Acqua nevata*.[29]

Even rarer were coherent remarks about Neapolitan art and architecture, though Bullen Reymes and his friends twice visited Artemisia Gentileschi and her daughter (who also painted) in March 1634 [Fig. 20]. In the spring of 1651 the self-exiled Royalist connoisseur,

20 Bullen Reymes's *Travel Diaries* (1633–36), open on fols. 129v-130r on which Reymes records his visit to Artemisia Gentileschi and her daughter ('who also paints') in Naples on Saturday 18 March 1634. [E. Chaney]

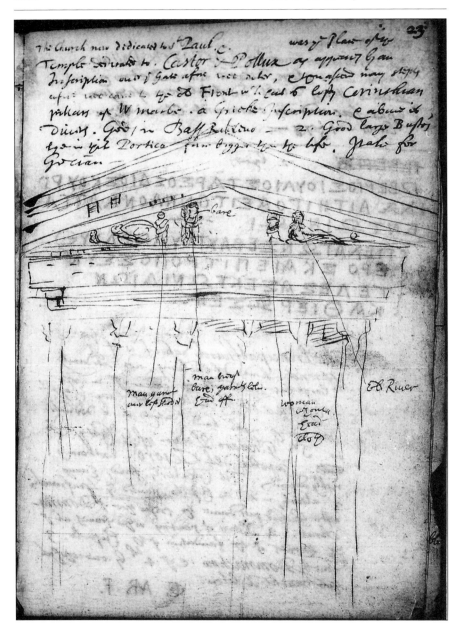

21 Richard Symonds, annotated sketch of the portico of the Temple of Castor and Pollux in Naples (which prior to the earthquake of 1688 stood in front of the Church of San Paolo Maggiore), from Symonds's 1651 travel notebook. [Bodleian Library MS Rawlinson D.121, p. 23]

Richard Symonds, surveyed the city with unusual thoroughness. He admired the works of Domenichino and Lanfranco in the Cathedral and Guido Reni and Ribera in the Certosa di San Martino. Like Inigo Jones almost 40 years earlier, Symonds also studied the Corinthian temple portico of San Paolo Maggiore, providing us with one of our most informative sketches of this no longer extant antiquity [Fig. 21]. Others such as John Evelyn, who used Raymond and Lassels to write up his account, were more derivative. In this respect the seventeenth-century French travellers were more sophisticated, Jean Jacques Bouchard and Maximilien Misson being particularly interesting for their sympathetic appreciation of the Neapolitan baroque before the weighty pronouncements of Muratori, Montesquieu and others on the subject of 'le bon goût' stifled such old-fashioned enthusiasms.[30] Lassels's thorough acquaintance with Vasari, however, had considerably enriched his (and thus the English) aesthetic vocabulary, even if it conditioned him to prefer 'the rare hand' of Domenichino in the 'moderne' and 'beautiful' Cappella di San Gennaro in the Duomo to that of the more Caravaggesque Ribera.[31] Indeed, for all the Huguenot Misson's criticisms of Lassels's 'Unexactnesses, Puerilities [and] gross Ignorances', it is clear that the Anglophile Frenchman learned a great deal from the guidebook whose title he merely updated.[32] On the subject of Fanzago's grey and white marble decoration at the Certosa di San Martino there is little to choose between the detailed praise both authors bestow on this 'most sumptuous thing in all *Europe*'.[33]

Though he may have been slow to appreciate both its art and its vital role in the *Settecento riformatore*, by the second half of the eighteenth century the travelled Englishman was as familiar with the city of Naples as he had been with Paris in the seventeenth.[34] Dr Johnson would have had it in mind when he declared that, 'A man who has not been in Italy, is always conscious of an inferiority, from his not having seen what it is expected a man should see. The Grand object of travelling is to see the shores of the mediterranean.'[35] One of the few distinguished men of his time who died without seeing Naples, Johnson would have chosen to tour Pompeii and Herculaneum with his 'companionable' biographer instead of the Hebrides, had he been 30 years younger. As it was, in late 1763 he accompanied the 22-year-old Boswell as far as Harwich but there parted with his new friend, who began his continental tour alone.

The next two decades – from the Treaty of Paris to the outbreak of war with revolutionary France – may be regarded as the climax of the Grand Tour, Naples in particular being visited by an extraordinary range of Boswell's celebrated contemporaries. As well as painters and sculptors such as J.R. Cozens, Thomas Jones, Henry Raeburn, Joseph Wright, Christopher Hewetson and Joseph Nollekens, these included the brothers and sons of George III, the millionaire aesthete William Beckford, the musicologist Charles Burney, the actor David Garrick, the historian Edward Gibbon, the philanthropist John Howard, the singer Michael Kelly, the connoisseur Richard Payne Knight, the surgeon Samuel Sharp, the novelist Laurence Sterne, the Catholic collector Charles Townley and Boswell's profligate politician friend John Wilkes.[36] Three female travellers, Lady Anna Miller, Hester Piozzi and Mariana Starke, published descriptions of Naples in this period, thereby establishing a literary precedent which Lady Morgan and the Countess of Blessington would improve upon in the next century.[37] Distinguished late eighteenth-century American visitors included the artist John Singleton Copley and his friends Ralph and Alice Izard, all of whom extended their tours as far as Paestum in 1775.[38]

From 1764 to the end of the century, the English community and the Grand Tourists were protected and entertained by their learned ambassador, Sir William Hamilton. Being an authority on both volcanoes and classical remains, Hamilton was frequently consulted, even by non-English visitors to the city such as Casanova and Goethe. The former knew Hamilton when his musically gifted first wife was still alive, but by the time of the latter's visit to Naples the major new attraction at the splendidly situated Palazzo Sessa was the voluptuous Emma Hart, soon to become the second Lady Hamilton and Nelson's mistress. 'Sie ist sehr schön und wohl gebaut', wrote Goethe, who could 'scarcely believe his eyes' when, thinly clad in a Greek costume which 'der alte Ritter' had designed for her, she performed her neoclassical 'poses plastiques' before a specially invited audience.[39]

Though the extreme poverty of the *lazzaroni* – Boswell's 'shocking race: eaters of garlic and catchers of vermin' – was frequently commented on, attention was chiefly focused upon the spectacular luxury of the Neapolitan court. The gilded carriages drawn by six or eight horses, the vast numbers of servants, the lavish receptions at Caserta and the operas and balls at San Carlo amazed even the wealthiest English visitors.[40]

Naples continued to be regarded as one of the grandest and most sophisticated cities in Europe until well into the nineteenth century. Arriving there in February 1817, Stendhal agreed with that 'Voltaire des voyageurs en Italie', Charles de Brosses, that it was 'la seule capitale de l'Italie'.[41] The Via Toledo, 'un des grands buts de mon voyage', was 'la rue plus peuplée et la plus gaie de l'univers'. It was not until he had 'couru les auberges pendant cinq heures', that he realized that 'il faut qu'il y ait ici deux ou trois mille Anglais', all taking advantage of the new era of peace – and of the new French-built roads – which Britain had secured by defeating Napoleon.[42] That Stendhal's estimate was not exaggerated is suggested by the statement published in the *Gentleman's Magazine* for the same month (less than two years before the arrival of Shelley and his growing family further swelled their numbers) that 'The emigration of our countrymen to Italy is so extensive, that 400 English families now reside at Naples alone.'[43]

In terms of travel literature, the climax of English enthusiasm for *ancien régime* Naples was Lady Blessington's still very readable *The Idler in Italy*, which appeared in two volumes in 1839. 'The more I see of the Neapolitans', she declared, 'the better I like them.'[44] But although in the same year in which these words were published Macaulay also formed a 'very favourable' impression of Naples, just a year later the headmaster of Rugby, Dr Arnold, was registering puritanical disgust with both the place and its inhabitants, and in this, as in much else, he anticipated the prejudices of his fellow Victorians.[45] Visiting Naples in 1845, Charles Dickens was no less critical though perhaps more broadminded. Where Arnold had waxed indignant that Naples 'stained the fame even of Nelson' (who had himself scorned this 'country of fiddlers and poets, whores and scoundrels'), Dickens was primarily concerned that 'lovers and hunters of the picturesque [should] not keep too studiously out of view the miserable depravity, degradation, and wretchedness, with which this gay Neapolitan life is inseparably associated!' Almost accusingly, he wrote from Genoa to Lady Blessington that the city had disappointed him greatly:

I expected something better than that long line of squalid houses which stretches from the Chiaja to the Quarter of the Porta Capuana . . . while I was quite prepared for a miserable populace, I had some dim belief that there were bright rags among them, and dancing legs, and shining sun-browned faces. Whereas the honest truth is, that connected with Naples itself, I have not one solitary *pleasant* recollection. The country round it, charmed me, I need not say.[46]

British concern over the increasing oppression of Ferdinand II's government was finally allayed in 1860, when Garibaldi entered the city 'by special train' and terminated the reign of 'King Bomba's' son, Francesco II.[47] With the disappearance of the Bourbons, however, Naples suddenly *did* become merely 'picturesque'. The lavish social life, in which the English had so actively and for so long participated, was at an end, while the *lazzaroni* seemed worse off than ever, many of them calling for the return of their king. With the taste for Neapolitan, or indeed any other kind of baroque, at its lowest ebb ever, the city's monuments offered no compensation for the loss. The American, George S. Hillard, informed his large readership that 'in Naples . . . there are very few objects of interest or curiosity. In architecture, there is almost nothing that deserves a second visit. There is not a church or a palace or a public building of any kind, of such conspicuous merit that one need regret not to have seen it.'[48]

With Baedeker and Murray's *Handbook for Travellers to Southern Italy* more or less at one with Hillard on the subject of Naples, it is not surprising that the city tended to become a place which tourists merely passed through *en route* to Pompeii or Paestum. Having fallen in love with Florence in the autumn of 1869, the following winter Hillard's fellow American, the 26-year old Henry James, 'conceived at Naples a tenfold deeper loathing than ever of the hideous heritage of the past'. Ruskin's influential enthusiasm for northern and 'pre-Raphaelite' Italian art and architecture evolved alongside growing contempt for Naples as 'the most loathsome nest of human caterpillars I was ever forced to stay in'. The terrible cholera epidemic of 1884, vividly described by Axel Munthe, seemed to confirm Ruskin's opinion of a decade earlier that Naples was 'certainly the most disgusting place in Europe'.[49] In 1897 Arthur Symons wrote that 'no city ever filled me with such terror as Naples'. By this time, as we may see from the architecture of some of the villas and grand hotels by the harbour, Sorrento had come into its own as an alternative resort; it was soon to be joined in this capacity by Positano and the once great city of Amalfi.[50]

In 1907 the wealthy American, Dan Fellows Platt, whose tour

Through Italy with Car and Camera was conducted in a large chauffeur-driven Fiat, introduced new, twentieth-century reasons for disliking Naples. The people, he writes:

> have made of this paradise a hell, in particular a motorist's hell. If Naples be distasteful to the railway tourist how much more so to the traveller by automobile. The roads of southern Italy are bad enough, but to reach even those, for the many excursions to the southward, one has to pass over the miles of pavement, filled with loitering beings, deaf to all sounds of warning.[51]

It is only relatively recently, with such works as Harold Acton's two volumes on the *Bourbons of Naples* and Peter Gunn's *Naples: A Palimpsest* (both of which exploit the travel accounts to excellent effect), that a serious re-evaluation of Naples, its people and its history has been attempted in the Anglo-Saxon world. With additional help from art-historical studies such as Anthony Blunt's *Neapolitan Baroque and Rococo Architecture* (1975) and exhibitions such as the Royal Academy's 'Painting in Naples: 1606–1705' (1982) and the British Museum's 'Vases and Volcanoes: Sir William Hamilton and his Collection' (1996), perhaps the city may eventually regain something of its once legendary appeal for travellers.

THE ENVIRONS OF NAPLES AND BEYOND

Though Naples was once a far more prestigious resort than now, its 'environs' always rivalled the city itself for the travellers' attentions. In 1648 Raymond wrote: 'Truly if a traveller Hyperbolize in any part of his voyage of *Italy*, the most fit theame he can take are the Wonders a little distant from Naples.'[52] As we have seen, Richard Lassels allocated a maximum of three days, out of a total of five, to be spent in the city itself. Thus, even before the excavation of Pompeii and Herculaneum and the subsequent 'discovery' of Paestum, almost half that which made the 15-day journey from Rome to Naples and back worthwhile lay outside the city walls.

Though Vesuvius was always a star attraction, before the mid-eighteenth century it was the area to the west of Naples, the Phlegraean Fields, rather than the now more popular south-easterly sites, which dominated the tourists' tight schedule.[53] Even after

Paestum and Sicily took over as the southernmost points of the Grand Tour, this exotic area, which provided the double attraction of freak natural phenomena and classical associations, continued to be very popular with the ever-growing numbers of British travellers. Indeed, after the frustrating interval caused by the Napoleonic Wars, the rush was so great that by 1825, when Lady Blessington inspected 'Virgil's tomb' at the entrance to the extraordinary Grotta di Posillipo (through which one used to ride to reach the Phlegraean Fields), the once legendary laurel tree which had crowned the tomb for centuries had disappeared. The tomb's Italian *custode* informed her that in their greed for souvenirs, 'the English travellers' had 'not only stripped it of its branches, but that when they all disappeared, cut the roots, so that no trace of it is left'. One should point out, however, that when the German traveller, Johann G. Seume, visited the already denuded tomb in 1802, 'der Gärtner' had blamed 'die gottlosen, vandalischen Franzosen' for the loss.[54]

The first, and not the least enthusiastic English account of the environs of Naples appeared in William Thomas's *Historie of Italie* in 1549:

> The countrey about is so pleasant, that in maner everie village deserveth to be spoken of, aswell for sumptuouse buildynges and noumbre of commoditees, namely, haboundaunce of delicate fruites, as also for the holesome ayre. For in most places it semeth alwaies (yea, at the deadest of the winter) to be continuall springe time.[55]

Just a few months after this was published, inspired by what they had already seen since leaving Rome as well as the relevant classical literature, and having 'taried a season within the citie', Thomas Hoby and his friends, 'thowght it behouffull to mak now . . . a jorney abowt the countrey called in times past Campania, and now Terra di Lavoro, so muche spoken of and renow[n]ed in all writers'.[56]

After visiting Virgil's tomb, they passed through the Grotta di Posillipo to the Phlegraean Fields. Hoby describes the Lago d'Agnano, already a health resort; the Grotta del Cane, where not only dogs, but 'catts, froggs and other lyving beastes' (including, on one occasion, slaves) were subjected to the sulphur fumes and then thrown into the lake to entertain the tourists; and the Solfatara, 'a poole of boyling sulphure water, owt of the which there arriseth a verie dark and black smoke'.[57] Constantly referring back to his Pliny,

Hoby then rode down into Pozzuoli, where he mentions the very well-preserved amphitheatre, the 'howses of pleaser' and the remains of Caligula's bridge across the bay. 'Keeping along by the seea side' he next describes Monte Nuovo, not yet crowned with umbrella pines for it had burst forth only 11 years before and indeed, 'with suche a terrible noise and suche violence that it cast stones as far as Naples . . . this hill a good space after burnt in the toppe and cast furthe stones, but yt hath ceased burning of late dayes.'[58]

Visiting Baia, he then passed on to the Lago d'Averno and hence to Cuma and the Sibyl's Cave – though by the latter he, like many a later tourist, would have actually meant the end of the larger Roman Grotta della Pace (or di Cocceio) which connected Cuma to the lake.[59] He refers to the cave as being 'of late dayes . . . stopped upp [as indeed both the Grotta and the genuine Sibyl's Cave still are] by the reason that two or three have perished there within'. Inspired, it seems, by descriptions in Livy, and in the company of the scholar Edward Stradling, Hoby next went on an excursion to Benevento, where he found '18 thowsand' Neapolitan exiles, and 'manie faire antiquities' including the Cathedral's thirteenth-century 'gate of brasse which is not muche inferior to Santa Maria rotunda in Roome' and the 'verie bewtifull triumphall arke of the Emperor Nerva [Trajan]'.[60] In making this tour and even more so in returning via Nola (where, just two years before, Giordano Bruno had been born) Hoby was unusual. He was truly exceptional, however, in choosing to tour Calabria on his way to Sicily:

> After I had well vewed whatsoever was to bee seen bothe within the citie of Naples and in the countrey abowt the same, I tooke a journey upon me to goo throwghe the dukedom of Calabria by land into Cicilia, both to have a sight of the countrey and also to absent my self for a while owt of Englishemenne's companie for the tung's sake.[61]

He left Naples on 11 February 1550, and having passed still-buried Herculaneum and Pompeii, travelled via Nocera to Salerno. With Paestum also still unknown – and Carlo Levi likewise – Hoby now left the coast and not even hesitating at Eboli, headed deep inland to Polla, the ancient *Forum Pompilii*. In doing so he soon found himself in 'the pleasant vale called valle di Diano'. 'At the entring into this vale on the right hand side' he immediately encountered its first major curiosity, the huge Grotta di Pertosa:

This cave is full of running cleere water, and in the middle of the water there is an altar which they call Altare di San Michael . . . Of this great abundance of water hathe a river his beginning called Negro [the Tanagro] . . . The hilles abowt it are so inhabited as it is wonder to behold. Yt bringethe furthe marvelous plentie of corn and all kindes of frutes.[62]

From Polla, Hoby rode, via Sala Consilina, to Padula where he inspected the huge and 'princelie' Certosa di San Lorenzo with its 'pleasant gardines and faire rowmes' (twice used in the twentieth century as a concentration camp). Though he comments on the wealth of the 364 'friers' ('as manie . . . as there are dayes in the yere'), Hoby does not mention the 1,000-egg omelette they had served the Emperor Charles V and his train 15 years before. Having entered Basilicata, soon after leaving Casabuono (which 'belongeth to the said Monasterie') Hoby entered 'a great thicke woode called Bosco del Pellegrino . . . verie jeapardous to passe. For there do the banisshed men of the kingdom lie for their praye, and many a man is there robbed and slaine in the yere by them.' Reaching picturesque Lagonegro – where Mona Lisa is supposed to have been buried – Hoby passed safely on to Lauria: 'Here be sharpe mountaynes to passe and wonderous to beholde on all sides with infinit springs of water.'[63] Taking the now unusual route, via Castelluccio and Rotonda, Hoby finally entered Calabria. He began 'to descende from the hilles throwghe a strait, sharpe roode and stonie waye . . . into a faire plaine, and on the right hand there is upon the hille's side the towne of Murano' (Norman Douglas's 'Old Morano' where, then as now, 'the white houses stream in a cataract down one side of a steep conical hill that dominates the landscape').[64]

From Morano, Hoby rode across the high plain to Castrovillari – the subject of another chapter of *Old Calabria* – where, according to mid-sixteenth-century gossip, the local Duke 'Giovan Battista Cariati . . . surrnamed Spinello . . . had Don Pietro de Toledo [the Viceroy] in great indignation . . . for keaping his syster as his concubine, making him beleave he wold marye herr.'[65]

From Castrovillari:

We descend a wondrous way downwards . . . By the way upon the right hand we may see Altomonte on the hill, within a mile wherof are the wonderous mines of salt. And a litle by yonde them are marvellous hige hilles upon the which is continuallie great abundance of snowe, which by the heate of the sonn dothe congele and becomme the cristall, wherof there there is great abundance upon those hilles.

In the vale that is over against Altomonte is manna gathered in the sommer time which fallethe from the aere in the night: . . . This manna is gathered upon trees that have leaves like unto a plumme tree . . . And of this they mak great merchandise.[66]

Hoby now entered the 'verie long but somewhat narrowe' valley of the river Crati, 'marvelouslie inha[bi]ted with townes and villages', along which one rode from Spezzano Albanese to Cosenza, 'the head of all Calabria' and at this date an intellectual centre of considerable importance.[67] After a lengthy description of Cosenza and its two rivers, backed up with quotations from Livy and Ovid, Hoby next describes his ascent into the mountains beyond, among which, 'upon a highe hill nighe unto the place called Golfo di San Eufemia, where the countrey is but xx miles in breadethe . . . a man may discern . . . the seeas that are on both sides of Italie.' The road to Sambiase passed through a forest which until recently had been 'most famous for robberies and murtheres . . . of all the rest within the realm . . . But now all the wood that was anie thing nig[h]e unto the high waye is burnt downe . . . some [trees] lying upon the earthe half burnt. This was done by th'Emperor's commandment when he passed bye there' (Charles V on his way from Reggio to Naples in 1535):

At owr cuming owt of this wood we may descern a faire plaine and a bewtiful countrey, full of plesant places abundant with sundrie kindes of frutes. And on the left hand we may see the towne of Nicastro with the countrey abowt yt well tilled and verie plentifull, which is a great delite to beholde.[68]

'Travailing thus upon the Apennine', it was not long before Hoby could see Stromboli 'and the [Æolian] yles there abowt within the see, and also Mongilbello [Etna] laden with snowe within Sicilia'. Descending out of the hills, he now travelled along 'the plaine valley betwext the Apennine and the seea' until he reached Reggio 'which is counted the verie end of Italie'. 'This towne', he writes, 'hathe often bine vexed, spoiled and destroied. And not long sith yt hathe received great damage by Barbarossa.' None the less he found it an attractive place, 'abundant with faire litle rivers and clere springs, and beset in everie place with pleasant gardines replenisshed with all kinds of frutes, and in especiallie aranges'.[69]

From Reggio Hoby crossed over to Messina, 'on[e] of the fairest portes in Europe', where he admired Montorsoli's unfinished 'fountaine of verie white marble' before setting off on a tour of the rest of Sicily.[70] He was dissuaded from continuing on to Malta when the knights of that island – its chief tourist attraction – 'arrived sodainlie' at Syracuse and an English gunner on one of their galleys informed him that they were on their way to join Andrea Doria in his attack on Tunis. He therefore joined the fleet as far as Messina and from thence 'sett forwardes in a shippe for Naples'. He had hardly arrived when a group of friends, perhaps inspired by his own adventures, persuaded him to sail with them back down to Salerno, 'a long the faire coost of Amalfi, which is praysed to be on[e] of the pleasantest peices of ground in all Italie'. At the 'pretie citie' of Amalfi itself they were lavishly entertained by the Duchess and her son, staying overnight in the castle which had probably been the setting for the murder of a more famous 'Duchess of Malfi' and her children (see above pp. 65–6). Their hosts also persuaded them to visit Ischia, of which Hoby provides the first account in English.[71]

When, earlier in the year, Hoby had gone on his excursion from Naples to Benevento, perhaps he had contemplated extending his tour into Apulia. In the event, however, it was to be more than 150 years before a British traveller would repeat Hoby's journey thus far, and then continue beyond Benevento across to Bari, head south and explore the 'heel' of Italy, leaving posterity a detailed record of the expedition.

George Berkeley had already published his most important philosophical works when, in the autumn of 1716, he agreed to accompany St George Ashe, son of the Bishop of Clogher, on his continental tour [Fig. 9]. The decision to travel so far from Naples, which was treated by most British travellers as a base only for the well-established day-trips, may have had something to do with Berkeley's interest in the tarantula and the related anthropological phenomena with which he was to fill his journals.[72] Perhaps, like Milton, he had originally contemplated going on to Greece. Most probably, however, Berkeley, who had visited Italy before, was prompted by an urge to outdo his friend Addison and other travelling predecessors, by breaking away from the stereotyped Grand Tour itinerary. On his return to Naples from Puglia, he was proud to announce that he had completed 'a tour through the most remote and unknown parts of Italy'. In one day he had seen 'five fair cities . . . the most part built of white marble, whereof the names are not known to Englishmen'.[73] It is not surprising that, *en route* between such 'cities', Berkeley and his young charge 'were stared at like men dropt from the sky'. Like the mid-nineteenth-century Calabrians, who issued forth 'a perfect hurricane of perchès' when Edward Lear explained that he wanted 'to make a drawing of [their] pretty little town' (Gioiosa), the early eighteenth-century Apulians were clearly at a loss to know what this Protestant clergyman and his wealthy-looking companion were doing so far from home, and why the former was for ever scribbling in his long, leather-bound notebooks.[74]

In these fascinating journals and in the more formal letters he wrote back to Pope and to his friend and patron, Sir John Percival, Berkeley provides us with an unprecedentedly detailed, intelligent and often lyrical account of these unexplored regions. Inspired perhaps by his friend Addison, he also spent four months on Ischia which he described as 'an epitome of the whole earth, containing within the compass of eighteen miles, a wonderful variety of hills, vales, ragged rocks, fruitful plains, and barren mountains, all thrown together in a most romantic confusion'.[75]

Though he started hunting for tarantulas and tarantella dancing at Bari, research seems to have been suspended (until arrival at Taranto itself) whilst he enthused over Lecce [Fig. 22]. Writing to Percival, whom he knew had completed only the conventional northern-dominated tour of the country, Berkeley announced that 'the most beautiful city in Italy' was to be found 'in a remote corner of the heel'.[76] The primary reason for his enthusiasm was the city's architecture and here as elsewhere his writings give the lie to the conventional notion that northern Protestants could not appreciate the Baroque, supposedly an exclusively southern and Catholic phenomenon. The remarks Berkeley jotted down during his visit to Lecce pre-date Sacheverell Sitwell's *Southern Baroque Art* (usually considered pioneering for its Anglo–Saxon appreciation of this style) by more than 200 years: 'Nothing in my travels more amazing than the infinite profusion of altorelievo and that so well done. There is not surely the like rich architecture in the world. The square of the Benedictines is the finest I ever saw.'[77] In his *Discursions on Travel, Art and Life*, published in 1925, a year after his

22 Achille Carducci and others, *San Matteo*, Lecce; late 17th century. [E. Chaney]

younger brother's book, Osbert Sitwell explained in detail 'the enormous advantage that Lecce possesses over all other towns' in having a

> great wealth of beautiful stone cropping up to the surface just beyond its walls. And this material is so swiftly quarried . . . that building is always cheap, while the actual softness of the stone when cut allows the rich imagination of the South an unparalleled outlet . . . The houses seem fashioned from snow.[78]

Though a few other early eighteenth-century travellers such as John Breval, Richard Pococke, Ellis Veryard and the 4th Earl of Sandwich went further afield, it was not really until the 1763–97 phase of the Grand Tour (after the Seven Years' War) that it became fashionable to 'wish', as Boswell did, 'for something more than just the common course of what is called the tour of Europe'. The result of Boswell's dissatisfaction was his *Account of Corsica* of 1768.[79] In the case of a fellow Scot, Patrick Brydone, it was the still more popular *Tour through Sicily and Malta* (1773) which was promptly translated into both French and German. Though this was a compliment which had rarely been paid to an English book on Italy in the century since Lassels's *Voyage* had been similarly honoured, it was not long before Henry Swinburne's illustrated *Travels in the Two Sicilies* – complete with a good account of Paestum – was also published in these languages.[80] As his own French was excellent, soon after war with revolutionary France broke out, Swinburne was chosen to go to Paris to negotiate on behalf of the government for the release of prisoners. Had he not died of sunstroke in Trinidad in 1803, he might have continued this work on behalf of those hopeful tourists who, having rushed abroad when the Peace of Amiens was signed in October 1801, found themselves trapped when war suddenly broke out again in the spring of 1803. Joseph Forsyth was at least fortunate in having completed his tour of Italy when this happened, for he was thus able to spend part of the 11 years' internment in France which followed turning his travel notes into the book he entitled *Remarks on Antiquities, Arts, and Letters during an Excursion in Italy in the years 1802 and 1803*.[81] Though the *Remarks* are based on the standard Grand Tour itinerary, perhaps influenced by Swinburne (who after John Berkenhout was the first Englishman to describe his impressions of the place in print), Forsyth had extended his tour to include malarial Paestum [Fig. 23]. A difficult journey

23 Antonio Joli, *The Temples at Paestum* from Thomas Major, *Les Ruines de Paestum* (London, 1768). [E. Chaney]

was more than compensated for by the view which he eventually obtained of the massive Doric temples standing in the deserted plain: 'These wonderful objects, though surveyed in the midst of rain, amply compensated our little misadventures . . . I do not hesitate to call these the most impressive monuments that I ever beheld on earth.'[82]

Inspired perhaps by this account to visit them, Shelley described the effect of 'the jagged outline of mountains [seen] through groupes of enormous columns on one side, & on the other the level horizon the sea' as 'inexpressibly grand', a phrase echoed by Sir Walter Scott's 'inconceivably grand' when he visited these 'sybarrite' temples in March 1832.[83] Forsyth's book was published in 1813 as if in anticipation of the long-term peace which followed two years

later. The rush to the continent which then took place was of such
proportions that Byron was to describe Rome in 1817 as 'pestilent
with English, – a parcel of staring boobies, who go about gaping and
wishing to be at once cheap and magnificent'. He hoped that 'this
tribe of wretches' would soon be 'swept home again', so that the
continent would again be 'roomy and agreeable'.[84] The remarks of
Lord Byron, whose entourage generally occupied five coaches, somewhat snobbishly refer to a new class of traveller, soon to be still more
clearly identifiable by surviving 'Grand' tourists as 'Cook's' tourists,
those who finally abandoned the coach as a means of transport in
favour of the steamship and the railway, which by 1845 had even
crossed the lagoon to Venice. When, in 1846, the railway-defending
Dickens published his somewhat superficial *Pictures from Italy* – combining as it did the now standard excursions to Pompeii and
Paestum with the relative novelty of a visit to Monte Cassino on the
return journey from Naples – he was consciously catering for the
same largely middle-class readership. He and they both used
Murray's new *Hand-Books for Travellers* as their principal sources of
information.

Meanwhile, at four a.m. on 29 April 1828, Craufurd Tait Ramage
left Naples, where he had been tutoring the sons of the British
consul and, consciously emulating Swinburne and Keppel Craven's
Tour through the Southern Provinces of the Kingdom of Naples (1821),
set off alone – where his predecessors had employed military escorts
– in search of the 'ancient remains and modern superstitions' of the
deep south. Very different in tone from the Grand Tour literature of
the previous century, Ramage's *Nooks and By-Ways of Italy* may be
classed together with Keppel Craven's *Excursions in the Abruzzi*
(1838) and Arthur Strutt's *Pedestrian Tour in Calabria and Sicily*
(1842). Highly individualistic and in this sense 'post-Romantic',
these works are yet enlightened, erudite and above all steeped in the
Magna Graecia which was their major concern. In the same genre,
though even more idiosyncratic, were the travel accounts of the
epileptic Edward Lear whose *Illustrated Excursions in Italy* (1846)
earned him the post – albeit a temporary one – of drawing-master
to Queen Victoria.[85]

George Gissing's *By the Ionian Sea* (1901) – considered by contemporaries to be his 'finest work' – is clearly a key transitional
text in the evolution of this genre. But the true heir to the great
tradition of the 'pedestrian tour' in our own century has been

'pagan-to-the core' Norman Douglas.[86] Having first visited the south of Italy with his brother in 1888, before he was 30 he had abandoned his pregnant Russian mistress and his job at the British Embassy in St Petersburg and purchased a villa at Posillipo. By then he had also published his first piece on the subject of southern Italy, a Foreign Office *Report on the Pumice Stone Industry of the Lipari Islands* which, he later claimed, led to the abolition of child labour there. By 1904 he had married, fathered two sons, divorced and settled alone on Capri, where 'during a serene period . . . with blissful streaks in between', he began work on the series of pamphlets which were eventually republished as *Capri: Materials for a Description of the Island* (1930), a task which helped earn him citizenship of his adopted home, an honour shared with Benedetto Croce but with no other Briton.[87] In August 1907 he made his first short visit to Calabria. His next was to be during the spring of 1909, when he delivered the money he had collected for the survivors of the terrible earthquake which had destroyed Reggio and Messina, claiming more than 90,000 lives.

Douglas's third and most important journey to Calabria was made in the company of a 12-year-old Cockney named Eric Wolton whom he had 'picked up' in London.[88] The diary which this hitherto untravelled youth kept of his tour deserves a place among the more unusual documents in the history of Anglo-Saxon travel in southern Italy. Like thousands of his predecessors, however, he too was attacked by bed-bugs. Like many of them also, he did not immediately take to southern food. 'Salami is a kind of sousage [*sic*] it is very beastly', he complained. Much of the touring was done on muleback after sleepless nights. Finally, both Douglas and Eric were attacked by a more deadly insect, Calabria's then still common malarial mosquito and, 'in a dazed condition', they just made it back to London in time to be properly nursed through the disease.[89] Douglas's first and in many ways his best travel book, *Siren Land*, which deals with Capri and the Sorrentine peninsula, had already been completed and accepted for publication before he and Eric left England in April 1911. This four-month journey to the deeper south was made with a new work in mind, that which is usually considered to be his greatest, *Old Calabria*, finally published in 1915. Perhaps Douglas felt guilty about not mentioning his young travelling companion in this book. If so, he made up for it when he dedicated *Looking Back* to him in 1933.[90]

Though *Old Calabria* was very well reviewed, it was only with the novel *South Wind* in 1917 that Douglas began to make any money from his writing. But perhaps this was to be expected. Not only were most of the places he was describing little known, but his idea of travel was an essentially elitist one, harking back to the days before Dr Arnold – 'that merciless pruner of youthful individualism' – destroyed 'singularity, the hall-mark of that older Anglo-Saxon'.[91] He may not have approved of William Beckford, whose eighteenth-century travelling entourage was once mistaken for the Emperor's, but he shared with that extraordinary eccentric the belief that everything which distinguishes man from animals was the result of leisure. The one or two years which the earlier travellers took off for their tours thus put them at an essential advantage over the twentieth-century tourist who attempts to 'do' everything in the same number of weeks. Of travel authors, Douglas's favourite, for all his sympathetic praise of Gissing, seems to have been the more robust Ramage, about whose *Nooks and By-Ways* he wrote: 'It reveals a personality. It contains a philosophy of life.'[92] Though the philosophy they contain is far more wilfully epicurean, much the same could be said of Douglas's own writings.

In June 1955, three years after Douglas ended his life on Capri, and just three weeks before his own ninetieth birthday, another admirer of Ramage, Bernard Berenson, was driven into Cosenza, having not seen the city for almost half a century.[93] When Hoby had described the same place more than 300 years before, little in the way of travel literature and certainly nothing in his own language had been available to condition his perception. Berenson's experience of what he saw, however, was both inseparable from and profoundly enhanced by a long-standing acquaintance with the best of a now vast literature on Southern Italy:

> I did not read up for this tour of ten days in Calabria. Yet memory retains impressions of much history and travel perused many years ago. For instance the Reverend Tate [*sic*] Ramage, who early in the nineteenth century roamed in these parts in the summer, carrying a huge sunshade, dressed in white nankeen trousers and a frock-coat, the ample pockets of which contained his entire luggage. Or Lenormant with the treasure trove of distilled information of every kind about every place in Calabria as well as Apulia. Or Edward Lear, the painter who accompanied his lithographed landscapes with very subtle annotations on

colour effects, on customs and inns and people. Gregorovius likewise and J.A. Symonds. And above all Norman Douglas's *Old Calabria*, now an English classic which, as Lenormant's *A travers l'Apulie et la Lucanie*, I have read again and again. While it would not yield up definite dates or names, memory trailed – so to speak – tapestries, faded but fascinating, of historical association, digested, assimilated, forming part of me as no recent reading ever could.

While Berenson was bidding farewell to Calabria, W.H. Auden was spending one of his last summers on Ischia. Though both men appealed to the past, when Auden came to write his more personal 'Goodbye to the Mezzogiorno', he chose to celebrate the south by invoking not the foreigners it had inspired, but its native talent – even if in doing so he borrowed a non-native name or two:

> . . . Go I must, but I go grateful (even
>   To a certain *Monte*) and invoking
> My sacred names, *Vico*, *Verga*,
>   Pirandello, Bernini, Bellini,
> To bless this region, its vendanges, and those
>   Who call it home: though one cannot always
> Remember exactly why one had been happy,
>   There is no forgetting that one was.[94]

A recent biography attempts to explain Auden's abandonment of Ischia for Austria in more or less mundane terms.[95] In concluding *Siren Land*, however, Norman Douglas insisted that 'No person of culture, however prosaic, will easily detach himself from such scenes and thoughts – is it not the prerogative of civilised man to pause and ponder before the relics of his past.'[96] After praise of Lenormant, for whom 'Italy proved fatal', *Old Calabria* ends on a similar note: 'The sage, that perfect savage, will be the last to withdraw himself from the influence of these radiant realities. He will strive to knit closer the bond, and to devise a more durable and affectionate relationship between himself and them.'[97]

After likewise enthusing over Lenormant, whose signature he had just discovered in the visitors' book of the museum at Reggio, the consumptive Gissing 'saw the evening fall on cloud-wreathed Etna, the twinkling lights come forth upon Scylla and Charybdis', and 'as I looked my last towards the Ionian Sea, I wished it were mine to wander endlessly amid the silence of the ancient world, to-day and all its sounds forgotten.'⁹⁸

Perhaps Auden doubted Douglas's assurance that the Sirens were 'not demons of putrefaction', and brooded instead on Circe's pre-Hellenic account of them sitting in a meadow 'piled high with mouldering skeletons of men, whose withered skin still hangs upon their bones'.⁹⁹ But 'certain persons have rated wisdom higher than domestic bliss' and though he was fully aware of the more sinister interpretations of the Sirens' song and of the legend that 'whoso hears these voices . . . nevermore returns to his home and family' – and had moreover witnessed the results of the worst earthquake of the century – in the end Douglas was enticed to 'stay and learn new wisdom from the wise': 'for I perceive in this lay no promise of any of those things which [the crowd covets], of gold and diamonds and fair women and long life and earthly honours and the joys of heaven; but only of enlightenment.'¹⁰⁰

NOTES

This chapter was first published in E. Chaney and N. Ritchie (eds), *Oxford, China and Italy: Writings in Honour of Sir Harold Acton on his Eightieth Birthday* (Florence and London, 1984). A shorter, unannotated version was originally published as an introduction to the *Blue Guide Southern Italy*, ed. P. Blanchard (London and New York, 1982), pp. 47–60. At that stage it benefited considerably both from the expertise of the *Festschrift*'s dedicatee and from the splendid collection of books on southern Italy he donated to the library of the British Institute, Florence. I would also like to thank Lisa Chaney, Mark Roberts, Michael Thomson-Glover and Professor J.B. Trapp for their help.

1. *Remarks on several Parts of Italy* (London, 1705), sig. A3r (Preface).
2. Ibid., p. 251. The influential Addison devotes an entire chapter to Capri but in 1785 Henry Swinburne was still wondering 'why so few of our mysanthropic countrymen resort to it' (*Travels in the Two Sicilies* (London, 1785), II, p. 8). For its seventeenth-century use as a posh penal colony, see the anonymous French travel account (1627–8) now in the Gabinetto Vieusseux, Florence, MS 33, folio 92v.
3. *A Voyage to Sicily and Malta* (London, 1776), p. 6, as cited in P. Kirby, *The Grand Tour in Italy (1700–1800)* (New York, 1952), p. 47. For Dryden in Sicily, see above pp. 20–2. For 'the first to apply the term "romantic" to natural scenery', see Norman Douglas's corrections to *Siren Land* (1911) in *Late Harvest* (London, 1946), p. 73 (though in transferring the credit for this from Addison to Evelyn – who uses 'romance' rather than 'romantic' – he does not mention candidates such as Dryden jr). For a more scientific survey, see H. Eichner (ed.), *'Romantic' and its Cognates: The European History of a*

Word (Toronto, 1972). I thank Hugh Honour for this reference. For George Berkeley's use of the word to describe Ischia, see below, p. 324.

4. Creuze de Lesser, *Voyage en Italie et en Sicile en 1801 et 1802* (Paris, 1806) as cited on p. 15 of A. Mozzillo, *Viaggiatori stranieri nel Sud*, 2nd edn (Milan, 1982). The latter is the best survey of its kind, but has nothing on the sixteenth- and seventeenth-century travellers and indeed next to nothing on any travel account before 1770.

5. *The Diary of John Evelyn*, ed. E.S. de Beer, 6 vols (Oxford, 1955), II, p. 354.

6. National Library of Scotland, Advocates' MS 15.2.15, p. 121. I thank the trustees of the library for permission to quote from this manuscript. For the complete text, see Appendix I of my *The Grand Tour and the Great Rebellion: Richard Lassels and the Voyage of Italy in the Seventeenth Century* (Geneva and Turin, 1985). The pagination given here is Lassels's own. The *procaccio* was the offical escort who organized transport and accommodation on a regular twice-weekly basis, while the *vetturini* ran a private, more flexible service.

7. National Library of Scotland Advocates' MS 15.2.15., p. 125. In early 1651 about 4 or 5 miles beyond Priverno, Richard Symonds encountered '4 Gallowses . . . furnisht with quarters of Banditis' (Bodleian Library, MS Rawlinson D.121, p. 4). On the same page of his illustrated travel manuscript he included a small pen and ink sketch of the 'Tre Taverni mentioned by St Paul'. The succeeding pages follow the route described here more or less precisely, including sketches of Terracina and Cicero's Tomb. For this journey in context see Mary Beal, *A Study of Richard Symonds* (New York, 1984).

8. Ibid., p. 126. The description of the Appian Way is taken from the printed *Voyage of Italy* (Paris, 1670), II, p. 262, the work in which the term 'Grand Tour' occurs for the first time in an English context; see the *Oxford English Dictionary* (OED) though cf. A. Frank-Van Westrienen, *De Groote Tour* (Amsterdam, 1983), pp. 1–3.

9. *Il Mercurio Italico*, or *An Itinerary contayning a Voyage made through Italy* (London, 1648), p. 127. Raymond merely introduces these hexameters with the words: 'as the Poet saith'. He had, however, lifted them from the best guidebook of its day, Pflaumern's *Mercurius Italicus* (Lyons, 1628), p. 424, which had in turn borrowed them from François Schott's popular *Itinerarii Italiae rerumque Romanarum libri tres* (Antwerp, 1600), p. 345. Both these specify that the Virgilian poet was a German; compare Goethe's lines about 'das Land, wo die Zitronen blühn' and 'Die Myrte . . . steht' in *Wilhelm Meisters Lehrjahre*, III, i, and Thomas Gray's 1740 letter to his mother describing 'the oranges in full bloom and myrtles in every hedge' (*Correspondence*, ed. P. Toynbee and L. Whibley (Oxford, 1935), I, p. 163.

10. Op. cit., p. 128. A small Sienese group portrait depicting Raymond and his two companions, Dr John Bargrave and Alexander Chapman, is preserved in Bargrave's collection of Italian souvenirs at Canterbury Cathedral Library [Fig. 17]. Bargrave probably helped his nephew write his guidebook; see my *Grand Tour*, op. cit., Chapter II and idem, entry in A. Wilton and I. Bignamini (eds), *Grand Tour: The Lure of Italy in the Eighteenth Century* (London, 1996), p. 99.

11. *Diary*, op. cit., II, p. 323.

12. Nat Lib. of Scotland Adv. MS. 15.2.15., p. 128. In 1815, Samuel Rogers 'passed the Garigliano [the ancient Liris] on a bridge of boats' (*The Italian Journal . . .*, ed. J.R. Hale (London, 1956), p. 249.

13. Nat. Lib. of Scotland Adv. MS. 15.2.15., p. 129. In March 1594 Fynes Moryson celebrated having survived the most dangerous stretch of his journey down from Rome, by treating himself to a 2½ giulii meal at Capua

not included in the 'forty foure Giulii' travel contract he had signed with his *vetturino*: 'And in deede we had excellent cheare, delicate wine, most white pure bread, and among other dainties, I remember wee had blacke Olives, which I had never seene before, and they were of a most pleasant taste' (*Itinerary* (London, 1617), I, ii, p. 106). Almost half a century later, in 1637, the sculptor, Nicholas Stone jr., travelling on a 50 giulii package-tour arrangement, paid just half a giulio more for his 'one meale extraordinary at Capua' ('The Joyrnall of N.S.', *Walpole Society*, VII (1919), p. 193). In April 1651, Richard Symonds also paid 3 giulii for 'Dinner at Capua' though his total payment to Carlino the *vetturino* came to 14 crowns for the '15 dayes voyage' (Bodleian Library, MS Rawlinson D.121, p. 150).

14. *Diary*, II, p. 324.
15. Ibid., II, p. 325; cf. Richard Symonds's 1651 experience in Bodleian Library, MS Rawlinson D. 121, p. 150: he stayed at the '3 Rè' for the standard 5 nights which cost him 5 crowns with an extra 3 giulii for breakfast. Bullen Reymes, Walter Montagu and the Earl of Carnarvon stayed at 'l'Aquela negro' in March 1634 (*Bullen Reymes Diaries 1633–36* [author's collection], fol. 127v). Nicholas Stone is clearly referring to the same institution in his accounts, paying 40 julios 'for 8 meales dyett att the Eagle at Naples' in 1639 (op. cit., p. 193). For the location of these inns, see E. Zaniboni, *Alberghi italiani e viaggiatori stranieri* (*sec. XIII–XVIII*) (Naples, 1921), pp. 157–67.
16. John Arthos, *Milton and the Italian Cities* (London, 1968), pp. 97–103 and G. Trease, *The Grand Tour* (London, 1967), p. 90.
17. *Diary*, II, pp. 353–4. Sir Sanders Duncombe obtained patents for the right to hire out sedan chairs in London in the mid-1630s. His clientele could have read about the way they functioned in Naples and seen an etching of one in action at the Solfatara in the popular *Relation of a Journey* (London, 1615) by the great translator and poet George Sandys, who had sailed up the coast of Calabria and the Campania on his way back from the Holy Land in 1611 (1670 edn, pp. 202, 209). Fynes Moryson also commended the 'seggioli di Napoli' for their ability to manoeuvre in the narrow streets of both Naples and Genoa in his *Itinerary* (op. cit., I, ii, p. 112).
18. Thomas's *Historie of Italie* was republished in an abridged edition by G.B. Parks for the Folger Shakespeare Library (New York, 1963). Quotations here are from the original now available in facsimile (Amsterdam and Norwood, NJ, 1977). *The Travels and Life of me Thomas Hoby* were published for the Royal Historical Society in 1902 by Edgar Powell (Camden Miscellany X). The Jacobean titles are the two already cited by Sandys and Moryson and *A True Relation of the Travailes and most miserable Captivitie of William Davies, Barber Surgion of London, under the Duke of Florence* (London, 1614), which includes details of the author's exploits in Naples and Sicily as a grand-ducal galley-slave in 1598. Perhaps Webster's *Duchess of Malfi* (first performed *c.* 1613) helped stimulate this interest on the part of publishers in things southern (and Spanish) Italian. Inigo Jones accompanied the Earl and Countess of Arundel to Naples in 1614; see below, chapter 7. For an unusually coherent medieval account of the south, see G.B. Parks, *The English Traveler to Italy . . . (to 1525)* (Rome, 1954), pp. 573–4.
19. J.W. Stoye, *English Travellers Abroad (1604–1667)* 2nd edn (New Haven and London, 1989), pp. 281–4 reminds one of the importance of Charles's treaty with Louis XIII in 1630; cf. R.S. Pine-Coffin, *Bibliography of British and American Travel in Italy to 1860* (Florence, 1974), p. 24. Corrections and additions to the latter appear in *La Bibliofilia*, LXXXIII (1981).

20. Op. cit., sig. D1.
21. Moryson, op. cit., I, p. 109 and Logan Pearsall Smith, *Life and Letters of Sir Henry Wotton* (Oxford, 1907), I, p. 17.
22. See Appendix V of my *Grand Tour*, op. cit., where the three English Catholics with whom Milton dined at the Jesuit-run English College, Rome, are identified and it is argued that the 'Selvaggi' who wrote the Latin distich which prefaces the 1644 *Poemata* was an Italophile English Benedictine; see also below, p. 313 n. 68.
23. *Historie*, op. cit., p. 113. For the life see above pp. 70-6 and p. 94, n. 55. Despite Adair's assertion to the contrary (loc. cit., p. 136) there is no reason to doubt that Thomas actually visited Naples.
24. *Travels*, op. cit., p. 26.
25. Ibid., pp. 26-7. *Aeneid*, VII, i: 'Tu quoque littoribus nostris Aeneia nutrix / Aeternam moriens famam Caieta dedisti'.
26. Ibid., p. 26. For Gaeta, see below, p. 198, n. 41, and Fig. 18.
27. Ibid., p. 29.
28. Ibid. and Burnet, *Some Letters* (Rotterdam, 1686), p. 193, as cited in my ' "Philanthropy in Italy": English Observations on Italian Hospitals, 1545-1789', in *Aspects of Poverty in Early Modern Europe*, ed. T. Riis (Stuttgart and Florence, 1981), pp. 183-217; cf. below, p. 261. The invariably enthusiastic travellers' accounts of this and other Italian hospitals make nonsense of W.K. Jordan's claim that the seventeenth-century London hospitals 'stood unrivalled . . . in the whole of the western world' (*The Charities of London, 1484-1660* (London, 1960), p. 195), while the tone which they adopt when describing institutions for the insane ill-accords with the thesis propounded by Michel Foucault in *Histoire de la Folie* (Paris, 1961); see, for example, Lady Blessington's remarkable account of the lunatic asylum at Aversa (*Idler in Italy* (London, 1839), II, pp. 250-7.
29. *Observations topographical, moral, & physiological made in a Journey* (London, 1673), p. 267. For his specimen collection (as admired by Edward Browne in Rome in 1665), see C.E. Raven, *John Ray, Naturalist* (Cambridge, 1942), p. 136. In the 1880s, Augustus Hare described an Italian dish which has since become almost as popular as the *pasta* mentioned by Ray: 'Very little . . . is needed to sustain life at Naples . . . the horrible condiment called *Pizza* (made of dough baked with garlic, rancid bacon, and strong cheese) is esteemed a feast' (*Cities of Southern Italy and Sicily* (London, 1896), p. 85).
30. *Bullen Reymes Diaries 1633-36* (author's collection), fols 129r-v. For Reymes, see Helen Kaufman, *Conscientious Cavalier* (London, 1962); Symonds's notebook, Bodleian Library MS Rawlinson D.121, p. 23; for Jones see below, Chapter 7. For the French, see Anthony Blunt, 'Naples as seen by French Travellers, 1630-1780', *The Artist and the Writer in France: Essays in Honour of Jean Seznec*, ed. F. Haskell, A. Levi and R. Shackleton (Oxford, 1974), pp. 1-14. Muratori's *Riflessioni sopra il buon gusto* (Venice, 1708) would surely have interested Montesquieu, who visited the author during his 1728-29 Italian tour; see Shackleton's *Critical Biography* (Oxford, 1961), p. 107 and cf. J. Ehrard, *Montesquieu, critique d'art* (Paris, 1965), *passim*. He was soon writing in his travel journal that 'A Naples, il me paroît qu'il est plus facile de se gâter le goût que de se le former' and beginning an *Essai sur le goût* of his own (ed. A. Gérard (Paris, 1766), pp. 265-306). The English had meanwhile caught up. Between Muratori and Montesquieu lay Shaftesbury's *Characteristicks* (London, 1711) which, by preaching the unity of morality and taste, provide the profoundest justification for a Grand Tour: that of becom-

ing a *virtuoso* in order to become *virtuous* in the modern sense. Shaftesbury left the 'great smoak' of London for Naples and died there after more than a year's residence in February 1713.

31. *Voyage*, op. cit., II, p. 273; compare the earlier manuscript of the *Voyage* in my possession (c. 1664, p. 486): 'The Domo is ancient but adorned with a new Chappel on the right hand, which is gracefull.'

32. *A New Voyage to Italy* (London, 1739 edn), I, ii, pp. 674-5.

33. Lassels, op. cit., II, p. 279 (MS *Voyage*, p. 490), compare Misson, op. cit., I, ii, pp. 408-9. Misson concluded that Naples was 'one of the most noble and perhaps finest cities in the world'; see Desmond Seward, *Naples: A Travellers' Companion* (London, 1984), p. 43. By the 1720s we find Edward Wright declaring that although the 'Profusion of Marble' in Naples 'is scarcely to be imagin'd . . . the Disposition of it in the Incrustations is not so well judg'd, as it is in the Churches of *Rome*' (*Some Observations* . . . (London, 1730), I, p. 150). Wright also interviewed the 'excellent Master' Solimena in his studio (H. Acton, 'The Bourbons as Patrons of the Arts', *Connoisseur*, CXCVI (1977), pp. 78-9). In the mid-1720s, the Irish painter, Henry Trench, studied with Solimena and in the following decade Allan Ramsay studied with this by then octogenarian artist. Compare L. Schudt, *Italienreisen im 17. und 18. Jahrhundert* (Vienna, 1959), p. 383.

34. As well as Franco Venturi's now completed trilogy of this title, see 'L'Italia fuori d'Italia' (*Storia d'Italia*, III (Turin, 1973)), p. 1069.

35. *Boswell's Life of Johnson* (Oxford, 1965), p. 742.

36. For Boswell in and around Naples, see *Boswell on the Grand Tour . . . 1765-1766*, ed. F. Brady and F. Pottle (London, 1955), pp. 54-62. For the other travellers, see the *DNB*, Pine-Coffin's *Bibliography*, op. cit. and, forthcoming, John Ingamells (ed.) *A Dictionary of British and Irish Visitors to Italy 1701-1800* (New Haven and London, 1997).

37. Miller, *Letters from Italy*, 3 vols (London, 1776), Piozzi (Mrs Thrale), *Observations*, 2 vols (London, 1789) and Starke, *Letters from Italy*, 2 vols (London, 1800). Other women who described Naples in this pre-revolutionary period were Cornelia Knight, Mary Berry, Elizabeth Wynne and Elizabeth Webster (Lady Holland). For further details see Pine-Coffin's *Bibliography*, op. cit., though not included therein is the useful edition of Piozzi's *Observations* by Herbert Barrows (Ann Arbor, MI, 1964).

38. Copley had been advised to visit Italy by his compatriot and master, Benjamin West, who had himself spent the years 1760-4 there; see *Letters and Papers of . . . Copley*, ed. C.F. Adams, G. Jones and W.C. Ford (Cambridge, MA (Massachusetts Historical Society, LXXI), 1914). He was encouraged to visit Naples, Herculaneum, Pompei and Paestum by the Izards. For his fine portrait of this couple, done on their return to Rome (now in Boston), see *The Lure of Italy: American Artists and the Italian Experience 1760-1914*, ed. T.E. Stebbins (Boston and New York, 1992), pp. 156-58. For early American travellers in general see G. Prezzolini, *Come gli Americani scoprirono l'Italia (1750-1850)* (Milan, 1933), Van Wyck Brooks, *The Fortunate Pilgrims* (Cambridge, MA, 1964), E. Amfitheatrof, *The Enchanted Ground. Americans in Italy, 1760-1980* (Boston and Toronto, 1980). C.R. Walker, *The Anglo-American Artist in Italy 1750-1820* (University Art Museum, Santa Barbara, CA, 1982) and William L. Vance, *America's Rome*, 2 vols (New Haven and London, 1992).

39. B. Fothergill, *Sir William Hamilton Envoy Extraordinary* (London, 1969), H. Acton, *Three Extraordinary Ambassadors* (London, 1983), pp. 43-60, Goethe, *Italienische Reise*, ed. H. von Einem (Hamburg, 1954), p. 209 and the W.H.

Auden and E. Mayer translation (London, 1962), p. 200. See Carlo Knight, *Hamilton a Napoli. Cultura, svaghi, civiltà di una grande capitale europa* (Naples, 1991); P. Griener, *Le Antichità Etrusche Greche e Romane 1766-1776 di Pierre Hugues D'Hancarville . . .* (Rome, 1992) and Ian Jenkins and Kim Sloan, *Vases and Volcanoes: Sir William Hamilton and his Collection* (London, 1996).

40. *Boswell on the Grand Tour*, op. cit., p. 19, and H. Acton, *The Bourbons of Naples (1734-1825)* (London, 1956), passim. See also A. Gentile, *Caserta nei ricordi dei viaggiatori stranieri* (Naples, 1980).

41. Stendhal, *Voyages en Italie*, ed. V. del Litto (Paris, 1973), p. 516; compare H. Harder, *Le Président de Brosses et le Voyage en Italie au dix-huitième siècle* (Geneva, 1981), p. 307. In an article entitled 'Quando l'Europa scoprì il sud', C.A. Anzuini claims that Stendhal defined Naples as 'La plus belle ville de l'univers', but I have not found where he did so (see *Viaggio in Italia*, I, 1983, p. 11).

42. *Voyages*, op. cit., p. 511. Despite his claims to have done so, Stendhal probably never visited Puglia, Calabria or Sicily; see A. Mozzillo, 'Stendhal in Calabria?', in *Storia e cultura del Mezzogiorno. Studi in onore di Umberto Caldora* (Rome and Cosenza, 1978).

43. Vol. LXXXVIII, p. 170, as cited by Pine-Coffin, op. cit., p. 11. The same source estimated there to be the relatively small number of 'between 500 and 600 English persons . . . resident at Rome'. For Shelley, see below, notes 45 and 85. Two years later Keats 'was profoundly depressed the day we went ashore at Naples, though he had been so eager to leave the ship and explore the beautiful city'; see William Sharp, *Life and Letters of Joseph Severn* (London, 1892), p. 59. It was in Naples, at the Hotel d'Inghilterra, that the dying Keats received Shelley's invitation to join him and Byron in Pisa, but he and Severn were already destined for Rome. Turner also visited Naples in 1819.

44. Op. cit., I, p. 102. In her edition of this section of the *Idler* (*Lady Blessington at Naples* (London, 1979), p. 10), Edith Clay gives an incomplete account of the editions, as does Pine-Coffin, op. cit., p. 192. There were in fact at least three distinct editions, all published in 1839. I quote here from the first, published in 2 vols by Henry Colburn.

45. Harold Acton, *The Last Bourbons of Naples (1825-1861)* (London, 1961), pp. 146-7. The headmaster's son, Matthew, on the other hand, writing to his wife 25 years later, judged Naples 'the most brilliant and lively place, brilliant and lively as Paris, only in a natural popular sort of way' (ibid. and Peter Gunn, *Naples: A Palimpsest* (London, 1961), p. 210). The reactions of a fellow poet with a more radical reputation were closer to those of Arnold senior. For Shelley's strictures on 'degraded, disgusting and odious' Italy with its 'filthy modern inhabitants' and on the garlic-eating women of Naples in particular, see *The Letters of Percy Bysshe Shelley*, ed. F.L. Jones (Oxford, 1964), II, pp. 67-9. He nevertheless abandoned an illegitimate daughter among them. She died in less than two years; see Richard Holmes, *Shelley: The Pursuit* (London, 1987), pp. 458-78.

46. H. Acton, *Last Bourbons*, cit., p. 150, Dickens, *Pictures of Italy*, ed. D. Paroissien (London, 1973), and *The Letters of Charles Dickens*, ed. K. Tillotson (Oxford, 1977), IV, pp. 302-3 (letter dated 9 May 1845). Though he had clearly read the *Idler*, Dickens was more influenced by the critical account of Naples in Louis Simond's, *Tour in Italy and Sicily* which appeared in French and English in 1828.

47. H. Acton, *Last Bourbons*, cit., pp. 489-91. The 'dungeon's eye view' of Naples which dominated British public opinion in the final decade of Bourbon

government was above all the result of Gladstone's 1850 visit and the *Letters to Lord Aberdeen* which he published in the following year. Herman Melville, however, was relieved to find 'Naples in the Time of Bomba' the 'Gayest city in the world' and discontent with the new regime continued through the 1860s and beyond.

48. *Six Months in Italy* (Boston, 1853), II, pp. 105-6. If Hillard seems insensitive in his remarks, most English visitors would probably have been more so. Hillard's own comments on their establishment of cricket and football in Rome, and fox-hunting in the Campania, conclude with the observation that 'the English . . . as a general rule, are not at home in the region of art. They are either not sensitive to the touch of beauty, or affect not to be . . . The most ignorant men I saw on the Continent . . . were Englishmen' (ibid., II, pp. 269-71).

49. *Henry James Letters*, ed Leon Edel, I (London, 1974), p. 182. Gunn, op. cit., p. 211 and Munthe, *Vagaries* (London, 1898), pp. 280-308.

50. Symons, *Cities of Italy* (London, 1907), p. 115. For early English enthusiasm for Sorrento, 'one of the most pleasant spots for a summer residence', see Blessington, op. cit., II, pp. 232-3. An American contemporary, Fenimore Cooper, hired a house 'on the cliffe within the walls and in plain sight of every object of interest in the bay'. He was told it was the house in which Tasso had been born; see *Excursions in Italy* (London, 1838), p. 245. Sir William Gell was meanwhile (1835) using notepaper headed with a lithographed scene of the 'Maison de Tasso a Sorrento' (*Sir William Gell in Italy: Letters to the Society of Dilettanti, 1831-1835*, ed. E. Clay (London, 1976), fig. XIII [a]).

51. Op. cit. (New York and London, 1908), p. 453.

52. *Itinerary*, op. cit., p. 142.

53. R.T. Günther, *Bibliography of Topographical and Geological Works on the Phlegraean Fields* (London, 1908). Still very useful and based on the traditional itinerary is A. Maiuri, *The Phlegraean Fields . .* , 3rd edn (Rome, 1958).

54. Blessington, op. cit., II, p. 90, and Seume, *Spaziergang nach Syrakus* (1803), ed. Jurgen von Hollander (Munich, 1962), p. 135. Another German, Marlowe's *Doctor Faustus*, was taken by Mephistophilis to view both 'learned Maro's golden tomb' and 'the way he cut an English mile in length / Through a rock of stone in one night's space' (Act III, Scene i). For the definitive study of 'The Grave of Virgil' and its *fortuna*, see the article by J.B. Trapp in the *Journal of the Warburg and Courtauld Institutes*, XLVII (1984); this is reprinted in Trapp, *Essays on the Renaissance and the Classical Tradition* (Aldershot, 1990) where fascinating supplementary material is to be found in 'Virgil and the Monuments' (chapter VI).

55. *Historie*, cit., fol. 113r.

56. *The Travels*, op. cit., p. 29. Though unacknowledged, Hoby's principal source for what follows was Leandro Alberti's *Descrittione di tutta Italia* (Bologna, 1550). The discovery of this permits us both to observe the future translator of the *Cortegiano* practising his skills and to distinguish that which is first-hand observation in the travel account from that which is merely plagiarized. My undocumented assertion that Alberti was Hoby's source (*Blue Guide Southern Italy*, op. cit., p. 52), has been confirmed in detail by Maria Grazia Padovan in her excellent *tesi di laurea: Il primo viaggio in Italia di Sir Thomas Hoby* (University of Pisa, 1982), a revised version of which we hope to publish.

57. *Travels*, op. cit., p. 32. Fynes Moryson tells us that Don Juan of Austria, not content with testing the toxic effects of the sulphur on mere dogs, 'forced a

Gally-slave into this cave, and he falling dead, forced another slave to fetch him out, who likewise fell dead, and that he killed the third slave with his owne hand, because he refused to fetch out his two dead fellowes' (*Itinerary*, I, ii, p. 114). In several other versions of this story, however, it is Don Pedro di Toledo who 'caused two offenders to be thrust thereinto' (Sandys, op. cit., p. 208. Compare Evelyn's *Diary*, II, p. 336, and Stone's 'Joyrnall', op. cit., p. 172, where the villain is Nero). The earliest printed source for the story would seem to be Scipione Mazzella, *Sito, et antichità . . . di Pozzuolo* (1590), 1606 edn, p. 78.

58. *Travels*, op. cit., p. 33.

59. Ibid., pp. 33–4. Hoby quotes Horace on Baiae: 'Nullus in orbe locus Baiis praelucet amoenis' (*Epistolae*, I, ii, l. 83). More than 150 years later George Berkeley writes to Percival of his visit: '*Nullus in orbe sinus Baiis praelucet amoenis* was the opinion of one who had very good taste'; *Works*, VIII, p. 103. The 'true' Sibyl's cave was discovered in 1932; see Maiuri, op. cit., p. 135.

60. *Travels*, p. 36.

61. Ibid., pp. 37–8.

62. Ibid., p. 38.

63. Ibid., p. 40.

64. Ibid. and *Old Calabria* (London, 1915), chapter XVII. Douglas seems not to have known of Hoby's Calabrian tour. Another early describer of Morano he might have enjoyed was the Reverend Brian Hill who, in 1791, travelled north along the same route as Hoby and concluded that Calabria was: 'a country, which though scarcely inferior to any other in climate and productions, and which for its sublime and magnificent views . . . perhaps exceeds every other, yet affords for travellers no one convenience whatever; but on the contrary, they have every real danger and misery to encounter . . . especially from the gangs of banditi, which have considerably increased, and become more desperate since the dreadful earthquake of 1783' (*Observations and Remarks in a Journey through Sicily and Calabria* (London, 1792), pp. xii–xiii).

65. *Travels*, op. cit., pp. 40–1; compare Douglas, op. cit., chapter XVI, 'Reposing at Castrovillari'.

66. Ibid. Sandys also believed the manna fell on the trees – he thought they were mulberry – 'like a dew in the night time' (*Relation*, cit., p. 195). In the chapter on Sandys in his *Paradise of Travellers* (London, 1964, p. 173, n. 13), A. Lytton Sells fails to identify this substance. H.V. Morton, however, explains that this 'mild aperient which is sold by every Italian chemist' is gathered by making incisions in the trunk of the Calabrian ash (*Fraxinus ornus*); see *A Traveller in Southern Italy* (London, 1969), pp. 323–4.

67. *Travels*, op. cit., p. 41. The then flourishing Accademia Cosentina included among its members the 40-year-old Bernardino Telesio, whose *De natura juxta propria principia* was to prompt Francis Bacon to hail him as 'the first of the moderns'.

68. *Travels*, p. 43.

69. Ibid., p. 44. The most recent Turkish attack on Reggio had occurred just seven years before Hoby's visit. The Turkish pirate-cum-admiral Barbarossa (Khayr-Ad-Dīn) died in 1546. In 1664 John Ray crossed over from Messina to Reggio and described it as 'an old City, but now very mean and poor'. He then 'took boat and went as far as *Scylla*, to see the fishing of the *Pesce Spada* or Sword-fish' of which he provides a detailed description (*Observations*, op. cit., p. 316; compare the modern account in Morton, op. cit., pp. 355–8).

70. *Travels*, p. 45. Hoby described the Orion fountain as 'graven with the storie of Acteon and such other, by on[e] Giovan Angelo, a florentine, which . . . is on[e] of the fairest peece of worke that ever I sawe. This fountain was appointed to be sett uppe before the hige churche where there is an old on[e] alreadie.' The latter remark raises a doubt about Vasari's report that in September 1547, Montorsoli had 'messo mano a fare il, condotto dell'acque che vengono di lontano' (*Le Vite*, ed. G. Milanesi (Florence, 1906), VI, p. 647).

71. Ibid., pp. 53-5. Capistrano had already shown Hoby and his friends 'great courtesie' in Siena and Rome. In the 'castle above [Amalfi] belonging to the duke', Hoby and Peter Whitehorn, the future translator of Machiavelli's *Art of Warre* (1560), were accommodated in 'a chamber hanged with clothe of gold and vellett'. The more famous Duchess of Amalfi was Giovanna d'Aragona who disappeared – presumed murdered by her brothers – in 1513. Bandello published the *Novella*, which was the ultimate source for Webster's great tragedy, in 1554; see G. Boklund, 'The Duchess of Malfi' . . . (Cambridge, MA, 1962). According to Giuseppe Gargano in D. Richter (ed.), *Alla Ricerca del Sud: tre secoli di viaggio ad Amalfi* . . . (Florence, 1989), p. 31, Hoby's host was Innico Piccolomini d'Aragona, son of Alfonso II (1499-1559) Duca d'Amalfi and Costanza d'Avelos d'Aquino (died 1575). Innico died in Rome on 18 August 1568 and is buried in S. Maria del Popolo.

72. There is still no self-contained English edition of Berkeley's remarkable travel journals and letters. All quotations here are taken from *The Works of George Berkeley, Bishop of Cloyne*, ed. A.A. Luce and T.E. Jessop (London and Edinburgh, 1955), VII and (1956) VIII. A recent Italian edition of the letters and journals, Berkeley, *Viaggio in Italia*, ed. T.E. Jessop and M. Fimiani (Naples, 1979), is disappointing, not least in failing to account for Berkeley's whereabouts between November 1718 and July 1720, 'un periodo di venti mesi di cui non sappiamo nulla' (ibid., p. 357). For the suggestion – based on the discovery of his signature in the visitors' book of the University of Padua – that he spent most of this period in the north of Italy, see my 'George Berkeley in the Veneto', *Bollettino del C.I.R.V.I.*, I, ii (1980), pp. 82-8; revised version below pp. 366-76. English fascination with the tarantula dates at least as far back as Sandys (op. cit., pp. 194-5) and is particularly evident in Misson's *New Voyage* (1714 edn, II, ii, pp. 598-604 and illustration on p. 396) which we know Berkeley used.

73. *Works*, VIII, pp. 104-5 (letter to Percival dated 18 June 1717).

74. Ibid., VIII, p. 105. The four surviving uniform volumes are now in the British Library (Add. MS 39307-10); others, including one on Sicily, are known to have been lost. For Lear's travels, see below, note 85.

75. *Works*, VIII, p. 107 (letter to Pope from Naples dated 22 October 1717). Despite Addison being 'more earnest in the Whig cause than Mr. Steele', Berkeley became a firm friend from c.1709. He was present with Mr Addison . . . in a side box (equipped with burgundy and champagne) on the first night of the latter's *Cato* ('a most noble play') in April 1713. Addison describes sailing to Ischia from Procida and quotes Virgil (and Dryden's translation) on the effect on the islands of the collapse of the Baian Mole; *Remarks* (London, 1705), pp. 275-8 and A.A. Luce, *The Life of George Berkeley* (London, 1949), pp. 58-9. Among earlier visitors (since Hoby) were Isaac Basire and his pupils, blown there in a storm in 1648; see above, p. 87, n. 2. Later eighteenth-century admirers of Ischia include William Bristow FRS, 'a great pretender to taste' who sought a health cure there in 1737 and Allan

Ramsay, who, on a visit there in 1776, also for the sake of its baths, drew the self-portrait now in the National Portrait Gallery, London; see Alastair Smart, *Allan Ramsay* . . . (New Haven and London, 1992), pp. 37–8 and 244.

76. *Works*, VIII, p. 104. Berkeley was particularly impressed by the fact that 'The meanest houses are built of hewn stone, have ornamented doors, rustics . . . in Lecce there is general good *gout*, which descends down to the poorest houses'. The recent Italian edition of this (*Viaggio*, op. cit., p. 226) renders 'The meanest houses' as 'Gli edifici principali'; see below, Chapter 13.

77. *Works*, VII, p. 284 (Journal entry dated 27 May 1717). In 1828, Ramage found at Lecce 'nothing to interest a stranger, except, perhaps, the church of Santa Croce, which is not a bad specimen of architectural design' (cf. N. Douglas, *Alone* (London, 1921), p. 248). Later in the nineteenth century, Gregorovius and Paul Bourget were considerably more appreciative. A pre-Sitwellian 'discoverer' of *il barocco leccese* was Martin S. Briggs (*In the Heel of Italy* (London, 1910)).

78. Op. cit., pp. 24–5; cf. V. Cazzato and M. Fagiolo, *Lecce* (Bari, 1984)

79. Op. cit., p. 263: 'Corsica occurred to me as a place which no body else had seen, and where I should find what was to be seen, and where I should find what was to be seen no where else, a people actually fighting for liberty.' Even before his *Account* was in print Boswell was encouraging friends to follow in his footsteps. In 1767 John Symonds wrote to him that everything was 'as You foretold – I never found a Person of a more liberal, improved Conversation, than the General' (Paoli); see M. Ambrosoli, *John Symonds. Agricoltura e politica in Corsica e in Italia (1765–1770)* (Turin, 1974), pp. 136–7. In this same letter Symonds refers to a recent 'Account of my Journey into Calabria' which had gone astray; cf. D. Grimaldi in ibid., p. 32. It has recently been suggested that one of the most important mid-century extensions of the conventional Grand Tour, James Stuart and Nicholas Revett's expedition to Greece, may have been partly inspired by Pococke and Stuart meeting at the Three Kings in Naples after the former's return from Athens in 1740; see Michael McCarthy, ' "The dullest man that ever travelled"? A re-assessment of Richard Pococke . . .', *Apollo*, CXLIII (May 1996), pp. 25–9.

80. In 2 vols (London, 1783–5). Hélène Tuzet writes that Brydone's *Tour* 'est une date dans l'histoire du récit de voyage, en tant que genre littéraire' (*La Sicile au XVIII*^{e} *siècle vue par les voyageurs étrangers* (Strasbourg, 1955), p. 33); cf. P. Fussell, 'Patrick Brydone: the Eighteenth-Century Traveler as Representative Man', in *Literature as a Mode of Travel*, ed. W.G. Rice (New York, 1964). Soufflot (and others) had visited Paestum before the Seven Years' War but publication of his drawings was postponed until the 1760s: see M. McCarthy, 'New Light on Thomas Major's *Paestum* . . .', *Paestum and the Doric Revival 1750–1830*, ed. J.R. Serra (Florence, 1986), pp. 47–52.

81. On the final page of the first edition of his *Remarks* (London, 1813), Forsyth recalls how he arrived in Turin on 25 May 1803: 'The next day I was arrested as a British subject, and I am now passing the TENTH YEAR OF MY CAPTIVITY. VALENCIENNES. 1 June, 1812'. By the time he was released, in the year following the publication of his book, his health was so impaired that he died after enjoying his freedom for just 18 months; see his brother Isaac's memoir which prefaces the later editions of the *Remarks*.

82. *Remarks*, op. cit., p. 343; compare Brian Hill's 1791 account (op. cit., pp. 259–64).

83. G. Massara, 'British and American Travellers and the Image of Paestum' *Paestum and the Doric Revival*, cit., p. 157; *The Journal of Sir Walter Scott*, ed.

W.E.K. Anderson (Oxford, 1972), pp. 690–713 and *Letters of . . . Shelley*, cit., II, p. 79. Cf. Charles Macfarlane, *Reminiscences of a Literary Life* (London, 1917), pp. 1–12. Macfarlane travelled from Naples to Paestum with Shelley in a two-horse *calèsse*. For Shelley's opinion of Forsyth's *Remarks* as 'worth reading', see *Letters*, II, p. 89. Byron presented a copy of the book to the Veronese poet Pindemonte, hoping its flattering references to his verse on p. 24 would please him (*Byron's Letters and Journals*, ed. L. Marchand, V (London, 1976), p. 233). Having established that both Byron and Shelley knew Forsyth's *Remarks*, I believe one can argue that its extraordinarily detailed account of Pisa, its institutions, poets, climate ('Winter is by far the finest season . . . fully as mild as our Spring') must have encouraged Shelley to abandon the 'infernal cold' of Florence for Pisa in January 1820, and helped persuade Byron to join him there.

84. Ibid., V, p. 187. Having ventured further south than Byron, in 1824 a honeymoon couple, Mr and Mrs Thomas Hunt, were murdered at Paestum; see William Gell, *Reminiscences of Sir Walter Scott's Residence in Italy, 1832*, ed. J.G. Corson (London, 1957), pp. 16 and 47, n. 46.

85. Vivien Noakes, *Edward Lear, the Life of a Wanderer*, 2nd edn (London, 1979), pp. 67–70. The *Illustrations* were mainly concerned with the Abruzzi which Lear claimed he saw more of 'than any Englishman has ever yet done' (ibid., p. 58). His *Journal of a Landscape Painter in Southern Calabria*, based on an 1847 tour, was published in 1852 with 20 lithographed plates. Ramage did not publish his *Nooks and By-Ways* until 1868. An abridged edition, including letters to his mother (1825–8), was published in 1965 by Edith Clay (introduction by Harold Acton).

86. Mark Holloway, *Norman Douglas: A Biography* (London, 1976). For praise of *Ionian Sea* as it appeared in the *Fortnightly Review* in 1900, see *George Gissing and H.G. Wells: their Friendship and Correspondence*, ed. R.A. Gettmann (London, 1961), p. 146.

87. *Late Harvest* (London, 1946), p. 18, and O. de Zordo, *Una proposta anglofiorentina degli anni trenta: the Lungarno Series* (Florence, 1981), pp. 61–77; see also ibid., pp. 191–203, for Richard MacGillivray [Dawkins's] still very useful *Norman Douglas*, published by Orioli in 1933.

88. Holloway, op. cit., p. 180. Douglas described Eric as 'A pick-up' in his diary.

89. Ibid., pp. 185–7. Douglas's 'nurse' in this instance was Joseph Conrad, a fellow *aficionado* of Capri, who had hitherto considered him 'one of my two most intimate friends'. According to Constantine FitzGibbon, however, the Eric 'scandal' lost Douglas this friendship; see *Man in Aspic* (London, 1977), pp. 27–8. It is amusing to note that 'Salami' already features in John Florio's *Queen Anna's New World of Words* (London, 1611), p. 459: 'any kind of salt, pickled, powdred or bloted and smoake dried meats . . .'

90. Wolton eventually became Chief Superintendent of the Tanganyikan Police. For the less fortunate Armitrano, with whom Douglas was living in 1908 when '*Siren Land* was begun', see *Alone*, op. cit., p. 182, and the more revealing tribute in *Late Harvest*, op. cit., pp. 74–6. The revelation that 'each of his books had ripened under the warm rays of some temporary attachment', recorded by Harold Acton in his contribution to *Grand Man. Memories of Norman Douglas*, ed. Nancy Cunard (London, 1954), p. 239, has recently been adapted by Paul Fussell as the title of his chapter on Douglas in *Abroad: British Literary Travelling between the Wars* (Oxford, 1980), pp. 119–36.

91. *Experiments* (London, 1925), p. 13 (review of Doughty's *Travels in Arabia Deserta*). For Douglas's writings in the context of Edwardian travel literature,

see J. Alcorn, *The Nature Novel from Hardy to Lawrence* (London, 1977), chapter 3.

92. *Alone*, op. cit., p. 246; compare what Douglas says about *Old Calabria* in the list of suggested superlatives he sends its prospective *TLS* reviewer (Holloway, op. cit., p. 212). Perhaps because *Ionian Sea* was uncomfortably recent, Douglas implied that Gissing was 'a dilettante traveller' (*Old Calabria*, op. cit., p. 82). More generous remarks appeared in *Late Harvest* (op. cit., p. 47) though even there he was still reprimanded for 'his lack of humour'. In *Calabria and the Aeolian Islands* (London, 1957), p. 65, E. and B. Whelpton write that 'In spite of all his peevish carping, Gissing came back to Calabria, and he died at Crotone in 1901', when in fact he died two years later in the south of France. This error is probably based on a misreading of *Old Calabria* (op. cit., p. 299). Referring to the 'amiable guardian of the cemetery' whom Gissing had described at Cotrone (Crotone), Douglas writes: 'Dead, like those graves he tended; like Gissing himself. He expired in February 1901 – the year of the publication of the "Ionian Sea", and they showed me his tomb near the right side of the entrance.'

93. *The Passionate Sightseer* (London, 1960), pp. 146–7. For Douglas's thoughts on suicide as man's 'inalienable right', see *How about Europe?* (Florence, 1929), pp. 134–6; compare the account of his death in Holloway, op. cit., p. 491.

94. *Collected Shorter Poems 1927–1957* (London, 1966), p. 341. In an earlier version of the same poem in *Homage to Clio* (London, 1960), p. 81, Croce's name appeared instead of Bernini's, and in a third, Leopardi's. All three versions, however, feature Bellini where perhaps Antonello (da Messina) might be thought more appropriate. It is clear, however, that Auden is thinking of music (and *Vincenzo* Bellini) rather than painting here.

95. Charles Osborne, *W.H. Auden: The Life of a Poet* (London, 1979), pp. 246–9. 'Monte' was the name of the Ischian landlord who tried to 'fleece' Auden when he considered purchasing the villa he had been renting after receiving prize money from Feltrinelli. Humphrey Carpenter quotes Auden as saying 'I don't like sunshine. I would like Mediterranean life in a northern climate', *W.H. Auden: A Biography* (London, 1981), p. 386.

96. Op. cit., 1929 edn, p. 312. More specifically on the subject of Ischia, Douglas's 'The Island of Typhoeus' first appeared in a 1909 issue of the *English Review* and was republished in *Summer Islands* (London, 1931).

97. Op. cit., p. 338. For the literally fatal influence of 'Douglas's splendidly sinewy pages' on the young scholar Felix Raab, who fell to his death climbing Monte Pollino, see H.R. Trevor-Roper's foreword to Raab's *English Face of Machiavelli* (London and Toronto, 1964), p. ix.

98. *By the Ionian Sea* (London, 1901), p. 203. See also P. Kirby, 'Norman Douglas, Gissing and Lenormant in South Italy', *Critical Dimensions*, ed. M. Curreli and A. Martino (Cuneo, 1978), pp. 397–418.

99. Homer, *The Odyssey*, XII, transl. E.V. Rieu (Harmondsworth, 1946), p. 190, compare Douglas, *Siren Land*, op. cit., p. 13.

100. Ibid., pp. 47–8 (referring to Pope's translation of the *Odyssey*, XII, lines 184–91). Finally, for accounts of Berenson in and around Naples, Auden on Ischia and Douglas on Capri (as well as Evelyn Waugh in Palermo), see the closing chapters of Harold Acton's *More Memoirs of an Aesthete* (London, 1970), those which cover the decade 1950–60, when the author divided his time between Florence and southern Italy in order to write his *magnum opus* on the Bourbons.

5

Robert Dallington's *Survey of Tuscany* (1605): A British View of Medicean Florence

⸎⸎⸎

IN THE CENTURY and a half which lay between the fall of the Florentine Republic in 1530 and the Glorious Revolution, it could be argued that the states of Tuscany and England moved in opposite directions – something of an irony in that much of the ideology motivating British politicians throughout this period was Florentine in origin. With the waning of the Renaissance, Florence drifted from republican prosperity, through intermittently effective and decreasingly democratic duchies and grand duchies towards the oppressive and superstitious régime of Cosimo III, who was finally granted 'royal' status in 1695. During the same century and a half, England lurched or, as Whigs and Marxists would have it, 'progressed' from the megalomaniac monarchy of Henry VIII, through Reformation, Civil War, regicide and Restoration, to settle for the 'mixed' (republican-influenced) constitutional government of the 'doge-like' William III, whose regal powers were strictly rationed by Parliament. Meanwhile, the British economy had so far flourished, and the Florentine so far declined, that although our monarchs had for centuries been obliged to borrow money from private citizens in Florence, by the 1670s new-rich British citizens could outbid the Grand Duke himself for works of art in Italian auctions.[1]

For all the fascinating evidence presented by Harold Acton in *The Last Medici*, Francis Haskell in *Patrons and Painters*, Eric Cochrane in *Florence in the Forgotten Centuries*, and the authors of the catalogues which accompanied the great Cinquecento and Seicento exhibitions of the 1970s and 1980s, it is clear that, apart from a few brief periods of revival, Florentine culture went the way of the Florentine economy.[2] Having attended meetings of the Svogliati and Apatisti Academies, and formed friendships with leading members of these Florentine societies during his Italian tour of 1638–9, back in revolutionary London John Milton protested against Parliament's reintroduction of Star Chamber-style censorship by citing the culturally disastrous consequences of such censorship in grand-ducal Florence.[3] Ridiculing in particular the licensing of books by 'imprimatur', Milton included in his *Areopagitica* translations of the four examples of such 'exorcism' he found in his copy of Bernardo Davanzati's *Scisma d'Inghilterra*, a work which had been published in Florence during his stay there. Later in the same pamphlet he returned to the case of contemporary Florence, 'lest som should perswade ye, Lords and Commons, that these arguments of lerned mens discouragement at this your order, are meer flourishes, and not reall':

> I could recount what I have seen and heard in other Countries, where this kind of inquisition tyrannizes, when I have sat among their lerned men, for that honor I had and bin counted happy to be born in such a place of Philosophic freedom, as they suppos'd England was, while themselves did nothing but bemoan the servil condition into which lerning was brought; that this was it which I had dampt the glory of Italian wits; that nothing had been there writt'n now these many years but flattery and fustian. There it was that I found and visited the famous *Galileo* grown old, a prisner to the Inquisition, for thinking in Astronomy otherwise then the Franciscan and Dominican licencers thought.[4]

As if acknowledging that Italian wits had indeed been 'dampt', at the very time that Milton was writing this *Speech . . . for the Liberty of Unlicenc'd Printing*, the Grand Duke Ferdinand II and his enlightened younger brother, Prince (later Cardinal) Leopoldo de' Medici, were taking advantage of the English Civil War by recruiting scholarly talent from this country to relatively tranquil Tuscany in an attempt to maintain standards. Though they failed to attract the great mathematician William Oughtred, despite the offer of £500 per annum, during the 1650s they employed several of England's most learned men, including the connoisseur of pictures and medals, Peter Fitton, the wandering humanist, John Price, Professor of Greek at the University of Pisa [Fig. 24], and the Padua-trained physician, John Finch, who was appointed Professor of Anatomy at Pisa in

24 R.A. Persyn,
John Price (c.1650)
from L. Apuleii
*Metamorphoseos
libri xi cum annota-
tionibus uberiobus
Ioannis Pricaei*
MDCL. [E. Chaney]

IOANNES PRICÆVS.

1659 and, like his lifelong companion, Dr Thomas Baines, was painted by Carlo Dolci.[5]

The causes of decline, however, were too deep-seated to be eliminated by a handful of academic appointments. Fitton died in 1656, his catalogue of the Uffizi medals and antiquities unfinished, and Finch returned to England and a knighthood at the Restoration, while the long-suffering Dr Price, having failed to find a post in England owing largely to his Catholicism, eventually settled in Rome to work for Cardinal Francesco Barberini. Significantly, in 1653 Price was already complaining that 'here in *Florence* is not so much as a Greek Stamp' (that is, a printing press with a Greek typeface). 'The Air of this place in winter', he wrote, 'is . . . most pernicious to me; the Conversation of this place, both in Winter and Summer,

A
SVRVEY OF
THE GREAT
DVKES STATE
of *Tuſcany.*

In the yeare of our **Lord**
1 5 9 6.

AT LONDON
Printed for *Edward Blount.*
1 6 0 5.

25 [Robert Dallington] *A Survey of the Great Dukes State of Tuscany in the yeare of our Lord* 1596 (London, 1605). [E. Chaney]

is most contrary to me, but the Great Duke's Civilities, rather than ought else, have made me thus long abide here.' Finally, in 1660, when even Venice had tried and failed to cope with its polyglot text, he published his folio *Critici Sacri* in London, notwithstanding its dedication to Prince Cosimo de' Medici.[6]

In 1654 the Roman Catholic travel writer Richard Lassels noted that 'Belle lettere have allwayes been much cherished' in Florence but apparently considered only one academy, the della Crusca, worthy of mention and that merely for having 'helpd to polish the Italian tongue'.[7] By 1685 Florentine scholarship had reached an all-time post-Renaissance low. Interviewing the famous librarian Antonio Magliabecchi after visiting the Laurentian Library, Gilbert Burnet, the historian and future Bishop of Salisbury, reported him as complaining that 'there was not one man in Florence that either understood Greek, or that examined Manuscripts'.[8]

Given that in the late fifteenth century, the English had had to travel to Italy, more often than not to Florence, in order to study Greek,[9] it is remarkable testimony to both the success of British education under the Tudors and the corresponding decline of humanistic scholarship in Italy that, long before Burnet commented on the phenomenon, an English schoolmaster, Robert Dallington, could report that in the University of Florence 'yee shall scarce finde two that are good *Grecians* without the which tongue, they holde in our Schooles in England a man never deserveth the reputation of learned.'[10]

Dallington's fascinating *Survey of the Great Dukes State of Tuscany* was first published in 1605 but, as its full title makes clear, it actually describes Tuscany as seen 'in the year of our Lord 1596' [Fig. 25]. Between 1594, when Fynes Moryson discreetly settled in San Casciano near Florence, and 1617, when his *Itinerary* finally appeared, Moryson laboured over a vast manuscript which he abridged drastically in order to publish what is still a massive folio.[11] Dallington's diminutive *Survey*, on the other hand, seems to have circulated in the form of an unrevised manuscript until his friend, Edward Blount, obtained a copy and published it in order, or so he claimed, to prevent 'one that loves you not so much' from seeing it through the press less conscientiously. Almost immediately it raised a storm of protest from Florence, its punning conclusion that 'Qui sub Medicis vivit, misere vivit' ('he who lives under the Medici (or doctors), lives wretchedly') causing Ferdinand I to demand that the king have all copies destroyed. Despite the fact that James was for ever borrowing money from the Medici and was considering a plan to marry Prince Henry to Ferdinand's daughter, only half-hearted attempts at fulfilling this request were made, just three copies of the *Survey* being burned in St Paul's Churchyard in the presence of the Tuscan Resident.[12] A second printing, moreover, appeared within the same year. Through the good offices of the Italophile 5th Earl of Rutland and Sir Thomas Chaloner, who has been defined as 'the principal agent in the formation of [Prince Henry's] circle' and who was also in Florence in 1596, Dallington was appointed gentleman of the privy chamber to the Prince.[13] Given that a Stuart–Medici marriage had been mooted as early as 1601, it is indeed possible that it was Henry who requested the *Survey* in the first place. In contrast to so many in Henry's circle whose careers collapsed when the young prince died in 1612, Dallington continued in the favour of the future Charles I, who in 1624 recommended him as Master of Charterhouse in which prosperous post he died (aged 76), 13 years later.[14]

Though not a Fellow of Peterhouse like the better-born Fynes Moryson, Dallington was nevertheless Cambridge-educated and, to judge from the *Survey* and several other publications, at least as learned as his younger contemporary. After working in Norfolk as a provincial schoolmaster, in 1592 he (probably) demonstrated both his originality and his knowledge of Italian by publishing a translation of part of the extraordinary *Hypnerotomachia Poliphili*, an illustrated novel supposedly written by a Venetian Dominican, which so seductively celebrates love and beauty in a vaguely neo-Platonic context that it has been accorded an exaggeratedly central place in Renaissance cultural history.[15]

It may have been the appearance of this work, *The Strife of Love in a Dreame*, albeit merely under the signature R.D., that brought Dallington to the attention of Roger Manners, 5th Earl of Rutland, who was then studying at Corpus Christi College, Cambridge, where Dallington had been a bible clerk. In September 1595 the 18-year-old Rutland was granted a 'licence to pass over the seas' but in January of the following year he was still receiving letters of travel advice from the Earl of Essex (to whom R.D. had dedicated his translation) apparently helped by Francis Bacon (who was related to Dallington's first patron, Thomas Butts).[16] It is not certain that the 35-year-old Dallington actually accompanied Rutland on his journey out to Italy, for an apparently eye-witness account in the *Survey* of an incident which probably took place in January 1596 suggests that he was already there before Rutland arrived.[17] By the end of the year, however, Dallington was cashing a bill of exchange in Florence 'with his L's consent' and by the time Rutland's younger brother Francis, the future 6th Earl, visited Florence two years later, the schoolmaster had become so senior a member of the household (which probably included Inigo Jones) that, after Francis returned home and all three Manners brothers were imprisoned for involvement in Essex's rebellion, Dallington joined them in the Tower [Fig. 26].[18]

Given that Dallington implies he was already in Florence in January, and that we know him to have been there again the following winter, the fact that he says he spent four months in nearby Prato means we can assume he spent most of 1596 in

26 Simon van de Passe (?), *Francis Manners, 6th Earl of Rutland.* [E. Chaney]

Tuscany.[19] The extended title of a manuscript Italian translation of his *Survey* in the Florentine archives emphasizes what is indicated in the original text, namely that a large part of this 'Falsissima

Relatione' was based on what he had been told by the Chancellor and Captain of the Guard of Prato, as well as disgruntled Sienese and Pisans.[20]

Though Dallington seems to have been predisposed to listen to criticisms of grand-ducal government, occasionally extending them to refer to Italy as a whole, he by no means depended on second-hand information. Indeed the very effectiveness of the *Survey* is due to his tendency to corroborate sophisticated statistical evidence with eye-witness accounts. At Prato, for example, having explained in only mildly patronizing tones the high esteem in which the city's prize possession, the Virgin's belt or girdle, was held, he goes on to describe the annual Lady Day Fair (7 September) at which this holy relic was displayed from Michelozzo and Donatello's exquisite, purpose-built pulpit on the façade of the Duomo:

> There came that day in devotion (to see me, not the Girdle) two English Gentlemen my friends; we observed (if it be not impertinent here to remember) that there were in view upon the Market place of people at the shewing of this Relicke, about eighteene or twenty thousand, where-of we judged one halfe to have Hattes of Strawe, and one fourth part to be bare legged; that we know all is not gold in *Italy*; though many Travellers gazing onely on the beautie of their Citties, and the painted surface of their houses, thinke it the onely Paradize of *Europe*.

If these travellers would look more carefully at the countryside instead of the city and actually enter the houses of the peasants, Dallington argues, 'they would surely graunt, that povertie and famine had not a greater kingdome in those countries where *Crassus* starved his Armie, then they have heere.'[21]

Drawing not merely upon those sources which the Florentine government accused him of exploiting but also on the works of Machiavelli, Guicciardini, Leandro Alberti, Buonacorsi and Paolo Giovio, Dallington puts the poverty of Prato into historical context, attributing it largely to the devastating sack of the city by the Spaniards in 1512 (though ultimately even this is described as 'an injurie of the *Florentines*').[22] Dallington is excellent on the other Florentine dependencies, Pistoia, Siena and Pisa, as well as on the rural economy, the silk industry, taxation, mining, monopolies, diet, banking, bureaucracy, brothels, methods of torture and local government. But what ultimately fascinates him is Florence's government and in particular the way in which one family, the

Medici, could from such humble beginnings in a relatively democratic state have acquired almost regal powers. One can imagine
Ferdinand I's furious reaction when he read his specially prepared
translation of the following occasionally judicious but ultimately
scathing account:

> The Government (to speake in one word, and not to use a harder terme)
> is meerely *Despoticall.* The Prince himselfe is of stature meane, of colour
> by complexion browne, by age grisled, of body corpulent, of age some-
> what about fiftie, his name *Ferdinando*, who (till his brothers death) was
> Cardinall, which dignity he hath since renounced, having attained this
> Scepter, whereof he had not beene capable, if he had before entered the
> order of Priest-hood. He is of the familie *Medici*, a noble house of *Florence*,
> the first raiser whereof was *Lippo*, not three hundred yeares since (whose
> Father, though a Colliar) yet he by his vertues and his posteritie also
> succeeding from time to time, advanced the reputation of this name to
> the greatnesse wherein now it is . . .
>
> The meanes how this house rose to such superioritie in a common-
> wealth, where was alwaies maintained such equallitie, is by the *Florence*
> historie easily discerned to be their popularity & insinuative stealing
> into the peoples good opinions; over whom they oftentimes in cases of
> insolencies & oppressions by the nobler sort, undertooke the Patronage,
> & became as it were the *Tribunes* of the people in *Rome*, or the *Avogadori
> del Commune* in Venice.[23]

As in most English accounts, from William Thomas's *Historie of Italie*
of 1549 to Samuel Lewkenor's *Discourse* of 1600, Cosimo il Vecchio
and his grandson, Lorenzo, are given a good press in the *Survey*,
Machiavelli and Guicciardini being Dallington's primary sources for
his account of the fifteenth century.[24] We are left in no doubt, however, that the steady rise of the Medici meant the conversely steady
decline and ultimate fall of Florentine liberty. In the second half of
the fifteenth century the Medici's 'plausible carriage towards the
meaner and baser rancke of Citizens, by whom they were chosen for
a head against the greater and more powerfull sort' enabled them to
build a power base which eventually proved impossible to destroy:

> And not contented with this preheminencie, their desires rested not:
> untill (as in the person of *Alexander* shall appeare) one of their house
> came to be Duke of so great a State, brother to a King of *France*, and
> sonne in law to an Emperour.[25]

Though it is clear from all this that he was not the stuff of which Royalists were to be made, neither was Dallington consistently radical. In view of his repeated criticisms of grand-ducal taxation, for example, you might expect him to criticize Ferdinand's court for its centralized extravagance, yet here he chauvinistically complains that, where the quantity of courtiers was concerned, 'it may hardly compare with the houses of the Nobility of *England*, comprehending in this number none but such as live and have their dyet in Court, whereof there be very few.'[26]

Perhaps, as the loyal servant of one of the great noblemen who in 1601 rebelled against Secretary Cecil's formidably centralized administration, Dallington preferred the idea of oligarchic rule. His apparent sympathy with the acorn-eating peasants, impoverished artisans and disinherited ('mere'?) gentry of Tuscany, however, also suggests democratic inclinations of the kind which would lead to Civil War. The following complaint, for example, could almost be that of a Leveller 50 years later:

> That glory and wealth there is, is in the Cittie, and in the hands of few, to whom all the fruites of the country are conveyed: as for the Artificer he can doe no more but live, whereof scarce one in a citty ever groweth rich, and the poore *Contadines* life is such, as if naturally he were not proud in this extreame miserie, it would move any stranger to pittie his estate.[27]

Typical of his free-trader's contempt for the grand duke's 'over-charging of his people by Taxations and impositions' is Dallington's account of the way in which the customs function at Florence's great gates. Since the whole operation is farmed out by the grand duke for 200,000 ducats,

> There is not that poore Asses burthen of dung that goeth out the gates, nor that Radish roote that commeth in, that paieth not his *Gabell*, except they have the cunning to deceive them that keepe the gates, men whose eyes will pearce what *Valigia* or basket soever: and if it chance they be detected, they loose the thing hidden without redemption.'[28]

As usual, Dallington supports his assertions with a first-hand account (in this instance one which encourages scepticism regarding the thesis that Breughel's peasants were depicted solely that the upper classes might mock them):

I saw a poore *Contadina* [or] Countrey-woman, who coming to the gate
to pay her tolle for a Basket of Lettice she brought in: one of the foxes,
who I thinke could smell a goose, for he could not possibl[y] see any,
searched under the hearbes, and finding one dead without feathers, sent
the poore woman away halfe dead for sorrow, without her goose. And
they told me, that if a Gentleman of Siena should come out at *Florence*
gates with a chaine of gold new bought about his neck, howbeit worne
betweene his doublet and Ierkin that it might not be seene to save the
gabell, that being discovered he should not loose his Chaine onely, but
his horse also.[29]

Even when Dallington writes in praise of Florence, there is often
an ironic sting in the tail referring to some aspect of repressive
government policy. Occasionally this is so mild one remains unsure
whether criticism is intended. Having experienced the notoriously
filthy, unplanned and unpaved streets of London, lined with
asymmetrical, timber-frame houses, Dallington could hardly deny
Florence's claim to be one of the best-built and most modern cities
in the world:

It hath the streetes very long, streight, large, and faire, paved with a
broad stone which they call *Lastra*, so as no weather makes them foule:
it is beautified with many stately Pallaces, which have more *del Reale*
then *del Cittadinesco*, as that of the *Signoria*, that of the *Pitti*, where is
always the great Dukes court: that of the *Medici* that of the *Strozzi* and
many others: it is graced with many large *Piazzes*, and in them many
Statues, some of Brasse [bronze], as that of *Cosme*, the first great Duke,
and others very many and very curious, some of Marble, some of
Alabaster.[30]

Thus he continues, praising the city's 'four faire Bridges of Stone'
and even its monasteries and churches, having caused us to hesitate
only in the light of what he says elsewhere, when he comments on
the palaces' regal rather than private or civic character. Even his
eulogy of Michelangelo's Laurentian Library concludes on a worry-
ing note, given Protestant attitudes to the Inquisition and its *Index
librorum prohibitorum*:

In the Cloisters of the Church of *San Lorenzo* is a very faire and beautiful Librarie, built and furnished with Bookes by the familie of *Medici*: the
roofe is of Cedar very curiously wrought with knots and flowers, and
right under each knot is the same wrought with no lesse Arte in the

pavement. In this Library I told three thousand nine hundred bookes very fairely bound in Leather, after one sort, all bound to their seates, which were in number sixtie eight: and, which is the greatest grace and cost also, very many of the bookes were written with the Authours owne hands. There is also at the farther end of this Librarie one other of prohibited bookes, which I could not see.[31]

'The repairing at the great Dukes charges' of the 'excellent Fabrick' of the Baptistery at Pisa after the 1595 fire sounds commendable until we hear that the salt tax throughout Tuscany will be raised by five *quatrini* in the pound to pay for the work and that 'it is thought (be examples too many of like nature in other places) that being once granted, it shall not then be ended.'[32] Such arguments, first in the form of propaganda but ultimately at his show trial, proved fatal for Charles I. Even the apparently uncritical and detailed description of the 'exquisite and rare invention of Water-workes' and the spectacular gardens at Pratolino is undermined when we are informed in a subsequent section how Ferdinando's brother, Francesco I, had raised the 300,000 crowns to pay for it all.[33]

Dallington's need to complete discussion of almost every aspect of Florence with a sometimes minor but more often devastating criticism ultimately extends even to puritanical disparagement of her artistic achievement. The letter which Essex and Bacon wrote to Rutland on the eve of his foreign tour recommended, as well as an appreciation of 'the beauty of many cities', the cultivation of an inward 'beauty of the mind'.[34] Such Platonic advice may have been more relevant to Rutland's pioneering patronage of Inigo Jones than to Jones's colleague Dallington. Though highly literate and politically sophisticated, he was also typically Elizabethan in his ignorance of art and architecture. Of Siena's immediately appealing Campo he was capable of remarking: 'I have not seen a Market-steede, excepting that of *Sancto Marco* in *Venice*, so beautifull.'[35] But when more elaborate aesthetic or historical terminology was required, Dallington's conceptual range proved totally inadequate. Though Henry Wotton, Inigo Jones, Henry Peacham and the Earl of Arundel were soon to discover Vasari's *Lives*, not until the publication of Lassels's *Voyage* in 1670 did an English book on Italy demonstrate some understanding of the history of art. The only artist actually named by Dallington is Brunelleschi, whom he rightly con-

siders an 'excellent Architeck'. This, however, is because he believes
him to have designed the whole of that 'most magnificent and
admirable Fabrick of the *Duomo*' rather than just its cupola.[36] That
he is stronger on historical geography than the history of style is
confirmed by his account of stone-quarrying and its banal conclusion:

> There is digged out of these hilles a kinde of Free-stone, passing hard, of
> colour according to the nature of the place whereout it is taken, white,
> redde, and black, or to say more properly, enclining to these colours: of
> all which sorts there be in *Florence* and elsewhere, very gallant and
> stately Pallaces builded. They have also in many places, pitts of Marble,
> white, blew and party-coloured excellent good: namely in the Territory
> of *Massa*, but especially in the Mountaines of *Carrara* and *Lunigiana*:
> hence dayly they dig for the building of their Churches and Pallaces of
> *Genoa, Florence, Bologna, Rome,* and *France* also.[37]

The careful effect of all this is spoiled by a failure – based on
ignorance – to acknowledge the great revival of classical style which
had been occupying Italian architects for almost 200 years. For,
according to Dallington's almost determinist thesis, the availability
of cheap marble 'is the reason the buildings of *Italy* so farre exceed
ours, especially their Churches: as for any other thing in that land,
the truth is they can no way compare with us, nor make good the
great opinion the world hath thereof'.[38] Later, he enlarges the range
of his compliment, but even this proves backhanded: 'Indeed it
cannot be denied, that in two faculties this towne hath had famous
men in Painting and Poetry and I verily thinke that herein *Italy*
generally excelleth. And no marvaile, when all their time is spent in
Amours, and all their churches deckt with colours.'[39]
   Implicit in much of the criticism is a commentary not just on
Florence but on Britain; a commentary of the kind that becomes
explicit in Milton's *Areopagitica* early in the Civil War, certain of
James Howell's writings and in Burnet's *Some Letters,* which goes
into great detail on the supposed causes of economic decline in Italy
and concludes with a eulogy of William of Orange on the eve of the
Glorious Revolution.[40] In this respect Dallington was a pioneer
exploiter of Italy as a means of persuading complacent English
readers to preserve and protect their ancient liberties. Behind his
criticisms of the city which more than any other may be credited
with the renaissance of classical learning, the visual arts, sciences

and the political thought which formed the basis of his own proto-democratic ideas, there must have lain a powerful feeling of disappointment. Neither travellers' tales of this 'onely Paradize of Europe', nor his own vicarious experience of Italy through its literature and history, had prepared him for the large numbers of poverty-stricken, barefoot peasants and their credulous devotion to relics, the ubiquitous taxation, the injustice, the stagnation of scholarship and the censored superficiality even of the hitherto celebrated wit of the Florentines.

Perhaps the best adjective for Dallington's politics would be that coined by the Italo-Dalmatian Protestant convert, Sir Giovanni Francesco Biondi, in the 1630s: 'aristodemocraticall'. In his *Istoria delle Guerre Civili d'Inghilterra*, Biondi described the horrors of the Wars of the Roses in the hope of averting another Civil War. As if consciously echoing Dallington (and certainly following their mutual source, Machiavelli), Biondi draws his English readers' attention to the sufferings of those who live under less benign regimes than their own. But whereas Dallington concluded optimistically on the 'blessed happinesse' that prevailed under James I's 'flourishing monarchy', Biondi was clearly concerned that the puritanically inclined subjects of Charles were insufficiently appreciative of their lot:

> [the English people] are not taxed or oppressed . . . And whereas the Country people in other parts walke bare foot and bare legged, with tattered cloathes and leane lookes; heere well cloathed and well liking, they in substance are, and in apparell seeme to be honourable and wealthy Citizens.[41]

Biondi concludes on an ominous note, strongly suggestive of his anxiety that the untravelled Englishman may yet provoke 'violent changes [which] draw after them slaughter, misery and destruction': 'But it is plainely seene . . . that men are weary of well doing. For ignorant of other mens miseries . . . they thinke themselves miserable, whilst in comparison of as many as I know, they are the happiest nation in the world.'[42]

NOTES

This is a revised version of an article which was first published in *Apollo*, CXXXVI (August 1992), pp. 90–4.

1. As, for example, Dr Richard Mead buying at the sale in Rome of Cardinal Massimi's collections in 1678; see F. Haskell, *Patrons and Painters*, 2nd edn (New Haven and London, 1983), p. 118, and cf. E.L. Goldberg, *Patterns in late Medici Art Patronage* (Princeton, 1983), p. 127.

2. *The Last Medici* (rev. edn, 1980); *Florence in the Forgotten Centuries, 1527-1800* (Chicago, 1973) and *Firenze e la Toscana dei Medici nell'Europa del Cinquecento*, various catalogues, Florence, 1980.

3. For a sceptical account of Milton's later remarks on his tour, see E. Chaney, *The Grand Tour and the Great Rebellion* (Geneva and Turin, 1985), pp. 243-41, and Chapter 12 below.

4. *Areopagitica* (1644).

5. Chaney, *The Grand Tour*, op. cit., *passim*; for the Dolci portraits, see C. McCorquodale, 'Some Paintings and Drawings by Carlo Dolci in British Collections', *Kunst des Barock in der Toskana* (Florence and Munich, 1976), pp. 313-20.

6. R. Parr, *The Life . . . of Usher* (London, 1686), pp. 595-8, unpublished Price correspondence in the Biblioteca Nazionale and Laurenziana, Florence, and Chaney, op. cit., pp. 274-5. For Greek studies in early seventeenth-century England, see H.R. Trevor-Roper, 'The Church of England and the Greek Church in the Time of Charles I', *From Counter-Reformation to Glorious Revolution* (London, 1992), pp. 83-111.

7. Lassels, *Description of Italy*, National Library of Scotland Advocates' MS 15.2.15, p. 112 (Chaney, op. cit., p. 170).

8. *Some Letters containing an Account of what seemed most remarkable in Switzerland, Italy, &c.* (Rotterdam, 1686) p. 175.

9. See above, p. 61.

10. *A Survey of the Great Dukes State of Tuscany in . . . 1596* (London, 1605), p. 62. For a similarly defensive assertion by the contemporary Catholic priest, Thomas Wright, see below, p. 320.

11. For Moryson's *Itinerary* and other published travelogues, see R.S. Pine-Coffin, *Bibliography of British and American Travel in Italy to 1860* (Florence, 1974). Part of the unpublished section of the *Itinerary* appeared in 1903 as *Shakespeare's Europe*, ed. C. Hughes. The rest remains in MS and belongs to Corpus Christi College Library, Oxford.

12. For the marriage negotiations, which 'haveva praticato il Re Jacopo, mentre era Re di Scozia' (that is pre-1603), see A.M. Crinò, 'Progetti di matromonio fra Medici e Stuart', *Fatti e Figure del Seicento Anglo-Toscano* (Florence, 1957), pp. 262-77, and idem, 'Two Medici-Stuart Marriage Proposals and an early Seicento Solution to the Irish Problem . . .', *Oxford, China and Italy: Writings in honour of Sir Harold Acton*, ed. E. Chaney and N. Ritchie (London, 1984), pp. 107-15. For the Florentine reaction to the *Survey*, see A.M. Crinò, 'Documenti relativi al libro di Sir Robert Dallington sulla Toscana', *Fatti e Figure*, cit., pp. 41-8. This includes a Latin memorandum by a Catholic exile, Thomas Dempster, recommending the death penalty for authors of libellous pamphlets such as Dallington's; for Dempster see below, p. 309, n. 42. Brief mention of the incident but ample documentation of the essential accuracy of Dallington's observations is to be found in F. Diaz, *Il Granducato di Toscana: i Medici* (Turin, 1976).

13. T.V. Wilks, *The Court Culture of Prince Henry and his Circle* (unpublished DPhil dissertation, University of Oxford, 1987), p. 4.

14. Dallington was knighted soon after his appointment (J. Nichols, *Progresses of James I* (London, 1828), IV, p. 1010). He is buried at Charterhouse. According

to the *DNB*, two years before he died, at his own expense, Dallington built a schoolhouse in his native village of Geddington. He is also 'said to have considerably improved the walks and gardens of Charterhouse'. The only study since the *DNB*, though he presents a more straightforwardly Italophile figure than here, is K.J. Höltgen, 'Sir Robert Dallington (1561–1637): Author, Traveler, and Pioneer of Taste', *Huntington Library Quarterly*, XLVII (1984), pp. 147–77. Professor Höltgen discovered an earlier MS version, dedicated to Prince Henry, of Dallington's *Aphorismes Civill and Militarie* (1613). A disappointing Italian edition of the *Survey*, by N.F. Onesti and L. Rombai, was published in Florence in 1983 as the *Descrizione dello Stato del Granduca di Toscana*. The *Survey* appeared in two variant printings in 1605. In 1974 Walter Johnson of Amsterdam and Norwood, New Jersey, produced a facsimile in their 'English Experience' series (no. 650). It is quoted extensively in H. Acton and E. Chaney, *Florence: A Travellers' Companion* (London, 1986).

15. For a detailed account of *The Strife of Love*, apparently written in ignorance of Professor Höltgen's article and thus not discussing Dallington's probable authorship, see D. Wilson, '*The Strife of Love in a Dream*, an Elizabethan Translation of Part of the First Book of Francesco Colonna's Hypnerotomachia', *Bulletin of the Society for Renaissance Studies*, IV, 1 (1986), pp. 41–53. Consistent with our view of Dallington is 'R.D.'s' omission of several passages in the *Hypnerotomachia* dealing with architecture and garden design. The dedicatees of the *Strife* were the late Sir Philip Sidney and the Earl of Essex, who married Sidney's widow. The latter's daughter, Elizabeth, who thus became Essex's stepdaughter, married Rutland, the patron of Inigo Jones, Ben Jonson and Dallington. Jones, whom Rutland employed as 'a picture maker' at this time, accompanied Dallington and the Earl to Denmark in 1603. Dallington returned to work for the 6th Earl after Prince Henry's death, travelling to Spa in 1620–2 on his behalf; see *HMC Rutland MSS*, i, pp. 454 and 467; iv, pp. 446 and 519. In August 1620, he wrote two letters to William Trumbull, British Resident in Brussels, and he is mentioned in several letters from his publisher, Edward Blount, to Trumbull, written between 1621 and 1623; see *Sotheby's Auction Catalogue of the Trumbull Papers*, 14 December 1989, pp. 20, 41–42. The Trumbull Papers are now in the British Library.

16. G.B. Parks, 'Travel as Education', in R.F. Jones, *The Seventeenth Century* (Stanford, CA 1951), pp. 264–91 and J. Spedding (ed.), *Letters and Life of Francis Bacon* (London, 1862), II, pp. 1–26.

17. On p. 57 of the *Survey*, Dallington describes (in gruesome detail) the torturing of a groom who was accused of throwing an English gentleman into the Arno 'this Ianuary past'.

18. From Dallington's *View of France*, of 1604, one can deduce that he was with a patron, briefly in Paris and for the rest of the summer of 1598 in Orleans; see J.W. Stoye, *English Travellers Abroad 1604–1667*, 2nd edn (New Haven and London, 1989), p. 21. It is clear that the patron was Francis Manners, who inherited the title from his brother in 1612. He toured Italy after France in 1599. Imprisoned with Francis and his brothers was the Earl of Southampton, also a crypto-Catholic, and a better-known patron of Shakespeare. Francis commissioned an *impresa* from Shakespeare and Burbage in 1613; see S. Schoenbaum, *William Shakespeare: A Compact Documentary Life* (Oxford, 1977). The youngest of the Manners brothers, Sir Oliver, returned to Italy and was ordained a Catholic priest on 5 April 1611 by Cardinal Bellarmine; see *John Gerard: The Autobiography of an Elizabethan*, ed. Philip Caraman (London, 1956), *passim*.

19. Dallington is almost certainly referring to his stay in Prato in his *Briefe Inference upon Guicciardines Digression* (London, 1613, p. 59): 'In a Towne of *Italie* where I abode foure moneths, was a poore Trades-man . . .' On the following page he also refers to having seen the Virgin's girdle, 'among many thousand moe that came to see it (as they yearely do upon the seventh of *September*)'. A passage on p. 65 of the *Survey* indicates that Dallington spent Lent and the Carnival period, presumably of 1597, in Venice. Given so many mutual patrons and acquaintances, and Shakespeare's fascination with Italy, it is probable he would have read the *Survey*. Dallington's criticisms of the vendetta in Italy culminate in his observation that in Venice 'there was almost every night one slaine, all that Carnevale time. The occasion of most these quarrels and mischiefes are from the *Burdello*.' If Cassio's wounding and the slaying of Roderigo in Act V, Scene i, of *Othello*, with Iago's explanation that 'This is the fruit of whoring' (line 115) were influenced by Dallington's account, this would be another argument for a post-1604 dating of *Othello* (unless Shakespeare read the *Survey* in MS or even dicussed it with Dallington).
20. Crinò, op. cit., pp. 43–4; Florentine officials were still referring indignantly to the *Survey* 12 years later; ibid., p. 45.
21. *Survey*, p. 16.
22. *Survey*, p. 17.
23. *Survey*, pp. 39–35 (sic; the *Survey* is mispaginated from p. 40, recommencing at p. 33).
24. See N. Rubinstein, 'The Posthumous Image of Lorenzo de' Medici', *Oxford, China and Italy* . . . cit., pp. 94–106, and J. Hale, *England and the Italian Renaissance* (London, 1954), *passim*.
25. *Survey*, p. 36 (second).
26. *Survey*, p. 38.
27. *Survey*, p. 29.
28. *Survey*, p. 51; cf. pp. 36–7 where, in a section on intensive farming, Dallington explains that 'there are those who all their life time doe nothing but with their Asses go up and downe the cities, gathering up the dung in the streetes, and carrying it to the land of those with whom they have bargained', who use it as manure, paying tax on it as they pass the gates.
29. *Survey*, p. 51.
30. *Survey*, p. 9. Dallington's praise of the paved streets makes for an instructive contrast to Giordano Bruno's disgust with the state of the Strand which obliged Londoners to suffer the ill manners of the Thames ferrymen; *Cena de le Ceneri* (1584), ed. G. Aquilecchia (Florence, 1955).
31. *Survey*, pp. 11–12. Perhaps it was Dallington's description of the Laurenziana that encouraged Prince Henry to ask for a model of its staircase. For this request, forwarded via the Tuscan Resident, Ottaviano Lotti, see Roy Strong, *Henry Prince of Wales* (London, 1986), p. 211.
32. *Survey*, p. 23.
33. *Survey*, pp. 12–13, 19, 23 and 42.
34. Spedding, op. cit. (n. 16 above), p. 7.
35. *Survey*, p. 26.
36. *Survey*, p. 9.
37. *Survey*, pp. 27–8.
38. *Survey*, p. 28.
39. *Survey*, p. 62.
40. *Some Letters*, op. cit., pp. 299–304.
41. *An History of the Civill Warres of England, betweene the Two Houses of Lancaster*

and Yorke . . . (London, 1641) introduction (translation by Henry Cary, Earl of Monmouth), quoted in Dianella Savoia, 'Giovanni Francesco Biondi: An Italian Historian of the Wars of the Roses', *Journal of Anglo-Italian Studies*, I (1991), p. 54. Dallington makes his comparison between the 'heavy *Dinasty* of small Tuscany [and] the happy government of great *Brittany*, on p. 49 of the *Survey*.

42. Ibid., p. 55. Cf. Rubens's comment in August 1629 that the English people were 'rich and happy in the lap of peace'; Chaney, *The Grand Tour* . . . cit., p. 56. Biondi left England in 1640 and died in his brother-in-law Sir Theodore de Mayerne's castle at Aubonne, near Lausanne, in 1644; see *DNB*; L. Pearsall Smith, *Life and Letters of Sir Henry Wotton* (Oxford, 1907), II, pp. 463–4; G. Benzoni, 'Giovanni Francesco Biondi: Un avventuroso dalmata del '600', *Archivio Veneto*, LXXX (1967), pp. 19–37 and idem in *Dizionario Biografico degli Italiani*, X, pp. 528–31.

6

Documentary Evidence of Anglo-Italian Cultural Relations in the Sixteenth and Seventeenth Centuries

I. A MINIATURE OF THE MAGI FOR KING PHILIP OF ENGLAND

WHILST COMPILING 'A Calendar of Royal Taste' for the National Gallery's exhibition of *The Queen's Pictures*, I decided to investigate a reference in Lewis Einstein's pioneering work, *The Italian Renaissance in England*,[1] which had long intrigued me. On page 206, having referred to the Duke of Urbino's gift of Raphael's St George to Henry VII (which provenance is now doubted), Einstein writes that 'Presents of a similar nature were made from time to time. The Grand Duke of Tuscany, for instance, sent Queen Mary a miniature of the Three Magi.' The relevant footnote refers the reader to 'Guardaroba Medicea, Florence, filza 34'. Not being able to get to the Archivio di Stato in the short term, I wrote asking my old friend and one-time protectress at the University of Pisa, Professoressa Anna Maria Crinò, to look up the complete reference for me. As the world authority on the Anglo-Italian contents of the Archivio, she was able to send back the following transcription by return: 'Quadro di minio di Don Giulio de tre Magi con ornamento d'ebano a uso di sp[h]era mandato al Re d'inghilterra con ordine della Sig.ra Duchessa portò Don Hernando de Sylva.'

It was immediately evident that this was a miniature by the celebrated Don Giulio Clovio, Croatian-born protégé of the Medici,

friend of Vasari (and subject of one of his *Lives*). It was not sent by
the grand duke (who was in any case not yet 'grand'), but by his
wife, Eleanor of Toledo, and it was sent not to Mary Tudor but to
her husband, Eleanor's cousin, Philip II of Spain, now King of
England. An earlier treatment of the Adoration of the Magi (a
subject especially favoured by the Medici), appears on folio 10 verso
of Clovio's illuminated Grimani Evangelistary in the Marciana
Library, Venice; see the illustration in Maria Giononi-Visani, *Clovio:
Miniaturist of the Renaissance* (London, 1993), p. 25. Professoressa
Crinò not only supplied a date for this reference but very kindly
added transcriptions of two related entries from the list of what was
acquired by and left the Guardaroba during the years 1554-5:

ENTRATA

> Tre quadri di pittura di mano di Don Julio miniator, uno fornito d'Ebano
> entrovi la historia de tre magi, li altri due forniti di noce, in uno il
> Crocfisso et nell'altro la Pietà.[2]

On folio 43 recto of the same filza, headed 'USCITA', is the following confirmation of the above:

> Un quadro de Magi di minio di mano di Don Giulio con ornamento
> d'ebano al Re d'Inghilterra a di 22 d'aprile 1555 con ordine della
> signora Duchessa portò don Hernando de Sylva.

II. TWO UNPUBLISHED LETTERS BY SIR HENRY WOTTON TO VINCENZO I GONZAGA, DUKE OF MANTUA[3]

These two hitherto unpublished letters written in 1606 by Sir Henry
Wotton, the first post-Reformation English ambassador in Venice
[Fig. 27], were first brought to my attention by Dr D.S. Chambers
(Warburg Institute, London), author of that fundamental study of
Anglo-Italian relations, *Cardinal Bainbridge and the Court of Rome,
1509 to 1514*,[4] and a widely published expert on Venice and
Mantua. He not only supplied me with photocopies of the original
texts but, on one of his frequent visits to the Mantuan archives,
checked my readings against the originals. I am very grateful to him
for his help. The only published reference to either of these letters I

27 Unknown artist, *Sir Henry Wotton* (1568–1639). [Eton College]

have found is in an article by A. Luzio, 'I carteggi dell'Archivio Gonzaga riflettenti l'Inghilterra'.⁵ In view of Wotton's crucial importance in the belated but rapid growth of interest in art under the early Stuarts, and the fact that the acquisition by Charles I of the Mantuan collection may have begun after Wotton helped arrange the Countess of Arundel's visit to the Mantuan Court in 1622 (with Van Dyck), this even earlier Anglo-Mantuan contact is of great interest.

The reference to Odoardo Fialetti in the second letter is also interesting here. Born in 1573, Fialetti was a Bolognese artist, who studied under Tintoretto and remained in Venice for the rest of his life. He was much patronized by Wotton who may have introduced him to Inigo Jones, as well as to Edward Norgate, Lord Roos and the Earl and Countess of Arundel, to whom he dedicated etchings. Jones was influenced by Fialetti, perhaps in person, but certainly by *Il vero modo et ordine per dissegnar*, an illustrated treatise on drawing, published in Venice in 1608, thus five years before Jones's last visit to Venice. In 1615 Fialetti illustrated Gigli's poem on Andrea Schiavone, *La Pittura trionfante scritta in IV capitoli*. Wotton acquired several pictures by Fialetti which he bequeathed to Charles I (they are now at Hampton Court and Kensington Palace). He left Fialetti's great bird's-eye view of Venice to Eton College, of which he became Provost in 1624 [Fig. 28].⁶

[On verso] 'Al Serenissimo Signore il Duca di Mantova . . .'

Serenissimo Signore

Io stavo apunto insul' risolvermi d'ispedire alla Corte della Gran Bretagna fra pochi giorni un gentilhuomo mio parente,⁷ quando mi sopragionse la L[ette]ra di V. Alt^zza. Serenissima con le annesse. Onde, per maggior sicurta ho preso la presuntione di ritinere da me cosi cari pegni della gratia et dall'affetto suo verso le Maestà loro insin' alla partenza di detto gentilhuomo et in tanto (accioché Lor Maestà sieno quanto prima raggualiate di questa congiontione delle Serenissime Case di Gonzaga et di Lorena da che riceveranno particolar consolatione, et anche augmento) Io feci l'ufficio hieri per la via ordinaria conforme alli commandamenti di V. Alt^zza Ser.^ma et conforme a quella benignissima confidentia che la s'e degnata d'havere nel mio povero servitio: obligo veramente supremo sopra tutti li altri.

Quanto poi a quelli due ufficii impostimi qua dal Sigr Residente di V.A.

28 Odoardo Fialetti, *A Bird's-eye View of Venice*, (c.1608) brought back by Sir Henry Wotton, ambassador to Venice, and given to Eton College. [Eton College]

in nome d'Essa. La si compiacerà di riceverne particolar risposta dal sudetto mio parente, che per questa occasione haverà l'honore di visitar la Corte di V. Alt.^{zza} Ser.^{ma} di passaggio, et potra (occorrendone) ricevere anche lo gratia di portar a lor Maestà li piu freschi commandamenti suoi. Finirò per ora col pregarle dal summo Dio a questa presente allegrezza una perpetua successione delle altre, et col dedicarmele per

di V. Altezza Serenissima
eterno servidore

Di Venetia alli 25 di
Marzo 1606

Arrigo Wottoni

[On verso] 'Al Serenissimo Prencipe et Signore il Duca di Mantova & Signor mio Oss.^{mo}'

Serenissimo Principe

Questo gentilhuomo mio Nipote presenterò a V[ostra] Altezza la mia divota servitù et particolar zelo verso la sua Serenissima persona, et insieme quelli ritratti che la si degnò di commandare quando questa povera casa fu honorata con la sua presentia. La cagione di non haverne ubidito prima alli suoi commendamenti è stata in vero una lunga infirmità dell'Odoardo Fialetti pittore qua di che mi soglio servire non volendo commetter la cosa a persona incognita che ne potesse forse haver fatto una copia per se, poi che pare che convenga alla Maestà di Prencipi che ne anche lor ritratti siano troppo familiari: Ma se ben gli ho mandati a V. Alt*zza*, così tardi mi rallegro pure di pensare che arriveranno in Corte sua sul giorno destinato costi al Sponsalitio della Prencipessa sua figliuola: et che per questa congiuntura d'accidenti la Regina della Gran-Bretagna col suo primogenito si ritroveranno presenti alle allegrezza della Serenissima casa Gonzaga almeno in ombra non potendovi essere in persona.

Quanto alli altri commandamenti suoi. Io ho già raggualiato la Maestà del mio Signore dell'affettuoso Voluntà di V. Altezza Serenissima Verso essa, et delle sue lettere che per maggiore sicurtà mi risolvevo di mandare per questo mio Nipote a chi m'e passo anche convenire il presentarsele ora di passagsio, acciò che la si degni d'honorargli di quanto più gliene occurrerà di commandare. Et così priegandole dal Cielo continuate allegrezza et consolationi con ogni debita riverentia le bacio le mani

Di Va Altezza Serenissima
eterno servidore

Di Venezia alli 22
d'Aprile 1606

Arrigo Wottoni

NOTES

This chapter was first published in the *Journal of Anglo-Italian Studies*, ed. E. Chaney and P. Vassallo, I (1991), pp. 156–9.

1. Lewis Einstein, *The Italian Renaissance in England* (New York, 1902). This 'Calendar' eventually provided the basis for 'Vignettes of Royal Collections and Collectors from Queen Elizabeth to Queen Victoria', in C. Lloyd, *The Queen's Pictures: Royal Collectors through the Ages* (London, 1991), pp. 28–42.
2. ASF Guardaroba Medicea 30 (Giornale della Guardaroba), folio 40 verso.
3. Archivio di Stato di Mantova AG. b. 1538.
4. D.S. Chambers, *Cardinal Bainbridge and the Court of Rome, 1509 to 1514* (Oxford, 1965).
5. A. Luzio, 'I carteggi dell'Archivio Gonzaga riflettenti l'Inghilterra', *Atti della Reale Accademia delle Scienze*, LIII, I (1917–18), pp. 167–82.
6. See Chapters 7 and 8 in this volume; and L. Pearsall Smith, *The Life and Letters*

of Sir Henry Wotton, 2 vols (Oxford, 1907), *passim*.

7. This is almost certainly Edward Partheridge, or Partridge, from Eridge, Kent, whom Wotton advises Lord Salisbury 'will arrive with other matter of much consideration through the way of France' in a letter dated 22 April 1606 (L. Pearsall Smith, op. cit., I, p. 346; see also ibid., p. 347 and II, p. 476. That Partridge was a nephew through Wotton's sister's marriage is suggested by a family letter dated 25 September 1590, in which he mentions having written 'to my sister Partridg' (op. cit., I, p. 240). On 16 June 1606, Salisbury wrote to Wotton of Partridge's arrival in England (p. 346n). Confirmation is to be found in his appearance in the 'list of English knights and gentlemen who were in Italy' during Simon Willis's visit there, dated to *c.* 1608 but in the light of the above, perhaps earlier: 'Mr Partherydg. A Kentysher gent, allyed to Sir Ha: Watton, his Ma^ta Ambassador at Venice' (HMC Salisbury MSS, XXIV, 1986, p. 147). Partridge evidently met Tobie Matthew in Florence in 1605 after a visit to Naples. In A.H. Mathew's edition of *A True Historical Relation of Sir Tobie Matthew* (London, 1904), p. 8n, Matthew's original identification of the 'English gentle-man' has evidently been mistranscribed as 'Mr Partridge, Sir Henry Weston's nephew'. Though described as 'a Protestant . . . of the purer sort', it is ironic that Partridge unwittingly encouraged Matthew's journey to Naples and subsequent conversion (which Wotton loudly deplored), by his presumably enthusiastic account of the liquefaction of San Gennaro's blood. The letter printed here addressed to 'Serenissimo Principe' is clearly that which Wotton's 'parente', now defined as his 'nipote', presented to the Duke of Mantua.

7

Inigo Jones in Naples

GIVEN HIS REPUTATION (as early as 1605) as 'a great traveller',
the Spanish-named Yñigo Jones may have visited Spain as
well as southern Italy around the turn of the century. But the
farthest south he is known to have travelled was to Naples in March
1614. Together with his patron Lord Arundel (and the latter's wife
who joined them there) [Figs 14 and 15], he stayed in this huge,
Spanish-dominated city for two months. Today, the church of S.
Paolo Maggiore looks much like any other post-Renaissance
Neapolitan church [Fig. 30]. Before the 1688 earthquake which
severely damaged it, however, it looked like the Roman temple
it essentially was, featuring a magnificent, hexastyle Corinthian
portico. Since Palladio had fully discussed and illustrated this, the so-
called Temple of Castor and Pollux, in the copy of *I Quattro Libri*
which Jones possessed and carried everywhere with him, Jones had
known of this building even before seeing the real thing. From the
annotations in his Palladio (now in Worcester College Library,
Oxford), we find the former painter and masque-designer and now
aspiring architect visited the church-temple at least three times,
judging it 'on[e] of the Best things that I have seen'. Towards the
end of his stay in Naples, Jones acquired another book which
survives at Worcester College, a then recently published history of
Naples. This contains a critique of Palladio's account of the temple,
which is illustrated by a more accurate engraving. This may have
encouraged Jones to return yet again to the site before returning to
Rome where he fully exploited his enhanced understanding of
classical building. The giant statuary which had stood on the pediment of the Neapolitan temple, and whose 'excellent' remains Jones

29 Francesco Villamena, *Inigo Jones* (probably done in Rome in 1614 when Jones already knew he had obtained the reversion to the Surveyorship of the King's Works and thus would be 'Architector Magnae Britaniae'). [Devonshire Collection, Chatsworth]

found lying beneath it, became a favourite feature of his most distinguished buildings in London.

* * *

Turning to Richard Lassels's *Voyage of Italy* in preparation for a journey from Rome to Naples, the late seventeenth-century Grand Tourist would find the following lyrical account of the Appian Way: 'The frequent passing of *horses* and *mules* (for so many years) upon this cawssey, have made it both so *smooth* and *shyneing*, that when the *Sunn* shines upon it you may see it glitter two miles off, like a sylver highway.'[1] In March 1614, the response of Britain's first classical architect, Inigo Jones, had been more pedantically archaeological. In the 1601 edition of Palladio's *Quattro Libri* – which he had brought along to help him and his patron, Thomas Howard, 14th Earl of Arundel, fully appreciate the buildings of Italy, along-

30 Antonio Joli, *The Church of San Paolo Maggiore*, done for Robert Lord Brudenell during his 1756-8 Grand Tour. [Viscount Montagu, Beaulieu]

side a passage on the Appian Way Jones wrote: 'This waye I obsearued in my voyage to Napels 1614 and yt remains much intyre.'[2] On the verso, next to the plate which illustrates the typical Roman road, with its central paved area for pedestrians, continuous cut-stone borders with regularly placed pedestals for mounting horses, and flanking, sand-covered tracks allocated to the equestrian travellers, Jones commented:

> The Via Appia w[ch] I saw in my Jorney to Napels is as this is but y[e] horse wais on the sydes are not deserned. The high stones stand upon y[e] Castrico marked D[B?] I immagin to gett up the esier.[3]

At about the same time, in Palladio's chapter on Roman wall-building, Jones annotated the illustration of *opus reticulatum*: 'In my Jorney to Napels I saw much of this opera ritticulata . . .'[4] On the following page, at the lower left-hand corner of Palladio's illustration of 'Pietre incerte', Jones noted that 'going to Napels I saw a wall of an Anticke house as this and yt did well'.[5]

Jones had already annotated this woodcut before leaving England. As in six other instances, he indicated at the foot of the page that the original drawing for the print belonged to Sir Henry Wotton: 'The drawing of thes wales S^r He Woo: and slyght sciczos of allter-tables.' Wotton had returned from his second Italian embassy in July 1612, nine months before Jones left England with the Arundels. Prior to his first appointment in 1604, Wotton had travelled throughout Italy, including Naples in 1592. By the time he returned from Venice in 1610 he had established himself as England's leading connoisseur of painting and architecture.[6] He was a major patron of Odoardo Fialetti, the artist who published a treatise on drawing which influenced Jones, befriended Edward Norgate and dedicated etchings to Lords Roos and Arundel. In 1608 Wotton was preparing for Lord Salisbury (with Anne of Denmark, Jones's principal patron prior to Prince Henry and Arundel) 'some things about the subject of architecture, [which] shall be within a few days sent you in picture [as] you command'. His scholarly interest in Palladio was to culminate in his sophisticated treatise, *The Elements of Architecture*, of 1624.[7] Meanwhile, it was no doubt he who encouraged Thomas Coryate [Fig. 12] to describe Palladio's buildings with unprecedented thoroughness in his *Crudities*, published, complete with a satirical introductory poem by Inigo Jones, in 1611.[8] Wotton was probably also responsible for Salisbury's son, Viscount Cranborne, visiting Vicenza and praising Palladio by name for the first time in an English context in his 1610 diary account.[9] Most interesting for our purposes, however, is that his collection of Palladio's drawings seems to have been known and at least partially acquired by Jones before his departure for Italy. Inspired by Wotton's example, once in the Veneto with Arundel, Jones expanded this collection to more than 200 items.[10]

Jones was to add one further comment to the first page of Palladio's chapter on walls. Highlighted by a pointing hand and in slightly darker ink, between the printed captions beneath the illustration of *opus reticulatum* and his previous annotation, he wrote:

1614 Baia: 17 January Like wise at ye Thearmi at Baia thear ar many wales wth mor courses of Brick and Sum great Bricke amongst for y^e

Romans varied thes things according to thear Cappriccio mingling on[e]
wth an other, so yt sheaud well.[11]

This technical point, which turns into a quasi-aesthetic one similar
to that elaborated in his *Roman Sketchbook* on 20 January 1614/15,
was probably prompted by his visit to the Palatium Imperiale at
Baia.[12] Jones is unlikely to have visited this in January 1614, when
he was still based in Rome, but very likely to have done so between
the beginning of March and May of that year, when, as we shall see,
he was based in Naples. For this reason it is almost certain that by
'1614 Baia: 17 January', 1615 new style was intended, and that
like several other entries dating from January and February 1615, it
was added in London after Jones's return home. Thus it dates from
just three days before the related entry in the *Roman Sketchbook*.[13]

Given Jones's importance as Britain's first professional architect
and connoisseur of the classical tradition, and Arundel's, as our first
great patron and collector of art and antiquities, it is surprising that
their formative journey to Naples together has not been studied in
more detail.[14] Having left England in order to accompany the newly
wed Princess Elizabeth to Heidelberg, as soon as they had accomplished this duty the Arundels headed surreptitiously for Italy.
Arundel himself had briefly visited the Veneto to take the waters
near Padua but had returned the previous November, apparently on
hearing that his wife threatened to join him for the winter.[15] His
journey home was hastened, however, on receiving news of the
death of Prince Henry. Now, some seven months later, the Earl and
Countess selected three of their most trusted and sophisticated
servants to remain part of a scaled-down Grand Touring entourage.
This included Arundel's cosmopolitan Catholic cousin, Robert
Cansfield, Thomas Coke, a great favourite of Lady Arundel's father,
Lord Shrewsbury, and the newly patronless Inigo Jones.[16] On 27
April 1613, ten days after leaving England, Jones had been granted
the reversion of the Surveyorship of the King's Works, making him
next in line for the most important architectural position in the
country. Though he had been Prince Henry's Surveyor for two years
and was now almost 40, he had built very little and was still known
less as an architect than as the leading designer of court masques
and 'a great traveller'.[17] It was indeed as the latter that Wotton's
successor as ambassador to Venice, Sir Dudley Carleton, described
Jones on 9 July in a letter to his friend John Chamberlain. Reporting

on the arrival of two gentlemen who had been with the Arundels and Princess Elizabeth in Germany, Carleton writes:

> They tell us my lord of Arundel and his lady, whom they left with the duke of Lennox at Strasburg, will return through France home without passing any further, but I rather believe they were so told to be rid of their companies, and the more because I hear my lord had taken Inigo Jones into his train, who will be of best use to him (by reason of his language and experience) in these parts.[18]

Even as he wrote, Jones and Arundel had left Basle and were crossing the Alps via the St Gotthard Pass. They arrived in Milan on 11 July and found it 'soe hott, as without danger, wee can not (they say) stirre, till some rayne fall'. In the event, however, they stayed little more than a week (just long enough to have celebrated Jones's fortieth birthday there), for, offended by the Spanish Governor's lack of respect for their presence, the Arundels suddenly left Milan, and via Parma reached Padua on 20 July.[19] Basing themselves in a villa two miles outside Padua, they spent the rest of the summer here and in Venice [Fig. 28], where they were lavishly entertained by the Doge and Senate. On 13 September Arundel wrote to Sir Robert Cotton from Padua, asking him to 'pick out some story of my Ancestors' which he could have painted in Venice, adding that Cotton should 'send it in writing and direct unto Mr Richard Willoughby in case I be not here.'[20] On 23 and 24 September, perhaps with one or both Arundels but certainly in the footsteps of his friend Thomas Coryate (who in 1608 had had Willoughby as his guide), Jones made his historic visits to the Villa Capra and the Teatro Olimpico in Vicenza.[21] On 30 September Carleton reported that, after a splendid farewell party given by Gregorio Barbarigo, 'My lord Arundel is gone privately to Florence, having left his lady at a villa hereby towards Cataio.'[22] He wrote back to her from Bologna on 1 October and from Florence on the 5th. Lady Arundel and her entourage followed him to Florence about three weeks later and then discreetly established winter quarters (complete with Italian lessons) in a monastery (delle Grazie) near Siena.[23]

By 2 January 1614 (and here he specifies 'new stille' in his annotation), Jones was in Rome studying large-scale classical remains for the first time since the late summer of 1609 when he had completed a tour of southern France, probably with Lord Cranborne.[24] As one who would continue to design royal masques until the Civil War,

31 Unknown artist,
engraving of Sir Tobie
Matthew, from John
Donne junior,
A Collection of Letters
(London, 1660).
[E. Chaney]

32 Sir Anthony Van Dyck,
*George Gage, connoisseur
and Roman Catholic priest*
(probably painted in Rome
in 1622). [National Gallery,
London]

Jones meanwhile maintained an active interest in Italian theatre. Twenty-one years later, the Papal Nuncio in London would suggest that the reason the machines in Jones's Shrovetide masque, *The Temple of Love*, were so 'maraviglie belle' was that 'l'Architetto' had been at Rome 'a tempo che il Principe Peretti fece quella sua festa tanto celebre'. This *festa* is identifiable as the spectacular wedding entertainment, complete with fictive sea and mobile boats laden with singers, given by Sixtus V's nephew on 8 February 1614.[25]

Arundel seems to have been anxious to see Naples after a relatively short stay in Rome. His haste may have been motivated by fear of recall. Like his previous Italian journey, when he reached no further than the Veneto, this 1613–14 journey was also to be concluded by news of a distinguished death, that of Arundel's uncle, the Earl of Northampton. Fortunately, this occurred only after the Arundels had spent almost a year in Italy and even then they did not hasten back, savouring the details of Northampton's generous will in Tuscany.[26] But premature recall may have been feared for another reason, one which would also account for the high degree of secrecy maintained. Although James I had signed his historic peace treaty with Spain ten years previously, there was still considerable concern regarding communication between English Catholics and their co-religionists abroad.[27] So far as the government was concerned, Arundel's father, grandfather, great-grandfather and

great-uncle (Lord Lumley) had all been Catholic traitors and Arundel himself, though favoured by James, was not to renounce the family faith for more than a year after his return to England.[28] On 26 May 1613 Arundel's father-in-law, Lord Shrewsbury, was already warning Thomas Coke in The Hague that 'four of our Court Bishops much noted that neither Lord Arundel nor my daughter have at any time been at prayers with her highness since they went hence.'[29] When Arundel returned to England he was investigated by the Calvinist Archbishop of Canterbury and later felt obliged to send a servant abroad to clear his name.[30] The official line is clear enough in Dudley Carleton's anxious report on hearing that the Arundels had arrived in Rome, a city still specifically excluded from the travel licences issued by the Privy Council:

> The common recourse of his Ma[ties] subjects to Rome, notwithstanding their direct inhibitions on their licences for travaile, to the contrarie, is continued wth th[t] freedom th[t] both the Earle of Arundel and his Lady

have spent many days in th' place: wch I could not beleeve uppon advertisements from thence, until I had spoken wth some who had seen them there. I heare of no English who did much resort unto them but Toby Mathew [Fig. 31] and George Gage [Fig. 32], neither of any course they took for the purpose than the satisfying of curiosity; yet the quality of their persons being so much above other travellers, I held it my duty to give this advertisment.[31]

Ironically, by the time Carleton was writing this in Venice, Arundel and Inigo Jones had left the Countess and most of their entourage and had established themselves in Spanish-dominated Naples, a fact which Carleton was not to report until 25 April.[32] It is only in mid-May, by which time he prematurely expected them back in the Veneto, that Carleton reveals that Lady Arundel had joined them in Naples, having left most of her servants 'divided betwixt Sienna and Luca'.[33] How horrified Carleton and the British government would have been had they known – as Arundel may have done – that throughout this period, George Gage and his friend Tobie Matthew, the Archbishop of York's convert son whom James eventually knighted, had been preparing for the Catholic priesthood.[34] Already acting as a travelling art agent, on 10 May Matthew wrote from Rome to Thomas Coke in Naples that 'if I can recover a little health, I think to go into a villa for the taking of some fresh air. If in the mean time you return[,] this letter will meet with you and also a roll of pictures I have left for Don Roberto [Cansfield].'[35] If, as Matthew clearly anticipated they might, the Arundel party arrived back in Rome by 20 May, it was as well that he had invented an explanation for his failure to appear, for on that day he and Gage were secretly ordained by Cardinal Bellarmine.[36] Interestingly, it had been nine years earlier in Naples (whose 'city and confines . . . for delicacy I esteem to be, as it were, the very spring and source of that whole world which I had seen'), that Matthew began the path to his notorious conversion. A conversation with Robert Cansfield in the Duomo at Fiesole had encouraged this process, as had another with a nephew of Henry Wotton who had witnessed the liquefaction of the blood of San Gennaro.[37]

Jones arrived in Naples by 8 March at the latest.[38] We can assume that Arundel travelled south with him via Gaeta [Fig. 18] and Capua and thence on the road that John Evelyn was to describe as 'of a huge breadth, swarming with travellers more then ever I remember any of our greatest, & most frequented roads neere London'.[39] That Arundel was accompanied by the minimum of servants and tolerated the maximum of discomfort, we know from the letter he sent back to his wife soon after his arrival:

> Sweet Hart, I can only let y^u knowe that I have done nothinge for a lodginge, Mr Wrath mette me the other day, and though I avoided him, he must needes see me, soe as I mean to be knowne to him, and some english heere, that may help me better in my business/ all that is heere to be seene you may in a short time dispach, soe as I would wish y^u to see Rome well, for there are noe more such, I wish yu could have bin there the Settimana Santa, wch I desire much to see (if I can) there. the Soccoloes for women (to my likinge) are much better at Rome than heere[.] in y^r way hither y^u shall finde vile Hosteriass, one Mattresse, & one blankette, and neyther any bolster, or any thinge els. in y^r way hither only Gayetta [Gaeta] (some two miles from mola), is worth y^r seeinge. there is a rocke w^{ch} (they say) clove at Christ his death just like that of Hierusalem, and, in the Castell, Bourbon his body, to be seene, wch y^u may see, askinge leave as strangers of Florence, to goe see, the Houses (though poore) alonge that shore, are very neate. Mr Coke should doe well, to put all his mony in Pistolles so the[y] be full of wayte, & Roman testony goe well heere too, if y^u send Shovanne [? presumably a servant] before, from Capua y^u may there stay, till wee eyther provide heere, or send a coach thither for y^u, as y^u shall like best, wee are yet at the Fontana de i Serpi, & there he shall eyther heare of us or else at Mr Wrath his lodginge, at the Orso del Oro.[40] Soe I ever rest commendinge us all to God his holy protection.
>
> Y^r most faithful husband
T. Arundell

Naples 14° Marzo

St° Rome 1614

If this letter come to y^r handes, before y^r cominge from Rome I shall be glad, where I wish wee might both have seen the Settimana Santa if it might well be, and after, I might come along with you hither in Easter weeke.[41]

Whatever Arundel meant by the latter he clearly cannot have meant that he had 'been wonderfully fortunate' in having spent

Holy Week in Rome.[42] Easter itself fell on the 30 March. Neither is it likely that he and Jones were in Rome in April when the great column in front of S. Maria Maggiore was raised.[43] Instead, having been joined by Lady Arundel, they seem to have remained in Naples for a full two months, an unusually long time in a city which, when visited at all by the English in this period, tended to be visited for a mere five days, with a total of ten more allowed for the journey to and from Rome.

When Christopher Marlowe's Doctor Faustus flew 'up to Naples, rich Campania', he saw:

> Buildings fair, and gorgeous to the eye
> Whose streets straight forth, and paved with finest brick,
> Quarter the town in four equivalents;
> There saw we learned Maro's golden tomb,
> The way he cut an English mile in length
> Thorough a rock of stone in one night's space.[44]

Even within the five-day package recommended by Lassels's *Voyage*, the typical tourist devoted more than half his time to what John Raymond, in an earlier guidebook, called 'the Wonders a little distant from Naples', rather than to the city itself.[45] Before the discovery of Pompeii and Herculaneum, this meant the area to the west of the city rather than the now more popular south-east. For the aspiring architect, the ruins around the Phlegraean Fields were, however, too ruinous to be very instructive. The brickwork at Baia has been mentioned. Like Fynes Moryson and George Sandys before him, Jones also explored Pozzuoli, and no doubt also the Solfatara and the so-called Sibyl's Cave, pausing, before entering the extraordinary Grotta di Posillipo, to contemplate the legendary tomb of Virgil (to whose magic Faustus attributed the mile-long tunnel).[46]

In Naples itself the architecture was mainly modern, albeit constructed on the ancient grid-plan referred to by Marlowe. There were the great triumphal arches such as Alfonso of Aragon's entrance to the Castel Nuovo, or Da Maiano's Capuan Gate, through which Arundel and Jones would have entered the city. There was an extraordinary range of churches, from the intriguing Quattrocento Cappella Pontano, with its composite pilasters and high attic, to Dosio's still unfinished cloister of the Certosa di San Martino. Jones would have been particularly interested in Domenico Fontana's massive new Palazzo Vicereale, having tried his hand at a similarly

33 Francisco d'Ollanda, *The Temple of Castor and Pollux*; from E. Tormo, *Os desenhos das antigualhas que vio Francisco d'Ollanda* (Madrid, 1940), fol. 45v. [Warburg Institute, London]

34 The Temple of Castor and Pollux, annotated by Inigo Jones in his copy of Palladio's *Quattro Libri* (Venice, 1601), vol. iv, p. 96. [Worcester College, Oxford]

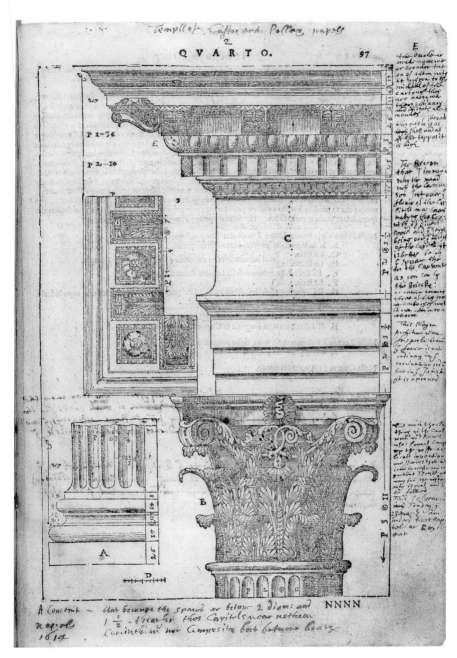

35 The Temple of Castor and Pollux, annotated by Inigo Jones in his copy of Palladio's
Quattro Libri (Venice, 1601), vol. iv, p. 97. [Worcester College, Oxford]

monotonous building, Lord Salisbury's New Exchange, as his first
known architectural design in 1608.[47]

But, in the words of Raymond's *Mercurio Italico*, 'the onely
Antiquity within the city' was the now all but forgotten Temple of
Castor and Pollux. When Jones and Raymond saw it, the body of this
temple had been incorporated into the church of S. Paolo Maggiore
by the distinguished Theatine architect, Fabrizio Grimaldi.[48] Before its
almost total collapse in the 1688 earthquake, its well-preserved
Corinthian portico stood proud of Grimaldi's proto-Baroque building,
functioning like those Roman porticoes still to be seen in Assisi and
Pola. This had been greatly admired even before the Theatines began
their 1580s rebuilding, most notably by the Portuguese-born artist,
Francisco d'Ollanda, who in drawing it around 1540 [Fig. 33]
deliberately omitted the medieval church which then crouched
behind it, but also by Giuliano da Sangallo, who commented upon
it in his notebooks.[49] Shortly before Grimaldi began work on the
church, Palladio devoted an illustrated chapter of his *Quattro libri* to
the temple, omitting in his woodcut the Greek inscription then still
visible on the frieze, but sketching a fanciful version of the relief
sculpture in the pediment and reinstating the three, by then already
absent, statues above [Fig. 34].[50] Even before setting out for Italy in
1613, Jones had studied this chapter, adding a translated paraphrase
of Palladio's praise of the intertwined acanthus stalks which support
the rosette on the abacus, in the margin alongside the relevant illustration [Fig. 35]:

> noat the clothing of the Cauliculi wth leaves whos branch beares up the
> rosse a delicatt inuention and sheaues thatt w[ch] is doo[n] by reason and
> is gratious Though y[t] varry fro[m] the useual way is good and to be
> folloed.[51]

It must have been thrilling for Jones to have seen the capitals
themselves soon after his arrival in Naples. Something of his excite-
ment is conveyed in the first of his on-the-spot marginal notes to the
left of Palladio's woodcut of the reconstructed temple façade: 'This
tempell I sawe on Satterday the 8 of March 1614.'[52] Beneath this we
find an early example of Jones's empirical criticism of Palladio:

> The desine of this Baso relevo is not as the originall is for thear is a flood
> and a Seagod on ye corners and on the on[e] sid 2 figures standing
> sacrifising the middell is broken.

Below this, referring again to the portico as a whole, he added: 'This is on[e] of the Best things that I have seen.'

Jones also observed that: 'Thear is a fine stair made up to this a squar and half pases, rails and ballester of marbell' [Fig. 39]. He then sketched a miniature plan of this post-Palladian stair. Leaving a space, so that what he wrote was roughly in line with what he was describing, he continued to document what Palladio had not, revealing that he had discussed the history of the building with one of the Theatine monks attached to the church: 'Underneath this Portico is a Valte wch is volted a medza botte 3 of them and at the ends a Crochura and Pillasters gros / onns this the friar tould mee was anticke.'

The extent of Jones's enthusiasm for the temple is indicated by the fact that a fortnight later he returned to survey it again, this time focusing his attention on those rich columns he had first admired in reproduction. Directly under his pre-1613 paraphrase of Palladio's account of the capitals, he announced: 'This I obsearved Sonday ye 23 March and indeed these capitels are Exelent.'

Carleton's report of 25 April implies that Arundel must still have been in Naples shortly before he wrote it. We can confirm this thanks to the survival of an elaborately illustrated two-part folio by the Sicilian gentleman-scholar, Don Vincenzo Mirabella e Alagona. Entitled *Dichiarazioni della pianta dell'antiche Siracuse . . .* , it had been published in Naples by Lazzaro Scoriggio only months before Arundel's arrival. On its title-page are inscribed the price, his name and the date, presumably in new style: 'Napoli Pre[zzo]: Carlini 13 T. Arundell. Aprile 23 1614.'[53] As well as the large, fold-out street plans of Syracuse, a detailed topographical text and a first-hand account of Caravaggio's 1608 visit to the 'Ear of Dionysius', this book contains the earliest illustration I know of a Greek Doric temple [Fig. 36]. Though its columns are no longer baseless and the absurdly over-size statues on the cutaway pediment look like seventeenth-century nightclub dancers, this was a gallant attempt to depict the Temple of Athene before its transformation into Syracuse's cathedral.[54] Perhaps an expedition to Sicily had been envisaged. If so, nothing further is known of one and, like Milton's projected expedition 15 years later, it must have been abandoned.[55] It was thus left to Isaac Basire and his pupils, in December 1648, to become the first British travellers known to have visited Sicily's Doric temples, and to John Breval, almost a century later, to publish the

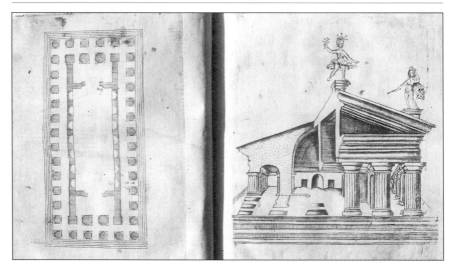

36 The Temple of Athene, from Vincenzo Mirabella e Alagona, *Dichiarazioni della Pianta dell'antiche Siracuse* (Naples, 1613), pp. 28–29. [E. Chaney]

first recognizable engravings of them in his *Remarks on Several Parts of Europe* of 1738 [Fig. 11].[56]

From another publication which Arundel purchased and inscribed during this tour, a catalogue of the Vatican Library now in the Beinecke Library at Yale, we know that he was back in Rome by 28 May at the latest.[57] Three days later, Jones embarked on his fullest study of a Roman building to date, that of the Pantheon, volunteering with unprecedented confidence opinions not vouchsafed by Palladio.[58]

Dudley Carleton's mid-May statement that the Arundels were, 'when I last heard from them, at Naples', is too vague to build upon, but as exceptionally 'curious' Grand Tourists, and Catholics to boot, the Earl and Countess may well have postponed their departure long enough to witness what John Raymond described as the 'famous Miracle of the bloud of Santo Gennaro, carryed in procession' on the first Saturday in May.[59] To judge from the autobiographical account of his conversion, Tobie Matthew for one would have encouraged them both to visit Naples in the first place and to stay for this spectacular event. So too, no doubt, would the proselytizing Robert Cansfield.[60] That the Arundels were indeed still in Naples at the beginning of May is suggested by yet another surviving purchase,

37 Inigo Jones's signature and date of acquisition in Giovanni Antonio Summonte, *Historia della Città . . . di Napoli* (Naples, 1601), title page of vol. II. [Worcester College, Oxford]

this time by Inigo Jones, of a two-volume history of the city, each of which he carefully inscribed: 'Napoli 1 Magio 1614: 14 Carlini 2 volls' above his newly improved italic signature. Probably it was the embarrassed heirs to his heir, John Webb, who obliterated Jones's signature from the title-page of volume I of this work when they sold it together with the rest of his library in the 1670s or 1680s. Fortunately, whoever it was forgot to check volume II where Jones had pedantically repeated the entire inscription [Fig. 37]. Both volumes are now in Worcester College Library, Oxford, together with almost all his other surviving books, and they are of special interest in shedding further light on Jones's response to the Temple of Castor and Pollux.

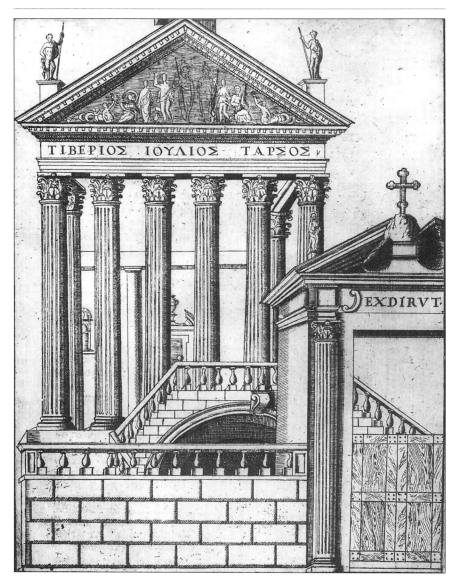

38 Giovani Antonio Summonte, engraving of the Temple of Castor and Pollux from his
Historia della Città . . . di Napoli (Naples, 1601) vol. I, opp. p. 90. [Worcester College,
Oxford]

39 Fabrizio Grimaldi, stairs of San Paolo Maggiore, Naples, late 16th century. [E. Chaney]

Giovanni Antonio Summonte's *Historia della città e regno di Napoli*, published in Naples in 1601–2, is a wide-ranging, informative work and carries the kind of illustrations which would have appealed to Jones. But I believe that one illustration would have been especially influential in persuading Jones to purchase the *Historia*. This is a full-page engraving of the Temple of Castor and Pollux, which, though less architecturally sophisticated than Palladio's woodcut, was considerably more detailed as to the current state of the temple [Fig. 38]. It depicts the relief sculpture in the pediment more precisely, and revises the *Quattro libri* in the light of the late sixteenth-century rebuilding of the church, illustrating in particular those additions to the temple which Jones admired: the 'fine stair', with its vaulted terrace and entrance beneath (eventually imitated at the Queen's House, Greenwich) [Fig. 39], and the great entrance gate, which is clearly visible in the painting of S. Paolo by Antonio Joli, commissioned by John Lord Brudenell in the 1750s as one of a series of topographical views of southern Italy [Fig. 30].[61] I would argue that this gate, and more specifically, Grimaldi's great door to the church itself [Fig. 40], which is only glimpsed through the central columns in Summonte's illustration, influenced Jones in designs he undertook

40 Fabrizio Grimaldi, door to San Paolo Maggiore, Naples, late 16th century. [E. Chaney]

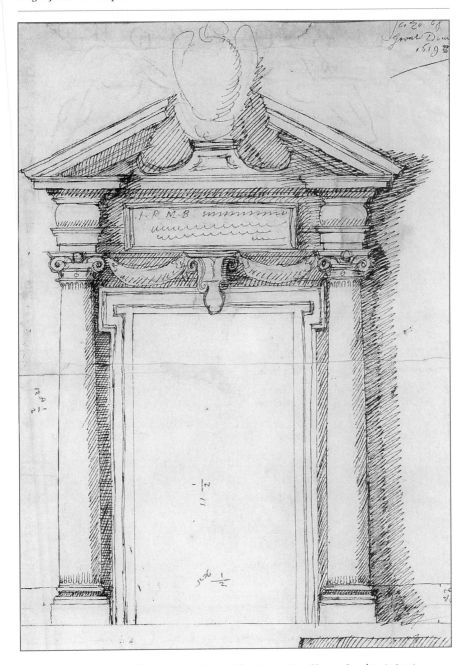

41 Inigo Jones, drawing for the great door of the Banqueting House, London (1619).
[RIBA]

on his return to England. In particular, his elevation for the 'Great
Door' of the Banqueting House of 1619, with its confident broken
pediment and identical surround [Fig. 41], is surely closer in style to
the door of S. Paolo Maggiore than it is to Scamozzi's doors in the
Sala di Consiglio in the Doge's Palace, the source usually cited for
Jones's design.[62]

After a long discussion of the pediment's Apollonian iconography,
based largely on Stefano Vinando's (or Pighius's) *Peregrinatio*,[63]
Summonte justly criticizes Palladio for the poor quality of his illustration of the sculpture and rather less justly – citing post-Palladian
archaeological discoveries – claims the credit for an aspect of his
etching which Palladio had in fact already hypothesized, the placing
of the free-standing statues on the marble pedestals on the roof:

> And although in his book of architecture, Andrea Palladio illustrated the
> said columns well, he nevertheless failed to illustrate the figures above
> [that is, in the pediment] properly, which are different from the way he
> has depicted them, but which we have had engraved with great care as
> anyone who doubts can go and see for themselves.
>
> In excavating the foundations for the rebuilding of this church in
> 1578, the two marble figures that one [now] sees leaning under the
> same columns were found, which suggests that they were the statues of
> Julius Caesar and the Emperor Octavian [Augustus] of those times, and
> that they would have stood on those marble bases which can be seen
> above the great cornice [pediment], in the way that we have had them
> engraved, which due to an earthquake, or for some other reason, fell
> and were spoiled.[64]

We have demonstrated the extent of Jones's interest in the Temple
of Castor and Pollux by documenting three distinct moments when
he consulted and annotated Palladio's chapter on the subject: first,
before setting out for Italy; second, on site on 8 March 1614
shortly after arriving in Naples; and third, a fortnight later, when
he returned to the temple to study its columns and capitals more
closely. I believe that the acquisition of Summonte's *Historia* may
have prompted him to return to S. Paolo Maggiore yet again. Jones's
criticism of Palladio's depiction of the pedimental sculpture need not
have followed his announcement that he first saw the temple 'on
Satterday the 8 of March 1614' as closely in time as in its position
on the page. It could have been added in May. Moreover, his
remarks that 'the desine of this Baso relevo is not as the originall

is' and that 'the middell is broken' are remarkably similar to Summonte's 1601 criticisms of Palladio as reinforced by the *Historia*'s representation of the 'broken' relief figures in the centre of the pediment in outline. By depicting them in this way Summonte clearly distinguished his version of the damaged or missing central portion of the relief from his corrected depictions of what Jones described as 'a flood', 'a Seagod on ye corners and on the on[e] sid[e] 2 figures sacrifising'. So apparently close a relationship could be the result of independent observation and given that Jones only acquired his copy of Summonte on 1 May, not long before leaving Naples, we might leave it at that. But if Summonte's more precise account of the pedimental relief sculpture might not have prompted Jones to return to the temple a third time, his specifically archaeological information might well have done. Certainly, he annotated the relevant pages of his *Quattro libri* again, even if only back in London. On the top left of page 96 of Book IV, above Palladio's hypothesized statues, he wrote: 'the Statues wch stand on the Tope ar lying on the ground beelow and wear exellent'.

About twenty years later, now the grand old man of English architecture, theatre design and connoisseurship (and incidentally, ex-J.P. and Member of Parliament), Jones returned for the last time to this page and to the memory of what he had seen in Naples [Fig. 42]. Squeezed between his enthusiastic remark about the statues and his dated declaration beneath, in darker ink, Jones inscribed the letter 'E' (referring to the one he had also placed to the right of Palladio's left-hand statue) and added: 'thes statues are in hight ¼ part of ye collome and architrave the statues I saw broken liing on ye ground'.

Jones's consciousness of the relative proportions of temple façade to roof-top sculpture was manifest even in his earliest architectural designs. Three of these, the preliminary side elevation for the Queen's House at Greenwich, the designs for the Prince's Lodging at Newmarket and the first scheme for the Banqueting House, date to within five years of his return from Italy, that is, between 1616 and 1619. Jones's fascination with the use of large-scale sculpture surmounting architecture never waned. One has only to think of his 1625 catafalque for James I, his design for a triumphal arch at Temple Bar and, most spectacularly, his massive Corinthian portico for the west front of St Paul's Cathedral, which carried two or three enormous statues though many more had been intended. It was probably Jones's work on the latter that prompted him to return to

42 William Dobson,
Inigo Jones (c.1644).
[National Maritime
Musuem, Greenwich]

Palladio's account of the Neapolitan temple and add this final remark.[65]

It is clear that Jones had been fascinated by the use of monumental sculpture in architecture for several years before his 1613–14 journey to Italy. One of his earliest surviving drawings, dated to around 1608, is for an archway – presumably intended for a masque or entertainment – upon whose pediment he has posed three large statues, if indeed live actors were not intended. A live tableau certainly featured in his 'House of Fame' which was constructed for the *Masque of Queens* in February 1609.[66] Jones's first truly architectural design, for Lord Salisbury's New Exchange, also dates from this period and features what would have been three huge classicizing statues on pedestals placed just as those in Palladio's engraving of the Temple of Castor and Pollux (and, it has to be said, several other temples as well as Palladian villas). Most prominent of all, in these early designs, would have been the giant trio on the stable building he designed soon after this, perhaps also for Lord Salisbury.[67] Here the statues would have been nearer a third than a quarter the height of the façade. According to the most recent study of this drawing, it should be dated several years earlier than hitherto, that is, to around 1610. This is approximately the same date given to Jones's earliest marginal comment on the Temple of Castor and Pollux. Already then, perhaps, and certainly later (after experiencing its portico in three dimensions), when Jones thought of monumental sculpture placed on pedestals above a classical pediment, he thought of the Temple of Castor and Pollux in Naples. Like the similarly sculptural 'Palais Tutele' at Bordeaux, which Jones and Cranborne so admired in 1609, this major classical monument deserves to be better remembered, for despite its virtual disappearance, it was once an inspiration to more than one great architect.[68]

NOTES

This chapter was delivered as a lecture to the Society of Antiquaries on 11 April 1991 and published in J. Bold and E. Chaney (eds), *English Architecture: Public and Private Essays for Kerry Downes* (London and Rio Grande, NJ, 1993), pp. 31–53.

1. R. Lassels, *The Voyage of Italy* (Paris, 1670), II, p. 262. This passage is not included in the *c.* 1664 manuscript of the *Voyage* in my possession and may therefore have been added posthumously to Lassels's text by fellow priest, Simon Wilson, who saw the printed *Voyage* through the press; E. Chaney, *The Grand Tour and the Great Rebellion* (Geneva and Turin, 1985), pp. 133–40 and 425–6.
2. A. Palladio, *I quattro libri dell'architettura* (Venice, 1601) (copy in Worcester College Library, Oxford), III, p. 9. I thank the Provost and Fellows of Worcester College for permission to consult, quote from and photograph this book. I am especially grateful to the former College Librarian, Mrs Lesley Le Claire, and her successor, Dr Joanna Parker, for their help and hospitality at all times.
3. Ibid., III, p. 10.
4. Ibid., I (though the running title on this page has 'Quarto'), p. 11.
5. Ibid., I, p. 12.
6. The standard work is still Logan Pearsall Smith, *The Life and Letters of Sir Henry Wotton*, 2 vols (Oxford, 1907); see also A.M. Crinò, 'Lettere autografe inedite di Sir Henry Wotton nell'Archivio di Stato di Firenze', *Fatti e Figure del Seicento Anglo-Toscano* (Florence, 1957), pp. 7–40. Jones's references to Wotton were first discussed by W. Grant Keith, 'Inigo Jones as a Collector', *RIBA Journal*, 33 (1925), pp. 94–108, and most recently by Gordon Higgott, 'The Architectural Drawings of Inigo Jones: Attribution, Dating and Analysis' (unpublished PhD dissertation, University of London, 1987), p. 226. For Wotton and Fialetti, see Chapters 6 and 8 of this volume. The 1614 etching (after Pordenone's *Diana*) which Fialetti dedicated to 'Baron e Cavalier da Rondel' is reproduced in D.

Howarth, *Lord Arundel and his Circle* (New Haven and London, 1985), p. 171. Fialetti dedicated the series entitled 'The Sport of Love' to Lord Roos. Four large three-quarter length Fialettis of Doges, probably including the portrait of Leonardo Donato which Wotton gave to Charles I, now hang above the doors in the King's Drawing Room at Kensington Palace. The influence on Jones of Fialetti's illustrated drawing manual, *Tutte le parti del corpo humano* (Venice, 1608), has been argued by John Peacock, in 'Inigo Jones as a Figurative Artist', *Renaissance Bodies*, ed. L. Gent and N. Llewellyn (London, 1990), pp. 154–79. Jeremy Wood has since drawn attention to sources via which Jones might have known Fialetti indirectly, whilst confirming that he used Oliviero Gatti's set of engravings after Guercino; see J. Wood, 'Inigo Jones, Italian Art and the Practice of Drawing', *Art Bulletin*, LXXIV (June 1992), pp. 247–70. See now, J. Peacock, *The Stage Designs of Inigo Jones* (Cambridge, 1995).

7. L.P. Smith, *Life and Letters of Sir Henry Wotton*, p. 412. For the *Elements*, see the facsimile edition by F. Hard (Charlottesville, VA, 1968).

8. See my entry on Coryate in the *Macmillan Dictionary of Art* (1996). This points out that the reason Coryate's account of Vicenza is so sophisticated, including a full account of Palladio's buildings, is that it is based on Fra Girolamo Gioannini da Capugnano's 1601 revision of François Schott's *Itinerarium Italiae* (Vicenza, 1601).

9. Cranborne's Italian diary is published (in French) in *HMC Salisbury MSS*, XXI (London, 1970), pp. 237–49; the references to Palladio are on pp. 242–3. See below, note 24, for the argument that Jones accompanied Cranborne through France in the previous year.

10. See W. Grant Keith, 'Inigo Jones as a Collector'; Douglas Lewis, *The Drawings of Andrea Palladio* (New York, 1981), p. 10 and and J. Harris and G. Higgott, *Inigo Jones: Complete Architectural Drawings* (New York and London, 1989), p. 25.

11. Palladio, I, p. 11.

12. For the complete text of Jones's January 1615 discursion on variety and decorum, see J. Alfred Gotch, *Inigo Jones* (London, 1928), pp. 81–2.

13. Before the work of John Newman and Gordon Higgott, these January and February '1614' dates confounded scholars despite Jones's more or less logical return to old-style dating after his return to England in late 1614. In mid-January 1615 he began a period of intense study of his Palladio, both the text itself, his own on-the-spot annotations and his fading memories of specific details; for further instances, see Higgott, 'Architectural Drawings of Inigo Jones', p. 247, n. 17. I am very grateful to both John Newman and Gordon Higgott for commenting on a draft of this essay.

14. The most detailed accounts available are given by M. Hervey, *The Life, Correspondence and Collections of Thomas Howard, Earl of Arundel* (Cambridge, 1921), J.A. Gotch, *Inigo Jones* (London, 1928) and D. Howarth, *Lord Arundel and his Circle* (New Haven and London, 1985). Jones had known the Earl since at least as early as 1606 when he designed Essex's wedding masque *Hymenaei* in which Arundel performed. In 1609 Jones designed the costume in which the Countess danced (as Atalanta) in *The Masque of Queens*; see S. Orgel and R. Strong, *Inigo Jones: Theatre of the Stuart Court* (London, Berkeley and Los Angeles, 1973), I, p. 149.

15. Letter from Carleton in Hervey (p. 67): 'He pretends his going home to be to hinder his Lady from a winter's journey, who had asked leave of the King to come hither at this time, to prevent her Lord's coming home before his cure was performed.'

16. The size of the entourages of the three peers, Lennox, Arundel and Lisle, delegated to accompany Princess Elizabeth, are given in British Library, Add. MS 64875 (Coke Papers), VI, fol. 90. (Formerly at Melbourne Hall, these papers were purchased from the Marquis of Lothian by the British Library in 1987.) The Earl's servants numbered 20, his wife's ten. I thank Professor K.J. Höltgen for photocopies of guest lists in Leiden and Germany which show that Cansfield, Coke and Jones (in that order and immediately under Francis Quarles) were part of the large Arundel entourage from the beginning of the continental tour. Thomas Coke had 'long served' the Countess of Arundel's father, Lord Shrewsbury, who confessed 'there neither is nor ever was any man towards whom I have or do more love or affect than I do this man'; see Howarth, *Lord Arundel and his Circle*, pp. 16–22, and his unpublished PhD dissertation, 'Lord Arundel as a Patron and Collector, 1604–1646' (University of Cambridge, 1979), pp. 228–31, though beware his confusion, following J.I. Whalley in *Apollo*, XCIV (1971), pp. 184–91, between the Earl of Exeter and his son, William Cecil, 3rd Baron Burghley, the Catholic traveller and connoisseur who suggested that Shrewsbury might use Coke in the acquisition of works of art in Italy. There is more detail in Howarth's dissertation where Cansfield, as 'Causfield', is documented as travelling with Burghley's son, Lord Roos, in 1612 and writing to William Trumbull about plants and Arundel's return from Ireland in 1616 (p. 244, n. 46). It seems likely that it is Cansfield (rather than 'Cannefield') who co-mortgages Arundel House in 1607 (Hervey, *The Life of Arundel*, p. 41).
17. During the royal visit to Oxford in 1605 a contemporary reported that, 'They hired one Mr Jones, a great traveller, who undertooke to further them much, and furnish them with rare Devices, but performed very little to that which was expected'; Gotch, *Inigo Jones*, p. 38.
18. Maurice Lee (ed.), *Dudley Carleton to John Chamberlain, 1603–1624: Jacobean Letters* (New Brunswick, NJ, 1972), pp. 144–5.
19. PRO SP 99/13, fol. 90. The Viceroy had offended Lord Cranborne and his entourage, arresting one of the latter, just three years earlier; see J. Stoye, *English Travellers Abroad, 1604–1667*, 2nd edn (New Haven and London, 1989), p. 85. Isaac Wake writes from Venice: 'To my assured good friend Mr Thomas Coke at Milan', on 20 July (BL, Add. MS 64875, VI, fols 97r–98v). For Arundel's indignation, see Hervey, *The Life of Arundel*, pp. 75–7. On 3 August Isaac Wake wrote to Coke saying he will come to Padua to pay his respects if the party postpones coming to Venice any longer (BL, Add. MS 64875, VI, fol. 101). A formal letter from Pietro Martire Martignone dated 18 September pursued Arundel to Padua, explaining away the writer's inability (and that of his daughter) to have 'far la dovuta riverenza et servitu, conforme all'obligo et desiderio mio . . .' HMC, *Cowper MSS*, I, p. 79. For Parma, see *I Farnese: Arte e Collezionismo*, ed. L.F. Schianchi and N. Spinosa (Naples, 1995) and *Aurea Parma*, lxxix, I–II, Jan.–Aug. 1995. Either en route to Padua or on their return journey, Jones and the Arundels visited Mantua. A decade later the latter were requesting an elaborate model of the Palazzo del Te 'with a clear description of the principal things to be seen inside'; see F. Haskell in A. MacGregor (ed.), *The Late King's Goods* (London and Oxford, 1989), p. 212.
20. Howarth, *Lord Arundel and his Circle*, p. 37
21. Palladio, II, p. 64, and *Coryat's Crudities . . .*, 2 vols (Glasgow, 1905), I, p. 299: 'Mr Willoughby a learned student in the University (of Padua)'. When Willoughby died in 1617, Henry Wotton described him as 'an infectious papist'; L.P. Smith, *Life and Letters of Sir Henry Wotton*, II, p. 114; see also A.

Lytton Sells, *The Paradise of Travellers: The Italian Influence on Englishmen in the 17th century* (London, 1964), p. 111. Galileo inscribed one of his astronomical treatises to Willoughby, who was Counsellor to the English Nation at the University of Padua in 1592-3. That Arundel visited the Rotonda and Theatre with Jones seems likely. That he knew both buildings later is clear from the MS 'Remembrances of things worth seeing in Italy' which he wrote for John Evelyn on 25 April 1646; see the edition by J.M. Robinson for the Roxburghe Club (1987), p. 23.

22. Lee (ed.), *Carleton to Chamberlain*, p. 148. Carleton describes the farewell party for the Arundels 'made by Signore Barbarigo, where were about 20 of the most principal women'. For Barbarigo and the villa near Cataio (perhaps the Castle of the Obizzi), see Jennifer Fletcher, 'The Arundels in the Veneto', *Apollo*, CXLIV, no. 413 (August, 1996), pp. 63-9.

23. Ibid., p. 149, and Hervey, *The Life of Arundel*, pp. 80-1. Coke wrote soon after, probably to Lady Kent (who studied Italian): 'Siamo qui in un paese vago e piacevole ed abondante. L'eccell[ma] Signora contessa sua sorella sta bene e qui in Siena e ogni di accarezzata e visitata di queste signori per dozzene a volta . . .' On 14 January 1614, Gilbert, 7th Earl of Shrewsbury, writes from his house in Broad Street, 'To my very lovyne frend Mr Thomas Coke':

> The last we hard from any of you, was a letter from my Lo: of Arundel to me dated at Sienna the 24 Novem: last w[ch] I receaved but a weeke synce . . . We heare y[t] [that] my Lo: of Ar: & my daughter have sent all theyr company to Pysa, except only 3 or 4 y[t] are of necessity to be aboute them, to th'end they may better learne y[t] language but this other day y[t] Lyttel dapp[?] Italian fellow y[t] fested my daughter Grey [the Countess of Kent] before Ascanio came last to her (Antonio they say his is [sic]) toulde my Wyfe, that he hard my daughter hadd put her selfe into a monastery for vj or viij weeks, the better to Learne y[t] Language. I doubt not but ther are many other Idle reports as well as this, spredd of you in this Towne, w[:ch] never cum to o[r] eares, but I trust no wyse man will gyve credite to them.

(BL, Add. MS 64875 Coke Papers, VI, fol. 109r; cf. summary in *HMC*, *Cowper MSS*, I, p. 80.) At this stage, Shrewsbury trusts that the Arundels will return home by midsummer.

24. Palladio, IV, p. 10. On the basis of a reference to Jones's arrival in Paris on the eve of Cranborne's tour of southern France I have argued that he was sent by Salisbury to accompany his son. This tour was distinct from Cranborne's visit to the Veneto in the following year; see my review of A.C. Fusco, *Inigo Jones Vitruvius Britannicus* (Rimini, 1985), in the *Burlington Magazine*, CXXX (1988), pp. 633-4. On 3 July 1609, the English ambassador, Sir George Carew, reported to Salisbury that he 'receaved his M[ties] letters of the 19 of the last . . . [on] the 28. of the same . . . At the same time, I also receaved your L[ps]. by M[r] Jones, for w[ch] I geve your L.[p] mine humble thankes' (PRO, SP 78 [France], 55/122). Previously it had been thought that the payment made to Jones on 16 June 'for carreinge Lres for his Mat's servyce into France' must have dated from after the completion of his journey (as such payments usually were). If both dates are old style, this payment seems to have been made in advance, a thesis supported by comparison with others of this period; see for example PRO, E 351/543, recording a payment to Mr Andrew Bussey 'for carreigne of lettres for his Majesties service into ffraunce and retornynge back againe wth letters of answere xxx li'. Jones was paid less than half this amount, no return task being specified; cf. G. Higgott, 'Inigo Jones in Provence', *Archi-*

tectural History, XXVI (1983), pp. 24–34. Higgott and Harris, *Inigo Jones: Complete Architectural Drawings*, pp. 40–2, have accepted this hypothesis as, implicitly, has Stoye in the revised edition of *English Travellers Abroad*, p. 332, n. 28.

25. Howarth, 'Lord Arundel as a Patron and Collector', pp. 43 and 245. Interestingly, Peretti had visited England in 1612. If Jones and Arundel visited the Villa Peretti Montalto they could have seen the magnificent pair of 2nd century Caryatids now in the Vatican and British Museum; see A. Wilton and I. Bignamini (eds), *Grand Tour* (London, 1996), pp. 226–7.

26. The news arrived in Siena and was immediately forwarded to Arundel in Rome in a letter dated 4 June 1614 by 'Frate Angelo Ing^se Cap^no Ind^o': 'Jesu+Maria Sta Most Right Honourable Lord, I making something bould to write these fewe lines only to guife your Honour to understand that Sig^r Ottaviano Perini hath newse out of England that the Earle of Northampton departed this life, and that he hath made your Honour his heare . . .' (BL, Add. MS 64875, fol. 131r). A letter of 17 August 1614 reveals that Arundel is in Genoa and has received details of Northampton's will. Anthony Tracy sends news and Robert Cansfield is with Arundel, HMC, *Cowper MSS*, I, pp. 86–7.

27. See Chapter 3 in this volume, pp. 83–7.

28. Hervey, *The Life of Arundel*, p. 112. Reporting on the death of Arundel's uncle, Northampton ('an obedient son of the Roman Catholic church') the Spanish ambassador, Gondomar, informed Philip III that his heir 'el conde de Arandel', was in Italy with his wife and children to see the country, 'but the more certain reason is to enable him to live as a Catholic in public'. A.J. Loomie (ed.), *Spain and the Jacobean Catholics* (Catholic Record Society, 68), II, 1978, pp. 37–9. Arundel reverted to Roman Catholicism before his death in Padua in 1646; see E. Chaney, 'Thomas Howard, 14th Earl of Arundel by François Dieussart', *Apollo*, CXLIV, no. 413 (August, 1996), pp. 49–50, n. 12.

29. HMC, *Cowper MSS*, I, p. 78; see also D. Mathew, *The Jacobean Age* (London, 1938), p. 134. Shrewsbury concludes: 'I have not heard that the King hath heard thereof.' In 1592, Shrewsbury had himself been reported to the Privy Council as maintaining a household of 'notorious papists and dangerous recusants' (*Cal. S.P. Dom.*, 1591–94, p. 174).

30. See p. 86 in this volume. Hervey, *The Life of Arundel*, p. 89, quotes a letter from Chamberlain to Carleton: 'It is whispered abroad that your Don Diego's master [probably Lord Roos] gave very malignant intelligence of the Lord of Arundel's being at Rome, and of his entertainment and conversation there; which being related to the King by the Ar[chbishop?], that had the advertisement, he was put to his answer, and gave very good satisfaction.'

31. Hervey, *The Life of Arundel*, pp. 83–4.

32. Ibid., p. 85.

33. Ibid., pp. 85–6. Carleton's reference to the Arundels' servants as 'theyre great family' suggests that more were brought with them from Germany than is sometimes thought and tends to confirm Gondomar's reference to their having children with them; cf. n. 28.

34. Chaney, *The Grand Tour and the Great Rebellion*, pp. 263–7. Especially useful on Matthew is J.P. Feil, 'Sir Tobie Matthew and his Collection of Letters' (unpublished PhD dissertation, University of Chicago, 1962). Jones and Matthew were no doubt well acquainted but Howarth's conclusion (*Lord Arundel and his Circle*, p. 100) that they were 'very close as a result of Jones' acting as gaoler to Matthew while he prepared for his banishment' is based on the mistaken assumption that the 'Master Jones' who acted as Matthew's guarantor in 1608 was Inigo Jones. It was in fact Edward Jones, MP, for whom

see the forthcoming volume of the *History of Parliament: 1604-29.*

35. *HMC, Cowper MSS,* I, p. 84.
36. J.P. Feil, 'Sir Tobie Matthew', pp. 78-9 and G. Anstruther, *The Seminary Priests* (Great Wakering, 1975), II, pp. 120-1 (where Gage is 'still alive in apr 52'). Jones would have re-met Matthew and Gage in the Veneto on his return there in late July (see his copy of Sarayna's *Verona* (Worcester College) inscribed 'Venetia 30 Juli 1614' and annotations in Palladio of 10-14 August; cf. Feil, pp. 81-4). Three years earlier, Bellarmine had ordained the younger brother of the Earl of Rutland, Sir Oliver Manners. Jones had probably travelled with Sir Oliver in the 1590s; see above, p. 158, n. 18. The Arundels were still socializing with George Gage in the 1630s. On the basis of a somewhat cryptic reference in a letter from 'the painter', Nicholas Herman, to Lionel Cranfield, to Gage as 'the Architect of Tart-halle', Howarth has transferred the traditional attribution of Lady Arundel's house from Nicholas Stone to Gage; Howarth, *Lord Arundel and his Circle*, p. 245, n. 38, but cf. Chaney, *The Grand Tour*, p. 264.
37. A.H. Matthew (ed.), *A True Historical Relation of the Conversion of Sir Tobie Matthew* (London 1904), pp. 12-15. Matthew's 1605 travels in Italy were in defiance of a parental veto; see Feil, op. cit., p. 15, and above, p. 167, n. 7.
38. Palladio, II, p. 96 (see below).
39. *The Diary of John Evelyn,* ed. E.S. de Beer (Oxford, 1955), II, pp. 324-5 (30 January 1645). It is worth noting here that early seventeenth-century Naples was one of the largest cities in the world with a population of approximately 250,000. It was only in this period that London overtook it in size.
40. A former diplomatic rival of Henry Wotton, John Wrath, or Wroth, was effectively British consul in Naples. On Monday 16 March (old style) his brother, Sir Robert Wroth, died leaving his wife Mary Sidney, daughter of the Earl of Leicester, and a month-old baby. On the death of the latter, John inherited his brother's estates (letter from Arundel's mother, BL, Add. MS 64875, VI, fol. 128) though Chamberlain describes these as encumbered with £23,000 of debt; T. Birch, *Court and Times of James I* (London, 1849), I, p. 237; cf. J. Nichols, *Progresses . . .,* II, p. 756. Sir Robert Wroth was a patron of Ben Jonson.
41. BL Add. MSS 64875 (Coke Papers), VI, fol. 126rv. The exterior of the folded letter carried an address to 'Tomaso Cocko. Nobile Inglese in Roma, Racc^ta al Sg Fr^co Ruggieri M^ro dell Poste di Firenza in Roma'. Jones's criticism of Scamozzi in his copy of *L'Idea* (now at Worcester College, Oxford; 1615, II, p. 111) confirms that the travellers recognized a Zoccolo as a platform-soled shoe: 'Scamotzio erres for the Dorik tēpels of ye greeke had no bases expressing a naked foote of a mā, and bases imitates a soccolo or sliper.' Lassels (who knew Arundel) summarizes the story of Bourbon's body from du Bellay's history (*Voyage of Italy* (Paris, 1670), II, p. 264). He says that 'it stands with its *clothes, bootes* and *spurrs* on, in a *long boxe* streight up, with this *Spanish Epitaph* over his head . . .' Arundel later purchased what he thought was a Titian portrait of Charles de Bourbon. It was engraved by Vorsterman; illustrated in Howarth, *Lord Arundel and his Circle*, p. 50. The extent to which Arundel's letter is typical of the educated (and not necessarily Catholic) tourist may be judged by comparison with Isaac Basire's account of his 1648 visit to Gaeta: 'In it wee saw some wonders, especially the thorow rupture of a rocky mountain by an earthquake, which tradition sayes, and Cardinal Baronius publishes, to have happened at our Saviour's passion; a stupendous sight . . . In the castle, wherein we saw the corpse of the Duke of Bourbon . . .'; see *The Correspondence of*

Isaac Basire, ed. W.N. Darnell (London, 1831), p. 90. Three years later, Richard Symonds sketched a 'Prospect of Gaeta from Mola' on his way to Naples (Bodleian Library, MS Rawlinson D.121, p. 15).

42. As stated by Howarth, ibid., p. 44.

43. Howarth, ibid., p. 49, says that the column in front of S. Maria Maggiore was raised 'while Arundel and Jones were there' and attributes Jones's skill in raising the drums for the columns of St Paul's portico to his having witnessed its construction. What Jones actually writes, alongside the *Quattro libri* illustration of the Temple of Nerva Trajanus (Palladio, IV, p. 24) is 'January ye 5. 1614 whilst I was in Roome the Pillors then stood of this Tempell was Pulled doune by Pau. V: to sett a figur on before St Maria Maiore.' Perhaps Jones encouraged Arundel to attempt to acquire the obelisk of Domitian which Bernini eventually erected in the Piazza Navona, then lying just off the Appian Way in the Circus of Maxentius, 'broken in three peices and neglected until that the noble Earle of Arondel and Lord Marshal of England offering to buy it, and having given threescore crownes [in] earnest, made the Romans beginn to think it a fine thing, and to stop the transporting of it into England . . .'; Richard Lassels, 'Voyage of Italy' MS of c. 1664, quoted in Chaney, *The Grand Tour*, pp. 407-8.

44. Marlowe, *Doctor Faustus*, III, i.

45. See Chapter 4 in this volume.

46. The best secondary account of contemporary tourists (albeit dealing mainly with Germans who are better documented), is Malcolm Letts, 'Some Sixteenth-Century Travellers in Naples', *English Historical Review*, XXX (1918), pp. 176-96. For the French, see G. Labrot, *Un instrument polémique: l'image de Naples au temps du schisme, 1534-1667* (Lille, 1978). The most relevant contemporary guidebook is Gioseppe Mormile, *Descrittione del amenissimo distretto della città di Napoli* (Naples, 1617); see also F. Schott's *Itinerarium Italiae* (post-1601 edition); G.C. Capaccio, *Neopolitanae historiae tomus primus* (1607) and above all, Carlo Celano, *Notitie del bello, dell'antico, e del curioso della città di Napoli*, 10 vols (Naples, 1692). The best contemporary plan is Alessandro Baratta's of 1627. Fynes Moryson's *Itinerary* (1617) is the most detailed English account, though it fails to mention the Temple of Castor and Pollux. George Sandys, *Relation of a Journey begun An; Dom: 1610* (London, 1615), is both less detailed and more derivative. For other relevant literature, see G. Alisio, 'L'immagine della città', *Civiltà del Seicento a Napoli* (Naples, 1984), pp. 77-90. That Jones visited Pozzuoli is confirmed by an annotation in his copy of Vitruvius (now at Chatsworth), *I dieci libri dell'architettura* (Venice, 1567), p. 268: 'of this Potsolano wch is a burned sulferous yearth I brought from Pottsioli/1614'. He also refers to having drawn 'the Temple at Putioli', in his Palladio (IV, p. 31). I thank Gordon Higgott for both these references. Arundel's grandson, Henry Howard, later Duke of Norfolk, built his own Grotta di Posillipo through a hill in his garden at Albury. John Evelyn designed this in 1667 (*Diary*, III, p. 496). What is presumably the work of Arundel (and perhaps Jones?) is visible beneath this spot in Hollar's etching, which dates from 1645; illustrated in Howarth, *Lord Arundel and his Circle*, p. 123. John Aubrey recalled that Arundel 'had many Grotts about his house [at Albury] cutt in the Sandy sides of hills, wherin he delighted to sitt and discourse'; *Brief Lives*, ed. O.L. Dick (London, 1950), p. 224.

47. In a review of the quatercentenary exhibition in the Banqueting House (*Op. Cit.*, n. 29, Naples, January 1974), Cesare de Seta argued that the Palazzo Vicereale must have influenced Jones's design for the New Exchange but the

buildings are only similar in general proportions and while the latter is pre-1613, the former was not complete when Jones was previously in Italy; see also de Seta's 'L'Italia nello specchio del "Grand Tour"', *Storia d'Italia*, annali 5, *Il paesaggio*, ed. C. de Seta (Turin, 1982), pp. 148–51. The Palazzo was illustrated in Garzia Barrionuevo, *Panegyricus* (Naples, 1616), p. 153. Perhaps Jones saw the University of Naples' academic assembly hall, built in the form of a theatre and apparently completed shortly before his visit to Naples. It is mentioned as a possible precedent for Christopher Wren's Sheldonian by Howard Colvin in *Unbuilt Oxford* (New Haven and London, 1983), p. 13. Perhaps Jones's so-called Cockpit Theatre design (Worcester College) might be considered as an intermediary between the Neapolitan hall and Wren's design though the former was illustrated in Barrionuevo, op. cit., pp. 149–51.

48. John Raymond, *Il Mercurio Italico: An Itinerary contayning a Voyage made through Italy in the yeare 1646 and 1647* (London, 1648), p. 141, transcribes the Greek inscription on the frieze, and refers to 'the Frontispiece, or Porch of ancient Pillars . . . as likewise the remnants of their two Statues yet standing'. This account provided the basis for John Evelyn's when he came to write up his '1645' *Diary* account several decades later (II, pp. 327–8). For Grimaldi, see A. Quattrone, 'P.D. Francesco Grimaldi C.R. architetto', *Regnum Dei*, 5 (1949), pp. 25ff. For the early history of S. Paolo, see L. Correra, 'Il Tempio dei Dioscuri a Napoli', *Atti della Reale Accademia di Archeologia, Lettere e Belle Arti di Napoli*, 23 (1905), pt 2, pp. 214–28; see also C. Celano, *Notitie*, II, pp. 151–77. There is a brief account in A. Blunt, *Neapolitan Baroque and Rococo Architecture* (London, 1975), pp. 39–41.

49. Correra illustrates d'Ollanda's then unpublished drawing in his 1905 article, 'Il Tempio dei Dioscuri'. The Escorial sketchbook has since been published twice in its entirety, most recently with commentary by Elias Tormo, *Os Desenhos das antigualhas que vio Francisco d'Ollanda, pintor Portugues* (Madrid, 1940), fol. 45v and pp. 199–203. Sangallo's comments are discussed in Cornel von Fabriczy, *Die Handzeichnungen Giuliano da Sangallo* (Stuttgart, 1902), p. 67. In 1648, Isaac Basire mentions S. Paolo, 'wch (they say) was Castor and Pollux, where there is a Greek inscription of Titus Vespatianus Settus in his passage through Naples at his returne from Jerusalem'; see *Travels through France and Italy (1647–1649)*, ed. L. Monga (Geneva and Turin, 1987), p. 94, and for attribution to Basire above p. 87, n. 2. The far more aesthetically aware Richard Symonds included an annotated sketch of the portico, complete with 1578 and Greek inscription, in his 1651 travel notebook; Bodleian Library, MS Rawlinson D.121, p. 23 [Fig. 21].

50. Palladio, *Quattro Libri*, IV, p. 96.

51. Ibid., IV, p. 97.

52. Ibid., IV, p. 96.

53. Sotheby's, 4 May 1925, lot 135. This sale was ordered by the President and Council of the Royal Society and consisted largely of books donated in 1667 by Arundel's grandson, Henry Howard, 6th Duke of Norfolk. Many were from Arundel's library, and a sizeable number therefore from Pirckheimer's. This item, according to the annotated copy of the sale catalogue in the British Library, was sold to W. Leith for £1 10s.

54. Vincenzo Mirabella, *Dichiarazioni della pianta dell'antiche Siracuse* (Naples, 1613), pp. 28–9. That Jones was to become aware that the Greek Doric was baseless is clear from the annotation in his copy of Scamozzi's *Idea*; see above, note 41.

55. For Milton's intended voyage from Naples to Sicily and Greece in 1638/9, see the Columbia edition of his *Works* (New York, 1933), VIII, pp. 125–6; for a

sceptical account of his intentions, however, see Chaney, *Grand Tour*, p. 249 and idem, 'Milton's Visit to Vallombrosa', Chapter 12 below.

56. See above Chapter 1, pp. 26–32. Before Breval, only George Berkeley seems to have appreciated the Sicilian temples for what they were; see below, Chapter 13.

57. *Bibliotheca Apostolica Vaticana* (Rome, 1591). It is inscribed: '28 di Maggio 1614. Roma. T. Arundell'; see Howarth, *Lord Arundel and his Circle*, p. 230, n. 47. In Siena Arundel acquired a MS Vitruvius, which he inscribed 'Thomae Comite de Arundel emptus Siennae 14 Junii 1614' (now BL Arundel MS 122).

58. Palladio, *Quattro Libri*, IV, p. 74: 'This Tempell I Obsearved exactly ye last of Maye 1614 and have noated what I found more than is in Palladio.' Jones criticizes Palladio's illustration of the Pantheon stairs, sketching in his own corrected version. According to the inscription on his drawing of the Castel Sant'Angelo, now at Chatsworth, Jones sketched it on 29 May 1614.

59. Raymond, *Il Mercurio Italico*, p. 141.

60. A.H. Mathew (ed.), *A true historical Relation of the Conversion of Sir Tobie Matthew . . .* (London, 1904), pp. 7–9. A mutual friend of both Jones and Matthew, the then Catholic John Donne, probably visited his exiled Jesuit uncle, Jasper Heywood, in Naples *c.* 1590. Father Heywood died there eight years later; R.C. Bald, *John Donne: A Life* (Oxford, 1986), pp. 45 and 52.

61. Summonte, *Historia della città e regno di Napoli*, I, illustration facing p. 90. The Joli is now at Beaulieu in the collection of Lord Montagu; see exhibition catalogue, *All'ombra del Vesuvio: Napoli nella veduta europea dal quattrocento all'ottocento* (Naples, 1990), pp. 186 and 400. I thank Lord Montagu for his permission to reproduce the painting.

62. Compare Per Palme, *Triumph of Peace: A Study of the Whitehall Banqueting House* (London, 1957), p. 227, and J. Harris, *Catalogue of the Drawings Collection of the Royal Institute of British Architects: Inigo Jones and John Webb* (Farnborough, 1972), p. 13, item 6, fig. 6, citing J. Charlton, *The Banqueting House, Whitehall* (London, 1964).

63. S.W. Pighius, *Hercules prodicius, seu principis inventutis vita et peregrinatio* (Antwerp, 1587), was the major source for Andrea (later François) Schott's *Itinerarii Italiae rerumque Romanorum libri tres* (Antwerp, 1600). This became the most influential seventeenth-century guidebook to Italy, translated into English by Edmund Warcupp in 1660, thanks to its being revised and expanded in 1600–1 by the Vicentine Dominican, Fra Girolamo Gioannini da Capugnano.

64. Summonte, *Historia della città e regno di Napoli*, I, p. 92:

'E se ben' Andrea Palladio nel suo libro de Achitettura [*sic*], fè essemplare le Colonne sudette, nondimeno le figure di sovra non l'esemplò bene, essendo diverse da quelle che con effetto vi sono, e da noi con gran diligenza fatte scolpire come ciascheduno che ne dubitasse ne potrebbe far saggio.

Nel Cavare i fondamenti per la renovatione di questo Tempio l'anno 1578. si trovaron due Busti di marmo, che si veggono appoggiate sotto l'istesse Colonne de quali si fa giuditio che fussero le statue di Giulio Cesare, e di Ottaviano Imperadori di quei tempi, e dovevano stare sopra quelle Basi di Marmo che si scorgono sovra del Cornicione, nel modo che l'habbiamo fatti ivi scolpire le quali per terremoto, o per altro accidente debbero cascare, e rovinare.'

65. For all these, see the relevant entries in Harris and Higgott, *Inigo Jones: Complete Architectural Drawings*.

66. Ibid., fig. 3 and S. Orgel and R. Strong, *Inigo Jones: The Theatre of the Stuart Court*, 2 vols (London, Berkeley and Los Angeles, 1973), I, p. 130.
67. Harris and Higgott, *Inigo Jones: Complete Architectural Drawings*, cat. no. 9.
68. Viewing the extraordinary 'Palais Tutele' (destroyed later in the century) together with the so-called Palais Gallien just outside Bordeaux, Cranborne concluded that they were 'remarques ancien[n]es de la grandeur et magnificence des Romains'; see his travel journal in *HMC Salisbury MSS*, XXI, p. 107. The argument that Jones's presence may have prompted such enthusiasm for architecture on the part of his patron's son and heir (see n. 24 above) is strengthened by his stage design for the first scene of Prince Henry's *Barriers*, 'The Fallen House of Chivalry', in which an almost identical ruined colonnade with arcade above appears in the middle distance on the right. Jones designed this in the winter of 1609 soon after returning from his tour of France. The most vivid pre-Jonesian illustration of Les Tutelles was the fold-out woodcut in Elie Vinet, *L'antiquité de Bordeaus* (Bordeaux, 1574), opposite sig. Bv. Probably via Perrault's engraving of this monument, Vanbrugh and Hawksmoor were inspired to introduce the unusual arched attic motif in their great corner pavilions at Blenheim; see J. Summerson, *Architecture in Britain 1530-1830* (New Haven and London, 1993), p. 265.

8

Pilgrims to Pictures:
Art, English Catholics and the
Evolution of the Grand Tour

eᒪᗢᏊᏬ

SURVIVING JEROME'S misgivings, Chaucer's irony and even
Erasmus's sarcasm, the phenomenon known as pilgrimage
lasted considerably longer than its successor, that which the
seventeenth-century priest and former pilgrim, Richard Lassels, first
identified as the Grand Tour. Moreover, though Lassels's pioneering
Voyage of Italy (1670), introduced innumerable influential Englishmen to 'art' and even Vasarian art history, within its shorter life-
span the Grand Tour was less consistently concerned with art and
architecture than the pilgrimage had been with relics and sacred
places. Even in Lassels's fascinating preface on the theory and practice of travel, art in the modern sense of the word hardly featured.
It had featured even less prominently in the mid-sixteenth-century
diary of Sir Thomas Hoby, the translator of Castiglione's *Cortegiano*,
who deserves no less fame as the first Grand Tourist. Evolving out of
and, in Protestant northern Europe, reacting against the medieval
practice of pilgrimage in response to demand for a non-superstitious
justification for travel, the Grand Tour began as an exclusively
educational phenomenon. Even in its maturity in the eighteenth
century, after the establishment of rules of 'taste', when the Grand
Tour became almost synonymous with artistic concerns, these
remained subordinate to an educational ideal of virtuosity, which
Lord Shaftesbury argued led to virtue in the modern sense of the
word.

Art's rise to its present, extraordinarily elevated status – though
unprecedented commercial value now threatens genuine concern –

is nevertheless inextricably linked to the history of the Grand Tour. Those primitive attempts at art appreciation on the part of pioneering Grand Tourists – and their first efforts at collecting – provide fundamental clues about the origins of our notions of 'art'.

In the immediate wake of the Reformation, before Calvinist and Jesuit extremists put an end to hopes of Erasmian compromise in Europe, mid-sixteenth-century British travellers such as Thomas Hoby, John Shute, author of the first English treatise on architecture, or William Thomas, author of the first Anglo-Italian dictionary and the precocious *Historie of Italie*, crossed the Alps with relative freedom and wrote about Renaissance Italy with the enthusiasm characteristic of discoverers. An earlier generation had studied with humanist teachers but had been blind to those visual aspects of Italian culture we now – almost too exclusively – associate with the *Quattrocento*. Like Erasmus in 1506, though vaguely aware of Italy's superiority in areas beyond textual criticism, these scholars scarcely noticed the artistic achievements of the great city-states they stayed in. Neither did indulgence-orientated pilgrims such as Sir Richard Guylforde or Torkington, who praised Venice in only the most general terms on their journeys to the Holy Land. Hoby, Shute and Thomas were the first to refer to specific buildings, and, in Hoby's case, a piece of Renaissance sculpture, Montorsoli's great Orion fountain in Messina, which he described as 'one of the fairest peece of worke that ever I sawe'. No doubt inspired by this, when he inherited his estate at Bisham in Berkshire he built a fountain of his own. Painting, on the other hand, was hardly noticed; when Hoby mentions Michelangelo, probably for the first time in English, it is with reference to negotiations for a proposed tomb of Paul III. A century later, British travellers such as John Evelyn, and even Lassels, still managed to describe the Sistine Chapel without mentioning the ceiling.

The aspiring courtiers, diplomats and professionals of an increasingly secularized nation-state justified their visits to papist Italy on the useful principle derived from Homer by Horace that Ulysses was wise 'For that he knew mens maners and saw many cities'. 'Curiosity', which had worried Petrarch as tending to undermine the piety of pilgrims, was now encouraged to the extent that a non-religious appreciation of art and architecture, even religious art, began to insinuate itself under the category of seeing cities. Such curiosity led to comparison and hence, eventually, to the cultivation of what became known as 'taste'. This was a slow and far from steady process, however, and nowhere more so than in Britain, whose visual culture suffered such traumatic setbacks at the hands of the more puritanical reformers. Had it not been for these isolationist philistines, a second generation of returned travellers might have carried through the Italianate transformation of the man-made environment which made so promising a start in the mid-sixteenth century. After the domestic disruptions of the 1550s, however, the 1560s and 1570s saw a dramatic deterioration in relations with the Spanish-dominated Catholic continent and a virtual end to the incipient Grand Tour. Pius V's excommunication of Elizabeth, 'Pretended Queen of England', in 1570, confirmed the cold war with Italy even if Venice remained accessible to a determined minority, one of whom was Philip Sidney. who had himself painted by Veronese. Although Sidney described mythological pictures in his *Arcadia*, and may even have sent his uncle, the Earl of Leicester, pictures from the continent, it is significant that this unusual record of the commissioning of a work of art by an Elizabethan abroad should be a portrait. Portraits were the only acceptable works of art in a post-iconoclastic culture permeated by Puritanism, Sidney's Venetian commission being thus rare as such but typical in its genre in the history of patronage between the ages of Holbein and Van Dyck. Where architecture was concerned, advising his brother, Robert, on the benefits of travel, Sidney recommended indifference, for 'houses are but houses in every place'.

Something of a thaw followed the failure of the Armada, but only after James I's 1604 peace treaty with Spain did English Protestants begin to travel safely to Italy again. Even then the fate of John Mole warned Protestants not to articulate their beliefs too openly. Travelling tutor to Lord Roos, Mole was arrested in 1608 for criticizing Catholicism in Florence and spent the rest of his life – more than 30 years – in a Roman prison. On the other hand, crypto-Catholic cosmopolitans such as Roos himself came into their own as patrons, collectors, cultural entrepreneurs, art agents and guides, returning to England from time to time despite the continued ban on visits to Rome. The new Grand Tourists were encouraged by the appointment of an ambassador in Venice who, in turn, greatly encouraged interest in Italian art. Sir Henry Wotton had already travelled extensively in Italy – albeit surreptitiously – and had emerged not only as one of the first Englishmen to be interested in Italian art and architecture but as a diplomat determined to improve his knowledge and exploit it for the furthering of his career [Fig. 27]. Unlike today's photo-calling ambassadors who can merely order up reproductions of Annigoni's latest image of the Queen, the seventeenth-century ambassador – 'sent to lie abroad for his country' – had to know something about portrait painting, likenesses of monarchs, prospective spouses and politicians being his stock in trade. Wotton collected drawings by Palladio, and sent books (including, on the day it was published, Galileo's *Sidereus Nuncius*), telescopes, sculpture, paintings, maps, models and mosaics back to the most powerful men in England. From Vienna in December 1620, Wotton provided Francis Bacon with a remarkable account of Kepler's *camera obscura*:

> In this man's study I was much taken with the draft of a landscape on a piece of paper, methought masterly done: whereof inquiring the author, he bewrayed with a smile it was himself . . . He hath a little black tent . . . which he can suddenly set up where he will in a field . . . capable of not much more than one man . . . exactly close and dark, save at one hole, about an inch and a half in the diameter, to which he applies a long perspective trunk, with a convex class fitted to the said hole, and the concave taken out at the other end, which extendeth to about the middle of this erected tent, through which the visible radiations of all the objects without are intromitted, falling upon a paper, which is accommodated to receive them; and so he traceth them with his pen in their natural appearance . . . to make landscapes by it were illiberal, though surely no painter can do them so precisely.

Four years after writing this, Wotton published the highly sophisticated *Elements of Architecture*, which told his conservative compatriots to abandon the pointed arch to its 'first inventors, the Goths or Lombards, amongst other reliques of that barbarous age'. Similarly, he ridiculed the English 'Fashion of colouring . . . even Regal statues'. More positively, he promoted 'irregular' garden design and the vocabulary of art criticism, along with Henry Peacham, introducing Anglo-Saxon readers to the lives of the (Italian) artists (though he was more Albertianly functionalist than Vasarianly historicist in his methodology). Above all though, Wotton introduced a significant selection of his travelling compatriots to Renaissance buildings and paintings *in situ*.

These travellers included not merely members of the courtly elite such as Prince Henry's 16-year-old favorite, Sir John Harington, who studied architecture and fortification alongside Wotton in Venice, but men of more humble origin who were at least as influential. It was, for example, as much thanks to Wotton as to da Capugnano's Vicentine edition of Schott's *Itinerarium Italiae* (1601) that Thomas Coryate discovered Vicenza's Palladian buildings in the summer of 1608. Earlier that year, on the eve of his appointment as Lord Treasurer, Lord Salisbury received a letter from Wotton which serves as a good example of the latter's role in Italianizing English taste. The ambassador began by thanking his patron for sending a portrait of himself by de Critz which he was to have copied as the fine mosaic eventually installed above the fireplace in the library at Hatfield. Wotton went on to request Salisbury's 'Coat armour in the true colours, with the mantling and the crest', proposing to turn this too into a mosaic. He suggests that 'it may afterwards be very fitly placed in the front of your buildings over the portal', by which he may mean either Hatfield, Salisbury House or the New Exchange, for which Inigo Jones prepared his first extant architectural design at this time and which indeed, according to Smithson's slightly later elevation, featured the Cecil coat of arms.

A few months earlier, Wotton had announced that he was preparing 'for your Lordship's own delight some things about the subject of architecture', perhaps a preliminary draft of the *Elements*. Now he promises 'to present unto your Lordship some drafts of architecture'. Having been unable as yet 'to make them ready', Wotton:

adventures to entertain your Lordship with two or three poor things . . . that are sent in a ship called the *Martha* . . . There is a picture of this famous Duke [Doge Leonardo Donato by Odoardo Fialetti; see above, p. 164], done truly and naturally but roughly, *alla Venetiana*, and therefore to be set at some good distance from the sight. There is also a figure (I take it) of Prometheus, devoured by the eagle [probably the *Tityus* now in the Royal Collection], done by Giacobo Palma in concurrence with Titiano, which for the emulation between two painters (both of no small name) I dare almost say to be worthy of a corner in one of your Lordship's galleries. I have added to these a map of Italy (the country where by your favour I have received my first credit), distinguished not by the provinces, but according to the estates and governments. They shall be brought unto your Lordship by one Harry Cogan [the most obvious candidate for having conveyed to Jones his copy of Fialetti's drawing manual, *Il vero modo et ordine*, published earlier in 1608].

By the time the mosaic portrait was ready, Wotton, with an eye to the future, decided to dedicate it to Salisbury's son and heir, Viscount Cranborne. Because Cranborne was travelling in France, however, he sent it to Salisbury. In his covering letter on the theme of how works of art should be viewed, Wotton forwarded the mosaicist's 'special suit and remembrance that it may be set in his true light, and at a little more height from the eye than a coloured picture would require'. Cranborne meanwhile, in fulfilment of his father's wishes, was keeping a travel diary in schoolboy French which reveals a surprisingly sophisticated interest in the Roman remains of Bordeaux and Provence. This is almost certainly because Inigo Jones was sent out in the summer of 1609 to act as his guide on the southern stretch of Cranborne's *tour de France*. Jones returned home to work for Salisbury and Prince Henry, while – after a brief return to England necessitated by the assassination of Henry IV – Cranborne continued his journey to Venice. Here Wotton awaited him, having postponed his own departure in order to act as Cranborne's host and show him the same sites his servant had shown Coryate. Like Coryate, Cranborne was taken to Vicenza and shown its 'belles maisons' and the Teatro Olympico, 'fait depuis 25 ans par ce grand Architecte Palladius'. Albeit unpublished diary entries, these jottings are highly significant as the earliest references to Palladio by an Englishman. The publication in 1611 of Coryate's accounts of these and other Palladian buildings, including the Villa Capra, was still more significant, as it must have encouraged his friend Inigo Jones to visit them – Palladio's *Quattro libri* in hand – two years later. Jones's familiarity with Coryate's text cannot be doubted because, along with Ben Jonson, Henry Peacham, John Donne and others, he contributed satirical verses to the *Crudities*.

Jones's 1613–14 tour of Italy was arguably the most significant Grand Tour ever undertaken. This is as much because it gave the impetus to his own pioneeringly classical work as because he accompanied the Earl and Countess of Arundel, the most important patrons and collectors of art in pre-eighteenth-century England. Arundel and his wife were still Roman Catholics and, like most of their servants, Jones may then have been one too. Certainly the rest of their English acquaintance in Italy were, most notoriously the convert son of the Archbishop of York, Tobie Matthew [Fig. 31], and his 'inseparable companion' George Gage [Fig. 32], the core of a 'knot of bastard Catholics' abhorred by Wotton. While Jones and the Arundels were in Naples, acquiring books such as Summonte's history of the city [Fig. 37], comparing its illustration of the Temple of Castor and Pollux with the real thing, and riding across the Phlegraean Fields, Matthew and Gage remained in Rome buying Counter-Reformation treatises to prepare them for the priesthood. Arundel and Jones arrived back in Rome within days of their compatriots' ordination, however – an event which took place on 20 May. Arundel acquired his catalogue of the Vatican Library (now in the Beinecke Library at Yale) in Rome on 28 May. Given that Matthew and Gage were ordained by none other than Cardinal Bellarmine, it is hard to believe that Arundel would have been unaware of such an event.

Although Matthew and probably Gage also joined the Society of Jesus, rumours to this effect did not prevent Arundel and those who imitated his example as collectors, including the King and the Prince of Wales, from exploiting their diplomatic as well as artistic expertise. Despite their unsuccessful outcome, the top-level negotiations on behalf of the proposed marriage between Prince Charles and the Infanta Maria of Spain earned Matthew a knighthood, and Gage a royal reward of £375 and the temporary status of ambassador in Italy. Their Catholicism proved equally advantageous when it came to negotiating both with great Italian collectors and Flemish painters such as Rubens and Van Dyck. Sir Oliver Millar was the first to identify Gage's arms in the altar-like pedestal in Van Dyck's National Gallery portrait of a virtuoso admiring a classical statue. If the sitter is indeed Matthew's 'fidus Achates', it is appropriate that he should be admiring an androgynous sculpted figure whose sexual parts (hidden by the head of the second, presumably Italian, figure) are apparently indicated by the black servant, who grins at us in much the same way as he does in Christ Church, Oxford's *Continence of Scipio*. As Van Dyck was a devout Catholic, joining a Jesuit con-fraternity in 1628, and like Gage had a sister in a Flemish convent, he no doubt knew that Gage was a priest. As well as being described as 'the chief of the Catholics' by the Venetian ambassador, Gage was regarded as the shrewdest English connoisseur of his day. It may indeed have been he, rather than Buckingham's brother, Lord Purbeck, who first recommended Van Dyck in England, after he and

Matthew arranged Dudley Carleton's acquisition of Rubens's pictures in 1617. Gage was said to have had great influence over Rubens. Lucas Vorstermann dedicated his exquisite engraving of Van Dyck's *Lamentation* to Gage and recommended him to Arundel, along with Van Dyck, as capable of touching up an important drawing. He may even have designed the suburban villa, Tart Hall, for Lady Arundel, who certainly patronised him *qua* priest. Only John Donne's probably mistaken remark in 1611 that Gage had lost an eye tells against Van Dyck's portrait being of him.

It is then no accident that, with the possible exceptions of William Petty (part-time Anglican clergyman) and Balthazar Gerbier (who was all things to all men), the early Stuart art agents were Roman Catholics. Like Matthew and Gage, Robert Cansfield (cousin of Arundel and companion of Roos), Anthony Tracy (servant of Arundel and brother-in-law of the fellow Catholic Wenceslas Hollar), Walter Montagu (convert son of the Earl of Manchester), Nicholas Lanier (royal musician and artist), David Codner (Benedictine and probably Milton's mysterious 'Selvaggi'), Daniel Nys (French-born art dealer), Peter Fitton (Richard Lassels's friend and fellow priest) and John Price (Anthony Wood's 'greatest critic of his time') were all effectively exiled at one time or another. This rendered them trustworthy in the eyes of their continental hosts whilst keeping them anxious to please their influential compatriots. A closely related class of occasional art agents were the more respectable royal servants, Endymion Porter, Sir Dudley Carleton, Sir William Hamilton, Basil, Lord Feilding and Sir Kenelm Digby, at least three of whom were also portrayed by Van Dyck and were Catholics.

Wotton's anxiety about such characters resurfaced during his third and last embassy to the Veneto between 1621 and 1623. Unfortunately for him, this coincided with the period in which the most active patroness of the most notorious of these, the formidable Countess of Arundel, was living there in order to bring up her sons as cultured Catholics. On her journey south she was painted, with Dudley Carleton in attendance, by Rubens. Meanwhile, Van Dyck had visited England for the first time (staying in the house of Edward Norgate, Lanier's brother-in-law, during the winter of 1620–1), before joining Gage in Rome in February 1622. Gage's portrait would thus have been painted between February and July 1622, when fellow ambassador (and Catholic) Sir Robert Shirley arrived and had his portrait, complete with the pendant of his Circassian wife, painted by Van Dyck. Gage left Rome at the end of July, no doubt calling on the Countess of Arundel on his way home. Later in the year Van Dyck too visited Lady Arundel and her sons in the Veneto. Wotton had maintained an artistic as well as a diplomatic correspondence with the Gonzagas since at least as early as 1606 (see above, pp. 162–7) and, despite the crisis in his relationship with Lady Arundel following the execution of Foscarini, it may have been he who first established contact between her and Chancellor Striggi of Mantua over the sale of the Mantuan collections, which she inspected with Van Dyck in late 1622. After a six-month tour of the rest of the northern Italian cities, she parted company with Van Dyck, who returned south for the rest of his six-year tour of Italy.

The Countess returned to London, bringing with her the collection of paintings Van Dyck had admired in her palazzo on the Grand Canal and her Palladian villa on the Brenta at Dolo ('del motcenigo al duolo'), a gondola, two black slaves, a variety of plants and a consignment of 'prodigious edible snails'. Significantly, she had also ordered a model of Giulio Romano's Palazzo del Te which Inigo Jones had admired in Mantua some ten years earlier when acting as her cicerone. In May 1625, within weeks of coming to the throne, Charles I dispatched his extraordinarily versatile Master of Music, Nicholas Lanier, 'to provide for him some choice Pictures in Italie', but in particular to negotiate the purchase of the Gonzaga collection, all under the pretext of a Holy Year pilgrimage so as not to 'enhance the prices'. It was doubtless at this time that Van Dyck painted his Italianate three-quarter length of Lanier in a seven-day sitting which would have begun with the black and white chalk drawing now in the National Gallery of Scotland. A 'retratto di detto Sig. Nicolo' features in the export licence obtained by Lanier later that year, and Sir Peter Lely is reported to have said that 'this was the picture wch being showed to King Charles ye first caused him to give order that V. Dyck should be sent over into England'. Now, and again in 1627, Lanier established himself in the mysterious Daniel Nys's house on Murano, acquiring one of the first English collections of old master drawings (some of which he later etched and published) whilst haggling for pictures with the *ancien régime* Mantuans on behalf of his nouveau-cultured patrons in England. For he was employed not just by the King but by the Duke of Buckingham, whose collection already rivalled Arundel's, thanks to the likes of Henry Wotton (whose gift of 'a great many pictures' and plans of Caprarola helped obtain him the Provostship of Eton), and Balthazar Gerbier, who in 1621 toured Italy on Buckingham's behalf to return home with a superb collection of Bassanos, Tintorettos and Titian's *Ecce Homo*, now in the Kunsthistorisches Museum in Vienna.

That even Lanier was a Catholic is suggested by the appearance of his name and that of his wife, Elizabeth – along with Lady Arundel's – among a list of Chiswick recusants drawn up after the calling of Parliament in 1640. He was less confidently established in continental Catholic circles than Gage, Matthew or Montagu, however, so that the 1640s were a disaster for him. It was probably during the siege of Oxford that he painted and presented his slightly melancholy self-portrait to the Music Faculty, where it is still to be found [Fig. 43]. By 1646 he was writing from Antwerp that he was 'old, unhappye in a manner in exile, plundered not only of his fortune, but of all his musical papers, nay almost of his witts and vertue'. When the magnificent royal collections he had helped create were sold following the execution of his master, he managed to buy back Van Dyck's portrait of him for £10 (as well as Bellini's *Concert* and other pictures) before returning abroad. In the 1650s we hear of him designing a low-budget entertainment for the exiled Marquis of Newcastle, who was renting Rubens's house in Antwerp. Van Dyck himself, meanwhile, had tried to leave England when he realized that the calling of Parliament signalled the end of civilization as he knew it. He died on a return visit from Antwerp in 1641.

Many who had taken advantage of the opportunities for travel in the 1630s found themselves travelling abroad in the following two decades whether they wished to or not. Meanwhile, a hundred years after Hoby's first mention of Michelangelo, the Interregnum tourist Francis Mortoft talked incoherently in his comparable travel journal of 'that rare engraver Isaac Angelo'. The aesthetic progress possible within a single tour is, however, demonstrated by Mortoft's getting 'Michael Angelo' right in Rome just three months after getting him wrong in Florence. By this time (February 1659) he was, moreover, discovering the sculpture of 'the famous Barnino' (whom Nicholas Stone junior had interviewed twenty years earlier). John Bargrave, Royalist exile, nephew of one of Wotton's heirs and ejected Fellow of Peterhouse, described himself as Bernini's 'neighbour and friendly acquaintance'. He did the best he could to educate his teenage pupils, Alexander Chapman and John Raymond, who with his help

43 Nicholas Lanier,
Self-portrait (c.1644).
[Faculty of Music,
Oxford]

composed the first English guidebook to Italy, the *Itinerary* (1649).
With the great patron-collectors either dead or in exile, Bargrave
collected for himself on a doll's-house scale. His fascinating cabinet
of curiosities – together with his riding boots – survives to this day
in the Library of Canterbury Cathedral. In contrast to Gage and
Lanier (who had exchanged paintings with Guido Reni and was
drawn by him), when Bargrave wanted his portrait done he had to
resort to Reni's relatively obscure but no doubt cheap Siena-based
follower, Matteo Bolognini [Fig. 17]. Pointing proudly to the map of
Italy, flanked by his Royalist protégés, it was nevertheless men
such as Bargrave, with Richard Symonds, note-compiling gentleman
connoisseur *par excellence*, and Richard Lassels, impoverished
Catholic cosmopolitan, who maintained English interest in art
through the traumatic middle years of the century. Even if the
Restoration failed to restore the appreciation of art in England to

quite the level it had achieved under Charles I, the efforts of the pioneering Grand Tourists were not in vain.

Charles II was, above all, concerned never to be sent 'on his travels again' and so, although pleased to receive diplomatic gifts in the form of paintings, he never went to the expensive lengths his father and his ministers had done in order to seek out works of art. The Grand Tour, on the other hand, flourished as never before and became increasingly art-orientated. Cromwell had established Britain's military might and despite degrading set-backs, particularly at the hands of the Dutch, Britain was becoming a major world power. Louis XIV still dominated Europe both militarily and culturally, however. Charles was a Francophile owing to his years in exile in his mother's country and, if anything, the French orientation increased under his openly Catholic brother, James II. The Glorious Revolution did little to undermine French taste in England, any more than war with France had done in Holland. As our understanding of the sources of post-Renaissance civilization deepened, however, so too did the significance of Italy as the ultimate destination for the Grand Tourist. This process was encouraged by the return of travellers such as Sir Thomas Isham and the 5th Earl of Exeter, laden with Italian prints and pictures. Albeit based largely upon French art-historical expertise, the publications of Jonathan Richardson, culminating in his and his more travelled son's *Account of some of the Statues, Bas-Reliefs, Drawings and Pictures in Italy*, together with Robert Samber's more specifically derivative *Roma Illustrata* (which also appeared in 1722), concentrated that focus upon the arts of Italy which remained the essential ingredient of our civilization until recent, more populist times.

NOTE

An abridged version of this chapter was first published as 'Pilgrims to Pictures' in the special issue of *Country Life* entitled 'The Age of Charles I' (4 October 1990), pp. 146–9.

9

Notes towards a Biography of Sir Balthazar Gerbier

❧

S IR BALTHAZAR GERBIER was born in Middelburg in Holland on
23 February 1592. His father was a Huguenot émigré by the
name of Anthony and Gerbier was to claim that his great-grandfather was 'Anthony Gerbier, Baron Douvilly', a title he used
himself on at least one occasion. He may have been a pupil of
Hendrik Goltzius (of whom he published a verse eulogy in 1620), but
seems to have come to the attention of Prince Maurice thanks to his
knowledge of the 'framing of warlike machines'. Gerbier's elaborate
pen and ink equestrian portrait of the prince, dated 1616, is in the
British Museum, as is his later drawing of Frederick of Bohemia.
On Maurice's recommendation, Gerbier accompanied the Dutch
Ambassador, Noël de Caron, to London in 1616 and in the same
year he painted the heir to the throne, Prince Charles. In his
Graphice (1658, p. 15), William Sanderson says that Gerbier 'had
little of Art, or merit; a common Pen-man, who Pensil'd the *Deca-
logue* in the *Dutch* Church LONDON; his first rise of preferment'.
 Within two or three years of his arrival in England, Gerbier
entered the service of George Villiers, Marquis and soon 1st Duke of
Buckingham, whose miniature equestrian portrait he painted in
1618 (Duke of Northumberland's collection). In 1619 he painted the
far more successful miniature of Prince Maurice in the Queen of the
Netherlands collection (G.C. Williamson, Plate XIX). In the same
year, 'he began to have the keeping of [Buckingham's] pictures and
other rarities' and was clearly instrumental in the spectacularly rapid
growth of the duke's collections. That he was initially employed for
artistic rather than diplomatic skills is indicated by his first major
mission on Buckingham's behalf. Bodleian Library, MS Tanner 73,

44 Paulus Pontius after Van Dyck, engraving of Sir Balthazar Gerbier (1634). [E. Chaney]

folios 122-3, 'Reckening what the pictures of Milord Admiral doe cost, whit the Charges and Fraemes', reveals details of a very successful journey to Venice in 1621 during which Gerbier acquired three Bassanos, Titian's *Ecce Homo* (now in Vienna) and Tintoretto's *Woman taken in Adultery*. It was probably in this year also that Gerbier made the copies of Raphael's frescoes in the Farnesina which Edward Norgate – a relative by marriage – praised in his *Miniatura* as 'The best Crayons that I ever saw'. (Gerbier also copied the Farnese Hercules so well that Norgate claimed that his drawing was 'the admiration of all the Italians who saw it'.) Meanwhile, he arranged for larger copies of the Farnesina frescoes to be made by a Florentine artist and purchased works by Guido Reni.

The following year, however, we hear of Gerbier keeping the duke's cyphers and being sent on his first diplomatic mission to Brussels. Buckingham seems to have sat for his portrait by Gerbier but the result was not deemed a success (Carpenter, p. 57). A measure of the esteem in which he was now held was that he was chosen to join Buckingham and Prince Charles on their initially secret journey to Spain in 1623. Here he painted the Infanta Dona Maria, whom the Prince was intending to marry, and arranged for the transport of Giambologna's *Samson slaying a Philistine* to the Strand Mansion, York House, which Buckingham had acquired from Francis Bacon, and its 'setting up before the new building' there. In 1624-5 Gerbier supervised major alterations at York House, in the wake of Inigo Jones's departure, and at Buckingham's country house, New Hall, in Essex, later implying that he had designed the former's 35-square-foot 'Great Chamber'. He insinuated that in 1628 Charles I praised this room as the equal of the Banqueting House, but this may merely be indicative of Gerbier's growing rivalry with Jones, to whose position as Surveyor of the King's Works, he aspired. (See Jacob Esselens's drawing in *King's Arcadia*, p. 202.) According to Gerbier, Jones himself came to York House 'pour veoir la Mayson et estoit comme confus et honteux, il ne me faudroit plus que la reversion de la passe pour luy faire aveoir la gravelle car il en est, fort jaloux'. Gerbier may have helped complete the once prominent York House Water-Gate, but Jones is more likely to have begun it (there is a later drawing of it by John Webb), and it was probably built by Nicholas Stone who, according to his nephew, 'desined' it as well. Gerbier was referred to by contemporaries as an architect and the possibility of his later involvement in architectural design is discussed by Howard Colvin in *The Canterbury Quadrangle, St John's College* (Oxford, 1988) as well as in his *Biographical Dictionary*.

By January 1625/6 Gerbier was important enough to be receiving ingratiating letters from the likes of Isaac Wake, the ambassador to Venice (Tanner MS 72, folio 68). In February 1625 he felt able to inform Buckingham that 'out of the amateurs, and Princes and Kings, there is not one who has collected in forty years as many pictures as your Excellency has collected in five.' Later that year, while accompanying Buckingham to Paris on the mission to bring Henrietta Maria to England, Gerbier met Rubens, who took time off from painting the Marie de Medicis cycle at the Luxembourg Palace to begin the great equestrian portrait of the duke destined for the Great Chamber. This commission would no doubt have been organized by Gerbier, who had eulogized Rubens in print – the first to do so – as early as 1620 in his poem on Goltzius. Though it is probable that they knew each other from the second decade of the century, it is only from the mid-1620s that we can document the friendship between these two artist/diplomats.

In about 1618 Gerbier had married Debora Kipp through whose father, the Utrecht-born jeweller and engraver, William, he was to inherit property in Bethnal Green ('Returns of Aliens', *Huguenot Society*, X, 3 (1908), p. 194; I thank Ole Grell for this reference). In view of Gerbier's later involvement in triumphal arches, it may be significant that William Kipp engraved Stephen Harrison's 1603 arches. Gerbier's father-in-law, with whom the newly married couple lived in Candlewick Street, is also referred to as one who could frame pictures. The Titian portraying Georges d'Armagnac and his secretary, which Gerbier acquired for Buckingham in France in 1624 and which Inigo Jones 'almost went down on his knees before' when he saw it in York House, was framed by Kipp. In December 1626 Buckingham sent Gerbier to Paris (*Calendar of State Papers Venetian*, p. 54) to sound out whether he would himself be welcome to Bassompierre and the Queen Mother. At the same time, it seems, another visit to Italy was being contemplated, 'the Duke sending . . . one of his gentlemen abroad very often'; A.M. Crinò, 'The Date of Orazio Gentileschi's Arrival in London', *Burlington Magazine*, CIX (1967), p. 533. In the summer of 1627, Gerbier and Rubens met again in Holland, 'walking from towne to towne upon theyr pretence of pictures' but, in fact, attempting to negotiate a peace treaty between England and Spain. A contract between Buckingham and Gerbier, now in the library of Lady Fairfax of Cameron, which must date from the first half of 1628, confirms that Gerbier had been given charge of Buckingham (York) House since 1619 at the latest and records that he had taken a 31-year lease on the house at the east side of the gatehouse, for which he would pay yearly on the birthday of Buckingham's new-born heir, George, Earl of Coventry. The agreement continues:

> It is also my pleasure that whensoever Orazio Gentileschi His Majesty's picture maker doth remove from the lodging . . . which are adjoining to this said house . . . that the two upstairs rooms towards the street which are in the same body of the said house shall appertain and be fully to the use of the said Balthasar Gerbier . . . with the kitchen and the great upper room in which the said Orazio Gentileschi is making at this present his pictures.

Following Buckingham's assassination in August 1628, Gerbier became a British citizen and was appointed 'esquire of his Majesty's body extraordinary'. He had remained in contact with Rubens whilst negotiating the acquisition of his great art collection for Buckingham, negotiations which acted as a cover for a secretly planned peace treaty between England and the Habsburgs. Thus, when Rubens came to England in May 1629 on the artistic/diplomatic mission which resulted in his knighthood, he and his brother-in-law spent most of the following winter (7 December–22 February 1630) in Gerbier's house. On Rubens's arrival, Gerbier had displeased the then Master of Ceremonies, Sir John Finet, by allowing Rubens 'one of his majestyes barges' to carry him to Greenwich to be introduced to the king when he was not a 'qualifyed ambassador' (Finet, p. 62). Gerbier seems to have divided his time between York House and Bethnal Green, which he gave as his address on at least two occasions that winter. It was in this period, while Gerbier was busy supervising the completion of Le Sueur's equestrian statue of Charles I and its garden setting at Lord Treasurer Weston's villa at Roehampton, that Rubens painted the famous group portrait of Gerbier's wife and children (Washington) which Gerbier later had copied and enlarged into the picture now in the Royal collection. (See the two interesting notes by George Vertue: British Library, Add MS 23090, fols 61–3, 105 and cf. C. Whitfield, *cit.* below.). Rubens also used George, Gerbier's eldest

son, as the model for Hymen in his *Allegory of Peace and War* for
Charles I.

As the trusted servant of Buckingham, Gerbier continued to be
shown great favour by Charles I, who stood godfather to his son
and, in the spring of 1631, appointed him 'His Ma.ies Agent' at
Brussels. (Instructions: PRO SP 77/20/27–35, issued 7 May and 7
June 1631.) In late June he arrived with 'all his Family' in Brussels,
where they found a house in 'new stryte' (SP 77/20/69). He soon
embroiled himself in a plot against the Spanish, then switched sides
to conspire against the French, and is said to have sold the names
of Belgian conspirators to the Infanta Isabella, an act which seems
to have resulted in several executions and compromised Charles. He
also failed to dissuade Marie de Medicis from going into exile in
England. He was more successful in obtaining overdue payment for
Rubens's canvases for the Banqueting House ceiling, so that these
were finally unrolled, retouched and sent off in October 1635.
Though the Hispanophile and crypto-Catholic minister, Francis
Cottington, probably knew of Gerbier's treachery, Charles I seems to
have been kept in the dark about it, for he knighted him in October
1638 and on 10 May 1641, shortly before his definitive return from
Brussels, appointed him Master of Ceremonies.

In 1636 Gerbier had sent back from Brussels a portrait of the Duke
of Lorraine and another of the Elector of Treves 'by a good Master
named Crayer' which 'his Majestie well liked'. As early as December
1631 he had sent Weston 'a very beautiful Virgin and St Catherine
by the hand of Van Dyck' as a New Year's gift for either the king or
queen. For various 'malicious' reasons, by March 1632 Van Dyck
was saying the picture was not by his hand and Gerbier was having
to defend himself to Weston. He insisted that 'Le Sr. Rubens . . .
knows it to be by the hand of Van Dyck; and, moreover, the said
Van Dyck, having an intention of going into England, thanked me
by word of mouth, for having sent this same picture, being the one
which the Infanta had caused to be placed in the chapel of the
Queen Mother, when she was at her court . . .' (Horne, p. 119
citing Carpenter, p. 507). In 1634, Gerbier and Rubens again combined forces to persuade an Antwerp printer to sell his Greek types
and matrices to Archbishop Laud (H.R. Trevor-Roper, *Archbishop
Laud 1573–1645* (London and New York, 1962), pp. 274–5).
Gerbier's last Flemish negotiation (1639–40), involved coordinating
between Inigo Jones (probably via John Webb; see the latter's copy

of Palladio in Worcester College, Oxford), the Abbé Scaglia and Jacob Jordaens, who had been commissioned to provide panels depicting the story of Cupid and Psyche for the Queen's House at Greenwich. Having ascertained that a landscape depicting the Escorial praised by Edward Norgate to Charles I as being by Rubens was in fact by Verhulst, Gerbier went on to acquire it for the king, having had it completed under the supervision of Rubens a month before the latter's death.

With his experience of international banking (and pawnbrokers), Gerbier now proposed that the bankrupt Charles I establish a national bank-cum-Monte di Pietà. Unfortunately, in giving evidence before the House of Lords on the treatment of English merchants abroad, Gerbier could not resist accusing Lord Cottington of high treason in betraying the secrets he had himself betrayed to the Habsburgs. With an aggressive Parliament already hounding him and his ministers, Charles was furious and Gerbier's reputation with the Royalists never recovered. He was effectively dismissed as Master of Ceremonies and his hopes of obtaining the reversion of the Surveyorship of the King's Works were ended, Jones having apparently always opposed his candidature, no doubt the source of an undercurrent of hostility towards Jones's work which pervades Gerbier's subsequent writings.

Questioned by Parliamentary commissioners over a Royalist plot in October 1642 and persecuted by Puritan neighbours who accused him of being a Papist, Gerbier finally left for France in 1643, taking his long-suffering family with him. He almost persuaded the French to adopt his banking scheme, but Royalist exiles such as Sir Kenelm Digby, who seduced his daughter, and William Crofts, who told Anne of Austria that Gerbier 'had destroyed all the King of England's affairs', helped prevent this and other schemes coming to fruition. Having sent advance publicity to be distributed by the educationalist Samuel Hartlib, and having established his Protestant credentials by publishing *A Letter . . . to his three daughters enclosed in a Nunnery at Paris*, Gerbier returned to England after the execution of the King, and on 19 July 1649 opened a continental-style academy in Bethnal Green for the sons of gentlemen. *The Interpreter of the Acadamie* of 1648 contains details of what was to be taught: foreign languages and 'riding the great horse', as well as anti-Copernican cosmography, more sophisticated architecture, perspective, drawing, limning, engraving and fortification. It also praises Italian art and architecture and classical sculpture, including the *Venus de' Medici* (then still in Rome). When insufficient numbers turned up to hear his lectures he published them, together with other pamphlets more specifically designed to curry favour with the new regime. These included a revised version of his banking project, a scheme proposed jointly with George Geldorp and Peter Lely to decorate the Banqueting Hall with military portraits, and the 'memorable achievements' of the Long Parliament. Most obnoxious of all, if it is indeed by him, was the anonymously published *Nonesuch Charles*, which disparages his former benefactor, at whose court 'great sums were squandered away on braveries and vanities; on old rotten pictures, on broken-nosed marbles'. The tone of this pamphlet is consistent with that of the letter to Cromwell and Bulstrode Whitelocke of 1 March 1652 and the accomanying *Summary Relation* of Gerbier's services to Parliament since 1642 (British Library, Add. MS, 32,093, fols 302–7). Given his superior knowledge and contacts, Gerbier no doubt made most of his money in this period from dealing in the pictures which had formerly belonged to Charles and Buckingham and which Parliament sold off or gave to its creditors in the early 1650s. Among others, he 'bought the picture of the late King on horseback [presumably the Van Dyck now at Buckingham Palace] for £200 and that of Charles V Emperor [Charles I's Titian] for £150'. On 18 June 1652 we catch a glimpse of Gerbier chatting with the poet and ambassador, Jacob Cats, in Chelsea (Huygens, *Journal*, p. 144).

Following his revelation of a supposed conspiracy against Cromwell's life, in 1658 Gerbier was paid by the Council of State to find out more by mingling with the Royalists in Holland. Not surprisingly, Clarendon considered him 'too infamous a fellow to be trusted even by the rebels', and he failed to obtain significant information. He therefore persuaded the Dutch government to finance a scheme to send him and his family to Guiana in search of a gold mine he had learned of in Spain in 1623. After an extraordinary voyage, from which he was sent back by the Dutch themselves and by mutineers who murdered his daughter Catherine, Gerbier once more published an indignant account, claiming to have been the victim of a conspiracy. In 1660 he also published two pamphlets promoting plantations in America.

Although official records show that he lost his post as Master of Ceremonies at the Restoration, Gerbier dedicated his *Brief Discourse concerning the Three Chief Principles of Magnificent Building* to Charles II in 1662, implying that the post was still his and reminding the king that 'the Place of Surveyor Generall was also intended to me (after late *Inigo Jones*)'. He may have designed the triumphal arches for the king's 1660 reception and he certainly proposed to level the London streets of Fleetbridge and Cheapside and to make a sumptuous gate at Temple Bar 'whereof he had presented a draught to his Majesty'. A year later he followed this with the more substantial *Counsel and Advice to all Builders* in which, among other things, he ridicules the heads of lions which were creeping through the (capitals of the?) pilasters on the houses in Great Queen Street built by John Webb. By the time the latter book was published, Gerbier had entered the employ of William, 1st Earl of Craven, in whose regiment his playwright son George had served, and was designing a large mansion for his patron (perhaps out of an earlier structure) at Hampstead Marshall in Berkshire. (The numerous drawings in Bodleian Library, MS Gough a.2 date from 1662 onwards.) Here, according to Gerbier's tomb in the local church, he 'built a stately pile of Building in the years 1662 to 1665 . . . the greatest part of which was destroyed by Fire in the year 1718. He died in the year 1667.' This account, however, is inaccurate for by 24 August 1663 Gerbier's daughters were already petitioning the king for relief, apparently six months after their father's death (PRO SP Dom Entry Book 44, xiii, p. 352). A few of the 40 dedications of the *Counsel and Advice* can be internally dated to the spring of 1663 at the earliest, as can that of the 1665 *Subsidium Peregrinantibus* to James, Duke of York, as a 'Princely Traveller' and Knight of the Garter (28 March 1663). Sir Howard Colvin has found further confirmation of the earlier date of death in a 1666 note by Elias Ashmole to the effect that Gerbier was buried at Hampstead Marshall but as yet without a monument (Bodleian Library, Ashmole MS 850, fol. 159). Hampstead Marshall was completed by William Winde, the last of the 40 dedicatees of the *Counsel and Advice to all Builders* and Craven's godson. There is a pre-1709 view of the building in Kip's *Britannia Illustrata*.

The contradictions inherent in Gerbier's disastrous diplomatic career were almost equally evident in his artistic and literary career. Whether or not he knew of his recent death, Samuel Pepys may be said to have provided his epitaph. Though he apparently admired Gerbier enough to have acquired a major collection of his original drawings, the 'Armoiries Royales', as well as proof engravings after his work, after purchasing the second of the two architectural treatises he expressed his regrets in no uncertain terms in a diary entry of 28 May 1663:

> At the Coffee-house in Exchange-alley I bought a little book, *Counsell to Builders*, written by Sir Balth. Gerbier; it is dedicated almost to all the men of any great condition in England, so that the epistles are more than the book itself; and both it and them not worth a turd, that I am ashamed that I bought it.

REFERENCES

Betcherman, Lita-Rose, 'Balthazar Gerbier in seventeenth-century Italy', *History Today* (May 1961), pp. 325–31.
— 'The York House Collection and its Keeper', *Apollo*, XCII (1970), pp. 250–9.
Bodleian Library, Tanner MSS 72, fols. 73, fols. 491v. and 510v.
British Library, Add MSS 32,093, fols. 302–7.
Brookes, Anne, *Sir Balthazar Gerbier . . .* (MA dissertation, Oxford Brookes University, 1992).
Carpenter, W.H., *Pictorial Notices, consisting of a Memoir of Sir Anthony Van Dyck* (London, 1844).
Cheetham, F.H., 'Hampstead Marshall and Sir Balthazar Gerbier', *Notes and Queries*, 118, VII (1913), pp. 406–8.
Colvin, Howard, *A Biographical Dictionary of British Architects 1600–1840*. 3rd edn (London, 1995).
Croft-Murray, E., and Hulton, P. *Catalogue of British Drawings in the British Museum* (London, 1960), pp. 328–30.
Davies, R., *The Greatest House at Chelsey* (London, 1914).
De Boer, M.G., 'Balthazar Gerbier', *Oud Holland* (1903).
Finet, J., *Ceremonies of Charles I: The Notebooks of John Finet 1628–1641*, ed. Albert J. Loomie (New York, 1987).
Freedberg, David, 'Fame, Convention and Insight: on the relevance of Fornenbergh and Gerbier', *Ringling Museum of Art Journal*, 1 (1983), pp. 236–59.
Grell, Ole, *Calvinist Exiles in Tudor and Stuart England* (Aldershot, 1996).
Goodman, Godfrey, *Court of King James I*, ed. J.S. Brewer, 2 vols (London, 1839).
Horne, Herbert, 'The Ventures of Sir Balthazar Gerbier . . .', *Hobby Horse*, no. 3 (1894), pp. 97–120.
Huygens, Lodewijck, *The English Journal 1651–1652*, ed. A.G.H. Bachrach and R.G. Collmer (Leiden, 1982).
Lockyer, Roger, *Buckingham* (London, 1981).
McEvansoneya, Philip, *The Houses of the Duke of Buckingham* (MA dissertation, Courtauld Institute, London, 1985).
— 'Some Documents concerning the Patronage and Collections of the Duke of Buckingham', *Rutgers Art Review*, VIII (1987), pp. 27–38.
Pepys Library, Magdalene College, Cambridge: 'Armoiries Royales (tant anciennes

que modernes) du Chevalier Balthazar Gerbier' (205 leaves of drawings in pen
and ink and watercolour). Also David Loggan engravings after Gerbier's drawings
before titles, etc. added in Ogilby's *Entertainment of Charles II.*
Philip, I.G., 'Balthazar Gerbier and the Duke of Buckingham's Pictures', *Burlington
Magazine*, XCIV (1957), pp. 155-6.
Power, M.J., 'Sir Balthazar Gerbier's Academy at Bethnal Green', *East London
Papers*, X, 1 (1967), pp. 19-33.
Public Record Office, E 178/5973.
Public Record Office, SP 105/7-18.
Rubens, Sir Peter Paul, *Correspondance de Rubens*, ed. M. Rooses and C. Ruelens, 6
vols (Antwerp, 1887-1909).
Sainsbury, W.N., *Original unpublished papers illustrative of the life of Sir Peter Paul
Rubens . . .* (London, 1859).
Stechow, Wolfgang, 'Deborah Kip, Wife of Sir Balthazar Gerbier, and her Children',
Studies in the History of Art, National Gallery of Art (Washington, DC, 1973), pp.
7-22.
Whitfield, Clovis, 'Balthazar Gerbier, Rubens, and George Vertue', *Studies in the
History of Art*, National Gallery of Art (Washington, DC, 1973), pp. 23-31.
Williamson, G.C., *History of Portrait Miniatures* (London, 1904), I.
Williamson, Hugh Ross, *Four Stuart Portraits* (London, 1949), pp. 26-60.

WORKS BY GERBIER

Balthazar Gerbier, Knight, to all men that loves trath [sic] (Rouen, 1646).
*The most humble expression of Sir Balthazar Gerbier concerning his integrity and zeale to
this state and nation* (London, 1649).
The Interpreter of the Academie for Forrain Languages and all noble sciences and exercises
(London, 1649).
A Manifestation by Sr Balthazar Gerbier Kt (London, 1651).
The None-such Charles his Character . . . (London, 1651).
A brief Discourse concerning the three chief Principles of Magnificent Building (London,
1662).
Counsel and Advise to all Builders (London, 1663) (dedication to Holles: 'if during
absence any of your habitations require Overseers' etc., implies post-July 1663
date).
Subsidium Peregrinantibus: or an assistance to a Traveller in his convers . . . (Oxford,
1665).

10

English Catholic Poets in mid-Seventeenth-Century Rome

A MAJOR STUDY of the closely linked group of English Catholics who lived and wrote poetry in Italy in the mid-seventeenth century is long overdue. Among them were some of the most highly respected Latin poets in Europe, true heirs to the international reputations of George Buchanan (1506-82), the 'Admirable' James Crighton (1560-82), John Owen (*c.*1560-1622), Thomas Dempster (1579-1625) and John Barclay (1582-1621), whose bust by François Duquesnoy is still to be found in the Museo Tassiano at S. Onofrio.

Though much has been written about Richard Crashaw in recent years and a volume of Patrick Cary's *Poems* is now in print (ed. V. Delany, Oxford, 1978), few today will have heard of James Gibbes. Douglas Bush, for one, fails to mention him when he names 'the only poets of British birth who achieved continental fame' in his introduction to the Latin and Greek poems of Milton (*A Variorum Commentary on the Poems of John Milton*, I (London, 1970), pp. 4-5). In his lifetime, however, Gibbes was regarded as the 'Horace of this age'. This phrase, which Wood adapted for his *Athenae* entry (II, pp. 338-42) occurred first in Lassels's *Voyage of Italy* (Paris and London, 1670, II, p. 231). As it is not to be found in Lassels's 1664 *Voyage* manuscript (now in the Beinecke Library, Yale University) it may have been introduced into the published text by Simon Wilson, who was resident in Rome contemporaneously with Gibbes from 1644-51 and there again soon after he received laureation. Having pointed out that both he and Dr Hart were Readers at the Sapienza, the *Voyage* also described Gibbes as 'a *Noble Caesarean Laureat Poët*'. This was a reference to the fact that the Emperor Leopold 'was pleas'd to honour him with the title of poet laureat; at the same time bestowing upon him a golden chain and medal to be worn upon all solemn occasions. The *Diploma* for this dignity bear's date *May* 2d 1667' (C. Dodd, *The Church History of England* (London, 1737), III, p. 274).

James Alban Gibbes was born in 1611 at Valognes, about 60 miles from Caen (see the *Dictionary of National Biography* (*DNB*) and confirmation in the Padua *Registro* entry cited below, though Dodd and Joseph Gillow's *Bibliographical Dictionary*, say he was born in Rouen in 1616). His father, William, who was from Bristol and eventually became physician to Henrietta Maria, had been converted to Catholicism by his wife, Mary Stonor. It was because of their religion that they were in France at the time of James's birth. The family returned to England in about 1620. Some five years later James was sent to study at St Omer's College (*Catholic Record Society* (CRS), LXIX (1979), p. 114). By the late 1630s he was tutoring Philip, the son of Endymion Porter 'wanting his money matters settled that he may go abroad to Padua or Bologna to complete his medical studies' (D. Townshend, *Life and Letters of Endymion Porter* (London, 1897), p. 129). He arrived in Padua late in 1641, signing the University *Registro* with William Pound on 1 November of that year. (H. Brown (ed.), *Inglesi e Scozzesi all'Università di Padova* (Venice, 1921), p. 153, does not give his signature exactly as it appears: 'Jacobus Gibbes Normanusmensis Cadomensis. Nov. 1° an° 1641'; see Biblioteca del Seminario Patavino Cod. 634, p. 64.) Having studied under the famous anatomist Veslingius for three years,

> In 1644 he removed to *Rome*; and was, soon after, made tutor to *Almericus*, son of *Francis*, duke of *Modena*. Having spent two years in this honourable employment, he was entertain'd in quality of physician by *Bernardini*, cardinal *Spada*, bishop of *Frescatti*; and after his death, was a domestick to prince *Justiniani*. (Dodd, III, p. 274)

According to Evelyn, in November 1644 Gibbes, whom he considered 'an incomparable Poet', also 'had dependance of Cardinal [Luigi] Cap[p]oni'. In January 1645 Evelyn was shown around the Ospedale di Santo Spirito by 'Dr Gibb's a famous poet & Countryman of Ours who had some intendency' there (see *Diary*, II, pp. 213, 311) and below, p. 258. On 20 February 1649, arriving back in Rome with his pupils after a tour to Naples, Sicily and Malta, Isaac Basire consulted Gibbes who instructed him to 'abstinere se a cibis, tempore quadragesimae, usitatis et vesci carnibus' (Durham Dean and

Chapter Library, Hunter MSS. 134, fol. 10, as cited by Colin Brennen in his unpublished PhD dissertation on Basire (University of Durham, 1987), p. 69). John Bargrave also mentions 'Dr. Gibbs, an English physician at Rome, who in his poems writeth himself Albanus Gibbetius, my worthy acquaintance, and one of the orators at the Sapientia, where I have heard him on several public affairs make learned orations with a graceful pronunciation'. He confirms that Gibbes was of Cardinal Spada's 'seguità . . . and much in favour with the Cardinal, as being both poetical, – he gave me this insuing hexastichon.' There follows: 'De Angliae Rege Necato . . .' in Gibbes's original and Bargrave's translation (see Bargrave, *Pope Alexander the seventh . . .* ed. J.G. Robertson, *Camden Society*, XCII (London, 1867), pp. 23–4).

> . . . in the year 1657, pope *Alexander* VII . . . made him professor of rhetorick in the noted school *Sapienza*. This employment brought him sixty pounds *per an.* which, together with certain perquisites, and a *sine cure*, made him very easy in his circumstances. All this while he was much admir'd for his ingenious performances in poetry, not only by the *Italians*, but by the emperor *Leopold* . . . (Dodd)

Dodd's account should be supplemented by the documents dis-covered and published by A. Bertolotti in an article almost as 'poco conosciuto' as its subject, 'Un professore alla Sapienza di Roma nel secolo XVII poco conosciuto', *Il Buonarroti*, ser. III, part ii, quaderno 8 (Rome, 1886), pp. 249–58, which identifies Gibbes as a patron of Pietro da Cortona. Da Cortona and Salvator Rosa contributed the portrait and frontispiece, respectively, for Gibbes's *Carminum* (1668).

In 1670 Gibbes presented his gold chain, his medal and a fair copy of his poems to the University of Oxford, who in turn made him an honorary MD: 'This ingenious author died 6. calend. *Julii* an 1677. aged 66, and was interr'd in the *Pantheon*, otherwise cal'd *St Maria rotunda*.' Dodd finishes his account with a short bibliography of Gibbes's writings of which a more complete list is given by Bertolotti (op. cit., pp. 11–12). Unnoticed by the latter, however, or by the *DNB*, is the interesting series of letters from Gibbes to Hill printed in *Familiar Letters which passed between Abraham Hill, Esq [FRS] and several eminent . . . persons . . .* (London, 1767, pp. 29–44). Beginning in January 1659 from Rome, the last of these is dated 1 December 1664 and addressed from Naples. In his second letter to Hill, dated Rome 15 February 1659, Gibbes writes: 'Father *Kircher* desires to be remember'd to you, as do the lords *Somerset* and *Gerard*, *Cavendish and Roscommon*. The two latter are procuring licences to visit Naples, which, if they obtain, in all likelihood I shall travel so far with them.' See *Francis Mortoft, His Book*, ed. M. Letts (Hakluyt Society, 1925, p. 76), though Letts is mistaken in stating that 'Lord Candish' is the future Duke of Newcastle; the latter was in Antwerp at the time. This is the 19-year-old future Duke of Devonshire, the builder of Chatsworth. Lord Roscommon is Wentworth Dillon, the numismatist and poet whom Dryden was to praise for his *Essay on Translated Verse* (1684); see *DNB*. The Jesuit scholar, Athanasius Kircher, whose 'cabinet' at the Sapienza was a major attraction at Rome, was to write commendatory verses in Gibbes's Horatian *Carminum . . . Pars Lyrica* (Rome, 1668). Gibbes's subsequent letters, dated Messina, 29 June 1661 (p. 37), 1 September, Naples, 1663 (p. 40) and, finally, Naples again, 1 December 1664 (p. 44), suggest that he remained in the south of Italy for about four years (but cf. P. Skippon, *Account of a Journey* (London, 1732), p. 650). In the last letter he writes:

> I have settled my affairs in such a manner as to set out next week for England. The pleasure I feel at the hopes of seeing my friends and yourself in particular is inexpressible [meanwhile he continues to collect coins and curiosities for Hill] and I shall see you, in all probability very soon.

That he had still not left Rome for the south in February 1661 is suggested by a letter in the Westminster Cathedral Archives (WCA) (Old Brotherhood Archives, II, doc. no. 68) dated the 22nd of that month. In it, Francis Gage, the clergy agent in Rome, writes – probably to John Sergeant in London:

> This inclosed for Mr Belson, I know not whether it be for the father or the sonne; it comes from one Doctor Gibbes, who heares that Mr Belson hath done him some favour in advancing his pretensions to the inheritance of Besse Gibbes his sister, as Mr Wright the painter tells him . . . the Dr is an honest fellow and will deserve their courtesy.

For Belson's visit to the English College during the late 1640s, see *Records of the English Province of the Society of Jesus*, ed. H. Foley, 7 vols (London, 1877–83), VI, p. 634. In view of the acquaintance with John Michael Wright revealed here it is tempting to identify Wright and Gibbes in the following 1642 *Pilgrim Book* entry (Venerable English College, Rome, Liber 282, p. 130): 'Die 12. 9bris pransi sunt D.N. Gibs et D.N. Wright Londinenses Catholici.' Unfortunately, Foley's 'Cornelius White, London, a catechumen', recorded as dining on 6 August, is based on a faulty transcription of 'Cornelius Wrigtus'. Foley (VI, p. 623) also omits a translation of the words 'posterior saepe pransus est in Coll.°'. Given both pieces of information, it is possible that the Mr Wright from London who dined with Mr Gibbs was Cornelius the catechumen and not J. Michael, the Catholic artist.

As we have noted, on 21 February 1649 Gibbes probably dined at the English College with Augustine Conyers, the Benedictine who helped convert Thomas Keightley. This is not, however, our only evidence that Gibbes was acquainted with Thomas Whetenhall's group of friends who shared the house in the Via Condotti in 1646. There is indeed an unusual source, a volume of seventeenth-century verse, first published in the early nineteenth century, which unites all the English Catholics mentioned in that note. In several cases it also provides new biographical insights. The volume in question is called *Tixall Poetry* and was published in Edinburgh in 1813 by Arthur Clifford, a Catholic colleague of Sir Walter Scott and a grandson of James, 5th Lord Aston. The poems contained in the volume were printed from a collection of mid-seventeenth-century manuscripts found by Clifford at Tixall, then home of the Aston family. Probably the largest number were written by the poet and future priest Edward Thimelby. But apart from occasional appearances in such places as 'his honoured friend' Serenus Cressy's *Church History* (Rouen, 1668), very little of Thimelby's verse was published in its author's lifetime, and in spite of the publication of *Tixall Poetry*, with the exception of three contributions to *Notes and Queries*, Thimelby's verse has remained unnoticed. David Mathew mentions other members of the family, but not Edward, in his note on the poems in *The Social Structure in Caroline England* (2nd edn, London, 1950, p. 118). See also Clifford's edition of *Tixall Letters* (London, 1815), *passim*.

Even the short articles in *Notes and Queries* (*NQ*) were concerned primarily with Thimelby's more famous colleague and contemporary, Richard Crashaw. First, N.W. Bawcutt in 'A seventeenth-century Allusion to Crashaw', (*NQ*, CCVII (1962), pp. 215–16) drew attention to Thimelby's praise of Crashaw in his 'Letters to Mr Normington' (*Tixall Poetry*, pp. 37–42). In 'Crashaw at Rome' (*NQ*, CCXI (1966), pp. 256–7), P.G. Stanwood expanded Bawcutt's account, noticing Thimelby's *Responsa* in the relevant volume of the CRS and Crashaw's appearances at the English College, Rome. He also drew attention to the four ejected Fellows of Peterhouse who all became Catholics and who were all to be found at Rome in the 1640s, mistakenly adding that John Cosin, the son of the former Master of Peterhouse, returned to England 'as a Jesuit priest' (E. Chaney, *The Grand Tour*, cit., pp. 97–8). In 1971, Kenneth J. Larsen published 'Some Light on Richard Crashaw's Final Years in Rome' (*Modern Language Review*, LXVI, pp. 492–6). This added new evidence to our knowledge of Crashaw's residence at the English College and pointed out that he was not a canon at Loreto but a 'beneficiatus' (a post which provided a living in return for singing the Office). Finally, in 1972, Hilton Kelliher published 'Crashaw at Cambridge and Rome' (*NQ*, CCXVII, pp. 18–19), which focused upon the friends Crashaw and Thimelby must have had in common, mentioning, among others, Normington (whom he calls Normanton) and the Keightleys. An unprinted source (Bodleian Library, Tanner MS. 65, folio 175) reveals that when Normington was obliged to leave Cambridge, William Dillingham, a friend of Crashaw, reported that 'Sr Keene junior is chosen into Mr Normington fellowship.' Kelliher suggests that Crashaw was already acquainted with Normington at Cambridge. Both attended Pembroke College during the early 1630s. One might add that both the Keightley brothers were at Cambridge in the second half of the 1630s.

From the 'Letters to Mr Normington', and a few other poems, it is clear that Thimelby and the future Benedictine were close friends. Remembering the words with which Weldon rounded off his brief obituary of Normington – 'an excellent poet both in English and Latin' – it is clear also that verse must have been an important ingredient in their relationship. Kelliher (p. 18) points out that on the two occasions when Thimelby mentions Crashaw to Normington he calls him familiarly 'our Crashaw', which suggest that all three men knew each other well. While Normington and Crashaw probably met at Cambridge, Thimelby seems to have got to know the other two in Rome during the late 1640s, perhaps via the English College. Certainly he was to be found dining there with Normington in early May 1647 and then again on 20 and 21 August later in the same year; see Foley, VI, p. 626 (in the first instance Normington is recorded under his alias of Clifton).

Edward Thimelby was born on 25 April 1615, the youngest son of Richard Thimelby of Irnham in Lincolnshire and Mary Brookesby. His maternal grandmother Eleanor was a daughter of William, third

Lord Vaux, and it was first she and then her sister Anne who
brought the boy up after his father's death in 1623 (at Tobie
Matthew's house in High Holborn). After his grandmother's
death, he went at the age of 9 to the secret Jesuit school run by his
great-aunt Vaux at Stanley Grange, West Hallam, Derbyshire. Then
at 13 he was sent to St Omer where he studied grammar, syntax,
poetry and rhetoric for four years; see his *Responsa*, CRS, LV (1963),
pp. 448-50; Anstruther, II, p. 316; idem, *Vaux of Harrowden*
(London 1953), pp. 388, 460; CRS, LXIX (1979), p. 260; and the
'Pedigree of Thimelby, Co. Lincoln' to be found at the back of
volume II of the *Chronicle of St. Monica's*, ed. Dom Adam Hamilton
(London, 1906). He arrived in Rome in November 1636, dining at
the English College with five other students ('Missione Audomarensi,
veniens Romam') on the 26th; see *Pilgrim Book*, p. 117 and Foley,
VI, p. 614. Four days later he entered the College as a convictor. A
later note appended to the relevant entry in the College *Annales*
records that 'Discessit ex Coll° die 12. Novembris 1639. et Romae
extra Collegium diutius commoratus est. Natura suavis [sed
Discipline parum observans, caeterum?] in studiis satis profecit'
(CRS, XL (1943), pp. 15-16). The unfavourable comment between
square brackets was subsequently heavily scored through but presumably represented someone's (probably the Rector's) opinion of
Thimelby during the 1640s. There is no record of his having taken
orders, but from later references it seems that he became a secular
priest some time in the late 1650s.

Meanwhile, 'for a long time he resided at Rome in the service of
a certain Cardinal' and thus became 'very well known at the Roman
Court'. He never went on the English Mission; see George Leyburn,
'Catalogus Spectabiliorum Sacerdotum qui in praesentarium
reperiuntur in Clero Seculari Angliae' (c.1667), *Douai Diaries*, CRS,
XI (1911), pp. 538, 551, who also describes Thimelby as 'a man
of great eminence . . . of very noble family . . . which is highly
regarded by the King of England'. Kelliher speculated that the
cardinal who patronized Thimelby 'could have been Giambattista
Pallotto, Crashaw's Anglophile patron' (*NQ*, loc. cit.), but a letter in
the WCA (XXXI, 112) reveals that he was Cardinal Ginetto whose
Latin Secretary Thimelby became sometime during the 1650s. By
1659 he was canon and provost of St Géry at Cambrai where he
seems to have remained for the rest of his life, dying there on 17
July 1676 (see Anstruther, loc. cit).

With a few noteworthy exceptions (in particular, poems by Dryden and Waller), the best verse in *Tixall Poetry* is Thimelby's and seems to date from the late 1640s and early 1650s. That Gibbes, like Crashaw, was known to both Normington and Thimelby is indicated by the latter's compliment to him in one of his 'Letters to Mr Normington' (loc. cit., p. 39):

> Had I, lyke Doctor Gibbs, some serious trade,
> It weir excuse sufficient to perswade
> That rime was all the play and sport I had.
> Yet made I but of verse each day a score
> Lyke his, I'd sweare he playd as much, and more,
> That sweats to hold a plow, or tugge an oare.

Later in the same poem, 'Our soft-pend Crashaw' is also praised. But of the group of English Catholics under discussion, it is not only Gibbes and Crashaw whose names occur in *Tixall Poetry*. To begin with, there is a series of poems dedicated to the 'Easterne Voyage' of Normington, 'Cononell Plater' and 'Mr Kitely on the same Voyage'.

Normington had met the exiled Royalist Colonel Thomas Playters at least as early as 24 June 1646, for on that day he dined with him at the English College. (Foley, VI, p. 632, omits the 'l' in the name 'Platter' though it is clearly visible in the original *Pilgrim Book*, p. 142. Normington is recorded under his alias of Clifton.) Presumably in the autumn of 1646, soon after the group at Via Condotti broke up due to the departure of Whetenhall and Sheldon, Playters, Normington and one or both of the Keightley brothers set out on their journey to Turkey and Greece (and Egypt and India?). None of their names occurs in the *Pilgrim Book* between September 1646 and August 1647. Thimelby's three poems on the subject seem to have been written immediately before his friends' departure. It is clear that he himself did not go with them. The first poem in the group, 'To Mr Normington upon his Easterne Voyage' begins:

> You that have tasted Rhodanus and Po,
> And now to Nilus and to Ganges goe;
> That Alpes and Apenines by stepps have past,
> And now to Caucasus and Athos hast;
> Who, leaving Roman eagles, equall runne
> With moones of Ottoman, and Sophis sunne;

it continues with advice to remember one's mortality and,

significantly, in view of Normington's later career, to be content
with a single point on earth for 'he, in this our passing, acting age,
/ Sees better in a cell then on a stage'.

> Goe you, but take my Normington along,
> Who'le equall your great action with his song;
> Whose pen can match your sword, and he out doe
> As much of Tasso's fame as Godfry's you; . . .
> Goe then, and take him with you, syr, and when
> You've seene as many, both of townes and men,
> In monthes no more then were Ulissees' yeares,
> Returne againe, and quitt us of our feares:
> Returne with shining conquest in your face,
> Unto your sad Penelopy's embrace;
> And lett him to our academy turne,
> Which, ah! till then must heere in silence murne.

It is unlikely that 'our academy . . . heere' signifies the English
College, as neither Normington nor Thimelby was a student there
any longer. It is more likely that it refers to a private and informal
poetical academy of the group's own devising.

The only clue we have as to which brother 'To Mr Kitely, on the
same Voyage' is dedicated, rests in the following lines:

> But you, whose vertue studyes equally
> Morall and physicall philosophy,
> And counts man rising even with his falls
> Must know your ends as well as principalls.

That Normington returned to Thimelby and their Roman
'academy' we know, for on 20 and 21 August 1647 they dined
together with Nicholas Mildmay in the English College vineyard
(Foley, VI, p. 636). By this time Normington must already have been
thinking of becoming a Benedictine, his religious conviction no
doubt strengthened by the miraculous cross he had seen in Turkey.
As we have seen, in the College *Annales*, after ceasing to be a
student, he spent some time in Rome and 'ingressus est Ordinem S.
Benedicti Placentiae'. Given that he was professed at Douai in
February 1650, we can therefore date another of Thimelby's poems
to between 1648 and 1649 by its dedicatory title: 'To Mr
Normington at Piacenza upon occasion of the overflowes of Po and
Tyber.'

A third member of the Via Condotti group and yet another who also had strong links with the Benedictines was John Caryll, the future playwright and Jacobite Secretary of State. In the poem 'To Mr Caril perswading him upon the death of Card. F. to leave the Court' Thimelby implies that Caryll too was one of the same informal academy of English Catholic poets resident in Rome:

> Caril, you see what baites the court now uses,
> With which the Graces steal you from the Muses . . .
> You're surely surfeited e're this,
> Of all that trust the court calls blis.
> Make you to port, like those who coast the main
> But to be sea-sicke, and turne home again.

That Caryll remained a friend of Thimelby's is indicated by the presumably much later letter he wrote about 'Mr Carell' allowing him time to spend in England at Lady Englefield's. He says that he is 'inserted' into Caryll's travel pass for Flanders 'there bing no other way of going over'. A manuscript poem which Clifford did not publish in full contains the lines:

> Come, Janus, thou shalt be my muse to day,
> While I this new yeares debt of verses pay,
> Unto my Normington's and Carrell's bay.

At first sight, the most interesting of the poems in *Tixall Poetry* in the context of this essay seemed to be 'On the Death of the Lady Catherine White, in Child-birth at Rome' ('Poems collected by the honourable Herbert Aston' (London, 1658), pp. 8-9). Given the approximate coincidence of dates, name and location, the death of the Lady Catherine Whetenhall (sometimes spelled Whitnall, White-hall, etc.) in childbirth at Padua sprang to mind. Subsequently, on reading H.W. Jones's 'Thomas White (or Blacklo), 1593-1676: New Data' (*NQ*, new series, XX (October 1973), pp. 381-8), it became clear that Blacklo's sister-in-law, Catherine, the daughter of Sir Richard Weston, first Earl of Portland, had a more convincing claim to the title. Mgr Shanahan, upon whose research much of Jones's article is based, sees 'signs of Thomas White's Latin style' in a monumental inscription (honouring Catherine White) near the Lady altar of the church attached to the English College, Rome. The epitaph informs us that with her husband, Richard White (Blacklo's brother and a frequent visitor to the English College; see Foley, V, pp. 624–37), Lady Catherine settled in Rome in 1642 (see H.W. Jones, op. cit., p. 387, and *Essex Recusant*, IV (1962), p. 127). She died there in 1645. For her sons, Jerome and Thomas, and three daughters, see Anstruther, II, pp. 348–9. In his book on Weston, Michael Van Cleave Alexander writes that Catherine 'is said to have been buried in the church of Santa Maria Maggiore', though he does not cite his source (*Charles I's Lord Treasurer* (London, 1975), p. 32). Lady Catherine's sister, the wife of Basil, Viscount Feilding, had died in Italy in 1635 during her husband's embassy in Venice. (Cecilia Countess of Denbigh, *Royalist Father and Roundhead Son* (London, 1915), pp. 96–104, and Lassels's *Description*, in E. Chaney, *The Grand Tour and the Great Rebellion*, cit., p. 368.)

ON THE DEATH OF / THE LADY CATHERIN WHITE, IN
CHILD-BIRTH, AT ROME.

Ladys, would you have combin'd
Beauty both of face and mind;
Would you marry, hand in hand,
Strict obedience with command;
Snatch the low and high degree
Of greatness with humilitye;
With chastetye calme appetite,
And with wisdome temper wit:
Would you reade the double story
Of beauty's wrack, and vertue's glory;
Teach lip-rethorik to yeeld;
Silent eloquence the field;
Heare the best philosophy,
To dye to live, to live to dye? –
Study in one Epitaph,
What all tongs and voloms have.
Would you lerne your thoughts to move
I' th'upper spheire of hevinly love;
To find your home in banishment,
In warfare peace, in woe content;
No change of minds in change of time;
Not altring hearts, though altring clime:
Or would you see, or would you know
The flowers that over graves may grow;

> What miracles can silence verse? –
> Goe sob and weepe o're yonder herse:
> For everye sigh and everye teare,
> There lyes a grace and vertue there.

Another poem which brings one nearer Lassels is 'On the death of the Countesse Rivers' (*Tixall Poetry*, pp. 43–4). The mother of Lady Anne Brudenell, Lassels's patroness in exile of the mid-1640s, died on 9 March 1650 (OS). The connection with Thimelby was through his eldest brother, Sir John, who married Elizabeth, a daughter of the Countess (*Responsa*, CRS, LV (1963), p. 450). The latter is surely the dedicatee of 'To the Lady Elizabeth Thimelby on New-Years-Day 1655 looking dayly for her sonne from travaile' a poem by Thimelby's sister-in-law, Mrs Henry Thimelby; *Tixall Poetry*, pp. 104–5. The son, Edward Thimelby's nephew, is surely the John Thimelby with whom he dines at the English College on 20 January and 8 and 9 February 1654; Foley, VI, p. 646.

Various presumably later commonplace-book poems worthy of mention, if only for their biographical interest, include (Waller's?) 'Mr Waller when he was at sea' (p. 219); (Thimelby/Dryden's?) 'Mr Henningham's Song' (p. 183), presumably indicating the Mr Heinegham/Heveningham who arrives in Rome with Ferdinand Hastings, 'habitu peregrinorum' in November 1646 and who thenceforth dines several times at the English College with Sir John Cansfield, the Catholic Royalist who had been badly wounded at Newbury (original *Pilgrim Book*, pp. 145–8 and Gillow); 'To Mr Nevill at his departure' (p. 272), probably referring to Dom Francis Nevill, the Procurator at Piacenza who, after staying at the English College for almost a month, returned to Piacenza with a companion on 5 May 1650 (Clifford, p. 394, thinks Henry Neville, the Republican, might be indicated here, but this seems unlikely in view of the *Pilgrim Book* reference in Foley, VI, p. 642). With so many Benedictine friends, it is not surprising that George Leyburn was to write that Thimelby 'valde gratus est omnibus Regularibus praesertim Patribus Societatis et Benedictinis Anglis . . .'; see 'Catalogus . . .', op. cit., p. 538.

I conclude this note with the transcript of a poem discovered at Stonyhurst College (Grene's Collections, N. II, no. 23, p. 49). It was written by Dom Leander Normington when he was still plain Mr Thomas Normington and 'On his Easterne Voyage' (therefore in

1646-7). I thank the Reverend F.J. Turner SJ, both for locating the original – on the basis of an incomplete reference I had found among the Farm Street archives – and for sending me a photocopy. Since the text of the poem is in the same hand as the footnote it seems unlikely, from the wording of the latter, that the manuscript is an autograph. The asterisk placed alongside the word 'Behold' refers to a small sketch, in the left-hand margin, of a mosque surmounted by a cross.

> Behold ye signe of Christ most strangly sett
> Above ye inconstant Badge of Mahomett
> Whose glorious beames (though distant farr) appear
> Whose aery substance non can feele, though neere.
> Sure t' is a wandring Ghost from England fledd
> Of some poor Crosse there lately murthered
> Which finding in that Christian Church noe roome,
> For refuge to this Turkish Mosque is come.
> Sunn of ye Ghospell, viewing thee our eyes
> The faithlesse Moone beneath thy feet, despise.

Mr Normington

made these verses of a crosse wch he saw in Turky placed in a half-moone upon a Mosque w^{ch} (the Turks often endeavouring to pull downe) became invisible, although a farre off most conspicuous.

NOTE

This chapter was first published as Appendix II in *The Grand Tour and the Great Rebellion* (Geneva and Turin, 1985).

11

'Philanthropy in Italy': English Observations on Italian Hospitals, 1545-1789

✦

'The Stewards . . . come to the Market-place at an appointed hour; and according to the number of those that belong to their Hall, they carry home Provisions. But they take more care of their Sick, than of any others, who are looked after and lodged in public Hospitals: They have belonging to every Town four Hospitals, that are built without their Walls, and are so large, that they pass for little Towns: By this means, if they had ever such a number of sick Persons, they could lodg them conveniently, and at such a distance, that such of them as are sick of infectious Diseases, may be kept so far from the rest, that there can be no danger of Contagion. The Hospitals are so furnished and stored with all the things that are convenient for the ease and recovery of their Sick; and those that are put in them, are all looked after with so tender and watchful a care, and are so constantly treated by their skilful Physicians; that as none is sent to them against their will, so there is scarce one in a whole Town, that if he should fall ill, would not chuse rather to go thither, than lie sick at home.

After the Steward of the Hospitals has taken for them whatsoever the Physician does prescribe at the Market-place, then the best things that remain, are distributed equally among the Halls in proportion to their numbers.'*

* From Gilbert Burnet's translation of Sir Thomas More's *Utopia* (London, 1684), pp. 92-3. More's *Utopia* originally appeared in 1516. In 1508, Henry VII, wishing to found a Royal hospital in London, obtained from Francesco dei Portinari a detailed manuscript account of Florence's then renowned Arcispedale di S. Maria Nuova. See note 19 below. Within a year of publishing his translation of *Utopia*, Burnet was travelling in Italy. In 1686 he published *Some Letters* which, in spite of the Protestantism of its author, contained the highest praise and several detailed descriptions of Italian hospitals; see above, p. 53, n. 6.

'There were then in the heate of the sickness, that thought to purge and clense theyr houses, by conveying their infected servants forth by night into the fieldes, which there starved and dyed, for want of reliefe and warme-keeping. Such mercilesse Canibals, (insteade of purging theyr spyrits and theyr houses) have thereby doubled the Plague on them and theyr houses. In Grayes-Inne Clarkenwell, Finsbury and Moore-fieldes, with myne owne eyes have I seene halfe a dozen such lamentable out-casts. Theyr Bretheren & their Kinsfolkes, have offered large summes of money, to gette them conveied into any out house, and no man would earne it, no man would receive them. Cursing and raving by the Highway side, have they expired, & their Maisters never sent to them, nor succourd them. The feare of God is come amongst us, and the love of God gone frome us . . .

In other Lands, they have Hospitals, whether their infected are transported, presently after they are strooken. They have one Hospitall, for those that have been in the houses with the infected, and are not yet tainted: another for those that are taynted, and have the sores rysen on them, but not broken out. A third for those that both have the sores, & have them broken out on them. We have no provision but mixing hand over heade, the sicke with the whole. A halfe-penny a month to the poore mans boxe, we count our utter empoverishing. I have hearde Travailers of credite avouch, that in *London*, is not gyven the tenth part of that almes in a weeke, which in the poorest besieged Citty of Fraunce is gyven in a day. What is our religion, all avarice and no good works? Because we may not build Monasteries, or have Masses, Dirges, or Trentals sung for our soules, are there no deeds of mercy that God hath enioyned us?

Their hospitals [at Rome] are more lyke noble mens houses than otherwise; so richly furnished, cleane kept, and hot perfumed, that a soldier would thinke it a sufficient recompence for all his travell and his wounds, to have such a heavenly retyring place.'*

'Now as I have spoken of the two deadly sinnes wherein [the Italians] exceed [i.e., murder and prostitution], so will I speake of one thing wherein some of them are to be commended, that is this. If there be any Christian, of what Nation soever poore and in distresse making his case knowne and asking for Christs sake, he shall be relieved, with all those necessaries whereof he is destitute, as apparrell, meat, and drink, and some money, though it be but little: if he is sick, then shall he be put in a Hospitall where he shall be choisely attended upon, having good lodging,

* From *The Works of Thomas Nashe*, ed. R.B. McKerrow (rev. edn, Oxford, 1958), II, pp. 160-1 and 285 (*Christs Teares over Jerusalem*, 1593 and *The Unfortunate Traveller*, 1594).

daintie diet, and comfortable Phisicke for the restoring of his health, whether he be Papist or Protestant.'*

* * *

I should explain at the outset that this chapter is concerned as much with the history of philanthropy in England as it is with Italian hospitals *per se*. It could even be regarded, in a primitive sort of way, as a 'comparative study'. By documenting the English travellers' almost invariably enthusiastic comments on the great philanthropical institutions of pre-industrial Italy, I have tried to show that there must be something wrong with the current image we have of early modern English philanthropy, and in particular with what we are told about the state of the latter, relative to the contemporary state of such things in the rest of Europe.[1]

The debate concerning the comparative merits of Catholic and Protestant charity is almost as old as the Reformation itself.[2] In a work which so thoroughly documents the achievement of a Catholic state's 'social institutions' in the late Renaissance period, one might therefore have expected a more thoroughgoing exposé of the long-standing myth regarding the Protestant north's supposedly superior philanthropic ideals and achievement, when the author touches briefly on this subject. But perhaps because he so carefully avoids polemic, Professor Brian Pullan's short historiographical survey provides us with the most suitable introduction to the issue:

> Certain generalizations made in the past about the differences between Catholic and Protestant attitudes to the poor have proved very persistent, although they originated with sociologists rather than with historians and although they have sometimes been partially discredited by the examination of philanthropy and poor relief as practised in particular European societies. To use Troeltsch's terminology, the Roman Catholic Church is associated with the practice of mere 'charity', and the Protestant churches in general are credited with the formulation of a more far-reaching 'social policy'.[3]

Pullan continues with a discussion of the 'far-reaching consequences [that] have been attributed to the Catholic doctrine that good works actually contribute to the salvation of the persons who perform them':

* From *A True Relation of the Travailes and most Miserable Captivitie of William Davies, Barber–Surgion of London, under the Duke of Florence* (London, 1614).

Hence, the charitable man in the Roman Catholic society is accused of being concerned chiefly with the acquisition of merit for himself, and of not caring whether the alms he gives have a demoralizing effect on the person who receives them.[4]

The Catholic Church, 'because of its anxiety to preserve opportunities for the rich to be charitable', is supposed to have had 'no desire to eliminate poverty':

> Allegedly, if constructive schemes for poor relief were ever devised in Roman Catholic societies of the sixteenth century, they were formulated in spite of the Church and not through its efforts. On the other hand, the Protestant Churches are supposed to have moved towards more rational poor relief, its value determined only by its beneficial effects on the poor and on the society of which giver and receiver form part.[5]

Having analysed in detail the numerous charitable foundations of Renaissance and post-Tridentine Venice, Pullan could, in conclusion, hardly remain within the camp claiming Protestant superiority in such matters. Where the subject of comparative merit occurs however, apart from conceding that institutional forms 'certainly differed substantially between one country and another', he goes no further than to state that 'general attitudes to the poor were often determined by a rather similar mixture of pity and fear, of genuine humanity and brutal paternalism . . . whether a given society had remained Catholic, or whether it had severed its allegiance to Rome'.[6]

The historians of the Protestant north have been less scrupulously relativistic. Johan Huizinga, for example, in his widely read *Dutch Civilization in the Seventeenth Century*, claimed that 'our precocious attempts to provide a measure of social welfare based on Christian charity . . . primitive though they were by modern standards, were far in advance of anything found in most other countries'.[7]

While it is doubtful that the Dutch hospitals were 'far in advance' of those in Italy, at least one seventeenth-century Englishman considered that Amsterdam was 'far advanced' over London in this respect.[8] It is unlikely that W.K. Jordan would have agreed with him. In his three-volume study of philanthropy in England between 1480 and 1660, Jordan claimed that before the end of the sixteenth century, Calvinism, in its distinctly English form, had generated the most advanced and comprehensive system of poor relief in the world.[9]

Although it has been much criticized, especially for its statistical methods, Jordan's work remains standard on the subject and its very clearly stated conclusions have had, and continue to have, a fundamental influence on students of the period.[10] Most now accept that the previous very grim view of 'rising' capitalism's attitude to the poor (a view deriving largely from Marx, and refined, via Max Weber, by R.H. Tawney, Margaret James and others) was highly exaggerated if not an anachronistic construct.[11] Jordan's apparently scientific documentation of the 'vast outpouring of charitable wealth' following the English Reformation seems to have discredited not merely the critical conclusions of his predecessors but also the contemporary testimony so effectively brought to bear by these earlier scholars. Since then, the debate has continued almost exclusively within the statistical terms of reference established by Jordan. His 'failure' to deflate his statistics has been alternately attacked and vindicated.[12]

But if anything has emerged from the controversy so far, it is that no conclusive results are likely to be achieved by further quantification of these same data. Even Jordan's most aggressive pair of critics, Professors Bittle and Lane, have been obliged to admit that neither their own research nor that of other doubters of what they call 'Jordan's "immense generosity" claims' had actually served to *refute* such claims. 'These studies', they write, 'merely fail to support Jordan's conclusions.'[13] It is hoped that here, by returning to contemporary testimony, one can show that what is perhaps Jordan's single most important conclusion, his claim that 'by 1580 . . . already in England an edifice of charity had been reared which stood incomparable in all Europe', is not only impossible to maintain, but that it is a claim which any late sixteenth- or seventeenth-century Englishman, who had travelled as far as Italy would have rejected as absurd.[14]

By focusing on the subject of hospitals one restricts conveniently the range of the discussion without, it is hoped, losing sight of the wider debate regarding comparative levels of charitable giving. Where England is concerned a further restriction is automatically provided, for despite its rapidly expanding population there was, throughout our period, only one city whose institutions could meaningfully be compared with those of the major Italian cities and that was London.

According to Jordan's second volume, *The Charities of London*, however, this city's philanthropical achievement was so remarkable that it guaranteed outstanding international historical status for England as a whole. Though his research had been limited to an analysis of the wills of just ten English counties, he felt he could claim that in terms of the 'immensity of [its] charitable wealth . . . London stood *solus* in England, and for that matter, in the western world'.[15]

Dealing specifically with the London hospitals, Jordan wrote that by 1660, the close of his period:

> These five great institutions . . . endowed . . . by the great generosity of London's benefactors . . . stood unrivalled not only in England but in the whole of the western world as a well-articulated and munificently supported system of hospitals designed to protect helpless men and women against the most grievous blows of fortune.[16]

In the way they financed and organized these 'great [philanthropical] institutions', 'the burghers of London were pioneering, not only for England but for the Western World'.[17]

In spite of his emphasis on the internationally pioneering nature of the London burghers' 'proud accomplishment', Jordan's solitary reference to an Italian charitable institution, 'the great hospital at Florence' (presumably S. Maria Nuova) reveals it as having been a thoroughly investigated model for London's Savoy Hospital.[18] The latter, moreover, was founded and generously endowed not by a Protestant bourgeoisie but by the Catholic monarch Henry VII. According to John Stow, it was 'againe new founded, indowed and furnished by Queene *Mary*'. Probably because of this, however, and also because it went into a steady decline after the Reformation, this important and, within England, truly pioneering institution is hardly mentioned again by Professor Jordan.[19]

Jordan, of course, denied that the dissolution of the monasteries deprived the community of an important source of relief.[20] This, he claimed, was a nineteenth-century tradition.[21] But Jordan's view has now so thoroughly supplanted this tradition that J.F. Hadwin has felt it necessary to suggest that 'the loss of monastic charity was more serious than is often now implied'.[22]

Of very much the same mind as Hadwin were the seventeenth-century antiquaries, men such as Sir William Dugdale and Sir Henry Spelman, whose professional familiarity with the ancient documents led them to form a no doubt idealized mental picture of English medieval charity, which contrasted dramatically with present-day reality and the deficiencies of the system they could see operating around them.

One such scholar, Spelman's pupil and trustee, Jeremiah Stephens, went so far as to express his disgust with the inadequacy of provision for the poor since the dissolution of the monasteries.[23] Compiling material for a major study of the subject, he wrote to the Vatican librarian asking for further information on the papal reaction to this aspect of the English Reformation. Then, his curiosity probably having been aroused by a travel account or the perusal of a recent guidebook, he continues:

> Further, if it be not too troublesome, I desire to know what Hospitals of note there are in Italy for reliefe of the poore. I have bin told much of a very great one att Rome called lo Spirito Santo; and an other att Naples worth 100 thousand crownes yearely, wherein 2000 poore children are maintained, besides other pious uses. In England we had anciently very many; and particularly appendant upon the Abbayes; whereof every great one, had 3 hospitalls belonging to it. We had 110 great hospitals (as appeareth upon record) demolished att one clappe in the tempest of King Henry the 8 his rage. By the losse of wch our poore att this day do suffer extremly in all partes.[24]

Jordan also denied that the Civil Wars had a devastating effect on facilities for the poor in general and the London hospitals in particular.[25] His views on the matter have proved influential even on the post-1960 writings of the Marxist historian Christopher Hill.[26] But if any should argue that Stephens's letter, written as it was in 1652, only three years after the execution of the King, can be dismissed as merely reflecting adverse post-war conditions, one need only quote the far more sweeping condemnation of Sir Matthew Hale written around 1659, that is, at the very end of Jordan's chosen period and after more than ten years of peaceful Puritan dictatorship. England was at this time, claimed Hale, 'more deficient in . . . prudent provision for the poor than any other cultivated and Christian state'.[27]

Where the Civil War period itself is concerned one can hardly do better than quote from the *True report of the great costs and charges of the foure Hospitalls in the City of London* . . . for the year 1645. The section on Christ's Hospital, for example, the country's major orphanage, clearly states that:

> In respect of the troubles of the times, the meanes of the said Hospitall hath very much failed for want of charitable Benevolences . . . by these and other meanes, the said Hospitall hath not beene able to take in any Children for three years past having a greater number already upon their charge, than they are any way able to maintain.

In spite of a much increased demand from war casualties, London's two general hospitals, St Bartholomew's and St Thomas's, were capable of accepting fewer inmates each year, the current figures being given as 246 and 226 respectively.[28] For the orphanage, the number currently maintained is given as 630, including all those children 'in divers places of this City and Suburbes, and with sundry Nurses in the Country'. This figure seems to have been average for the entire 1640-60 period.[29]

It is interesting to compare these statistics with those given in 1595 by the Anglo-Irish traveller, Henry Piers, when he encountered the Ospedale degli Innocenti on his way to Rome.[30] Florence, with a population of little over a third that of London, was apparently already catering for three times as many orphans:

> There are three hospitalles in the same Cittie, whereof one is for orphantes which are in number one thowsande eight hundred; another of men where there is in one Roome one hundred and thirtie beddes, in everie of which were lodged two; the thirde of women, where there are three score beddes, in each of them three women.[31]

Comparing the second part of Piers's account (which presumably refers to S. Maria Nuova) with the information contained in the 1645 London *Report*, we see that the numbers catered for by the combined resources of England's two largest hospitals only just matched those accommodated by the Florentine hospitals 50 years before. By 1666, with the situation in London much the same, a remodernized S. Maria Nuova could apparently handle more than 1500 patients [Fig. 45].[32]

Not long before Piers noticed the Florentine hospitals, a well-travelled and relatively objective Italian, Petruccio Ubaldini, felt obliged to include a comment on the hospitals of London in order to complete the 'Descrittion' of that city, which formed part of his

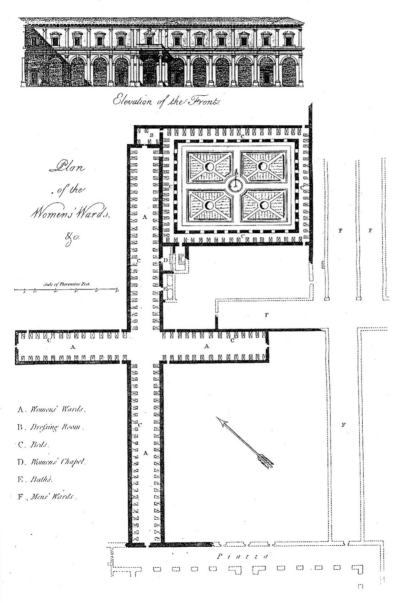

FLORENCE.

Hospital of St. MARIA NUOVO.

Elevation of the Front.

Plan
. of the
Women's Wards.
&c.

Scale of Florentine Feet.

A . Womens' Wards.

B . Dressing Room.

C . Beds.

D . Womens' Chapel.

E . Baths.

F . Mens' Wards.

Piazza

45 The Hospital of Santa Maria Nuova, Florence, from John Howard, Account of the Principal Lazarettos (Warrington, 1791) plate 17, see below, note 32. [E. Chaney]

revised *Relatione d'Inghilerra*. And although Ubaldini was writing after the date by which England's 'edifice of charity' had become, in Professor Jordan's words, 'incomparable in all Europe', he seemed if anything embarrassed that a city which could boast 'un ponte di pietra dei più belli che si veggono in Europa', should have only three small and badly maintained hospitals: 'Di spedali non si può dir troppo perché sono tre piccoli et mal tenuti, dei quali son mandati via tutti gl'incurabili'.[33] Only Christ's Hospital, according to Ubaldini, was adequately maintained. And if any should argue that our Poor Laws were already eliminating the need for large-scale hospital relief, Ubaldini's account of the new laws in operation shows that at least in this period (*c.*1580), the combined resources of voluntary and compulsory poor-relief contributions were not sufficient to clear beggars and even the dying from the streets of London:

> Le limosine che si fanno nella città sono richieste per via di tassa delle case et son pagate ogni mese et quei che le risquotono si dicono Colletori. Questi hanno da provvedere ai poveri della loro parrochia et il resto dei denari va allo spedale di quell'orfani. Montono queste lemosine assai, ma pur si veggono spesso persone per le strade non solo mendicare, ma morirvi ancora.[34]

If there are no English accounts of Italian hospitals dating from as far back as Luther's praises for the (Florentine?) institutions he saw on his way to Rome in 1510,[35] S. Maria Nuova was enthusiastically reviewed not so much later (and 40 years before Henry Piers was to admire it) in the first English book exclusively devoted to Italy, William Thomas's *Historie*.[36]

Unlike Piers, Thomas was so dedicated a Protestant that he was eventually executed for rebelling against Queen Mary and her Spanish husband. Neither his religion nor his politics, however, prevented him from admiring grand-ducal Florence in 1545, and after praising the 'houses' of the Medici and Strozzi and the 'stretes: which are verie faire, large and straight [and] paved with flatte stone', he continues:

> But amongst all other thei have divers goodlie hospitals for relieve of the sicke and poore, and one verie faire, so well ordred that it receiveth a great number of men and women, but into severall houses, where they are applied with good phisicke and their beddes, their shetes, and everie other thyng so cleane that manie tymes righte honest men and

women be not ashamed to seke their health there. For that hospitall alone maie dispende yerelie above 20,000 crownes: by reason wherof they have excellente phisicions, good poticaries, dilygente ministers, and everie other thyng necessarie.[37]

So utopian a description must have been read with great interest when it was published in 1549, for it was at this moment, during the short reign of Edward VI (whose adviser Thomas became), that the decaying hospitals of London were being refounded.[38]

Thomas's account of the Venetian institutions corroborates Pullan's conclusions.[39] Dwelling on the practical and long-term nature of the charity, it counters the traditional view of the Catholics as having been haphazard and indulgent in their philanthropy in contrast to Protestant far-sightedness and superior consciousness of social consequences:

Furthermore there are certaine hospitalles, some for the sicke and diseased, and some for poore orphanes, in whiche they are nourisshed up till thei come unto yeres of service: and then is the man childe put unto a craft, and the maidens kept till they be maried. If she be fayre, she is soone had, and little money geven with hir: if she be foule, they avaunce her with a better portion of money.[40]

By way of comparison here it might be mentioned that Jordan failed to find any apprenticeship endowments in London before Elizabeth's accession, and admitted that 'the growth of these funds was very slow indeed through the remainder of the sixteenth century.'[41]

The next English description of an Italian hospital dates from just a year later and occurs in the *Booke of the Travaile and Lief of Me Thomas Hoby*, the trainee diplomat who was to achieve lasting fame with his translation of Castiglione's *Il Cortegiano*. Following the death of Pope Paul III in November 1549 and while the conclave was taking a particularly long time to select a successor, Hoby 'determined in the mean time to make a journeye to Naples'. And among other items of interest in this 'verie beawtifull citie' he found:

a very bewtifull and large hospitall [presumably the Annunziata], wherea[t] are continuallie both gentlemen and poore men and in like maner women which are placed according to their disease and served according to their degree, with a good order and cumlie to behold; great revenwes are belonging unto yt, and a great multitude of people alwais within yt.[42]

46 Courtyard of Filarete's *Ospedale Maggiore* (Milan). Aquatint 18 × 22.2 cm; drawn by
F. Durelli, engraved by Angelo Biasioli, for *Nuova Raccolta delle Principali Vedute Interne
ed Esterne della Città di Milano disegnate da F. Durelli . . . ed incise da Angelo Biasioli ed altri
volenti artisti* (Milan, 1820–21). [E. Chaney]

Finally, in 1555, the anonymous member of a Marian embassy to
Rome recorded his admiration for Filarete's Ospedale Maggiore in
Milan [Fig. 46] a century after its foundation by Francesco Sforza.
This ever-expanding institution:

> may dispend 25,000 crowns a year, the provision whereof passeth all
> other; for at present, we saw one hundred fat oxen in a stable, one
> hundred vessels of wine, every one containing five tons, in one cellar;
> the diet so cleanly and daintily prepared for the sick as can be, by the
> recourse of surgeons and physicians, that it is a goodly thing to see.
>
> In this hospital are five hundred nurses to look to the sick, and to
> bring up children.[43]

While it is evident from these brief accounts that the authors
are impressed by what they see and perhaps, by implication, that
things are not of the same high standard in England, it is only
with the next author that we encounter that degree of enthusiasm

which became commonplace in the next century. The fact that this author, Gregory Martin, was a Catholic priest is not necessarily, as we see later when we encounter numerous instances of Protestant enthusiasm for Italian charitable institutions, the primary explanation for his praises (though professional familiarity with his subject may well account for the unrivalled detail with which he was able to describe them). In the years which lay between Thomas's and Hoby's mid-century travels and Martin's 1576–8 presence in Rome, the full impact of the Counter-Reformation had been felt by the hitherto existing institutions and many new ones had been founded. That this process continued can be seen by the comparison between the 1575 and 1600 Holy Years drawn by the important Italian commentator on these matters, Camillo Fanucci, in his *Trattato di tutte le opere pie dell'alma città di Roma* of 1601. He had been 'maravigliato' by the great works of charity he found existing in Rome at the time of the former Jubilee. By the time of the latter, however, he claims to have been 'stupefatto, e quasi fuora di me stesso, havendo visto le grandissime e immense opere di Carità, e pietà fatte dalle Confraternite di detta Città . . . e quasi da tutti li habitatori di essa Città'. Rome, he concludes, if formerly known as 'Madre pietosa', should now be called 'pietosissima fuor d'ogni misura'.[44]

Before Fanucci published this *Trattato*, Gregory Martin's manuscript *Roma Sancta* (1581) probably contained the most thorough survey of the city's charitable institutions in existence. Although it seems that Martin used the 1574 edition of *Le Cose maravigliose dell'alma città di Roma*, his chapter on hospitals was largely the product of original research. As such it included all ten institutions later to be listed by Fanucci, where *Le Cose* had mentioned only eight. Martin's descriptions, moreover, contain many important details, particularly on the actual organization and conditions of the Roman hospitals, which even Fanucci did not include.[45]

Book II of *Roma Sancta*, 'The Charitie of Rome', runs to more than 150 pages in the modern edition. Apart from the account of hospitals proper, it also includes an interesting series of shorter chapters on the Orfanotrofio at SS. Quattro Coronati (chapter 10), the Miserabili in Piazza Capranica (chapter 11), the 'Malmaritatae' at S. Marta started by Loyola 'for wemen so called by occasion of misliking, displeasure, or falling out betwene their husbands and them' (chapter 12), the Pazzi, cared for by the 'Company of the

Pietà' – at this time next to S. Maria della Pietà in the Piazza Colonna but later incorporated in the Arciospedale di S. Spirito (chapter 13) and finally the Monti di Pietà (chapter 14).

In his description of the hospitals Martin is careful to include only those ten institutions which are for 'the sicke and sore'.[46] This contrasts with Jordan's freer use of the term which enables him to arrive at the figure of five 'great' hospitals for London (which, it should be noted, by the turn of the century had a population more than twice that of Rome). Bridewell, for example, one of these 'five great institutions', in spite of Jordan's definition of it as 'a most notable landmark along the road of man's humanity to man', has recently been described in less flattering terms by a scholar who none the less admires Jordan's work.

> Its chief function [she writes, referring to Bridewell in the mid-seventeenth century] remained penal: a common gaol with its barbaric accompaniments of public whippings, boring through the ears, branding, carting through the streets, working the treadmill, and forced labour generally.[47]

Martin starts his account with S. Salvatore, or the Ospedale di S. Giovanni, which still functions today:

> This was first built by Jhon Columna Cardinal and citizen, of that noble familie, nere the Church of S. Jhon Laterane, whereof it hath the name. afterward by other Cardinals and charitable persons so enriched, that it hath in revenues of houses, lands and vineyards every yere 12000 crownes in gold, and sometime 13000, when the yere is fruitful.[48]

It is useful to bear in mind this 'landed' aspect of the hospitals when we come to consider their continued maintenance of high standards long after the economies of the Italian cities had otherwise seriously declined. Although one is dealing with much smaller amounts where Jordan's London hospitals are concerned (for all that his rhetoric implies otherwise), the same 'inflation-proof' principle applies with regard to their revenues. Jordan's figures, which did not seem to allow for the sweeping inflation of the period and were consequently much criticized, have been vindicated in this respect by Charles Wilson.[49]

After discussing the strict segregation at S. Giovanni, men and women being served exclusively by members of their own sex, Martin goes on to provide the statistics for each department: 120

beds for men and 30 for women but 'in the summer double for both sexes, bicause of more sicknes then'. The staff consisted of:

> Three Physicions, one Surgeon for them that have sores or hurts called *Feriti*. Servants sixtene, A Prior, and a Prioresse: wardens and overseers, of the *Companie de Salvatore*, whose Charity is emploied to the good administration of this Hospital . . . Al other provision of potecarie wares [are] within the house in a shoppe for the purpose.

At the end of the account he points out that this hospital and that of S. Spirito are peculiar in that 'they live wholy by their rents and not upon dayly almes'.

Turning next to the Ospedale di S. Spirito itself, Martin writes:

> This is of al other the greatest, as it were a little parish in it self for buildings and distinct roomes: begonne by Pope Innocentius 3 and augmented by Sixtus 4. The rents are 30000 crownes in gold and above. Gesse thereby the number of beddes for the sicke, which stand in most goodly order and in a stately roome for the greatnesse and building therof. And this is for the common sort of sicke persons. There is an other place for *Feriti*, that is, the wounded and sore, never lesse then thirtie. Also faier chambers above with their galleries for gentlemen. And this Hospital is so universal and without exception, that if his disease be according (for some diseases are for other places) there may come gentlemen and gentlemens servants, who in their owne lodgins neither should nor could be so conveniently attended. A great pothecarie shoppe, foure Physicions, and two Surgeons: which byside al incident and urgent necessities, keepe their ordinary course to visite every one and to prescribe their diet, at certaine houres of the day. Servants for these sicke and sore, 40 . . . Here are also those children both men and wemen of whom I numbered . . . 401 . . . which are called *Expositi*, that is imediatly after their birth laid forth in the night by some frend in a place of the Hospital for that purpose, where they are found ordinarily in the morning and receaved as their owne children: these are such as the parents are either ashamed of as begotten in fornication, or not able to keepe them, and therfore but for this provision they should perish: wheras now whatsoever become of their lewd parents, which are not knowen, they are brought up til they be made scholers or artificers, according as they are apt and towardly: and the girles kept by vertuous wemen in good order . . . til they either mary with their dowries also of the Hospital, or enter into Religion if they be so disposed. [A note in

the margin here indicates that there are sometimes 70 girls ready for marriage, all of whom are supplied with a dowry of 50 crowns.] The Nources for so many, living al upon the Hospital, are of necessitie very many. Over them al is a grand Prior called *Commendatore* or *procuratôre de S^{to} Spirito*, such an one as of late hath built there a goodly Church even from the ground.[50]

The third hospital dealt with by Martin is that of the Consolazione in Piazza della Consolazione between the Capitol and the Palatine:

This is also a famous Hospital, governed by the nobles of Rome. Beddes for men, alwaies fiftie; for wemen, ten, in the summer, they are in al an hundred. Physicions, Surgeon, servants proportionably to the number. Upon Al Holand day every yere there are twelve poore men new apparailed through out. To this Hospital belongeth a Church adjoyning thereunto, called *Our Ladies of Comfort* [S. Maria della Consolazione].

'Adjoyning to this renowned Church of much devotion' Martin next mentions the Ospedale di S. Antonio near S. Maria Maggiore in the Via Carlo Alberto. Here, he says, 'be many sicke wel provided for'. There follow four more short accounts of, 'The Hospital of our Ladie del Horto. For al the diseases of that Societie, for such poore folke as sel herbes, rootes, sallets, and by digging dampish and wette gardens . . . and (as I have heard) for the botemen'; 'the Hospital of S. Rooke' (S. Rocco delle Partorienti), 'for the sicke of that confraternitie' and others, including expectant bargees' wives; 'Our Ladies Hospital of Loretto' (S. Maria di Loreto), 'for the Companie of bakers, a very fine Hospital'; and the Hospital of S. Lazarus (S. Lazzaro), 'For such as be Lazars and have foule diseases'.

None of these accounts supplies much more detail than *Le Cose Meravigliose* had done. Martin returns to a fuller description with the fourteenth-century Ospedale di S. Giacomo degli Incurabili, situated between the Via Ripetta and the Corso:

That is, for such as are almost uncurable. As the lesser Hospital of S. Lazarus is for such diseases as require a several place from common sicknesses and sores, so this is a very goodly and large Hospital for the same purpose, both for men and wemen . . . The rents of the foundation are 1500 crownes by the yere, but there are spent in almes every yere 8000 crownes. The ordinarie number of men and wemen 150. Servants very many, Physicions and Surgeons. Al things very commodious and plentiful and cleanly, and it is a place much affected and liked of al

straungers for the charitie shewed there, and therefore straungers also
here bestow their almes, as the first founder him self was a Spaniard.
Here specially doe they exercise their charitie and humility in serving
and dressing them, that are of the perfecter sort, either Religious, or of
Confraternities.

The last of the ten hospitals described is that of SS. Trinità de'
Convalescenti e Pellegrini opposite the Monte di Pietà. Martin, of
course, dwells at length on the facilities for the pilgrims, all of whom
were entitled to three days' board and lodging. More interesting for
us here, however, is the hospital's other function as a convalescent
home and its coordination with the institutions already described. He
tells us that when the patients from any of the latter

> be so recovered that they can walke, and the daunger is past, bicause
> they may geve place to others, and yet not be wel to sone for feare of
> recidivations, they are removed into this, therfore called *de Convalescenti*,
> that is of such as are recovering. Al such out of al other Hospitals (when
> they neede not now keepe their beddes) are here kept for certaine weekes
> and daies, til they be fully recovered, and be able to returne to their
> former functions abrode.

As far as the funding of such an institution is concerned, although
one cannot produce the sort of detailed documentation which Jordan
manages, the general impression, even allowing for a predictable
degree of exaggeration on Martin's part, is that the Roman hospitals
faced none of the economic problems with which their 'unrivalled'
London equivalents had to deal throughout this period. Martin knew
of

> one noble matron that gave at one tyme 6000 crownes. Yea it is
> general and usual to these Hospitals, that wood, and wine, and victuals,
> and mony be sent thither past expectation, they know not whence, nor
> from whom, because the gevers looke for reward of him onely that seeth
> in secrete.[51]

If it should be objected that Rome was, as ever, a special case, a
show-piece and a receiver of taxes from all over Europe, and therefore no fair comparison with Protestant London, it can be pointed
out that the next English traveller and commentator on Italian
charity, Fynes Moryson, considered none of the Roman institutions
to be up to the standards of S. Maria Nuova at Florence. This

hospital, he reports, 'is said to passe all others in *Italy*, for all necessaries to cure and nourish the sicke, and for orderly attendance, where to that purpose are ninety six beds in one roome'.[52] Moryson was also impressed with the Venetian almshouse-cum-hospital of S. Lazzaro, which he claimed fed 'foure hundred, or five hundred poore people; for all that beg are sent thither, and they have many of these houses'. These figures are consistent with those arrived at by Pullan for the year 1601.[53]

The next hospital to be admired by an Englishman was Milan's 'very magnificent' Ospedale Maggiore [Fig. 46] which, despite Jordan's thesis that the secularization of charity was a post-Reformation phenomenon, was already under lay control in the fifteenth century. If Thomas Coryate, travelling in 1608 and describing his travels in print in 1611, fails to express quite that degree of enthusiasm which became commonplace from the mid-seventeenth century on, it is because only a part of the huge structure which Raymond, Lassels and those who travelled after 1642 were able to describe was then in existence. Before 1621, when work began on the great court, the hospital consisted only of Filarete's southern part of the buildings now existing, the southern side of the present great court forming the then northernmost perimeter of the whole.[54] In spite of this, Coryate's account suggests that he had not seen the like in England. After commenting on the hospital's outward magnificence, he informs his contemporaries (thinking perhaps especially of Henry Prince of Wales to whom his book was dedicated), that within it 'are an hundred and twelve chambers, and foure thousand poore people are relieved . . . The yearelie revenues of it are said to be at least fifty thousand crownes', that is, twice the amount recorded by the Marian ambassador in 1555.[55] When John Raymond saw the hospital with its completed great court in 1647, his enthusiasm was such that despite his Protestantism he momentarily forgot the Reformation's theological demotion of Charity and of 'Good Works':

> The fairest Pallace in *Milan* (*I may say in Italy*) is the great Hospitall, a square of Columnes and Porches six hundreds Rods about; fitter to be the Court of some Kings then to keep Almes men in; yet no use can it be put better then to feed the Hungry and cloath the naked.[56]

By 1652, when Jeremiah Stephens was writing the letter to Rome quoted above, he could in fact have derived his information on Italian hospitals from one or more of a host of possible English sources. Apart from the descriptions already cited, there were now the Royalist exiles to correspond with and, with the expansion of the 'Grand Tour' phenomenon (and the published advice of Sir Francis Bacon, James Howell and others to the effect that the traveller 'must always have a Diary about him when he is in motion'), a greatly increased number of English accounts of Italy available, both manuscript souvenirs of specific journeys and published, or publishable, descriptions intended to be of use to future 'tourists'.[57] In a manuscript which clearly comes within the former category, written by Richard Lassels in 1650 and presented to his patron Thomas Whetenhall at the end of their journey together, we find a short but enthusiastic account of the Ospedale di S. Spirito at Rome, from which Stephens might have learned, for example, that its annual revenue was now 'seaventie Thousand Crownes'.[58]

Further information about this and other charitable institutions was included in Lassels's more formal *Description of Italy*, written in 1654 as the next best thing for a Scottish aristocrat who had failed to procure his personal services as a guide. As well as describing the 'Common Hospitals' and those that 'every nation hath . . . for those of its owne country', Lassels mentions several other less well-known Roman institutions:

> every particular body of Artists allmost have their hospitals for themselves. The servants of the Court, that of *S. Martha* behinde S. Peters Church: the Apothecaries, *S. Lorenzo* in foro Romano: the bakers, that of *S. Elizabeth* neere the campo di ffiori: the very Coachmen have theirs allso in Campo Martio.
>
> Neere S. Peters Church there is a house where the Pope commandes 13 poore men to be treated dayly at dinnar by his two Priests appointed for the office.
>
> Every friday in honour of our Saviours passion bread and wine are given to 2000 poore by the Pope: and dayly to a world of deserving gentlemen and prelats by his holyness.
>
> The Hospital of S. Anthony giveth dayly two loaves to every poore that cometh. The Hospital of S. Salvator neere S. John Laterans, giveth as much bread to all comers as would serve a man a whole day. The hospital of San Spirito . . . giveth dayly to all comers, bread and wine. And because some men out of shame will not beg, and yet are in great want, there stands a great chest in the Church of the 12 Apostles [SS. Apostoli] into which poore men throw their billets with their name and

dwelling place, and the nombre of their familie and every Saturday it is opened by the Confraternity of the 12 Apostles; and men are sent to carry almes to them who are ashamed to beg it.

Lassels refers later on once again to the Ospedale di S. Spirito when discussing the charitable reception afforded to 'Infants whom cruel mothers . . . expose to hide their shame'. 'Fooles too, so much the more miserable, as not knowing what they want, or where to find reliefe, are charitably taken care of in the Pazzarella, and provided for according as their humour and necessity require.'[59]

In his posthumously published *Voyage of Italy*, Lassels included a 14-page section devoted entirely to Roman charity, an expansion of the two earlier manuscript accounts. It is rounded off with an account of 'La Compagnia de' Morti, whose office is to bury the dead. . . . After which *charity* can do no more to man: and therefore I will conclude that . . . such singular acts of *charity* both for *body* and *minde*, are practised no where so much as in *Rome*.'[60]

If Lassels, who like Gregory Martin was a Catholic priest, might for this reason be accused of a predisposition to favour Roman institutions, John Evelyn, his more famous contemporary, as a staunch Anglican and would-be scientist, cannot. Yet he gave an even more detailed and no less enthusiastic account of the Ospedale di S. Spirito, around which he was shown by the English Catholic physician and poet Dr James Gibbes 'who had some intendency' there.[61]

Evelyn concluded that 'Indeede 'tis altogether one of the most pious and worthy Foundations that ever I saw, nor is the benefit small which divers Young Physitians & Chirurgions reape by the experience they learne here among the sick, to whom those students have universal accesse.' Like Lassels, he also admired the department for the care of exposed children:

Here are 40 Nurses who give suck to such Children as are accidentaly found expos'd & abandon'd: In another quarter are Children of bigger Groth 450 in number, who are taught letters, In another 500 Girles under the tuition of divers Religious Matrons, in a Monastry as it were by it selfe. I was assurd there were at least 2000 more maintain'd in other places: I think one Appartiment had in it neere 1000 beds: These are in a very long rome having an inner passage for those who attend, with as much curiosity, sweetenesse and Conveniency as can be imagin'd, the Italians being generaly exquisitely neate: Under this

Portico the sick may walke out and take the ayre: Opposite to this are other Chambers for such as are sick of maladies of a more rare & difficult cure, & they have roomes apart: At the end of the long Corridor is one of the fairest & well stord Apothecarys shops that I ever saw.[62]

At least as remarkable, however, was the recently founded *farmacia* mentioned by Lassels in his manuscript *Description*:

In fine (to omitt a world of such like knowne and unknowne charityes) here you shall finde an Apothecary shop founded and endowed with 12000 crownes a yeare (every mounth a thousand crownes) onely to furnish the poore with physick for nothing; and this in perpetuum. This is the charitable foundation and guift of our noble protectour Cardinal Francis Barberin [Francesco Barberini, styled Cardinal-Protector of England], who not content to give many secret charityes, hath found out a way to make his charity as common as the Sunn, and as lasting as the world.[63]

If much of Evelyn's account of S. Spirito is based on Pompilio Totti's *Ritratto di Roma Moderna* (Rome, 1638, 1645 and 1652), an earlier though unfortunately anonymous English account – which also remained in manuscript during the seventeenth century – managed to be both more detailed in terms of hospital procedure while at the same time less dependent on easily available guidebook material:

When you come in, you shall see right out before, on both sides, three-hundred beds standing, all hung with very fair curtains, the bedsteads carved, nightgowns, pantables, and other necessaries in order placed by every bed. So soon as a sick body comes thither (for none are refused) he is set on a bench, until the doctors and surgeons are brought to him, with the apothecaries, by whom the sick are visited. He is presently accepted, his bedding appointed, and immediately a clean sweet shirt is given him. His cloaths are laid up, till he recovers, or dies; and, as soon as the sick person is any whit amended, they give him another lodging, where he is well attended fourteen days, and more, until he be well recovered. In this hospital are thirty persons always maintained, only to give diligent attendance on the sick that resort thither.

In the midst you shall see as many beds, as in the room you came in at; and there is an altar and tabernacle, where mass is read to the sick, every morning. Both sides are hung with arra in winter-time, in summer with gilded leather, from the ground to the top. There are continually found at this hospital, above the three-thousand persons, as, children, nurses, widows, and other poor people, that are there maintained. This hospital, as is credibly reported, hath had every year income, more than two-hundred thousand crownes; but the popes of late have taken it away, so that the yearly revenue now is one million seven hundred thousand crowns [*sic*, presumably an error for 'one *thousand* seven hundred' which suggests that the author's source here was an Italian one].[64]

If the high standards of the Italian hospitals were clearly a novelty to sixteenth- and seventeenth-century English travellers, Englishmen were at least familiar with hospitals *per se*. This was clearly not the case with the Monti di Pietà, a notable example of which Francis Mortoft paused to admire at Rome in January 1659:

> On the Afternoone wee passed by a place that is called Monte della Pieta, and takes that name upon this Account. Pope Xistus Quintus appointed this house out of Charity to decayed Men, that is if any wanted money, and brought any goods or Jewels to this house, those things soe brought should be valued at the Best Rate, and the Owner should have the third part in money of what they were valued for, and at 9 months end, if he had noe mind to lay downe as much money as he tooke up, they should be sold to the full value, and he to have all the money without paying any use for the former.[65]

After a short account of Santissima Trinità, across the piazza, Mortoft goes on to describe another and less easily identifiable institution, perhaps the recently founded Ospedale di Santa Galla:

> Close by this place in an Hospitall Appointed by the same Pope [Innocent X] for all Inhabitants in Rome that are not able to worke; that is to say Either Blind, Lame, or Aged, and they may come, soe they have been Borne in Rome, and lawfully claime maintenance as long as they like.[66]

In Naples the hospital of the Annunziata (almost entirely destroyed by fire in 1757) was, according to the anonymous author of the early seventeenth-century *Description*, comparable to that of S. Spirito at Rome for the quality of its treatment of the patients and for the fact that such treatment was given free of charge: 'This is a wondrous fair hospital wherein are continually a great number of sick attended. Every nation is there entertained and accepted; each one has a clean bed, with all necessaries and attendance, as if he were at home in his own house, until he recovers, all gratis.'[67]

If we cannot be sure about this author's religious persuasion (the internal evidence being somewhat contradictory), about the orthodox Protestantism of Gilbert Burnet there can be even less doubt than there has been concerning Mortoft's or Evelyn's. Under William III, Burnet was to become the Bishop of Salisbury and, as an opponent of the Catholic regime in England, his 1685-6 travel letters were more than conventionally anti-papal.[68] When he came to describe the Annunziata, however, even though up to that point he had been condemning the excessive wealth of the Neapolitan monasteries and convents, he could not refrain from praising this Catholic institution in the most enthusiastic terms:

> The riches of the Annunciata are prodigious: It is the greatest Hospital in the World, the Revenue is said to be four hundred thousand Crowns a year: the number of the Sick is not so great as at Milan: Yet one convenience for their sick I observed in their Galleries, which was considerable, that every Bed stood as in an Alcove, and had a Wall on both sides separating it from the Beds on both hands, and as much void space of both sides of the Bed that the Bed it self took up but half the Room. The young Children that they maintain are so many, that one can hardly beleeve the numbers that they boast of: for they talk of many thousands that are not seen, but are at Nurse.[69]

The number of children had already been 'boasted of' in the 1654 edition of François Schott's *Itinerarium Italiae*, a work which had first appeared in Latin at Antwerp in 1600 but had been transformed into the first useful guidebook by a Vicentine Dominican, Fra Gioannini da Capugnano, in the following year. This re-revised Italian version was in turn translated into English (though without acknowledgement and somewhat clumsily) by Edmund Warcupp in 1660. According to the latter, the Annunziata was built

> like a spatious Castle, wherein are maintained as their condition, age, and health require, two thousand souls; therein are also brought up children of the poorer sort, more than eight hundred, between orphane and exposed infants as well as males as females: instructed in letters and art, according to their inclination till they become great. 'Tis a pleasure to see and observe their several diligent exercises and works.

It is noteworthy that as well as commending 'this custome of Christian Charity', the author discusses several classical precedents, observing that it 'resembles *Platoes* Republique in part'.[70]

By the time Burnet visited the Ospedale Maggiore at Milan in
1686 [Fig. 46], there were, besides Warcupp, at least four other
published accounts available in English. As well as those of Coryate
and Raymond already cited, there were now also the descriptions in
Lassels's *Voyage of Italy* (1670) and John Ray's *Observations* of 1673.
Lassels's description, like Coryate's 60 years before, starts with
rhetorical praise for the building's magnificence:

> The great *Hospital* built in a quadrangle upon arches and round pillars
> is a most magnificent thing. Really if sickness where not a little unwhole-
> some and troublesome, a man would almost wish to be a little sick here,
> where a *King*, though in health, might lodge hansomely. The place
> where the sick people are kept, is built crossewise, and in the middle of
> that crosse, stands an open *Altar* where all the sick people from their
> several quarters and from their very beds, may heare the *Divine service*
> at once. Four thousand men are entertained dayly in this *Hospital*, and
> therefore it hath great revenews. *S. Charles* [Carlo Borromeo] was a great
> benefactor to it, and gave away to it, and other pious uses, in half an
> hour, five and twenty thousand crownes of inheritance.[71]

Ray's account is similar enough to have been influenced by it; we
know that he used Lassels elsewhere. However, the ultimate source
for facts such as the number of poor who received assistance from
the hospital was, in both cases, probably Schott's *Itinerario*. Certainly
Ray seems to have derived his figure for the annual revenue from
this guidebook:

> The great Hospital is the largest and most magnificent, I think, in *Europe*,
> more like a stately Cloyster or Princes Palace than an Hospital. There is
> one great square Court, surrounded with a double *portico*, the one below,
> the other above stairs; besides four or five other smaller Courts. The
> Revenues of this house amount to more then 50000 crowns yearly;
> and there are maintained in it about 4000 poor, infirm and sick
> persons.[72]

If such figures are at all reliable, when we come to Burnet's account
we find almost a hundred per cent increase in the annual revenue:

> The Hospital is indeed a Royal Building, I was told it had ninety
> thousand Crowns Revenue: The old Court is large, and would look noble
> if it were not for the new Court that is near it, which is two hundred
> and fifty foot square, and there are three rows of Corridors or Galleries

all round the Court, one in every stage according to the Italian manner, which makes the lodgings very convenient, and gives a Gallery before every door: It is true these take up a great deal of the Building, being ordinarily eight or ten foot broad; but then here is an open space that is extream cool on that side where the Sun doth not lie, for it is all open to the Air, the Wall being only supported by Pillars, at the distance of fifteen or twenty foot from one another. In this Hospital there are not only Galleries full of Beds on both sides, as is ordinary in all Hospitals; but there are also a great many Chambers in which persons whose condition was formerly distinguished are treated with a particular care.

Burnet goes on to describe the Lazaretto which Fynes Moryson, three generations previously, had also paused to admire on his way through Milan:[73]

There is an out-house which is called the Lazarette, that is without the Walls, which belongs to this Hospital, it is an exact quarter of a mile square, and there are three-hundred and sixty Rooms in it, and a Gallery runs all along before the Chambers, so that as the service is convenient, the sick have a covered walk before their Doors. In the middle of this vast square there is an Octangular Chappel, so contrived that the sick from their Beds may see the elevation of the Hostie [sic] and adore it: This House is for the Plague or for infectious Feavers, and the Sick that want a freer Air, are also removed hither.[74]

Here as elsewhere, if England's hospitals were so well financed (whether by Professor Jordan's wills or by the Webbs' '£250,000' per annum rate-borne relief), it is strange that an Italian hospital such as this should make such a great impression on the cosmopolitan and reluctant-to-praise Burnet.[75]

In spite of the fact that economically Italy was in decline during this period, its philanthropical institutions managed to maintain their high standards, and this, as ever, was freely acknowledged by Catholic and Protestant visitors alike. Admiration on the part of the English tourists, now citizens of the wealthiest Protestant nation in Europe, continued well on into the eighteenth century, long after they had built Italian or French-style hospitals of their own, such as those at Chelsea and Greenwich. The latter, incidentally, were initiated not by Protestant burghers for their fellow citizens but by a crypto-Catholic monarch and his niece, for their military personnel. It was nevertheless only with these, and with the refounding of

Bethlehem Hospital in 1674, that England began to 'rival' the continent in such matters.[76]

Italy's ongoing philanthropical enterprise and the travellers' continuing admiration for it are both apparent in an interesting letter dated 3 January 1705, probably addressed to Sir Thomas Frankland. It mentions several of the hospitals already discussed and ends by revealing that major institutional construction was still being carried out, in this case on the great Albergo dei Poveri at Genoa, soon to be imitated on an even grander scale by Carlo di Borbone at Naples. This must already have been of a considerable size in 1684 when the French bombarded Genoa, for Misson, who travelled through the city four years after this disaster, reported that while the attack was under way

> The Doge with thirty thousand Persons more, took Shelter in the great Hospital called the *Albergo*; which being very high and large, not only afforded a safe Retreat to a great Number of the Inhabitants, but preserved a considerable Part of their Goods; for they brought thither all that could be carried.[77]

It thus comes as no surprise that the unknown author of the 1705 letter considers the Albergo to be the largest hospital in Italy:

> As the religious houses are great conveniences in Italy so their charities are very commendable. The *Convertiti* for cast mistresses at Venice is a noble foundation; there were three hundred and eighty women in it as I passed through. The *Pietas* for bastards are in every town in Italy; that at Rome is the largest; there is a fine one at Florence, and two in Venice, where upon laying the child in a window and ringing a little bell, it's immediately taken in and well taken care of. At Venice, the girls are brought up to all manner of needlework and music, and after they are fourteen years old are shewn every Whitsuntide to tradesmen in order to marry, and have a portion of 200 silver ducatts, but if they prove good musicians the hospital seldom parts with them. The boys are put out to prentice, but mostly employed in their arsenal and on board their galleys in the Morea. The hospitals of the *Incurabile* for all manner of sick people, and *Mendicantis* for all aged and decrepit are *very noble things and worthy to be imitated* [my italics]. I went into the *Incurabile* of Bolognia and was charmed to see so many sick people so well looked after; nurses with broths at every bed, their linen, even the curtains of the beds, very clean, in one corner priests confessing dying people, and in

another surgeons and doctors according to the disease. The largest in Italy and the best indued of this kind is at Genoa; it cost above fifty thousand pounds sterling building, and is not quite finished yet.

The writer continues with an observation which is not correct (as we saw from Martin's and Lassels's accounts of Rome, there were in fact institutions for 'i Pazzi'), but which seems worth quoting, if only for its primitive conception of the origins of insanity:

> You will be surprised when I tell you that amongst all their charities there is not a Bedlam in all Itally, nor have they occasion for any, for I do not remember in all my travels to have heard of either a down-right fool or a madman in Italy. Whether its the regular diet, their keeping good hours in going to bed, or the happiness of the climate, I don't know.[78]

The decline of Italy's social institutions is another story and no doubt directly related to the country's economic collapse. As we have seen, however, this decline was so considerably postponed that even towards the mid-eighteenth century Johann Keysler, a respected cosmopolitan and Fellow of the Royal Society, could conclude, after much detailed discussion of the comparative merits of hospitals throughout Europe in his four-volume *Travels*, that 'No country in the world equals Italy in the care of the poor and sick.'[79]

On the more general theme of the respective merit of Catholic and Protestant nations in matters philanthropical, few were better qualified to sum up than Keysler. His testimony is all the more valuable (if reluctantly pronounced) for being that of a convinced Protestant:

> As to hospitals, *Lazaretti*, and other charitable foundations, it must be owned that the protestant countries cannot come in competition with those of the *Romish* persuasion. This difference I partly impute to the prevalency of some doctrines among the latter, whereby the laity are not only incited to large contributions for such establishments, but even as it were constrained to it; among the motives that put them upon it, the dread of purgatory is not the least.[80]

Whether the latter observation, if in fact valid by the mid-eighteenth century, detracts from the Catholic achievement, or indeed excuses the backwardness of the English prior to this period, it is for the reader to decide.

EPILOGUE

Writing in 1786–9, John Howard, FRS, philanthropist and self-appointed inspector of prisons and hospitals throughout Europe, was far less impressed with the Hôtel Dieu at Lyons than he had been a decade earlier since he had meanwhile visited the Italian institutions. He concluded that 'having not then seen the well-regulated hospitals of Italy and Spain, perhaps I was now too much struck with the difference'.

Taking this author's very detailed accounts collectively, however (and excepting Florence which, under Pietro Leopoldo, had considerably improved its social institutions between the dates of Howard's two major reports), it becomes clear that the decline of the Italian economy was at last adversely affecting the quality of Italian philanthropy. Only now would England truly surpass Italy in such matters. It is thus only now that we find an Italian medical student travelling to England in something like the spirit with which Thomas Linacre had gone to Italy three centuries before.[81]

In the preface to his 1789 *Account of the principal Lazarettos*, though he was still calling for a 'reformation' of the English institutions, Howard nevertheless acknowledged that 'many changes for the better ha[d] been made' in his own country since the publication of his highly critical comparative study, the *State of the Prisons*, nine years before. It is certainly not extravagant to claim that some of the credit for the long overdue improvements in England's social institutions were specifically due to Howard's influence. Perhaps one might also claim a small share of such credit for Howard's travelling predecessors who, for more than two centuries, insistently drew their contemporaries' attention to the exemplary, for some 'Utopian' state of the Italian hospitals.

NOTES

This chapter was first published in *Aspects of Poverty in Early Modern Europe*, ed. T. Riis (Florence, 1982), pp. 183–217. Research for this and other work completed during the academic year 1978–9 at the European University was made possible by a grant from the Leverhulme Trust Fund which I gratefully acknowledge. An Italian version of this paper, 'Giudizi inglesi su ospedali italiani: 1549–1789', was published in the *Atti* of the conference on *Pauperismo e assistenza negli antichi stati italiani* held at Cremona in March 1980: *Timore e Carità: i poveri nell'Italia moderna*, ed. G. Politi, M. Rosa and F. della Peruta (Cremona, 1982), pp. 62–82.

1. For the published material see R.S. Pine-Coffin, *Bibliography of British and American travel to Italy to 1860* (Florence, 1974). There is as yet no comprehensive bibliography of the travel manuscripts. A select list, for the seventeenth century only, can be found in J.W. Stoye, *English Travellers Abroad 1604–1667*. 2nd edn (New Haven and London, 1989), pp. 362–3. I have found only one previous attempt to examine foreign observations on Italian hospitals: Mario Battistini, 'Viaggiatori stranieri in Italia nei sec. XVIII e XVIIIe e impressioni sull'assistenza ospitaliera', *Rivista di Storia Scienze Mediche e Naturali*, IX–X (1929), pp. 199–203. The Italians were conscious of foreign efforts in the field from at least as far back as Francesco Guicciardini who in 1511 admired the facilities in Barcelona: 'There is a large hospital with large numbers of sick in fine and well decorated rooms. As far as I could see they were well cared for. In the same hospital they care for foundlings and lunatics are there too'; see *The Travel Journal of Antonio de Beatis*, ed. J.R. Hale (London, 1979), p. 52.

2. For our purposes, the most interesting of the early controversies relating to charity and the hospitals is that surrounding the publication at Oxford in 1687 (probably by Obadiah Walker and with the implicit approval of James II) of a work entitled *Pietas Romana et Parisiensis or a faithful relation of the several sorts of charitable and pious works eminent in the Cities of Rome and Paris*. This was in fact a compilation of two earlier studies, Theodor van Meyden, *De pietate Romana libellus in quattuor partes divisus* (Rome, 1625), and Thomas Carre (also known as Miles Pinckney, a convert Catholic priest), *Pietas Parisiensis, or a short description of the pietie and charitie comonly exercised in Paris which represents in short the pious practises of the whole Catholic Church* (Paris, 1666). In his introduction to the joint edition of these works, Abraham Woodhead, the Catholic convert tutor and controversialist, provocatively invited his English readers to imitate the 'great variety of patterns of wisely-disbursed wealth' to be found in Rome and Paris. In the following year an indignant James Harrington, barrister-at-law, published, also at Oxford, his *Some reflections upon a treatise call'd Pietas Romana & Parisiensis lately printed at Oxford to which are added I. a Vindication of Protestant Charity* (etc.). In the course of rejecting the claims of the three Catholic authors, Harrington provides us with an impressive bibliography of the relevant post-Reformation literature on the issue.

3. Brian Pullan, *Rich and Poor in Renaissance Venice. The Social Institutions of a Catholic State, to 1620* (Oxford, 1971), p. 11. For Venice, see also B. Aikema and D. Meijers (eds), *Nel Regno dei Poveri. Arte e storia dei grandi ospedali veneziani in eta moderna, 1474–1797* (Venice, 1989).

4. Op. cit., p. 11. See the works cited in note 31 on the same page.

5. Op. cit., p. 12 and note 32 for the relevant bibliography.

6. Op. cit., p. 638.

7. Johan Huizinga, *Dutch Civilization in the Seventeenth Century*, transl. A. Pomerans (New York, 1968), p. 77.

8. Hugh Peters, *Good Work for a good Magistrate* (1650), p. 28. Conrad Russell, who cites this in his *Crisis of Parliaments* (Oxford, 1971, p. 373), states that the Leveller, Richard Overton, was of a like mind on the matter.

9. W.K. Jordan, *Philanthropy in England, 1480–1660* (London, 1959), *The Charities of London, 1480–1660* (London, 1960) and *The Charities of Rural England, 1480–1660* (London, 1961).

10. Even Pullan was persuaded by Jordan that 'the role of the individual philanthropist was, if anything, more conspicuous in England than in either France or Italy.' See Brian Pullan, 'Catholics and the Poor in early modern Europe', *Transactions of the Royal Historical Society*, 5th Series, XXVI (1976), p. 21.

11. Max Weber, *The Protestant Ethic and the Spirit of Capitalism*, transl. Talcott Parsons (London and New York, 1931); R.H. Tawney, *Religion and the Rise of Capitalism* (London, 1926); Margaret James, *Social Problems and Policy during the Puritan Revolution, 1640–1660* (London, 1930). See also S. and B. Webb, *The Old Poor Law* (London, 1927) and, on the more general subject of the supposedly fundamental differences between Catholic and Protestant attitudes to the poor, E. Troeltsch, *Social Teaching of the Christian Churches*, transl. O. Wyon (New York, 1931).

12. The articles criticizing Jordan's statistical methods are too numerous to list here, starting with the first reviews of *Philanthropy in England*. One of the most convincing supporters of Jordan's general thesis in these early reviews was Charles Wilson (*English Historical Review*, LXXXV (1960), pp. 685–7). He was able to point to a recent publication of his own which had proposed a similar critique of the Tawneian view of early capitalism's attitude to the poor; see 'The other Face of Mercantilism', *Transactions of the Royal Historical Society*, 5th series, IX (1959), reprinted in D.C. Coleman (ed.), *Revisions in Mercantilism* (London, 1969).

13. The article by W.G. Bittle and R. Todd Lane in the May 1976 issue of *Economic History Review*, 'Inflation and Philanthropy in England . . .', 2nd series, XXIX, pp. 203–10, revived the controversy by prompting articles by J.F. Hadwin, D.C. Coleman and J.D. Gould, all of whom attacked these latest critics of Jordan's statistics and, with reservations, defended *Philanthropy in England*; see *Economic History Review*, 2nd series, XXXI (1978), p. 105 ff. Bittle and Lane replied to *their* critics in turn in: 'A Re-assessment Reiterated', op. cit., pp. 124–8, from which I take the above quotation.

14. See W.K. Jordan, 'The English Background of modern Philanthropy', *American Historical Review*, LXVI (1961), p. 407. For the original 'documented' version of this claim, see *Philanthropy in England*, p. 230.

15. Jordan, *The Charities of London*, p. 20.

16. Ibid., p. 195. Jordan claims that these foundations 'are as interesting as they are worthy, because they represent the first really significant advance towards the assumption of civic responsibility for the cure of illness and the care of completely helpless persons' (op. cit., p. 186). Jordan suggests that thanks to 'the incredible generosity of a relatively small but faultlessly responsible burgher society', around 33,000 human beings 'were in 1660 being lifted and maintained above the slough of utter social disaster, if not death . . . These men and women had raised up institutions which were then and remain among the noblest of those the spirit of man has ever brought into being' (op. cit., p. 135).

17. Ibid., p. 195.

18. Ibid., pp. 136–7 and note 236.

19. Henry VII gave 10,000 marks to secure the foundation of this hospital-cum-almshouse which, when it was finally completed in 1519, became the largest institution of its kind in England and the only one with a cruciform plan. Henry VIII, who remained some sort of Catholic (to the detriment of Jordan's thesis) half-heartedly continued his father's funding of the Savoy but the Puritanical government of Edward VI suppressed the hospital in 1553. It was refounded three years later by Henry's Catholic daughter Mary; see John Stow, *A Survey of London* (1603), ed. C.L. Kingsford (Oxford, 1908), p. 144 and R. Somerville, *The Savoy* (London, 1960). For the fascinating description and *regolamento* sent on request to Henry VII by Francesco Portinari, see Luigi Passerini, *Storia degli stabilimenti di beneficenza e d'istruzione elementare gratuita della città di Firenze* (Florence, 1853), pp. 304n and 851–67 and J. Henderson and K.P. Park,

' "The First Hospital among Christians": The Ospedale di Santa Maria Nuova in early 16th-century Florence', *Medical History*, XXV (1991). For the hospital's architectural influence on the Savoy, see H. Colvin (ed.) *The King's Works*, III, pt 1 (London, 1975), pp. 196–206. For the true extent of the royal contribution to the London hospitals – a considerably larger one than Jordan would have us believe – see J.F. Hadwin, 'The Problem of Poverty in Early Modern England' in *Aspects of Poverty in Early Modern Europe*, ed. T. Riis (Florence, 1982), pp. 219–51.

20. Jordan, *The Charities of London*, p. 57 ff.
21. Ibid., p. 58.
22. See note 13 above.
23. For Stephens, see *Dictionary of National Biography* and under 'Spelman' in *Biographica Britannica*, 6 vols (London, 1750). Stephens was continuing his master's massive project, only ever partially published, as *The History and Fate of Sacrilege* (London, 1698 and 1853); see *DNB*, XXVIII, p. 740.
24. Biblioteca Vaticana MSS. Barberini Lat. 3539, fol. 155 (a letter dated 1/11 Nov. 1652 and probably intended for Lucas Holstenius). I was led to this source by Roman Transcripts 31/9/95 in the Public Record Office, London. My thanks to Peter Mack for transcribing the original headed 'The coppy of part of Mr Jeremy Stephens his letter to me'. For a detailed letter introducing Stephens to Holstenius, dated 2 February 1650, see J.G. Fotheringham, 'Unpublished letters written by Sir Kenelm Digby to Signor Luke Holstein', *The Antiquary*, XXXVI (1900), pp. 12–14.
25. Jordan, *Philanthropy in England*, pp. 137–41.
26. See the several references to Jordan's work in 'The Poor and the Parish', in Christopher Hill, *Society and Puritanism* (London, 1964), and compare with the same author's article on William Perkins in 'Puritans and the Poor' (*Past & Present*, 2, 1952). For a post-Jordan summary of the relevant historiography on the specific subject of poor relief between 1640 and 1660, Valerie Pearl, 'Puritans and Poor Relief, the London Workhouse, 1649–1660', in D. Pennington and K. Thomas (eds), *Puritans and Revolutionaries: Essays . . . presented to Christopher Hill* (Oxford, 1978), pp. 206–8.
27. Quoted in B. and S. Webb, op. cit., p. 95.
28. It was probably the lack of funds available for the successful running of Christ's *qua* orphanage that encouraged the policy whereby it eventually emerged as a grammar school; see Valerie Pearl, op. cit., pp. 213–14. The fact that the intake of both children and adults into the London institutions was decreasing can be seen by comparing the 1645 *Report* (Wing 13092) quoted from here, with that for the previous year, reprinted as Appendix XIV in E.M. Leonard, *The Early History of English Poor Relief* (Cambridge, 1900).
29. By 1775 in one London parish 'Three quarters out of the twelve hundred babies born every year in the parish died, many being exposed or overlaid by "nurses".' In the 14 parishes investigated, Jonas Hanway, the Russian merchant and social reformer, calculated 'that the death-rate amongst infants entering or being born in the workhouses that had sprung up since 1720 was 88%'; see Charles Wilson, 'The other Face of Mercantilism', cit., pp. 91–2. Professor Pearl (op. cit., p. 211) estimates that between 1640 and 1660 Christ's provided annually for between 450 and 900 orphans, St Thomas's and St Bartholomew's combined for over 2,000 sick and aged persons, and Bridewell for about 1,000 vagrants and other offenders, as well as around 200 apprentices.
30. Thomas Frank, *An Edition of a Discourse of HP his travelles* (MS Rawlinson D83),

(unpublished B.Litt. thesis, University of Oxford, 1954). I am very grateful to Professor Frank for the loan of a copy of his dissertation.

31. Ibid., p. 149. Whilst preparing his doctoral dissertation on the Innocenti for the University of Michigan, Ann Arbor, Philip Gavitt kindly informed me that the figures given by Piers were fully in accord with his own estimates for the same period; see now Dr Gavitt's excellent *Charity and Children in Renaissance Florence: The Ospedale degli Innocenti 1410-1536* (Ann Arbor, 1990). The figures are further confirmed by L. Passerini, op. cit., p. 707, who also deals with the 1640s. Venice at around the time of Piers's travels 'claimed to be supporting about 3000 children or *creature*' in three of its major hospitals (that is, around 2 per cent of its total population); see Brian Pullan, *Rich and Poor*, p. 374. Observing the decline in intake during a difficult period in the case of the London hospitals makes one doubt the general applicability of Professor Pullan's suggestion that an *increase* in the number of children accepted 'può essere considerato un riflesso del deterioramento economico'; see Professor Pullan's chapter on 'Poveri, mendicanti e vagabondi: secoli XIV-XVII' (*Storia d'Italia*, Annali I, Turin, 1978), p. 1026.

32. Conte Gualdo Priorato, *Relatione della Città di Fiorenza* (Cologne, 1668), p. 56. If this figure is accurate it would certainly have involved accommodating more than one to a bed. For the 1661-3 completion of Buontalenti's loggia, see *Lo Spedale di S. Maria Nuova . . .*, ed. Guido Pampaloni (Florence, 1961). It is this that is depicted, together with the influential cruciform plan of the women's dormitory (which interlocked with the original men's wards) in John Howard, *Account of the principal Lazarettos in Europe . . .*, 2nd edn (Warrington, 1791), plate 17. [Fig. 45]

33. A.M. Crinò, 'Il testo di quella che Petruccio Ubaldini considerava la redazione definitiva della sua Relatione d'Inghilterra', *Annali della Scuola Normale Superiore di Pisa*, series III, 9, 2 (1979), pp. 729-32. For the visitor from Italy, which had numerous institutions devoted specifically to the 'incurabili', the rejection of these must have seemed particularly outrageous. The maintenance of syphilitics and other mortally ill patients (the sixteenth-century equivalents of the medieval lepers) was, of course, truly charitable, there being no possible economic return on those who would never work again.

34. Crinò, op. cit., p. 732.

35. Without supplying any concrete evidence, Mariano da Alatri in V. Monachino (ed.), *La Carità Cristiana in Roma* (Rome, 1968), pp. 151-2, argues that the passage from Luther's 'Tischreden' refers to the Roman rather than the Florentine institutions. There is a marked similarity, it is true, between the relevant passage in the *Liber regulae* of the Ospedale di S. Spirito and Luther's account; but then the *regolamenti* of hospitals such as S. Maria Nuova (see note 19) were also similar. Luther's account is of great interest and must have served as a considerable encouragement for English Protestants to eulogize the Italian hospitals. Its translation into English in 1652 by Captain Henrie Bell (*Dris Martini Lutheri Colloquia Mensalia*, or *Dr Martin Luther's Discourses at his table* (London), p. 233) caused it to be still more widely known and it is from this that I quote here:

> In Italie (said Luther) the Hospitals are very well provided, fair buildings, good meat and drink, they have diligent attendance, and learned physicians, the bedding and furniture are clean and neat, the dwelling places fairly painted. So soon as a sick person is brought in, they take off his Cloths in the presence of a publique Notarie, who truly taketh notice thereof in

writing, they are well and warily laid up, and they put upon him a white coat, and lay him in a well prepared bed. Soon after they bring two physicians, and the servants bring meat and drink in pure glass vessels and cups, which they touch onely with one finger. Then also certain married Matrones and women (whose faces are covered) do come and minister to the poor, as unknown, and afterwards go home again.

The Protestant moral is, of course, supplied by way of conclusion: 'Now (said Luther) these works are good and laudable, onely, the mischief is, that thereby they think to merit Heaven, and to bee sustained and saved by reason of such their works, which spoileth all.'

36. *The Historie of Italie* . . . (London, 1549). For Thomas see above, pp. 70–6. He also published the first Anglo-Italian grammar-cum-dictionary, 'for the better under-standynge of Boccace, Petrarche, and Dante' (London, 1550). There is in fact an earlier English account of an Italian hospital than this, but it is more rhetorical than informative. It occurs in the *c.*1476 poem 'Meditations at Tivoli' by Robert Flemmyng. This appears, translated from the Latin, in George Parks, *The English Traveller to Italy* . . . *to 1535* (Rome, 1954), pp. 601–6. The poem praises Sixtus IV's rebuilding of the Ospedale di S. Spirito.

37. *The Historie* . . ., op. cit., p. 138. Priorato (op. cit., p. 56) bears eloquent witness to S. Maria Nuova's continuing high standards and secular support from the 'pii Cittadini, in modo tale, che ora si trova così ricco, che sorpassa 70. mila scudi di annuale entrata'.

38. See P. Slack, 'Some Comparative Problems in the English Case', in *Aspects of Poverty in Early Modern Europe* (op. cit.) and by the same author 'Social policy and the Contraints of Government 1547–1558', in J. Loach and R. Tittler (eds), *The Mid-Tudor Polity, c.1540–1560* (London, 1980), pp. 94–115.

39. Pullan, *Rich and Poor*, op. cit., pp. 11–13 and 638, and the same author's 'Catholics and the Poor in early modern Europe', *Transaction of the Royal Historical Society*, 5th series, XXVI (1976), pp. 15–34.

40. Thomas, op. cit., p. 82.

41. Jordan, *The Charities of London*, p. 168.

42. Sir Thomas Hoby, *The Travels and Life* . . . *1547–1564*, ed. Edgar Powell, Camden Miscellany, X (London, 1902), p. 29.

43. 'The Jurney of the Queenes Ambassadours unto Roome Anno. 1555', *Miscellaneous State Papers, 1501–1726* (London, 1778), p. 82; cited in E.J. Baskerville, *The English Traveller to Italy, 1547–1560* (Ann Arbor, MI, 1982), p. 66. For the Ospedale Maggiore see also Evelyn S. Welch, *Art and Authority in Renaissance Milan* (New Haven/London, 1995), chs 6 and 7.

44. Fanucci, p. 6 (A3v), 'Alli lettori' and Gregory Martin, *Roma Sancta*, 1581, ed. G.B. Parks (Rome, 1969), preface, *passim* and p. xxix. One post-*Roma Sancta* institution enthused over by Fanucci, San Sisto, is viewed in a more sceptical light by Bronislaw Geremek in 'Renfermement des pauvres en Italie (XIVe–XVIIe siècle)', *Histoire économique du monde méditerranéen 1450–1640: Mélanges en l'honneur de Fernand Braudel*, I (Toulouse, 1973), pp. 212–21. In the Vatican Archives there is a list of charitable institutions, with numbers maintained, dating from the late 1550s; see A.S.V. Armadio II, Politicorum, 78. I thank Dr Ruth Liebowitz for this reference. Father Gregory Martin was an MA from St John's College, Oxford (where his somewhat severe portrait is still to be seen). He had been tutor to the sons of Thomas Howard, 4th Duke of Norfolk, and was the principal translator of the Douai Bible. As such he would have been distressed to find himself referred to as a Protestant (and as 'Graham'

Martin) who gloated over the ruins of Rome for anti-Roman reasons, in an otherwise useful article on sixteenth-century French travellers and their sources: Margaret M. McGowan, 'Impaired Vision: the Experience of Rome in Renaissance France', *Renaissance Studies*, VIII, 3 (1994), pp. 244–55.

45. Martin, op. cit., p. xxx and note on p. 184.
46. Martin, op. cit., p. 184.
47. W.K. Jordan, *The Charities of London*, p. 195, and Valerie Pearl, op. cit., p. 212. Although Professor Pearl's article is about philanthropical progress, as seems to be customary where English social history is concerned no reference is made to continental developments in the same field, with the result that London tends to retain its 'pioneering' reputation; see, for example, pp. 210 and 218 for Rice Bush's 'anticipatory' recommendation of free medicines for the poor, when such facilities already existed in Rome and other Italian cities.
48. Gregory Martin, op. cit., p. 184. The quotations that follow are all taken from pp. 184–9, the chapter entitled 'A Breefe description in particular of all the *hospitals* in Rome, *for the sicke and sore*'.
49. 'Poverty and Philanthropy in Early Modern England', in *Aspects of Poverty*, ed. T. Riis (cit. in headnote), pp. 253–79. Wilson already showed in 1958 ('The other Face' . . ., published 1959, cit. above n. 12, pp. 92–3), that for every £1 of miscellaneous charitable investment there was a £5 investment in land. No survey of the considerable landed wealth of the Italian hospitals seems to have been made. See, however, for Florence, the interesting documentation in Ginori Lisci, *Cabrei in Toscana* (Florence, 1978) (I thank Sir Harold Acton for this reference), and for Venice, Brian Pullan, *Rich and Poor*, pp. 412–21.
50. For the hospital generally see the numerous publications of P. de Angelis; see also A. Canezza, *Gli arcispedali di Roma nella vita cittadina, nella storia e nell'arte, I: Santo Spirito in Sassia* (Rome, 1933). For the specific role of Sixtus IV in creating an institution which was clearly ahead of anything England was to have for a century or more, see the PhD dissertation by Eunice D. Howe, *The Hospital of Santo Spirito and Pope Sixtus IV* (Johns Hopkins University, 1977, published London and New York, 1978) which has a useful bibliography. Innocent III founded the hospital in the borgo formerly occupied by Anglo-Saxon expatriates and pilgrims; hence the suffix 'in Saxia' and hence also an ongoing tradition by which English visitors to Rome joined the confraternity; see G.B. Parks, op. cit., *passim*; Robert Brentano, *Rome before Avignon* (London, 1974), pp. 19–22, and W.J. Moore, *The Saxon Pilgrims to Rome and the Scuola Saxonum* (Fribourg, 1939). In 1596, Henry Piers (op. cit., p. 185) described S. Spirito as 'the most famous and Lardgeste hospitall in the whole worlde'. Though occasionally worried that the institutions for receiving unwanted children might 'encourage licentiousness', most English travellers strongly commended them. Sir John Reresby, probably thinking of the Innocenti, which he had seen in Florence in 1657, wrote: 'I am sure they prevent the barbarous murder of one's own children, too often here [in England] committed with violence both to nature and conscience, for want of some such salve for reputation' (*Travels and Memoirs* (London, 1813), p. 107) For the continuation of this practice in Victorian England, see George K. Behlmer, *Child Abuse and Moral Reform in England 1870–1908* (Stanford, CA, 1983). For pre-Renaissance abandonment of children see John Boswell, *The Kindness of Strangers* (New York, 1988).
51. That such (secular) generosity was not confined to Rome (or London) is shown by note 32 on p. 23 of Pullan's article on 'Catholics and the Poor'. There are few of Jordan's London burghers whose generosity rivals that of Bartolomeo Bontempelli, the Brescian mercer who gave 36,000 ducats during his lifetime

and 100,000 by his 1613 will to the beggars' hospital in Venice; see *Capitoli della veneranda congregazione dell'Hospitale di Santo Lazaro et Mendicanti della città di Venezia* (Venice, 1619), pp. 7–8.

52. *Itinerary written by Fynes Moryson gent.* (London, 1617) (but referring to travels undertaken during the first half of the 1590s), I, ii, p. 151.
53. Ibid., I, ii, p. 84 (N.B., there are two pages numbered 84), and Brian Pullan, *Rich and Poor*, p. 370: 'At the end of 1601, the governors reported that they had in the course of the year dealt with about 800 paupers, and disposed of more than half of them through apprenticeship (etc.) . . . This left about 370 inmates, old people and small children, lepers and sick persons. In 1605, and 1618, the Mendicanti was again described as having about 400 inmates.'
54. See the footnote in Evelyn's *Diary*, ed. E.S. de Beer (Oxford, 1955), II, p. 495 note 8, which is based on G. Caimi, *Notizie storiche del grand'ospitale di Milàno* (Milan, 1857), pp. 33–7, and the essays in *La Ca' Grande*, exhibition catalogue (Milan, 1981). Evelyn himself, probably the most derivative of the travellers under discussion, describes the building as it had been when Coryate saw it merely because he used out-of-date sources (in spite of having actually visited Milan in 1646).
55. *Coryats Crudities Hastily gobled up in five Moneths travells in France, Savoy, Italy* . . . (London, 1612), p. 102. The Italian section of Coryate's travelogue is indebted to Fra Girolamo da Capugnano's edition of François Schott's *Itinerarium Italiae* (Vicenza, 1601).
56. John Raymond, *An itinerary contayning a voyage made through Italy, in the yeare 1646, and 1647* (London, 1648), pp. 244–5.
57. Bacon, *Of travel*, in *Essays* (London, 1625); Howell, *Instructions for Forreine travell (1642)* (London, 1869 edn), p. 20.
58. British Library, Add. MS. 4217, folio 24r-v. There is an annotated edition of this part of Lassels's manuscript in my M.Phil. thesis (Warburg Institute, University of London, 1977). I thank Professor J.B. Trapp for originally suggesting I work on this manuscript. The most detailed contemporary account of S. Spirito is P. Saulnier, *De Capite Sacri Ordinis Sancti Spiriti dissertatio* (Lyons, 1649), which is also illustrated with engravings. Lassels's praise of 'the particular and better accommodations for Gentlemen that those whom fortune had privileged by bettre birth, might not be involved in common miseries', probably refers to Urban VIII's important foundation for *i poveri vergognosi*, praised and described in greater detail by C.B. Piazza in his *Eusevologio romano* . . . (Rome, 1698), I, pp. 120–2.
59. National Library of Scotland, Advocates MS 15.2.15 (formerly catalogued as anonymous), pp. 166–7. I include a complete transcript of this manuscript in my PhD dissertation ('Richard Lassels and the Establishment of the Grand Tour: Catholic Cosmopolitans and Royalist Exiles in Italy 1630-1660', Warburg Institute, University of London, 1982); cf. *The Grand Tour and the Great Rebellion* (Geneva and Turin, 1985). Both the sympathetic tone which Lassels adopts and the humanitarian attitude he ascribes to the institution he is dealing with ill accord with the thesis advanced by Michel Foucault in *Histoire de la Folie* (Paris, 1961), *passim*. For a detailed early nineteenth-century account of the lunatic asylum at Aversa, still less in accord with Foucault's thesis, see Lady Blessington, *Idler in Italy* (London, 1839), II, pp. 250–7; cf. *Lady Blessington in Naples*, ed. Edith Clay (London, 1979), pp. 131–3. For the best recent account of the major (for 400 years the *only*) English institution for the insane, see Christine Stevenson, 'Robert Hooke's Bethlem', *Journal of the Society of Architectural Historians*, LV, no. 3 (1996), pp. 254–75.

60. Richard Lassels, *The Voyage of Italy* (Paris, 1670), II, pp. 6–20. For those interested in the history of 'access to justice' or legal aid, there is an account on ibid., II, pp. 16–17, of the Congregation of Advocats who 'meet once a week to examin poor mens *law sutes*; and either to dehort them from proceeding in bad causes; or prosecute good causes for them at the cost of this *Congregation*'. For a discussion (with bibliography) of the *advocatus pauperum deputatus et stipendiatus*, in its historical context, see Mauro Cappelletti, 'The Emergence of a Modern Theme' in M. Cappelletti, J. Gordley and E. Johnson (eds), *Towards Equal Justice* (Milan and New York, 1952), pp. 13–15.

61. Lassels, op. cit., II, p. 231, calls Gibbes 'the *Horace* of this age', as does (following him?) Anthony à Wood, '*Fasti Oxonienses*' in P. Bliss (ed.), *Athenae Oxonienses*, II (London, 1820), pp. 326 and 338–42; Wood was presented with a copy of Lassels's *Voyage* by his Catholic friend and patron Ralph Sheldon; see also above, pp. 226–30.

62. *The Diary of John Evelyn*, ed. E.S. de Beer (Oxford, 1955), II, pp. 311–12; cf. P. Totti, *Ritratto di Roma Moderna* (Rome, 1638), pp. 41–2 which is the main source for Evelyn's account. L. v. Pastor, *La Storia dei Papi* (Ital. edn by P. Cenci, XIII, Rome, 1961), p. 981, writes of the hospital at this period as having 'due sale per malatti, contenenti mille letti . . . Annesso all'ospedale . . . era un'ospizio di trovatelli ed un istituto di educazione per 450 ragazzi e 500 ragazze'.

63. National Library of Scotland, Advocates' MS 15.2.15, pp. 167–8 (Chaney, *Grand Tour*, cit., p. 182). There is an article by the Barberini's biographer, P. Pecchiai, specifically devoted to this 'Apothecary shop': 'Una farmacia fondata dal Cardinal Francesco Barberini seniore per la compagna dei SS. Apostoli', (*Pantheon*, IV (1950), nos 9–10, pp. 159–60, and nos 11–12, pp. 201–2).

64. J. Malham (ed.), *The Harleian Miscellany*, 12 vols (London, 1808–11), XII, pp. 99–100. The recent reduction in revenue, if a fact, is probably accounted for by a return to reasonable running expenditure after the hospital's expansion during the late sixteenth century; I have not, however, found any reference to it elsewhere. After listing a few minor complaints and problems encountered by S. Spirito and the other Roman hospitals during the course of the seventeenth century, M. Petrocchi in his *Roma nel Seicento* (Bologna, 1970), p. 108, concedes that 'La vita ospedaliera di Roma seicentesca ha avuto cioè alcune difficoltà.' He concludes, however, with the observation that 'tutti gli stranieri sempre testimoniarono la preparazione tecnica e l'assistenza precisa nel campo materiale e la pietà spirituale'.

65. *Francis Mortoft: his book*, ed. M. Letts, Hakluyt Society, 2nd series, no. 57 (London, 1925), p. 105. On the Monti di Pietà of Venice and elsewhere, see Brian Pullan, *Rich and Poor*, part III, *passim*. There is a useful short account and bibliography for Rome in Petrocchi, op. cit., pp. 82–4.

66. Mortoft, op. cit., p. 106.

67. *Harleian Miscellany*, op. cit., pp. 118–19. For the reputation of the Ospedale dell'Annunziata see R. de Maio, *Riforme e miti nella Chiesa del Cinquecento* (Naples, 1973), pp. 245–53.

68. Burnet, *Some letters containing an account of what seemed most remarkable in Switzerland, Italy etc.* (Rotterdam, 1686). For an interesting analysis of Burnet's criticisms of late seventeenth-century Italy, see V.I. Comparato, 'Viaggiatori inglesi in Italia tra Sei e Settecento' (*Quaderni Storici*, XLII (1979), pp. 850–86). See also F. Venturi, 'L'Italia fuori d'Italia' (*Storia d'Italia*, III, Turin, 1973), pp. 990–6.

69. Burnet, op. cit., p. 193. Between 1680 and 1730 the Annunziata almost

doubled its annual intake of children (from 600 to 1110); see Brian Pullan, *Poveri, mendicanti e vagabondi*, p. 1026. It is worth noting that in the year before writing this Burnet had published his translation of Sir Thomas More's *Utopia* with its description of an ideal hospital.

70. Warcupp, *Italy, in its original glory, ruine and revival* . . . (London, 1660), pp. 264–5. This book and its source are discussed by E.S. de Beer in *The Library*, 4th series, XXIII, nos 2, 3 (1942).

71. Lassels, *Voyage*, I, pp. 121–2. Of unpublished accounts of the Ospedale Maggiore most noteworthy is that to be found in the 1610 British Library, Sloane MS 682, (fols. 10v–12r). This was probably written by Sir Thomas Berkeley or one of his train; see Stoye, op. cit., pp. 339 and 362.

72. Ray, *Observations . . . made in a journey through part of the Low Countries, Germany, Italy, and France* (London, 1673) (describing travels of 1663–66), p. 243.

73. Moryson, op. cit., I, ii, p. 171. Lassels also provides a good description of Milan's famous Lazzaretto (op. cit., pp. 112–13), for a contemporary print of which see J.D. Thompson and G. Goldwin, *The Hospital: A Social and Architectural History* (New Haven and London, 1975), figure 55.

74. Burnet, op. cit., pp. 108–9. Burnet probably derived his figure of 90,000 crowns for the hospital's annual revenue from a revised edition of F. Schott's *Itinerario d'Italia*, or from a guide, basing his estimate on the updated figures contained therein: 'Ha d'entrata ogn'anno 50. mila scudi; è ben vero, che alle volte passa 60. & anco. 90. mila. Mantiene anime 4000 . . .' (Schott, (Padua edn., 1659), part I, pp. 134–5). The Ospedale Maggiore continued to receive the highest praise throughout the first half of the eighteenth century. Even the somewhat bigoted, Protestant account, dating from *c.*1711, to be found in the anonymous MS in the Brotherton Collection, University of Leeds, praises the hospital, though it estimates a total of only 2,000 inmates (*Journal of Travels in Europe*). By the late 1770s, however, the philanthropist John Howard, travelling specifically to investigate the prisons and hospitals of Europe comparatively, confessed to being disappointed, his expectations having been 'too much raised by the accounts of travellers'; 'Most of the wards are on the ground floor, and not lofty, as there are rooms over them. They are also dirty and offensive, though provided with spacious drains. They have a middle row of beds, and in many of the beds were two persons: but care was taken to separate patients in fevers from those who were attended by surgeons.' John Howard, F.R.S., *The State of the Prisons* . . . (2nd edn, Warrington, 1780), p. 105.

75. For the Webbs' estimate of £250,000 (which contrasts rather dramatically with Jordan's £3,000 per annum estimate for the same period), see J.F. Hadwin, 'The Problem of Poverty', op. cit. It has recently been demonstrated that more than half the money spent on poor relief in at least one mid-seventeenth-century London parish came from the rates; see Valerie Pearl, op. cit., p. 208, citing R.W. Herlan, 'Poor Relief during the Great Civil War and Interregnum, 1642–1660' (unpublished PhD dissertation, State University of New York, Buffalo, 1973), chapter IV.

76. For Bethlem, see above, note 59. For the 'Economic decline of Italy', see the article of that title by Carlo M. Cipolla, in Brian Pullan (ed.), *Crisis and Change in the Venetian Economy* . . . (London, 1968). Two more recent works by Professor Cipolla have not been cited hitherto as they do not relate directly to philanthropy as such. They should perhaps be mentioned, however, as having clearly documented Italian superiority in the field of public health in the

seventeenth century. Both works, moreover, make good use of the evidence of English travellers; see *Cristofano and the Plague* (London, 1973) and *Public Health and the Medical Profession in the Renaissance* (Cambridge, 1976). See also Cipolla's *I pidocchi e il Granduca. Crisi economica e problemi sanitari nella Firenze del '600* (Bologna, 1979), which describes how the Florentine hospitals dealt with the 1620-1 outbreak of typhus.

While England imitated Italy's hospitals during the Renaissance and seventeenth century, Italy, having fallen behind during the past 200 years, recently chose to adopt a National Health-type system derived, at least in part, from the English model. It is arguable that with the establishment of the National Health Service, Britain's hospital system at last became, in Jordan's words (referring to an earlier period), 'unrivalled . . . in the whole of the western world'. But so far as the foundation of hospitals in London is concerned, the golden age was the first half of the eighteenth century. The foundation of Westminster Hospital followed soon after the formation of the charitable society of that name in 1719; Guy's was founded in 1724; St George's in 1733; the London in 1740; and the Middlesex in 1745.

77. François Misson, *A New Voyage to Italy* (London, 1739 edn), II, part I, p. 373. For the proportion of wealth belonging to charities and religious institutions in late eighteenth-century Genoa, see C.H. Wilson and G. Parker (eds), *An Introduction to the Sources of European Economic History 1500-1800* (London, 1977), pp. 32-3. For the Albergo itself, see E. Grendi, 'Pauperismo e Albergo dei poveri nella Genova del Seicento', *Rivista Storica Italiana*, LXXXVII, 4 (1975), pp. 621-63.

78. *Historical Manuscripts Commission Report on Manuscripts of Mrs Frankland-Russell-Astley* (London, 1900), p. 173. That the author of this letter was clearly a Protestant can be seen, for example, by his references to the Madonna and superstition generally on p. 172.

79. Johann G. Keysler, *Travels . . .* (London, 1756-7, English version of the second German edn), II, p. 345, cited along with other travellers' enthusiastic comments on Roman charity, in Herbert Thurston, *The Holy Year of Jubilee* (London, 1900), pp. 282-95. For a glowing account of late eighteenth- and early nineteenth-century hospitals in Tuscany see Eric Cochrane, *Florence in the Forgotten Centuries 1527-1800* (Chicago and London, 1973), pp. 431-3. Evidence to support Cochrane is to be found in John Howard, *Account of the principal Lazarettos . . .*, 2nd edn (Warrington, 1791), II, p. 57: 'At Florence, in 1786, in the *Prisons* and *Hospitals* which I had seen about seven years before, I found the most pleasing alteration had taken place, in consequence of the great care and attention of the *Grand Duke* [Pietro Leopoldo].'

80. Keysler, *Travels*, I, p. 336, in a comparison between the hospitals of Leiden and Milan. For Keysler's detailed praise of S. Maria Nuova in Florence, see II, p. 64 (1760 ed.).

81. Brian Moloney in his *Florence and England* (Florence, 1969), p. 161, notes the example of Lorenzo Nannoni, a surgeon like his father, travelling to England in the 1780s 'to observe hospitals and operating techniques'. For Linacre's twelve years in Italy see Charles B. Schmitt in F. Maddison, M. Pelling and C. Webster (eds), *Linacre studies . . .* (Oxford, 1977), pp. 36-75: 'What Linacre brought back with him from Italy to Britain was a high-level education in both humanistic and medical studies, which was superior to anything he might have obtained in his native land.' By the late 1840s when that mistress of the comparative study of such matters, Florence Nightingale, visited the Italian hospitals, conditions had deteriorated considerably. At S. Giacomo in Rome, she

found four rows of beds all in one ward: 'the stench dreadful, the locale cold, airless, dark . . . it seemed a physical impossibility for anyone ever to get well there . . . There are but 9 nuns to the whole concern, who relieve each other every 6 hours through the 24 . . . they seemed hopeless and worn out'; Mary Keele (ed.), *Florence Nightingale in Rome: Letters written in Rome in the winter of 1847–1848*, Memoirs of the American Philosophical Society, CXLII (Philadelphia, 1981), p. 190. For the reluctant-to-praise Dr Samuel Sharp commending the bug-resistant iron bedsteads of S. Maria Nuova in the 1760s and confirmation of Howard's enthusiasm for Pietro Leopoldo's reforms in the 1785 *Travels* of President Charles Dupaty, see H. Acton and E. Chaney, *Florence: A Travellers' Companion* (London, 1986), pp. 129–32.

POSTSCRIPT

At the time of going to press in 1981 a short article appeared which drew attention to a group of seventeenth-century manuscripts in the British Library which include hospital descriptions. The only one of these not mentioned above which may be of relevance is Sloane MS 1385. This is anonymous and contains an account of Santo Spirito written in 1687. It is described as one of the finest hospitals in Europe; see J.D. Alsop, 'Some notes on seventeenth-century Continental hospitals', *British Library Journal*, VII, 1 (Spring 1981), pp. 70–4. In 1996 one should mention Brian Pullan, *Poverty and Charity: Europe, Italy, Venice, 1400–1700* (Aldershot, 1994), which reprints his most relevant articles, and Sandra Cavallo, *Charity and Power in Early Modern Italy: Benefactors and their Motives in Turin, 1541–1789* (Cambridge, 1995), which conveniently cites much of the relevant bibliography published between these two dates. For the English background see Nicholas Orme and Margaret Webster, *The English Hospital 1070–1570* (New Haven and London, 1995). Roy Porter's *Mind-Forg'd Manacles: A History of Madness in England* (London, 1990) begins with the Restoration so does not cover Bethlem Hospital prior to its 1674 relocation. With regard to the Anglo-Italian comparison, however, and the egregious influence of Foucault (see note 59 above) it might be worth quoting an early sixteenth-century Milanese merchant traveller on Bethlem a century and a half before it left Bishopsgate: 'In Londres in uno borgho apresso ad una porta a cantto ad una chiesietta appellata Bethelem li he uno hospitale de matti ove sono molte camere et ciaschuna ha uno matto entroví, et glien'è de ogni sorte: he cosa paurosa ad vedere'; Luigi Monga (ed.), *Un Mercante di Milano in Europa: Diario di Viaggio del primo Cinquecento* [1517–19] (Milan, 1985), p. 84. Finally, two collections of essays relevant to many of the issues raised here: Lindsay Granshaw and Roy Porter (eds), *The Hospital in History* (London, 1990), and J. Barry and C. Jones (eds), *Medicine and Charity before the Welfare State* (London, 1991).

12

Milton's Visit to Vallombrosa:
A Literary Tradition

Vallombrosa! of thee I first heard in the page
Of that holiest of Bards . . .

W. Wordsworth, 'At Vallombrosa'[1]

MORE THAN A thousand metres above sea-level, on a pine-clad prominence at the north-western edge of an impressive chain of hills known as the Pratomagno, is perched a somewhat austere building known as the 'Paradisino'. From here, on a clear day, one can peer westward across the complex valleys and streams which wind down into the upper Arno and make out Brunelleschi's cupola some 20 miles away in Florence. In exceptional weather, other features of the great city through which the Arno flows on its journey to Pisa and the Mediterranean may also be discerned. 'Col sereno', says the guidebook (though here a lively imagination is surely a prerequisite), it is even possible to perceive the sea itself.[2]

There is no doubting the real presence of the buildings immediately beneath one, for the Paradisino perches directly above the spreading bulk of the monastery to which it belongs, the once great convent of Vallombrosa which gave its name to one of Italy's most powerful religious orders. Between the date of its foundation in the early eleventh century and its decline and suppression in the nineteenth, this monastery became the home of innumerable distinguished clerics and played host to travelling clergy and laity alike. Among the latter, especially during the last 200 years, have been many well-known foreigners whose visits to Vallombrosa and its Paradisino are well documented. But although the Paradisino

47 Unknown artist, early 19th-century etching of the convent at Vallombrosa, Tuscany, with (centre) the *Paradisino*, where Milton stayed, allegedly. [E. Chaney]

functioned for centuries as the monastery's retreat and guest-house – latterly indeed as a hotel – only one commemorative plaque is affixed to its façade. Erected in the summer of 1925, this late (pre-war) example of Anglo-Italian collaboration – the work of American sculptor, Henrik Andersen, and Fascist literary critic, Ugo Ojetti – fulsomely celebrates the visit of a seventeenth-century English Protestant, albeit a significantly Italianized one:

Nel 1638
Qui dimoro
il sommo poeta inglese
Giovanni Milton
studioso dei nostri classici

devoto alla nostra civiltà
innamorato di questa foresta e di questo cielo
30 Agosto 1925[3]

Both the erection and wording of so prominent and confidently specific a plaque was, and is still, consistent with contemporary scholarship. In the then standard, six-volume life of Milton, the great Scots scholar, David Masson, powerfully endorsed the notion that Milton visited Vallombrosa. 'Among all Milton's excursions round Florence', he wrote,

> none seem to have been remembered by him more fondly; his mention of it has added much to the prior poetical celebrity of the spot; and in the Convent of Vallombrosa they still cherish, it is said, the legend of his visit, and profess even to show relics in authentication.[4]

As if referring the reader to a primary source, Masson then cites Wordsworth's notes to 'At Vallombrosa', a subject to which I shall return. More recently, William R. Parker's still standard two-volume biography further supports the view that Milton returned to England enriched with 'memories of . . . "autumnal leaves that strow the brooks / in Vallombrosa, where th'Etrurian shades / High over-arched embower".' Indeed, Parker seeks to confirm this by asserting that 'the excursion [to Vallombrosa] was popular with travellers'.[5] Almost all subsequent accounts have taken the visit for granted.

*   *   *

In this chapter I shall argue that Milton never actually visited Vallombrosa but merely borrowed its picturesque name, probably from Ariosto's *Orlando Furioso* – which by September 1644 he had read at least twice – to promote an appropriate atmosphere in a particular scene of *Paradise Lost*.[6] I believe that Ariosto's references to the 'rich and beautiful badia' of Vallombrosa – or Valspinosa as he had even more arbitrarily named this fictive French abbey in the first two editions of *Orlando* – however inviting ('cortese a chiunque venia'), would never have sufficed to persuade Milton to depart from his otherwise entirely conventional Grand Tour itinerary and make the extremely arduous detour to the remote monastery which genuinely went under this name.[7] Parker could see 'no reason to doubt that Milton actually visited Vallombrosa', because he thought that an excursion there was a relatively routine part of the seventeenth-century tourist's itinerary. But far from being 'popular with travellers' and thus part of a general pattern into which Milton's particular pilgrimage might have fitted unobtrusively (albeit uncomfortably, given Parker's conventional view of Milton's inflexible Protestantism), no Englishman is known to have visited Vallombrosa during the whole of the sixteenth and seventeenth centuries.[8] Nor, with the fascinating exception of Don Enrico Hugford, who in 1743 went so far as to become Abbot of Vallombrosa, have I found evidence of any Englishman, or woman, visiting the monastery in the first three-quarters of the eighteenth century.[9]

Merging with a rapidly evolving European travel literature of the late eighteenth century, the legend that Milton actually visited Vallombrosa spawned its own literary tradition, stimulating count- less cultured, and subsequently less cultured tourists to follow in the allegedly holy bard's supposed footsteps. The earliest travelogues to include accounts of Vallombrosa seem to have been French. Curiosity might have been stimulated by Ariosto's implicit Franco- philia, Orlando – post-Pulci and Boiardo – being the Italianized name for the *Chanson*-singing Roland, and Vallombrosa being a similarly Italianized monastery somewhere in Charlemagne's France. More significant, however, may have been the fact that Benedictinism in France enjoyed a strong revival in seventeenth-century France, especially after the foundation of the scholarly congregation of Maurists in 1618. This revival encouraged a renewed religious and antiquarian interest in ancient monasteries such as Vallombrosa, which was unparalleled in post-Reformation England.[10]

Only one of the French accounts of Vallombrosa I have found pre- dates Milton's Italian journey, but its place and date of publication (Paris, 1634), and its distinguished provenance and popularity throughout Europe make it a major rival to Ariosto's *Orlando* as the possible source for Milton's famous reference. Written by a servant of the zealously anti-Protestant Henri de Bourbon, Prince de Condé, the *Voyage de Monsieur le Prince de Condé* describes a tour of Italy begun in Montpellier in the summer of 1622 and completed a year later. Richard Lassels, an English Catholic priest who worked for Cardinal Richelieu in the late 1630s and visited Rome a year before Milton, frequently referred to Condé's *Voyage* in his accounts of Italy. Even Father Lassels, however, never seems to have been persuaded by its account of Vallombrosa to make the pilgrimage there himself.

Condé's concern to demonstrate the extent of his eschewal of his family's Huguenot past may partly explain his inclusion of Vallombrosa, La Verna and Camaldolí in an otherwise conventional itinerary. In this respect, it conforms to the pious tradition to which Benvenuto Cellini may have subscribed when, in the summer of 1544, he ostentatiously asked for an eight-day leave of absence to visit the same monasteries, 'continually thanking God' for having helped him cast his bronze *Perseus*.[11] Condé and his entourage spent the night of Friday, 27 January 1623, at Vallombrosa. As if echoing Ariosto, the *Voyage* account describes the 'tres-belle Abaye dans de tres-fascheuses montagnes pleines de neige' as 'fort beau & riche.' It was noticed that higher up there was a hermitage, 'd'une seule cellule, fort beau, mais la demeure en est afreuse'. The monks belonged to the Benedictine order, 'reformez par Sainct Gualbert', and it was observed that the beautiful church contained some fine relics.[12]

In 1691, the renegade Franco–Italian priest, Gabriel d'Emiliane, to help demonstrate that he was now a good Protestant in exile, worthy of the Whiggish patronage of the Earl of Nottingham, published a travelogue with the sensational title of *The Frauds of Romish Monks and Priests, set forth in eight letters*.[13] Just as Jean Mabillon and Michel Germain had done in April 1686, d'Emiliane approached Vallombrosa from Camaldoli. After the thick snow which surrounded the latter, the initial descent into warmer and more fertile terrain was welcome. It also encouraged d'Emiliane to notice variations in the type of tree which grew at the different altitudes, providing us with useful seventeenth-century evidence for our encounter a century later with Enlightenment concern about the scarcity of 'fallen leaves' in a predominantly coniferous area.[14] As this best-selling account seems to have been the earliest in English and was probably the first full-length traveller's description of Vallombrosa published in any language, it is important as a source for the increasingly elaborate setting into which Milton *qua Wandervogel* was to be placed. After his brief simmering by Johnsonian sceptics, this nature-trekking Milton was stirred into a leafy setting, brought to the boil by disbelief-suspending Romantics, to end up so solidly fixed in a gelatinous accumulation of detail contributed by unquestioning nineteenth-century scholars and literati that it was not until the age of deconstruction (by coincidence), on the three-hundred-and-fiftieth anniversary of his Italian journey, that the historical poet was finally lifted free of the legend. In view of its potential value in understanding the evolution of the legend, I quote from d'Emiliane's *Frauds* at length:

> knowing that the Abby of *Valombrosa*, which is chief of another Order of Monks, very famous in *Italy*, was not above a days Journy from thence, we all of us Travelled thither. We went down Hill for some miles, and afterward, coasted about the *Apennin*, by a very pleasant Way . . . All these sides of the Mountains are exceeding rich, as abounding with all sorts of *Fruit Trees* . . . After half a days Journy, we were obliged to mount the *Apennin*, for four Miles together, through very stony and rugged ways, until we came to Vallombrosa, in Latin *Vallis Umbrosa*. This Place in indeed a Vally with respect to the Tops of the Mountains, that raise themselves a great height above it; but if we compare it with the level of the Country that lies beneath it, it is a very high Mountain, and very cold, for there are no Fruit-Trees to be seen here, except only some *Chesnut-Trees*, and a few *Apple-Trees*. The great Forests of *Pine* and *Fir-Trees* that encompass it, in former times rendred the place very Dark and Shady, which was the occasion of giving it the name of *Valombrosa*.

At this point, d'Emiliane gives the reader a potted account of San Giovanni Gualberto's commendable refusal to avenge the death of his brother, which led instead to his becoming a monk and founding the Vallombrosan Order.[15] D'Emiliane then returns to 'my Solitude of Vallombrosa' and provides us with an exceptionally detailed description of the Paradisino, then still known as the Hermitage, though since the visit of the Prince de Condé, together with the monastery itself, considerably enlarged:

> We arrived at this famous Abby, where are some of the most magnificent and sumptuous Buildings that can be. One of the *Florentine* Gentlemen that was with me had a Brother there, who was the chief Person there, next to the Abbat, for whose sake we were very Civilly received. The Monks here lead a very commoditous and pleasant life; when they are weary of living in this Desert, they make an Enterchange with the Monks of *Florence*, and thereby enjoy the pleasing variety of living one part of the year in the Country, and other in the City. They have cut down for a quarter of a League round their Monastery all the great Fir-Trees that Shadow'd it, to give themselves more air, and to make the place more Healthy. The next Morning we were led to the Hermitage of S. *John Gualbert*, which is about half a League distance, from the point of a

little rock which lifts up it self in the midst of a Vally, being very craggy on every side. In getting up to it, we went round the Rock, as by a winding Stairs, for the space of one quarter of an hour, at the end of which, we found our selves at the Top of the Rock, where the Hermitage is; which consists of a very neat Chapel, curiously gilt and painted all over, and a very handsome Set of Lodgings, well Wainscoted and Painted all within, with a Garden of a moderate size, so that the whole is a meer Jewel. There is no monument left here of the ancient Cell of this Saint, all the building being new and modern: there is always a Father Hermit that dwells here, with a Converse Brother to serve him. Whenever the Hermit dies, the Abbots of that Congregation *Valombrosa*, at their general Chapter, make choice of a Monk of Exemplary Life, and a lover of Solitude, to reside there. The great Abby is to furnish him all necessaries of Life: He has a very fine Library full of choice Books when he has a mind to Study; and indeed the Hermit that was then in possession of the place, was a Man of competent Learning, and appeared to me a very honest Man. He made us a very fine Discourse about the Contempt of the World, and the Advantages of Retirement and Solitude: Tho' indeed there was no great need of it, for we were already, without all that, so Charmed with the Beauty of this Hermitage, that in case there had been more of the same cut, Nature, rather than Grace, would easily have persuaded us to become Hermits, in order to enjoy an easie and pleasant Life, without either care or trouble. The Monks of *Valombrosa* have extremely relaxed their strictness of their first Institution. They are Clothed in Black, and profess the Rule of S. *Bennet,* tho' indeed they observe but little of it. The next day we set out very betimes in the Morning towards Mount Alverne [La Verna].[16]

Despite the frequent republication of d'Emiliane's account during the first half of the eighteenth century, the earliest evidence of native English interest in Vallombrosa I have found is a letter written by Horace Walpole in May 1752 to one of his favorite correspondents, the British Envoy to the Court of Tuscany, Sir Horace Mann. It is highly significant that Walpole attributes the recent 'passion' for Vallombrosa to Milton's having 'mentioned it' in *Paradise Lost,* our first indication that those apparently topographical lines were to become an essential part of the poet's biography. He asks Mann for a copy of a print of the monastery which he has recently seen at the house of a friend, though he writes: 'I don't think it gives much idea of the beauty of the place.'[17] If by the latter remark Walpole were trying to persuade Mann, who in 13 years' residence in Florence had never visited Vallombrosa, that during his 13 months in the same city (between 1739 and 1741), he, Walpole, *had* done so, he was to be more candid as an old man.[18] Replying in 1791 to a letter from Mary Berry, who had been 'disappointed of going to Volombroso' on her Grand Tour, Walpole admits that he had never been there himself. Now that 'Milton has made everybody wish to *have seen it*', he also regretted this, though half a century earlier it had probably never occurred to him to undertake the journey.[19]

Notwithstanding Walpole's mid-century reference to a Milton-induced passion for Vallombrosa, the earliest manifestation of such a passion dates from the 1780s. The fact that this occurs in what was to have been the grand literary début of that self-consciously original travel writer, novelist and collector, the millionaire dilettante, William Beckford, suggests that there cannot have been many British travellers who had preceded him to this remote spot. Based on his European tour of 1780–1, after a complementary second tour in 1782, Beckford completed his extraordinarily precocious *Dreams, Waking Thoughts, and Incidents; in a Series of Letters* early in the following year.[20] One of these 'Letters', ostensibly written in Florence on 23 October 1780 and addressed to an unnamed but idealized amalgam of Alexander Cozens, his charismatic art teacher, and William Courtney, the boy with whom he had fallen in love the previous year, began as follows:

> Do you recollect our evening rambles last year, upon the hill of pines; and the dark valley [at Fonthill], where we used to muse in the twilight? I remember, we often fancied the scene like Valombrosa; and vowed, if ever an occasion offered, to visit its deep retirement. I had put off the execution of this pilgrimage from day to day till the warm weather was gone; and the Florentines declared I should be frozen if I attempted it. Every body stared, last night at the opera when I told them, I was going to bury myself in fallen leaves, and hear no music but their rustlings. Mr ———— [the Revd John Lettice, Beckford's necessarily complaisant tutor] was just as eager as myself to escape the chit-chat and nothingness of Florence: so we finally determined upon our expedition, and mounting our horses, set out this morning, happily without any company, but the spirit which led us along.[21]

Beckford describes the difficult journey in characteristically melodramatic style. At one stage, slowed down by 'rocky steeps shattered

into fragments', the travellers were tempted to turn back; the
temperature indeed dropped when they ascended into 'the forests of
pine', but their 'fresh aromatic odour' revived Beckford's spirits.²² His
imagery (if not his proto-Romantic prose style) becomes more
Miltonic as he approaches the sacred spot, so that on arrival,
the reader is presented with a fully fledged example of the literary
tradition which enshrines Milton's Vallombrosan visit as historical
fact at the very birth of that tradition. So 'advanced' is Beckford's
imaginative description that it raises – as if deliberately – almost all
the issues which are addressed in the course of this essay (including,
given the absence of the passage from the relevant surviving manuscript, even a degree of doubt about his own expedition). Even his
laboured emphasis on the prevalence of deciduous autumn leaves,
the reward for his deliberate postponement of the excursion from
Florence, seems intended to counter the later, leaf-related scepticism
about Milton's visit:

> The cold to be sure was piercing; but, setting that at defiance, we
> galloped on, and issued shortly into a vast amphitheatre of lawns and
> meadows, surrounded by thick woods beautifully green. Flocks of sheep
> were dispersed on the slopes, whose smoothness and verdure equal our
> English pastures. Steep cliffs, and mountains, cloathed with beech to
> their very summits, guard this retired valley. The herbage, moistened by
> streams which fall from the eminences, has never been known to fade;
> and whilst the chief part of Tuscany is parched by the heats of summer,
> these upland meadows retain the freshness of spring. I regretted not
> having visited them sooner, as autumn had already made great havock
> amongst the foliage. Showers of leaves blew full in our faces as we rode
> towards the convent, placed at an extremity of the vale, and sheltered
> by remote firs and chesnuts, towering one above another. Alighting
> before the entrance, two fathers came out, and received us into the
> peace of their retirement. We found a blazing fire, and tables spread very
> comfortable before it, round which five or six over-grown friars were
> lounging, who seemed, by the sleekness and rosy hue of their counte-
> nances, not totally to have despised this mortal existence.²³

Escaping from the 'friars' (*vere* monks), 'who made a shift to
waddle after', Beckford soon found himself at liberty among decaying beeches, 'listening to the roar of the waterfall which the wood
concealed.' There follows a passage which was retained with only
minor alterations in the widely read 1834 edition:

The dry leaves chased each other down the steeps on the edge of the torrents with hollow rustlings; whilst the solemn wave of the forests above, exactly answered the idea I had formed of Valombrosa,

> where the *Etrurian* shades
> High overarch't imbowr.

The scene was beginning to take effect, and the Genius of Milton to move across his favourite valley, when the fathers arrived puffing and blowing, by an easier ascent than I knew of.[24]

At this point, anticipating Coleridge's reaction to the person from Porlock, Beckford adds another sentence he was later to suppress: 'Pardon me, if I cursed their intrusion, and wished them as still as Gualbertus.' 'You have missed the way', cried one of Beckford's puffing monks, adding, significantly for our purposes, 'the Hermitage, with the fine picture by Andrea del Sarto [now in the Accademia in Florence] *which all the English admire* [my italics], is on the opposite side of the wood; there! don't you see it on the point of the cliff?'

With marriage and a potential peerage in the offing, both of which were already threatened by the homosexual scandal which was to destroy his hopes of a career, on 15 April 1783 Beckford instructed his printer not to distribute any copies of his completed book. It seems, however, that it was not until 1801 that he had most copies of *Dreams* destroyed. Though this helped the book acquire charismatically mysterious status, it is very difficult to assess its influence in general, and passages such as that on Vallombrosa in particular, in the period prior to the first published (i.e. public) edition of 1834. In 1783, stray pages were almost immediately snapped up by interested parties such as Henry Fuseli, whence they must have circulated freely. Referring to this phenomenon on 22 January 1797, the diarist, Joseph Farington, also seemed relatively well informed about the general quality of the *Dreams*:

> They were written with genius, – full of reflections on Individuals & on nations – malevolent & expressive of a bad heart. – The descriptions of Lanscapes &c were admirable, – throughout the whole there was a spirit like Champaigne prevailing, sparkling everywhere.

Roderick Marshall argued persuasively that it was Beckford's 1783 account of Venice, rather than Mrs Piozzi's, which inspired Mrs

48 J. R. Cozens, *Conifers at Vallombrosa* (24 September 1783). [Whitworth Art Gallery, Manchester]

Radcliffe's lurid style in *The Mysteries of Udolpho,* first published in 1794. (Mario Praz meanwhile pointed to the possible influences of Beckford's *Vathek* on Radcliffe's *The Italian.*) As we shall see, Mrs Piozzi, herself an admirer of *Vathek,* seems to have been aware of more than just Beckford's description of Venice in the *Dreams.* Vallombrosa and Venice combine in a suspiciously Beckfordian manner in the anonymous novel entitled *Vallombrosa: or the Venetian Nun,* published by the Minerva Press in November 1804. The copy of *Dreams* (one of the five known to have survived) given to the indiscreet banker-poet, Samuel Rogers, would no doubt have been shown to all and sundry in the literary world. Since it cannot have been presented long before Rogers's 1817 visit to Fonthill, however, although important for having encouraged Rogers's own enthusiasm for Vallombrosa, this particular copy cannot have influenced

49 J. R. Cozens, *Villa Salviati on the Arno* (25 September 1783). [Whitworth Art Gallery, Manchester]

eighteenth-century taste. The passage in Rogers's *Table-Talk* recalling his visit reveals both a likely method of influence and the name of yet another whose work may already have benefited from that influence:

> The other visitors at that time were Smith, who published *Views in Italy*, and a French ecclesiastic . . . In the evening Beckford would amuse us by reading one of his unpublished works.[25]

When, in November 1821, Rogers asserted that 'nobody I know has been to Vallombrosa', he may have been stimulated to do so by his friend Wordsworth's soon-to-be-published *Memorials of a Tour*, *1820*, which expressed an as yet unfulfilled longing 'to slumber, reclined on the moss-covered floor' in the 'shadiest wood' of Vallombrosa. (Ironically, this is not only reminiscent of Beckford's recollections of his conversations in Fonthill gardens, but uncannily like the style he had parodied in *Modern Novel Writing* of 1796: 'Here stretched supinely on a bed of moss, the late Lord Mahogany would frequently pass the sultry hours of the day.')[26] In the process of promoting himself as pioneer, however, Rogers may either have forgotten Beckford's 1783 account (not to speak of cousin Peter Beckford's 1787 one), have regarded Beckford as so extraordinary as not to count or, conceivably, have suspected Beckford's account to be fictional.[27] In any event, it seems likely that directly or by report, Beckford's vivid Vallombrosan set-piece became known soon after it was printed and encouraged incipient English interest in a place already rendered sacred by Miltonic citation. It is indeed probable that Beckford was in the minds of Miss Berry and Walpole when they articulated their regrets at not having visited 'Volombroso'.

We know of at least one eighteenth-century Vallombrosan visit undertaken as a direct result of Beckford's interest (if not instructions), that of the great landscape painter, John Robert Cozens, the unstable son of the exotic Alexander. Almost two years after the ostensible date of Beckford's description, and 12 months after separating from Beckford in Naples during the latter's second great Italian tour, Cozens travelled north to Florence and then rode out to Vallombrosa to spend 24 September sketching in the vicinity of the monastery.[28] To an unrealistic extent, almost all Cozens's Vallombrosan drawings depict decidedly deciduous trees, which might suggest that Beckford was conscious of an otherwise unrecorded debate on Milton's fallen leaves a decade or so before Mrs Piozzi referred to the problem in print. That the exception among the handful of these drawings is so specifically a sketch of a group of conifers (dated 'Valombrosa – Sept^r: 24') only reinforces this impression [Fig. 48]. The following day Cozens was back in Florence, sketching the Villa Salviati (though not the one I believe Milton had in mind when he remembered 'the Tuscan artist' and his 'optic glass' in *Paradise Lost*) [Fig. 49]. A month later he rejoined Beckford, now on his third Grand Tour, in Geneva, where he was sighted alighting from a coach by Miss Berry.[29]

While we can be reasonably sure that Cozens's 1783 expedition was inspired, and probably patronized, by Beckford, we can only hypothesize that knowledge of his *Dreams* may have encouraged William Parsons, Bertie Greatheed, John Biddulph and Gabriel Piozzi to form a 'party of pleasure' and travel from Florence to Vallombrosa two years later. Relevant to this hypothesis may have been Mrs Thrale's visit to Fonthill on 27 June 1784, just two months before

her departure for Italy with her Italian husband.[30] With the publication of Parsons's poem 'Vallombrosa' in his *Poetical Tour* of 1787,
and, two years later, of Mrs Piozzi's own *Observations and Reflections*,
with its report of this somewhat sceptical Vallombrosan expedition,
the excursion-stimulating legend of Milton's visit really got under
way.[31] By 1837, when the defiantly unsceptical, 68-year-old William
Wordsworth came and composed 'At Vallombrosa', which he
prefaced with the relevant lines from *Paradise Lost* in exactly the way
Parsons had done, the legend had become a fully established feature
of Grand Tour mythology, featuring prominently even in the French
and German travel literature.[32] Lamartine included mention of
Milton with Dante, Boccaccio and Michelangelo among the great
poets, artists and political refugees whose cells he was shown.[33]

By Wordsworth's day, the popular guidebooks and travelogues
such as Joseph Forsyth's and Eustace's, both based on 1802 tours
but not published till 1813, included accounts of Vallombrosa and
of Milton's visit as a matter of course. Most quoted *Paradise Lost*,
while some, such as the anonymous *Mementoes . . . of a Tour*,
published in two volumes in 1824, incorporated into their descriptions their own full-length poems, the *Mementoes'* surprisingly good
40-line meditation 'Written at Vallombrosa, 1821' in rhyming
couplets being, I believe, a hitherto unnoticed precedent for Wordsworth's contribution to what by 1837 was a 50-year-old genre.[34]
Indeed, if justice is to be done (given the priorities of our originality-
obsessed century), this poetic (and artistic) tradition should be
extended still further back to Beckford's 1783 account (that he felt
this himself might lie behind his decision to publish the revised
edition of *Dreams* in 1834). Beckford once commended Rousseau's
'prose poems in praise of nature'. Whatever Milton would have
thought of Rousseau, or, for that matter, of Beckford, all three
merged in the latter's Vallombrosan 'Letter', which surely qualifies
as a 'prose poem' of great originality.[35]

In the wake of Beckford and Parsons, but still prior to the
Napoleonic Wars, it seems to have been the ladies who responded
most warmly to the literary legend. And once the British had
rendered Italy safe for tourism again, it was again the female travellers who seemed keenest to write about Vallombrosa. Admittedly, the
radical Lady Morgan was responding to the Roman Catholic
Reverend J.C. Eustace in her account, and like Mary Berry (and
perhaps Mariana Starke, who also corrected Eustace's exaggerated

accounts of French destruction) failed actually to scale the hills to reach the monastery. As an admirer of Milton and the author of the pioneering biography of Milton's more genuinely freedom-fighting contemporary, Salvator Rosa, her account of Miltonic Vallombrosa (annotated by a 15-line political biography) is nevertheless of interest:

> Commanding this beautiful vale, rise the woods of Vallombrosa, with all that magnificence of scenery which left on the mind of Milton images which recurred to cheer his spirit, to freshen his fancy, and enrich his page, when blindness shut out nature from his view; and the persecution of despotism had left him lonely and unhonoured, in solitude, and in neglect.
> The scenery of Vallombrosa, caught even in the mistiness of distance, still has the character which, in Milton's days, distinguished its 'Etrurian shades', and which, in far remoter times, lured the hermit's steps to its profound solitudes, and gave it its melodious name.[36]

Intrepid as ever (though now past 60), Frances Trollope, with least famous son, Thomas, in tow, thought nothing of the journey to Vallombrosa.[37] On an early May morning in 1841 she rode out of Florence, complaining first of her companions for rising so late and then of the 'frightful' heat they all had to suffer as a consequence. She comments on Ariosto's praise of Vallombrosan hospitality but notes that the ladies were not permitted to enter the monastery, apparently being entertained instead in the Foresteria (or Paradisino) above. Still more forcefully than Forsyth, she concludes from its 'wonderful exactitude of description' that Milton's 'sylvan scene' account of Eden in *Paradise Lost* '*must* have been written as a record of Vallombrosa'. Quoting the relevant lines, she bestows on them the highest praise: that they surpass even Walter Scott's in 'painting scenery with words'.[38]

Published within a year of her visit, Mrs Trollope's account may just have been known to Mary Shelley, who, though it was late October and 'not the season for excursion', 'could not resist the temptation of visiting Vallombrosa' in the autumn of 1842. Two years later she published a popular account of her visit which incorporates an observation on autumnal leaves to which I shall return.[39] Perhaps misled by references in Mary's *Rambles* to a 'new and good road' and the 'accommodation' laid on for women at the monastery's 'forestiera', Elizabeth Barrett Browning, complete with

Flush, Wilson and the ever-indulgent Mr Browning, was soon having herself hauled up to the monastery 'along a "via non rotabile" through the most romantic scenery . . . in basket sledges drawn by four white oxen'; only to be drawn ignominiously back down again when the male chauvinist monks refused to let her stay the three summer months she had intended.[40]

*   *   *

Far from motivating Milton to seek out the real Vallombrosa, Ariosto's popularizing choice of this effective signifier of a non-specifically signified location was surely in *itself* sufficient explanation for Milton's incidental use of the name in *Paradise Lost*. It would not have taken an especially learned or imaginative Grand Tourist, let alone one familiar with Greek, Latin and Italian, to conjure up classically leaf-strewn brooks when he read and probably heard of a place known as 'shady valley'.[41] No doubt proud Florentines would have informed Milton that the real Vallombrosa, the original monastery of their prestigious Vallombrosan order (which their greatest living architect was rebuilding at considerable expense), was not in France but in their Grand Duchy, the recently revived ancient Etruria; hence its corrected location among 'the Etrurian shades' in Milton's poem. (With Don Diego de Franchi's monograph on San Giovanni Gualberto wending its way through the Florentine censors, collecting those 'proud', 'exorcising' *imprimaturs* Milton so abhorred, Vallombrosa would have been much talked of in the academic circles he frequented in late 1638 and early 1639.)[42] But like Ariosto, Milton was primarily interested in the effect the name would have on his readers. Whether these were familiar with the relevant classical or Renaissance sources for the fallen leaves simile, they would have even less knowledge of the real Vallombrosa than himself. In his *Epitaphium Damonis* Milton refers to the River Himera; in *Lycidas*, the Fountain of Arethuse; and in *Paradise Lost*, to 'that fair field of Enna', all three of which are in Sicily. Thanks to the well-known passage in *Defensio secunda* – in which Milton creates the false impression that he rushed home from Naples in order to fight for liberty in the Civil Wars (three years before they began) – we know he never visited Sicily or Greece as he claimed to have intended. Were it not for this, we might still be speculating whether Milton travelled in the footsteps of William Lithgow or George Sandys, whose inspiring accounts of those countries he would surely have read. Conversely, it may have been on the basis of a reading of Poliziano's *Rusticus* that Milton mentioned Fiesole in *Paradise Lost*, but in this case he also wrote, in a letter to Benedetto Buonmatthei, that he 'loved often to visit your Arno and these hills of Fiesole'. Milton nowhere claims to have visited Vallombrosa, or for that matter Paradise, so that in contrast to the debate as to whether he visited Galileo – which he specifically claims to have done – here the burden of proof lies not with the sceptics, but with those who subscribe to what is merely an eighteenth-century tradition.

As with most such traditions, 'documentation' to underpin the legend was soon forthcoming. If Milton could write fulsome thank-you letters to the Catholic convert librarian, Holstenius, for hospitality and for arranging a meeting with a cardinal, would he not have thanked his Vallombrosan hosts with a similarly Ciceronian epistle or two? Our first recorded 'sighting' of such letters dates from just before the 1866 dissolution of the monastery and was made by an incipiently redundant monk. Dating from a few decades earlier, the original manuscript version of 'At Vallombrosa' reveals that Wordsworth had initially paused to wonder 'if local traditions speak truth' on the subject of Milton's visit and indeed residence in a cell up at the Paradisino. Somewhat naively, he seems to have been won over by 'the pride with which the Monk, without any previous question from me, pointed out [Milton's] residence', and thereupon decided to upgrade the legend to historical status in the published version of his poem, exclaiming almost impatiently:

> The Monks still repeat the tradition with pride,
> And its truth who shall doubt? for his Spirit is here
> In the cloud-piercing rocks doth her grandeur abide,
> In the pines pointing heavenward her beauty austere;
> In the flower-besprent meadows his genius we trace . . .[43]

By the mid-1860s these monks must have been still more desperate to promote the international prestige of their convent in a last-ditch attempt to avert the forthcoming crisis. Thus we find one of them informing the gullible-sounding James Henry Dixon that 'they had several letters that Milton addressed to the convent after his return to England. He said they were written in the purest Latin, but he could not show them, as he was not aware in what part of the library they had been placed.'[44] Though apparently no relation to

Wordsworth's eponymous gardener, James Dixon would certainly have read the Laureate's poem and accompanying note, his enthusiasm for the topic being such that he soon sent in another contribution to *Notes and Queries*. In this he recalls being shown 'a small organ on which Milton used to play':

> The keyboard was worn away. The venerable custodian said 'We do not have a new one, out of respect to Milton'. He then said, 'It is the only old part: all the interior is new'. The chapel which contains the organ is on the summit of the hill or mount called il Paradisino di Miltone.[45]

Meanwhile, however, a certain C.J.H. claimed to have outdone Dixon by seeing the letters themselves which were now in Florence. Prompted by an appeal for their discovery which had been published in *Notes and Queries* soon after Dixon's original article, C.J.H. writes: 'A few years ago, when residing in Florence, I was shown two letters to the convent of Vallombrosa, both in an excellent state of preservation.' 'What became of these', C.J.H. continues nonchalantly, 'I know not; probably they have been given away.'[46]

I vividly remember a lecture at the Warburg Institute given by Dr Neil Harris, who wittily put the case for Milton's having visited Vallombrosa. In order to counter the sceptical argument first put forward by Mrs Piozzi's friends that the brooks of Vallombrosa could never have been leaf-strewn because 'the trees are all ever-green in those woods', Dr Harris concluded his lecture by flinging handfuls of recently gathered Vallombrosan beech-leaves at the stunned academic audience to demonstrate that devil-like deciduous 'autumnal leaves' do in fact fall in Vallombrosa.[47] Today, Vallombrosa is indeed rich in beeches and other deciduous trees, but the extent to which this was always the case is not entirely clear. As we have seen, Gabriel d'Emiliane, writing in 1691, described the monastery as encompassed by 'great Forests of Pine and Fir-Tree', a few chestnuts and apple trees excepted. As early as 1637, topographical engravings depict the monastery as surrounded almost exclusively by conifers, though the presence of oaks, chestnuts and, as we shall see, one beech in particular, was an integral part of the story of S. Giovanni Gualberto's eleventh-century foundation of the monastery being completed by Don Diego de Franchi at the time of Milton's visit to Florence [Fig. 50].[48] A recent documentary history of *Vallombrosa e le sue Selve* shows that forestry was the monastery's major industry from the earliest times, the composition of the

50 Vallombrosa: the convent and centre (below) the '*Faggio Santo*', from Don Diego de'
Franchi, *Historia del Patriarca S. Giovanni Gualberto* (Florence, 1640). [E. Chaney]

surrounding woods changing in response to economic demand from generation to generation. Between 1750 and 1753, during the prosperous abbacy of Enrico Hugford, the monks not only distributed 229,761 loaves of bread to the local poor but, I was pleased to read in Augustus Hare's *Florence*, also planted 40,300 beeches 'on the neighboring mountains'.[49] Unfortunately, the new history contradicts my less respectable source, recording that these beeches were in fact 'abeti' or pines.[50] Be this as it may, when the Reverend John Chetwode Eustace visited the abbey in 1802, he was still characterizing the woods as consisting 'of firs thick and lofty' and, quoting Pope (as if to demonstrate that Vallombrosan imagery could be created independently of a Vallombrosan visit), 'darksome pines that o'er yon rocks reclin'd'.[51] In the second edition of his *Classical Tour*, Eustace appended to his account of Vallombrosa a virulently anti-French report taken from the *British Review*, which, in language itself borrowed from the first edition of Eustace's *Tour*, announced that the Napoleonic invasion had in the meantime been responsible for the total destruction of 'the majestic abbey, the enchanting Paradisino' and the 'sylvan scene' generally:

> The forests and dells resound no more with the sound of the *church-going bell*, the wide spreading cedar, the darksome pine, the mournful cypress, no longer wave their aged brows to the embalmed air.[52]

Subsequent to this supposed destruction, however, Mariana Starke, the anonymous author of the *Mementoes*, Wordsworth, Frances Trollope, Mary Shelley and Elizabeth Barrett Browning all seem to have found both monastery and surrounding woods in reasonable condition, with the latter still characterized by conifers (though in 1837, Wordsworth, provoked perhaps by Crabb Robinson's scepticism, drew attention to the presence of beeches in a letter to his daughter).[53] Mrs Browning indeed, no doubt jaundiced by her reception at the hands of those unfriendly monks, consoled herself for her expulsion from Paradise by remembering how ghastly the food had been, complaining to Mrs Jameson that, 'they make their bread, I rather imagine, with sawdust of their fir trees.'[54] Back in Florence, however, writing 'Casa Guidi Windows' (and, no doubt, rereading her Wordsworth), her imagination reasserted itself more positively in favour of Miltonian Vallombrosa, not merely by belatedly emphasizing the prevalence of beeches there, but by bringing autumn forward a few months:

> The Vallombrosan brooks were strewn so thick,
> That June-day, knee-deep, with dead beechen leaves,
> As Milton saw them ere his heart grew sick,
> And his eyes blind . . .

'We must think', she writes, addressing the mountains and the forests, that:

> Your beauty and your glory helped to fill
> The cup of Milton's soul so to the brink
> He never more was thirsty . . .
> He sang of Adam's Paradise and smiled
> Remembering Vallombrosa. Therefore is
> The place divine to every English man and child,
> And pilgrims leave their soul here in a kiss.[55]

According to the third edition of Hare's *Florence*, by 1890 large numbers of Eustace's aged trees had indeed been destroyed:

> But nowhere has the mad destruction of old trees in Italy been carried to such an excess as at Vallombrosa. An Englishman vainly offered to pay the fullest timber price for some of the finest trees which adorned the ascent from Pelago if they might be left standing in their places; his offer was refused, and every tree of any age or beauty was destroyed. The noble wood on the ridge of the hill, which sheltered all the young plantations, has been ruthlessly annihilated in the same way.[56]

I have not discovered who Hare's anonymous Englishman might be – though the millionaire Anglo-Florentine exile, John Temple Leader, is a possible candidate. He or Hare may have been inspired by Wordsworth's 'The Pine of Monte Mario'. This single pine tree (presumably of the 'umbrella' type) was 'saved from the sordid axe by Beaumont's care', an act which stimulated in the poet 'a gush of tenderness'.[57]

An American who merits a mention in this context is George P. Marsh, the former United States minister at Constantinople and Turin, who spent the last 21 years of his life in Florence and then in Rome – when the capital was transferred there – as minister to the new kingdom of Italy.[58] He was a pioneering ecologist and author of a fascinating book entitled *Man and Nature*, first published in 1864, which included detailed documentation of the failures and achievements of the Italian authorities in the field of conservation in general, and warnings of the dire effects of deforestation in particular.[59] It was partly thanks to his influence that the National School of Forestry (Istituto Superiore Forestale Nazionale) was established in the monastery at Vallombrosa in 1867 (transferred to Florence in 1913), and it was here in the hotel which was established by the Croce di Savoia in the ancient Foresteria that he died on 23 July 1882. His friend, Thomas Adolphus Trollope, Anglo-Florentine brother of the novelist, describes what happened next in terms not entirely irrelevant to our theme:

> the *very inaccessible nature of the place* [my italics] made it a question of some difficulty how the body should be transported in properly decorous fashion to the railway station in the valley below – a difficulty which was solved by the young scholars of the School of Forestry, who turned out in a body to have the honour of bearing on their shoulders the remains of the man whose writings had done so much to awaken the Government to the necessity of establishing the institution to which they belonged.[60]

To complete this saga with a definitive argument against Milton having seen even a thinly strewn layer of autumnal leaves on a Vallombrosan brook, I should like to conclude with a second distinguished American Italophile who died at Vallombrosa, the sculptor and man of letters immortalized by Henry James, William Wetmore Story.[61] In an informative if somewhat belletristic essay entitled simply 'Vallombrosa', first published in the April 1881 issue of *Blackwood's Magazine*, Story describes how, 'in the latter part of last October', he was invited by an unnamed lady (probably his daughter Edith, wife of the Marchese Peruzzi dei Medici) to spend a few days with her and her family in 'an old deserted house, built centuries ago by the Medici as a stronghold and hunting-box' about three miles from the famous monastery.[62] Story's account of this once castellated *villino*, whose flanking towers had been 'cruelly' levelled by the present government, as well as that of the monastery itself, are well worth reading, but what is of primary interest here is that although this was late October, the autumnal leaves, even those of the most decidedly deciduous chestnuts, had not detached themselves from their trees. Story would no doubt have preferred them to have been strewing the brooks for, having quoted the inevitable lines, he refers frequently to the season as if willing nature to respond to art. But though it was mid-autumn, both birds and trees persisted in behaving as if it were summer. On one side of the monastery, 'the sloping hills are dark with miles of serried firs; on the corner, they are golden-brown with glowing chestnuts'.[63] Elsewhere in the same essay the leaves may have changed colour but have clearly not yet lost their grip:

> Magnificent chestnuts throng the autumnal slopes, their yellow leaves glowing in the autumn sun. Sombre groves of firs, marshalled along the hillsides for miles, stand solemn and dark. Beech-trees rear at intervals their smooth trunks, or gather together in close and murmurous conclave.[64]

Meanwhile Vallombrosa's most distinguished tree, *il Faggio Santo*, supposedly flourishing after almost nine centuries, was famous for being even more reluctant than its non-miraculous colleagues to part with its leaves. From early in the eleventh century it would 'put forth its leaves long before the others', thus sheltering S. Giovanni and his hut, and 'was the last, when winter came, to shed its leaves on the ground'.[65]

All this, of course, has been by way of emphasizing the impossibility of Milton's having seen – as distinct from having imagined – Vallombrosa's leaves in their fallen state, even if, for some unknown reason, he had ventured so far as Vallombrosa itself. That 1880 was not climatically unique is indicated by Mary Shelley's discovery of the same conditions in late October 38 years earlier. She had hesitated to embark on the excursion from Florence, considering that autumn was 'too far advanced' but when she arrived at Vallombrosa 'the branches on noble forest trees . . . spread over our path . . . were [still] in the sear and yellow leaf', a state of affairs which prompted the observation that 'the place [as distinct from its botanical behaviour?] was the more consonant with Milton's verse'.[66] No more than other nineteenth-century travellers, however, was she inclined to doubt so attractive a tradition as Milton's visit, quoting the inevitable lines with the best of them. Even after Masson's Methuselan *Life* had, in the form of an unprecedentedly precise chronology, unwittingly supplied the means to undermine the myth, the romantic Story was to implicitly postpone Milton's autumn to an impossibly late date – and describe conditions he had not seen himself – rather than forgo the chance to dream (in print) of his hero's hillside wanderings:

Here, among others, came Milton, in the flower of his youth, to gaze on this magnificent panorama, to store his mind with images and pictures – that long remained vivid when the outer windows of his sight were closed – to study in the library, to pace the terraces, to ponder the grand poem of his later years, and to leave behind him a memory dear to all who love English poetry. The landscape is still the same as when he saw it, and the leaves strew the hillsides as thickly as when he wandered among these shady groves. His shadow walks with every English traveller through the long corridors, where once the monks who are now but dust listened to his silvery tones, and wondered perhaps at this fair youth, with long and golden hair, who came from a far-away country, and spoke softly if brokenly in their tongue. The charm of this place long lingered in his mind . . . the impression made on his mind never left him.[67]

Milton was in Tuscany twice in his life, first during the summer of 1638, for a period of approximately two months ending some time around mid-September, and second, during early spring of the following year. By the end of October 1638, a time of the year when – as Mary Shelley and Story both so eloquently testify – the deciduous leaves of Vallombrosa change colour but do not yet fall, Milton and his servant had long since left Tuscany and were in Rome, being wined and dined by the English Jesuits.[68]

APPENDIX

'Written at Vallombrosa, 1821' from Anon., *Mementoes, historical and classical, of a Tour through part of France, Switzerland, and Italy in the years 1821 and 1822 . . .*, 2 vols (London, 1824), I, pp. 264–5.

> In these lone shades, where solitude e'er reigns;
> Far from the world, and all its sick'ning pains,
> Here let me muse, and hush'd be every strife,
> Remote from man, and vain, delusive life:
> Mid scenes which, erst, the classic muse did sing
> And Milton soaring with sublimer wing.
> Here may the heart, when sadd'ning thoughts inspire,
> Flee from mock mirth, and into self retire;
> Friendship betray'd may here some solace find

To heal the wound still rankling in the mind.
Here too may some fond youth of generous mould,
Whose heart responded to the tale he told,
Whose idol mistress to adore was pleasure,
His heart's chief life, and soul's best treasure,
Find a fit place to mourn his hapless lot
And sigh o'er love profaned and vows forgot.
Some one unfit to feel, just fit to feign,
A mimic love, to give another pain.
Whose fashion-phrase, or mode, or dress more spruce,
Or dashing vice, may offer some excuse
To show the bitter slight, or cold disdain,
Or words of scorn to love that pleads in vain;
To sink the soul, oppress it more and more,
And bleed the fainting heart at every pore.
Or here, perchance, may flee some maiden true,
Firm of resolve to bid the world adieu;
Of him she fondly loved, by fate bereft,
No hope, no joy, or peace, to her is left;
To memory's woes she gives the live-long day,
Weeps oe'r the past, and sighs her soul away.
Or here may pine some yet more hapless maid
Honour abused, and virgin faith betray'd:
Retirement best suits with wounded pride,
And woe that springs from shame who would not hide?
Like some fair vase of alabaster hue,
Of purest form, and exquisite to view,
If once defaced, deform'd, by hands profane,
Or lustre lost by some foul, tainted, flame,
The beauteous object, late the general pride,
To pity, scorn, neglect, is thrown aside.

NOTES

This chapter is based on a paper first given at the Third International Milton Symposium, Vallombrosa, in June 1988. It was first published in Mario A. Di Cesare (ed.), *Milton in Italy: Contexts, Images, Contradictions* (Medieval & Renaissance Texts and Studies, Binghamton, NY, 1991), pp. 113–46.

1. *Memorials of a Tour in Italy, 1837* (London, 1842).

mistaken in saying that Cozens was not released by Beckford until early December (*Alexander and John Robert Cozens: The Poetry of Landscape* (New Haven and London, 1986), p. 150). Her source, Thomas Jones's *Memoirs* (*Walpole Society*, XXXII (1946-48), p. 114), is quite specific in recording that Beckford 'left *Naples* for *Marsailles* leaving behind his Draughtsman Cousins Once more a free Agent and loosed from Shackles of fantastic folly and Caprice –' on 10 September 1782. The sketch of the Villa Salviati was done on 25 September 1783, the day after the Vallombrosan sketches; see *Walpole Society*, XXIII, nos 387-93. Galileo stayed with Filippo Salviati at the Villa delle Selve to the west of Florence and wrote his letter on sunspots there in 1612. Beckford owned a copy of Giuseppe Zocchi's *Vedute delle ville e d'altri luoghi della Toscana* (Florence, 1744) which includes an etching of the larger Villa Salviati on the Via Bolognese (see Clive Wainwright's summary of the Sotheby's sale held in October 1975: *Times Literary Supplement* (19 Dec. 1975), p. 1524). It is this villa, which lies beneath Fiesole across the Mugnone valley and has a massive tower, which Milton would have seen on his way in and out of the north of Florence, that I believe he had in mind when referring in all but name to Galileo. The Miss Berrys' interest in Vallombrosa may have stimulated several others', not least that of Charlotte Bury who in 1833 published a long poem illustrated by her late husband, the Revd Edward Bury: *The Three Great Sanctuaries of Tuscany, Valombrosa, Camaldoli, Laverna* . . . For Lady Charlotte's connection with 'Miss Berries', see her daughter's diary: Harriet C.B. Campbell, *A Journey to Florence in 1817*, ed. G.R. de Beer (London, 1951), pp. 90, 91, 107, 116-17.

30. *Thraliana*, ed. K.C. Balderston, 2nd edn, 2 vols (London, 1951), I, p. 598. In view of what Beckford and James Wyatt were to do with Fonthill a decade later, Mrs Piozzi's comparison between the old (i.e., Palladian) Fonthill and the eventually Wyattized Wilton is worth quoting in full: 'We went to Wilton and also to Fonthill; they make an admirable & curious contrast between ancient Magnificence and Modern Glare: Gothic & Grecian again however, a Man of Taste would rather possess Ld Pembroke's Seat, or indeed a single Room in it – but one feels one should live happier at Beckford's.' That Mrs Piozzi was certainly aware of Beckford's literary talent is revealed by her praise of *Vathek*; at the same time, however, she more than once condemned the man as a 'Professor of Paederasty' (*Thraliana*, I, p. 969, n. 2).

31. Parsons, *Poetical Tour* (London, 1787), pp. 84-101 (2nd edn, 2 vols, 1807, I, pp. 125-48) and Hester Lynch Piozzi, *Observations and Reflections made in the course of a journey through France, Italy, and Germany* (1789), ed. H. Barrows (Ann Arbor, MI, 1967), p. 164. See also Peter Beckford's 1787 account of Vallombrosa ('the convent . . . enclosed in a forest of firs') in *Familiar Letters from Italy* . . . 2 vols (London, 1805).

32. Though his critical method apparently does not call for mention of Beckford, Parsons, nor the other precedents dealt with here, I cite, as the most recent study of this poem, Robin Jarvis, 'Shades of Milton: Wordsworth at Vallombrosa', *Studies in Romanticism*, XXV (1986), pp. 483-504.

33. See Charles Dedeyan, *Lamartine et la Toscane* (Geneva and Turin, 1981), p. 24. In a letter to Virieu, dated 1 March 1827, Lamartine described Vallombrosa as: 'un immense monastère, au sommet d'une montagne de l'Appenin, entouré de forêts de pins et de chataigniers. Voilà ou j'irai souvent, comme y allait Milton, pour passer des journées au printemps [*sic*; no thoughts of fallen leaves here]; mais je t'y voudrais!' Lamartine was persuaded that 'tous les grands poètes et tous les grands artistes de l'Italie y sont-ils venus tous chercher un asile

temporaire contre les misères, contre le désespoir ou contre les proscriptions dont la vie des hommes mémorables est toujours travaillée. On y montre la cellule de *Boccacce*, celle de *Dante*, celle de *Michel Ange*, celles de différents proscrits des maisons rivales qui se disputèrent la liberté ou la tyrannie pendant les luttes des républiques du moyen âge' (op. cit., p. 75). Three years after his visit, Lamartine published his poem 'L'Abbaye de Vallombreuse' (see *Harmonies poétiques et religieuses*, no. 11, in *Oeuvres poétiques complètes*, ed. M.-F. Guyard (Paris, 1963), pp. 332–4, and N. Harris, op. cit., p. 194). While on the subject of famous foreigners, one might mention that even Nietzsche visited Vallombrosa, by this time Milton's 'visit' having become so well known as to inspire Austrians and Germans (*L'Abbazia di Vallombrosa nel Pensiero Contemporaneo*, cit., pp. 28–30). Mrs Piozzi's *Reflections* had been published in German in 1790.

34. *Mementoes, historical and classical, of a Tour through part of France, Switzerland, and Italy in the years 1821 and 1822 . . .* 2 vols (London, 1824), I, pp. 265–6; see Appendix (above) for the complete text of this poem. In his more down-to-earth text, the author merely explains that Vallombrosa is 'a spot which Milton is said to have visited, and from which he is supposed to have painted some of the scenic imagery in Paradise Lost'. The *Mementoes* was a widely distributed book which it is difficult to believe Wordsworth did not know. It was reissued with 14 quality engravings and a cancel title-page as *A classical and historical tour through France [etc]*, in 1826, and again, as *A Tour through France [etc]*, in 1827; see R.S. Pine-Coffin, *A Bibliography of British and American Travel in Italy to 1860* (Florence, 1974), pp. 186–7. I would greatly welcome any suggestions as to who the author might have been. In all three issues, his or her preface is subscribed: 'London, Nov. 1823.'

35. The extent to which Beckford and his family were indeed anxious to maintain a low profile by the suppression of the edition, during and after the time of the Courtney scandal, is poignantly suggested by the aspiring author's original ambitions for *Dreams*: 'You know', he wrote to his tutor, Lettice, in 1781 shortly before finalizing the Vallombrosan passage, 'I have set my heart upon the success of this book' (*Dreams*, R.S. Gemmet edn. p. 19). For the possible influence of Philippe Jacques de Loutherbourg's *Eidophusikon* or 'Moving Pictures' on Beckford, see Bruce Redford, *Venice and the Grand Tour* (New Haven and London, 1996), pp. 108–11. In January 1782, de Loutherbourg concluded his theatrical programme with 'Satan arraying his Troops on the Banks of the Fiery Lake, with the Raising of Pandemonium, from Milton'. Given the apparently Miltonic content of the spectacle that Beckford commissioned from de Loutherbourg the previous Christmas, it is likely that this aspect was due to Beckford's influence; see J.W. Oliver, *The Life of William Beckford* (Oxford, 1933), pp. 88–91.

36. Lady Sydney Morgan, *Italy*, 2 vols (London, 1821), II, pp. 145–6. No doubt in part because she praises him in it, Byron praised Lady Morgan's book as 'really *excellent*' in August 1821 (*Born for Opposition: Byron's Letters and Journals*, ed. L.A. Marchand (London, 1978), VIII, p. 186). For a brief life, see E. Suddaby and P.J. Yarrow, *Lady Morgan in France* (Newcastle-upon-Tyne, 1971). The 8th edition of Mariana Starke's Baedeker-like *Travels*, complete with reference to Vallombrosa's del Sarto and Perugino, appeared in time for Wordsworth's 1837 tour.

37. Mrs [Frances] Trollope, *A Visit to Italy*, 2 vols (London, 1842), p. 219. I thank Mildred K. Abraham, of the University of Virginia Library, for informing me of Mrs Trollope's expedition.

38. Ibid., pp. 222-3.
39. Mary Shelley, *Rambles in Germany and Italy*, 2 vols (London, 1844), II, p. 137.
40. *The Letters of Elizabeth Barrett Browning*, ed. F.G. Kenyon, 3 vols (London, 1897), I, pp. 332-3; cf. several subsequent letters to others describing the same excursion with different emphases and details, e.g., two oxen instead of four (p. 341). Mary Shelley (op. cit.) had written that: 'No women are admitted within these sacred walls, but a *forestiera* is built adjoining for our accommodation', meaning in her case, coffee and the opportunity to dry her clothes. See the related problems encountered by George Eliot and *her* devoted escort at nearby Camaldoli in 1861 as told by Thomas Adolphus Trollope in *What I Remember*, 2 vols (London, 1887) II, pp. 275-8. For a relevant guide-book owned by the Brownings, see Maggs's catalogue 849 (London, 1958), p. 20: *Nuova Guida ovvero descrizione storico-artistico critica della Città e contorni di Firenze*, compilata de Federigo Fantozzi (Florence, 1852). The Brownings owned a lock of Milton's hair, given them by Leigh Hunt; see *Letters of Robert Browning*, ed. T.L. Hood (London, 1933), pp. 49, 347.
41. If more learned or imaginative explanations are required to account for Milton's Vallombrosan imagery, several are supplied in Sergio Baldi 'Folte come le foglie (e lo scudo di Satana)', *Critical Dimensions . . . Essays in honour of Aurelio Zanco*, ed. M. Curreli and A. Martino (Cuneo, 1978), pp. 221-41 (now reprinted in the very useful, if index-less, *Studi Miltoniani*, collected as a posthumous tribute to Professor Baldi by his colleagues at the University of Florence (1985), pp. 65-97). See also Neil Harris, op. cit., especially pp. 260-1, for Alexander Ross's 1658 reference to the 'order of *vallis umbrosa* or the Monks of the Shadowy Valley'.
42. Gherardo Silvani is described as 'Florence's greatest 17th-century architect' by Rudolf Wittkower in *Gothic vs. Classic* (New York, 1974), p. 80. Given his pre-publication knowledge of Buonmattei's *Della lingua Toscana* in September 1638, it is not impossible that Milton knew of de Franchi's book, with its detailed illustrated account of Vallombrosa, prior to publication (see below, note 48). In 1629, Averardo Nicolini, the Abbot responsible for employing Silvani for the rebuilding in progress at the time of Milton's visit, had published the folio: *Rituale Monasticon secundum consuetudinem monachorum, & monialium ord. S. Benedicti. Congreg. Vallisumbrose*. 'Etruria' carried a variety of connotations for the cultured, the most ancient being somewhat sinister and thus suited to the satanic context Milton intended. More mundanely, however, as in Leandro Alberti's *Descrittione di tutta Italia* of 1550 (which, according to J.C. Boswell's survey of his library, Milton probably owned), Etruria was simply the classically correct term for Tuscany, which a poet was all the more bound to use since Cosimo I had lent it powerful, archaeologically supported political prestige in the mid-sixteenth century. It is surely worth noting in this connection that the world's foremost Etruscologist – the posthumous publication of whose book *De Etruria Regali* effectively pioneered the subject – was a British Catholic who had died in Italy little more than a decade before Milton's visit. Thomas Dempster (*c.*1579-1625) was a Latin poet, the well-known editor and author of several distinguished books on subjects of great interest to Milton, a professor at Pisa and Bologna favored by Medici grand dukes and the Barberini Pope, Urban VIII, the colleague of Galileo, teacher of Giovanni Battista Doni and the focus of several Anglo-continental scandals, including one involving the Earl of Leicester's son, Sir Robert Dudley, the most distinguished Englishman resident in Tuscany at the time of Milton's visit. Milton would thus surely have known of Dempster and his works even if he may not have had access to his as yet

unpublished treatise on the Etruscans, which had been commissioned by Cosimo II but awaited its 'discovery' at the hands of Thomas Coke, the early eighteenth-century Earl of Leicester, before being published. The most detailed post-*DNB* accounts of Dempster are to be found in A.M. Crinò, 'Inediti su alcuni contatti Tosco-Britannici nel Seicento', *English Miscellany*, XII (1961), pp. 158–70 and R. Leighton and C. Castelino, 'Thomas Dempster and Ancient Etruria: A Review of the Autobiography and *De Etruria Regali*', *Papers of the British School of Rome*, LVIII (1990), pp. 337–52. Several recent studies deal with his pioneering place in Etruscology: G. Cipriani, *Il mito etrusco nel rinascimento fiorentino* (Florence, 1980); M. Cristofani, 'Sugli inizi dell'Etruscheria. La pubblicazione del De Etruria Regali di Thomas Dempster', *Mélanges de l'Ecole Française de Rome 90* (1978), pp. 577–625; idem, *La Scoperta degli Etruschi* (Rome, 1983); and, in the year of the major Etruscan exhibitions in Florence, F. Borsi (ed.), *La Fortuna degli Etruschi* (Milan, 1985) and G. Morolli, '*Vetus Etruria*': il mito degli Etruschi nella letteratura architettonica . . . (Florence, 1985). Dempster's most important poem, *Musca Recidiva*, went through three editions during his lifetime which would in itself justify adding his name, along with that of James Gibbes, to those of Buchanan, Barclay and John Owen, whom Douglas Bush cites as 'the only poets of British birth who achieved continental fame'; see *Variorum Commentary on the Poems of John Milton* (London, 1970), I, pp. 4–5 and Chapter 10 above. In the *Ragionamento funebre* published by the Accademia della Notte di Bologna in 1626, a year after his death, Dempster was praised by Ovidio Montalbani as the equal of Homer. As someone who would so assiduously recruit similar eulogies during his Italian tour 12 years later, perhaps Milton sought out Dempster's tomb in the great church of San Domenico on his way through Bologna.

43. *The Poetical Works of William Wordsworth*, ed. E. de Selincourt and H. Darbishire, 5 vols, 2nd edn (Oxford, 1940–9), III, p. 223. Wordsworth begins 'At Vallombrosa' (1842) by quoting the lines with which he had begun 'Composed in the Simplon Pass', published in 1822 in *Memorials of a Tour on the Continent, 1820*: 'Vallombrosa! I longed in thy shadiest wood / To slumber, reclined on the moss-covered floor.' If there is any similarity between these lines and the anticipatory spirit of the lines with which Beckford began his Vallombrosan set-piece, it should be remembered they were first published prior to Beckford's *Italy* of 1834, which would lend support to the hypothesis that Wordsworth had access to the original *Dreams*, perhaps via their mutual friend Rogers. Though in their accounts of this tour, the standard biographies do not mention the fact (see M. Moorman, *William Wordsworth: A Biography*, 2 vols (Oxford, 1965), II, pp. 524–6; and S. Gill, *William Wordsworth: A Life* (Oxford, 1989), pp. 394–5), Crabb Robinson declined to accompany the 67-year-old Wordsworth on his horseback pilgrimage to Vallombrosa, apparently leaving him at Pontassieve and excusing himself on the basis of having been there before (see *The Letters of William and Dorothy Wordsworth*, ed. E. de Selincourt, rev. edn A.G. Hill (Oxford, 1982), VI, p. 406). Robinson may even have helped provoke Wordsworth's indignant tone in 'At Vallombrosa' by articulating his doubts about the Miltonic connection. He had joined 'a party of pilgrimage' to Vallombrosa on 2 August 1830, and was to describe his experience in more down-to-earth, dare one say, intelligent terms than Wordsworth. Vallombrosa, he wrote, was: 'of interest to English travellers, chiefly because one of our great poets has introduced its name into a simile . . . It must be the delight which the sound gives to every ear susceptible of the beauty of verse, that excites a curiosity concerning the place, the name of which is so introduced. But as far

as expectation is raised, that can only suffer disappointment from the visit, for with the present appearance of the valley, the description does not in the least agree. I could see but one little stream in it. It is by no means woody, and all the trees now growing there (I presume that twenty years have produced no change) are pine or fir-trees, and of all trees the least adapted to arched bowers are the fir and larch' (*Diary, Reminiscences, and Correspondence of Henry Crabb Robinson*, ed. T. Sadler, 2 vols (London, 1872), II, pp. 98–9).

Wordsworth might almost be responding to his friend (the deserved dedicatee of the *Memorials*) when he writes: 'The fault-finders are themselves mistaken; the *natural* woods of the region of Vallombrosa *are* deciduous, and spread to a great extent; those near the convent are indeed mostly pines; but they are avenues of trees *planted* within a few steps of each other . . . plots of which are periodically cut down . . . My guide, a boy of about fourteen years old, pointed this out to me' (*Poetical Works*, III, p. 498). Privately, however, Wordsworth confessed to having been 'somewhat disappointed at Vallombrosa'. He was also to excise the description of Milton as 'Holiest of Men' from the 'Prospectus' to *The Recluse*.

44. *Notes and Queries* (*NQ*), 4th series, XI (1873), p. 62: 'I have passed three winters at Florence . . . when I was at Vallombrosa one of the Fathers stated that they had several letters . . . Since I was at Vallombrosa the convent has been disolved, and the buildings are now used for a Botanical and Agricultural College.' The latter information enables us to date Dixon's Vallombrosan visit to before 1866.

45. *NQ*, 5th series, VIII (1876), p. 306. It is amusing to remember that Beckford claims to have 'made a full stop at the organ' in Vallombrosa, 'perhaps the most harmonious I ever played upon'; *Dreams*, p. 182. This is no doubt the 'old' one mentioned on fol. 8v of an early nineteenth-century manuscript collection of Vallombrosan inscriptions in my possession: 'L'organo antico era del celebre autore Onofrio che li trova dalla Congregazione[?] in Bibbiena[.] l'attuale e del Fronci Benedetto, fatto nel 1819 . . .'

46. *NQ*, 5th series, VIII (1877), p. 117. Defenders of Milton *qua* Vallombrosan visitor, mainly against Todd's *Milton* (1801), II, p. 40, who quotes Mrs Piozzi, and Brewer's *Dictionary of Phrase and Fable*, continued to appear in *Notes and Queries*, e.g., Jonathan Bouchier, *NQ*, XI (1879), p. 463, and his supporters, pp. 488–9. The last of these was 'H.W. New Univ. Club', who writes: 'I visited Vallombrosa in the spring of 1867, in company with a son of the poet Wordsworth, and can testify to the truth of Beckford's description of the convent as "sheltered by firs and chestnuts towering one above another".' See also Aldo Sorani in *Saturday Review of Literature*, 2 (1925), p. 318, which confirms that no trace of the letters survives but lends credence to their existence more than a century earlier.

47. For more detail, see Neil Harris's PhD dissertation, cited above, note 3.

48. *Historia del Patriarca S. Giovanni Gualberto primo abbate et institutore del monastico ordine di Vallombrosa* (Florence, 1640). This book took almost three years to wend its way through the bureaucratic procedures required to obtain the necessary imprimaturs. For the etchings, at least one of which seems to have been by Stefano della Bella, see A. Gabbrielli and E. Settesoldi, *Vallombrosa e le sue selve: nove secoli di storia* (Stia: Ministero dell'Agricoltura e delle Foreste, 1985). For a later and superior depiction of Vallombrosa, see that by Cicci dated 1750, from the set of aquatint views published by Charlotte Bury (see above, note 29), illustrated in Nello Puccioni, *La Vallombrosa e la Val di Sieve inferiore*, Italia artistica no. 81 (Bergamo, n.d.), pp. 27–8.

49. A. Hare, *Florence* (London, 1884), p. 217.

50. Gabbrielli and Settesoldi, p. 118.

51. J.C. Eustace, *A Tour through Italy*, 2 vols (London, 1813), II, pp. 227–31. The Pope quotation is from *Eloisa and Abelard*. The author writes that *Paradise Lost* 'is considered as the model of modern parks'. For Eustace in Italy, see J.H. Whitfield, 'Mr Eustace and Lady Morgan', *Italian Studies Presented to E.R. Vincent* (Cambridge, 1962), pp. 166–89. While Mariana Starke took care to disabuse her readers of Eustace's exaggerated account of French destruction, Lady Morgan was so incensed as to launch a satirical onslaught on both him and *The British Review* (*Italy*, II, p. 146 n.)

52. Eustace, *A Classical Tour through Italy, An. MDCCCII*, 2nd edn, 2 vols (London, 1814), II, p. 215. *British Review*, no. 10, p. 383; compare Beckford's *Italy; with Sketches of Spain and Portugal*, 2 vols (London, 1834 – but based on journeys of 1780 and 1782).

53. Wordsworth, *Letters*, op. cit., VI, p. 406.

54. Ibid., p. 333.

55. E.B.B., *Poems*.

56. Hare, *Florence*, 3rd edn (London, 1890), pp. 23–32. Hare, like Eustace and the earlier key Italian travel writers, e.g., Richard Lassels in the seventeenth century and Henry Swinburne in the eighteenth, was a Roman Catholic. For milder mention of Vallombrosan trees 'felled by order of the Government' in 1891, see Virginia W. Johnson, *The Lily of the Arno* (London, 1891), pp. 110–11.

57. Wordsworth's note to this poem, which precedes 'At Vallombrosa' in *Memorials of a Tour in Italy, 1837*, explains that 'a price had been paid for it by the late Sir G. Beaumont, upon condition that the proprietor should not act upon his known intention of cutting it down'; see F. Owen and D.B. Brown, *Collector of Genius: The Life of Sir George Beaumont* (New Haven and London, 1988).

58. *Dictionary of American Biography*, XXI, pp. 297–8.

59. This book was described by Lewis Mumford in *The Brown Decades* (New York, 1931), p. 78, as 'the fountainhead of the conservationist movement'. It was republished in a revised edition as *The Earth as Modified by Human Action* in 1874.

60. T.A. Trollope, *What I Remember*, 2 vols., 2nd edn (London, 1887), II, pp. 262–6.

61. H. James, *William Wetmore Story and his Friends*, 2 vols (London, 1903); see also *Dictionary of American Biography*. Story died in his daughter's house at Vallombrosa in 1895 and, like Marsh, was buried in the Protestant Cemetery in Rome.

62. Op. cit., p. 483. As noted by James, Story's essay was 'reissued as a volume of scarce more than a hundred pages in 1881' (II, pp. 330–3). The British Institute of Florence possesses a rare copy for notice of which I thank its librarian, Mark Roberts. James also notes that three miles for the distance between the monastery and the house at Lago is something of an exaggeration. Vallombrosa provided what James calls the 'undertone' for Story's 'short idyllic novel *Fiammetta*', published in 1886. It was written at the Lago di Vallombrosa during the summer of 1885 and, 'in memory of those happy days in the "Etrurian shades"', dedicated to Story's wife and daughter, to whom it had been read 'on three beautiful mornings as we sat under the shadows of its whispering pines'. For Medicean interest in (and presence at) Vallombrosa dating back to Landino's *Camaldulese Disputations*, see G. Volpi, 'Lorenzo de'Medici e Vallombrosa', *Archivio Storico Italiano*, XCII (1934), 2, pp. 121–32,

and C. Elam and E. Gombrich, 'Lorenzo de' Medici and a Frustrated Villa Project', in *Florence and Italy: Renaissance Studies in Honour of Nicolai Rubinstein*, ed. P. Denley and C. Elam (London, 1988), pp. 481–92.

63. Story, 'Vallombrosa', p. 487.
64. Ibid., p. 484.
65. Ibid., p. 490.
66. M. Shelley, pp. 135–7.
67. Story, op. cit., p. 408. in *Pascarel* (London, 1873), Ouida outdoes Story by combining two traditions, having Milton gaze towards Vallombrosa from Galileo's tower in Arcetri: 'here Galileo learned the story of the sun; and here Milton, looking on Valdarno, dreamed of Paradise' (op. cit., II, p. 93). It is odd that Miltonists pursuing his two best-known but worst documented Italian visits (to Vallombrosa and to Galileo – though at least Milton claimed to have visited the latter) have failed to combine forces and note that Galileo actually studied at Vallombrosa as a novice; see R.N. Vasaturo et al., cit. above in note 3, pp. 132 and 152–3.
68. For identification of those with whom he dined and of the 1645 *Poems*' 'Selvaggi' see *The Grand Tour and the Great Rebellion*, pp. 282–3 and Appendix III. In the unpublished second section of my paper at Vallombrosa I attempted to strengthen my hypothesis that Selvaggi was David Codner, OSB (*alias* Matteo Selvaggio) by pointing out his connection with Jane Savage, the Catholic subject of Milton's 1631 *Epitaph on the Marchioness of Winchester*.

ADDENDUM, MAY 2000

Partly due to the reflected glory of fellow Vallombrosan Henry James, the sculptor of Milton's plaque, Hendrik Andersen (above, p. 279), is receiving unprecedented attention. Though his family tomb in the Protestant Cemetery seems as abandoned as ever, this American of Norwegian origin was last winter honoured by the creation of 'The Hendrik Andersen Museum' in his former home, the Villa Helene, Via Mancini 20, Rome. His (quasi?) affair with Henry James, meanwhile, is documented by the publication by Rosella Zorzi of the letters James wrote to him between 1899–1915, under the title *Amato Ragazzo* (Venice, 2000). As well as Story's 1881 essay on Vallombrosa, no doubt both men also knew Adeline Sergeant's *In Vallombrosa* (1897), which was dedicated to 'Leader Scott', *nomme de plume* of Mrs Lucy Baxter, the scholarly daughter of the Dorset poet, William Barnes, who worked for John Temple Leader, rebuilder of the Florentine castle of Vincigliata When Barne's friend, Thomas Hardy, visited Florence, Leader Scott acted as his guide as she no doubt did when Henry James visited Vincigliata. Other relevant recent literature includes, Francesco Salvestrini, *Santa Maria di Vallombrosa* (Florence, 1998) and the fascinating biography by David Lowenthal of *George Perkins Marsh, Prophet of Conservation* (Seattle and London, 2000).

I might not have made a less excusable omission had I had access to the facility now available on the *Dictionary of National Biography*'s CDRom, which provides one with every *DNB* citation of the place, even unto Alexander Munro's 1869 bust of the 'Duchess of Vallombrosa'. I owe my knowledge of this pioneering Vallombrosan visit, however, to my friend Anna Eavis of the late-lamented RCHME (now part of English Heritage). In 1765, the Winchester- and Oxford-educated William Benson Earle (future philanthropist and man of letters) set off on his Grand Tour, accompanied by his exemplary Grand Touring friends, Henry Penruddocke Wyndham and Joseph Windham of Earsham. On his return home, as well as writing an account of the 1766 eruption of Etna, Earle published 'A Description of Vallombrosa' in the *Monthly Miscellany*. Meanwhile I find that John Talman visited in 1719.

13

George Berkeley's Grand Tours: The Immaterialist as Connoisseur of Art and Architecture

IN THE SUMMER of 1711, having finally seen the first edition of his *Characteristicks* through the press, Anthony Ashley Cooper, the consumptive 3rd Earl of Shaftesbury, left the 'great smoak' of London for Naples, which had been the southernmost point of his Grand Tour 23 years earlier [Fig. 51].[1] Though still only 42 when he died in Naples little more than a year later, since that first tour Shaftesbury had established himself as an immensely influential arbiter (and merger) of morality and taste.[2] Thus, although the ten-page *Letter concerning Design* he wrote to Lord Somers whilst confined to his grand Palazzo during the first months of 1712 was not published until much later, Shaftesbury's reputation was such that, within weeks of arriving in England, it was circulating in manuscript and had joined his other canon-creating writings on the shelves of the (largely Whig) intelligentsia.[3]

With the Hanoverian Succession and freedom from the French military threat more or less assured by diplomacy and the Duke of Marlborough respectively, Shaftesbury argued that Britain could at last look forward to the uninterrupted Parliamentary-limited monarchy for which he and his grandfather had so vigorously campaigned, and should now turn her attention to the arts of peace. 'I can', he wrote:

> with some assurance, say to your Lordship in a kind of spirit of Prophecy, from what I have observed of the rising Genius of our nation, That if we live to see a Peace any way answerable to that generous Spirit

51 John Closterman, *Anthony Ashley Cooper, 3rd Earl of Shaftesbury* (1671–1713). [The Earl of Shaftesbury; photo: National Portrait Gallery, London]

with which this War was begun, and carry'd on, for our *own* liberty and that of Europe; the Figure we are like to make abroad, and the increase of our Knowledge, Industry and Sense at home, will render *united* Britain the principal Seat of Arts.[4]

Continuing the theme of competition with the France of Louis XIV into a brief though highly politicized survey of the state of each of the major arts (or 'sciences' as he calls them), Shaftesbury remembered the time when,

> in respect of music, our reigning Taste was in many degrees inferior to the *French*. The long reign of Luxury and Pleasure under King Charles the Second, and the foreign Helps and study'd Advantages given to *Musick* in a following reign, cou'd not raise our Genius the least in this respect. But when the Spirit of the Nation was grown more free . . . we no sooner began to turn ourselves towards *Musick*, and enquire what Italy in particular produced, than in an instant we outstrip'd our neighbours the French, enter'd into a Genius far beyond theirs, and rais'd ourselves an *Ear*, and *Judgement*, not inferior to the best now in the World.
>
> In the same manner, as to painting. Tho we have as yet nothing of our own native Growth in this kind worthy of being mention'd; yet since the Publick has of late begun to express a Relish for Engravings, Drawings, Copyings, and for the original Paintings of the chief *Italian* schools . . . I doubt not that, in very few years we shall make an equal progress in this other Science.[5]

Coming finally to the subject of architecture, as a deeply committed Whig and self-conscious exponent of the purest 'Greek' classicism, Shaftesbury had more complex things to say, for England's two greatest living practitioners of this science were the venerable but still dominant Royal Surveyor, Sir Christopher Wren, and the unorthodox ex-playwright and Clarenceux King-at-Arms, John Vanbrugh, who in Swift's rhyme had, 'without thought or lecture / hugely turned to architecture', and in particular to what we now call 'baroque' architecture.[6] Shaftesbury attacked both men in all but name. 'As for architecture', he wrote,

> 'tis no wonder if so many noble Designs . . . have miscarry'd amongst us; since the Genius of our Nation has hitherto been so little turn'd this way, that thro' several Reigns we have patiently seen the noblest publick Buildings perish (if I may say so) under the hands of one single Court-Architect . . . But I question whether our patience is like to hold

much longer. The Devastation so long committed in this kind, has made us grow rude and clamorous at the hearing of a new Palace spoilt, or a new Design committed to some rash or impotent Pretender.[7]

Whether or not Shaftesbury approved of the Italianate Inigo Jones for the sake of his Palladianism, he could only have disapproved of Jones's status as a courtier and Royalist who, even worse, was then thought to have died a Roman Catholic.[8] He might have been embarrassed, moreover, by the role the mid-seventeenth-century Parliamentary revolution had played in bringing the progress of architectural classicism to a near standstill (a role which writers such as John Aubrey, Evelyn, Roger Pratt and Anthony Wood had criticized).[9] Neither Jones nor the exemplary standards of taste achieved towards the end of the personal rule of Charles I were mentioned in Shaftesbury's misleading account, even during his discussion of the two 'noblest subjects for architecture: our Prince's Palace and our House of Parliament', those still unbuilt projects for Whitehall which Jones would have completed for Charles I had he not been dismissed as a 'delinquent' and his master executed. With the early Stuart cultural achievement and its destruction by the proto-Whig Puritan establishment conveniently excluded from his potted cultural history, Shaftesbury was able to wax optimistic that 'Our State . . . may prove perhaps more fortunate than our Church, in having waited till a national taste was formed' before the rebuilding of Whitehall was undertaken.[10] He regrets that 'the zeal of the nation could not . . . admit so long a delay in their ecclesiastical structures'. Following this disparaging reference to Wren's rebuilding of the city churches after the Great Fire with another to the recently announced Commission for Building Fifty New Churches, he laments that:

> since a Zeal of this sort has been newly kindled amongst us, 'tis like we shall see from afar the many Spires arising in our great City, with such hasty and sudden growth, as may be the occasion perhaps that our immediate Relish shall be hereafter censur'd, as retaining much of what Artists call the *Gothick* kind.[11]

Having implicitly criticized Wren, Vanbrugh and Hawksmoor, Shaftesbury now explicitly attacked Hampton Court and St Paul's Cathedral.[12] Then, as if to confirm that by the 'new design committed to some . . . new pretender' of his previous paragraph he had meant

Vanbrugh's still incomplete Blenheim Palace, he pronounces in almost populist terms on the 'common censure' which 'national monuments' were liable to receive even when 'raised by private men' (a probable reference to Shaftesbury's one-time money-lender, the Duke of Marlborough):

> when a great Man builds, he will find litle Quarter from the Publick, if instead of a beautiful Pile, he raises, at a vast expense, such a false and counterfeit Piece of Magnificence, as can be justly arraign'd for its Deformity by so many knowing Men in Art, and by the whole *People*, who, in such a Conjuncture readily follow their Opinion.[13]

Clearly it was not just the Gothic – whether surviving or reviving – that Shaftesbury abhored, but what we now call the baroque. Joseph Rykwert has coined the not very catchy term 'High Tory Gothic-baroque' to describe the English version of the style which Shaftesbury and his like-minded contemporaries found so offensive.[14] Given the language's then still very limited aesthetic vocabulary, when confronted with any rule-breaking style they failed to appreciate, these critics resorted simply to the pejorative 'Gothic'. In 1672, Giovanni Pietro Bellori had condemned Borromini as a 'Gothic ignoramus' but had more scrupulously commended many less 'corrupt' contemporaries.[15] Shaftesbury commandeered the casual moralism of continental criticism of the Gothic, of mannerism, of Caravaggist realism and the baroque, and forged it into a respectably theoretical but easily understood 'moral aesthetic', which gave the likes of Colen Campbell greater confidence when they applied such judgements to modern architecture. In 1715, this ambitious ex-lawyer (and Grand Tourist) introduced his enormously influential *Vitruvius Britannicus* with a blanket condemnation of the entire Seicento. The works of Bernini and of James Gibbs's master, Carlo Fontana, were 'affected and licentious', while Borromini (whose designs Jones's friend Henry Cogan had praised as 'ingenious and excellent') had 'endeavoured to debauch Mankind with his odd and chimerical Beauties'.[16] Clearly, in post-Glorious Revolution Britain, neither Borromini's 'wildly Extravagant . . . Designs' nor those of Guarino Guarini were to become the liberating aesthetic influence they became in central Europe, where the extraordinarily eclectic Fischer von Erlach drew on sources as diverse as Chinese pagodas and Inigo Jones's 'Roman' Stonhenge.[17] Instead of the 'Absurdities' of the still unnamed baroque, Campbell commended:

those Restorers of Architecture, which the Fifteenth and Sixteenth Centurys produced in Italy . . . But above all, the great Palladio, who has exceeded all that were gone before him . . . With him the great Manner and exquisite Taste of Building is lost; for the Italians can no more now relish the Antique simplicity, but are entirely employed in capricious Ornaments, which must at last end in the *Gothick*.

Campbell's assumption that an over-elaborated classicism inevitably degenerates into the Gothic now seems crudely historicist. As with Shaftesbury, who condemned Bernini as 'wicked', it also blinded him to the fact that Bernini, the greatest of the artists he condemns, had fully shared his admiration for both the ancients and for Palladio and had indeed exploited the latter's 'great Manner' (or 'maniera') to produce 'baroque' masterpieces.[18]

Although the aesthetic priorities announced here conformed to those of the so-called 'new Junta for Architecture', consisting of Thomas Hewett, Sir George Markham, Lord Molesworth and his son John, the recently returned ambassador to Florence, the readiness of these Whig patrons to bestow major commissions upon foreign architects worried Campbell. Clearly he was interested in obtaining such commissions for himself; he no doubt found the arrival in London in 1714, at Molesworth's suggestion, of the talented neo-classical architect, Alessandro Galilei, a far from welcome addition to the ever-present competition from Gibbs.[19] Perhaps this is why, despite having benefited from a Grand Tour himself, Campbell added a warning to his 1715 introduction:

The general Esteem that Travellers have for Things that are foreign, is in nothing more conspicuous than with Regard to Building. We travel, for the most part, at an Age more apt to be imposed upon by the Ignorance or Partiality of others, than to judge truly of the Merits of Things by the Strength of Reason. It's owing to this Mistake in Education, that so many of the *British* Quality have so mean an Opinion of what is performed in our own Country: tho', perhaps in most we equal, and in some Things we surpass, our Neighbours.[20]

Though the latter claim – if intended to refer to architecture – was only just becoming plausible, patriotic (not to say paranoid) Protestants had been arguing something similar since the first signs of a thaw in relations with the Catholic continent at the end of the sixteenth century. By 1604 even the Catholic priest and one-time traveller in Italy, Thomas Wright (albeit writing his *Passions of the Minde* in prison), was arguing that:

> in some one or other trade, the Italians surpasse us, but they be such as eyther England regardeth not at all, or prizeth not very much: but, in such as our Countrie esteemeth, wee may, eyther equall or preferre our selves before them.[21]

The claim that British buildings were as good as foreign ones was exploited by the Puritanical tendency in its campaign against foreign travel, epitomized in its most respectable form by Joseph Hall's *Quo Vadis? or a just Censure of Travel*, first published in 1617.

*   *   *

Elizabeth I founded Trinity College, Dublin, in 1591, soon after the failure of the Armada, in order that

> knowledge and utility might be increased by the instruction of our people there, whereof many have usually heretofore used to travel into France, Italy, and Spain, to get learning in such foreign universities, where they have been infected with popery and other ill qualities, and so become evil subjects.[22]

If the humanities flourished as a result of such attempts at self-containedness, where architecture was concerned, the much-travelled Inigo Jones was the exception that proved the rule that it was only in the late seventeenth century, when influential travellers such as Gilbert Burnet could at last cite the likes of Chatsworth and returned Grand Tourists such as the Earl of Carlisle could build so confidently as at Castle Howard, that such claims could be taken seriously. It is ironic that late twentieth-century theorists, whose supposedly sceptical methodology prides itself on alerting us to the dangers of anachronistically canonical aesthetic judgements, should in practice be pushing us back to the relativism of the 'we're just as good as them' bigots of the pre-Enlightenment. Even the *Spectator* published an article which sought to assure its classical–liberal readership that cosmopolitan visitors to Elizabethan England would have found much to admire in British buildings.[23] Surely this tendency tells us more about our own sophisticated ability to appreciate styles as diverse as Gothic, classic, Baroque, neo-Gothic and modernist simultaneously, than about highly competitive and more single-minded early modern cultures groping towards a vocabulary with which they might disparage rival groups and the despised barbarism of the pre- and extra-Renaissance.

Having thus defended my right to exploit traditionally progressivist (even historicist) terminology, I would argue that it was really only in the eighteenth century, after the delays caused by Protestant Reformation and Puritan rebellion, that Britain could be said to have caught up with the Catholic continent. Unfortunately for the anti-travellists, however, the process of catching up, which included learning to mislike Gothic and Baroque, required an enhanced appreciation of ancient architecture. In order to acquire the correct taste and, in the manner of Lord Shaftesbury, to become virtuous by becoming a virtuoso, despite the best efforts of Inigo Jones and John Webb to promote Stonehenge as a Roman ruin, there was no alternative but to travel to southern France and Italy to study the better-known classical remains. An ever-expanding understanding of archaeology, combined with a kind of connoisseurial one-upmanship, eventually necessitated travel even further afield to the very sources of classicism in Sicily, Paestum and Greece itself.

* * *

Famous as a philosopher of extraordinary originality and depth, as a prose-writer of classic quality and one of the most universally liked men who ever lived, George Berkeley is, however, little known for the quality of his artistic judgement or as an arbiter of taste [Fig. 9]. And yet, for all that its influence might have been personal rather than public, wherever we are able to document it, his aesthetic judgement stands the test of time far more satisfactorily than either that of Shaftesbury (whose taste was conventional and patronage second-rate, and whose comments on individual artists were commonplace), or of his increasingly dogmatic contemporaries and followers.[24]

For Shaftesbury and the New Junta were hardly pioneering in their call for classical order. John Webb had continued his master Jones's Palladian project well into the Restoration. Roger Pratt praised Palladio in his projected treatise on architecture and by 1706, John Evelyn was looking forward to 'some perfect Edition of what remains of the incomparable Palladio'. Sir Howard Colvin has drawn attention to the precocious Palladianism (post-Inigo Jones) of the Scots ex-Catholic James Smith, the probable master of Colen Campbell.[25] The Dean of Christ Church, Oxford, Henry Aldrich, had died in 1710 a fully fledged Palladian theorist and architect. His friend George Clarke had succeeded him both in the latter capacity and as patron and promoter of such neoclassical masterpieces as Hawksmoor's Clarendon Building, completed prior to the publication of Campbell's *Vitruvius Britannicus*. Meanwhile in Hanover, despite close links with Von Erlach's Vienna, Lambert Corfey's Palladianism was encouraged by the Elector several years before, as George I, he became the patron and dedicatee of Campbell's first two volumes and of Leoni's translation of Palladio's *Quattro Libri*.[26]

In the process of becoming the principal consolidator of the taste for Vitruvian plainness and the patriotic promotion of Inigo Jones, Richard Boyle, 3rd Earl of Burlington, influenced in particular by Campbell, returned to Italy to inspect those Palladian buildings he had ignored during his 1714–15 Grand Tour and bring back original drawings by the Vicentine master and an English painter named William Kent, who would help him establish the new Rule of Taste.[27]

Given the presence of Berkeley's previously unnoticed signature in the University of Padua visitors' book earlier in the same year, it is possible that Berkeley first met Burlington during the latter's 1719 visit to the Veneto (see Appendix) [Fig. 52]. Certainly, the two men were closely associated by 1721, having been brought together by their mutual friend Alexander Pope, with whom Berkeley corresponded throughout both his Italian journeys. According to Joseph Warton's *Essay on Pope*, Berkeley won Burlington's friendship 'not only by his true politeness and the peculiar charms of his conversation, which was exquisite, but by his profound and perfect skill in architecture'.[28] Decades later, as Bishop of Cloyne, Berkeley wrote to Lady Burlington of being 'haunted with a taste for good company and fine arts that I got at Burlington house, the worst preparative in the world for a retreat at Cloyne'. Despite familiarity with the work of Aldrich and Clarke, followed by such close association with this most powerful Palladian of them all, Berkeley retained an admirably independent aesthetic spirit, selectively eschewing the fashionable orthodoxies in a way that undermines those Foucaultist, Spenglerian or, indeed, Pevsnerian theorists who exaggerate the extent to which an *episteme* or *Zeitgeist* conditions the judgement of all who live in a given period.[29]

By the second half of the eighteenth century, boredom with Palladianism had set in and, in the wake of Hogarth's example, the

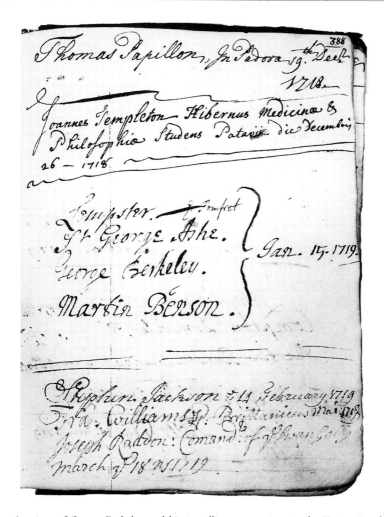

52 The signature of George Berkeley and his travelling companions in the University of Padua's visitors' book-cum-matriculation register. Biblioteca del Seminario Patavino, codice 634, p. 388. [European University Institute, Florence]

likes of Horace Walpole, William Chambers, the Adams, William Beckford and even Sir Joshua Reynolds were articulating a new, more pluralistic appreciation of the serpentine line, the Gothick, Chinoiserie and the picturesque, thus laying the foundations for the Romanticism which would sweep away the objective canons so carefully established by the Augustans. Reynolds – who might have used the still unborn term Baroque in a positive sense – wrote of Vanbrugh's having apparently 'had recourse to some principles of the Gothick architecture', but this no longer prevented him from praising the former playwright as 'a poet as well as an architect' capable of 'a greater display of imagination, than we shall find perhaps in any other'.[30]

George Berkeley anticipated such imaginative freedom. At the same time, without being merely eclectic, he developed such a deep regard for the classical that he deserves recognition as a discoverer of Greek Doric architecture, decades before the discovery of Paestum and half a century before the so-called Greek Revival.[31] His originality, like his extraordinary theory of knowledge, was based on an equal emphasis on the mind, with its imaginative generalized preconceptions or ideas (in this case, his profound knowledge of Greek history and literature), and on those particular objects which he claimed depended for their existence on our perceiving them (in this case, the Doric temples of Sicily). It is thus only an apparent paradox that the inventor of immaterialism was one of the most perceptive and visually sensitive observers both of nature and material culture.

As well as enthusing over Greek Doric, Berkeley exported books, prints, medals, sculpture and *scagliola* from Rome and Florence,[32] pioneeringly praised Baroque Lecce as 'the most beautiful city in Italy'[33] and the landscape of Ischia as 'thrown together in a romantic confusion',[34] and commended the 'sweetness, grace and beauty' of pre-Raphaelite Perugino.[35] Proto-anthropologically, he investigated tarantism – the state of hysteria allegedly induced by the bite of the tarantula – by interviewing peasants in southern Italy who had survived by having danced the tarantella. He introduced Palladianism into America by borrowing a design from Kent's *Designs of Inigo Jones* for the door-case of his house in Rhode Island [Fig. 53].[36] He also brought to New England John Smibert, the British artist he 'discovered' in Italy, who is generally regarded as the founding father of American portrait painting.[37] At Cloyne he had a collection of mainly Flemish pictures and encouraged painting in the locality.[38] He drew up detailed plans for an ideal city he intended to build on Bermuda, having already published proposals '*preventing the Ruin of Great Britain*' (beginning with a new 'Parliament house') in 1721,[38] and advised Irish landowners on how to build their country houses, most notably designing 'two fronts' for Speaker Conolly's

53 George Berkeley's house 'Whitehall' in Middletown near Newport, Rhode Island, featuring an Ionic doorcase derived from William Kent's *Designs of Inigo Jones* (London, 1727). [E. Chaney]

Castletown in 1722. Berkeley's widow remembered him as 'an excellent architect'.[39]

The moment at which we realize that Berkeley considered he had become fully competent in matters architectural is epitomized by the letter he wrote to one such aristocrat, his life-long friend and patron, Sir John Percival, the future 1st Earl of Egmont, in the summer of 1718 [Fig. 54].[40] Though he was aware of Percival's own expertise – based on a Grand Tour completed a decade earlier – as well as his patronage of the two ablest Italianate architects of the period, James Gibbs and Colen Campbell, confident in the knowledge that he had now travelled more extensively than any of these, Berkeley wrote somewhat rhetorically, but with only a modicum of irony, that he longed for liberty to return from Italy,

54 Vincenzo Felici, *John Percival, later 1st Earl of Egmont* (Rome, 1707). [National Portrait
Gallery, London]

that I may have a part in the contrivance of the house you design to build this winter, for you must know I pretend to an uncommon skill in architecture, as you will easily imagine when I assure your Lordship there is not any one modern building in Rome that pleases me, except the wings of the capitol built by Michael Angelo and the colonade of Berninies before St Peter's. The Church itself I find a thousand faults with, as indeed with every other modern Church here. I forget the little round one in the place where St Peter was beheaded [*sic*] built by Bramante, which is very pretty and built like an ancient temple. This gusto of mine is formed on the remains of antiquity that I have met with in my travels, particularly in Sicily, which convince me that the old Romans were inferior to the Greeks, and that the moderns fall infinitely short of both in the grandeur and simplicity of taste.[41]

If Berkeley sounds more Palladian than the Palladians here, his praise of Bernini both in this passage and elsewhere is indicative of a far richer and more tolerant taste. By examining Berkeley's letters and notebooks, from the time of his arrival in England from Dublin in January 1713 to his return from Italy in 1720, we can study the development of this taste in illuminating detail.[42]

Berkeley seems to have become the popular figure he remained from the moment he arrived in London, forming friendships with Addison, Swift and Steele almost immediately, and with Pope soon after. The physical aspect of London appealed to him less than the social, however. During his journey east from Holyhead in early January 1713, Berkeley was pleasantly surprised by the landscape, but, he wrote, 'if the country outdid my expectation, the towns fell short of it, even London itself seems to exceed Dublin not so much in the stateliness or beauty of its buildings as in extent'. In June he settled for the summer in Oxford, the city in which he was to die half a century later.[43] Although, even after seeing France and northern Italy he would continue patriotically to praise Dublin as 'one of the finest cities in the world', where its buildings were concerned the Oxford which Aldrich, Clarke and Hawksmoor were busily modernizing clearly impressed and influenced him more. Trinity College Chapel and Queen's College Library had both been completed in 1694; the Fellows' Building at Corpus Christi College in 1712. Aldrich may have been responsible for all three of these buildings but was almost certainly the designer of All Saints, complete except for its spire when Berkeley first saw it, and certainly for Christ Church's

Peckwater Quad. Begun in 1706, Aldrich's three-sided main block was being completed during the time of Berkeley's visit. By the time George Clarke completed the fourth side of the quadrangle as a library (1717–38), Berkeley had seen and admired the building which inspired it, Michelangelo's Capitoline Palace. In 1706 Clarke had designed, paid for and now occupied the Warden's Lodgings at All Souls. As has been said, he also advised on Hawksmoor's Clarendon Press Building which, in its almost complete state, was the most impressive modern building in Oxford (and one of the most impressive neoclassical buildings in Britain) in the summer of 1713. Berkeley wrote to his friend and patron Sir John Percival:

> I have been now almost a month in this town and think it to be the most delightful place I have ever seen, as well as for the pleasantness of its situation, as that great number of ancient and modern buildings which have a very agreeable effect on my eye, though I came from London and visited Hampton Court and Windsor by the way.[44]

The 'very agreeable effect on my eye' is surely an interesting choice of expression, given the subjectivist theory of perception so recently articulated in Berkeley's *New Theory of Vision*, published with a dedication to Percival in 1709. This letter was written to Percival on 19 July 1713. It was just three months later that Berkeley wrote to his friend from London to announce that he was about to leave for the continent:

> I have just time to take my leave of you and let you know that I am now on the point of going to Sicily, where I propose seeing the new king's coronation. I go Chaplain to my Lord Peterborough who is the ambassador extraordinary sent thither on this occasion. We take France, &c. in our way. There is not any place that I have a greater curiosity to see than Sicily.[45]

In the light of later evidence, we can read into Berkeley's anticipatory enthusiasm for Sicily a pioneering interest in Sicily's Greek remains and its Doric temples in particular. He would already have come across references to these in Clüver (referred to in his travel journals), or in Tommaso Fazello's even earlier *De Rebus Siculis* (which he cites in *Alciphron* to demonstrate parallels between the pretensions to great antiquity of foreign-dominated Ireland and Sicily). But ultimately his awareness of their existence must have originated in that deep grounding in Greek literature and history suggested by his lectureship in this subject and epitomized by his subsequent presentation to Trinity College of its first font of Greek type, and his institution and endowment of the Gold Medal for Greek, now named after him.[46]

For all this anxiety to see Italy and his belief that Ireland was 'the place in the World . . . least furnish'd with Virtuosi', Berkeley had been about to return to his Junior Fellowship at Trinity College, Dublin, when his Anglo-Irish friend Swift had arranged this far more attractive appointment.[47] On 25 October he set out from London with the Earl of Peterborough's aide-de-camp, Colonel du Hamel, arriving in Paris, via Calais and 'many instances of poverty and distress', on the evening of 17 November (new style). From Paris he reported back to Percival that he had just dined with the Sicilian ambassador, was about to meet the 75-year-old Nicolas Malebranche, 'a famous philosopher in this city', but that for the most part he was busy 'viewing the noble buildings and pieces of painting and statuary, which are here very numerous, and so far as I can judge excellent'.[48] Among the buildings he had seen since arriving five days earlier were:

> the place de Vendome, le place de Victoire, and le place Regale and the Louvre, le convent des Capucins, le Feuillant, l'Eglise des Minims, l'Eglise des Celestins, where are the tombs of the ancient kings. Yesterday we saw the monastery of Ste Genevieve, with its library and cabinet of rarities; the English college where the body of King James and that of his daughter are still to be seen exposed in their coffins . . . We saw likewise the Irish College, and the Sorbonne, where we were present at the Divinity disputations. All is wonderfully fine and curious, but the finest of all is the Chapel in the Church of the Invalides, which the Abbé d'Aubigne assured me was not to be surpassed in Italy.[49]

Berkeley left Paris after about a month, and the next we hear is on 28 December from Lyons, which he describes to Percival as 'a very noble city, and more populous and rich in proportion than Paris. It has several fine buildings and antiquities, which made the week I have spent here pass very agreeably. The opera here is magnificent enough, but the music bad.'[50] In this letter Berkeley mentions the future Jacobite, Theophilus Oglethorpe, 'an ingenious English gentleman that goes with us to Sicily', and announces that they are to 'set forward tomorrow morning for Turin and thence to Genoa, where we meet my Lord [Peterborough], who goes by sea from Toulon'.[51] In his next letter, dated Turin 6 January 1714, he wittily describes his New Year's Day crossing of the Alps via the Mont Cenis pass, over which he and his fellow travellers were 'carried in open chairs by men used to scale these rocks and precipices'. He had 'received no other damage than the breaking my sword, my watch, and my snuff-box'. He was now 'hardened against wind and weather, earth and sea, frost and snow; can gallop all day long, and sleep but three or four hours at night'. Nevertheless, he advised his friends 'that they do not pass the Alps in their way to Sicily'.[52]

The court at Turin, where he spent a full week, Berkeley described as 'polite and splendid, the city beautiful, the churches and colleges magnificent, but not much learning stirring among them'.[53] It is interesting to compare this with Edward Gibbon's decline-conscious comments about 50 years later: 'The servility of the courtiers revolts me and I view with horror the magnificence of the palaces which have been cemented with the blood of the people.'[54]

The major bombardment that Genoa had received from a French fleet in 1684 – often said to have ended the city's seventeenth-century reputation as one of the finest in Italy – was not mentioned by Berkeley, who on the contrary seems to have liked it even more than Oxford: 'I have not seen any town that pleased me more than this. The churches, palaces, and indeed the ordinary houses are very magnificent.'[55] Knowing that Percival had already completed a Grand Tour, Berkeley refrained from going into more detail (though he did so in the missing notebooks). He nevertheless echoed almost all his travelling predecessors in complaining that the 'streets of Genoa are very narrow'.[56] In this respect he preferred his next major destination, Livorno, praising it as 'the neatest and most regular [town] that I have seen in Italy . . . There are several English families of merchants, who are very rich and live at a much greater rate than the Italian nobility.'[57]

By 19 February, when Berkeley wrote this, Lord Peterborough (who had joined the party at Genoa) had left Livorno for Palermo, 'where he designs to stay but a short time, and put off his public entry till his return'. Unfortunately, mainly because of extraordinary delays in the arrival of the necessary coaches and equipages from England, the ambassador never made a public entry into Palermo but returned to Livorno the following May, having completed his negotiations informally.[58] As well as improving both his French and

Italian, Berkeley had meanwhile taken the opportunity to visit the other principal cities of northern Tuscany – Pisa, Lucca, Pistoia and Florence. Perhaps because he had been based too long in the mundanely modern port of Livorno (where he preached in the English church), and had seen Renaissance and Seicento Italy rather than its classical remains, he expressed a somewhat frustrated sense of relief at returning homewards. Probably rationalizing his disappointment at having travelled no further than Florence, having thereby failed to see the rich Campagna and the legendary scenery of southern Italy, even the landscape disappointed him: 'The descriptions that we find in the Latin poets make me expect Elysian fields and the golden age in Italy. But in my opinion England is a more poetical country.'[59]

Berkeley returned to Paris from Genoa in the company of John Molesworth, 'the late envoy at Florence, and the Col. his brother and . . . had a very pleasant journey in their company'. These were the sons of Robert, soon to become 1st Viscount Molesworth, who in October 1717 was to define 'the new Junta for Architecture' as consisting of 'Mr [Thomas] Hewett My eldest son [John,] Sign[r] [Alessandro] Galilei & I, & (if you can engage him Sr George Markham'. Given that John Molesworth invited Alessandro Galilei to follow him to England in 1714 and to Ireland four years later, it seems likely he would have discussed with or even introduced the architect to Berkeley, with whom Galilei was to collaborate, in a way which has yet to be clarified, on the design for Speaker Conolly's mansion at Castletown.[60] In Paris Berkeley met 'an Irish gentleman of my acquaintance' with whom he decided to take the Brussels coach and explore Flanders and Holland (whence Burlington had gone the previous month) before returning finally to London at about the time of Queen Anne's death in August 1714.[61]

No doubt endlessly encountering those who had seen so much more of Italy, Berkeley soon began to regret what he had missed. Then, in the autumn of 1716 – once more on the point of having to leave London for Dublin – he found a second opportunity to visit Sicily, this time as travelling tutor to St George Ashe. As this rather frail 16-year-old was the son and heir of the wealthy Bishop of Clogher, who was also Vice-Chancellor of the University of Dublin, this post was doubly convenient in that it facilitated the extension of his sabbatical leave and may even have helped in his promotion while still abroad to a Senior Fellowship at Trinity College.[62] Berkeley and his protégé left London in October and were carried over the Mont Cenis pass in a blinding snow storm, encountering 'a huge dark-coloured Alpine wolf' and two avalanches along the way. (Berkeley's use of the word avalanche pre-dates the *OED* first date by several decades.) They arrived in Turin on the evening of 22 November. Travelling south via Milan, Parma, Modena, Bologna, Florence and Siena, by the beginning of January 1717 Berkeley was at last in Rome, having now seen, as he thought, 'the best part of the cities of Italy'.[63] Though probably born in 1685, the same year as Bach and Handel, Berkeley describes himself as having 'eyes but no ears' in Rome. 'I would say that I am a judge of painting though not of music', he wrote to Percival on 1 March and it is indeed as a connoisseur of art and architecture that he now comes into his own.[64]

Though he travelled the length and breadth of the peninsula on this tour, the four long, leather-bound, pocket notebooks which are preserved in the British Library are most detailed on two places whose very distinctiveness provides us with excellent means by which to study the development of his taste and compare his responses to a wide range of styles. Although, therefore, reference to what we know he saw in Sicily and elsewhere will be made, discussion will largely be restricted to Rome, concluding with his comments on Puglia.[65]

Despite having now seen all the major cities of northern Italy, Berkeley was clearly most fascinated by Rome. From a slightly later entry in his diary we discover that, like the majority of tourists from long before the visit of John Evelyn to long after the death of Keats there, Berkeley, Ashe and their servant took lodgings near the cosmopolitan Piazza di Spagna at the foot of the hill upon which stands the French convent church of S. Trinità dei Monti.[66] Francesco de Sanctis's now famous Spanish Steps, though much needed, were still five years in the future, so that the area retained a considerably more rural aspect than it does today. The morning of 7 January, on what was probably his first full day in the city, apparently alone, Berkeley walked down to the Tiber, crossed it by the Ponte Sant'Angelo, manoeuvred his way along the medieval streets which were replaced in the 1930s by Mussolini's vast Via della Conciliazione, to find himself suddenly embraced by Bernini's arm-like colonnades in front of St Peter's.[67] As we have seen, even after his journey to Sicily Berkeley was to retain his admiration for the colonnades, which I believe may have influenced those at Castletown. The church itself, however, he was to was to find 'a thousand faults with'. Even now he was clearly not tempted to fall on his knees on the steps of St Peter's, like T.S. Eliot on his first visit. He was more impressed by the Vatican next door and, in particular, the great library, the first building he describes in the first of his four surviving notebooks. As Fellow Librarian of Trinity College (and most likely a major force behind the rebuilding of what was to rival the Vatican Library as the largest single-chamber library in the world), as well as future benefactor of the libraries of Harvard and Yale, Berkeley's enthusiastic response to the modernity of the shelving and well-designed readers' facilities in Domenico Fontana's papal library are of considerable interest:

> This morning I paced a gallery in the vatican four hundred & eighty eight paces long. We saw the Famous Library in that Palace. It contains seventy two thousand Volumes MSS. & printed. The building surely is not to be equalled in that kind being nobly proportioned & painted by the best hands. It is in this form T the greatest length about eight hundred feet. The books are all contained in desks or presses whose backs stand to the wall. These desks are all low of an equal heigth so that the highest books are within reach without the least straining.[68]

Plans for Thomas Burgh's library at Trinity College, Dublin, were first formulated in 1709.[69] On 26 November of that year, Berkeley wrote to his friend Molyneux of his appointment as librarian 'in a disconsolate Mood, after having passd the better part of a sharp & bitter day in the Damps and mustly [sic] solitudes of the Library without either Fire or any thing else to protect Me from the Injuries of the Snow that was constantly driving at the Windows & forceing its Entrance into that wretched Mansion'.[70] Burgh submitted an estimate for £7,140 in 1710 (excluding wainscotting), the foundation was laid in 1712 and £11–2s worth of scaffolding pole, paid for in April 1713, indicates that building had commenced.[71] But it was not until after Berkeley's return from his second Italian journey in 1723 that even the exterior was finished.[72] The interior, including the kind of furnishings to which Berkeley refers in his account of the Vatican, was not completed until 1733, the final cost being £20,000. He was thus in or near Dublin during all the crucial moments of its development.[73] Quite independently of any reference to Berkeley, significant similarities between Trinity Library and Castletown have recently been remarked upon. Both buildings are tall, have balustraded roofs, narrow, closely spaced windows and Palladian rusticated basements.[74] Given Berkeley's documented involvement in both, it is surprising how little has been made of the likelihood that he was at least partly responsible for their designs. No sooner had the library been completed than the first estimate for the Doric Printing House was submitted.[75]

Like most visitors Berkeley was shown the Vatican Library's most sensational holdings, from the earliest illuminated manuscripts of Virgil's *Aeneid* (whose 'pictures' he subjected to comparative study in order to ascertain their respective age) to Henry VIII's lascivious love-letters to Anne Boleyn (which had long been shown to the English as the sordid source of their so-called Reformation but which had now appeared in print) and the anti-Lutheran treatise which earned Henry and his successors the title of Defender of the Faith. In the afternoon Berkeley returned to the Vatican and inspected the sculpture arranged around the courtyard of the Belvedere: 'The principal are Cleopatra, Apollo (found in the Baths of Caracalla), the Famous Laocoon & Antinous. These are all Masterpieces of Antiquity. The Apollo & Laocoon can never be enough admired.'[76]

Most of the next morning was taken up with a formal visit to the Anglophile (and Jacobite-supporting) Cardinal Antonio Gualtieri, but that afternoon Berkeley and his pupil 'went to see the Villa Borghese'. Having been accustomed to the great formal layouts of Hampton Court and Versailles, one might have expected an unsympathetic reaction to this Villa's more natural seventeenth-century garden plan. It is now clear, however, that even the so-called English garden was ultimately derived from Italian models and an incipient taste for such artistic freedom can be traced back to proto-Tories, such as Richard Lassels, and proto-Whigs, such as Gilbert Burnet, alike.[77] (Berkeley may have brought with him Burnet's 1686 journal-cum-guidebook, *Some Letters. Containing an Account of what seemed most remarkable in Switzerland, Italy, &c*; for he makes fun of its disparagement of the Tarpeian Rock in his entry of 15 January.[78]) Even more than these, Berkeley, a liberal Tory, was almost defiantly enthusiastic: 'I liked the gardens, they are large, have fine cut walks, white deer, statues, fountains Groves, nothing of the little French gout, no parterres. If they are not so spruce and trim as those in France and England, they are nobler and I think much more agreeable.'[79] The Villa Pamphilia (now Doria Pamphili) beyond the Porta San Pancrazio, its nine-acre park laid out for Prince Camillo Pamphili by Algardi in the mid-seventeenth century, was to appeal to him for similar reasons: 'It stands to the West of the Town, in a very delightful situation. The garden's [*sic*] are neat spacious and kept in good order, adorned with Statues, Fountains, &c. But the prospect with the Variety of risings and vales made the greatest part of the beauty.'[80] The next evening, Berkeley walked in the 'very spacious' gardens of the Villa Montalto, which he concluded, 'like the [other] gardens in Italy is not kept with all that neatness that is observed in French and English gardens'.[81]

Where the Villa Borghese itself was concerned, that afternoon of the 8 January 1717, Berkeley noted it was

> noble and hath the richest outside that I have anywhere seen being enchased with beautiful relievos of Antiquity. The portico was furnished with old chairs very entire being hard stone colour'd red in some places, and gilt in others, carved too with several devices. It was too dark to see the pictures, so we put off viewing the inside to another time.[82]

The next morning, Berkeley's first visit was to the Augustan Pyramid of Gaius Cestius [Fig. 55], the great marble tomb next to the Porta San Paolo (the ancient Porta Ostiensis) which in the third century was incorporated into the Aurelian Walls. Although the area immediately behind the Pyramid, inside the walls, was already being used as a burial place for foreign Protestants (including Jacobites), Berkeley remarked only upon the architectural or archaeological aspects of the tomb itself and – as at the Vatican, somewhat Gulliver-like – upon its sheer size:

> This building is pyramidal, of great smoothed pieces of marble. A considerable part of it is now under ground but what appears is about a hundred foot in length, each side of the square basis, and about a hundred and fifty the side of the pyramid. There is a chamber within in which there have been [found?] not many years ago several antique figures painted in fresco. They are now defaced and the entrance made up.[83]

Walking next to the top of the nearby Monte Testaccio, 'from whence we had a fair prospect of Rome', Berkeley now focused on the purely historical interest in what he was standing upon, ancient Rome's riverside rubbish-dump: 'This Mount was formed in the time of old Rome by the Potters who had this place appointed them for

55 Richard Symonds, *The Pyramid of Cestius*, sketch at the beginning of his 1651 notebook.
[Bodleian Library MS Rawlinson D.121, p.1]

heaping together their rubbish to prevent their choaking the Tiber. You see the mount to be made up of bits of broken potsherds.'

Returning through the Porta San Paolo, Berkeley now walked along the Via Ostiense, 'of w[hi]ch we cou'd still see some remains', past the now demolished oratory with its fifteenth-century 'bas relief representing the parting embrace between S: Peter and S: Paul', to San Paolo fuori le Mura, prior to the Renaissance rebuilding of St Peter's the largest church in Rome, but since the great fire of 1823 a rather frigid reconstruction. Here Berkeley again demonstrates unusual independence of mind, this time attempting to use architectural connoisseurship to make a Vasarian (and proto-Gibbonian) judgement on artistic decadence under Constantine:

> S: Pauls church which stands above a mile out of the towne was built by Constantine; there are nevertheless two ranges of noble Corinthian pillars on both sides of the great Isle that seem too elegant for that age in wch the arts were much on the decline. Probably they belonged to some more ancient building. On the floor of this church we saw a Column of white marble in shape of a Candlestick for wch purpose it had been made in Constantine's time. It was all over adorned wth very rude sculpture. Under the great altar there lie one half of the bodies of S: Peter and S: Paul (the other half being under the great altar of St: Peter's).[84]

Where the huge paschal candlestick was concerned, Berkeley was out by almost a millennium, for it dates from the twelfth century. He also dismissed the thirteenth-century mosaic in the apse, now heavily restored, as deserving 'no regard'. The rest of the day was taken up with visits to the octagonal Santa Maria Scala Coeli and to San Paolo alle Tre Fontane, in which Berkeley praised Guido Reni's 'finely painted' altarpiece (the Caravaggesque *Crucifixion of St Peter* now in the Vatican).[85]

On 10 January, Berkeley went with Ashe, Charles Hardy and an Abbate Barbieri 'to see the Famous Farnesian Palace'.[86] It was not until 24 January that Berkeley noted that in the courtyard 'the Ionic pillars are placed above the Corinthian tho it was built by M: Angelo.'[87] A fortnight earlier, however, it was clear that the Farnese's famous collection of ancient sculpture and Annibale Carracci's frescoed gallery had been the principal reasons for his visit. Again responding initially to scale, his expectations no doubt conditioned by the numerous engravings of 'the gallery so much spoke of', Berkeley recorded that it 'proved smaller than I expected, but the painting is excellent, it is all over done in fresco by Annibal Carache'. Both in the gallery itself and elsewhere in the palazzo, Berkeley spent most of his time admiring the sculpture, the bulk of which is now in the Museo Nazionale in Naples. In particular, he was intrigued by the then famous Farnese Bull:

> an admirable groupe of Zetus, Amphion, Antiope Dirce and a Bull all out of one stone done by two R[h]odians, the two young men Sons of the Theban King, tie Dirce to the Bull's horns in order to precipitate her into a well (as the Inscription on a tablette hung by the statue tells you). The Bull and the men are incomparably well done, but there is little expression in the face of Dirce whh [*sic*] makes me suspect the head to be modern.[88]

Restored on the advice of Michelangelo soon after its discovery in order to make it conform more closely to the sculptured group described by Pliny, the Farnese Bull had lost a little of the enormous prestige which had reached its peak in 1665, when Louis XIV had attempted to acquire it. By British standards, however, Berkeley's critical remarks are sophisticated, anticipating those of Edward Wright, who about a decade later wrote that 'the expression in the Countenance of *Dirce* is not such as one might expect on the Occasion: it is quite without Passion'.[89] Berkeley's conclusion goes significantly further than Wright's and, indeed, the Richardsons' 1722 *Account*, in suspecting the head to be the result of modern restoration, a line of argument not fully developed until Winckelmann, who nevertheless thought the work as a whole to be Greek rather than Roman. Berkeley concluded his account with further praise of the Hercules, the Flora and the bust of Caracalla Farnese: 'flesh and blood. nothing can be softer'.[90]

That afternoon the same group 'drove out of town through the porta Collatini, leaving Lucullus's gardens on the left hand and Sallustius's on the right', and by this roundabout route returned to the Villa Borghese. Having previously inspected the garden and the exterior, they now viewed what he called the apartments. 'The greatest part of the pictures are copies', wrote Berkeley, 'I remember some some [*sic*] good ones of Corregio and the famous Battel of Constantine by Julio Romano.' But it was again the sculpture that most interested him:

In the apartments of this villa we saw several excellent statues, those most remarkable of the Antique are the Hermaphrodite, the Gladiator, and, on the outside of the wall that of Curtius on horseback leaping into the Cavern. I must not forget three statues of Bernini in these apartments, that raise my idea of that modern statuary [i.e. sculptor] almost to an equality with the famous ancients Apollo & Daphne. Aeneas with Anchises on his shoulders. David going to fling the stone at Goliah. The grace, the softness, and expression of these statues is admirable.[91]

After leaving the grounds of the Villa Borghese they 'took a walk round part of the walls of the City. Both walls and Turrets were pretty entire on that side. They have stood since Justinian's time, having been built by Bellisarius.' Re-entering the city from the north, they 'steped into the Victoria [S. Maria della Vittoria] a beautiful Church incrusted with ornaments of the richest stones as Jallo Antico, Verde antico, Jaspers &c. In this are hung up trophies taken from the Turks.'

Berkeley must literally have merely 'stepped into' this church for it is not large and half-way down on the left-hand side is the lavishly decorated Cornaro Chapel which features the floating figure of St Teresa in ecstasy, carved and designed in the late 1640s by the same Bernini whose earlier work he had just been praising as equal to the ancients. Ten days later, having no doubt been informed of his omission, he returned and 'spent some time in surveying the statues and pictures of that beautiful little Church. particularly the Statue of the Angel aiming a dart at the heart of S: Teresa, wonderfully well done by Bernini'. Berkeley also praised 'the Madonna col Bambino & other figures, an excellent picture of Dominiquins'. By this he clearly intends the altarpiece of 'St Francis receiving the Christ Child from the Virgin' in Domenichino's Merenda Chapel.[92] In this connection it is interesting that almost exactly two years earlier, on 13 January 1715, the young Lord Burlington purchased from the church for 1500 crowns the Madonna della Rosa now at Chatsworth. Rudolf Wittkower says that Burlington's acquisition was the result of his determination 'at all costs to secure a genuine Domenichino for himself'. Unfortunately, this rather feeble picture is now thought to be only partially by Domenichino, who probably touched up an assistant's copy whilst working on the Merenda Chapel c.1630 in order to replace his earlier original.[93]

Continuing their return journey towards the Piazza di Spagna, going only a little out of their route, they then paid what Berkeley calls 'a second visit to Diocletian's Baths, admiring the lofty remains of that stupendous Fabrick which is now possessed by the Carthusians'. Unless he had arrived in Rome earlier than 6 January, this must mean that he had visited the Baths, as tourists tend to do today, on first entering the city.

During the morning of 11 January Berkeley shopped for Greek books with 'Mr Domvile' (almost certainly Compton Domvile rather than Swift's friend, William, as claimed by Berkeley's editors). The same afternoon 'we took the air on the Mons Quirinalis, drove by Montalto's gardens towards S: Maria Maggiore and S: John de Lateran'.[94]

On 12 January, again it seems alone, Berkeley took a walk up the slope of the Pincian Hill behind his lodgings, whence he 'had a good prospect of Monte Cavallo, S: Peters and the Intermediate part of the towne'. Then, having as he says, 'amused [himself] some time here', remembering how impressed he had been with the Piazza del Popolo on entering Rome a week before, he decided to return for a closer look, taking in what he describes as the 'handsome Facade' of the Longhis' Sant'Ambrogio e Carlo al Corso, and the less handsome housing of the Corso itself on the way. In terms of his future involvement in architecture or, more precisely, urban design, his description of the Piazza with its radiating trident of streets laid out by Latino Manetti, both Fontanas and Bernini is especially interesting, for in the late 1720s Berkeley drew at least two plans for his utopian university city of Bermuda. One of these was described by his widow, but the other survives in an engraving which was included in the first collected edition of his works, published in 1784 [Fig. 56].[95] Looking at the latter and reading his account of the Piazza del Popolo it becomes clear that, for all that it incorporates elements of Inigo Jones's Covent Garden (in the type and position of the church), the Appian Way (for the tomb-lined 'Walk of Death'), the great Corinthian pillar in the main piazza in Lecce for the same feature here, as well as peculiarly English features such as the private and communal gardens behind the houses, the principal inspiration for Berkeley's ambitious scheme was this Roman walk in January 1717:

The Piazza del Popolo is contrived to give a traveller a magnificent

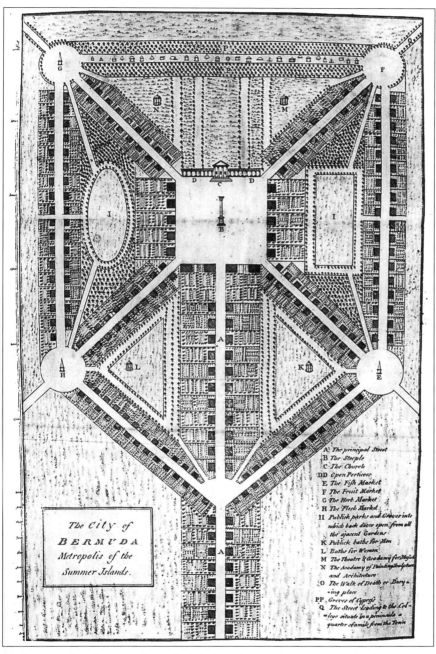

A The principal Street
B The Steeple
C The Church
DD Open Porticoes
E The Fish Market
F The Fruit Market
G The Herb Market
H The Flesh Market
II Publick parks and Groves into
  which back doors open from all
  the adjacent Gardens
K Publick baths for Men
L Baths for Women
M The Theatre & Academy for Musick
N The Academy of Painting Sculpture
  and Architecture
O The Walk of Death or Bury-
  ing place
PP Groves of Cypress
Q The Street Leading to the Col-
  lege situate in a peninsula a
  quarter of a mile from the Town

The City of
BERMUDA
Metropolis of the
Summer Islands.

56 George Berkeley's proposed plan for 'The City of Bermuda' from the 1784 edition of his *Works*. [E. Chaney]

impression of Rome upon his first entrance. The Guglio in the middle, the two beautiful Churches of the same architecture that front the entrance standing on either side of the end of the Corso, or great street directly opposite to the gate carrying the eye in a strait line through the middle of the city almost to the Capitol. While on the sides there strike off two other straight streets, inclined in equal angles to the Corso, the one leading to the Piazza d'Espagna, the other towards the Piazza Navona. From the Guglio your prospect shoots thro these three streets. All this I say is contrived to produce a good effect on the eye of a new comer. The disposition it must be owned is pleasing & if the ordinary houses that make up the greatest part of the streets were more agreeable and regular, wou'd make a very noble prospect.[96]

Berkeley then goes on to comment in detail on the first century BC 'Guglio' or obelisk (originally set up in the Circus Maximus by Augustus, who had brought it to Rome from Heliopolis) and to commend 'the most spirited' Sixtus V for re-erecting both it and others as landmarks in the major piazzas of the city in just the way he was soon to propose for Bermuda. Also worthy of note in his plan is its prominent provision in the communal parks for an Academy of Music and another of Painting, Sculpture and Architecture, which John Smibert was probably intended to direct.[97]

The almost Shaftesburian role Berkeley envisaged for these arts in a civilized society he most clearly expressed in the *Essay towards the Preventing the Ruin of Great Britain* which he published in 1721, within a year of returning from Italy and discovering the disastrous effects of the collapse of the South Sea Company:

> Those noble arts of architecture, sculpture, and painting do not only adorn the public but have also an influence on the minds and manners of men, filling them with great ideas, and spiriting them up to an emulation of worthy actions. For this cause they were cultivated and encouraged by the Greek cities, who vied with each other in building and adorning their temples, theatres, porticos, and the like public works, at the same time that they discouraged private luxury; the very reverse of our conduct.[98]

In a later, more specifically nationalistic publication, the first edition of the *Querist* of 1735, Berkeley extended suggestions he and Percival had made for founding an Italian- or French-style British Academy to teach these traditional subjects, and pioneeringly pro-

posed that Ireland should resolve its economic problems by insti-
tuting an 'Academy for Design':

Query 64. Whether those same manufactures which England imports
from other countries may not be admitted from Ireland? And if so,
whether lace, carpets, and tapestry, three considerable articles of English
importation, might not find encouragement in Ireland? And whether an
academy for design might not greatly conduce to the perfecting those
manufactures among us.

Query 65. Whether France and Flanders could have drawn so much
money from England for figured silks, lace, and tapestry, if they had not
had academies for designing?

Query 66. Whether, when a room was once prepared, and models in
plaster of Paris, the annual expense of such an academy need stand the
public in above two hundred pounds a year?

Query 67. Whether our linen-manufacture would not find the benefit of
this institution? And whether there by anything that makes us fall short
of the Dutch in damasks, diapers, and printed linen, but our ignorance
in design?

Query 68. Whether those who may slight this affair as notional have
sufficiently considered the extensive use of the art of design, and its
influence in most trades and manufactures, wherein the forms of things
are often more regarded than the materials?[99]

There is much else in the notebooks on Rome. Berkeley praises
Raphael's 'life and grace' in the Palazzo Odescalchi, his 'excellently
well expressed' details in the Farnesina, Titian's portraits 'that
seemed to breath' and the 'fine soft graceful pieces of Coreggio' in
the 'vast' Palazzo Borghese, which featured 'one fine vista through
nine rooms that is lengthened by a hole cut thro an adjacent house
(wch the prince bought for that purpose) to a fountain and a
beautiful passage'. He praises both the classical and the baroque,
even Padre Pozzo's illusionist ceiling in Sant'Ignazio, which
'wonderfully deceives the eye as one walks towards it from the door
along the great Isle', and Maderno and Bernini's 'magnificent'
Palazzo Barberini, though here he fails to mention Pietro da Cortona.
Interestingly, although Berkeley considers this to be 'the noblest
palace in Rome', he laments the lack of a good old English long
gallery in which to display pictures. The Palazzo Barberini, he writes,

hath many noble chambers & salons, being of great extent, but without a gallery. I much wonder this defect shou'd be so common in the Roman Palaces, a gallery being a thing of less expence and more beauty as well as a fitter repository for pictures than a suite of Rooms which serve to no use, their families [i.e., their households] being not proportioned to their Palaces.[100]

Both parts of the palace were 'extremely well furnished with Pictures and Statues, especially the latter' but Berkeley singles out 'an incomparable Madeleine of Guido Reni, reckoned the best piece that he ever did'. More originally, he also praised a Perugino 'Madonna and holy family' as 'the most valuable piece of that painter that I have seen'. Berkeley says 'he knew nothing of the chiaro oscuro. But for sweetness, grace and beauty there is enough in this piece to render it admirable.'[101] 'The antique Statue of Brutus holding the heads of his two sons' and another of Diogenes showed that 'the ancients had indifferent statuarys as well as the moderns'. Two large pieces, the Diana and Adonis, by the still-living, ultra-baroque sculptor, Giuseppe Mazzuoli, Berkeley considered 'equal to Bernini'. Since in Berkeley's judgement even Bernini was not the greatest of the moderns – 'the best statue in St Peter's' being 'the dead Christ of M. Angelo Bonaroti' – the ancient sculptors, in as much as their work survived (and this applied still more to painting), were rivalled by the moderns in a way the ancient builders were not. On the great staircase on his way out of the Palazzo Barberini, however, Berkeley encountered 'the noblest antique Lion in stone that I have any where seen'.[102]

Berkeley returned a third time to Diocletian's Baths and measured the granite columns, now praising Michelangelo's great work of conversion there. He visited many other Roman remains: the Temple of Minerva Medica, which before 1828 when its vault collapsed was an extremely influential building, the Castel Sant'Angelo and the Mausoleum of Augustus. 'The eye', he wrote, 'is never weary with viewing the Pantheon [though he would no doubt have preferred the Parthenon]. Both the rotonda itself and the vestibule discover new beauties ever[y] time we survey them.'[103] At the Theatre of Marcellus, he writes that 'the Doric & Ionic order in two ranges are still to be seen. The Corinthian and perhaps the Composite being destroy'd.' He did not hesitate to criticize the rare surviving antique painting known as the Aldobrandini Wedding: 'the attitudes are very well, the colouring seems never to have been good, and the drapery but of an indifferent gout'. He took particular notice of this, he says, because he had heard that 'those shewn for ancient paintings in the palace Barberini' were in fact the work of Polidoro da Caravaggio.[104] On a second visit to San Giovanni in Laterano he noticed '4 noble fluted pillars of bronze gilt in an altar of the church in one end of the same which was built by Constantine'. As earlier in San Paolo fuori le Mura, he is over-ambitious in his attempts to criticize the magnificent thirteenth-century Cosmatesque cloisters of San Giovanni as decadently Constantinian, thus detecting 'a great tendency in that age to the Gothic'. With more than a touch of irony, however, he writes that 'the most valuable things' in San Giovanni

> are the sacred antiquities brought back from Jerusalem. as the Column – this, I think, was of porphyry – on which the Cock stood when he crow'd and Peter deny'd Xt. Another pillar of white marble that was rent in two on the suffering of our Blessed Saviour. Here is likewise a flat porphyry stone set in the wall, on wch, they tell you, the soldiers threw lots for our Saviour's garment.[105]

Taking Ashe beyond the southern wall of the city, Berkeley described the Appian Way and the vast first-century Tomb of Cecilia Metella.

The Roman journal ends on 25 January 1717, simultaneously with the premature conclusion of a play Berkeley and his friends were watching, caused by 'the principal actor's being run thro the leg on the stage by accident'. After some delay caused by 'the extreme rigour of the season . . . and since that by the illness of our valet de chambre', Ashe and Berkeley, accompanied by Thomas Tyrwhitt and Compton Domvile, left Rome for Naples in mid-March.[106] The second surviving journal begins, in Latin, on 5 May 1717 and describes Berkeley's remarkable journey from Naples into Puglia. On 1 March he had informed Percival – in the hope that it 'may possibly have escaped your observation' – about 'the original of your Danae, which is esteemed one of the finest pieces that ever Titian did', and which he remembered seeing the previous December when he had visited the gallery of the Duke of Parma.[107] In Rome itself he was never sure whether Percival might have seen what he was describing. Now, knowing that Percival had not travelled as far as Naples, he anticipated being able 'to tell you of something you have not seen'.[108] Like the bishop in Norman Douglas's *South Wind*, the further south this future bishop travelled, the more enthusiastically lyrical he became. He had at last discovered the Claudian Campagna and had been obliged to revise dramatically his previous opinions of the Italian landscape. From Naples on 6 April he wrote trying to persuade Percival to bring his growing family there, extolling the potential benefits for everyone concerned:

> The air of this happy part of the world is soft and delightful beyond conception, being perfumed with myrtle shrubs and orange groves [Goethe's 'Das Land wo die Zitronen bluhn' and 'Die Myrte . . . steht' being ultimately based on sources also used by Berkeley] that are everywhere scattered throughout the country; the sky almost constantly serene and blue; the heat tempered to a just warmth by refreshing breezes from the sea . . . If enchanting prospects be a temptation, surely there are not more and finer anywhere than here, rude mountains, fruitful hills, shady vales, and green plains, with all the variety of sea as well as land.

'Prospects are the natural ornaments of this Kingdom', he concludes, and quotes Horace ('one who had very good taste') on the Bay of Baia.

> Every hill, rock, promontory, creek, and island, is sung by Homer and Virgil, and renowned as well for having been the scene of the travels of Ulysses and Aeneas as for having been the delicious retreat of all the great men among the Romans, whenever they with-drew from the fatigue of public affairs . . . surely nothing can be more beautiful than the wild Apennine on one hand and the boundless plain without enclosures on the other.[109]

If this letter expressed sentiments which Addison's experience and Pope's imagination could perhaps rival, Berkeley's next surviving letter to Percival – written again from Naples but just over two months later – brimmed with the confidence that what he was now describing was, at last, exclusively original:

> My Lord
>
>   I am lately returned from a tour through the most remote and unknown parts of Italy.
>   The celebrated cities your Lordship is perfectly acquainted with. But perhaps it may be new to you to hear that the most beautiful city in Italy lies in a remote corner of the heel. Lecce (the ancient Aletium) is the most luxuriant in all ornaments of architecture of any town that I

have seen. The meanest houses are built of hewn stone, have ornamented doors, rustics. Doric, Corinthian, are ornaments about the
windows, and balustrades of stone. I have not in all Italy seen so fine
convents. The general fault is they run into a superfluity of ornaments.
The most predominant are the Corinthian, which order is much affected by the inhabitants, being used in the gates of their city, which are
extremeley beautiful.[110]

As much as the 'barocco leccese' itself, what impressed Berkeley here
was what he had criticized as lacking in the urban design of Rome
around the Piazza del Popolo – the architectural attention paid to
what he calls 'the meanest houses': 'You know that in most cities
of Italy the palaces indeed are fine, but the ordinary houses of an
indifferent gusto. 'Tis so even in Rome, whereas in Lecce there is a
general good *gout*, which descends down to the poorest houses.' On
the arduous journey to Lecce, Berkeley boasted of having seen 'many
other remarkable towns, amongst the rest five fair cities in one day,
the most part built of white marble, wherof the names are not
known to Englishmen'.[111]
A careful reading of Berkeley's detailed second journal functions
as a fascinating complementary background to this letter. Not surprisingly, we find that Berkeley and his long-suffering pupil 'were
stared at like men dropt from the sky' by the natives. They passed
through Caserta, prior to its transformation into the Bourbon show-
piece, and Benevento, whose Arch of Trajan Berkeley described as
'one of the finest remains in Italy'.[112] As the journey progressed –
apparently conducted in two small chariot-like chaises – the pencil
notes reverted to English but became less decipherable, as if jotted
down whilst in motion. At Canosa, which he knew from Livy's
account of the Battle of Cannae, Berkeley must surely have been the
first northern European to describe the remarkable twelfth-century
Tomb of Bohemond, son of Robert Guiscard, which is attached to the
Cathedral (though entered from within it). At Barletta they saw
what Berkeley calls the 'Colossus of Heraklius, 20 palms high, this
brought from Constantinople in 1204' [Fig. 57]. Recently restored,
this fifth-century bronze is now considered more likely to represent
Marcian or perhaps Valentinian. Searching constantly for evidence
of tarantulas and the tarantella dancing thought to cure the spider's
bite, they journeyed via Trani, Bisceglie, Molfetta, Bari, Monopoli
and Brindisi, until finally, on 27 May, they arrived at Lecce.[113]

57 Fifth-century AD bronze statue of Roman Emperor Marcian or perhaps Valentinian, Barletta, Puglia. [E. Chaney]

Lodging that night in what he described as 'a miserable camera locanda', the next morning Berkeley noted briefly that Corpus Christi was to be celebrated and then launched – stream-of-consciousness style – into an extraordinary account of what he saw about him, enthusing first about the festival and then the no less volatile architecture, as he realized that he had discovered a remarkable city:

> standards, images, streamers, host, rich habits of priests, ecclesiastics of all sorts, confraternities, militia, guns, squibs, crackers, new cloaths. Piazza in it an ancient Corinthian pillar sustaining the bronze statue of S: Orontius, protexi & protegam, marble statue on horseback of Charles the 5th, another on horseback of a King of Spain on the top of a fountain adorned with many bad statues; Jesuites college most magnificent / fine buildings of hewn stone, ornamented windows, pilasters &c large streets divers piazzas façades of churches &c / Inhabitants 16,000 / 8 miles from the sea / oil only commodity / convents 14, nunneries 16 / streets open, pleasant but crooked / several open places / situate in a most spacious plain / gusto in the meanest houses, no where so common ornamented doors & windows, balconies, pillars, balustrades all of stone / the stone easily wrought / incredible profusion of ornaments

in the facades of churches convents &c / pillars or pilasters (mostly composite or corinthian) festoons, flowerpots, puttini, & other animals crouded in the chapiters above the foliages / double freezes filled with relievo i.e. beside the common frize another between the chapiters / took particular notice of the Jesuites church that of the Dominicans, nunnerie of S: Teresa, convent of the Benedictines, of ye Carmelites, nunnerie of S. Chiara. These & many more deserved attention / most of 'em crouded with ornaments in themselves neat but injudiciously huddled together / The façades of the church and convent of the jesuites noble and unaffected, the air & appearance wonderfully grand, two rows of pilasters, first composite, 2d or upper Ionic with mezzoninos above the second row of windows . . . Façade of the Benedictines convent & church wonderfully crouded with ornaments. as Likewise the altars generally adorned with twisted pillars flourished all over and loaden with little puttini, birds and ye like in clusters on the chapiters and between the wreaths along the fusts of the columns. Nothing in my travels more amazing than the infinite profusion of altorelievo and that so well done. there is not surely the like rich architecture in the world. The square of the Benedictines is the finest I ever saw; the cloisters have a flat roof & balustrade supported by double beautiful pillars with rich capitells.[114]

In a slightly calmer frame of mind, Berkeley described the mid-sixteenth-century hospital, 'rustic at bottom, double pilasters. Doric below, Ionic above', but continues to express wonder at the 'bold flights of Architecture, as in the façade of S: Matteo a nunnery [Fig. 22]. / garlands and coronets often round their pillars and pilasters'.[115] Finally, in an attempt to explain this extraordinary phenomenon, he concludes by returning to his beloved Greeks:

In no part of Italy such a general gusto of Architecture / environs well inhabited / Gates Corinthian & composite / Jesuites convent vaste building for 14 fathers / no river / their gusto too rich & luxuriant, occasion'd without doubt by the facility of working their stone / they seem to shew some remains of the spirit & elegant genius of the Greeks formerly inhabited these parts.[116]

As we have seen in Chapter 1, Berkeley soon encountered genuine fifth-century BC Greek architecture in Sicily. For all Shaftesbury's and the New Junta's talk of 'Greek taste', it seems that only Berkeley actually visited the Doric temples of Agrigento and appreciated them for what they were. Isaac Basire had indeed seen them with his pupils in December 1648, but their travel journal reveals little of aesthetic interest.[117] To judge from Berkeley's surviving journals, Joseph Warton was referring to a very precious document in the evolution of the Grand Tour when he wrote in his 'Essay on Pope' that Berkeley:

> went over Apulia and Calabria, and even travelled on foot through Sicily, and drew up an account of that very classical ground, which was lost in a voyage to Naples.[118]

NOTES

This chapter is ultimately based on a paper read at the Art Historians' Association Annual Conference held at Trinity College, Dublin, in March 1990. The conference title was 'Challenging the Canon', hence the defensive tone of the introduction and its somewhat elementary account of Campbell and Shaftesbury. The paper was originally entitled: 'Architectural Taste and the Grand Tour: George Berkeley's Evolving Canon' and published as such (without footnotes) in the *Journal of Anglo-Italian Studies*, I, ed. E. Chaney and P. Vassallo (University of Malta, 1991), pp. 74–91. The relevant session of the conference was chaired with inimitable wit by Professor Alistair Rowan and I should like to thank him and his wife, Ann Martha, for most generous hospitality. Since then I have received further hospitality in Dublin, most notably from Alistair's successor at University College, Michael McCarthy, who has shared with me his considerable knowledge of architectural taste and the eighteenth-century Grand Tour. The Appendix, 'George Berkeley in the Veneto', is a revised version of a review article first published in the *Bollettino del CIRVI*, I, ii (1980), pp. 82–8.

1. Robert Voitle, *The Third Earl of Shaftesbury, 1671–1713* (Baton Rouge, LA and London, 1984), chapter IX and Sheila O'Connell, 'Lord Shaftesbury in Naples, 1711–1713', *Walpole Society*, LIV (1988), pp. 149–219.
2. It is clear from Shaftesbury's 1687–89 travel diary (PRO 30/24/21/240) as summarized in Voitle, pp. 21–37 that the then Lord Ashley's principal source was Gilbert Burnet's *Some Letters* . . . first published in Amsterdam in 1686 (for Berkeley's use of this, see below, note 78). Burnet's Whiggishness may ultimately have proved less influential than Addison's, however, though eventually Addison and Shaftesbury influenced each other. Gibbon criticized both for claiming that 'after despotism was duly established at Rome, not a statue, picture or medal, not a tolerable piece of architecture afterward appeared.' The related notion that the man-made environment affects social behaviour was not new. Most influential regarding the present discussion was probably John Evelyn's introduction to Roland Fréart de Chambray's *Parallel of the Ancient Architecture with the Modern* (London, 1664): dedication to Sir John Denham: 'nothing costs dearer, and displeases more, than our undigested contrivances, and those intollerable defects which we have enumerated. It is from the *Assymetry* of our *Buildings*, want of *decorum* and

proportion in our Houses, that the irregularity of our *humours and affections* may be shrewdly discerned.' Evelyn's political angle on all this was not, however, to be adopted by Shaftesbury: 'But it is from his *Majesties* great Genius and the choise he had made of such an *Instrument* [i.e. Denham] . . . that we may hope to see it all reform'd' (ibid., 1707 ed., Sig. cIV.).

3. The *Letter* was almost certainly not published until 1732 in the 5th edition of volume III of the *Characteristicks*. Its appearance in some copies of the 1714 *Characteristicks* is probable due to a bookseller adding the relevant signatures retrospectively to unsold stock; see K. Downes, *Architectural History*, CXXIV (1985), pp. 519-23.

4. *Characteristicks* (Birmingham, 1773 edn), III, p. 398.

5. Ibid., p. 399.

6. See the several works of Kerry Downes on Wren and Vanbrugh and, for the most recent bibliography on these and others mentioned below, Howard Colvin, *A Biographical Dictionary of British Architects 1600-1840*, 3rd edn (New Haven and London, 1995) but see also Giles Worsley, *Classical Architecture in Britain: The Heroic Age* (New Haven and London, 1995).

7. *Characteristicks*, III, p. 400.

8. George Vertue notes that a Dr Harwood reported Sir Christopher Wren to have said that Jones died a Catholic at Somerset House (Walpole Society, XVIII, p. 105) though there is no independent evidence for either of these claims. Edward McParland has drawn attention to Shaftesbury's specific condemnation of the court: ' 'Tis not the Nature of a Court to improve but rather [to] corrupt a Taste.' Moreover, his statement that Britain 'has her models yet to seek' suggests that he was not an admirer of Jones; see 'Sir Thomas Hewett and the New Junta for Architecture', in *The Role of the Amateur Architect*, ed. G. Worsley (Georgian Group, London, 1994), pp. 21-6. Shaftesbury's ignorance, even of the nature of Jones's achievement, however, should not be underestimated. The increasingly well-informed cult of Jones fostered by George Clarke, John Talman, Campbell, Kent and Burlington succeeded the revival of Palladio, which was itself scarcely under way when Shaftesbury died.

9. Writing at the Restoration (a decade after his long period of voluntary exile in France and Italy), Pratt insisted on foreign travel for aspiring British architects due to the scarcity of suitable models at home: 'having nothing remarkable but the banquetting house at Whitehall and the portico at St Paul's'; *The Architecture of Sir Roger Pratt*, ed. R.T. Gunther (Oxford, 1928), p. 23. Combined with stray remarks which confirm that he more than merely completed Coleshill himself, Pratt's choice of Jones's two grandest and most classically ornate buildings, both the result of royal patronage more than a quarter of a century earlier, tends to contradict recent emphasis on continuity during the Civil Wars and Interregnum. In particular, Timothy Mowl and Brian Earnshaw argue for a Puritan Jones actively providing the model for 'Puritan Minimalism' in *Architecture without Kings* . . . (Manchester, 1995); cf. E. Chaney, 'A New Model Jones', *Spectator*, 13 January 1996, pp. 34-6 and J. Newman in *Society of Architectural Historians of Great Britain Newsletter*, no. 58 (1996), pp. 14-15.

10. *Characteristicks*, III, p. 400. For the long-delayed rebuilding of Parliament and Berkeley's proposal, see below, note 39.

11. Ibid., p. 401.

12. Ibid., p. 402.

13. Ibid. For details of Marlborough's loan to Shaftesbury and the latter's

difficulties in repaying it, see Voitle, op. cit., pp. 260–2. His references to Marlborough may be prominent among the reasons that Shaftesbury's executors 'unaccountably suppressed' the *Letter concerning Design* until 1732; cf. Downes, loc. cit., p. 519.

14. Rykwert, *The First Moderns: The Architects of the Eighteenth Century* (Cambridge, MA and London, 1980), p. 154. Rykwert rightly points out, however, that there was no neat party division on the matter and that baroque Vanbrugh was a Whig and a member of the Kit-Cat Club, knighted by George I. Meanwhile the Palladian Lord Burlington can no longer be read as representative of a Whig aesthetic, Jane Clark in particular arguing for a reinterpretation of him and his buildings as imbued with Jacobitism; see *Lord Burlington, Architecture, Art and Life*, ed. T. Barnard and J. Clark (London and Rio Grande, 1995).

15. Bellori, *Le Vite de' Pittori, Scultori e Architetti moderni* (Rome, 1672; ed. E. Borea, Turin, 1976).

16. Campbell, *Vitruvius Britannicus*, I (London, 1715), Sig. B1r. and Henry Cogan's *Court of Rome* of 1654 (essentially a translation of two works by Girolamo Lunadoro and Fioravante Martinelli). Cogan was a trustee of Jones's will in 1650.

17. Rykwert, op. cit., pp. 68–70.

18. E. Chaney, 'On the Progressive Side', *Times Literary Supplement*, 24 October 1986, p. 1198; review of J. Varriano, *Italian Baroque Architecture* (Oxford, 1986).

19. Prior to the collapse of the Tories and the Jacobite Rising of 1715, Gibbs's position was perhaps stronger than Campbell's. By January 1716, however, Gibbs was complaining of 'a false report of a Countrayman of mine that misrepresented me as a papest and a disaffected person . . . done purly out of a designe to have gott him self into the place I have now lost' (i.e. fellow Scot, Colen Campbell, who indeed succeeded Gibbs as one of the two surveyors to the commissioners for building Fifty New Churches); see Terry Friedman, *James Gibbs* (New Haven and London, 1984), p. 10. Berkeley's Anglo-Irish friend Sir John Percival patronized both Gibbs (whom he met in Italy in 1707) and Campbell. Despite his deep interest in architecture (he was also a subscriber to *Vitruvius Britannicus*, Kent's *Designs of Inigo Jones* and Gibbs's *Book of Architecture*), Percival's tendency to Toryism renders him an unlikely associate of the New Junta; see below, notes 39–42. For the Molesworths, Berkeley and the New Junta, see below, note 60.

20. *Vitruvius Britannicus*, Sig. B1r.

21. Wright, *Passions*, ed. T.S. Sloan (Chicago, 1971), p. lviii. For Joseph Hall, see the biographical study by F.L. Huntley (Cambridge, 1979). There is more than an echo in Campbell's complaint about the English tendency to overvalue the foreign of Hall's 1617 assertion that: 'We are still ready to under value our owne, and admire forrainers'; see Sara Warneke, *Images of the Educational Traveller in Early Modern England* (Leiden, 1995), p. 96.

22. Trinity College Foundation Charter.

23. Richard Hewlings, 'Jones the Baroque', *Spectator*, CCLXIV (3 February 1990), pp. 35–7.

24. A.A. Luce's standard life of *George Berkeley, Bishop of Cloyne* (London, 1949) has recently been reissued with a new introduction by David Berman (London, 1992); see also Berman's *George Berkeley: Idealism and the Man* (Oxford, 1994). The standard edition of the *Works* by A.A. Luce and T.E. Jessop is in 9 vols. (London, 1948–57); see also Benjamin Rand, *Berkeley and*

Percival (Cambridge, 1914). There is no self-contained edition of the travel journals integrated with the relevant letters in English. There is an Italian edition by T.E. Jessop and M. Fimiani: *George Berkeley: Viaggio in Italia* (Naples, 1979) for which see the Appendix below. The most inspiring treatment of several of the topics dealt with here is the Marcus Whiffen's 'George Berkeley', *Architectural Review*, CXXIII (1958), pp. 91–3; cf. also now, my entry on Berkeley in the Macmillan *Dictionary of Art* (London, 1996).

25. Colvin, op. cit., pp. 892–6. For Pratt's unpublished treatise, see Gunther (cit. note 9), especially the unindexed reference to 'those houses designed by that excellent architect Palladio' (p. 290). For Evelyn's anticipation of an edition of Palladio (perhaps he knew of Aldrich's plans), see the 2nd edition of his Fréart (cit. above note 2); *Account of Architects and Architecture* (London, 1706), p. 16.

26. See Barbara Arciszewska, 'A Villa fit for a King: The Role of Palladian Architecture in the Ascendancy of the House of Hanover under George I', *Revue d'Art Canadienne/Canadian Art Review*, XIX, 1–2 (1992), pp. 41–59; see also Dr Arciszewska's unpublished PhD dissertation (University of Toronto, 1994); I thank Michael McCarthy for bringing both these items to my attention. For Aldrich, Clarke and Hawksmoor, see most recently Colvin, *Biographical Dictionary* and idem, *Unbuilt Oxford* (New Haven and London, 1983).

27. The most recent and complete works on Burlington are John Harris, *The Palladian Revival: Lord Burlington, His Villa and Garden at Chiswick* (New Haven and London, 1994), and Barnard and Clark, cit. above in note 14. Kent remains inadequately covered. It seems not to have been noticed that Kent signs the University of Padua visitors' book on 1 September 1714 (see below p. 375), in the company of Henry Trench, who describes himself as 'Pictoro Hibernese / Amatore di Italia per le Picture sue'). For Trench and much else of relevance, see: Nicola Figgis, *Irish Artists, Dealers and Grand Tourists in Italy in the Eighteenth Century*, 3 vols. (unpublished PhD thesis, National University of Ireland, 1994), I, pp. 50–54 and II, pp. 91–99 and her article in the *Irish Arts Review Yearbook*, 1994, pp. 217–22. Trench, a pupil of Maratta and Solimena who had worked for Shaftesbury, and later decorated Thomas Hewett's 'greek Tempietto' (Colvin, s.v.) may be listed among the numerous artists and musicians whom the somewhat ruthless Burlington took up and then dropped: a select list might include Campbell, Castell (who died in a debtors' prison), Gay, Gibbs, Guelfi and Leoni. Recent scholarship qualifies the previous view that Handel and even Kent were dropped, though the sacking of loyal secretary, Richard Graham, author of the *Short Account of the Most Eminent Painters* (1716), may now be added to the list; see Jane Clark, 'Lord Burlington is Here' in Barnard and Clark, cit., pp. 287 and 309.

28. Op. cit. (London, 1782), II, p. 200.

29. For a critique of the notion of *Zeitgeist* in this context, see David Watkin, *Morality and Architecture* (Oxford, 1977). For an examination of its Hegelian (historicist) origins, see Roger Scruton, *The Aesthetics of Architecture* (London, 1979). Another contemporary of Berkeley's capable of appreciating both the purest Palladian and the richest baroque was the crypto-Catholic John Talman, first director of the Society of Antiquaries. After many years in Italy between the 1690s and 1716, he too seems to have returned there in 1719 (Colvin, *Biographical Dictionary*, and Figs 58 and 59).

30. Reynolds towards the end of his 13th Discourse (1786), quoted in Kerry Downes, *Vanbrugh* (London, 1977), p. 94.

31. See above, pp. 24–6.

32. On 20 July 1720 (N.S.) Berkeley wrote Lord Percival a detailed letter from Florence which epitomizes this side of his activities (*Works*, VIII, pp. 114–15). He has procured his friend '*serie mezana* of brass medals from Julius Caesar down to Galienus . . . fifty odd heads fair, about a dozen copies'. The reason for the copies was the falling through of a previous arrangement: 'you know how tedious it is to deal with Italians. I never knew people so ready to promise and so slow to perform.' He negotiates with Bianchi (curator of the Uffizi) in order to obtain copies of 'the painters' heads' (presumably the self-portraits), but 'the great Duke being very jealous in that point lest they should be made public' renders this project impracticable. The favour from Cosimo III that Percival had enjoyed during his 1706–7 tour should have helped in this respect. In his still unpublished autobiographical sketch (British Library, Add. MS 47072, fol. 22r), Percival recalled how he travelled from Hanover via Augsburg to Venice, Rome and Florence, 'where the good old Duke Cosmo 3 remembering the Civilities he had rec^d from Old Mr Southwell Sr Roberts [Percival's guardian and uncle's] father when cast by stress of weather into Kinsale [in Ireland in 1669] receaved Sr John with much curtesie, and made him the usual presents given to strangers of distinction. He also wrote him a letter with his own hand offering the best pictures he had in his collection, which Sr John handsomely declined, but in return for his favours sent him two volumes finely bound & gilt all the Mezzatintos engraved by Mr Smith the greatest artist that has been in that way, & which were much esteemed in Italy.' In his edition of *The English Travels of Sir John Percival and William Byrd II: The Percival Diary of 1701* (Columbia, 1989), p. 32, the editor, Mark R. Wenger, states that 'Cosimo presented the young Englishman with a set of gold medals' but according to the manuscript this seems to be a confusion with the gift of Princess Sophia the previous June in Hanover, where Percival was presented 'with a set of Court medals in gold and M^r [Francis] Clerk[e] in silver' (BL Add. MS 47072, fol. 21r though cf. Add. MS 47205, fol. 89v); cf. more generally, W.B. Stanford, *Ireland and the Classical Tradition* (Dublin, 1976). As well as commissioning a portrait bust of himself by Vincenzo Felici in Rome (see Fig. 54), Percival ordered other sculptures by Massimiliano Soldani. Berkeley is presumably referring to this when he writes: 'I have been with Soldani to know what the busts were which he did for you, but having at different times done things for English gentlemen, he remembers nothing in particular which he did for you' (Lord Burlington had meanwhile collected two bas-reliefs from Soldani in Florence in early 1715; Jane Clark, 'Lord Burlington is Here', *Lord Burlington . . .*, ed. Barnard and Clark p. 257; cf. Soldani's work of the previous year for Lord Strafford at Wentworth Castle; T. Friedman, op. cit., p. 123). Berkeley then goes on to write that since sending certain busts to Percival he 'had got some others much finer being made of scaglione (a hard composition that looks and shines like marble)', an interesting early reference to scagliola, later to be associated with the Anglo-Italian Abbot of Vallombrosa, Enrico Hugford, for whom see above, pp. 281 and 304, n. 9. John Bargrave acquired a scagliola ('cast marble') table during his mid-17th-century travels (unpublished inventory brought to my attention by David Sturdy). The second surviving scagliola table still at Canterbury was acquired subsequently.

33. *Works*, VIII, p. 104.

34. Describing Ischia to Percival on 1 September 1717, Berkeley writes: 'Nothing can be conceived more romantic than the forces of nature, mountains, hills,

vales and little plains, being thrown together in a wild and beautiful variety';
Works, VIII, p. 106 (cf. the similar account to Pope quoted above, p. 123).
Unfortunately, he adds, the locals 'have got an ugly habit of murdering one
another for trifles.' For John Dryden junior's even earlier application of
'romantic' in connection with Capri, see above p. 102. For Addison on Ischia,
p. 139, n. 75.
35. *Works*, VII, p. 254.
36. Desmond Guinness and J.T. Sadler Jr, *The Palladian Style in England, Ireland and
America* (London, 1976), pp. 81–3. Berkeley's source seems to be plate 56 in
volume I of Kent's *Designs*, which was published the year before he left and
included among its subscribers his friend Lord Percival. No doubt Berkeley
would also have helped introduce another book to which Percival subscribed,
James Gibbs's *Book of Architecture* (London, 1728) to the colonies. For its
'massive' influence there, see H.-W. Kruft, *A History of Architectural Theory*
(London and New York, 1994), pp. 241–2.
37. See Richard H. Saunders, *John Smibert: Colonial America's First Portrait Painter*
(New Haven and London, 1995). Saunders concludes that Berkeley was 'the
most important acquaintance of [Smibert's] career'. The two seem to have
met in Florence in late 1719 or 1720, Smibert painting Berkeley's portrait
soon after [Fig. 9]. For Smibert as a potentially crucial link between a group
of intellectuals in Edinburgh (which he left in 1719) and Berkeley, who
'offered to adopt them into his famous design of erecting a college at
Bermudas', see M.A. Stewart, 'Berkeley and the Rankenian Club', *Hermathena*
(TCD Dublin), no. CXXXIX (Winter 1985), pp. 25–45.
38. Charles Smith's *Antient and present state of the County and City of Cork* (Dublin,
1750), I, p. 146, records that the Bishop has 'successfully transplanted
the polite arts, which heretofore flourished only in a warmer soil, to this
northern climate. Painting and musick are no longer strangers to Ireland, nor
confined to Italy. In the episcopal palace at Cloyne the eye is entertained with
a great variety of good paintings as well as the ear with concerts of excellent
musick. There are here some pieces of the best masters, as a Magdalen of Sir
Peter Paul Rubens, some heads by Van Dyck and Kneller, besides several good
paintings performed in the house, an example so happy that it has diffused
itself into the adjacent gentleman's houses'; see Luce, *Life*, p. 179.
39. See below, note 95. Maurice Craig and the Knight of Glin quote from the
relevant correspondence between Berkeley and Percival (first published by
Rand; see next note) in the first of their important trilogy of articles on
'Castletown, Co. Kildare', *Country Life* (27 March 1969), pp. 722–6. In July
1722 Berkeley reported on the dimensions of the house, the 'fine wrought
stone' (superior to Portland) of which it was to be made, and the proposed
'outhouses joining to it by colonnades' (colonnades similar to those at
Burlington House and those Berkeley had admired in front of St Peter's in
Rome). Percival's reply is still more interesting: 'I am glad for the honour of
my country that Mr Conolly has undertaken so magnificent a pile of building,
and your advice has been taken upon it. I hope that the execution will answer
the design . . . I shall be impatient until you send me a sketch of the whole
plan and of your two fronts.' He goes on to recommend the use of Irish
marbles, oak and 'stone stairs . . . of black palmers stone' with a buffet
'adorned with the choicest shells our strands afford . . . But I forget that I
write to a gentleman of the country who knows better what is proper and
what the kingdom affords.' On 7 September 1722, Berkeley wrote that building had commenced 'before they have agreed on any plan for the elevation

or facade. Several have been made by several hands, but as I do not approve of a work conceived by many heads so I have made no draught of mine own. All I do being to give my opinion on any point, when consulted'; *Works*, VIII, p. 125. Given that Berkeley would know Galilei and Lovett Pearce (the professional architects involved), as well as other members of the New Junta for architecture, only the extent of his clearly significant contribution to the design of Castletown can be in doubt. For Berkeley's proposal of a Parliament house in context, see *The History of the King's Works*, V, *1660–1782*, ed. H. Colvin (London, 1976), pp. 416–33. When in 1733 Edward Gibbon's father moved that His Majesty build a new house, Percival (now Lord Egmont) recorded his approval and Lord Burlington immediately 'projected a plan' (ibid., p. 419). For Berkeley's Italian notes on architecture, appended to his 1717 travel diary (BL Add. MS 39308), see below, note 113.

40. See *The English Travels* . . . (cit. above in note 32), for the most recent life and bibliography, albeit brief on his 1705-7 Grand Tour. The emphasis on Percival's involvement in America (he became President of the Society of Georgia, having co-founded the State with James Oglethorpe), enhances our understanding of Berkeley's 1728-31 residence on Rhode Island. Still largely unpublished are the interesting Percival manuscripts including his letter-book and autobiographical sketches in the British Library, Add. MSS 47025 and 47072; the latter includes the summary of his 1706-7 Grand Tour (fols 21r–22r; cf. fol. 103v). See also Edwin S. Gaustad, *George Berkeley in America* (New Haven and London, 1979), though this makes no reference to Berkeley's prior acquaintance with Oglethorpe's brother Theophilus (see below, note 51).

41. *Works*, VIII, p. 111; letter dated Rome, 18 July 1718. The round 'church' by Bramante is the 'Tempietto' uniquely honoured by Palladio by inclusion among the ancient buildings in Book II of his *Quattro Libri*. It marks the place on which St Peter was supposed to have been crucified upside-down rather than beheaded. There may be a relationship between Berkeley's pioneering appreciation of Greek Doric in Sicily and John Breval's (discussed above, pp. 25-8). Percival's letter-book (BL Add. MS 47025, fols. 13r and 15r; letters dated 2 June and 10 August 1698) reveals that a Dr Breval, presumably Breval's father (a prebendary at Westminster) but conceivably the young Breval himself, was Percival's tutor. The antiquity of Berkeley's topos on the superiority of the ancients to the moderns (and an uncannily similar context) is revealed in its use by William Cecil, 3rd Lord Burghley, writing to Lord Shrewsbury about the Cappella dei Principi in Florence in 1609: 'Your Lordship knows these parts better than I though I have been there twice. This notwithstanding is my opinion that the ruins of the Ancient Romans both at Rome and at Provence are fairer than the greatest buildings in all Europe that are not ancient.' (J.I. Whalley, 'Italian Art and English Taste: an early 17th-century Letter', *Apollo*, XCIV (1971), pp. 184-91). For clarification of the authorship of this letter, see above, Chapter 7, note 16. Percival was 'in advance' of Lord Burlington and others in his Palladianism by commissioning from Colen Campbell a design for a villa based on Palladio's Poiana with a double hexastyle portico based on the loggia of the Villa Cornaro. A plan and elevation of this unexecuted design were published by Campbell in *Vitruvius Britannicus* (plates 95-7). For his relationship with Gibbs, see T. Friedman, op. cit., *passim*; cf. an interesting letter to the artist Edward Gouge, dating from soon after his return from Italy, in which Percival refers to Gibbs, Henry Trench, the Farnese ceiling and 'the ivory Caesars head which I brought at Rome' (*HMC Egmont MSS*, II, p. 217). In September 1709, Berkeley wrote to

Percival sympathizing with the loss of 'your statues, medals, etc. that you had coming from Italy' (*Works*, VIII, p. 20). In his letter-book (BL Add. MS 47205, fol. 133v) Percival merely annotates Berkeley's comments: 'My collection lost which I made abroad.' In his autobiographical sketch, however, he writes that soon after October 1707, he 'had news of the loss of a valuable collection of books, paintings, statues, antiquities drafts & musick he had made abroad, things that he took much delight in and enterd into the study of in Italy: they were put on board two merchant vessels and both taken by French Privateers, whereby the Academy of young painters & sculptors erected by Sr Godfrey Kneller the Queens Painter was frustrated of many good Patterns for emproving the Schollars, it being Sr John's Design to make them a present of them' (BL Add. MS 47072, fol. 23r). Significantly, in view of Berkeley's proposals for an Irish Academy, Percival's later (?) version of this differs in an important respect. In the chronology of his life (BL Add. MS 47072, fol. 103v) he writes that soon after October 1707 he 'had an Ac^t of the loss of valuable collections he made abroad of pictures, statues, books busts medalls drawings &c which he designed for the use of an Academy of painters which he purposed to forward the erecting *in Ireland*' (my italics). Given Burlington's second title of 4th Earl of Cork, it is perhaps worth noting that Percival was elected without opposition to represent the County of Cork in the Irish House of Commons in 1713. During his 1701 English tour Percival visited the Boyles' principal estate of Londesborough in Yorkshire, commenting somewhat oddly that the 'Small brick Seat . . . is neither bewtyfull on the outside nor in, having no gardins nor furniture, So we Soon were Sattisfy'd we came out of our way for nothing'; *English Travels*, ed. cit., pp. 106–7. 'Sr John Percivale 9th Oct^{br} 1706. of Ireland. now 23 years old' is the entry to be found on p. 347 of the Padua University matriculation register-cum-visitors' book; *Inglesi e Scozzesi all'Universita di Padova*, ed. H.F. Brown (Venice, 1922), p. 188. On his return from abroad in 1707, Percival 'fell into Country Improvements' at the family home of Burton, near Cork, but by late 1718, had turned his attention to a new house in Pall Mall, which must be that referred to by Berkeley. Writing after his return to Virginia, William Byrd also refers to this house, looking forward to seeing his friend 'settled in the most elegant house in town' (*English Travels* . . . p. 33).

42. Mark Wenger comments on 'Percival's tolerant – even positive – attitude toward later Gothic architecture', contrasting it with Roger North's 'classical dogmatizing' and speculating that it may have resulted from the time he spent at Westminster School and at Oxford. Though Berkeley and Percival shared tolerant temperaments, in this instance the degree of Percival's acceptance of Gothic may merely be attributable to the immaturity of his 'taste'; *English Travels* . . . p. 31.

43. *Works*, VIII, pp. 66–8.

44. *Works*, VIII, p. 68. For praise of Dublin, written in Livorno, see *Works*, VIII, p. 79. For Oxford architecture, see note 26 above.

45. *Works*, VIII, p. 73: 15 October 1713.

46. See Luce, *Life*, pp. 42 and 159, and, for more detail on Berkeley's donation of 220lb of Greek type in 1733 (which enabled the first books in Greek to be printed in Ireland), Vincent Kinane, *A History of the Dublin University Press 1734–1976* (Dublin, 1994). That Berkeley's donation immediately anticipated the building of the Doric Printing House supports my hypothesis that he was a crucial influence on its design. For Berkeley in Sicily, see above, pp. 22–6. For evidence of his visits to both Agrigento and Catania during the

winter of 1717, see his letter to Thomas Prior on 'Petrifactions', dated Cloyne, 20 May 1746; *Works*, IV, pp. 251–2. In 'The Notes on the Government and Population of the Kingdom of Naples and Berkeley's probable route to Sicily' (*Berkeley Newsletter*, no. 11 (1989–90), pp. 20–7), Louis E. Alfonso draws attention to the reference by Joseph Stock in his *Account of the Life of George Berkeley* (London, 1776), p. 55 to friends who 'remember to have heard from him, that in the town by Virgil called palmosa Selinus, Aeneid III – 705, he found the ruins of a most significant temple'. If Berkeley actually disembarked to inspect the ruins of Selinunte on the south-west coast of Sicily, he would be the first British traveller known to have done so, the nearest precedent being Isaac Basire and his pupils in early 1649, who merely sailed past 'Terra de li Pulice . . . anciently called Selinunte, for the abundance of parsely, called in Greek Selinonte, built by those of Megara, Virg.: Teque datis linquo ventis palmosa salinis [*sic* for Selinus] now left disinhabited by reason of the poisonous aire. There are severall antiquityes and gyants bodys found often'; see *Travels through Fance and Italy* (*1647–1649*), ed. L. Monga and C. Hassel (Geneva and Turin, 1987), p. 131. For my attribution of these *Travels* to Basire and his pupils, see above, p. 87, n. 2. Though he makes no reference to Basire, Breval or Berkeley, there is much of interest in Arnaldo Momigliano 'La riscoperta della Sicilia antica da T. Fazello a P. Orsi', *Studi Urbinati di Storia, Filosofia e Letterture*, Lettere Italiane (1978), nuova serie B, nos 1–2, and 'The Rediscovery of Greek History in the Eighteenth Century: The Case of Sicily', *Studies in Eighteenth Century Culture*, IX (1979), pp. 167–87, both reprinted in Momigliano, *Settimo Contributo alla Storia degli Studi Classici e del Mondo Antico* (Rome, 1984).
47. *Works*, IX, p. 29.
48. For the meeting with the Oratorian Cartesian, Malebranche, see *Works*, IX, pp. 12 and 30. In October 1710, Percival had informed Berkeley that he was being compared to Malebranche and John Norris (Rand, *Berkeley and Percival*, cit., p. 87).
49. *Works*, VIII, p. 74; letter to Percival dated 'Paris, 24th Nov. N.S. 1613'. The next day Berkeley was due to see Versailles. No doubt, like most tourists, he would also have visited nearby Marly, J.-H. Mansart's château for Louis XIV whose layout, incorporating two rows of six pavilions, may have influenced Berkeley's plans for Bermuda. Marly was destroyed in the Revolution.
50. *Works*, VIII, p. 76.
51. *Works*, VIII, p. 77. For this Oglethorpe, see the biography of his brother, James Edward Oglethorpe (whose Georgia scheme was to receive money scheduled for Berkeley's Bermuda project) by Amos Attinger (Oxford, 1936). For a more positive, albeit brief portrayal, Eveline Cruickshanks, *The Oglethorpes: a Jacobite Family: 1689–1760*, Royal Stuart Papers, XLV (1995). Lord Oxford sent Theophilus to Sicily with the aim of having him appointed envoy, but Bolingbroke refused to accredit him. He was still there when Anne died in August 1714. For a long letter from Theophilus to Berkeley, see B. Rand, *Berkeley and Percival* (Cambridge, 1914), pp. 275–9.
52. *Works*, VIII, pp. 77–78.
53. *Works*, VIII, p. 78.
54. E. Chaney, 'Architectural Taste and the Grand Tour: The Case of Guarino Guarini', *Bollettino del CIRVI*, XX (1989), pp. 317–26.
55. *Works*, VIII, p. 79.
56. Ibid., p. 79. Berkeley's brief stay in Genoa also prompted the following comment to Percival on the state of Italian scholarship: 'I made it my busi-

ness to visit the colleges, libraries, booksellers' shops, both at Turin and here, but do not find that learning flourishes among them. Nothing curious in the sciences has of late been published in Italy. Their clergy for the most part are extremely ignorant; as an instance of it, they shewed me in the library of the Franciscans in this town a Hebrew book, taking it to be an English one'; cf. the observations of Dallington, Milton and Burnet quoted above, pp. 144–6.

57. Ibid., p. 80. Livorno had been a favorite city of the English since the sixteenth century. In the early seventeenth century, Lord Leicester's self-exiled son, Sir Robert Dudley, took an active role in developing the free port under the Grand Duke. John Evelyn is usually credited with first noticing that Inigo Jones's inspiration for Covent Garden was Livorno's Piazza Grande. An unpublished travelogue by the New College Fellow, Daniel Vivian, pre-dates this by almost a decade, being more or less contemporary with the completion of Jones' piazza in 1637: 'Ligorne is a very rare new built Cittie . . . the chiefe markett place, or Exchange ye which is very large and spacious, after ye forme of yt in Coven garden in London, haveing a curious Church, standing after the same manner, at one end of ye same, built, and porcht alike, so yt, theirs doubtlesse, was ye patterne of this' (Bodleian Library, New College MS 349, fol. 38v. I thank Professor Gerald Aylmer for bringing this manuscript to my attention).

58. *Works*, VIII, p. 80.

59. *Works*, VIII, p. 84. To Percival, dated Leghorn, 1 May 1714. On the same day, however, Berkeley wrote to Pope, congratulating him on the *Rape of the Lock* and encouraging his 'half formed design of coming to Italy' for the sake of its climate and Alpine landscape; *Works*, VIII, p. 83. Berkeley's preaching in Livorno may have been connected with the recent departure on the grounds of ill-health (caused by the climate) of Basil Kennett, the first chaplain to the British factory there, author of *Romae Antiquae Notitiae* (London, 1696) and former tutor to Percival's brother (see Kennett's 1703 letter in the letter-book: BL Add. MS 47025, fol. 62r). Berkeley later wrote of Kennett that the 'chaplain to the factory at Leghorne in Queen Anne's reign was esteemed and called a Saint by the papists themselves as the English merchants there assured me' (*Works*, VII, pp. 150–51). Luce (*Life*, p. 72) seems to have interpreted this as evidence that Kennett was still in Livorno when Berkeley preached there, but he was by this time at Corpus Christi College, Oxford, where he was elected President prior to his death in January 1715. Two of Berkeley's extant sermons are marked 'preached at Leghorne' (BL Add. MS 39306, fols 26 and 75).

60. *Works*, VIII, p. 85. For the New Junta, see Colvin, *Biographical Dictionary*, s.v. Galilei, Hewett and Lovett Pearce, and E. McParland, 'Sir Thomas Hewett and the New Junta for Architecture', *The Role of the Amateur Architect*, ed. G. Worsley (London, 1994), pp. 21–6 and idem, 'Edward Lovett Pearce and the New Junta for Architecture', in *Lord Burlington . . .*, ed. T. Barnard and J. Clark, cit., pp. 151–66. Further to Dr McParland's interesting analysis of styles and allegiances, an essay by a philosophical colleague at Trinity College, Dublin, confirms that Robert Molesworth was no friend to Berkeley, sympathetically receiving a denunciatory letter from a rival candidate for the living of St Paul's, Dublin. Robert and John Molesworth had both been intimates of Lord Shaftesbury and, in Robert's *Account of Denmark* (1694) the former had explicitly criticized the now suspect ('slavish') doctrine of 'passive' or 'blind obedience'; see David Berman, 'The Jacobitism of Berkeley's Passive obedience', *Journal of the History of Ideas*, XLVII (1986), pp. 309–19 and idem,

George Berkeley: Idealism and the Man (Oxford, 1994), pp. 71–97. Berman suggests that Berkeley's failure to obtain St Paul's and the increasing dominance of the Molesworth Circle 'which flourished in Dublin in the 1720s' encouraged his decision to 'spend the residue of [his] days in the Islands of Bermuda' and found a new St Paul's there. Molesworth senior and junior in fact died in 1725 and 1726 respectively, Hewett dying likewise in 1726; but since Berkeley was already planning his voyage in 1722, the thesis works even though Berkeley did not leave for another six years. Later in the century it seems that a strong connection between the two families was established, Mrs Eliza Berkeley requesting in 1797 that 'Dr Berkeley's noble relation, the excellent Lord Molesworth now on a visit to Ireland' deliver a letter to the Provost and Fellows of Trinity College, Dublin (Luce, *Life*, cit., p. 245).

61. *Works*, VIII, pp. 84–5; letter to Percival dated Paris, 13 July 1714. At least two Irishmen were in the entourage of Lord Burlington, who had arrived in Brussels on 2 June 1714, visited the Duke of Marlborough in Antwerp nine days later and was in The Hague from 15 June until 7 August; see Jacques Carré, *Lord Burlington (1694–1753): le connaisseur, le mécène, l'architecte* (unpublished doctoral thesis, University of Dijon, 1980). Jane Clark ('Lord Burlington is Here . . .', cit.) argues that Burlington was fraternizing with Jacobites throughout this period. Marlborough was certainly lending the Stuarts large sums of money (though we have also seen him lending money to Shaftesbury; note 13 above), and the exiled 2nd Earl of Ailesbury, whose son married Burlington's sister, Juliana, was resident in Brussels. The identities of Burlington's Irishmen is confirmed in the University of Padua Visitors' Book on 21 February when Burlington signed above 'Alexander Sandilands MD' and 'Henry Isaac Gervais of Lismore Ireland S.T.P.'; H. Brown (ed.) *Inglesi e Scozzesi*, cit., p. 193). The latter has often been confused with the painter Charles Jervas but he was the Huguenot-born graduate of Trinity College, who became Vicar Choral of Lismore and one of Berkeley's closest friends. Burlington and Berkeley could thus have met on either of their Grand Tours, albeit recommended to each other by Alexander Pope; see also below, pp. 371 and 375.

62. Luce, *Life of Berkeley*, ed. cit., p. 75. Ashe died in Brussels in 1721 almost a year after Berkeley had returned to London (Rand, *Berkeley and Percival*, cit., pp. 175–86).

63. *Works*, VIII, p. 101 (letter to Percival).

64. It seems that our only authority for Berkeley's date of birth, though given specifically as 12 March 1685, is Joseph Stock's 1776 *Life*. A.A. Luce (*Life*, cit., p. 211) seems uninterested in the fact that the date of birth engraved on Berkeley's memorial in Christ Church Cathedral, Oxford (set up by his widow who was then still resident in Oxford) is 1679, with his age given consistently but incorrectly (?) as 73.

65. The original notebooks are in the British Library (Add. MSS 39307, 39308, 39309 and 39310). For the standard (though unannotated) edition, see above, note 24.

66. *Works*, VII, pp. 249–50 (12 January 1717), here transcribed with minor corrections from the original diary: BL Add MS 39307, fols 2r–2v. Berkeley's account of walking 'on the mount behind our Lodging on which stands the Church & convent of La Trinita', suggests that they stayed in one of the row of houses in which still stands the Keats–Shelley Museum (on the northern side of the Piazza, now adjacent to the steps). From October to December

1714, Lord Burlington was confined – seriously ill – to 'Mr Brown's' rooms in the Albergo dei Tre Re on the Piazza; see also note 94.
67. *Works*, VII, p. 245. Berkeley would either have taken the Borgo Vecchio or the 1490s Borgo Nuovo, each of which flanked La Spina, the strip of medieval housing swept away by the Fascist plan. The northernmost Borgo Nuovo would have taken him past the Renaissance Palazzo Torlonia, once the property of Henry VIII; for which see above, pp. 42 and 52, n. 5.
68. *Works*, VII, p. 245.
69. For the evolution of the New Library, see Anne Crookshank, 'The Long Room', *Treasures of the Library, Trinity College, Dublin*, ed. P. Fox (Dublin, 1986), pp. 16–28.
70. *Works*, VIII, p. 24. Berkeley's appointment as Librarian is dated 20 November 1709; Luce, *Life*, p. 41.
71. Paid to John Barkey, 11 April 1713 for New Library, Trinity College, Dublin, Muniments P/2/25, item 1.
72. More than a year after his return from Italy, in October 1722, Berkeley demonstrated his continuing concern, writing to Percival from the early seventeenth-century library (on the site of the later Theatre), 'it is at present so old and ruinous, and the books so out of order, that there is little attendance given' (*Works*, VIII, p. 126). The two spiral staircases at the end of the Long Room came from the old library, having been erected there in 1651.
73. A Crookshank, cit. above note 69.
74. G. Worsley, *Classical Architecture in Britain*, cit., p. 163.
75. Trinity College, Dublin, Mun P/2/65 (1–8); there is an ambiguity between 1733 and 1744 but item 8 is clearly dated 18 March 1733/4.
76. *Works*, VII, p. 245; for the sculpture see F. Haskell and N. Penny, *Taste and the Antique* (New Haven and London, 1981). For a detailed account of Henry VIII's letters (said to have been brought to Rome by Cardinal Pole), see William Champney's unpublished travel notes; Douai Abbey MS CCXIX, p. 217. I thank Fr Geoffrey Scott for a photocopy of this MS.
77. For the most detailed treatment of the relevant period, see J. Dixon Hunt, *Garden and Grove: The Italian Renaissance Garden in the English Imagination 1600–1750* (London and Melbourne, 1986). Although Francis Bacon had said something approaching this, the earliest English promoter of informal features in early modern gardening seems to have been Sir Henry Wotton in *The Elements of Architecture* (London, 1624), p. 109: 'For as Fabriques should bee *regular*, so Gardens should be *irregular*, or at least cast into a very wilde *Regularitie*.'
78. *Works*, VII, p. 253: 'we all agreed [it] was high and steep enough to break either the late Bp. Burnet's or any man else's neck who should try the experiment by leaping down'. Burnet's *Letters* may thus be added to Misson's more detailed *New Voyage to Italy* (4th edn, London, 1714) which it is known Berkeley used. For other possible sources, both guidebooks and works such as Vasari's *Lives*, as well as architectural treatises by Palladio, Scamozzi and others, see Réné Maheu, 'Le Catalogue de La Bibliothèque des Berkeley', *Revue d'histoire de la philosophie* (1929), based on the 1795–6 Sotheby's sale catalogues of the bishop's grandson, George Monck Berkeley.
79. *Works*, VII, pp. 246–7. In the light of such an account, perhaps Jacob More's late 18th-century remodelling of part of the Borghese Gardens in the English style (following Sir William Hamilton's similar intervention at Caserta), may be interpreted as the enhancement of an existing aesthetic.
80. *Works*, VII, pp. 253–4 (15 January 1717).

81. *Works*, VII, p. 255 (16 January 1717).
82. *Works*, VII, p. 247. When this way of displaying ancient inscriptions and bas-reliefs was no longer fashionable they were enclosed or transferred inside. It is still possible to gain an idea of the original effect at the Villa Doria-Pamphili, which Berkeley also praised.
83. *Works*, VII, p. 247; the Pyramid is now nearer 120 feet above street level. It already features in Inigo Jones's design for the *Barriers* (a masque of 1610) and was sketched by Richard Symonds as the frontispiece to his 1651 note-book (Bodleian Library, MS Rawlinson D 121) [Fig. 55]. In October 1716, Berkeley's companion in Rome, the Jacobite Dr Roger Kenyon, wrote to the Duke of Mar, about Dr Arthur, who 'after escaping a thousand dangers in the King's cause, met his death where he came for safety by eating a few figs, which threw him into a dysentry . . . We had permission to bury him by the sepulchre of Cestius, a piece of antiquity well known here and within the walls which is esteemed a favour to us sort of people, and was procured by means of Cardinal Gualterio [*sic* for Gualtiero]; *HMC Stuart Papers* (London, 1907), III, pp. 92–3. For help in identifying Berkeley's 'Dr Chenion' as Kenyon I thank John Ingamells whose *Dictionary of British and Irish Travellers in Italy 1701–1800* (New Haven and London, 1997) includes an entry on him. During the course of the eighteenth century the pyramid became the identifying landmark of Rome's Protestant Cemetery; see the 1791 painting by Jacques Sablet exhibited in the Tate Gallery's Grand Tour exhibition in 1996, catalogue no. 82. It is now best known for its memorials to Keats and Shelley. Interestingly, Florence, despite its popularity with the British, had no equivalent until the second half of the 19th century; see H.C.B. Campbell, *A Journey to Florence in 1817*, ed. G.R. de Beer (London, 1953), p. 133: 'There is no protestant burial ground here.'
84. *Works*, VII, p. 247.
85. D. Stephen Pepper, *Guido Reni* (Oxford, 1984), p. 215; cf. Misson, ed. cit., II, p. 257.
86. *Works*, VII, p. 248. My identification of the 'Mr Hardy' as Charles here is due to the combination of his appearing again with Berkeley, this time with 'Mr Terwhit', on 18 January (at the Farnesina; *Works*, VII, p. 256) and then sign-ing the Padua University visitors' book on 13 May 1717 as 'Chas. Hardy' beneath the signature of 'Thomas Tyrwhitt'; H. Brown (ed.) cit., p. 196. He was often in Berkeley's company in Rome, on three occasions with 'Dr Chenion' or Kenyon who seems to have been his travelling companion at this stage (*Works*, VII, pp. 251, 253, 255 and above, note 83).
87. *Works*, VII, p. 264. The palace was in fact begun by Antonio da Sangallo and completed by Michelangelo and Giacomo della Porta.
88. *Works*, VII, p. 248.
89. E. Wright, *Some Observations made in Travelling throught France, Italy &c in the years 1720, 1721 and 1722*, 2 vols. (London, 1730), I, p. 284; cf. Haskell and Penny, op. cit., pp. 165–7.
90. *Works*, VII, p. 249. Berkeley's somewhat surprising description of the Caracalla's softness is perhaps ultimately derived from a reference to its 'morbidezza'. For the bust, sometimes suspected of being a Renaissance work, see Haskell and Penny, op. cit., no. 18.
91. *Works*, VII, p. 249. For the sculpture of Bernini, see monographs by Rudolf Wittkower and Howard Hibbard. For the 'Curtius flinging himself into the Gulf', see Haskell and Penny, op. cit., no. 27. This very high relief was removed to its present position inside, above the door facing the entrance,

during the 1770s for Prince Marc Antonio IV Borghese. Bernini's father, Pietro, may have been responsible for restoring the work (and transforming the antique horse) for Cardinal Scipione Borghese in 1617; see C. d'Onofrio, *Roma vista da Roma* (Rome, 1967), pp. 255–8. In admiring the Curtius, perhaps Berkeley remembered Percival's philosophical letter to him dated 29 November 1709. Percival commented upon 'the force of enthusiasm which ever works strongest in the weakest minds' (citing the Civil War regicides among others), and continued: 'Empedocles would be thought a god, & threw himself into Etna, and Curtius leaped into the chasm, to have a year's enjoyment of the fairest women, which is no such strange thing for a heathen to do, when even Christians who are better convinced of a future state are seen to make themselves away often because disappointed of a single woman'. (Rand, *Berkeley and Percival*, cit., pp. 65–6).

92. *Works*, VII, p. 262; cf. Richard E. Spear, *Domenichino*, 2 vols (New Haven and London, 1982), pp. 282–3, plate 248.

93. R. Wittkower, 'Domenichino's Madonna della Rosa', *Burlington Magazine*, XC (1948), pp. 220–3; cf. Spear, op. cit., p. 285.

94. *Works*, VII, p. 249. In this year, 'Monsù Donvil' and 'Monsù Trencer' (presumably Compton Domvile and Henry Trench) were registered as living in 'Seguita Strada Paolina v° Li Greci mano destra, Dal Vicolo del Carcioffolo' in the Parish Registers of San Lorenzo in Lucina (note in Brinsley Ford Archive, Paul Mellon Centre for British Art, London). A Mr 'Dumville' was also in Naples in March 1717 with Berkeley, Ashe and Tyrwhitt (see note 106 below); but it is specifically 'Compton Domville' who signs the Padua University visitors' book on 27 March 1719 two years later, between 'Lord Lempster' and Martin Benson, both of whom add: 'per la 2da volta', having signed the same book two and a half months earlier with Berkeley and Ashe. Horatio Brown (ed.) cit., p. 199, identifies him as Sir Compton Domville who died in 1768. He was born *c.*1686, educated at Trinity College, Dublin, and succeeded his father as 2nd Baronet of Templeogue in 1721. He was Sheriff of County Dublin in 1724 and MP for the same from 1727. He was a second cousin of Lord Leominster. See also Appendix.

95. In her comments on and corrections to the second edition of Stock's *Life* of Berkeley in *Biographia Britannica*, III (London, 1784), sig. *d r., Mrs Anne Berkeley wrote:

> Dean Berkeley was an excellent architect, and he had completed elegant plans of his projected town, as well as his seminary. The last edifice [St Paul's College] was to have occupied the center of a large circus; and this circus was to have consisted of the houses of the Fellows, to each of which in front a spacious garden was allotted. Beyond this academical circus was another, composed of houses for gentlemen, many of which houses had been actually bespoken, and the Dean had been requested to superintend the building of them. Beyond this circus was one more, which was calculated for the reception of shops and artificers. Dr Berkeley disliked the custom of burying in Churches; for which reason a Cypress Walk, called 'The Walk of Death', was to be solemnly appropriated to the sole purpose of interment. There monumental urns or Obelisks might be erected.

96. *Works*, VII, p. 250, with minor corrections from the original diary: BL Add. MS 39307, fols 23r–25r. The 'two beautiful Churches' were those commissioned by Alexander VII from Carlo Rainaldi: S. Maria dei Miracoli, 1675–8 (on the left) and S. Maria di Monte Santo (on the right). As Berkeley

would have noticed (and perhaps implies in his repeated use of the word 'contrived'), they were not literally 'of the same architecture'. Santa Maria di
Monte Santo, which is on a narrower site, was given an oval dome which,
however, matches its companion's round dome when seen on entering the
Piazza. Both are fronted by identical classical porticoes based on Bernini's
1673 revision of Rainaldi's original designs. Bernini had already rebuilt the
inner face of the Porta del Popolo in preparation for the grand entry into the
city by the convert Queen Christina of Sweden in 1655, hence the punning
inscription: 'Felici fauso ingressui' ('For a happy and blessed entrance'). With
spaces reserved for the fish market, herb and flesh market, public baths for
men and women, and the two academies, Berkeley's aspirations were mani-
festly more practical than Alexander VII's baroque priorities, for all their
shared insistence on a beautifully planned, classicizing symmetry. Berkeley's
disapproval of the irregularity of the ordinary houses around the Piazza del
Popolo may be reflected in the mathematical precision with which he lays out
his houses and gardens in the Bermuda plan, a hierarchy of three sizes with
the grandest reserved for the 14 residences grouped facing into the main
square. His use of the expression 'good effect on the eye' echoes that used in
relation to Oxford (see above, p. 328). Another possible influence on Berkeley
might have been Louis XIV's Marly (see above, note 49). For a contemporary
bird's-eye view with the argument that Marly may also have influenced the
layout of the University of Virginia, see W.H. Adams (ed.), *The Eye of Thomas
Jefferson* (National Gallery of Art, Washington, 1976), p. 131.

97. For Smibert, see R.H. Saunders, cit. above in note 37.
98. *Works*, VI, p. 80.
99. *Works*, VI, pp. 110–11. This, the slightly revised text of the 1752 *Miscellany*
     edition, carries Berkeley's note: 'Since the first publication of the Query, the
     art of design seems to be more considered and countenanced among us.' In
     Query 67 here, Berkeley sounds like the similarly patriotic Percival in the
     remainder of his letter suggesting the use of Irish materials at Castletown (see
     note 39 above): 'I would even carry my zeal to things of art: my hangings,
     beds, cabinets and other furniture should be Irish.'
100. *Works*, VII, p. 254.
101. Two Reni *Magdalens* feature in the 1738 Barberini inventory. This must be
     either cat. no. 118 (now in a private collection) or 137 (Galleria Nazionale
     d'Arte Antica: Corsini Gallery, Rome), in D. Stephen Pepper, *Guido Reni*
     (Oxford, 1984). The Perugino may also be the one now in the Galleria
     Nazionale d'Arte Antica in Rome: *The Madonna and Child enthroned*.
102. *Works*, VII, p. 255. The large bas-relief lion is still *in situ*.
103. *Works*, VII, p. 252.
104. *Works*, VII, p. 259. Of the fresco, Berkeley interestingly observes: 'The bed is
     without curtains and like enough to the modern beds one meets with now in
     Italy' (ibid., p. 261).
105. *Works*, VII, pp. 262–3.
106. *Works*, VII, p. 266. For their arrival in Naples, see PRO SP Foreign, 93/35;
     John Fleetwood to the Rt. Hon. P. Methuen, Naples, 19 March 1717
     (reference in Brinsley Ford Archive, Paul Mellon Centre). Fleetwood reports
     that Mr Ashe, son to the Bishop of Clogher, has arrived that week 'With him
     are come Messrs Berkeley Terret & Dumville.' Tyrwhitt evidently returned
     north rather than accompany Berkeley and Ashe on their epic journey to
     Puglia for he signs the Padua *Register* with Charles Hardy on 13 May 1717
     (above, note 86).

107. *Works*, VIII, p. 101. For Titian's *Danae*, now in Naples but then in the Palazzo del Giardino in Parma after removal from the Palazzo Farnese in the late seventeenth century, see H.E. Wethey, *The Paintings of Titian: Complete Edition*, 2 vols. (London, 1975), III, pp. 132-5, cat. no. 5 and Charles Hope (confirming that this erotic picture was painted for Cardinal Alessandro Farnese rather than Ottavio), 'A neglected document about Titian's "Danae" in Naples', *Arte Veneta*, XXXI (1977), pp. 188-9.
108. *Works*, VIII, p. 102.
109. *Works*, VIII, p. 103.
110. *Works*, VIII, p. 110.
111. *Works*, VIII, p. 105.
112. *Works*, VII, p. 270.
113. *Works*, VII, pp. 273-82. Berkeley discussed the tarantella with a Theatine in Barletta who claimed that he had cured by this means a Franciscan 'whom he cou'd not think wou'd feign for the sake of dancing'. Meanwhile the admirably empirical Berkeley was still not entirely convinced that the spiders were poisonous: 'one peasant at Canosa was affraid of 'em while his companion laugh'd & said he had taken them without harm in his hands' (*Works*, VII, p. 236). Either Berkeley or Dr John Freind, author of the *History of Physic* (London, 1725-6) to whom he later sent a detailed account of the tarantula (Luce, *Life*, pp. 60-1) seem to have been inspired by the similarly anthropological approach to the phenomenon adopted by Maximilian Misson in *A New Voyage of Italy* (4th edn, London), 1714, II, pt ii, pp. 396-7 and plate 15 illustrating the spider. Not published in *Works*, VII, pp. 276-7 are the notes which Berkeley copied (in paler ink, probably later) 'ex Georgii Baglini disputatio de anatome, morsu et effectibus Tarantulae' (BL Add. MS 39308, fols 52r-55v). Similarly unpublished are Berkeley's notes in Italian on architecture, which included a table of comparative measurements of the five orders in the same manuscript (ibid., fols 92v-93v).
114. *Works*, VII, pp. 283-4.
115. *Works*, VII, p. 284, referring to the Ospedale Civile (founded by S. Filippo Neri) and Achille Carducci's rebuilding of San Matteo (not completed until 1700), perhaps the most genuinely Baroque building in Lecce. In view of Colen Campbell's use of the word Gothic to describe the Baroque, it is interesting that in his pioneering published account of Lecce, Martin S. Briggs comments on San Matteo's interior being: 'remarkably like proportions of an English Gothic church, with triforium and clerestory'; see *In the Heel of Italy* (London, 1910), p. 345. For more recent accounts of *barocco leccese*, see V. Cazzato and M. Fagiolo, *Lecce* (Bari, 1984) and John Varriano, *Italian Baroque and Rococo Architecture* (New York and Oxford, 1986), pp. 278-84.
116. *Works*, VII, p. 285.
117. See above, p. 30.
118. *Essay on the Genius and Writings of Pope* (London, 1782), II, p. 201. Another subsequently recorded insight into Berkeley's travels in Sicily, tending to confirm their almost legendary status, is to be found in the *Memoirs of the Court of Augustus* (II, p. 277). Remembering that Berkeley almost persuaded him to join his expedition to Bermuda, Thomas Blackwell recalled in 1755 that the great philosopher had 'travelled through a great part of Sicily on foot, clambered over the mountains and crept into the caverns to investigate into its natural history, and discover the causes of its volcanoes' (Luce, *Life*, cit., p. 193).

APPENDIX

GEORGE BERKELEY IN THE VENETO

In the autumn of 1716, the 31-year-old George Berkeley, his greatest philosophical works already in print, set out for Italy for the second time. On his first journey he had travelled as chaplain to the Earl of Peterborough, but only got as far as Tuscany. This time, travelling as tutor to the delicate St George Ashe, son of the Bishop of Clogher, Berkeley more than compensated for the limitations imposed on his previous itinerary. In particular, his second Italian journey is noted for its unusual and apparently predominant bias towards the south of the country.

The letters and journals in which Berkeley wrote of his travels were first published in the nineteenth century by A.C. Fraser and then more comprehensively by A.A. Luce and T.E. Jessop in the 1950s.[1] They have now, for the first time, been translated into Italian, and for the first time in any language have been collected together and arranged as a consecutive narrative within the pages of a single volume.[2] Some minor improvements to Luce's reading of the third and fourth of the British Library journals have been effected, especially where Italian words and place-names are concerned.

Although one must pay tribute to this largely Italian enterprise – something of a reproach to British scholarship, which should long ago have produced a similarly self-contained edition of the original texts – it is a pity that the opportunity to improve the annotation provided in the *Works* and to supply a more relevant and informative introduction has not been better taken. The Italian translation, moreover, is seriously unreliable.

If the lack of an index, inexcusable in a work of this kind, is primarily the fault of the publishers, responsibility for the most serious omission in the new edition lies with the editors themselves. Though it might in itself seem a trivial one, this omission carries with it wider implications which affect our total conception of Berkeley's Grand Tour and his vision of Italy.

The conventional reconstruction of Berkeley's itinerary – one that is accepted by the editors of the volume – is that, having crossed the

Alps in late 1716 and reached Rome via Turin, Milan, Parma (and, presumably, Bologna and Florence) by early January, he and Ashe stayed in Rome until March 1717. They then moved south to Naples and after a tour of Apulia and a four-month stay on Ischia, they wintered in Sicily. Though it is not true that 'il materiale documentario è, da questo punto, *lacunosissimo* [my italics]', it is the case that, after a journey from Naples to Rome which we know took place in mid-April 1718, and three subsequent letters from Rome dated April, July and November of the same year, an apparent lack of further documentation, before a letter from Florence dated 20 July 1720, has meant that more than a year and a half of Berkeley's life has been left 'a total blank'. It is thought that he eventually reached London in the late autumn of 1720.[3] Berkeley's latest editors summarize their reading of the second half of his *Viaggio* – that is, from the 1718 stay in Rome – as follows:

La comitiva ha, così, deciso di trattenersi ancora qualche mese in Italia. Solo, il 13 novembre, infatti Berkeley annuncia a Percival il suo rientro in Inghilterra, si prevede una tappa a Venezia e l'arrivo per la primavera. Ma nel luglio del 1720, dopo un intervallo di ventidue mesi, una quarta lettera a Percival da Firenze.[4]

They repeat that it is 'lacunosissimo il materiale che documenta quest'ultima fase del viaggio'.[5] More specifically, in a note on the July 1720 letter we are informed that 'la lettera da Firenze interrompe un lungo silenzio, un periodo di venti mesi di cui non sappiamo nulla.'[6] We are left to assume that the party remained (in Rome?) for about a year longer than intended, perhaps, as Luce suggested, because of Ashe's poor health, and then travelled north to Florence preparatory to leaving Italy.[7] A French scholar, René Maheu, has even hypothesized that Berkeley travelled to Spain during this period, drawing attention to the number of post-1716 Spanish publications in Berkeley's library.[8]

Only one scholar, Benjamin Rand, ever seems to have taken seriously Berkeley's own references to a proposed journey to the Veneto. Thus, in his edition of the *Correspondence of Berkeley and Percival* (Cambridge, 1914, p. 28) he suggested that 'Berkeley may well have spent the year 1719 in the cities of Venetia, and thereby have completed a tour with Ashe of the whole of Italy.' Rand knew that on the 5 June 1719, Trinity College, Dublin, granted Berkeley a new leave of absence for two years. He may also have been

58 John Talman, sketch and motto in University of Padua visitors' book (12 February 1713, Biblioteca del Seminario Patavino, codice 634, p. 368). Consul Smith's future wife, the singer Catherine Tofts's signature is at the top of the page. [European University Institute, Florence]

influenced by the knowledge that Percival had himself completed a Grand Tour which included a trip to Venice.'[9] In fact, more substantial evidence was already available, buried in Berkeley's last publication: *Farther Thoughts on Tar Water* (1752). In this he recalls a detailed discussion regarding anatomy and the circulation of the blood with Giovanni Battista Morgagni 'the celebrated professor at Padua . . . above thirty years ago'.[10]

Just eight years after Rand published his speculation regarding a possible visit to the Veneto, Horatio Brown published a document which fully, though unwittingly, confirmed it.[11] Since then, how-

59 Drawing by Giuseppe Grisoni (probably commissioned by Anthony, Lord Harrold) with signature of John Talman 'per la quinta volta' in the University of Padua visitors' book: Biblioteca del Seminario Patavino, codice 634, p. 377. Talman brought Grisoni back to England with him. [European University Institute, Florence]

ever, although the standard *Life* of Berkeley was written,[12] the *Works* were re-edited, numerous related articles appeared and a volume exclusively devoted to the travels has been produced, none of the relevant authors or editors seems to have consulted this primary source for the study of British travel in Italy. The original manuscript contains more than 2,000 autograph signatures of British visitors to the University of Padua recorded between 1618 and 1765.[13] Though it began life as a relatively formal students' matriculation register, it soon became a Grand Tourists' visitors' book, almost an *album amicorum* with its inclusion of the occasional motto or drawing [Figs. 58 and 59]. No sustained attempt to identify the signatories was made by Brown, however, and numbers 1597–1601 [Fig. 52], all grouped together beside the date 'Jan. 15. 1719', were thus printed without editorial comment:

> Lempster
> E. Pomfret
> St. George Ashe
> George Berkeley
> Martin Benson.

As is clear from the original, 'E. Pomfret' has in fact been added alongside the signature 'Lempster' and the briefest investigation establishes that it must have been added in or after 1721 when Thomas Fermor, 2nd Baron Leominster, was created Earl of Pomfret. St George Ashe is of course Berkeley's charge, while Martin Benson is Berkeley's friend, the future Bishop of Gloucester.[14] On the next page of both manuscript and printed edition, beside the date 27 March 1719, we again find the signatures of Lempster and Martin Benson (both 'per la 2da volta' in the manuscript) together with that of a certain Compton Domvile.[15]

Although the discovery of Berkeley's dated signature only reduces the 'intervallo di ventidue mesi' to one of 18 months, the fact that it appears at Padua completely transforms the conventional view of Berkeley's Grand Tour. When next we hear of him, in Florence on the 20 July 1720, he is writing that 'Every month these six months we have designed to begin our journey and have been as often disappointed. We are now resolved to set out in two days.'[16] If, as seems probable, the 'six months' referred to here began with Berkeley's arrival back in Florence from the Veneto, we may conclude that out of a total of three and a half years in Italy (January 1717–summer

1720), approximately the whole of one of them (January 1719–
January? 1720) was spent in the Republic of Venice.[17]

The route Berkeley was most likely to have taken on his way from
Rome to Padua and Venice was the one chosen by most travellers
of the period, whether Catholic or Protestant, the north-easterly one
via Loreto, which meant continuing on to Ancona, joining the old
Via Flaminia as far as Bologna and turning off towards Venice via
Ferrara. Though Berkeley's most recent editors are correct in claiming that he was not as vituperative about modern Italy and its
religion as many of his contemporaries, Berkeley was surely
Addisonian enough not to have wanted to miss that supreme
monument to Italian 'superstition', the then world-famous *Santa
Casa*. Recent speculation about Lord Burlington's clandestine contact
with the Jacobites, focusing on James III's marriage to Maria
Clementina Sobieska at Montefiascone on 1 September 1719,
encourages similar speculation regarding Berkeley's movements and
a perhaps similar reason for their being so poorly documented.
Berkeley's acquaintance with semi-exiles such as Dr Roger Kenyon
(Chenion) reinforces this impression.[18]

As has already been suggested, the implications of Berkeley's
1719 presence in Padua are more far-reaching than appear at first.
Even in the terms set by the new introduction to the *Viaggio*, it must
now be acknowledged that talk of Palladio's influence on Berkeley
qua architect, for example, literally takes on a new dimension with
the realization that he probably inspected Palladian Vicenza itself.[19]
It now seems likely that some of the architectural treatises cited by
Professoressa Fimiani in this connection, and in the appendix on 'La
biblioteca di Berkeley e l'Italia', were actually purchased in Venice,
which in most cases was their place of publication. One can argue
more forcefully for Berkeley as one who contributed to the design of
Castletown. Perhaps more might now be made of the still-
unpublished architectural notes in the back of the fourth travel
journal and such as, for example, the 'Instance of praying ultimately
to Saints and of an office recited at certain times in the church called
il hospito [?] di S. Antonio di Padua'.[20]

Turning more generally to the introduction and annotation of the
new edition of Berkeley's *Viaggio*, it is immediately clear that the
editors did not, as they might well have done, take as their model
E.S. de Beer's edition of John Evelyn's *Diary*.[21] Rather than con-
centrate on Berkeley's sources and other relevant contemporary

literature, the editors have preferred here to dwell on recent inter-
pretative secondary literature. Unfortunately, though they are for
the most part long and detailed, their contributions are too often
beside the point or inadequately informed. If, for example, one is to
have learned comment on 'il giudizio corrente del gusto inglese su
Michelangelo',[22] instead of the somewhat eccentric bibliography
supplied, the reader should surely have been directed to Giorgio
Melchiori's *Michelangelo nel Settecento Inglese. Un capitolo di storia del
gusto in Inghilterra* (Edizioni di Storia e Letteratura, Rome, 1950).
John Hale's *England and the Italian Renaissance* (London, 1954) would
have demonstrated to Professoressa Fimiani that so far from having
'riassunto bene' current English prejudice against Michelangelo,
William Aglionby's *Painting Illustrated . . .* (1685), cited at one
remove from Paul Kirby's *Grand Tour in Italy* (New York, 1952), was
atypical in departing from contemporary Vasarian enthusiasm for
the artist.[23] Here the editors have exaggerated Berkeley's originality
in matters of taste. Had they looked at such near contemporary
works as John Dryden junior's turn-of-the-century *Voyage* (London,
1776), Edward Wright's *Some Observations made in travelling through
France, Italy, &c. in the years 1720, 1721 and 1722* (London, 1730),
or Jonathan Richardson's *An Account* of 1722 or John Breval's
Remarks of 1726 and 1738, they would have been able to judge
Berkeley's enthusiams and prejudices against those of his peers.[24]

Having made much ado about Berkeley's remarks concerning
Michelangelo, Professoressa Fimiani tends also to exaggerate the
significance of his comments on Bernini, meanwhile confusing
'Caravaggio' with Polidoro da Caravaggio.[25] Berkeley's ability to
appreciate both the antiquities in the Cortile del Belvedere and 'il
Bernini ellenizzante' was in fact shared by many mid-seventeenth to
late eighteenth-century travellers in Italy.[26]

The genuine originality of what Berkeley wrote in southern Italy
has been appreciated since at least as long ago as 1946, when
Alice Brayton published her *George Berkeley in Apulia* (Boston). The
editors of the *Viaggio* rightly point out that Berkeley's enthusiastic
praise of Lecce as 'the most beautiful city in Italy' is a 'giudizio . . .
assolutamente isolato agli inizi del secolo XVIII'. Only with
Sacheverell Sitwell's *Southern Baroque Art*, we are told, was there
'una rivalutazione del barocco leccese'. John Steegman (here mis-
spelt Stegman) is recruited to explain that 'il barocco, legato ai con-
trasti della natura mediterranea e a uno stravagante splendore, cui

è estraneo lo spirito protestante . . . non avrebbe mai potuto diventare uno stile populare in Inghilterra.'[28] It is a pity, after the detailed psychological and aesthetic interpretation, that when we turn to the text itself it should be mistranslated. When Berkeley writes of the Leccean churches as being 'most of 'em crouded with ornaments in themselves neat but injudiciously huddled together', Professoressa Fimiani merely tones down what is primarily a criticism when she translates this as 'carichi di orna-menti, tutte immagini ben distinte ma un po' affastellate insieme'.[29] When, however, 'the *meanest* houses are built of hewn stone, have ornamented doors, rustics' is translated as 'gli edifici *principali* sono costruiti in rustico, con pietra tagliata, hanno tutte le porte decorate' (my italics),[30] a more serious mistake has been made. This is then exacerbated by a footnote to the introduction referring to the same passage, which informs the reader that 'l'uso del "rustico" . . . tipico, secondo Berkeley, dei *principali* edifici di Lecce . . . era un elemento innovativo introdotto soprattutto dal Serlio' an art-historical assessment which does less than justice to Serlio's predecessors, from the fifteenth-century Florentines who so self-consciously rusticated the Palazzo Pitti, Medici and Strozzi, to Bramante and Raphael whose Roman townhouse proved so influen-tial throughout Europe.[31]

NOTES

First published in the *Bollettino del Centro Interuniversitario di Ricerche sul Viaggio in Italia*, I, ii (December, 1980), pp. 82–8.

1. *The works of George Berkeley, D.D.*, ed. A.C. Fraser (Oxford, 1871), IV ('Journal in Italy') and *The Works of George Berkeley, Bishop of Cloyne*, ed. A.A. Luce and T.E. Jessop (London and Edinburgh, 1955), VII (journals) and VIII (letters) (1956). In vol. IX of the latter edition there are some notes to the letters sent from Italy.
2. *George Berkeley. Viaggio in Italia*, ed. T.E. Jessop and M.Fimiani (Istituto Italiano per gli Studi filosofici, serie testi V, Bibliopolis, Naples, 1979). A note on page 6 explains how the task of editing was divided up: 'Thomas E. Jessop ha curato la revisione dei manoscritti, la scelta e la disposizione dei testi, la ricostruzione degli itinerari. A Mariapaola Fimiani si devono la traduzione dei testi e le note, l'introduzione e il saggio conclusivo sulla biblioteca berkeleiana.'
3. Ibid., p. 141, following *Works*, Luce and Jessop, op. cit., IX, pp. 41–4 and 144. 'A total blank' are the words used by A.C. Fraser to describe the year 1719 in his introductory preface to the Journals; see *Works* (edn 1901), IV, p. 222.
4. Ibid., p. 244.

5. Ibid., p. 353.

6. Ibid., p. 357.

7. Luce's unsubstantiated suggestion occurs in his *Life of George Berkeley . . .* (London, 1949), p. 80. It is repeated by Jessop and Fimiani, op. cit., p. 141: 'Il ritorno in Irlanda è deciso già nella primavera del 1718 [*sic*; actually planned in November 1718 for the spring of the following year] ma poi rinviato all'anno successivo. La partenza avverà non prima dell'estate del 1720, forse per le gravi condizioni di salute del giovane Ashe.'

8. R. Maheu, 'Le Catalogue de la Bibliothèque des Berkeley', *Revue d'Histoire de la Philosophie* (Paris, 1929), p. 181.

9. See note 14 below for Percival plus travelling companion visiting the University of Padua in October 1706.

10. Berkeley's 1752 recollection of his 1719 conversation with the great anatomist Morgagni is reprinted in *Works*, V, p. 213.

11. Horatio R.F. Brown, *Inglesi e Scozzesi all'Università di Padova . . .* (Venice, 1922).

12. A.A. Luce, op. cit.

13. Biblioteca del Seminario Patavino, Codice 634. Brown's transcript reproduces all the names more or less accurately but omits a variety of marginalia, additional comments and sketches, including one pornographic drawing (p. 44) and an elaborate allegorical drawing done by Giuseppe Grisoni, above John Talman's signature: 'Giov: Talman per la quinta volta'. Immediately above, Anthony [Lord] Harrold's signature is dated 31 August 1716 [Fig. 59].

14. H. Brown, op. cit., p. 198 (p. 388 of the manuscript). Martin Benson (1689–1752) remained a life-long friend of Berkeley after they met in Italy. Benson became Royal Chaplain in 1727 and Bishop of Gloucester in 1735. The two bishops were famously linked in Pope's *Epilogue to the Satires*: 'Manners with candour are to Benson giv'n, To Berkeley ev'ry virtue under Heav'n.' See T.H. Cocke, 'Bishop Benson and his Restoration of Gloucester Cathedral', *British Archaeological Association: Conference Transactions for 1981*, VII (1985), pp. 130–5. There are indications, often in the form of sarcastic remarks, that the visitors' book's signatories were in the habit of turning back its pages to discover the names of their travelling predecessors. One can guess at certain friends and acquaintances in whom Berkeley would have been particularly interested, for example William Bromley, former Speaker and Secretary of State of whose 'Hanoverian-Tory' Commons speeches Berkeley approved and whose exceptionally sympathetic account of Italy, *Remarks in the Grand Tour . . .* (1692 and later edns) he would certainly have known. Bromley signed the visitors' book on 20 December 1695 on his second tour, after which he published another travel account (*Several year's travels . . .*) in 1702. Inspired by Richard Lassels's *Voyage of Italy* (1670) this was so sympathetic to Roman Catholicism that it cost him the Speakership of the House of Commons. Apart from many well-known politicians and aristocrats such as Charles Montagu, the Duke of Manchester (1698), Wriothesley Russell, 2nd Duke of Bedford (1698), Bolingbroke, the Pretender's Secretary of State (1699) and James Graham, 1st Duke of Montrose and Secretary of State (1700), Berkeley would surely have noted the signature of Joseph Addison, dated August 1700 (Brown, p. 182). Of still greater personal interest must have been the autograph of: 'Sr. John Percival 9th Octbr 1706. of Ireland. now 23 years old', Berkeley's life-long friend and patron (Brown, p. 188). Signing alongside Percival was 'Francis Clerke . . . Angloise. now 23 years old', who is clearly the 'Mr Clerke' often referred to in Berkeley's correspondence, eventually a baronet, whom previous editors have failed to identify (see *Works*, IX, pp. 4 and 20). As Percival's 'intimate

friend', Clerke had embarked on the Grand Tour with him, starting in Utrecht, in August 1705; see *The English Travels of Sir John Percival* . . . ed. M.R. Wenger (Columbia, 1989), p. 7 and BL Add. MS 47072, fol. 21r.

Of those travellers who signed the book in the years immediately preceding Berkeley's own visit to Padua, one might mention William Kent, 'Pittore Inglese Sept. I. 1714', whose signature succeeds that of the Irish painter Henry Trench and is followed by an inscription not printed by Brown: 'Quae Cytherea tibi fert milita [*sic*; milia?] munera Triton / Haec musis prima Kentius arte vovet' (MS, p. 368), Thomas Coke of Norfolk and his tutor Thomas Hobart on 3 October 1714 and Richard Boyle, Lord Burlington ('Feb. 24. 1715', Brown, p. 193) who, after first meeting Kent in Italy at around this time, became his life-long friend and patron. Having been introduced by Pope, Berkeley also became a friend and protégé of Burlington, whose more celebrated passion for Palladio was confirmed during a visit to nearby Vicenza which dated from the same year as Berkeley's. Interestingly, Kent had done a picture of Hercules and Iole for Lord Leominster at the end of the previous year; see Kent's letter to Massingberd, 15 November 1718, in M. Jourdain, *The Work of William Kent* (London, 1948), p. 31. The presumed meeting between Kent and Martin Benson may have led to the latter commissioning Kent's Gothick screen in Gloucester Cathedral in 1742; engraving in J. Vardy, *Some Designs of Inigo Jones and William Kent* (London, 1744), plate 49, and T.H. Cocke, cit. It might be noted also that Berkeley later collaborated with 'Gui. Kent' on the Wainwright tomb in Chester Cathedral (see *Works*, VII, pp. 377-9).

15. Brown (op. cit., p. 199) identifies the latter as Sir Compton Domville who died in 1768. Probably he, rather than the William Domville indicated by Luce and Jessop (*Works*, IX, p. 31) and Professoressa Fimiani (*Viaggio*, p. 280) following them, is the 'Mr Domvile' with whom Berkeley had gone book shopping in Rome in January 1717 (see *Works*, VII, p. 249), and above, pp. 340 and 363.

16. *Works*, VIII, p. 115.

17. The travellers' January arrival was probably so timed in order not to miss the Venetian carnival. As well as Venice, Padua and Vicenza, Berkeley would almost certainly also have visited Verona to see the *Arena*. Perhaps Mantua was also visited during the course of the year. Berkeley owned a history of the city; see item 975 of the 'Valuable Library', *Viaggio*, p. 366.

18. For the conventional nature of the tour to Venice via Loreto, see J.W. Stoye, *English Travellers Abroad 1604-1667*, 2nd edn (New Haven and London, 1989), pp. 131-3. For the possibility of Burlington (and indeed William Kent, who was rumoured to have painted Maria Sobieska) attending James III's wedding; see J. Clark 'Lord Burlington is here', *Lord Burlington: Architecture, Art and Life*, ed. T. Barnard and J. Clark (London, 1995), pp. 251-310. For 'The Jacobitism of Berkeley's *Passive Obedience*', see note 60 above.

19. *Viaggio*, p. 63. See also Professor Jessop's *Prefazione*, p. 14.

20. BL Add. MS 39310, fol. 83v.

21. *The Diary of John Evelyn*, 6 vols (Oxford, 1955). For the travels in Italy see especially II.

22. *Viaggio*, p. 65.

23. Hale, op. cit., pp. 67.

24. See R.S. Pine-Coffin, *Bibliography of British and American Travel in Italy to 1860* (Florence, 1974), a work apparently unknown to Professors Jessop and Fimiani, pp. 100-4. It might be mentioned that Breval's name occurs on p. 201 of Brown's list of visitors to the University of Padua alongside that of his charge, George Cholmondeley, Viscount Malpas, on 2 September 1721.

Richardson, op. cit., p. 270, wrote a detailed comparison between Michelangelo's *Last Judgement* and the Sistine Ceiling. Berkeley mentions neither in the surviving documents, though he visited both St Peter's and the Vatican.

25. *Viaggio*, p. 66, where Berkeley's enthusiasm for 'il chiaroscuro del Guercino e di Caravaggio' is discussed on the basis of a reference (*Works*, VII, p. 259) to work by 'Polidore Caravagio' at the Castel S. Angelo.

26. Ibid., p. 66. In a footnote on the same page, Professor Cesare Brandi's *La prima architettura barocca* (Bari, 1970) is brought in as evidence that only now, since Gestalt psychology has been thought of, can we fully appreciate Bernini's caricatures (and this in spite of the fact that Berkeley nowhere mentions Bernini's caricatures). According to Professoressa Fimiani, Brandi's application of Gestalt theory helps explain 'l'apparente paradosso della sensibilità berkeleiana per la scultura di Bernini'.

27. *Works*, VII, p. 284, and *Viaggio*, pp. 72–3.

28. *Viaggio*, p. 73 n. 224. In fact the Sitwells' 'discovery' of Lecce and Southern Baroque generally is heavily indebted to Martin S. Briggs, *In the Heel of Italy* (London, 1910).

29. *Works*, VII, p. 283, and *Viaggio*, p. 200.

30. *Works*, VIII, p. 104, and *Viaggio*, p. 226.

31. *Viaggio*, p. 73 n. 224.

14

Epilogue:
Sir Harold Acton 1904–94

꧁ഊ꧂

SIR HAROLD ACTON died on Sunday 27 February 1994 in the magnificent Florentine villa in which he was born almost 90 years earlier. The Villa La Pietra, its priceless contents and its exquisite gardens, created by Harold's father at the beginning of this century, will go neither to his old college of Christ Church nor to Oxford University as Sir Harold originally hoped, as neither institution had the imagination to accept his offer. Instead, maintained in perpetuity by an endowment of 25 million dollars, the entire estate has gone to New York University. Complete with five villas on the periphery of the 57-acre estate, as well as property in Florence, estimated to be worth up to 500 million dollars, the bequest is said to be the largest ever received by an American university.

Although it has (re?)discovered the art of fund-raising, Oxford has not changed much since Harold came up in 1922. He had already made his mark at Eton where, with Brian Howard, he edited the precocious *Eton Candle*. His familiarity with the arts went far beyond that of pupils and teachers alike. In the *Festschrift* for Harold's eightieth birthday (cit. above, p. 131), Peter Quennell remembered how at Oxford he upstaged even that generation, which included Robert Byron, David Cecil, Kenneth Clark, Cyril Connolly, Graham Greene, Anthony Powell and Evelyn Waugh:

None was quite so entertaining and original a character as Harold Acton . . . The leader and favourite figure-head of the contemporary Aesthetic Movement . . . he taught us a good deal. He differed from most of his friends, not only because he was unusually well-read . . . [He] had had a cosmopolitan youth, brought up at a famous Florentine villa, amid the

60 Sir Harold Acton with Jessica Chaney in the gardens of Villa La Pietra, Florence, c.1983. [E. Chaney]

> Sienese Primitives that his father had collected . . . I remember seeing on his table the magnificent golden coins Benvenuto Cellini had designed for a fastidious Renaissance Pope.

Christopher Hollis confirmed that 'he was enormously our superior in his knowledge of Continental literature, pictures or architecture', and Christopher Sykes that 'Harold Acton was the Arbiter Elegantiarum'. His familiarity with the French symbolists stimulated his early appreciation of T.S. Eliot whom he (now rather too famously) promoted through a megaphone from his Meadow Buildings balcony at Christ Church. He and Quennell were expected to become Britain's leading poets, but the latter paid homage to 'the advice and encouragement' Harold gave him at this time. Evelyn Waugh dedicated *Decline and Fall* 'in homage and affection' to Harold and asked him to be best man at his wedding with 'She-Evelyn'. (To the day he died, Harold kept a framed photograph of the couple on his bedroom wall.) In 1925, Graham Greene wrote to his future wife: 'The person I miss most now that I'm away . . . is Harold . . . Although I wouldn't admit it to anyone else his attack on me in *The Cherwell* was the best and most useful criticism I've ever had, and any alterations I try to make in my stuff is founded on it.' Twenty-five years later, Greene wrote to Waugh of having visited their mutual friend in Florence: 'How nice & dear he is, & how I didn't realise it at Oxford.'

Compared with such friends, however, he failed to live up to expectations on leaving Oxford. With his artist brother William he moved into a house in Lancaster Gate which their father, a dealer as well as collector, had furnished with Florentine antiques, some of which were for sale. But Harold soon migrated to Paris, where he renewed his acquaintance with Gertrude Stein and met Picasso, Cocteau and many others. He gradually abandoned poetry for the Firbankian prose of *Cornelian* and *Humdrum* (1928) which Cyril Connolly reviewed unfavourably by comparison with Waugh's *Decline and Fall*.

Just as he had pioneeringly promoted Victorian taste when his 'Georgian' and Bloomsbury elders were still rubbishing anything to do with that era, Harold now turned his attention to seventeenth- and eighteenth-century Florence and the 'decadent' Medici in particular. *The Last of the Medici* (1930) was an eccentric production, consisting of a learned if facetious preface by Harold Acton, his translation of a scurrilous early eighteenth-century account of the Grand Duke Gian Gastone's bizarre private life, the whole appropriately introduced by Norman Douglas. This signed and limited edition was published by Pino Orioli in Florence and got him into almost as much trouble as *Lady Chatterley's Lover* had done.

Harold published what would be his last book of poems, *This Chaos*, in Paris in January 1931, but by then he was hard at work completing *The Last Medici*. Published by Faber in 1932, after they insisted on cutting 30,000 words, *The Last Medici* sold badly and, despite the praise of Bernard Berenson, was in general not well received. In his diary, Waugh dismissed it as illiterate and dull, explaining: 'There are long citations from Reresby, Evelyn and contemporary travellers. Also endless descriptions of fetes and processions.' It is just these now fashionable ingredients, articulated in Harold's appropriately baroque style, which today make this one of his most appreciated books. It could indeed be argued that *The Last Medici* inspired the school of cultural history epitomized by Francis Haskell's *Patrons and Painters*.

Apparently not in demand in Europe, Harold left for China, where he might have remained for ever had the prospect of war not prompted his return. He taught English at Peking University, translated Chinese poetry and plays, wrote a still-standard article on Chinese theatre and what is probably his best novel, *Peonies and Ponies* (1941). This and the *Memoirs* reveal the full extent of his love of pre-Communist China. So profound was his commitment to his adopted home, his friends and students, that he remained in Peking during the hated Japanese occupation. Even when he returned to Europe in June 1939 he fully intended to return to China, having left behind his collection of precious painted scrolls and sculpture. Then the Japanese bombed Pearl Harbour and he never saw his possessions again.

Serving in RAF intelligence in India during the war, Harold was indignant that narrow-minded Foreign Office suspicion of his previous lifestyle meant that no use was made of his knowledge of China. Shortly before he was demobilized he heard the news of his brother's tragic death in Ferrara. By the sullen welcome he received on his return to La Pietra, Harold felt that his parents would rather he had died than his younger brother. This is all but articulated in his *Memoirs*, the first volume of which he now settled down to write. Sensing continued parental disappointment (due partly to his bachelordom), whilst deciding not to leave them entirely to return to China, he resolved nevertheless to live far from Florence for at least part of each year. Thus he took a villa at Posillipo and, with admirable determination, resumed the study of eighteenth-century Italy, focusing now upon the Kingdom of the Two Sicilies. He also travelled in America, translating the superb *Peach Blossom Fan* (in collaboration with his old friend Chen Shih-hsiang) at Berkeley and, in the wake of Oxford's rejection, finding an alternative destiny for his estate. After the death of his American mother in 1962, he signed the historic agreement with New York University.

As an historian of (and apologist for) the Bourbons of Naples, Harold was an anti-Whig revisionist *avant la lettre*. Into the political and biographical narrative, however, he also wove a social and cultural history of the kingdom of Naples which may never be superseded. Though there are a few footnotes, both substantial volumes are so exclusively based on skilfully exploited primary sources that the end product has itself the aura of a primary text. When I asked the then Professor of Modern History at Cambridge, Charles Wilson, to write on 'Harold Acton as an Historian' for the *Festschrift*, he responded enthusiastically. He concluded that the author possesses a profound and unique understanding of the subjects with which he deals. Other scholars might have attempted this task; but they lacked his erudition. Those who had the erudition had neither the courage nor imagination to venture on his approach to history. Unfashionable as this may – in some quarters and for the time being – seem to be, Harold Acton has put every student of the Renaissance and, above all, of the *ancien régime* in Italy irredeemably in his debt.

After the excellent *Tuscan Villas* of 1973, *The Pazzi Conspiracy* (1979) and introductions to various major exhibitions of Florentine and Neapolitan art, the last piece of historical writing of this quality was the essay with which Harold introduced *Florence: A Travellers' Companion*, an anthology he asked me to edit for Constable & Co. in 1984. Though he was now in his eighties, I know of no better summary of the history of Florence, and Gibbon could hardly have written a more stylish one. Despite the unhappy management of the final year or two of his life and the cheap sneers of much of the posthumous comment, Harold will be remembered by visitors of all nations, classes and ages as the great host of La Pietra. He was the last great Anglo–Italian in that romantic tradition which stretches back to the Catholic exiles of the sixteenth century, epitomized by Lord Leicester's illegitimate son, Sir Robert Dudley, 'Duca di Northumbria', who became one of the principal attractions in Tuscany for seventeenth-century Grand Tourists.

Despite his privileged background, Harold worked hard, albeit with *sprezzatura*. He wanted to succeed as a writer and thus break free of family support. In the end he combined creative, historical and critical writing of the highest order with dedication to his parents (and latterly their villa) and the most generous but intelligent hospitality. As his *Memoirs* so vividly reveal, he was always interested in other people, if mischievously so then all the more entertainingly.

Some who scarcely knew Harold Acton considered him a snob but this, in any conventional sense of the word, he never was. A streak of insecurity (due perhaps to uncertainty about his father's parentage if not deeper anxieties) may have encouraged his taste for titles and, latterly, royals. But his enthusiasm for these was never uncritical. He remained in essence a meritocrat. One had merely to reciprocate his almost invariably positive approach, whether conversationally, in one's writing or gossip about those things which interested or entertained him: music, literature, art, architecture, history and scandal. Together with his memoirs, Harold Acton's historical writings will probably survive best (though it has apparently still not occurred to publishers to reprint *The Bourbons of Naples*). His fascinating letters from Oxford, China and Italy should also be published, for they will help perpetuate the memory of one of the most charming, cultivated and hospitable personalities of the twentieth century.

NOTE

This chapter was first published as an obituary in *Apollo*, CXXXIX (June 1994), pp. 52–3.

15

Bibliography:
A Century of British and American Books on the Evolution of the Grand Tour, 1900–2000

⊷⊙⊙⊶

C HRISTIAN 'constructions' though both may be, the turn of a century, let alone that of a millennium, encourages the spirit of retrospection. Given that the post-medieval evolution from pre-dominantly religious to educational travel is so fundamental to an understanding of the origins of the Grand Tour, it seems appropriate to begin a survey compiled in the year 2000 by celebrating the centenary of **Herbert Thurston**'s quintessentially retrospective *Holy Year of Jubilee: An Account of the History and Ceremonial of the Roman Jubilee* (London, Sands & Co., 1900). Concerned above all with pilgrimage from the time of the first Holy Year of 1300 to his own of December 1899, this learned Jesuit nevertheless quotes so interestingly from several hundred years of travel literature that he almost incidentally documents the development of curiosity as a justification for travel in its own right. He also documents and to some extent analyses the praise of travellers for Roman hospitals, a topic he privileges partly because of his historical controversies with contemporary Protestant historians such as **G.G. Coulton**. Sands & Co. published an abridged version of Father Thurston's *Jubilee Year* in 1925.

Meanwhile, also in 1900, the romantically named **Walter Raleigh**, newly promoted to the Chair of English at Glasgow and in 1904 to become the first Professor of English literature at Oxford, published a reprint of **Sir Thomas Hoby**'s 1561 translation of *Castiglione's Cortegiano: The Book of the Courtier* (London, David Nutt, 1900). Raleigh's introduction is a model of its kind, summarizing the life

and works of Castiglione and of Hoby, before going on to discuss
the extraordinary impact of the *Courtier* on both Italian and English
culture. For our purposes, however, most significant is Raleigh's use
of Hoby's manuscript autobiography in the then British Museum
Library (now BL MS Egerton 2148). At least one late-nineteenth-
century copy of this survives in the Osborn collection in the Beinecke
Library at Yale (Osborn MS D.184), but it was then so little known
that the author of the *Dictionary of National Biography* entry on Hoby
was unaware of it. Raleigh recommended that, 'for its historical
value, if for nothing else, the Diary certainly deserves to be set in
print. It is the chief source of the ensuing life of Hoby.' More than
half of this manuscript describes Hoby's fascinatingly proto-typical
Grand Tour and, although Raleigh failed to identify Hoby's principal
source for his description of Italy, Leandro Alberti's *Descrittione di
tutta Italia* (1550), his comments, such as that on Hoby's Strasbourg
sighting of 'the first English historian of Italy', **William Thomas**, are
always illuminating. Raleigh's suggestion that the BL manuscript
should be published was taken up by **Edgar Powell** and the Camden
Society two years later (see above, p. 137, n. 56).

By the beginning of the last century, therefore, long before the
academic coining of 'reception theory' and related subjectivist
methodologies, both the permanent and the evolving aspects of Italy
were already being interpreted on the basis of an evolving variety of
religious and secular responses. Increasingly, the interpreters themselves, the travellers, were also being interpreted, not merely for
what their texts revealed of Italy and its institutions but for their
own mentalities and the contexts whence these emerged. Now, in
2000, it is the turn of the historiographer to survey those secondary
interpreters who pioneered the deconstruction of these travelogues
and, notwithstanding the alleged 'death of their authors', their full
and fascinating lives.

In 1901, in immediate succession to Thurston's *Holy Year*, the
same enterprising London publishers, Sands & Co., produced the still
more lavish *In Sicily* by the novelist and travel writer **Douglas
Sladen**. Weighing in it at some 4.8 kilos, with over a thousand
glossy and profusely illustrated pages in two volumes, Sladen begins
his account with a preface on previous writings, from the ancient
classics, via Brydone's eighteenth-century *Tour* (but not Hoby's) to
Freeman, Mrs Elliot's *Diary of an Idle Woman* and Cardinal Newman's
youthful letters. He concludes, as if warning the would-be historio-

grapher from his present project: 'I feel it would be bad taste in me to discriminate between recently published books on Sicily.' He shows less restraint, however, in the discursive text itself, echoing Richard Coeur de Lion when he disparages modern Messina on the eve of its terrible earthquake: 'Richard erected a gallows for thieves outside the gates of Messina; it ought to be there still.'

Presumably in order to divert his readership, **Sladen** included much bantering dialogue between himself and a not quite Jamesian mother and daughter on tour from America in occasionally unsuitable Sicily. In the following year, 1902, it was the turn of the more serious Columbia University Press to publish the work of the more learned American diplomat, **Lewis Einstein** (who later retired to one of those Fiesolan villas thought to be the setting for Boccaccio's *Decameron*; now part of the European University Institute), *The Italian Renaissance in England* (New York, 1902). As well as being a compact but comprehensive masterpiece on Anglo-Italian cultural relations during the fifteenth and sixteenth centuries, this work merits recognition as the pioneering study of the evolution of educational travel to Italy. No doubt encouraged by such interest, the same year saw the Camden Society's publication of Hoby's auto-biographical manuscript which Raleigh and now Einstein had both featured in their studies: *A Booke of the Travaile and Life of Me Thomas Hoby* (BL MS Egerton 2148). The editor, **Edgar Powell**, built usefully on the work of Professor Raleigh but added little of significance.

Although **Lewis Einstein** was not a university academic, his book was published in the 'Columbia University Studies in Comparative Literature'. Given that comparative literature was one of the few university 'disciplines' able to accommodate the study of travel, it is inevitable that publications on the subject continued to be the work either of American academics or of more or less scholarly amateurs, and that no British university press was to publish on this subject for several decades. The disproportionately large contribution to the subject made by Americans generally, especially if one includes the likes of **Henry James** and **Edith Wharton,** may be attributed to an identification between their encounters with historic Europe and the English 'discovery' of historic Italy after the Renaissance. Their experience as 'passionate pilgrims' is echoed by the late twentieth-century Australians (and Japanese?) who in their quest for European culture were the last (if often less than) 'Grand' Tourists.

In 1903, the London publisher, Grant Richards (major rival of

J.M. Dent for quality guidebooks and other Italiana), issued an edited anthology which, while it did not pretend to academic status, made available a mass of little-known material which still 'delights as it instructs' (as travel itself was held to do): **Henry Neville Maugham**'s *The Book of Italian Travel, 1580-1900* (London, 1903). Maugham's 110-page introduction attempts a survey of the entire history of descriptions of Italy, concluding Ruskinianly that 'it has taken 400 years for the northern races to arrive at a full conception of [Italian] civilization'. Also in 1903, Sherratt & Hughes of London published most of what **Fynes Moryson** (or rather, John Bale, his original printers in 1617) had omitted from the vast manuscript of his *Itinerary* (Corpus Christi, Oxford, MS 94). Together with a short introduction and index, the editor, **Charles Hughes** (or perhaps Sherratt & Hughes), chose to entitle the whole: *Shakespeare's Europe* (London, 1903).

This ever-growing Anglo-American interest in the history of European travel may have encouraged the Scottish publishers Maclehose & Son to include in their handsomely produced series a two-volume edition, with index and short introduction of **Thomas Coryate**'s *Crudities*, originally published in 1611 (Glasgow, 1905), the 1632 edition of **William Lithgow**'s *Total Discourse of the Rare Adventures and Painefull Peregrinations* in one volume, also with index and inaccurate introduction by the publisher (Glasgow, 1906) and, finally, Moryson's *Itinerary* itself (Glasgow, 1907), in four volumes. Coryate has since been published in edited Italian translation in 1975 and reprinted in facsimile by the Scolar Press (London, 1978), and Fynes Moryson appeared in the English Experience series: *Teatrum Orbis Terrarum* of Walter Johnson Inc., who also published the facsimile of **Robert Dallington**'s *Survey of the Great Dukes State of Tuscany* of 1605 (Amsterdam and Norwood, 1971 and 1974). The third edition of Lithgow was reprinted by the Folio Society (intro. Gilbert Phelps, London, 1974) and, for completeness' sake, we cite the disappointing Italian edition of Dallington: *Descrizione dello Stato del Granduca di Toscana*, edited by N.F. Onesti and L. Rombai (Florence, All'Insegna del Giglio, 1983).

While Maclehose were busy republishing these early seventeenth-century travelogues, in 1907 the Clarendon Press of Oxford brought out the first major monograph on a contemporary who, thanks to the experience and languages he gained on his European travels, obtained the first post-Reformation English ambassadorship in Italy:

Logan Pearsall Smith's two-volume *The Life and Letters of Sir Henry Wotton* (Oxford, 1907). Just as the Somersetshire Coryate was encouraged to visit early-seventeenth-century Venice by Wotton's presence there, the Oxford-educated Philadelphian **Pearsall Smith** was encouraged to visit early-twentieth-century Florence by the presence there of his sister Mary, **Bernard Berenson**'s wife. A bedroom at Berenson's Villa I Tatti (now an illustrious outpost of Harvard University) is still named in his honour. **Pearsall Smith**'s superb edition of Wotton's letters, lithographically reprinted by Oxford University Press in 1966, is unlikely to be superseded.

In 1911, another American, **Ernest S**. **Bates**, published the relatively light-hearted study of Montaigne, Moryson, Coryate and their contemporaries entitled *Touring in 1600: A Study in the Development of Travel as a Means of Education* (Boston and New York, Houghton, Mifflin and Co., 1911). It is probably no accident that Bates completed this as a PhD in 1908 for the same Columbia University whose press had so recently published Einstein's *Italian Renaissance in England* (see also Baskerville, 1967, below). Bates's less thoroughly researched study was reprinted as a Century paperback with an introduction by George Bull in 1987, while Hughes's *Moryson* was reissued in 'Second edition with a new index' by Benjamin Blom of New York in 1967.

Published in Oxford (1913) by the Clarendon Press (like Pearsall Smith's *Wotton*), the now almost forgotten volume II of the 'Oxford Historical and Literary Studies' series was 'issued under the direction of C.H. Firth and Walter Raleigh' (Hoby's biographer). Entitled *Anglo-Roman Relations 1558-1565*, this was written by **C.G. Bayne** C.S.I., who based it mainly on the correspondence between Philip of Spain and his ambassadors in Rome, and the Vatican transcripts in the Public Record Office.

Clare Howard wrote more specifically than Bates on *English Travellers of the Renaissance* but wore her superior scholarship lightly: 'This essay was written in 1908-10 while I was studying at Oxford as Fellow of the Society of American Women in London.' She describes her theme as 'the evolution of travel for study's sake' and, adopting a lively, anecdotal and mainly biographical approach, covers this subject quite comprehensively. First published by John Lane, the Bodley Head, in London, New York and Toronto on the eve of the Great War in 1914, her book was reprinted in facsimile by Burt Franklin of New York in 1968.

The established period of the Grand Tour (not covered by this essay) was first surveyed by yet another American, **William Edward Mead**'s *The Grand Tour in the Eighteenth Century* and also published in 1914, by the same Houghton Mifflin Co. of Boston, who had published Bates. Despite its title, this slightly bland survey, covering travel throughout Europe, has made relatively little impression, though it was reprinted by Ayer Co. in 1972. Also published on the eve of the First World War, a relevant study to judge from its main title, **Peter Guilday**'s *The English Catholic Refugees on the Continent 1558-1795*, turns out even from its subtitle to be disappointingly narrow in scope: vol. I (vol. II never apparently appeared): *The English Colleges and Convents in the Catholic Low Countries* (London, 1914). It is useful, however, inasmuch as several of the principal characters in our evolutionary story pass through its pages.

Although guidebooks (albeit inadequately revised) are often published immediately after a period in which travel has been rendered impractical, travelogues or histories of travel take longer to appear. (Martin Secker published **Norman Douglas**'s *Old Calabria* in 1915 on the basis of pre-war travels.) With such a huge number of the literate population killed either by war or by the subsequent flu epidemic, it took longer than usual for either genre to recover, even if several more primary texts were published or re-edited. Though most biographies of travellers are not included here, exceptions should be made for **Archibald Malloch**'s *Finch and Baines: A Seventeeth-Century Friendship* (Cambridge, Cambridge University Press, 1917) and **Mary Hervey**'s *Life, Correspondence and Collections of Thomas Howard, Earl of Arundel* (Cambridge, Cambridge University Press, 1921; facsimile reprint, New York, Kraus, 1969). The author of a highly original and well-documented monograph on *Holbein's Ambassadors* (1900), Mary Hervey (only daughter of Lord Alfred Hervey, son of the 1st Marquess of Bristol) was an independent scholar, who just managed to complete the manuscript of *Arundel* before her death in 1920. Although **David Howarth** added many interesting details (and interpretations) in his *Lord Arundel and his Circle* (London and New Haven, Yale University Press, 1985), Hervey's *Life* remains essential reading, if only for its transcription of so much primary material. As a good Protestant herself, the biographer's only fault is to have trusted to the genuineness of Arundel's abandonment of Roman Catholicism after his return from Italy with **Inigo Jones** in 1614. She thus misses the significance of

Arundel's essential loyalty to the 'old religion', both at the deepest level, in the enhanced sympathy for the visual arts which it engendered, and in terms of his network of friends and clients in England and abroad. Neither Hervey nor Howarth was aware that when Arundel died in self-imposed exile in Padua in 1646 he died 'in the bosom of the Catholic Church' (see E. Chaney, 'Thomas Howard, 14th Earl of Arundel by François Dieussart', *Apollo*, August 1996, pp. 49–50, and ibid., p. 35, n.162).

Though primarily concerned with the voyages associated with the man after whom it is named, the Hakluyt Society has occasionally published edited transcriptions of European travelogues. Only slightly relevant are *The Travels of Peter Mundy, IV: Travels in Europe 1639–1647*, ed. **R.C. Temple**, 2nd series, LV, 1924 (*sic*; though the preface is signed by Temple in 1925). A more relevant Hakluyt volume is the scholarly Hampstead solicitor, **Malcolm Letts's** edition of *Francis Mortoft: His Book* (2nd series, LVII, London, 1925), an account of a journey through France and Italy in 1658–59, which, by its conventional tone, supplies us with a useful yardstick against which to measure that minority of more enterprising and artistically sophisticated travellers (see also above, p. 199, n. 46).

In 1932, the 27-year-old **Harold Acton** published *The Last Medici*, a work which drew very interestingly on seventeenth- and early-eighteenth-century accounts by foreign visitors to Florence. Three years later, his publishers, Faber & Faber, evidently thought the *Grand Tour* was of sufficient interest to justify publishing a light-hearted collection of essays under this title, edited by **Richard S. Lambert** (see also Hale, 1954, below).

Although only marginally concerned with the Grand Tour as such, an important book which remains standard on its subject is **E.G.R. Taylor**, *Late Tudor and Early Stuart Geography 1583–1650* (London, 1934; facsimile reprint: New York, Octagon Books, 1968). Subtitled *A Sequel to Tudor Geography, 1485–1583*, this continues above all to deal with the geographical thought and nautical theory 'that formed the setting of the English Voyages for Trade and Discovery'. Much of this setting and bibliography is relevant, however, to the emergence of European travel for educational profit and pleasure; indeed, **Eva Taylor**'s penultimate chapter is devoted to what she calls 'The Urbane Traveller', who was neither pilgrim, merchant nor explorer in the normal sense.

Borrowing Eva Taylor's nomenclature for his title (but narrowing down her period), the American **Boies Penrose**, who had previously published a study of the itinerant Shirley brothers, named his somewhat unreliable study *Urbane Travelers 1591-1635* (Philadelphia, University of Pennsylvania Press, 1942). It is primarily useful in summarizing the journeys of some of the contemporaries of Moryson, Coryate and Lithgow. Already a major theme in this study, Penrose subsequently published almost exclusively on early-modern travel beyond Europe, accumulating a distinguished library on this subject which was sold by Sotheby's in 1971.

Penrose apart, the Second World War, and indeed the years immediately preceding it, while seeing many English and American books on Fascist Italy – several pre-war publications taking the form of enthusiastic travelogues – signalled a hiatus in the historiography of the Grand Tour similar to that longer pause in Anglo-Italian contact caused by Napoleon a century and a half earlier. Moreover, unlike the rush into print of travelogues which began even before Waterloo, in 1945 post-war weariness and poverty in Britain at least seem to have prolonged this hiatus through the 1940s. The only relevant publication of the decade seems to have been **Dorothy Carrington**'s excellent edited anthology, *The Traveller's Eye* (London, The Pilot Press, 1947; reissued in 1949 by the Readers Union 'in complete conformity with the authorised economy standards'.)

In 1937, **E.M. Hutton** had completed a wide-ranging PhD for the University of Cambridge entitled 'The Grand Tour in the 16th, 17th and 18th Centuries', but it was never published. Not until around 1950 were two equivalently relevant PhDs completed, one at Oxford on the seventeenth century and the other for the University of Columbia (?) on the eighteenth century. Published by Jonathan Cape in 1952, from his almost unaltered dissertation, **John Stoye**'s *English Travellers Abroad 1604-1667: Their Influence in English Society and Politics* probably deserves the accolade of being the finest of all the books under discussion, and is indeed one of the most enlightening books written on any aspect of the seventeenth century. Though succinct in its referencing, it supplies enough hitherto unpublished data and ideas for a dozen doctorates, if only university departments were less conventionally disciplinary. A hopeful sign is that in 1989 Yale University Press was persuaded by Stoye's admirers to publish a second, revised edition. By the time I met **Paul Franklin Kirby** (a colleague at the University of Pisa who had served with the American forces in the war in Italy, where he met the woman he married), he seemed to be finding teaching more difficult than fighting had been. Still incurably romantic about his adopted country, however, and indeed about the historic English 'love affair with Italy', he seemed pleased to meet someone who had actually read his PhD, *The Grand Tour in Italy, 1700–1800*, which a small New York-based Italian publisher named S.F. Vanni (Ragusa) had agreed to print in 1952.

When, in 1950, **Richard S. Lambert** completed a single-authored book, *The Fortunate Traveller: A Short History of Touring and Travel for Pleasure*, Faber & Faber apparently did not choose to continue the pre-war relationship they had established with his *Grand Tour* collection, and it was published in London by Andrew Melrose. An anthology of travel accounts, presumably pitched at a similar market, appeared in the following year: **Helen Barber Morrison**'s *The Golden Age of Travel: Literary Impression of the Grand Tour* (New York, Twayne, 1951). When, two years after the publication of John Stoye's masterpiece, however, fellow Oxford scholar **John Hale** produced his perhaps less thoroughly researched but wider-ranging *England and the Italian Renaissance: The Growth of Interest in its History and Art* (1954), Fabers were apparently willing to emphasize the cultural connections, reasserting this relationship with Hale's somewhat eccentric edition of *The Italian Journal of Samuel Rogers* (1956). This included a long introduction to Rogers generally, and his travels in 1814–15 in particular. *England and the Italian Renaissance* was reissued in a slightly revised Grey Arrow paperback in 1963 and then again in 1996 with an introduction by Nicholas Penny.

While it is not the intention of this essay to discuss travel accounts unless they or their editorial apparatus are relevant to the evolution of English travel to Italy, exception might be made for John Hale's last contribution to the history of European travel, his translation (in collaboration with J.M.A. Lindon) and edition of *The Travel Journal of Antonio de Beatis 1517–1518* (London, Hakluyt Society, 1979). **De Beatis** was chaplain and amanuensis to Luigi, the Cardinal of Aragon, during the latter's tour through Germany, Switzerland, the Low Countries and France. The Cardinal went out of his way to visit the 64-year-old Leonardo da Vinci in his villa near Amboise, viewing three of his pictures (including, it seems, the *Mona Lisa*) and describing him as 'the most outstanding artist of our day'. In Milan on his return journey, he noted that Leonardo's *Last Supper* was 'excellent though already beginning to deteriorate'. Equivalent

English interest in the visual arts would not be apparent for another century.

Published in the same year as Hale's still unsurpassed survey of English responses to the Italian Renaissance was the American **George Bruner Parks**'s survey of the period immediately prior to Hale's, focused more exclusively on *The English Traveler to Italy. Vol. I: The Middle Ages to 1525* (Rome, Edizioni di Storia e Letteratura, 1954). Having begun his academic career by specializing on *Richard Hakluyt and his Voyages*, in the last two decades of his life Parks concentrated exclusively on European travel. Unfortunately, he died before he could complete his projected second volume of *The English Traveler in Italy*, only managing to publish his editions of **William Thomas** and **Gregory Martin** (see below) and a few fine articles on English 'Italianateness' and the travels of John Evelyn.

The mid-1950s saw the publication of several editions of eighteenth-century diaries and correspondence, some of which had been planned before the war. **Warren Hunting Smith** began working on Yale University Press's *Horace Walpole's Corrrespondence with Sir Horace Mann* in 1940, before America joined the war. This part of W.S. Lewis's 48-volume Walpole project was put on hold while Smith served in the army and was only resumed again, now in collaboration with Dr **George L. Lam**, in 1947. Though Lewis anticipated three volumes, eleven were eventually published (New Haven, and London, Oxford University Press, 1954-71; second printing 1975).

Although they also fall outside the 'evolutionary' scope of this survey, it seems worth mentioning, if only from the publishing point of view, the 1950s editions of **James Boswell**, **Edward Gibbon** and **George Berkeley**. Boswell's travels were usefully (though by no means exhaustively) edited by **Frank Brady** and **Frederick Pottle** for Heinemann in 1955 under the title *Boswell on the Grand Tour: Italy, Corsica, and France 1765-1766*. In the following year, Gibbon's not very revealing letters from Italy appeared in volume I of *The Letters of Edward Gibbon*, edited by **J. E. Norton** (London, Cassells, 1956), while the entire text of his travel diary, largely written in French, was published with superior notes by **Georges A. Bonnard** as *Gibbon's Journey from Geneva to Rome: His journal from 20 April to 2 October 1764* (Edinburgh and London, Thomas Nelson and Sons Ltd, 1961, in a numbered, limited edition of 105 copies on Millbourn paper in pseudo-vellum and individually boxed; commercial edition of same year; followed by a bizarre, undated Italian edition, whose preface is signed 'G.A.B.' but which otherwise makes no reference to Bonnard, and whose entire critical apparatus is nevertheless translated. The title page reads: 'Edward Gibbon / Viaggio in Italia / Edizione del Borghese'). Though neither Norton nor Bonnard comments on the matter, the absence of any mention of Pompei or Herculaneum in either the letters or the travel journal, despite Gibbon's acquaintance with Sir William Hamilton in Naples, leads one to conclude that the unadventurous author of *The Decline and Fall of the Roman Empire* never rode out to the excavations beneath Vesuvius.

Nelson and Sons were also responsible for publishing the complete text of **George Berkeley**'s letters and travel journals as volumes VII and VIII of *The Works of George Berkeley*, edited as a nine-volume set by **A.A. Luce** and **T.E. Jessop**, these 1955 and 1956 volumes being Luce's responsibility alone. The co-edited volume IX, which includes the index to the whole, also includes notes to the letters (Edinburgh, 1957). Where the travels are concerned these are merely adequate, while the journals themselves, despite providing a unique insight into Berkeley's brilliant, yet extraordinarily virtuous personality, are scarcely annotated at all. This task was thus left to a philosophy lecturer at the University of Naples, **Mariapaola Fimiani**, in collaboration with Jessop (as if in belated acknowledgement of the significance of the journals), to re-edit them in Italian translation: *George Berkeley. Viaggio in Italia* (Naples, Istituto Italiano per gli Studi Filosofici, serie testi V, Bibliopolis, 1979).

But just as **Logan Pearsall Smith**'s monograph on **Henry Wotton** may be regarded as the supreme edition of the letters of an early modern traveller and indeed resident in Italy, so the supreme edition of an early modern travel journal and one of particular relevance to the evolutionary theme, must be the second volume of **E.S. de Beer**'s edition of *The Diary of John Evelyn* in six volumes (Oxford, Clarendon Press, 1955). Although the *Oxford English Dictionary* continues to credit Evelyn's *Diary* for the first use of several Italianate terms, by scrupulous examination of his sources de Beer demonstrated that most of what purports to be a journal was in fact a memoir written up from notes decades after the events described. This was especially apparent in the European travel diaries, where **John Raymond**'s *Itinerary* of 1649, **Monconys**'s *Journal des Voyages* of 1665–66 and **Richard Lassels**'s *Voyage of Italy*, which was not published until 1670, are plagiarized in order to create an account of Italy purporting to date from 1644-45.

Though neither British nor American, tribute should here be paid to two Anglophile Italians who both published their major contributions in 1957. The late **Anna Maria Crinò**, my former boss at the University of Pisa, spent a lifetime searching Florence's then Uffizi-based Archivio di Stato for anything of English interest, publishing a selection of her essays in 1957 as *Fatti e Figure del Seicento Anglo-Toscano: Documenti inediti sui rapporti letterari, diplomatici, culturali fra Toscana e Inghilterra* (Florence, Olschki, 1957). This includes important information on Wotton and Robert Dallington among others. Crinò seems to have transcribed some of her discoveries in a hurry and the fascinating classical-republican friend of Cosimo III, **Henry Neville**, is given a knighthood that so facetious a republican would never have been granted, but occasional eccentricities are far outweighed by the usefulness of this collection by a scholar who never received the recognition she deserved from her more conformist academic colleagues.

Only that even more devoted disciple of the great Mario Praz, **Vittorio Gabrieli**, former Professor of English at the University of Rome, has made an equivalently important contribution to this subject, above all with his biography *Sir Kenelm Digby: un Inglese Italianato nell'Eta della Contrariforma* (published by G.B. Parks's Roman publishers, Edizioni di Storia e Letteratura, in 1957). Finally, although even less English, mention must be made of the masterly, *Italienreisen im 17. und 18. Jahrhundert*, by the one-time director of the wonderful Hertziana library in Rome and bibliographer of guidebooks to that city, **Ludwig Schudt** (Vienna and Munich, Schroll-Verlag, 1959).

Independent gentlemen and women scholars have made major contributions to a subject which universities have hesitated to accommodate but for which a wider public, however restricted in size, provides some sort of market. Few scholars were more gentlemanly than **James Lees-Milne**, whose apartment in Bath was part of **William Beckford**'s post-Fonthill house (complete with the collector-traveller's bookcases) and whose own essays and books on Beckford, Lord Burlington (in *Earls of Creation*), *Baroque in Italy*, *Roman Mornings*, *The Last Stuarts*, *The Age of Inigo Jones* and *Adam*, if not primary sources such as his *Diaries* have become, were almost as original. Though superseded in some respects by more recent scholarship, Lees-Milne's most relevant contribution to our subject was his *Tudor Renaissance* (London, Batsford, 1951). At a time when the Italophile Keeper of the Queen's Pictures, Sir **Anthony Blunt** was recruiting spies for the Soviet Union, his colleague **Lesley Lewis** was in the process of writing her fascinating *Connoisseurs and Secret Agents in Eighteenth-Century Rome* (London, Chatto & Windus, 1961). Then it was the Jacobitism of Lees-Milne's *Last Stuarts* rather than Communism that was the perceived threat to the Whig ascendancy that still prevails.

    G.B. Parks's useful edition of **William Thomas**'s *History of Italy* (1549) appeared in 1963 in the Folger Documents of Tudor and Stuart Civilization series (New York, Cornell University Press). Given Parks's modernization of Thomas's black-letter text as well as his abridgement of the latter's long summaries of the history of each major city, the publication of a good-quality facsimile in the Theatrum Orbis Terrarum series published by Walter Johnson (Amsterdam and Norwood, 1977) was also very welcome.

    An English Research Professor of Languages working at Indiana University, **Arthur Lytton Sells,** had already published a respectable study of *The Italian Influence in English Poetry from Chaucer to Southwell* (London and Bloomington, 1955) but in 1964, Allen & Unwin published his *The Paradise of Travellers: The Italian Influence on Englishmen in the Seventeenth Century*. Given the refreshingly non-disciplinary choice of subject and promising title, this proved disappointingly dependent on well-known sources while the projected companion volume, on 'The Italians in Stuart England', never materialized.

    The second relevant Anglo-Italian project of 1964 was alliteratively entitled *Famous Foreigners in Florence 1400–1900*, being an alphabetically arranged biographical dictionary compiled by long-term resident **Clara Louise Dentler** and published, with a subsidy from Azienda Autonoma di Turismo di Firenze, by Bemporad Marzocco. Democratically allocating approximately one page to each visitor, Dentler is not always entirely accurate but includes a good deal of little-known information, especially about those not-so 'famous foreigners' whom she was old enough to have remembered.

    Though he made no pretence of being an academic, **Geoffrey Trease,** published his unfootnoted but wide-ranging and well-written *The Grand Tour* with Heinemann of London and Holt, Rinehart and Winston, of New York, in 1967. In the same year, the enterprising

Paul Elek published what is physically the widest of the books under discussion (though one which deals only with the 1720–1820 period): *The Age of the Grand Tour*. Featuring fine essays by **Anthony Burgess** and **Francis Haskell**, numerous illustrations and a rich but somewhat random collection of Grand Tour quotations, if legs were attached to its four corners it would itself make a handsome coffee table.

The American chemist turned humanist, **Edward John Baskerville** submitted his pioneering dissertation on *The English Traveler to Italy, 1547–1560* in the same quasi-revolutionary year of 1967 (published as a facsimile at Ann Arbor, 1982). Developing the empirical tradition pioneered by Lewis Einstein, Baskerville wrote his dissertation for Columbia University (Einstein's publisher) but dug more deeply in archives, in both the British Museum Library and the Public Record Office, finding more new material on mid-sixteenth-century travellers than any previous scholar. Another original product of an American campus, **John Arthos**'s *Milton and the Italian Cities* (London, Bowes and Bowes, 1968) is especially informative on the cultural scene encountered by Milton in Italy and on the music and spectacle in particular.

Though not ostensibly about travel, **Brian Moloney**'s *Florence and England: Essays on Cultural Relations in the Second Half of the Eighteenth Century* was published by Leo Olschki (Florence, 1969), if not to replace, then at least to supplement his stock of Crinò's *Fatti e Figure*, which had been depleted by the 1966 flood. Also published in Italy in English and in the same year, **G.B. Parks** made another major contribution to our understanding of the Cinquecento generally, and the Counter-Reformation in particular, when he edited **Gregory Martin**'s manuscript *Roma Sancta* (1581) (Rome, Edizioni di Storia e Letteratura, 1969). Martin was an exceptionally learned Catholic priest and one of the translators of the *Douai Bible*. His account of Rome as the charitable centre of the world would no doubt have thrilled Thurston had he known the manuscript, which is now in the Australian National Library in Canberra.

The year 1969 also saw the publication of a less esoteric survey by the professional author of dozens of readable and reliable historical studies, **Christopher Hibbert**. Perhaps because Trease's 1967 book on the Grand Tour had been favorably reviewed but had been illustrated somewhat sparsely in black and white, whereas the Burgess and Haskell volume had likewise stimulated interest but was unwieldy and expensive, Hibbert's publishers, Weidenfeld & Nicolson, decided to fill the gap in the market by producing a more practical (and affordable) colour-illustrated survey, yet again entitled *The Grand Tour*.

In 1974, Olschki rendered Grand Tour studies his third and perhaps most significant favour (after Crinò and Moloney) by publishing the extremely useful, chronologically arranged *Bibliography of British and American Travel in Italy to 1860*. On the staff of the then British Museum Library and married to an Italian, the memorably named R.S. Pine-Coffin was well placed to produce what remains the standard work of reference. This was supplemented in 1981 by his 'Additions and Corrections' in *La Bibliofilia*, LXXXIII, pp. 237–61. I have interlined relevant references in my own Pine-Coffin in the hope of one day producing an equivalently useful bibliography of travel manuscripts. Modern editions of historic travel accounts are not always cited by Pine-Coffin and one should perhaps mention **Guy Chapman**'s scarce (Cambridge U.P. for Constable & Co. and Houghton Mifflin Company, 1928) edition of **William Beckford**'s even more scarce (because self-suppressed) 1783 printed but not published *Travel Diaries* (see now the edition by Robert J. Gemmett, Rutherford, NJ, Farleigh Dickinson University Press, 1971); **Herbert Barrows'** useful edition of **Hester Piozzi**'s *Observations and Reflections* (Ann Arbor, University of Michigan Press, 1967) and, most comprehensive of all, **Sliva Klima**'s edition of **Joseph Spence**'s 1730s *Letters from the Grand Tour* (Montreal, McGill–Queen's University Press, 1975).

Jonathan Sumption's *Pilgrimage: An Image of Medieval Religion* (London, 1975) includes coverage of those formative centuries of travel which make Thurston's 1300 institution of the Holy Year seem modern. It is especially interesting on the pre-modern collecting of relics. **P.J. Ayres**'s edition of **Antony Munday**'s *The English Romayne Life of 1580* (Oxford, Oxford University Press, 1980) suggests some of the potential interest of a Catholic apostate's account of the community at the English College in Rome. See also **J.G. Links**'s *Travellers in Europe: Private Records of Journeys by the Great and Forgotten from Horace to Pepys* (London, Bodley Head, 1980).

Though not exclusively about the Grand Tour, **Francis Haskell** and **Nicholas Penny**'s *Taste and the Antique: The Lure of Classical Sculpture 1500–1900* (London and New Haven, Yale University Press, 1981; second printing with corrections 1982) is so uniquely useful to the subject, in documenting the development of the taste for ancient art, that it must be included in this survey. In view of the premature demise of Francis Haskell earlier this year, one might also mention his pioneering, yet still unrivalled *Patrons and Painters* (London, Chatto & Windus, 1963; 2nd edition, New Haven and London, Yale University Press, 1980).

The *Festschrift* for Sir **Harold Acton**'s 80th birthday, edited and produced in Florence in 1984 by **Edward Chaney** and **Neil Ritchie**, included a substantial collection of Anglo-Italian essays by the likes of **John Fleming, Michael Grant, Peter Gunn, Francis Haskell, Hugh Honour, Carlo Knight, John Pope-Hennessy, Amanda Lillie, Peter Quennell, Sacheverell Sitwell, Denys Sutton** and **Charles Wilson**. Entitled *Oxford, China and Italy* (in order to echo Stendhal but signal the three places most closely associated with the dedicatee), it was published privately in 1984 in a limited edition of 250 copies. A further 900 were then run off (in the same letter-press by the excellent Stamperia Editoriale Parenti of Florence) with the Thames & Hudson logo on the title page and dust jacket. Alexander Zielcke's black and white photograph of Acton replaced the colour reproduction of a watercolour portrait by Luciano Guarnieri, and the copies boxed and dispatched to the Thames & Hudson warehouse in London at £4.63p each (to be retailed at £18).

Meanwhile, at Harold Acton's request, but having to maintain secrecy about preparations for the *Festschrift*, I was editing an anthology of historical texts and travelogues to be entitled *Florence: A Travellers' Companion*, for Constable & Co. With Harold's superb introductory essay on the history of Florence (into which the history of travel to Florence is deftly woven), the *Companion* was finally published in 1986. Other relevant volumes in the series were **Desmond Seward**'s *Naples* (1984) and **John Julius Norwich**'s *Venice* (1990).

Given the importance of his earlier edition of **John Locke**'s travels in France, **John Lough**'s *France Observed in the Seventeenth Century by British Travellers* (Stocksfield, Oriel Press, 1984) was disappointing in both scope and reliability. A more original work, concentrating on Italian gardens observed by British travellers in more or less the same period, is **John Dixon Hunt**'s *Garden and Grove: The Italian Renaissance Garden in the English Imagination, 1600-1750* (London, J.M. Dent, 1984).

Written at the European University Institute in Florence but registered as a PhD at the Warburg Institute in London, my own 1982 dissertation on **Richard Lassels**, author of the posthumously published *Voyage of Italy* (Paris, 1670), attempted to use a biography as the basis upon which to explore the effects of Catholic and then Royalist exile on the political and artistic culture of the seventeenth century. It was published as *The Grand Tour and the Great Rebellion*, by the Centro Interuniversitario per Ricerche sul Viaggio in Italia, Moncalieri, in 1985. CIRVI, a quasi-autonomous body connected to the University of Turin through its founding director, Professor Emanuele Kanceff's chair in French literature there, publishes edited travelogues and secondary studies on the history of travel in Italy (see above, p.87, n. 2). In the same year, **Jeremy Black** published his first book on European travel: *The British and the Grand Tour* (Brighton, Croom Helm, 1985). Based on extensive exploration of archives throughout Britain, this work illustrates the variety of experiences of eighteenth-century travellers by means of previously unpublished diaries and correspondence (see also below, Black, 1992).

A more commercially successful enterprise than either of these, the rewritten, 1987 version of **Christopher Hibbert**'s *Grand Tour*, announces in its acknowledgements that 'This book has been written to accompany the Thames Television series, "The Grand Tour", with whose producer, Richard Mervyn, I have enjoyed long and profitable discussions while we were writing the scripts together.' Something of an oddity in being neither an entirely new book nor a second edition, *The Grand Tour* is, nevertheless, more historically informative than the television series, which featured Hibbert riding around modern Italy on a horse.

The last decade of the millennium, particularly the last five years, saw a dramatic increase in books on both the history of travel and Anglo-Italian cultural relations. More in the latter category than the former but with important essays relating to travel by **Sydney Anglo, Nicolas Barker, Michael Baxandall, D.S. Chambers, Ernst Gombrich, K.J. Höltgen, Charles Hope, Ronald Lightbown, Jennifer Montagu, Graham Pollard, Dennis Rhodes, Sergio Rossi** and **Roy Strong**, the *Festschrift* for the sixty-fifth birthday of the then director of the Warburg Institute, Professor **J.B. Trapp**, *England and the Continental Renaissance*, was edited by **Edward Chaney** and **Peter Mack** and published by Boydell Press (Woodbridge, Suffolk) in 1990 (second, corrected printing 1994).

In 1991, the first issue of the *Journal of Anglo-Italian Studies* was launched by the University of Malta (founding editors, **Edward Chaney** and **Peter Vassallo**). Volume I included travel-related essays by **John Woodhouse, Sergio Rossi, Dianella Savoia, John Stoye, Alan G. Hill, Michael Hollington** and myself, while the second volume of the following year included relevant contributions by **Malcolm Kelsall, Stephen Lloyd, William Collier, Vittorio Gabrieli** and **Hugh Trevor-Roper**'s piece on Sir Robert Dudley, the self-exiled son of Elizabeth's Leicester.

The Canadian historian, **Kenneth Bartlett**'s *The English in Italy 1525–1558* (Slatkine, Geneva and CIRVI, Moncalieri, 1991) is a useful account but apparently written without the benefit of E.J. **Baskerville**'s Columbia PhD (see above). It thus complements rather than supersedes the early work on more or less the same subject. The following year saw Jeremy Black's considerable enlargement of his 1985 publication, now entitled *The British Abroad: The Grand Tour in the Eighteenth Century*, this time published by Alan Sutton of Stroud in Gloucestershire. A paperback edition followed in 1997 with a reprint in 1999. No doubt Professor Black's book encouraged the Folio Society of London in 1993 to produce their illustrated anthology, edited and succinctly introduced by **Roger Hudson**, *The Grand Tour 1592–1796*.

The autumn of 1992 also saw the launch at the Boston Museum of Fine Arts of the magnificent exhibition *The Lure of Italy: American Artists and the Italian Experience 1760–1914*. From Boston this moved to Cleveland and then to Houston, where it finally closed in August 1993. The beautifully illustrated catalogue was expertly edited by **Theodore E. Stebbins, Jr,** but owed much to the contributions of several scholars, including **William L. Vance**, whose two-volume magnum opus on *America's Rome* (New Haven, Yale University Press, 1989) should be especially commended here, despite its focus on the post-evolutionary period.

The distinguished Professor of History at the University of Warsaw, **Antoni Maczak,** had seen two editions of his lively account of *Travel in Early Modern Europe* through the Polish press, but an unwieldy translation circulated in a battered typescript for more than a decade before Polity Press published an inadequately revised version in 1995.

In 1990, the year in which the New Zealand-born **J.B. Trapp** received his *Festschrift* (see above), 'Variorum', part of the Gower Publishing Group at Aldershot, reprinted a selection of his *Essays on the Renaissance and the Classical Tradition*. This included several classic articles, including his brilliant historiographies of the so-called tombs of Ovid and of Virgil. The first Australian to publish a book on the early years of the Grand Tour (if one discounts Felix Raab's *English Face of Machiavelli*, London, 1962) was **Sarah Warneke**. Her *Images of the Educational Traveller in Early Modern England*, published by the Leiden publishers E.J. Brill in 1995, had been written as a PhD for the University of Adelaide. Stylishly original, it is as much an analysis of the abundant sixteenth- and seventeenth-century theory of travel as about travel itself, underlining the significance of the largely negative domestic response to the evolution of educational travel. Also stylish in its late-twentieth-century concerns was the collection of essays edited by **Chloe Chard** and **Helen Langdon** as volume 3 of the Mellon Center's 'Studies in British Art': *Transports: Travel, Pleasure, and Imaginative Geography, 1600–1830* (New Haven and London, Yale University Press, 1996).

In 1993, **Michael Brennan** had edited the fascinating manuscript *Travel Diary (1611–1612) of an English Catholic* **Sir Charles Somerset**, for the Leeds Philosophical and Literary Society. Also fascinating but, because of its more mercantile flavour less relevant to the formation of the Grand Tour, was Dr Brennan's edition of *The Travel Diary of Robert Bargrave, Levant Merchant (1647–1656)* (Hakluyt Society, 1999). Robert was the son of **Isaac Bargrave**, chaplain to **Sir Henry Wotton** in Venice between 1616–18, and thus first cousin to John, subject of the methodologically eclectic study by **Stephen Bann**, *Under the Sign: John Bargrave as Collector, Traveler, and Witness* (Ann Arbor, University of Michigan Press, 1994). Neither Brennan nor Bann seems to have known **Mary Beal**'s Courtauld Institute PhD, *A Study of Richard Symonds* (1978, published by Garland, New York, in 1984), which pioneeringly promoted **John Bargrave**'s Italian travel manuscripts and his cabinet of curiosities. **Anne Brookes** is currently completing a PhD on **Symonds**'s other travel manuscripts for the University of Nottingham, and has contributed a excellent article on his print collection for the volume I am editing for the Mellon Center, *The Evolution of English Collecting* (New Haven and London, Yale University Press, 2001).

With interest in the subject attracting an ever-widening public and scholars from a growing range of disciplines, Olivetti agreed to fund a huge exhibition proposed by **Cesare de Seta** in Naples, in collaboration with **Pierre Rosenberg** at the Louvre and **Francis Haskell** in Oxford. The British venue for the exhibition was to have been the Royal Academy but its exhibitions officer is said to have vetoed the project as too 'elitist'. **Andrew Wilton** and **Ilaria Bignamini** (who was already gathering together contributors' wish lists) rescued a much-abridged version of the show, focusing more exclusively on eighteenth-century art and antiquities, and it was finally shown at the Tate Gallery during the winter of 1996–97. The exhibition and catalogue contained a much scaled-down selection of exhibits, my own section on the origins of the Grand Tour, to have included items associated with the likes of Hoby, Thomas, Coryate, Arundel, Inigo Jones, Milton, Hobbes, together with John Bargrave's cabinet, books and riding boots, being reduced from about 100 items to a mere dozen. Although in 1984 the Canadian, **John Towner**, had written a PhD for the University of Birmingham on 'The European Grand Tour, 1550–1840', the book that evolved from this placed the Tour in an even broader (and less elitist) context: *An Historical Geography of Recreation and Tourism in the Western World 1540–1940* (Chichester, John Wiley & Sons, 1996).

Implicitly aware of *fin-de-siècle* subjectivism even in his title, **Manfred Pfister**'s impressively wide-ranging collection of travel accounts is nevertheless appreciative both of the intrinsic value of the descriptions of his travelling predecessors and of the twentieth-century historiography which he lists in detail. Professor Pfister's *Fatal Gift of Beauty: The Italies of British Travellers. An Annotated Anthology*, appears as no. 15 in a German series entitled Internationale Forschungen zur Allgemeinen und Vergleichenden Literaturwissenschaft, but is published as an inadequately attractive paperback by Rodopi in Amsterdam and Atlanta, Georgia, 1999. One of its many virtues is a 'Gazeteer of Travellers' which includes biographies of all those cited, to some extent thereby continuing beyond the eighteenth century Sir **Brinsley Ford**'s great project, as seen through the press by **John Ingamells** for the Mellon Centre, *The Dictionary of British and Irish Travellers in Italy 1701–1800* (New Haven and London, Yale University Press, 1997; reprinted in 1999). Also published for the Mellon Centre by Yale University Press, and containing many relevant entries, was the 3rd edition of Sir **Howard Colvin**'s exemplary *Biographical Dictionary of British Architects 1600–1840* (1995, with corrections and additions in *Architectural History*, XXXIX, 1996, pp. 236–41).

Meanwhile, at Yale's Beinecke Rare Book Library, **John Marciari** organized a fascinating exhibition of its holdings on *The Grand Tour*. An elegant catalogue was produced to accompany this exhibition (which included the autograph manuscript of **Richard Lassels**'s *Voyage* I once possessed), but more important is Marciari's subsequent *Grand Tour Diaries*, a complete catalogue of the travel manuscripts in the Osborn Collection, published as the second in a series of 'Occasional Supplements' to the *Yale University Library Gazette* (ed. **Stephen Park**, 1999). Closely (albeit informally) associated with Yale's Mellon Centre in London (partly thanks to its director, Professor **Brian Allen**'s crucial role in both) is the long-established Walpole Society, which has published many volumes fundamental to our under-standing of the evolution of the Grand Tour, from the *Diary of Nicholas Stone Junior* in 1919 to *The John Talman Letter-Book* in 1997.

Jonathan Woolfson's excellent *Padua and the Tudors: English Students in Italy 1485–1603* (Toronto, University of Toronto Press, 1998), like Baskerville, Bartlett and Pfister before him, includes a 'Biographical Register' as an Appendix, this one documenting 350 students and visitors to Padua during the Tudor period. Beginning more or less where this study of visitors to the Veneto leaves off is the phenomenon documented in the book of the exhibition held at the Palazzo Barbaran in Vicenza's newly relocated 'Centro Internazionale di Studi di Andrea Palladio': *Palladio and Northern Europe: Books, Travellers, Architects*, ed. **Guido Beltramini, Howard Burns** *et al.* (Milan, Skira, 1999). In the Middle Ages, pilgrims visit-ed Venice on their way to Rome or the Holy Land. During the Renaissance, they came to Verona and Padua to study. Subsequently, they came to Vicenza to see the buildings of Palladio. **Wotton, Cranborne, Coryate, Arundel** and **Jones** are among the ear-liest north European admirers of Palladio, each in their own way indebted to the Dominican Inquisitor and art historian **Fra Girolamo da Capugnano**, whose greatly enlarged edition of **Franz Schott**'s *Itinerario* was published in 1601 in Vicenza. Curiously, catalogue entries on these topics bear an uncanny resemblance to work sent by the present author to one of the editors several years ago, unac-knowledged then as now (though documented in the *Yorkshire Georgian Society Annual Report* for 1995, under the title: 'The Real Discovery of Palladio', pp. 43–5).

The major Irish contribution to eighteenth-century Grand Tour studies, by Professor **Michael McCarthy** and Dr **Nicola Figgis** among others, lies outside the scope of this survey. Having been privileged to attend the launch of her fine book and the associated conference at the National Gallery of Ireland, however, I should like to commemorate the late **Cynthia O'Connor**'s courageous completion of *The Pleasing Hours: The Grand Tour of James Caulfield, First Earl of Charlemont (1728-1799) Traveller, Connoisseur and Patron of the Arts* (Cork, The Collins Press, 1999).

The year 1999 also saw the publication by the Cambridge University Press of two books of essays which are less informative on the Grand Tour than their titles might suggest: *Italian Culture in Northern Europe in the Eighteenth Century*, edited by **Shearer West**, and *Roman Presences: Receptions of Rome in European Culture, 1789-1945*, edited by **Catherine Edwards**. Meanwhile, also in 1999, Manchester University Press published a single-authored book by one of Catherine Edwards's contributors, **Chloe Chard**'s *Pleasure and Guilt on the Grand Tour: Travel Writing and Imaginative Geography 1600-1830*. This is a sophisticated account, but more concerned with imaginative geography and the language of travel writing than with travel (in any historical sense) itself. Almost as methodologically up-to-the-minute as Edwards and Chard, albeit beginning at the beginning with the ancient world, is **Jaś Elsner** and **Joan-Pau Rubiés** eds, *Voyages and Visions: Towards a Cultural History of Travel*, published in the 'Critical Views' series (London, Reaktion Books, 1999). Although one appreciates that an article entitled 'Looking for Virgil's Tomb' is no longer likely to be about looking, nor indeed about Virgil's Tomb, it still seems odd that **J.B. Trapp**'s classic article on the looking, the legend and the tomb itself, first published in the *Journal of the Warburg and Courtauld Institutes* in 1984 and reprinted in his *Essays* cited above, is nowhere mentioned.

Continuing the momentum accumulated during the penultimate year of the millennium, spring 2000 sees Philadelphia and Houston's Museums mount a major exhibition entitled 'The Splendour of 18th Century Rome'. Though this will not travel to Europe, the magnificent accompanying catalogue, *Art in Rome in the Eighteenth Century*, edited by **Edgar Peters Bowron** and **Joseph J. Rishel**, is published in London by Merrell Publishers. Symmetrical with the appearance in 1900 of **Herbert Thurston**'s *Holy Year of Jubilee* is **Judith Champ**'s similarly lively yet appropriately pious *The English Pilgrimage to Rome* (Leominster, Gracewing, 2000). Armed with these and the other titles all too briefly cited above, readers in the new millennium may, I hope, feel encouraged to break through the academic barriers still maintained by our educational systems and explore the fascinating world of our multi-disciplinary travelling forebears.

Index

✦

Note: Italicized page numbers denote illustrations.

n43, 312 n57
Wotton, Sir Henry, xvi, 86, 109, 154,
    163, 171, 176, 194 n6, 198 n40,
    212; and gardening, 361 n71; and
    Italian architecture, 205–11; letters
    to Vincenzo I Gonzaga, 162–7
Wrath (Wroth), John, 198 n40
Wrath (Wroth), Mary, 198 n4
Wrath (Wroth), Sir Robert, 198 n40
Wren, Sir Christopher, 200 n47,
    316–17, 351 nn6 and 8
Wright, Cornelius, 230
Wright, Edward, 135 n33, 338
Wright, John Michael, 229–30
Wright, Joseph, of Derby, *ii*, 114

Wright, Thomas, 319–20
Wriothesley, Henry (3rd Earl of
    Southampton), 158 n18
Wroth, *see* Wrath
Wyatt, Sir Thomas (poet), 54 n21, 92
    n32
Wyatt, Sir Thomas (conspirator, son of
    the above), 64, 70, 91 n22, 95 n57
Wyndham, Henry Penruddocke, 313
Wynne, Elizabeth, 135 n37

Yaxley, Francis, 69
Yonge, Nicholas, 93 n48
Young, John, 46